ABOUNDING IN MERCY

MOTHER AUSTIN CARROLL

The author thanks Jose Garcia for reproduction of this historic photograph.

ABOUNDING IN MERCY

MOTHER AUSTIN CARROLL

BY

SISTER MARY HERMENIA MULDREY, R.S.M.

HABERSHAM

New Orleans

1988

Printed in the United States of America

Art Direction by Wayne Miller

Library of Congress

Muldrey, Mary Hermenia, RSM
    Abounding in mercy, Mother Austin Carroll
    Bibliography index
    1. Carroll, Mary Teresa Austin, 1835–1909
2. Sisters of Mercy I. Title
BX4705   271.92 [B]

ISBN #0-944784-01-1

DEDICATION

"To the Sisters of Mercy in every land,"
this life and
"these records of their Institute
are affectionately dedicated
by their sister,
who, as the best reward for her labors,
covets their prayers."

The words of Mother Austin Carroll
on December 12, 1881,
in the *Annals of the Sisters of Mercy*

CONTENTS

1. THE CARROLLS OF CLONMEL   1
    County Tipperary, 1835–1853

2. TRAINING FOR MERCY SERVICE   15
    Cork, Ireland, 1853–1856

3. PILGRIM IN NEW ENGLAND   31
    & New York, 1856–1859

4. RESEARCH, TRAVEL, TRAVAIL   51
    Manchester & Omaha, 1859–1865

5. PRISONERS & PUBLICATION   73
    Saint Louis, 1865–1869

6. MOLLIE ABLE & MARY AUSTIN   91
    River & Riverfront, 1869–1870

7. IRISH CHANNEL CONVENT   111
    New Orleans, 1871–1874

8. INCREASE & EXPANSION   131
    The Gulf Coast, 1875–1878

9. YELLOW FEVER & GOLDEN JUBILEE   161
    The Deep South, 1878–1881

10. ANTAGONISM, BRANCHES, COMPLAINTS   199
    Irish Channel, 1881–1886

11. ORPHANS, ANNALS, FRIENDS   249
    At Home and Afar, 1887–1890

12. OLD AGE & NEW WORKS   287
    Alabama & Florida, 1891–1909

    Abbreviations   341

    Notes   343

    Bibliography   437

    Mary Austin Carroll Bibliography   441

    Index   447

ILLUSTRATIONS

Mother Austin Carroll   Frontispiece

(The following illustrations may be found after page 242)

The West Gate of ancient walled Clonmel
National Model School, Clonmel
St. Maries of the Isle, Cork

St. Alphonsus Convent, New Orleans
Mercy-staffed black school, Birmingham
Mercy High School, St. Martinville, La.

Austin Carroll's friends from the Northeast

St. Katharine's College, New Orleans
Mercy convent and school, Belize
Group from the Newsboys' School, N.O.

Several Southern friends of Austin Carroll

Austin Carroll's Creche, New Orleans
St. Michael Convent, School, and Church, N.O.
Tomb of Mercy yellow-fever martyrs, N.O.

A few of Austin Carroll's scattered friends

Girls near St. Katharine's College, N.O.
Coolock House near Dublin in the 1890's
Austin Carroll's grave (large cross) Mobile

Letter of Austin Carroll

Plan 1: An Irish Channel Neighborhood

Plan 2: Mercy Square

Mother Austin Carroll

ACKNOWLEDGEMENTS

Gathering together the scattered threads of words and events was the fascinating preliminary to the weaving of the multicolored lifecloth of an exceptionally compassionate, literate, and courageous woman of God called Mother Austin Carroll. To relate her story just as it unfolded from Irishtown, Clonmel in Tipperary to the Irish Channel in New Orleans and to other towns, along the Gulf Coast was the goal of the biographer. Certain aspects of the life of this dynamic Sister of Mercy complicated the undertaking, for Mother Austin Carroll worked not only on both sides of the Atlantic Ocean, corresponded with Sisters of Mercy on three continents, and taught in several areas of the United States, but she had also given freely of her time and talent throughout a forty-year period of service to the people of Louisiana and the other states bordering the Gulf of Mexico.

Furthermore, because Mother Austin Carroll was the primary archivist, biographer, and chronicler of the Sisters of Mercy, the ABCs of her life and that of the community tend to intertwine occasionally. This fact made it possible for her biographer to rely most heavily upon the thousands of Austin Carroll letters, documents, and other original writings located in dozens of convent, diocesan, and other archival collections. While gradually acquiring copies of this mass of material during several decades, this researcher depended upon the assistance of many fellow archivists, historians, and librarians as well as numerous other officials who made their documents available.

Although it is impossible to record their various services in detail or to thank adequately, or even to name, the innumerable persons in several countries who have aided this research project, this writer extends her sincere gratitude to each individual who has contributed in any of a thousand ways during the long quest for data. Heartfeld thanks go to all who furnished the bits and papers which, like the pieces of a giant jigsaw puzzle, interlocked to reveal a vibrant twentieth-century woman amidst her nineteenth-century environment. In order to make as real and authentic a presentation as possible, the words of Mother Austin Carroll and those of her correspondents are quoted in their original spelling and format, retaining even the awkward or dated usage.

Because the encouragement of her religious sisters who also work with archives and community history has sustained the researcher through the years, her deepest appreciation goes to these followers of Catherine McAuley. Cordial gratitude goes to the Sisters of Mercy everywhere who granted such a warm welcome, gave access to their archival coffers and the literary wealth of their libraries, and finally, who wrapped this researcher in the comfortable cloak of their generous hospitality.

The writer is particularly grateful to the following groups of Sisters of Mercy. In Ireland to those in Carysfort and Dublin, in Athy, Birr, Carlow, Charleville, Clifden, Clonmel, Coolock, and Cork; in Ennis, Galway, Kinsale, Limerick, Moate, Naas, and Passage West; in Shannon, Tuam, Tullamore, Waterford, Westport, and Wexford; and through correspondence, to Dundrum, Cobh, Newry, and Roscommon. In Great Britain to those in Bermondsey, Harewood Avenue, and Crispin Street in London; in Birmingham and Coventry in Warwickshire and in Liverpool in Lancashire, and through correspondence, Newcastle-upon-Tyne in Northumberland, Shrewsbury in Shropshire, and Sunderland in Durham; Belfast in Northern Ireland; and in Australia to those in Lesmurdie near Perth in the west, in Toowong and Red Hill near Brisbane in the east, and in Erindale near Adelaide in the south. In American to those in Albany, N.Y.; Baltimore, Md.; Belmont, N.C.; Biloxi, Miss.; Brooklyn, N.Y.; Buffalo, N.Y.; Cresson, Pa.; Dallas, Pa.; and Dobbs Ferry, N.Y.; in Erie, Pa.; Frontenac, Mo; Hartford, Conn.; Jeanerette, La.; Manchester, N.H.; Merion, Pa.; Mississippi City, Miss.; and Mobile, Ala.; in New Orleans, La.; Omaha, Neb.; Orchard Park, N.Y.; Pensacola, Fla.; Pittsburgh, Pa.; Providence, R.I.; Rochester, N.Y.; Savannah, Ga.; and Silver Spring, Md.; in St. Louis, Mo.; St. Martinville, La.; Vicksburg, Miss.; Warrington, Fla.; Windham, N.H.; and Worcester, Mass.; and through correspondence, in Burlingame, Calif.; Cedar Rapids, Iowa; Chicago, Ill.; Cincinnati, Ohio; Cuero, Tex.; Denver, Colo.; Detroit, Mich.; Durango, Colo.; Laredo, Tex.; Little Rock, Ark.; Oklahoma City, Okla.; Portland, Maine; San Diego and San Francisco, Calif.; Slaton, Tex.; Belize in Central America; and St. John's in Newfoundland, Canada.

Grateful appreciation for their helpful correspondence is offered to the Dominican nuns of St. Mary's in New Orleans and Cabra, Dublin; the Presentation nuns of Cork, Dublin, and Galway; the Visitation nuns of Georgetown and Mobile; the Religious of the Sacred Heart of Dublin, London, and St. Louis; the Ursuline nuns of St. Louis and New Orleans; the Sisters of the Blessed Sacrament in Cornwell Heights, Pa; the Daughters of Charity of St. Vincent de Paul in Albany, N.Y.; the School Sisters of

Notre Dave in St. Louis and New Orleans; and the Sisters of the Sorrowful Mother in Milwaukee, Wis.; and Wichita, Kan.

It would be impossible to forget the genuine interest and the assistance of Mother Austin Carroll's relatives in Ireland, England, America, and Australia who furnished family information for the opening chapters, who lent their aid in the time-consuming task of procuring copies of the official documentation of family marriages and deaths, and who generously shared their family letters, traditions, and memories along with the proverbial Irish warmth and traditional Irish tea. Countless prayerful mementos go out to the grand and the great-grand nieces and nephews and to the cousins and connections in Clonmel, Lisronagh, and Tobernaheena in County Tipperary; in Dublin and Dundrum in the County of Dublin; in Belfast in Northern Ireland; in Selsdon in Surrey, and Felpham in West Sussex in England; in White Plains in New York; and in Freemantle in Australia.

Sincere gratitude is extended to the archbishops, bishops, and chancellors, to the archivists, pastors, and other members of the clergy who allowed the use of their records and services in the archives of a dozen dioceses in the United States, in several parishes within the archdiocese of Cashel and Emly and within the diocese of Waterford and Lismore, in the espicopal papers, particularly those of the archdiocese of New Orleans, housed at the University of Notre Dame; in the archdiocese of Baltimore, Hartford, Mobile, New Orleans, Omaha, and St. Louis; and the dioceses of Buffalo, Jackson, Little Rock and Savannah.

Directors, archivists, librarians, and their staffs in the archival or special collections of several colleges, universities, and other institutions offered invaluable assistance concerning pertinent materials. Grateful recognition goes to the personnel staffing the following institutions: Catholic University of America, Georgetown University, the Marist College, the Library of Congress, the National Archives, and the Immigration and Naturalization Service—all in Washington, D.C.; the College of the Holy Cross in Worcester, Mass.; the archives of the American Catholic Historical Society in Overbrook, Pa.; St. Louis University in St. Louis and St. Mary's Seminary in Perryville, Mo.; the T.P. Thompson Collection in the University of Alabama in Tuscaloosa, Ala.; the University of Southwestern Louisiana in Lafayette, La.; Louisiana State University and the Louisiana State Archives and Library in Baton Rouge; Loyola University, Notre Dame Seminary, Tulane University, the University of New Orleans, the New Orleans Public Library—all in New Orleans; in Rome the Pontifical Irish College and the Vatican Library; in Ireland, St. Patrick's in Maynooth, the National Library, the Registry of Deeds, and the Office of Registrar-General—all in Dublin; the Tipperary (South Riding) Registry of Births, Deaths, and Marriages in Clonmel, the *Nationalist* newspaper files in Clonmel, the Clonmel Museum, the Cork City Library; the Irish newspaper collection in the research annex of the British Library and to the Public Records Office at Kew, Surray.

Reserved for the conclusion of a list lengthened unduly by the decades of research are a few individuals who cannot be omitted. Special recognition goes to the late Thomas T. McAvoy, CSC, of the Archives of the University of Notre Dame; Emmett M. Bienvenu, SJ, of Loyola University for the translation of Latin documents; Sister Judith Supreys, FMA, for the translation of Italian documents; to those without whom the biography could not have seen completion, the successive provincial superiors of the St. Louis Province of the Religious Sisters of Mercy, Sisters Mary Roch Rocklage and Jeanette Noonan, who, with their councils, commissioned the biography, made it possible for the writer to get to original sources, and provided the time needed for the organization of the mass of documentation and the writing of the manuscript; the dozens of contributors of such essential services as reading, correcting, or proofreading some of the chapters; for critically reviewing matter concerning Ireland, Sr. M. Magdalena Frisby; concerning the Mercy foundress, the late Sr. Joanna Regan; the early chapters, Srs. M. Silverius Shields and Regina Werntz; and the entire manuscript. Monsignor Henry C. Bezou, Srs. M. Alma Musy, Anne Brady, Kevin Trower, and Denise Fortier; for photography, José Garcia and Sr. Mary Anne Brady; for secretarial service, Jane Arvin. Finally, to Mother Austin Carroll's grandniece, Mrs. Joseph McCarthy, who allied her curiosity with that of the biographer and became a veritable detective chasing genealogical leads down ancestral lanes and lines, go the heartfeld thanks offered to all of those mentioned.

Sister M. Hermenia Muldrey, RSM
December 12, 1987

1

THE CARROLLS OF CLONMEL
County Tipperary
1835–1853

Clonmel in southern Tipperary was a hardy marketplace as the eighteenth century came to a close; and by the first quarter of the nineteenth century, it was to become a bustling transportation center. Much of the energy which started Clonmel's financial wheels whirling originated in the horse-drawn carts of Charles Bianconi, "who began his career as a pedlar of pictures and died a millionaire."[1] This creative entrepreneur from Lombardy had started with several short mail routes — one westward to Cahir and one east to Carrick-on-Suir. Before long his routes fanned out in all directions and transformed a quiet medieval town into a hustling hub from which the spokes of his transportation system stretched 4,000 miles.[2] While the cars of Charley Bian, as he was affectionately known, criss-crossed the nation, one business generated others as needs grew for more blacksmiths, wheelwrights, and drivers. Then all of these workers, along with their families, needed to be fed and housed. Thus, the thriving town beckoned to ambitious young men.

William Carroll, who was destined to be the father of Margaret Anne a few years later, was alert to the call from Clonmel.[3] He was to heed it, also, but not until after he had won from Waterford one of its young colleens, the lovely Margaret Mary Strahan,[4] who was in God's own time to have a namesake in her second daughter. Like everyone else involved in marketing or production in Ireland, William Carroll could scarcely have been unaware of the wheels awhirring in Clonmel. He was to establish his business there within a few years after his marriage. Hence, he was on the spot when shopkeepers became merchant princes. For instance, Bianconi's first assistant, Dan Hearn, became the High Street innkeeper, Hearn's Hotel still bearing his name. A gazeteer[5] of the time listed Clonmel as the largest inland town in Ireland, with a population of 15,890. This figure dates from 1839, when it was estimated that the nation had 8,000,000 people and that

1

two-thirds of Ireland's families still derived their living from agricultural pursuits, many in the Tipperary plain.

The ancestors of both Carrolls and Strahans came from the very heart of County Tipperary, "the Golden Vale" guarded by the Celtic towers of Cashel to the south and Roscrea to the north. In and about this central plain and as far south as the city of Waterford were to be found in the nineteenth century numerous relatives and more distant "connections," each and every-one of whom had lived through the harsh realities of the Penal Code. The Irish historian John N. Murphy explained that

> the Irish Catholic was prohibited the possession of landed property . . . denied all political and municipal privileges. . . . Not only was his religion proscribed by law, but he was bound under pain of fine and imprisonment . . . to testify on oath where and when he heard the Mass celebrated and the names of the persons celebrating and present at it. . . . Papists were forbidden to teach school . . . or send their children to foreign countries to be educated under penalty of disability to sue in law, or to be guardian, executer, or to take a legacy or a deed or a gift or bear office, and forfeit goods and lands for life.[6]

Of course, the Irish people found ways to celebrate the rites of their Catholic faith and discovered means for the giving and receiving of Catholic instruction as well as other subject matter. Penal times, "the hard years," were described by parents and grandparents in the Carroll home.

> The people worshipped God in mud-hovels, under mass bushes and beneath the friendly shelter of pillar stones. Illiteracy was more common among them than ignorance, and yet, in a quiet way, they had been most persistent law-breakers in the article which made it felony or death for the Irish Catholic to teach or learn.[7]

The thirst for "learning was so strong that there were hundreds of hedge schools in which Latin and 'figures' were the principal branches taught."[8] This was the era of William's parents or Margaret's grandparents, and theirs were the clandestine classes of the hedge and ditch schools.

When the government decided to offer rewards to each captor of a Catholic teacher, educational life in a way became a game — with the "popish masters" and their students as the hares and the fanatic priest-hunters as the hounds.[9] Pupils, alert to the danger of a stranger on the road, must have taken turns serving as "lookout." Their senses alive with the excitement, students may well have experienced a sharpening of intellectual aptitude. In any case, both schools and scholars thrived. "It is impossible not to admire and venerate a race which displayed such inextinguishable love of science and letters," stated Cardinal Newman.[10] It almost seemed that the harsh laws of the penal code strengthened the appreciation of the Irish for learning. That was certainly the case in the family of Margaret Carroll. They had set their priorities for several generations before her arrival. Like her father in his turn, they placed education second only to fidelity to the Catholicity of their forefathers.

William Carroll was born in the Ballynahinch which lies in the shadow of the great Rock of Cashel. He was born in 1795,[11] a dozen years after the prejudicial laws of the penal code began to be changed. The Relief Act of 1782 finally brought a minimal measure of relaxation with regard to the stringent laws against Catholic education.[12] Under the new rules a Catholic might teach legally once he fulfilled two requirements. He had to take an oath of allegiance and also acquire a license from the Church of Ireland Vicar or, more likely, his representative in the vicinity. These regulations were partially responsible for the increase in Catholic schools. William's school, like the Carroll forebears, was probably situated in the area of Cashel or Thurles, but uncertainty shrouds the exact location.

A fact that is quite certain, however, is that William was noted throughout his long life for an extraordinary knowledge of the faith.[13] This implies that heading the curriculum of whatever school he attended was Christian Doctrine. His later business successes would certainly indicate that he had a thorough grounding in such essentials for a tradesman as grammar and mathematics. Tradition adds that he was well versed in several languages.[14] Be that as it may, he undoubtedly knew all the nuances of the language of supply and demand. His first enterprise was located in the port of Waterford, where success crowned both his business ventures and his suit for the hand of the gracious and lovable Margaret Mary Strahan.

William Carroll and Margaret Mary Strahan were married on March 3, 1829, in St. Patrick's Church in the city of Waterford,[15] and the celebrant for the marriage was none other than the bishop of the diocese, Right Rev. Dr. Patrick Kelly.[16] The wedding ceremony had enough éclat or the participants enough lineage to rate an announcement on the front page of the *Waterford Chronicle* that week.[17] The youthful couple must have enjoyed their years in Waterford because it was home to many family connections like the Murphys, O'Keefes, Nagles, and Fitzgeralds. Several of these, along with friends like the Burkes, Walshes, Reids, and Brophys, acted as sponsors for the Carroll children baptized in Waterford. The three oldest of the nine children born to William and Margaret Mary were all carefully registered at baptism in the massive volumes of the Cathedral of the Holy Trinity in Waterford. Father Dixon, one of the curates of Trinity Within,[18] baptized the eldest son on March 29, 1830. The baby, Michael James, did not survive infancy, and the grief-stricken mother confided her memories of this first-born "laid beneath the grey willows" to her namesake Margaret years later.[19] Father Dixon also officiated at the baptisms of the second child, John Mary, on September 19, 1831, and the third, Catherine Mary, on May 22, 1833.[20] This first little girl would be called Katy by the family.

William seems to have moved his family to Clonmel in 1834. The exact date would have fallen somewhere between Catherine's birth in mid-1833 and Margaret's in early 1835. In any case, the couple was settled in well before February 23, 1835,[21] the birthday of Margaret Anne, the second daughter who was destined as Mary Austin to do magnificent work for God in the Institute of Mercy. According to local custom, the new baby was carried to the parish church for baptism on the day following her birth. This was the first child of William and Margaret Mary to be baptized in St. Mary's in the Irishtown section of Clonmel. The pastor himself, Rev. John Baldwin, performed the ceremony that February 24, 1835.[22] Immediately thereafter, this event and the names of the sponsors or godparents, Maurice Donahoe and Julia Denny, were faithfully recorded for posterity.

William's family, like his businesses, continued to thrive and prosper in Clonmel. Four-year-old Margaret had a sister who was baptized Johanna on February 12, 1839. Two years later Margaret witnessed the christening of William Francis on January 31, 1841. Mary and Anne, Margaret's youngest sisters, were the next arrivals, with Mary baptized on May 7, 1843, and Anne on December 20, 1846. Patrick, the ninth and last child in William's family, was born in 1849.[23] Eighteen sponsors were needed for the children of William and Margaret Mary. That was a dozen and a half, but County Tipperary, even more than Waterford, was native turf peopled by many family connections in the 1830s and 1840s. There were Strahans in Ballycormack, Carrolls in Lisroon, Nagles in Cahir, and some of each in Clonmel.[24] Just a score of Irish miles down the road from Waterford, the family was able to stay in touch with the relatives and friends there also. At the same time, Clonmel neighbors named Ryan, Everard, Guiry, Cantwell, Egan, and Cleary began to serve as godparents, too.

Only one of Margaret's four brothers was to outlive her. Michael James had died as an infant, William and Patrick were to die as young men, and John alone would carry the family name onward. John found his career in the civil service in England, where he and wife, Jenny, reared three children — Charles, Maureen, and young John.[25] At the time of Margaret's death, John and his grown sons were residing in Liverpool.[26] William Francis, the brother affectionately called Willie, was probably Margaret's favorite. He entered the military service of Great Britain and drew an assignment in India. Unfortunately, the young soldier contracted tropical fever which caused his death there. Shortly after the news of his untimely early death reached Margaret, by then in New Orleans in the early 1870s, she received the following note of condolence.

> I need not tell you how grieved I was to hear of poor Willie's death. You must have felt it greatly. I do remember well how fond you were of him. Somehow, it always seems as if we loved the one who is taken away more than all who are left behind.[27]

Heightening Margaret's grief were two considerations — this was the first death in the immediate family in her lifetime and, also, she was separated by an ocean of distance at the time from those whom she most wished to console.

As events happened, this death was the forerunner of two more soon to follow. On December 3, 1875, Margaret's mother, Margaret Mary Strahan Carroll, died rather suddenly, even though Willliam had seen his wife's strength gradually ebbing away for some years.[28] Mrs. Carroll's death was not unprepared, for it occurred one morning immediately after husband and wife returned home from daily Mass. The unexpectedness certainly caused her namesake in New Orleans to feel it more intensely. Patrick, the youngest of the children, "quickly followed" his mother to the grave.[29] Margaret's sympathy went out across the waves to her elderly father. The old gentleman, in his eighties at the time, had lost his wife and two sons within a four-year period. Earlier, his wife had hoped that Patrick would be the family priest, but perhaps she was solaced by the fact that four of her daughters — Margaret, Katy, Johanna, and Anne — dedicated their lives to God as religious women. Before noting the adult life of the Carroll girls, it might be well to see Margaret and her sisters as youngsters.

Among Margaret's earliest recollections was her parents' teaching that "the Divine Child lived in my heart and that He would stay there forever, if I did not drive Him out." Although this thought stayed with her, she was carried away now and again by her mischievous spirits until she felt the pangs of correction. But no matter how much she had fallen from parental grace on a given day, there was always full pardon before time for bed — a kiss from her Mama and a "fond father's hand rested in benediction on my head."[30] The Carroll children knew that they could keep Christ in their hearts even when they were being naughty. Basking in this gentle, caring love of her family, Margaret grew in age — sturdy in body, strong in pride and determination, quick in mind, mischief, and laughter. Nurtured by her parents' deep faith and generous charity, she also grew in openness to God. Wisdom was to come much later, both through the acquisition of experience and "as good an education as Ireland had to offer."[31]

Margaret later attended several schools, but her first teachers were her parents. When she was still a pre-schooler, Margaret's father evidently realized how bright she was. Hence, he related the history of Ireland and the Carroll ancestors in short tales for her, thus fostering her predilection for both history and literature. There was the O'Kerbhail or O'Carroll prince of Eli, which covered part of Ballybrit, Clonlish, and the present barony of Lower Ormond in County Tipperary. The O'Carroll sept, progenitors of many barons, were the Lords of LochLain who ruled for four centuries as history was made from Birtown Castle down through the plains of the Golden Vale. O'Heerin referred to these O'Carrolls as "the powerful lords to whom great men submit."[32] Even so, the family crest illustrated the Carroll submission to God with their escutcheon motto: "Staunch in faith and strong in war."[33] Margaret truly loved her father's patriotic tales and was never to outgrow either her flair for literature or her partiality for history.

Comparatively little is known of the Waterford period of William Carroll's family, but once they moved to Clonmel quite the opposite is true. Besides assisting the proprietor of the grain mill there, William also maintained his own flour shop in Clonmel's Irishtown. The sturdy Carroll home on Bolton Street in the center of the thriving town still does good service as a family dwelling. The building wears its age as proudly as many others of the same vintage in the "quaint streets and flowery suburbs of the old town," which Margaret wrote, "had triple walls battered by Cromwell and the hireling troops of Orange William."[34] In such a locale it takes more than a century to make a structure ancient. Strong and neat in appearance, the two-story Bolton Street home amply provided space for the growing family. And because the walled town had been compact, it is easy to trace the various routes that Margaret and other children took as they ran errands in and about the old city.

To attend school, the children had a five-minute walk down Queen Street and Western Road. To make a purchase in the shops in town, they went a square and a half southward to High Street. To reach the parish church, they passed through that relic of the old wall called the West Gate. And it stood then as it stands now, legs arched over the main thoroughfare. Several streets beyond the gate was the old chapel from the penal days, which "rose within a few feet of the Suir, was surrounded by shade trees, and commanded a beautiful view of hill and dale, pasture and moorland." Margaret went on to state that "My earliest and fondest memories" clung to the old chapel with its floor the bare ground because "it was a link between the times of persecution and those of peace." Even the grandest city churches awakened in her "no greater sentiment of reverential awe than devotions in the old chapel so beautifully situated vis-a-vis with the loveliest isles of the Suir."[35] Then she saw all this transformed as she herself changed from tot to rambunctious schoolgirl.

The first meetings to plan the new church, St. Mary's, were held in 1836, when Margaret was just a year old, and its generously proportioned walls grew taller through the years even as she did. Rev. John Baldwin and his curate, Rev. Patrick Meaney, saw the church completed in 1850; and thanks to the overwhelming generosity of the parishioners, the funds for construction kept pace with the builders. Although Margaret bemoaned the loss of "the trees that almost hid the chapel, all cut down to make room for the spacious new edifice," she lauded the beauties of the tessellated ceiling and the magnificent marble altar.[36] "Beautiful scenery is rendered doubly beautiful by hallowed associations," Margaret said as she fondly described the geographical setting of her beloved hometown.

> Clonmel, Vale of Honey, nestles in the windings of the silvery Suir, with the Mount of Fair Women on the north and the Waterford Hills on the south. From every one of its bridges and every opening of its ancient streets, one sees green hills, pleasant gardens, fragrant meads, and fair trees whose branches kiss the crystal river.[37]

This was the scene Margaret admired daily on her way to school. For elementary classes she attended the Cannings' School, which was situated just a square from her home. The two Misses Cannings taught in their large home on Mary Street, and the school was considered both private and Catholic.[38] Margaret obtained an excellent foundation as the teachers were quite strict, yet experienced at the same time the dual joy of friendship and scholarship. "I was taught to store up useful erudition, . . . but my mind was not cultivated at the expense of my heart."[39] Like youngsters the world over, however, Margaret had her school troubles and her "bad days," also, as she recalled,

> If I happened to think my teachers too severe, and desired to change them for more lenient ones, my father used to tell me that it is a great advantage for young people to meet with superiors who are strict and insist on their improvement, and who even misunderstand, contradict, or falsely accuse them occasionally, because such little annoyances are excellent preludes to the great battle of life.[40]

On more than one occasion in subsequent years, this advice of her wise parental mentor was to serve as one of Margaret's bulwarks against discouragement.

The Carrolls, like other Catholics of the merchant class, invested their income in their businesses, shops, and mills. Hence, if one concentrated only on cash flow, William and Margaret Mary Carroll might not have been tremendously rich, yet they were absolutely affluent in faith and piety and vastly wealthy in virtue. And even though she often did not care for some rule or regulation in her home, Margaret realized how fortunate she was to have her own particular parents. As a young girl she said, "Good parents are, beyond comparison, the greatest of earthly blessings."[41] In a book dedication written twenty years after she left home, Margaret gave public testimony to the influence of her mother and father,

> who still retain as in childhood, the first place in my affection and esteem; whose unobtrusive sanctity and unvarying tenderness have inspired their children with a degree of reverence and love which time and distance but intensify, . . . these pages are affectionately dedicated with the certainty that . . . they will shed a new joy on their declining years.[42]

This dedication was penned in 1869, but Margaret's parents were in their prime in most of her reminiscences of family scenes. In the evening after supper, for instance, her Mama generally heard the children recite their catechism and often enlivened the lessons with stories about the saints. It was Margaret who would pop up with a question at each pause in the action. Then the lively little Willie sent all the others into such gales of laughter with his clowning and inept answers that his mother "adopted for a while the plan of teaching him alone . . . careful never to laugh at his drolleries if they had any reference to sacred subjects."[43] Margaret's favorite brother Willie was filled with a natural generosity and affection just as she was. His sister appreciated these qualities in the youngster, but also felt a special kinship with his mischievous gaiety. Always fun-loving herself, Margaret had a quick sense of humor and a ready wit even at school. A childhood friend, recalling classes shared with Margaret, termed her spirit of fun irrepressible. This probably did not make her the most popular student with the teachers, but her loyal friends were legion. Her classmate adds, "How we did enjoy life then!"[44] Another friend later wrote of Margaret, "Being exceptionally bright and talented, Margaret advanced rapidly in all her studies, but was especially proficient in music."[45] Another might have said languages and history, but Margaret herself seldom alluded to her intellectual gifts.

On the other hand, she was most willing to brag about an encounter with the Great Liberator, Daniel O'Connell himself. There could be no doubt of her nationality as she related the event.

> In his journeys through Ireland, O'Connell nearly always visited the schools on his route. On these occasions his reception was a kind of ovation . . . and addresses were read by the pupils. To a young girl who had

delivered a flattering address, he said very graciously that he regretted that her sex precluded her from the distinguished place in the senate to which her elocutionary abilities entitled her. Then, glancing at the girls who surrounded the oratress, he continued with emotion: ". . . You shall be free; you shall not become the mothers of slaves; your country shall yet be a nation!" It is unnecessary to add that the children who listened to this outburst of patriotism became Repealers on the spot.[46]

Since the author keeps her secret, there is no way of knowing if she were the honored speaker or just one of the "repealers."

Margaret obtained her "normal school," or teacher training in the Clonmel National Model School. Erected quite near her home, the school was opened in 1849, and she enrolled that first year. Like many other schools across Ireland, this one was established under Lord Stanley's Board of Commissioners for Education. His Grace, Dr. Daniel Murray, the archbishop of Dublin, together with many other Irish bishops, welcomed the plan because it entitled Catholics "to enjoy the blessings of education"[47] without any danger of proselytism. Dr. John McHale of Tuam, however, denounced the plan even as Daniel O'Connell hailed it as the greatest step forward since the Catholic Relief Bill. In such towns as Clonmel, where parents were alert to their rights under the new system, Daniel Murray and Daniel O'Connell were probably correct in their estimate of the value of the National Board. Yet vigilance was needed to maintain the justice of the original plan. School readers, for instance, were later published containing anti-Catholic literature. Immediately the parents in Clonmel objected to the use of such books as an infringement of their religious rights, and in the face of this vocal opposition, the local Inspector thought it the better part of valor to ban the texts. Thus, while the Irish bishops formally objected in 1850 to the anti-Catholic readers sent to many schools, the Catholic students in Clonmel continued to receive a fine non-partisan education.[48]

Margaret's sisters, also, were enrolled in turn in the preparatory classes and the final National Teacher Course, both offered in the National Model School. With the teacher certification the young women were able to hold good positions for a time before choosing their lifelong endeavor. Two of the Carroll girls opted for marriage and gave their parents grandchildren closer to their Clonmel home than John's trio in England. Mary was the fourth daughter of William Carroll, one of the many descendants from those "Lords of LochLain" who ruled the Golden Vale. Mary added more historical lineage to her children's ancestry by marrying Charles Patrick Byrne, son of Gerald Byrne and grandson of centenarian Charles Byrne of Sleaty near Carlow. This Byrne Family could trace a direct ancestral line from the great Irish King of Leinster, Fiach MacAoidh O'Bryne. Genealogists know just how often they meet such royalty as they trace Irish-American lines, for it certainly abounds in Ireland.[49]

Most of the progeny of Margaret's parents, approximately one hundred twenty in various parts of the world in the 1980s, are also the descendants of Charles Patrick Byrne and Mary Carroll. Four of their seven children — Willie, Charles, Joseph, and Clare died without offspring. The other three, however, Gerald,[50], Mary,[51], and Margaret Mary,[52] each married, put down roots, and added branches to the family tree. Anne Carroll, the youngest of Margaret's sisters, married James Cleary in St. Mary's Church in Clonmel in 1872. In great contrast to Mary Carroll Byrne's large family and numerous descendants, Anne had only one little girl who did not marry. For a time the Cleary couple lived in Clonmel with family members close, but they left County Tipperary about 1880 and moved to the United States. There Anne's husband and little daughter Mary died relatively young, and Anne joined the Sisters of Mercy in New Orleans in 1885.[53] Her story thereafter as Sister Mariana, the name she received along with the habit of the Sisters of Mercy, mingles with that of her sister Margaret, Mother Austin by then, in New Orleans and Mobile on the Gulf Coast.[54]

Before settling Margaret and her sisters into their life's work as Sisters of Mercy and followers of Catherine McAuley, there are two cameo appearances of Margaret which her devoted family have bequeathed to the reader. Both concerned Margaret's ability to "speak out" when she felt that the occasion demanded it, and the first incident also involved historical accuracy. Through the years since her father had given her the first delightful taste of Irish history, Margaret had added volumes both at home and at the Cannings' School. She both expanded the scope and pursued with intensity her real penchant for history until she became quite expert. During a history session at normal school, one of Margaret's teachers made an error, "which Margaret, who was good at history, corrected. The teacher was, naturally, I suppose, annoyed and afterwards referred to her as 'Margaret Carroll, the Historian.' "[55] Other youngsters in the class enjoyed the event and brought it home to the Carroll family, but there is no record of the young scholar's reaction. Probably, after the indignation over the historical error wore off, she enjoyed the whole occasion as much as her classmates.

One final view of Margaret, a last cameo appearance before she leaves her home and family, presents her strength and courage under fire even more than the ability to speak out. And the incident is the more remarkable because she was only about twelve at the time. It happened, according to the family records, during the 1846 season of potato blight. The townspeople had not been seriously affected as yet, but the farmers across the whole countryside began to find their crops a loss. One day as Margaret and a number of friends were playing outside William Carroll's Flour Shop at 17

Irishtown, a group of teenagers came into town to raid the provision stores. As the noisy band of young people approached, all the children except the Carroll youngster fled to safety. Dauntless Margaret Anne Carroll not only stood her ground, but also had the audacity to talk the youths into bypassing her father's shop. While several newspapers in the United States carried items concerning the thefts of provisions in Waterford and Cork, or a report of the "Food Riot in County Tipperary," the press seems to have completely missed the story of just how the William Carroll Shop escaped the looters.[56]

Although the facts about Margaret's courageous stand are still carefully stored among the other treasures of the family heritage, a good part of the girl's success in the adventure was most certainly due to her father. It is only fair to mention that William's charity to the needy of the area was so consistent and generous that he had in all likelihood already aided the families of the looters. As Margaret often served as a messenger for these regular benefactions from her father, she may have brought this to the attention of the excited youths that day. Somehow, what she said to turn the group away was not preserved, but repeatedly through the years numerous comments were recorded by witnesses of the exceptional social consciousness and conscientious charity of her father. These qualities, together with his piety, became his distinguishing characteristics. One record states, "He was remarkable for his piety and extraordinary charity for the poor. He was a daily communicant when such a wonder was rare. His charity to the poor was so great that he often returned home minus boots and stockings."[57]

Undoubtedly, Margaret acquired her special appreciation of Irish history and her pride in her native land from her father. But even more than these gifts, she received from him a deep compassion for, even an alertness to the needs of, the poor and suffering. Her frequent service as courier during the famine years, when her father sent out from the shop a steady stream of sustaining packages of meal and flour, might have been of great influence in her decision to serve the poor as a religious. Years later a friend would sum up the influence of Margaret's parents upon her with the brief comment: "They taught their children to love virtue and to be kind and generous to the poor and sick."[58] William Carroll had a long life, and Katy wrote Margaret at its close,

> Our poor dear Father got very ill just before Christmas on the cold frosty mornings. Just imagine him on his way to church at five o'clock a.m. in very severe weather though the first Mass would not be until seven. . . . [Then Katy's letter was interrupted for several days.] When I had written the foregoing, I little thought our beloved and saintly Father was so near his end. He died a death worthy of his life on Friday the 7th [of January

1887]. . . . He was a Franciscan Tertiary and was laid out in the brown habit and cord of St. Francis and looked beautiful in death. We have a saint in heaven to intercede for us. . . . Many are praying to him already, but surely he will do more for us than for all the others. His saintly example for more than half a century has drawn many to serve God. . . . May we henceforward not be unworthy of such a father.[59]

Margaret, like Katy, believed that their father was a saint. An obituary mentioned the remarkable intellectual ability of the "venerable and patriotic Irishman,"[60] but neglected to record his generosity to the needy. Margaret noted this for she was closely akin to him in mentality and patriotism, and especially like him in charity toward the poor. Forty years before his death she had been attracted to the benevolent activities of a new group of religious. Sisters of Mercy, followers of Catherine McAuley of Dublin, spread out across the famine-ridden countryside in the wake of the potato blight. Thereafter, notices such as the following became commonplace in the papers, and it seems highly unlikely that Margaret with her compassionate nature was left unaffected by them. Of course, the style is the highly rhetorical mode that was ordinary press fare at the time.

Thousands would have perished unvisited had not the Sisterhood of Mercy blessed the poor with their presence and attention. For the last year and the dreary months of this calamitous one, hundreds would have starved in their pestilential garrets but for the unwearying vigilance of these handmaidens of Heaven. Prostrate from sickness, enfeebled by want, wretched, ragged, and unvisited by others, the poor have received from them food, fire, raiment, and relief, and passed from this earth to another world soothed and sustained to the last moment by their aid — or lived to signalize their Charity.[61]

The Sisters of Mercy had high visibility in Clonmel by the time that Margaret was sixteen because they were working in nine towns within a fifty-mile radius of the Carroll home. Mercy convents were flourishing in a regular circle about Clonmel, in Carlow, Wexford, Waterford, Cobh, Cork, Mallow, Charleville, Limerick, and Birr.[62] The work of these "walking nuns" caught Margaret's attention to such an extent that she was soon to become one of them, and led three of her sisters into the same community. Katy was the first to follow Margaret to the Convent of Mercy in Cork, entering at St. Maries of the Isle on the feast of Our Lady of Mercy in 1854 when Margaret was a novice. Katy received the Mercy habit and her name, Mary of Mercy, the following January, then professed her vows in March of 1857. Sister Mary of Mercy taught in Cork for a dozen years before being sent on a new foundation in 1865. Besides teaching at the new house, St.

Joseph Convent of Mercy in Passage West, County Cork, Mary of Mercy was the Mistress of Novices. A frequent correspondent of Margaret's throughout her life, Katy's last letter was dated January 6, 1887 — less than a week before her sudden death. Her obituary read,

> The deceased religious, like all of her remarkable family, was endowed with intellectual gifts of a high order; and was, moreover, a model of the religious virtues. Her dedication to the education of youth, to the succouring of the poor, and the comforting of the sorrowful was notable, even for a Sister of Mercy.[63]

One of Margaret's Clonmel classmates had written her some years prior to the death of Katy, confiding that she had always pictured Katy as the "Canticle of Canticles" because of her joyful disposition. She also confessed that she considered that the "Miserere" was especially appropriate for Johanna, Margaret's next sister to become a nun. Probably, Johanna had tagged after the older girls as a youngster and been as unwelcome as such tag-along siblings usually are in any country. Following the older girls to Cork, also, she entered in 1857, was received as Mary Dominica, and became a vowed religious in 1859. Because Johanna had trained at Cabra to teach the sign language,[64] she found her lifework when Cork opened a school for the deaf in September of 1858. Sister celebrated her golden jubilee in 1909, her sixtieth anniversary in 1919, and her advent into the eternal Mercy community on May 12, 1921, at the age of eighty-two.[65]

Religious were such an ordinary occurrence in this Levitical family that it was considered the normal everyday thing for four sisters in the William Carroll family to become members of a religious community. From the earliest generations of Margaret's family right down to the present, so many aunts, uncles, and dozens of cousins served as religious that there are far too many to list — except for one special "connection."[66] These were Margaret's favorite cousins, Marguerite and Jane Nagle. Their mother was Mary Jane Byrne, their father a grandnephew of Nano Nagle, the saintly foundress of the Presentation Nuns. In fact, he was named Garrett for Nano's own father. Margaret had such admiration for Nano's work for the poor that she was perfectly delighted to have the family connection, even though she and Nano were several generations apart.[67] Margaret Carroll and Jane and Marguerite Nagle had a special affinity and affection, and correspondence kept the trio close for a lifetime. Jane joined the Religious of the Sacred Heart and spent over sixty years as a nun, in England and Ireland for several decades, then on the foreign missions in Argentina and Chile. Like Margaret Carroll, she served others for a lifetime.[68]

So numerous were the relatives who served God as priests, prelates and religious that Margaret once wrote that there "was scarcely a convent in the south of Ireland which has not been aided" by relatives either as members, donors, or chaplains. Besides the Sisters of Mercy thus assisted, Margaret mentioned on other occasions relatives who were Presentation Nuns, Christian Brothers, Jesuits, Religious of the Sacred Heart, Dominicans, and Franciscans. Margaret knew personally innumerable religious aunts, uncles, and cousins, sometimes remarking upon certain ones as administrators or writers.[69] The greater number, however, simply spent themselves on the home or foreign missions for the people of God. With this kind of background in the family, it is not strange that the same trend has continued among Margaret Carroll's nieces and nephews, grandnieces and nephews, and even the great-grandnieces and nephews.[70] With the next generation as yet too young to select a pathway in life and the earlier generations hidden in the haze of time, any collection of specific statistics will be left to God's accountants. When teenager Margaret was ready to choose a particular religious congregation in which to spend her life, she certainly examined those in which her aunts and cousins served. Yet her eyes kept focusing on the Sisters of Mercy who worked to improve the conditions of the poor. The works of mercy caught Margaret's attention and Catherine McAuley her heart.

2 TRAINING FOR MERCY SERVICE
Cork, Ireland
1853–1856

Although Margaret Carroll left no autobiography among her works, it is quite easy to follow her footsteps through the ancient lanes of Irish town and the dusty streets of the Irish Channel, or to find her footprints in the New England snow as well as in the New Orleans silt. To discover her spiritual trek is much more difficult as she, like many another quarry of the "Hound of Heaven," passed through a maze of ways as she spent herself for others. Intimate acquaintances of Margaret probably gave a few hints as they repeatedly noted as her distinguishing characteristics: a compassionate kindness, an all-embracing charity, and a truly prodigal generosity. These traits are more hidden than the bright intellect and fun-loving nature that casual observers saw. Several friends spoke in typical hyperbole of Margaret in her teens, "Her future prospects were brilliant in the extreme, and her coming life looked like a long summer's day. But her mind's eye, undazzled by the flitting lights of the world, penetrated to the unchanging glories of the future."[1] Friends also described her idealism just at the time that she planned her lifework.

> Her heart soared to higher aims. She resolved to forego the world's promises and to dedicate her life to God. . . . She selected as the sphere of her labors the Order of Mercy . . . because the members devoted their lives to the service of God's poor.[2]

More than one congregation served the poor, however, and Margaret certainly knew of Nano Nagle's Presentation nuns, where she had six close relatives, and Mary Aikenhead's Sisters of Charity who performed the works of mercy. Margaret mentioned both in her biography of Catherine McAuley, and the book might also present the reason for the choice Margaret made. One factor in Catherine's aims is presented much more frequently than the others of the three special works: education of poor girls, care of the sick, and the protection and instruction of needy women. The third aim clearly demonstrated that these disadvantaged women were to be given instructions in both religion and work skills. The latter would enable them to support themselves and their families because disease and involvement in political conflict frequently left the whole family dependent upon the earnings of the women of the home. Catherine McAuley did not merely hand out money. Instead she hoped to assist the women to raise their own standard of living as a permanent measure. Catherine's assistant in working out the Mercy Rule, Rev. Myles Gaffney,[3] stated in his early history of Catherine McAuley and the Mercy Institute that the education of the poor was most valuable because of "the means which it affords them of improving their condition in the world."[4] Surely Catherine's trusted advisor understood her aims and intentions, and most certainly, this facet of the work of the Mercy Institute greatly impressed Margaret Anne Carroll. Whether or not it was the deciding factor in her choice, however, only Margaret would know.

Although Margaret did not offer the key to unlock the door to her spiritual life, she occasionally allowed a peek through the keyhole, as it were, to reveal in small measure the Source of her compassionate zeal and driving energy. "Love is the only key that can give us access to happiness in this world and heaven in the next." Or, "Kindness is the greatest of all apostles, the most eloquent of all preachers, and the surest road to happiness and holiness."[5] This is the road that teenage Margaret decided to take, in hopes that it would lead her to the proverbial pot of gold, the elusive goal of holiness. Nurtured in a family singled out by their deep piety, Margaret knew that they would joyfully accept her decision in spite of the natural sorrow her departure would cause. Once she had made her decision, Margaret herself embraced it with all the munificent generosity so natural to her. Liberality was of the essence in the William Carroll family—liberality to both God and man. Margaret's mother had prayed for years for religious vocations for some of her "jewels," as she liked to call her children. Perhaps as the "pearl" among the gems, Margaret was the first to choose a life of vowed service to God's people.

Like other aspects of her genealogical heritage, Margaret's faith contained the diverse elements common to southeast Ireland. Fiery Gaelic asceticism, along with other facets of the national culture, had bonded to the more formal piety of the Anglo-Normans. Historians vividly relate the glorious, and often gory, conflict with which the fusion of cultures was accomplished. Attesting to the fact that the bonding was not always through violence was the apartheid law which mandated separate villages for the Gael and the Norman. Remnants of this historical anomaly can be seen today in the numerous "Irishtowns" extant beyond the medieval walls of many older cities throughout Ireland. Just such a site was the Irishtown near the old wall of Clonmel, so dear to Margaret's heart. Yet to enter religious life, she deliberately chose to leave Tipperary. As a child she had treasured her father's tales of Irish heroes and Carroll ancestors. As a young woman, her choice to serve God's people afar was a much keener sacrifice because of her patriotism. Like the fibers of her being, this love of her land was woven of the proud warp of family ancestry and the loyal woof of Irish history.

People of other ages and other nations might find it difficult to fathom the depth of Margaret's feelings or to see her visualization of a portrait combining love and pride for her God, her family, and her homeland. Yet, Pope Leo XIII considered love of country and Church "twin forms of charity springing from the same eternal principle, for of both the author and cause is God."[6] As Margaret prepared to relinquish forever both her hearth and her homeland, she expressed her love equally for "Ireland's bright, sad past and its stirring present. . . . Not a country in all the world appeals to the poetry of one's nature or to the affection and imagination"[7] as Ireland does. Once Margaret decided on her vocation, her love of neither family nor country could deter her. After all, the decision to leave home and heartland was the additional test passed by each and every Irish missionary from time immemorial. Margaret simply gathered all her lovely memories in her heart, where faith and ancestry and history were interwoven into a single fine tapestry to be cherished as long as her heart would beat.

Margaret certainly felt keenly, also, the final parting from her circle of friends. Thirty years later one of her closest classmates, Sister Juliana Purcell, reminisced, "I feel as if I never got over that lonely home-coming when I parted from you."[8] And Margaret herself recalled an overwhelmingly happy childhood in company with friends who "divided their time between books and fun, . . . friends who were frank, bright, engaging, . . . honorable, truthful, but not particularly pious."[9] Quite possibly Margaret's concept of piety was heightened by the example of her parents' asceticism, for she led six of her schoolmates into religious life, four of them into Catherine McAuley's Institute of Mercy.[10] Margaret's sorrow at leaving her affectionate companions was keen, but sharper pangs were hers as she bid her family farewell.

Her departure was to wrench the first arc from the family circle, and the loving sensitivity of her parents filled the void by fostering in each child the deepest appreciation of both Margaret's generous heart and her precocious mind. As to the Carroll children—each goodbye was different. Margaret might have sent a note to John who was away at school, and had a huge embrace for twelve-year-old Willie struggling mightily to hold back the tears. But torrents of tears would have presented no problems for Johanna and the little girls. Johanna might have enjoyed a hearty cry as adolescents do, even as she felt ready to step into her popular sister's shoes. Then Mary, all of ten, and her shadow, Anne at seven, were likely to have found the leave-taking at once sad and exciting. And the talk of a future visit to Cork to see Margaret "take the veil" would have immediately evaporated their tears. All the hugging and laughing and crying was more than likely a source of amusement to pre-schooler Patrick. Secure in his lifetime experience of five happy years as the pet of the whole family, the chubby youngster probably enjoyed all the noise and commotion without really understanding the cause. The sister closest in age and heart to Margaret was her friend and confidante, Katy; and the two girls are very likely to have exchanged their adieux in private before the final gathering began that December 7th in 1853.

Farewells over, William and one of the clan's clergymen, and perhaps Katy also, escorted aspirant Margaret to the Convent of Mercy in Cork, where the practical arrangements would have been completed a fortnight earlier. The coach, Bianconi's of course, would have run the usual route westward through Cahir to Michelstown, then rumbled south through Fermoy to the southern port. The convent, St. Maries of the Isle, was right on the River Lee, where the final parting was a quick one as William needed to catch the returning coach. Little did he guess that he was soon to repeat the practical arrangements about the dowery, the farewells, and the trip down to Cork with a second daughter and, again later, with a third. The three eldest daughters of Margaret Mary Strahan and William Carroll were all to enter into religious life in the same convent, where the Superior was the gracious Mother Mary Josephine Warde, one of Catherine McAuley's first lieutenants.[11]

Like most of the superiors appointed by Catherine McAuley, Mother Josephine Warde was kept in the position which she fulfilled so well for the greater part of her religious life. Thus on December 7, 1853, it was she who welcomed from Clonmel young Margaret Carroll, an attractive colleen with mischievous eyes. Throughout her life Margaret was to keep the seventh, the eve of the feast of Mary Immaculate, as a day specially commemorating her entrance into the Mercy Institute. She felt, evidently, that she had made a special consecration of herself on the very day of arrival. Technically, such a commitment does not take place the day a girl walks into the cloister, and the community might even have considered her formal entrance date to be the eighth of December. As a major feast of Our Lady, it was an appropriate one on which to receive the postulant's cap, that symbol of the status of one aspiring to become a member of the Mercy Institute.[12]

Actually, in any religious congregation including the community of St. Maries of the Isle in Cork, the period of candidacy or postulancy is a period of orientation and mutual consideration. The youthful aspirant must have a chance to study the Rule and lifestyle of the particular order. Even though she hears the call of God, this might really be a beckoning toward some other type of service. During the same period the community needs a chance to decide if the qualifications and dispositions of the postulant fit her for the work to be done in the particular congregation. Regardless of all this practicality, Margaret Carroll seems to have offered her own private commitment on her initial day in the Convent of Mercy in Cork. Another important point about that first day was meeting the particular sister who was to be her superior throughout her novitiate in Cork. Margaret Carroll was of such a buoyant spirit and outgoing personality that it would be especially difficult for her to succeed under the direction of a narrow-minded or excessively rigid Mistress of Novices. But with Mary Josephine Warde as her guide, there was to be challenge and blossoming forth, not stifling — just a bit of pruning the branches and polishing the fruit.

To see how well Margaret Carroll qualified for the Mercy Institute it might be well to check out the list of requirements which Catherine McAuley enumerated as those "generally requisite for a Sister of Mercy."[13] Because of her own zealous nature and her home environment, Margaret should have rated well on the first two — "an ardent desire to be united to God and also to serve the poor." While Candidate Carroll had already had practice in these, she probably had none at all on the third — "a particular interest for the sick and dying." This she would have to acquire during her period of training, but her inexperience would vanish after a few "sick calls," as the home visitation was called. Next, the foundress looked for the postulant to "be healthy." Though slightly built, Margaret was strong in both body and will, and she often needed the latter strength to overcome periodic bouts with illness. Later, when she lived with the freezing snow of lengthy winters in New England, western New York and eastern Nebraska, she seemed to have developed an acute sensitivity to the extreme cold. Of course, this kind of weather was in great contrast to southern Tipperary's mild winters. In any case, she would not have scored as well healthwise as with the other requirements.[14]

Since Catherine McAuley hoped to receive candidates with "an impressive manner of speaking and reading," she certainly would have been delighted with the ability of that probable "oratress for the Great Liberator." This quality had become one of Margaret's fortes, thanks to a fine education and her natural talent. Lastly, Catherine McAuley listed as desirable a face "expressive of sympathy and patience," and this would have given the candidate a split decision. Margaret was keenly sympathetic and could have scored an "A" easily, as her face immediately mirrored her feelings. Since she was naturally inclined to impatience and had difficulty hiding her feelings, however, she could just as readily have rated a "D" in that category. She was certainly going to have to concentrate on acquiring patience because her impetuosity was just as much a part of her as the dimple in her chin or her dark curly hair. From personal experience Catherine McAuley knew that youth gave a tremendous advantage to any postulant. There was so much to be acquired "for a suitable manner passing through the public ways" plus the necessary "caution and prudence in the visits"[15] to the sick that it would be easier if candidates began rather young.

Blessed with the boundless energy of teenagers and a cheerful disposition which made her life lightsome, Margaret took the candidacy in stride. From day one this enthusiastic aspirant gave every evidence that she would have a successful postulancy. Evidently, she did, for the usual term of six months was shortened for her. The reason for this might simply have been that it was easier to have one ceremony for four candidates than to have two separate events just a few months apart. Whatever the reason, Margaret Anne Carroll was included with the three other postulants scheduled to receive the Mercy habit on May 16, 1854. The quartette had more than a month of special preparation during which the usual occupations, such as teaching, were taken over by others so that the young women could focus all their time and attention on their coming commitment. Then came the special day, and the entire Carroll clan probably gathered at St. Maries of the Isle to see the bridelike Margaret Anne receive the Mercy habit and her name in religion, Sister Mary Teresa Austin. This event was newsworthy enough to reach the United States, for the *Boston Pilot* contained the announcement that "Miss Lalor of Killarney, Misses Daly and Murphy of Cork, and Miss Carroll of Clonmel received the white veil on Monday the 16th."[16]

Earlier the *Cork Examiner* had published an account of the interesting ceremony attended by eight or so priests and prelates. A few of the many details include the following:

> Yesterday the touching and impressive ceremony of a reception took place at the Convent of Mercy . . . and was witnessed by a numerous and fashionable gathering of the friends of . . . the young ladies who have become aspirants for the honour of association in the deeds and virtues of this order. . . . The ceremony of reception was performed by the venerable prelate of the diocese, and a discourse of a most solemn and affecting character on the beauties of a cloister life, and the perfection . . . which may be attained therein, was delivered by the Reverend Dominick Murphy. . . . After the conclusion of the ceremony, . . . a sumptuous dejeuner was provided for the occasion.[17]

It is noteworthy that the bishop was the same William Delaney to whom Catherine McAuley referred in her letters, and the speaker was Cork's accomplished Rev. Dominick Murphy. As the biographer of Nano Nagle and the lecturer on other Irish foundresses, the Dean was an especially appropriate choice for speaker on the day that the future biographer of Catherine McAuley was received into the Mercy Institute.

If one might be allowed to speculate upon the family visit after the ceremony, it is probable that Margaret, now Mary Austin, bubbled over with joyous gaiety as she and her family enjoyed their visit. Her parents would have noticed that there was a more mature manner about her, and the younger children must have been fascinated with the transformation in appearance. Margaret seemed prettier because of the coif framing her elfin face and accentuating her rosy cheeks and happy smile. Katy would have studied her sister's expression and sparkling eyes and noted the inner contentment and deep peace. Possibly, Katy had an opportunity to confide that she, too, had decided to spend her life performing the works of mercy, for in just four months Katy joined Novice Mary Austin in St. Maries of the Isle in Cork.[18] There Margaret and Katy, along with the other young sisters in the noviceship, were gradually initiated into all the works of mercy performed by the community. These were legion in Cork. For instance, there were schools of all kinds — poor, industrial, pension, infant, primary, and secondary, plus adult catechetical instruction. The apostolate of visitation was primarily for the sick poor, but there were also visits to the gaol, the workhouse, and the hospital. Mother Mary Josephine Warde had learned from Catherine McAuley herself that Mercy was limited only by need.

This was the large view to which Mary Austin Carroll fell heir, and one of her favorite quotations was Faber's "There's a wideness in God's mercy like the wideness of the sea." Breadth of vision was only one of the many fine characteristics which Mother Josephine demonstrated regularly to the edification of the novices. Years earlier Catherine McAuley had noticed that, while Mary Josephine was "a rock as to propriety and composure," prudence and tact; she was also "full of affection."[19] No wonder that Novice Mary Austin thought her a wonderful superior and never mentioned her name without paying tribute to her. "She kept strict discipline" and could be severe about observance of the Rule, especially anything dealing with thoughtfulness for others. Yet, Mary Austin also testified that Mother Josephine "enforced the rules with all possible gentleness" and was as particular about the manners of the sisters as the Foundress herself. A sense of humor always appealed to Mary Austin, and she found one in her superior. Mother Josephine not only thoroughly enjoyed the joyfulness of others, but was even inclined to let a delinquent off easily if she came up with a witty remark. The Carroll novice had probably been just such a culprit on more than one occasion.[20]

Even as Mary Austin appreciated her superior's gentle, loving nature so did she admire Mother Josephine's outstanding executive ability, her talent and achievement having made Cork remarkable among the Mercy Institutions in Ireland. As the basis of her superior's successful administration, Mary Austin noted two points. The first was Mother Josephine's "keen appreciation of ability in her subjects, and the discrimination with which she employed each in the most fitting sphere." The second was Josephine's practice of letting all important decisions await the result of consultation and prayer, seeking the words of her sister advisors on the one hand and reflecting for several days on the word of God on the other. This system seemed to render successful the projects that Mother Josephine originated,[21] and the city of Cork enjoyed numerous works of mercy — all emanating from St. Maries of the Isle in the River Lee.

Mary Austin was no stranger to the large southern port, for the Carrolls had numerous family connections in the dioceses of both Cork and Cloyne. Mary Austin's writings give evidence that she visited relatives in more than one of the convents and monasteries in the area prior to entering the Convent of Mercy. Quite naturally, "Margaret the Historian" delighted in the historical associations there, the staunch loyalty to the church of the ancient city, and the fact that the island site of St. Maries of the Isle had been revered through the centuries. She related that the Dominican priory there gave hospitality to the ill-starred James II in 1689, but a thousand years earlier the same isle housed the monastery and witnessed the deeds of the saintly Bishop Finbar. Mary Austin delved in, thoroughly enjoyed, and presented at great length the historical Catholic background of both the city and the convent site in her Mercy *Annals*. Since their publication a century ago, so many have read Mary Austin Carroll's Mercy *Annals* and enjoyed the vivid descriptions of the magnificent Mercy Convent situated between two branches of the Lee that it need not be repeated here.[22]

Although Mary Austin admired the structure "celebrated far and near for its chaste beauty," she appreciated even more "its perfect adaptation to the purposes for which it has been erected."[23] Yet by her own accounting, she made her first contact with the Cork Sisters of Mercy in the old Rutland Street convent more than a year before she joined them. The sisters had moved into the new building on October 2, 1852. The convent was so new when Mrs. Sarah Peter, Lady Bountiful of Cincinnati, Ohio, visited in her quest for Mercy missionaries that she called it not only a "most pleasing specimen of monastic Gothic," but also "hardly completed." Like Austin herself, Mrs. Peter found the Cork superior to be "a most charming woman" even though she had no sisters to spare. Favorably impressed with the gentleness of Mother Josephine's refusal, the lady moaned, "What a pity we can not be so happy as to have them in Cincinnati." Josephine found Mercies for Mrs. Peter, however, by suggesting that she apply to the convent in Kinsale, where Mother Teresa Maher accepted the mission to Cincinnati.[24]

Sister Mary Austin missed Mrs. Sarah Peter by a mere six months. However, the novice met so many fine women during her novitiate years that she concluded God had blessed her specially by guiding her to this particular Mercy community. A number of the senior sisters had been instructed during at least a part of their noviceship by the foundress herself, for Catherine McAuley had spent three months in Cork in 1837. She then made two more visits in the two successive years. Totaling these weeks demonstrates that the Cork foundation was one of those assisted the longest by the presence of Catherine McAuley.[25] Mary Austin was thus able to get the impressions of the senior members about the foundress and to learn from them the origins of the Mercy Institute. To her great surprise, the novice saw a chronological parallel in the beginnings of her family and the Institute.

Just at the time that Catherine McAuley was building her House of Mercy in Dublin, William Carroll had established his home in Waterford. In 1829 William married, and his first child was born in 1830, when Catherine began her novitiate. In 1831, Catherine professed her religious vows and William's second infant was born. By 1833, when Katy Carroll was baptized, Catherine was training her co-workers in the religious life. In the year that Margaret Carroll was born, Rome gave its approval to the Institute of Mercy and Josephine Warde was one of the sisters taking her vows. When Margaret was a toddler in 1836 and 1837, Catherine McAuley took her Mercies to Tullamore, Charleville, Carlow, and Cork. Between the birth of Margaret's sister in 1838 and her brother in 1841, Catherine saw her followers established in Limerick, Naas, the Bermondsey District of London, Wexford, Galway, Birr, then Birmingham, England. If the foundress had met the dark-eyed Margaret Carroll, she would hardly have guessed that the lively youngster was one day to become one of her most prominent adherents and devoted biographers. In 1841 Margaret was six and could have read Catherine McAuley's obituary easily, but life rather than death probably occupied her full attention at the time.[26]

Thereafter, while Margaret was attending school, Catherine McAuley's early lieutenants carried her torch onward. Each of these co-workers like Josephine Warde, leaders of the first Mercy generation and about the age of Margaret's mother, were in turn to develop Catherine's spirit in the sisters of the next flame-bearing generation, that of Margaret Carroll. Novice Mary Austin was to be introduced to conventual life by the gently strict superior and fine administrator Josephine Warde; but it was as the close companion and friend of Catherine McAuley that Josephine was to imbue the novice with the ideals and hopes and dreams of the foundress. Anyone familiar with the Olympic symbol can easily envision the Mercy torch, afire with flaming spirit, being passed from Catherine McAuley to Josephine Warde to Austin Carroll. Later missioned by Mother Josephine to assist her sister, Frances Xavier Warde in Providence, the novice united her flame with that in Rhode Island. Austin Carroll was to serve twelve years with one or the other of the Warde sisters before she would be declared an emissary to carry Catherine McAuley's spirit down the Mississippi River to New Orleans.

As yet on the River Lee in Cork, however, Novice Mary Austin had miles to row before she was to set sail for America. During her formation days in Cork, like any good novice, Mary Austin kept busy receiving impressions. Besides those from Josephine and the other sisters who had known the foundress, the young Mercy was also affected by the advice and direction of several priests. Rev. John Pius Leahy, OP, prior at St. Dominick's and later bishop of Dromore, conducted the annual retreat in 1854. Mary Austin could recall fifty years later the depth of his lectures on the spiritual life and how they had influenced her relationship with God. Another retreat which had special impact for her was that of Rev. Dominick Murphy, "the Dean of Cork" as the vicar general was known. He was not only an eloquent preacher, but had a special interest in Catherine McAuley.[27] As a researcher of Ireland's religious orders and foundresses and the author of an earlier article on Nano Nagle, he was greatly interested in the Cork manuscript life of Catherine McAuley. This had been initiated by Sister Mary Teresa Wildridge, but left incomplete at her early death. "The Dean continued her work," explained Mary Austin a few years later, noting that "his connection with the Order as friend, benefactor, or confessor, gave him ample opportunities of learning facts connected with the foundress." His position at St. Maries of the Isle during her novitiate also made it possible for Mary Austin to get to know this author and his works.[28]

Cork has always been a literary center, and the sisters serving there, like Mary Vincent Deasy and Mary Teresa Wildridge, were among the first Mercy translators and biographers in Catherine McAuley's congregation.[29] Hence, it follows logically that the Cork novices learned of the appropriateness of literary pursuits for those spare moments between other duties and prayers in community. Although Mary Austin's first translation, that of the life of Margaret Mary Alacoque, was published only in 1867, it is highly probable that the work was begun earlier. From the number of references in Austin's preface to the people and places in and about Cork, that part of the work seems definitely to have been written on the spot—either before her entrance into the Mercy community or, perhaps, while she was in the noviceship. Undoubtedly, Mary Austin's previous inclination to literary pursuits was encouraged by the very environment at the convent which housed many of the books from the legendary library of Right Rev. John Murphy, the previous bishop of Cork.[30]

Even with Austin Carroll's interest in the works of mercy in Cork, the island community of St. Maries of the Isle, and the literary occupations, she did not become insular. Several events occurred during her noviceship which alerted her to the far-flung Mercy missions on opposite sides of the world. First a pair of visitors arrived with news of Mercy activity in New York City. Sister Mary Austin Horan accompanied Mother Mary Agnes O'Connor, superior of the New York community, in her search of a cure for her failing sight. While Mother Agnes recuperated in the Cork convent, the young sisters heard many details of the apostolic works in the huge American port. Austin Carroll's attention was riveted on the accounts of Sister Catherine Seton's prison work in the Tombs,[31] the usefulness of their sodality and circulating library, and the pastoral of Archbishop John Hughes, which stated that the 1854 collection of alms was to be distributed to the poor by the Sisters of Mercy in their "work of charity without parallel in the United States."[32] Such news enabled Mary Austin and her novice companions to appreciate the opportunities open to the Sisters of Mercy in America.

Shortly after these visitors departed for their mission to the West, community attention was directed to the East, the Near East where the Turkish border coincided with that of Russia. "The Government applied for the Sisters of Mercy to attend the sick and wounded soldiers at the Crimea, and ecclesiastical authority acceded to the request," wrote the convent annalist. Mother Vincent Whitty, superior at Baggot Street, had sent a circular seeking volunteers to nurse at the battlefront. A week after this appeal arrived Sisters Mary Paul Rice and Aloysius Hurley of Cork, "laden down with everything their dear companions imagined useful," left St. Maries of the Isle for Dublin "amid the tears, prayers, and blessings" of the professed sisters and the novices.[33] For two years the newspapers were full of details from the Eastern front. These items, along with the letters from their own sisters, kept Mary Austin and the other Mercies at home informed of the progress of this special mission of mercy—more precedent-setting than any of its participants ever dreamed.

Then, as suddenly as it began, the involvement of the Sisters of Mercy was over. The convent annalist explained: "The Crimean War being happily come to an end," the volunteers returned on May 20, 1856, to their convent in Cork where they were "joyfully and affectionately welcomed." Mary Austin was one of the senior novices when the community celebrated the safe return with "solemn Te Deums, Masses of thanksgiving, and other religious ceremonies" — and by what no novice could ever forget, "a first-class recreation day."[34] During the eighteen months that the two Cork sisters nursed on the battlelines, events had progressed normally on the home-front. Mother Josephine had instituted several new works, an industrial work-room and an infant school on Clarence Street. Even with two sisters in the East there were always enough sisters for Cork's multiplicity of works. For one thing, the number in the novitiate remained stable. When three novices took vows and moved out of the noviceship, three postulants, Katy Carroll among them, were accepted.[35] And soon to advance another rung up the ladder to profession was the senior novice, Mary Teresa Austin Carroll.

First, there was the mutual assessment and interchange, Mary Austin requesting the community to allow her to take religious vows and Mother Josephine and the other sisters approving her plea. Then there was the period of "distant retreat" in which the cessation of outside activity allowed time for meditation on the approaching life-time vows. A ten-day profession retreat followed the preliminary preparation, and judging by the copious notes which Mary Austin recorded during the time of spiritual discernment, she embraced her vowed commitment with her usual enthusiasm and zeal. Mid-summer brought the family and the profession day. Exactly two years and two months after her reception, Austin Carroll vowed poverty, chastity, and obedience and a life of Mercy service on July 11, 1856.[36] This was the day the jubilant young sister had been awaiting for two and a half years, zealously impatient to offer everything "for the greater glory of God." Mary Austin rejoiced that day in the public avowal of all that she had given in her heart the very day of her arrival in the Convent of Mercy. From this day forward "Ad majorem Dei gloriam" was her motto and the *raison d'être* for each and every good work, regardless of the location to which she was appointed.

Austin's location was soon to change, for hardly had the sister nurses returned from the East when an SOS came in from the West for sister teachers. Josephine Warde received a special appeal from her sister, Frances Xavier, in New England. It seems that Mother Xavier, as the sisters in America called her, had expanded to such an extent that she had "an urgent need of experienced members." Once again the younger sister, as she had done since childhood, turned for help to her older sister Josephine, "begging her to give or lend a few professed members." Present when the "touching letter" was read aloud for the community, newly-professed Mary Austin Carroll said "that it excited in many a burning zeal for the foreign missions." The total number of volunteers does not seem to have been recorded, but Mother Josephine announced that the selection of two missionaries would follow a period of prayer and consideration.[37] Repeatedly, the early Mercy convents noted instances in which similar appeals elicited a generous tabulation of responses. On one of these occasions Catherine McAuley expressed her joy that so many young women who were "happily circumstanced could leave their friends and country to enter on a mission so contrary to natural inclination." Attributing the great generosity of the response to the Author of all appeals, Catherine said, "The fire that Christ cast upon them is kindling very fast."[38]

In 1856 Josephine Warde saw this flame burning in a number of her sisters, but was to choose only two. The older was described by her younger companion as "a professed member of fifteen year's standing, highly educated, a brilliant musician, and very eager for the foreign missions. . . . She had been sighing for years to labor among the Indians and also to suffer martyrdom." In answer to Xavier Warde's request Mother Josephine replied that she was sending, to her "own great loss," Sisters Mary Francis Meade and Austin Carroll. The former was already known to Mother Xavier, and the latter was described as "most valuable regarding the schools, but also fully capable of any duty in the Order."[39] This assessment of the qualities of Mary Austin, Cork's most recently professed Sister of Mercy, illustrated Mother Josephine's ability to select the appropriate person for a specific assignment. With her legendary prudence and wisdom Mother Josephine knew that the talent and adaptability of young Sister Mary Teresa Austin Carroll would be tremendous assets in any new undertaking.

Josephine Warde also realized, however, that each sister chosen for the foreign missions would need intense zeal and deep spirituality. Even though Mary Austin had yet to serve her two-year term as a "black novice," the superior was confident that she would continue her precocious pace of development in the religious life. Already Mary Austin was exceptional in her assimilation of Catherine McAuley's spirit of compassion. An additional advantage was to be found in the boundless energy and "the lively and most amiable disposition" of Mary Austin, truly abounding in mercy. Although without the beauty of her fair sister Katy, now Mary of Mercy, Mary Austin attracted friends everywhere she went. Her button of a nose tilted even more during her lilting laughter.[40] Her sense of humor was keen, but no sharper than her appreciation of the feelings of others. In fact, this sensitivity was not only one of her most noticeable gifts, but also the most probable support underlying her ability to relate so readily with people of all ages and, as time was to demonstrate, of every conceivable background.

Mother Josephine's choice of missionaries might not have been announced until after the annual retreat in August. That still would have left ample opportunity for necessary preparations before the October departure for Providence, Rhode Island, and time for Mary Austin to bid her family, especially Katy, a final farewell. Also during this interval, the preliminary arrangements seem to have been completed with several promising candidates for Mother Xavier. Both of the Wardes had the grace of attracting girls to the religious life, and Mary Austin made that point quite humorously by quoting one of the County magnates, who allegedly said of Josephine,

> "That woman will not leave a bright girl in the County for a man to marry."
> "True," was the comment returned, "Madame Warde in Cork is bad enough, but she had a sister who was transported for it!"[41]

Mary Austin also explained that "Mother Xavier Warde's pen" was known to send cordial invitations far and wide to announce "the advantages of the Providence house for intending novices." Thus, chance was hardly the piper that called a number of Irish postulants to follow so closely upon the heels of the two Mercies from Cork. The leave-taking of these Tipperary aspirants was briefly recorded in the newspapers in the United States: "A number of well-dressed young girls left Clonmel" for Liverpool and the lengthy voyage to America.[42]"

The newspapers gave the facts, Mary Austin added the feelings in her *Annals*.

> The Sisters were all young, ardent, and affectionate, and keenly alive to the sorrow of parting from their dear friends . . . but never did they waver a moment. . . . Though deeply grateful to God for choosing them, there was not a dry eye . . . as they steamed away . . . leaving forever the land they loved.

As to transatlantic journeys, Mary Austin recounted for posterity many details of Xavier Warde's coterie from Carlow in the 1843 *Queen of the West*, of Agnes O'Connor's ladies from Lower Baggot Street in Dublin in the 1846 *Montezuma*, and of the nuns from Naas in the 1850 *John O'Toole*. In spite of her willingness to include even insignificant details about others, Mary Austin was inclined to be silent about her own crossing and crosses. On the other hand, she left ample evidence that the parting from Ireland was an unforgettable sacrifice, no matter how lovingly the Columban penance of perpetual exile was embraced. Again and again the *Annals* preserve that moment of poignant grief as missionary Mercies sail from the shores of their homeland.

> They leave behind parents, brothers, and sisters who love them, the friends of their youth, the companions of their riper years. . . . Can ever country become more sacred to them than that which contains the crumbling bones

of their sainted forefathers? . . . The Sisters, sustained by zeal for the glory of God and the salvation of souls . . . were ready to make any and every sacrifice for His sake.[43]

Partially responsible, along with the grace of God, was the fact that a certain amount of social grace was one of the requisites for Catherine McAuley's Mercies. The distinguished Mother Clare Moore, whose quiet dignity charmed Florence Nightingale in the Crimea, preserved the oft-quoted reminder from the foundress that "A perfect religious is a perfect lady." This social polish has even been credited to a certain extent for the speed with which the Mercy order spread. The social background of Catherine herself and "some of her early lieutenants . . . was that of the Irish gentry. They were able to give the nascent order an aristocratic cachet which had more than a little to do with its phenomenal expansion."[44] This may have been one factor in rapid growth, but newspaper items at the fiftieth anniversary of the Mercy Congregation suggested another. From publications as distant as the *London Tablet* and the *New Zealand Times* from the *New Orleans Picayune*, the press honed in upon the same point. One journalist, for example, concluded after a lengthy listing of numerous works of mercy, "This variety of functions is eminently suited to the intellectual, moral, religious, and industrial wants of a Catholic community; hence the popularity of the Order and the unexampled rapidity of its extension."[45]

So the press had noted what Catherine's letters show — the tremendous adaptability of her Institute to the needs of the place. Mary Austin realized this point, but would later be criticized roundly by those who seemed unaware that the foundress had written that: "Observances not in our Rule . . . were subject to any alteration that place or circumstances might require."[46] Catherine's spirit had been contagious for Mary Austin, and it was for others also to such an extent that psychological timing was suggested as the cause for the sweeping Mercy expansion. It was said that Catherine's compassion for the poor appealed to those awaiting just such an opportunity of serving others. It was as if "Divine Providence used Catherine McAuley to give an impulse to a movement which swelled into a mighty stream by gathering into itself the charitable yearnings of thousands of hearts."[47]

One last cause for the phenomenal rapidity was that given by and about bishops. An English prelate closely acquainted with the foundress commented, "The Institute was expressly founded for independent houses, and that is why the Bishops took it up so quickly. I was in Ireland soon after its commencement, and saw the eagerness with which it was adopted."[48] Although that reference was to the 1830s, Irish-born Andrew Byrne, Bishop of Little Rock, stated the identical reason in the 1850s for his enthusiasm for the Mercy Rule, "The Bishop of each Diocese is their only Superior under the Holy Father, and therefore, everything progresses well."[49] No matter how erroneously this idea was to be applied by bishops like John Timon of Buffalo and Augustin Verot of Savannah or St. Augustine, it seemed to persist.[50] Even in the 1870s, to look ahead for a moment, American-born William Henry Elder, bishop of Natchez, commented, "The Bishops commonly find great advantages in having Sisters who belong to the Diocese. The Bishop himself can see the wants of the various places, and choose among the Sisters those who are best suited."[51] Just as most Mercy superiors would have disagreed with this opinion, they would have been of one accord that, erroneously or not, the opinion of the bishops was certainly a factor in the spread of the congregation.

Whatever the combination of causes, Catherine McAuley's Sisters of Mercy from Ireland encircled the globe quite rapidly, reaching London in 1839, Canada in 1842, eastern United States in 1843, Australia in 1846, Scotland in 1849, New Zealand in 1850, the Pacific Coast in 1854, and South America in 1856.[52] In this year that Mary Austin herself joins the outward movement, she could say that the sun never set upon the convents of the Mercy Order. Perhaps the sisters had spread to other continents as speedily as they did because they were compelled by the mighty current of a psychological stream. Or possibly, the Mercies were propelled across an ocean, on occasion, by the velocity of an enthusiastic episcopal whirlwind. More probably, however, the followers of Catherine McAuley, like their foundress before them, were impelled by the gift of dynamic zeal from the Holy Spirit and the gentle enlightenment and loving inspiration of Christ the Divine Light.

3 PILGRIM IN NEW ENGLAND & New York 1856–1859

ister Mary Austin Carroll and her companion, Sister Mary Frances Meade, left St. Maries of the Isle in October of 1856, and crossed the Irish Sea, quite probably, in one of the fine Cork ships which regularly steamed from Cobh to Liverpool. Austin recorded that the two Mercy missionaries made only one brief stop on the journey to America, and that was a short delay in Liverpool while travel arrangements were completed. During this layover at the Mount Vernon Convent of Mercy, Mary Austin had the good fortune to meet Mother Aloysius Consitt, who had known Catherine McAuley personally. Austin, ever "the historian," discovered in this affectionate sister a primary source of information about Catherine McAuley's final weeks. Austin mentioned the fact that Mother Mary Liguori Gibson was away from Liverpool during her stopover, thus pinpointing the time of this visit to the Mount Vernon Convent just before her ocean voyage started.[1] Delighted by the cordial hospitality of the English Sisters of Mercy, excited by the new data concerning Catherine McAuley's legacy of love, and sustained by her own thirst for the salvation of souls, Mary Austin Carroll began her pilgrimage to the United States in the middle of October in 1856.

Pilgrimage it truly was because she was headed for a city just forty miles from Plymouth Rock and a scant ten miles farther from the town of Salem, Massachusetts. In the dimensions of both time and place, however, the Sisters of Mercy in Providence, Rhode Island, were nearer to the fagot-waving fanatics who burned the neighboring Ursuline convent than to the witch-searing citizens of eighteenth-century Salem. Rather than bewitching superstition, it was a wave of anti-Catholic propaganda from the Nativists that instigated the attempt at the violent destruction of the Convent of Mercy in Providence, Rhode Island. This aborted endeavor against the religious, however, stifled for a time the more rabid elements of the local

31

"United Americans," who kept their masonic secrets so well that they became generally known as the Know Nothing Party. In any case, the resulting hiatus allowed the remainder of the community to note the civic advantages of having religious serving in their town, and by the time that Mary Austin and her companion arrived from Cork, the political atmosphere had cleared somewhat in the interval.[2] The excesses of the movement, however, certainly had a negative influence upon the two Irish Mercies who had come over so enthusiastically to aid the poor in this land of opportunity.

Quite possibly, Mary Austin Carroll had previously learned of the burning of the Ursuline convent near Boston and the firing of several Philadelphia churches; but in the single year of 1854, Know Nothingism accounted for the complete or partial destruction of more than a dozen buildings from Maine to Ohio. Austin thought that the loss of property was certainly a light thing, however, when weighed against the several hundred Irish Americans maimed or killed. The Irish Sisters of Mercy were encouraged to see that the lawlessness and critical excesses of the fanatics so disgusted fair-minded Americans that the national Know Nothing candidates were roundly defeated in the 1856 presidential elections.[3] Respected political leaders and journalists had repudiated Know Nothingism from its inception. Lincoln pointed out that its aims violated the Constitution, Horace Greeley called it "that swindle," and Orestes Brownson referred to it as "contemptible prejudice." The strong prudence of such ecclesiastics as Francis Patrick Kenrick and Martin J. Spalding prevented retaliation on the part of the abused. The violence against Catholics was not that of real Americans, explained Bishop Spalding, but merely that of "unprincipled demagogues who as little represented the American people as did the mobs whom they incited to bloodshed and incendiarism."[4]

The Sisters of Mercy, along with Catholics across the country, embraced this viewpoint. And Mary Austin Carroll, after recovering from her initial shock at seeing the Know Nothing hatred, was able to admire the numerous opportunities available in the United States for the pursuit of the charitable work of the Church and the Mercy Institute. Austin pictured these favorable circumstances in her *Annals* as well as the annoyances which the Mercies endured from the anti-Catholic party. Experience has shown that young people tend to exhibit defiance while their elders are fanning their prejudices with violence, and 1856 New England was no exception.

> In their daily walks to and from the parish schools and on the visitation of the sick, insults and opprobrium were heaped upon the Sisters. The epithets which the Providence exponents of liberty and equality bestowed on them will not bear repetition. . . . Time and again the windows of their

poor dwelling were smashed, and one bright midnight the glass of every window was completely shattered.[5]

Austin thus described the battered convent to which she and Sister Frances Meade were brought upon their arrival in America that fall of 1856.

Sister Mary Austin was surprised at the intense warmth of their convent welcome in Providence until she learned that the Mercies there had feared the missionaries had been lost at sea. Such had been the fate of the Bishop of Hartford earlier that year when Bernard O'Reilly and all aboard the *Pacific* had vanished without a trace. The bishop had been a fatherly protector for the Sisters of Mercy, who still felt the shock of the tragedy. Just the preceding year the sisters had been saved from mob violence "by the courage and determination exhibited by the Catholic Bishop." Delighted with the expanding work of the fast-growing Mercy community, Bishop O'Reilly had himself recommended several postulants from his former parish in Rochester even as Mother Xavier Warde was procuring candidates from both Ireland and New York.[6] The sudden death of such a kind friend had profoundly affected the sisters, who could now rejoice that their reinforcements from Cork had not met a similar fate.

For Mary Austin and her companion who had just left Ireland, that prolific bastion of the ancient Catholic faith, some degree of culture shock was inevitable in Providence in the midst of puritanical New England during the Know Nothing turmoil. For one like "Margaret the historian," who had so reveled in the antiquities of her own country, the youth of the parish structures and the diocesan organization must have been a real surprise. Her initial comment in the *Annals* focused on this very point, as she noted that the oldest parish church in the city was begun only in the year that she was born and that the first bishop arrived almost a decade later. The expanse of the American Sees demanded missionary life so rugged that episcopal miters were transferred frequently, and Hartford witnessed the death of each of its first two bishops after just five years. Members of the Irish episcopal hierarchy, Mary Austin knew, usually experienced lengthy reigns with the assistance of generous allotments of clergy and religious. Austin quickly realized that more laborers were needed for the Lord's harvests in the United States, as early death also stalked the Mercies in these rugged missionary days. One of the Mercy teachers in Providence had died the previous spring, and that fall a second young sister was dying in the branch convent in Hartford, Connecticut.[7] Even before Thanksgiving Day arrived, Austin herself was feeling the rigors of a climate quite different from that of her home in southern Ireland.

The conditions under which the Mercy sisters taught differed vastly also, Mary Austin found, for many of the pioneer Catholic schools in

Rhode Island and Connecticut were first established in the cellars of the parish churches. Historians have referred to this period of early schools in temporary locations as the catacombic era. Actually, they were also the basement foundations of the educational structure which became one of the finest parochial school systems in the nation. The Sisters of Mercy were fortunate enough, as entrepreneurs might say, "to have gotten in on the ground floor" of the project. Even so, Austin found the classes "in close, crowded, dingy quarters" with pupils whom political unrest had made "rough and rude" to be in glaring contrast to the "bright, airy classrooms of St Maries of the Isle" filled with students whose faults were minimal.[8] Remembering the Cork school in which she had taught brought little contrast, however, when compared to that of the two convents.

Since the two newcomers, Sisters Mary Austin and Frances Meade, were fresh from the grandest Convent of Mercy in Ireland, they certainly had to find their New England home "a cradle of poverty." Sleeping quarters for all were in the attic dormitory, which "was freezing in winter and scorching in summer." Even so, sleeping arrangements did not provide as much contrast to their former home as did the size of rooms like the chapel and the novitiate. From the contrasting details in the *Annals* it is quite obvious that Austin missed her former community of sisters, the pupils there, and even St. Maries of the Isle itself; but with youthful enthusiasm she quickly settled into the life of her new convent, community, and school. Such was not the case for her older companion, Mary Frances Meade, who had come over to this country with the hope of carrying God's word to the savages. Instead of fulfilling her ideal of teaching the Indians, Mary Frances had to endure the daily pressure of nerve-racking harassment from the Know Nothing element, some of them quite savage. Sister became so affected by these experiences that, after consultation with Mother Xavier Warde, she agreed that it would be best to return to Cork. Although her stay in America was brief, Mary Frances Meade continued to work in Ireland for more than half a century.[9] Mary Austin Carroll was also to serve God's people for over fifty years, but seemed to know instinctively that she was in America to stay.

Both of these missionaries understood clearly that they could return to St. Maries of the Isle if they so wished, for the nineteenth-century Mercies had a definite understanding about the rights and duties of the sisters who were sent out to new foundations. The Ecclesiastical Superior of the Convent of Mercy in Cork at the time that Sisters Mary Austin Carroll and Frances Meade were selected for the mission to Providence was Bishop William Delaney of Cork, who carefully explained,

Before entering on the arduous mission . . . it is right to have a clear understanding on every point. And first, as regards the nuns whose heroic piety leads them so far from their native land into distant countries for the glory of their Creator, they are to be encouraged by knowing the usage of this diocese in all the missions hitherto undertaken. The religious always retain the right of returning to the convent for which they were professed.[10]

Thus Austin Carroll knew that Frances Meade could return to Cork with full confidence of retaining her place in the community. Austin was also to give long years of service elsewhere, not like Frances Meade in the south of Ireland, but in the United States — forty years in the deep South bordering the Gulf of Mexico.

For the 1850s however, Austin Carroll was in the Northeast where Mother Xavier Warde was always on the move, and so were the sisters who kept pace with her. Austin's varied abilities were a veritable treasure trove for Xavier Warde, enabling her to assign and reassign the talented young sister as frequently as community needs required. Hence, Austin was soon to serve in Hartford, Rochester, Manchester, and Omaha at Xavier Warde's direction. Mary Austin, recently professed, was to complete her formation period primarily in Hartford and Rochester, but later there were to be other missions from future superiors. Mercy Chronicles, which were called *Leaves from the Annals of the Sisters of Mercy* by their author, Mary Austin Carroll, furnish insights into her experiences on various missions as she forthrightly speaks of the people, the joys, the sorrows — all with surprising frankness. When urged to soften the wording here or there, the author replied, "I do not think that anyone's labors or character should be exalted at the expense of the truth; I have a perfect abhorrence of anything untruthful." One can readily see in the *Annals* Austin's attempt to present both the positive and the negative aspects of various situations.[11] While this type of presentation in the twentieth century is considered fair and accurate, Austin was often called a radical in nineteenth-century circles where unpleasantness was omitted as "better left unsaid."

Wintry weather, for instance, was a problem for Mary Austin in Providence; and in the chronicles are listed the cold details of the sisters' daily hikes, often through sleety rain or snow, out to the distant schools where there were as yet no convents. On the other hand, Austin recalled also the warm memories of the housekeeper who often brought the sisters a pot of hot tea at noon and of the kindly undertaker who gave the sisters a lift in his carriage when he had no funeral scheduled. Affronted by the lack of beauty in the convent chapel, Austin termed the makeshift decorations "hideous," then added that the chapel was truly beautified by the streams of novices professed there, God's presence sending forth Mercy teachers for generations of His New England people. The memories of these early days in Providence were preserved also in some alumnae notes. The girls of Sts. Peter and Paul School recalled the transfer of their class from the dark church basement to the second floor of the Lime Street building. The girls found the new location "big as a barn and just as airy" and wondered if Austin had been the moving force in their improved situation. Her pupils were exceptionally fond of Austin and believed her to be not only the "possessor of every virtue, but of every intellectual acquirement too." Probably, this was the natural response of affectionate children to such a jolly, creative, and challenging teacher.[12]

According to the records, Mary Austin "adapted herself to the circumstances of the country and took an active share in every duty." Her first convent responsibility was instructing the novices as to the fine points in the art of teaching. The schools were the primary assignment for the Mercies in Providence at the time, but they had such ancillary duties as visiting the sick and leading Sunday School classes or Sodality sessions. There was a circulating library which had its inception the year of Austin's arrival, and under her care a small collection and its patrons grew by leaps and bounds. In the following semester both the library patrons and the students lost Mary Austin to another school. The books became the responsibility of the Sunday School youths, and the affectionate pupils transferred their attentions to the next teacher. For the rest of their lives, however, the twenty novices were to remember both Austin's instructions on the imparting of knowledge and her creative approach to the enkindling of the desire to learn.[13]

The Hartford branch of the Mercy Community in Providence suffered the loss of Sister Mary Camillus O'Neill just as Advent approached in 1856. Having been taught by the Congregation of Notre Dame in Montreal, Camillus had such fluency in French that the Hartford Mercies thought her irreplaceable. To their great surprise, Mother Xavier Warde announced that she had a teacher capable of maintaining the high standards of St. Catherine Academy in Hartford. It was Mary Austin Carroll, talented linguist as well as historian, who was transferred to Hartford for the next semester. The New Year of 1857 and Austin probably moved ahead together, although the exact date of the trip is not available. The distance from Providence along the Connecticut Pike was really not far, Austin decided, especially when made by sled across the snow to Hartford. The superior, Mary Pauline Maher, the cousin of Mother Josephine Warde, and all the sisters had such a warm welcome for their new French teacher that Austin soon felt right at home. Most of the convent and school arrangements were quite similar to those in Providence, with the exception being that St. Catherine Convent in Hartford housed orphan girls rather than Mercy candidates as did St. Xavier Convent in Providence.[14] Austin did not find the wintry cold in Hartford as devastating as that in Providence. She was to continue to feel the cold keenly, but she thought that in Hartford there was either some decrease in wind, dampness, and chill factor or that she had become somewhat acclimated.

The large four-story St. Catherine Convent of Mercy in Hartford had been absolutely spacious when it was opened in 1855, but it seemed small and close by 1857, when Mary Austin found the house "full of work, poverty, and devotion." It was also filled with people—the sisters who staffed two schools, about twenty orphan girls, a number of boarders, and during the school hours, forty or more pupils of the academy. Space was certainly at a premium, there was no garden, and this was no Eden; but Mary Austin soon discovered that the close quarters and the real charity combined to produce an extraordinary spirit of Mercy unity and resultant happiness. Years later the alumnae members could recall this "together-ness." Although Austin had the unenviable task of following a teacher idolized by her students, this new teacher thrived on challenge, and her classes soon found that she led them to enjoy the experience of learning. In fact, the girls of St. Catherine Academy considered Austin an exceptional teacher because she stimulated their delight in great literature and in their own intellectual accomplishment. Her students managed to learn that "Sister Mary Teresa Austin," as they always addressed her, had been personally selected by Mother Josephine Warde to help her sister, Mother Xavier. In Jubilee "Retrospection" an alumna enumerated as hallmarks of those early days at the academy a spirit of courage and true culture.[15] The courage of that hardy young Margaret Carroll holding her own against a crowd of looters was felt here against Know Nothing antagonism, and the young nun's excellence in both music and literature had evidently left a permanent impression upon the girls.

Mary Austin herself mentioned neither of these points, however, as her fond memories of Hartford dwelt instead on the close-knit Mercy community with its charity and sharing. She found the association with a pair of friends, Sisters Mary Pauline Maher and Angela Fitzgerald, doubly rewarding as they became her friends also. Remarkably complementary in their giftedness, the pair became life-long correspondents of Austin Carroll. School-principal Angela Fitzgerald was filled with energetic determination and intellectual brilliance and close to Austin in both age and character. Superior Pauline Maher, the gentle and motherly possessor of joyful sanctity was the spiritual tutor of black-novice Mary Austin. In her Mercy *Annals* Austin paid similar compliments to Mother Josephine Warde and her cousin in Hartford, Pauline Maher, as she praised their virtue and named them as ideal Mercy superiors.[16] Austin's joy truly flowered that spring as the snow melted, and everything about St. Catherine Convent seemed to suit her perfectly. Then suddenly that sacrifice upon which Mercy expansion was built was thrust upon the Mercies as a fourth of the St. Catherine community learned that they had been selected to be missioned elsewhere. Although there was no rapine in the holocaust, Mary Austin and her sisters sorrowed as they realized that this unified Hartford community would probably never be together again. They were right. But Most Rev. John Timon, the bishop of Buffalo, had appealed to Mother Xavier Warde for a foundation, and she had happily agreed to the sacrifice of dividing the community and promptly began the exciting task of planning the foundation.

Mary Austin learned later that during the previous year Bishop Timon had applied for Sisters of Mercy in Pittsburgh, New York City, Brooklyn, Chicago, then Pittsburgh and New York again. The bishop's request for enough sisters to establish a motherhouse in Rochester was refused by his episcopal friends because they believed that the Sisters of Mercy in their dioceses were already overtaxed and their institutions understaffed. Once the canvassing bishop was directed to Providence, however, his search was over, for Mother Xavier Warde did not share the worries of other Mercy superiors about either novices or numbers. Several other relevant factors probably contributed to the rapidity with which the new foundation was arranged. The late Bishop O'Reilly of Hartford had not yet been replaced, and his brother, interim administrator Rev. William O'Reilly, could hardly refuse as he was deeply indebted to his former bishop, John Timon.[17] Additionally, and probably the weightiest reason, was Xavier Warde's special predilection for new foundations—a characteristic which her friend Catherine McAuley described as "a genuine ardour and a kind of real innocent pious anxiety to be engaged in such works." Catherine McAuley certainly understood Fanny Warde well because that propensity for finding "innocent pious anxiety" in the excitement of sending her sisters out on new foundations was to remain with Xavier Warde as long as she lived.[18]

While Mary Austin reveled in the joyful unity of St. Catherine Convent of Mercy in Hartford, a community which was fulfilling Catherine McAuley's ideal of a group with one heart, Bishop Timon met Xavier Warde in May 1857. Evidently, the two shared a kindred missionary spirit. Timon arrived in Providence on May 16, and obtained a promise of help the following day.[19] Xavier Warde and this new-found "brother in spirit"[20] had both embraced the frequent journeys, the discomforts of pioneer transportation, and the other hardships incidental to the establishment of new institutions. In any time or place, be it twentieth-century professional convention or this 1857 meeting of two administrators, participants generally find it invigorating to share experiences with others in their field. On May 17 Timon visited with the Mercies in Providence and "arranged for Sisters to go to Rochester," then went over to Hartford on May 18, where Austin assisted at his Mass on May 19. By May 21, Timon was back in Rochester "to preach at St. Mary's' " and to make arrangements for the "coming of the Sisters of Mercy."[21] Thus in less than a week he had completed the preliminaries for the Mercy foundation soon to be established in Rochester, New York.

Destined to be a member of the Rochester community, Mary Austin was to learn more about the bishop so frequently compared with St. Paul. Of course, Paul of Tarsus was also Paul of Damascus, of Jerusalem, of Antioch, of Syria, and some four dozen other places on or near the Mediterranean. Yet without taking one jot or iota away from the tremendous apostolic work of the martyred Paul, it seems no exaggeration to say that Timon's itinerary turned Paul into a homebody. In his early years Timon covered wilderness areas by horseback and "shank's mare," and during his episcopal career he was towed in canal packets, propelled in river paddlewheelers, and "staged" down the postroads and turnpikes. In his treks to finance his projects, Timon made voyages to South America and Europe and traversed North America from Canada to Mexico.[22] When it came to the Diocese of Buffalo, no begging effort was too great for Timon; and when he described his See city, his affection was apparent.

> The climate of Buffalo is more agreeable than that of any other American city in the same latitude. The winter and spring months are boisterous; but in winter, the thermometer never sinks as low as it does in other cities much to the south of Buffalo. The summers are cool and pleasant. Owing to this, and to the admirable system of sewerage, Buffalo is a very healthy city.[23]

Mary Austin was soon to learn that both the clergy and religious working with Timon found themselves, now and again, twirled about or tumbled painfully by the winds of the precipitous prelate's wake. Xavier Warde was excited by that whirling draft in 1857, as she hastily selected sisters from both Hartford and Providence for the new foundation. First she decided that the superior was to be Mary Baptist Coleman, a native of Dublin and an experienced religious. After that decision, choosing four or five sisters to accompany Mary Baptist was easy. Her selection included two young choir sisters or teachers, Sisters Mary Austin Carroll and Regis Madden, and two older lay sisters to assist with the apostolate of the sick, Sisters de Pazzi Kavanagh and Raymond O'Reilly.[24] Preparations moved ahead rapidly as copies had to be made of the prayers not yet printed, and cloaks and bonnets had to be readied as disguises for the religious travelers in this period when personal safety demanded such camouflage. Austin recalled the journey as having begun just as the spring semester neared the end of May. Perhaps, she and the other sisters destined for Rochester were summoned to Providence in May, in order to complete more quickly the preparations necessary before their departure in two weeks. Or possibly, Austin found this parting from her loving community in Hartford so painful, what Catherine McAuley had termed "a bitter sorrow," that she recalled the date as arriving sooner than it had in reality.[25]

Either way, by the beginning of June, Mary Austin and the other sisters chosen to establish the Mercy community in Rochester were as ready to make the transfer as they would ever be. Rev. William O'Reilly, administrator of the Hartford Diocese since his brother's death, was to escort the Mercies all the way to St. Mary's parish in Rochester because the safety of the sisters demanded such precautions in Know Nothing times. From Providence to the western tip of New York state was no quick trip in 1857. Austin wrote that the first stage of the long journey brought the group to Albany, where they remained overnight at the Delevan House on the corner of Columbia and Broadway. This hotel, just around the block from St. Mary's Church at Pine and Chapel Streets, was conveniently located for Mass the next morning. Father O'Reilly, gracious as he always was, recalled Austin, "made their stay in the capital very pleasant, for he took them to see all the religious houses in it." Thus, Austin visited the Sisters of Charity from Emmitsburg who staffed St. Mary's School on Pine Street and Sts. Vincent's Asylum and St. Joseph's on North Pearl. Whether or not the Mercies went out to Troy Road to see the Academy of the Sacred Heart is not clear from the annals.[26] The sisters all agreed that Father O'Reilly had planned wisely to allow them a period of relaxed visiting between the two lengthy days of jolting on the coaches.

After the group left the capital, Mary Austin related, "Bishop Timon met them on the road . . . and insisted that they should see his grand cathedral at Buffalo, and thither he escorted them . . . to the Clarendon." Austin, quick with compassion and treasuring the memory for three decades, stated that she visited the sick wife of the proprietor and managed to do a few things which contributed to her comfort. The next day was Trinity Sunday, June 7, the first full day that the Sisters of Mercy spent in the Diocese of Buffalo.[27] As Austin assisted at Mass in the beautiful cathedral, she was struck with the sense of mission imparted by the words of the Gospel: "Going therefore, teach all nations . . . to observe all things whatsoever I have commanded you; and know that I am with you all days, even to the end of the world."[28] Austin knew that this was a glorious day for herself and the other followers of Catherine McAuley, for they were being solemnly missioned to teach in the name of the Triune God and being promised that He would stay with them forever. Later, the Mercies dined at the cathedral rectory with the bishop and his confrere, Rev. John Joseph Lynch. These two Vincentians gave the sisters a tour of the Catholic institutions in the city, described as one of

> broad streets, handsome squares, fine buildings . . . and a harbor full of steamboats. Each boat had its band of music playing on the deck to attract the passengers as they came in on the mail-coaches or canal-boats. Buffalo in summer was a lively as well as a cool and lovely place . . . with steamboat excursions . . . sometimes fifty miles up the lake and back . . . or twenty miles down the Niagara, making the circuit of Grand Island, and boldly steaming across the river on the very edge of the rapids.[29]

This grand cataract was that which Bishop Timon wanted the visiting sisters to see. As an enthusiastic tour guide, he escorted Father O'Reilly and the Mercies out to view the magnificent Falls. Mary Austin described their trip across the suspension bridge to the Canadian side, where Timon pointed to his dream-site for a convent at some future date. The tour group then stopped at the Vincentian college, newly established on a hundred acres midway between Lewiston and Suspension Bridge. Austin was delighted to hear Father Lynch, the future Archbishop of Toronto, planning to double his land there, for he could envision the fine university his seminary was to become. But that June of 1857, Austin enumerated just twenty "little boys" who graciously entertained the visiting sisters. Thereafter, Timon took the sisters to Rochester, where he was displeased that the pastor of St. Mary's, Rev. Thomas McEvoy, was not at the rectory. Timon noted in his diary, "No one to receive, M. McEvoy kept away. Scold him—much trouble." Austin remembered it differently.

> The Sisters were escorted to Rochester, a pretty town near the Genesee Falls. Here they took possession of a small convent prepared for them by a good, zealous priest, Reverend Thomas McEvoy, who did not allow them to want for anything.[30]

Austin was referring to the general attitude of the kind pastor, of course, and not to the single event of their unheralded arrival. One might assume that Father McEvoy had expected the Mercies on the previous Saturday when Timon had whisked them away to Buffalo to admire his cathedral.

The Rochester community, following their usual Mercy tradition, immediately began to arrange the best room in their convent as the chapel, Mary Austin chronicled, and the bishop offered Mass there on Tuesday, June 9, 1857. This date of their first Mass in Rochester has been considered

Foundation Day. On Trinity Sunday the sisters had heard God's promise to remain with them, and on the ninth He came to their little chapel. He also sent a candidate to join them—none other than the pastor's own sister, Catherine McEvoy. Already Rochester, the City of Flowers, was blossoming for the sisters, and Austin recorded that classes were organized and the school opened that very day.[31] Austin's account in the Mercy *Annals* of this new foundation and subsequent recountings by Mercy historians from Providence, Rochester, and Buffalo have all emphasized the point that it was the persistent Timon who was the moving force behind the venture.[32] Even contemporary news items emphasized that fact. "At the earnest solicitation of the Bishop of Buffalo, the parent house of the Mercy Order in Providence, has been induced to establish . . . that excellent institution in Rochester."[33]

Be that as it may, credit must go to the efficiency of the founding group of Mercies. This organization of the school and convent progressed so smoothly that in less than three weeks Xavier Warde, who had accompanied the foundation community, was ready to leave for Providence. The bishop and Rev. Peter Bede accompanied Mother Josephine's sister aboard the canal packet on June 27 for a leisurely ride home, as Mary Austin and her companions waved their farewells. Perhaps Xavier Warde recalled her midwinter journey ten years earlier, when she traveled by stage across country from Chicago to Pittsburgh. How different was this ideal trip as she floated smoothly down the Erie Canal through the bright summer countryside. Also in contrast to the former experience, this time she had no worry about the youth of the founding superior, for Mary Baptist Coleman, in her thirty-sixth year, had with her two lay sisters her age, de Pazzi Kavanagh of County Kildare and Raymond O'Reilly of Dublin. Balancing their years of wisdom was the youthful enthusiasm of the two teachers, Mary Austin then twenty-two, and Mary Regis Madden. Also assisting in Rochester in the early days was another Mercy from Providence, Sister Anastasia Marnell, who arrived either with the original group or very shortly thereafter. In either case, however, she was temporary help, and like Mary Austin Carroll, would later return to one of Xavier Warde's convents.[34]

Just as Cork had detailed the rights of the sister sent on new foundations, so too, did Providence make clear the freedom of choice in this respect for each sister.

> No Sister is ever sent on these [foundations] unless she assents. . . . She is perfectly free to go, or to decline. . . . Should she consent to go, she is given a certain time in which she can satisfy herself if she will be able to work as well there for the salvation of her own soul and for those of others at the same time as in the Convent to which she originally belonged. If she is not

satisfied . . . she can return. . . . The services of the Sisters have frequently been lent to houses of the Institute. . . . The same rule applies here; the same liberty exists as for a foundation.[35]

Thus with both temporary and permanent assistance, Mary Baptist Coleman opened the doors of the Mercy schools in Rochester on June 9, and publicity soon appeared in the Catholic press. The *Boston Pilot*, for instance, announced that the Sisters of Mercy had been "received with every mark of attention. . . . A free school, pension school, and industrial school have been already opened, the sick visited, etc."[36] The small pension, or tuition, school established in the convent was dedicated to Mary and entitled the Academy of the Immaculate Conception.

It did not take historian Mary Austin long to learn that this title was especially appropriate because it coincided with the name of the original outpost in the area when New York was seeded with the blood of the seventeenth-century missionaries. A series of small mission stations, like stepping stones, marked the Jesuit pathway across the "Iroquois Mission," called the "Mission of Martyrs" by the intrepid French priests. The Genesee Valley mission, located just south of the site later to become the city of Rochester, was entitled *Gandachiorago* or *La Conception*.[37] One of the widely traveled blackrobes of the period considered the land in and about the Finger Lakes and western New York the most beautiful that he had seen anywhere in America.[38] Even though Austin certainly appreciated the natural beauty of the fertile area, she was profoundly touched and deeply awed by her presence in the land of martyrs. Her Gaelic asceticism never allowed her to forget the privilege of having, even for a relatively short time, trod the paths and followed the footsteps of the sainted missionaries. Mary Austin began to feel that here at last was a kinship joining this new land of faith and her beloved "old sod" of Clonmel, also trodden by the feet of priests who were martyred for their faith.[39]

With patriotic pride Mary Austin learned that it was from Ireland that many nineteenth-century missionaries came to western New York. In the 1820s Fathers Pat McCormick and Patrick Kelly had organized the Irish construction crews and built the first Rochester church — St. Patrick's, naturally. In 1835 young Father Bernard O'Reilly, later the Bishop of Hartford, became pastor in Rochester, where he worked for a dozen years before the Diocese of Buffalo was instituted. As one historian expressed it, the Irish immigrants digging the Erie Canal were also "working on the foundations of three" dioceses and selecting sites for some 500 parishes. By the time that the Mercies arrived, there were Irish parishes in all the towns near the Erie Canal and almost 7,000 Irish residents amid Rochester's booming population of 40,000.[40] These people, especially the parishioners of St. Mary's near the Convent of Mercy on South Street, welcomed the Sisters of Mercy who so willingly walked to their homes to visit the bedridden. The apostolate of visiting the sick poor, like the schools which held classes throughout that first summer, was also an immediate response to need. Austin enjoyed even the lengthy walks to see the sick because of the lovely trees and gardens everywhere. Visitors to the prosperous "Flower City" were often taken on tours of the suburban nurseries and orchards with their rows upon rows of flowers and fruit trees.[41]

Amid this budding environment the tiny Mercy community began to blossom in the remaining months of 1857. Several candidates arrived to join them; Catherine McEvoy received the veil of the novice in the first Mercy reception ceremony held in western New York; and Sisters Raymond and de Pazzi prepared to profess their vows for life.[42] Just as these sisters were moving ahead in their religious development, so was Mary Austin settling down into the community structure which made it possible to bring God's mercy to His people. In each school where she had served Mary Austin had felt pride and satisfaction in the improvement of her students, but most of all with the youthful Mercies she had taught in Providence. Among her greatest joys in each Mercy community was the pleasure of companionship and fun with her sisters, but most of all the warmth in friendship she had experienced with Sisters Pauline and Angela in Hartford. But Austin had to serve in Rochester to share a mutual affection with the sick, the needy, and the aged that she visited. It surprised her to realize that her feeling for these poor Irish immigrants in the shanties of Rochester was even stronger than her attachment to the poor she had visited in Cork. In New England she had evidently missed her countrymen more than she had realized, for she now reveled in their presence. Austin fell in love once again, this time with her countrypeople in the fair city of Rochester.

Although Mary Austin did not record the fact, she might have been the influence in the choice of the academy name, for Our Lady under the title Immaculate Conception was especially dear to her. It was just three and a half years since Candidate Margaret Carroll had consecrated herself to God on that feast, and only one year from her arrival in colorful Rochester to the day on which she made her vows. Even so, the newly established mother-house bore several indications that Austin was a leading influence in the Mercy community there. In its variety of the works of mercy, for instance, this new convent resembled that of Mother Josephine Warde in Cork rather than those houses founded by Xavier Warde in New England. Instead of concentrating on excellence in a few works, like Xavier's academies and convert programs, Josephine Warde embraced the broadest possible view of bringing mercy to the needy on as many fronts as possible. Josephine's view included health care and social work as well as education. With this background as her initiation into Mercy service, Mary Austin tended to follow the lead of Josephine and encourage the establishment of all the works needed. In the Rochester section of the *Annals*, Austin enumerated with an obvious pride their various projects, "the fine industrial school . . . the Mercy Home . . . the employment bureau . . . and the creche," where infants and young children were received while their mothers were working, the numerous visits to the sick and the dying, and "the hundreds of adults" instructed and baptized in the convent chapel.[43]

The sight of this wonderfully successful Mercy center in operation so rapidly caused the bishop to decide shortly that Buffalo needed the same type of Mercy institutions. "With Bishop Timon to resolve was to act . . . and he began canvassing the older Mercy foundations for volunteers. . . . On August 30, he applied to Chicago for a Sister to govern a house."[44] Evidently, Timon had already decided that, since no motherhouse could spare an entire foundation group, he would borrow a few sisters here and there and from newly established Rochester, then place them under an experienced superior from one of the older communities. Austin knew that Rochester really had no members to spare because, although several candidates had entered, two of the three were lay sisters and could not assist with the teaching. Timon thought that he had a commitment of help from "M R" of Pittsburgh, but the agreement had dissolved when he wrote on December 27. Timon's frustration is clear from his diary, as he notes that he "chides" Bishop Michael O'Connor because the bishop of Pittsburgh was not supporting his request either for a few sisters or for a superior for the Buffalo foundation.[45]

Because of his previous experience, Michael O'Connor tended to be cautious about the preparations and numbers necessary for a successful motherhouse in the United States. Already he had witnessed the ill effects upon the sisters' health when foundations were made with too few sisters to handle the community commitments. Timon was not the only one that O'Connor tried to warn against establishing foundations composed of too unprepared, too inexperienced, or too few sisters. In the following letter Michael O'Connor tried once again to explain these views to Xavier Warde.

> I would recommend you very earnestly to be slow in spreading. . . . It is better to mature things well, and then your progress will be more safe. . . . I think you ought not to consent to the establishment of even a branch house unless you have at least three experienced Sisters to put in it, leaving a sufficient number at home.[46]

By these criteria of the fatherly protector of the Sisters of Mercy in the United States, Buffalo would have had to wait quite some time before the

Rochester motherhouse was prepared to part with enough sisters to establish a branch. But how could the sisters there convince Timon, when his fellow bishops often could not withstand his determination and persistence.

In certain matters Timon was like Paul the Apostle, but in other ways like another Paul, the American wizard of the international chess world, Paul Morphy. Bishop Timon frequently shifted his pieces—the sisters, their superiors, the curates, and their pastors—according to his master plan. In that age so long before collegiality, that plan was not shared with the clergy or religious of the diocese. As a result they often found the sudden moves disconcerting, and on occasion, too difficult to accept. Rather than continue as pawns, several religious communities and individuals withdrew from the area. In January of 1858, the bishop's plans called for sudden shifts in personnel because he had decided to transfer to Buffalo several members of the thriving Mercy community in St. Mary's parish in Rochester. The Sisters of St. Bridget, the poor sisters who had already been transferred from St. Mary's in Rochester and sent to St. Bridget's parish in Buffalo,[47] were now to be shifted once more, this time to the town of Medina. Then reassigning his pastors for the new arrangement of sisters, Timon notified Father Martin O'Connor of Medina to swap parishes with Father Charles McMullen of St. Bridget's in Buffalo.[48] Austin was not as startled by all the swapping as by its unexpectedness and immediacy.

On January 12, 1858, Timon met with Father McEvoy, then with Baptist Coleman, and "arranged for a colony at St. Bridget's" in Buffalo. According to the diary there was no question of using either of the black novices, Mary Austin or Regis Madden, for the superior. Instead, Timon took Baptist Coleman to New York City "to plead for a sister to govern." At first Mother Agnes O'Connor refused, but persistence won her reluctant agreement on his third appeal several days later, and Sister Mary Elizabeth Callanan returned to Rochester with Baptist Coleman on January 23. With only two weeks to complete preparations for the new branch, participants must have been selected quickly. To have a list of their names would certainly be helpful, as Austin was probably in the number. However, the Timon diary does not mention the chosen personnel; and the original records of the Rochester Sisters of Mercy burned, along with their motherhouse, just after the turn of the century.[49] As a result, the hiatus in archival data has led to a divergence, even a diversity, in the assumptions made to reconstruct the establishing of the Convent of Mercy in Buffalo. Timon's chronological notes recount his early start from St. Mary's South Street convent and the total lack of preparation in the new branch at St. Bridget's.

Rochester 5:50 a.m. — to convent of Sisters of Mercy, Mass — M. Evoy absent, M. Lynch present — instructions — start with four Sisters, the Sister I brought from New York had gone back on the tenth — on to Buffalo — nothing fixed or provided — sent to get beds, bedding, etc.[50]

The date of all this activity was February 11, 1858, the very day, as Mercy historians noted, that God gave the world the hope of Lourdes through the instrumentality of poor, sickly Bernadette Soubirous.[51]

In the Mercy *Annals* Mary Austin Carroll once again took the long view as she mentioned Buffalo along with the other convents established from the Rochester motherhouse, which

> within a year . . . had to take charge of St. Brigid's Schools, Buffalo. The Buffalo house, though founded in the greatest poverty, became a flourishing establishment. Reverend Martin O'Connor . . . was their sincere and devoted friend to his latest breath.[52]

Typically, Austin glossed over the lack of bare necessities rather than point a finger of blame. After all, the new pastor, like the sisters, had received his orders to move to St. Bridget's quite suddenly, and it was only the following Sunday that the bishop presented both the pastor and the religious to the parishioners. This poor, spindly branch convent, like the sickly and impoverished Bernadette Soubirous, was to bring hope and consolation to vast numbers in years to come. The Buffalo community was eventually to unite with Batavia, another young branch from Rochester, intertwine roots, then mature in strength and send out green shoots of its own. In spite of the premature partition of the tiny community and the resulting shortage of personnel, Rochester was gradually to accomplish wonders as it flowered in profusion over New York state.[53] In 1858, however, Mary Baptist Coleman was desperate for help, as Sister Mary Florence Sullivan points out: "The Rochester community was left in straitened circumstances because of the diminished number to carry on the extensive program of teaching and visitation work in the parish."[54]

Mercy tradition in the area holds that Mary Austin Carroll, professed for a year and some months, was the last-minute substitute as superior for the elusive Elizabeth Callanan, who had been borrowed specifically to serve as the superior in Buffalo. Austin learned later that this remarkable sister who was so timid about accepting leadership in Buffalo, was reluctant on several other occasions to take the captain's helm, but eventually served as the Reverend Mother in New York City. Although Elizabeth Callanan left the Convent of Mercy in Rochester on February 10, it would seem that she returned later to assist until May. According to the New York chronicles,

Mother Agnes O'Connor recalled Elizabeth Callanan that month, and she arrived in New York on May 11, 1858. Obviously, Baptist Coleman had to make some changes when the New York teacher was recalled in order to keep her institutions even minimally staffed. With the borrowed expert gone, Baptist would have logically called as replacement her own exceptional teacher, Austin Carroll. Tradition states that Austin was back in Rochester "shortly after the reception" ceremony there in mid-April. Thus both logic and tradition place Austin in Rochester right at the time that her assistance was needed.[55] Evidently, Regis Madden was assigned to St. Bridget's, for she is listed there in the *Catholic Directory* published the following year.

Suppositions aside, there is factual data that found its way into contemporary newsprint. Within ten days of her arrival at St. Bridget's Convent in Buffalo, substitute Mary Austin sent out a plea for assistance through the pages of the *Buffalo Express* of February 21, 1858. This item explained that the Sisters of Mercy "most cheerfully gave their labor, their time, and their tenderest attention" to helping the destitute; but that, since they were so poor themselves, they were forced "to beg the charitable to aid them in their work."[56] Buffalo's cool summer breezes were icy cold in winter, however, and prosperity hibernated.

> The whole army of industry went into winter quarters . . . The canal was closed to navigation, the lake was frozen over from end to end, the ice forming two feet in thickness around the ships in the harbour. Navigation was ended; and there was nothing for the steamboat men and the canallers, and the mercantile interests generally to do . . . but wait for the opening of navigation, which might be early in March or late in May, according to the season.[57]

That spring Austin saw the ice gradually disappear, commerce improve, and the season for Mercy ceremonies arrive. Austin noted that several papers published the details of the reception as a novice of the American candidate, Mary Ann McGarr, who had joined the Irish Mercies. The imposing rite was "performed in St. Bridget's Church and attended by a large crowd," which included clergymen from the different parishes.[58] Following the report on the "very feeling address," was the news that the pastor was "already negotiating for a lot of ground to erect a new parochial church, much needed in this important parish."[59]

As both the substitute superior Mary Austin and the new pastor moved ahead, so did the Pauline bishop. "Urgent business of great importance to the church and to this diocese calls me to Europe," Timon announced and ordered the prayer "Pro Peregrinantibus" to be said daily until his return.[60]

On his way through Ireland, the bishop spent time and effort in his quest for Irish Mercies, but the motherhouses, like that of Waterford in August, had no sisters to spare. This search for a whole community for Buffalo seems to imply that the Rochester sisters were there temporarily until other sisters could be found to staff the promising mission. Throughout the summer news items heralded the steady progress of such events as the Ladies' Fair to aid the Rochester House of Mercy and the rapidity with which St. Mary's church was rising.[61] Not all the news chronicled so regularly was good. On August 31, Austin and the other Mercies shared the grief of Mary Clare McEvoy when she learned of the death of her brother Tom. Father Thomas McEvoy, the thirty-five year old pastor, had died suddenly in New York, where he had gone to purchase furnishings for his new church. Three weeks after the funeral was held in the handsome new church, Timon returned with the news that there were no Irish Mercies available.[62]

The final data of the year was positive again as the *Catholic Directory* listed the increased enrollment in the Mercy Academy of the Immaculate Conception in Rochester and in St. Joseph's Academy of Our Lady of Mercy in Buffalo.[63] Mary Austin and the other sisters were delighted with these statistics and the great success of the House of Mercy in spite of the continued hardship of insufficient numbers for two houses. For over a year, however, attempts to obtain more sisters met with refusals—from Providence in March 1858, from Waterford and other Irish convents that summer, and from Pittsburgh in March 1859. Yet, Timon applied to the last community again in January 1860, because it was the first and largest Mercy community in the United States. Success finally crowned his persistence. Sister Mary Philomena Devlin was accompanied to Buffalo by Bishops O'Connor and Timon, who installed her as the superior of the Mercies in Buffalo on January 24, 1860.[64] This superior obtained more sisters from her Pittsburgh motherhouse in August that year, and "the few sisters from Rochester, who still remained in St. Bridget's, gradually withdrew."[65]

Among the lifelong correspondents of Mary Austin Carroll were several of the Pittsburgh Mercies who came to lend aid and insure stability in Buffalo until candidates could reinforce the community. One was Austin's correspondent Mary Baptist Hearne, who served in Buffalo until 1871, when she returned to Pittsburgh.[66] Another, Mary Elizabeth Strange, became a warm friend of Austin and, like her, served in Buffalo only briefly. Elizabeth returned to Pittsburgh and Austin to Xavier Warde in Manchester, both reporting back to the superior who had assigned them to help in the diocese. Treasuring their mutual friendship, Elizabeth Strange and Austin Carroll kept in touch by letter until Elizabeth's death in 1900. Austin had little to say in the *Annals* about her three months at St. Bridget's. Of course, nearly all of her two and a half years in western New

York had been spent in service to the people of Rochester, and there she left her heart. Concentrated on the numerous works of mercy and the many poor sick she visited, Austin's memories remained as bright as the colorful gardens of the Flower City.[67]

Just before her return to Mother Xavier Warde, Mary Austin published an article on the Rochester apostolates.[68] The item praised the various institutions, mentioned that June 9, 1857, was the opening date of the Academy, and described

> its increasing number of pupils . . . the large free school . . . which is infusing . . . religious principles . . . into the minds and hearts of these youthful and impressionable beings; the House of Mercy . . . for the protection of females . . . where servants out of place are received . . . and provided with suitable situations. . . . The Industrial School, in which needlework is taught . . . not only hemming, running, stitching, and all that enters into the mystery of shirtmaking, but also . . . embroidery of the rarest kind, crochet . . . and lace that would do credit to Valenciennes or Brussels.[69]

The news item concluded, as Austin so frequently did, with the wish for every success in the truly Christian enterprises, which instead of giving monetary and momentary relief, helped all of society by aiding women to attain permanently a certain amount of self-sufficiency. In Austin's opinion, this was one of the finest aspects of Catherine McAuley's carefully laid plans. It had caught Austin's attention from the very beginning of her fascination with the Mercy Institute and its foundress. During her next assignment with Xavier Warde, Austin Carroll was to receive a special commission to research and to write the life of Mother Catherine McAuley, the first Sister of Mercy.[70]

While Mary Austin worked to collect the data which she needed to portray the saintly spirit and personal charm of Catherine McAuley, Austin Carroll's own fascinating personality filtered through her letters requesting information. Of course the written word conveys but faintly the unique combination of tender sympathy and brilliant understanding which attracted people of all classes to her. Religious leaders, especially, could appreciate not only Austin's idealism and zeal, but her breadth of view and depth of compassion as well. What matter that her assignments in Providence, Hartford, Buffalo, and Rochester happened to be brief, for each gave rise to friendships that lasted as long as life itself. These first four assignments were also, in a way, a foreshadowing of the events to come. In each locale in which she served, Austin Carroll's understanding of America grew and challenged her to find new ways of aiding poor girls, boys, and women to attain greater self-sufficiency.

4 RESEARCH, TRAVEL, TRAVAIL
Manchester & Omaha
1859–1865

While Mary Austin Carroll was serving in the Rochester area, a few changes which were to affect her next assignment occurred in the diocese of Hartford. After an interregnum of two years the diocese was to have as its new bishop Francis Patrick McFarland. Bishop Timon, in Providence to assist with the consecration on March 14, 1858, introduced the new prelate to the Sisters of Mercy and tried unsuccessfully to obtain more help for Buffalo.[1] He was not alone in seeking Sisters, however, because Bishop Byrne of Little Rock was trying to find Mercies for his friend Archbishop Antoine Blanc, who wanted them for several parishes in his Archdiocese of New Orleans. Newark's bishop, James Roosevelt Bayley, also hoped to locate a community of Mercies for his diocese as did Bishop David William Bacon of Portland, Maine.[2]

With so many requests at the same time, one might wonder why it was that the Bishop of Portland was able to win from Mother Xavier Warde the single positive answer amidst a flurry of negative ones. There was most probably a combination of reasons, one of which would have been the practicality of Mother Xavier. She must have been swayed by the fact that, of all the prelates issuing invitations, only Bishop Bacon had both convent and school built and ready for occupancy. The *Catholic Directory* had already announced that the "Ladies of Notre Dame were expected to take possession" of the facility shortly. When these Canadian religious found it necessary to withdraw their commitment, the disappointed bishop turned to the Sisters of Mercy, as happened again later in the city of Portland.[3] Bishop Bacon had visited the Providence motherhouse in both March and April with the news of his "new and commodious convent." In May Xavier Warde had completed her term as superior and was free to move ahead to Manchester, New Hampshire, where the empty convent beckoned. This was

51

especially true as she knew the Rhode Island and Connecticut Sisters of Mercy were well established. It would be written of these sisters that all who accept "the precept of fraternal love, must confess themselves beholden to this great company of heroic Christian women."[4]

Xavier Warde received another impetus to move from Sister Martha Mallon, who was mortally ill that May and envisioned the future of her superior "in a newly-built convent . . . large and handsome, with long corridors . . . on a rising ground, and built all for God . . . with a great number of Sisters . . . and you will do more for God than ever you did before."[5] Reinforcing Sister's unusual vision and the practicality of a completed convent were the pleas of the pastor of St. Anne's in Manchester, Reverend William McDonald. Father wrote several letters to Providence that spring about the urgent need for teachers for his beautiful new school, and his appeals would most certainly have touched Mother Xavier Warde's heart. She decided to leave Rhode Island for Manchester, in the diocese of Portland, Maine. Transferring with her on July 16, 1858, were her chosen companions, Sisters Mary Philomena Edwards, Gonzaga O'Brien, Joanna Fogarty, and Agatha Mulcahy.[6]

The school building "recently completed by the Catholics of Manchester" was described as "extremely light and airy in architectural style . . . an institution highly creditable to those who have so liberally contributed to its erection and endowment."[7] Since the building afforded the opportunity of teaching more students than she had anticipated, Mother Warde wrote in every direction for help. Sisters Mary Rose Davis and Veronica Dillon came from Providence right away. Later, candidates from Hartford, Providence, New York, plus a number sent over from Ireland by Josephine Warde, arrived in Manchester. So, too, did her earlier gift from Cork, Mary Austin Carroll, who had just completed her two years in the diocese of Buffalo.[8] Austin found that Xavier Warde was extremely fond of this New Hampshire town of Manchester, formerly Derryfield. It was not much larger than her own Mountrath in Ireland, but was surrounded by steeper hills and close to a large city. Mother Xavier explained its convenience. "It is only two hours ride in the cars to Boston and you can go there from here three times each day. We never were in any place where it seems so much good can be accomplished by us."[9] To these works of mercy Austin gave a generously detailed one hundred twenty-seven pages in the *Annals*, enumerating the various educational institutions. Besides Mount St. Mary's Academy and the instructions for adults, there were also free parish schools and evening classes for the young people who worked during the day.[10]

The devout Father McDonald would later make social works possible by providing a home for orphans and another for elderly women, where the Sisters of Mercy could give them the needed care. Mary Austin never tired of praising the zeal and quite evident holiness of this energetic pastor, and published several articles of tribute to him after his untimely death.[11] One said.

> As soon as he finished one good work he began another, and splendid churches, convents, schools, orphanage, home for old ladies, etc., remain as monuments of his zeal . . . and administered by the Sisters of Mercy, to whom he was a most generous benefactor.[12]

The unlimited charities of Father McDonald impressed even the anti-Catholics, who said that he and his congregation "deserved well of our citizens for contributing ornamental buildings to our young city."[13] Father's spirit of prayer and his life of mortification were so extraordinary that even his young people "deemed him a saint" and tried to cooperate with him by joining parish societies and striving to live lives pleasing to God.[14] Austin's letters frequently referred to Father McDonald as "the holiest priest" she ever knew.[15]

It was also in St. Anne's Parish in Manchester that Mary Austin had a new experience in the democracy of the United States, for she was deeply impressed by the independence of the spirited young women. Many were members of the sodality of Our Lady, most attended either evening or Sunday classes, and nearly all worked in the mills. The Irish girls lived frugally so as to send money home or, in many cases, in order to bring over other family members. This type of generosity was quite natural to the Irish, and Mary Austin was not surprised by it. What she found to be quite unexpected was the way in which the Irish girls had imbibed the independence of the Yankee mill workers together with their reservations about the control of the factory owners. Austin Carroll was not the only writer who noted this.

> It was at their peril that the factory corporations added half an hour to their work, or took six pence from their weekly wages. The girls would turn out in procession, hold a public meeting, make speeches, pass a resolution, and hold the whole manufacturing interest at their mercy. Every mill was stopped; there were no other hands to be had . . . the officers had nothing to do but quietly knock under.[16]

Austin wondered if there were any way to help the Irish girls who worked in the hotels and boarding houses of Boston and New York to organize as these mill girls had done.

The tremendous independence of these young women increased in Mary Austin a positive evaluation of the virtues of America and its democratic way of life, while she was finding Manchester quite a contrast to her earlier New England experiences with the prejudices of the Know Nothing adherents. Thus, Austin Carroll, who was one of the most patriotic Irishwomen ever to leave the beauty of her homeland to serve God's people elsewhere, continued down the gradual road of almost imperceptible, and certainly an unconscious, "Americanization" amid the color of a New Hampshire fall. Her joyous self-fulfillment in Providence and Hartford had been found both in her Mercy companions and with her students. She found it in Rochester also through contributing services in several other works of mercy. Finding assistance to aid the sick and the poor she visited there allowed Austin to see both the opportunities for improvement open to the immigrants, especially the English-speaking, and the generosity of the Americans. She took another step forward into democracy in the New Hampshire town grown from the village of Derryfield, the Manchester she was never to forget. Twenty-five years after her arrival in 1859, she reminisced in a letter to Sister Mary Gonzaga O'Brien, her Manchester "comrade-in-arms," sent like herself by Josephine Warde in Cork to Mother Xavier in Providence.[17]

> Do you remember when I was your faithful ally, playing the melodeon, teaching your boys to sing, etc., going after the backsliders, etc., in our happy young days? Only 'twould keep us too long out of heaven, I would like to go over them again.[18]

For enthusiastic Austin Carroll who admired the independence of the young women and enjoyed playing the melodeon for her friend's class of boys, Manchester was a perfectly lovely assignment. It became magnificently memorable, also, when Austin was commissioned to write the biography of her beloved Catherine McAuley.

Just as Margaret "the historian" had become involved years earlier with the story of Ireland, now she immersed herself in the history of the foundress and her Mercy Institute. To gather her data Mary Austin wrote the early companions of the foundress under the sponsorship of Xavier Warde. Many of Catherine's first lieutenants were still serving in 1859, just eighteen years after Catherine's death. With these personal acquaintances of Mother McAuley, in large measure untapped sources in Ireland, England, Australia, New Zealand, and America, Austin Carroll initiated her voluminous correspondence concerning Catherine and her Institute. This stream of letters was to cease only when Austin's fingers could no longer hold a pen; and in 1859, that time was fifty years into the future. Austin also sent out appeals for information to all the convents founded during the lifetime of Catherine. Generally, Austin made a two-fold request of each motherhouse. First, would it be possible for her to obtain copies of any of Catherine's extant letters held by any Sister in the house and, secondly, copies of any references to the foundress in the convent annals, chronicles, retreat notes, and the like. When the Sisters could not get to the copying, Austin would offer to handle that chore herself if they preferred to send her the original correspondence. Of course, the letters penned by the hand of Catherine herself were always considered too precious to risk to the mails. Frequently, and most unfortunately, the material arrived edited as it was copied. This is apparent, especially from the collection quoted in the "Appendix of Letters" at the conclusion of Austin's life of Catherine.[19]

Catherine McAuley left her followers neither photograph nor portrait, as she refused to sit for an artist during her life. Thus the Sisters of Mercy treasured even more the word pictures of Catherine by those who knew her as quoted in Austin's works. During the thirty years which elapsed between the publication of the *Life of Catherine McAuley* in 1866 and the fourth volume of the *Annals*, Austin had gathered together a veritable art gallery of the word paintings, the memoirs of the early Mercies who had known and loved Catherine. To one of these, Mother Catherine Maher of Carlow, Austin said: "How happy are you who saw her! Please write a description of her for us as you remember her."[20] When the letters were not those of Catherine herself but of one of the early Sisters, they were sometimes mailed. On one occasion when Austin had received a hefty packet of letters from the brother of a bishop, she sent her gratitude and her method of handling such correspondence. "The letters have come — a thousand thanks — I went through them before going to sleep last night as I am a rapid reader, and found much that will be of use. I will make such extracts as will be needed, and return all in a few weeks."[21]

In her opening preface Mary Austin carefully listed the individual sources which, besides the letters of the foundress, furnished the heart of her material. "Narrations of several of the early companions" of Catherine can be readily identified by the use of the data they contained: the Derry Manuscript with the story of Mother Mary Anne Doyle, the first young woman to join Catherine; the Bermondsey Chronicle, an integral part of the convent annals there, and probably the contribution of Mother Mary Clare Moore, one of the first four Sisters professed in Baggot Street; and the Dublin Manuscript of Clare Moore's sister, Mary Clare Augustine Moore of the Dublin community. Creative and alert to the value of recording personal reminiscences of those who knew Catherine McAuley, Clare Augustine forethoughtfully collected information with both patience and persistence over a period of years from Derry, Cork, and Bermondsey, as well as Dublin. This material is Clare Augustine's *first* legacy to the Sisters of Mercy everywhere. Her *second* magnificent gift to her community is the exquisite illumination work and the delicate paintings in the Register and Records at Catherine's Convent of Mercy on Baggot Street.[22]

Austin's preface to the biography of the foundress enumerated, besides the above manuscripts, "a Memoir specifically written for this work by the godchild of the Foundress," the delicate little Camillus Byrn who served in Baltimore at the time.[23] Austin's gratitude was also extended to a "venerable Religious . . . one of the oldest members of the Order," Mother Mary Xavier Warde, "for several incidents of the early life of the Foundress," and for the use of Mother Warde's collection of Catherine's letters.[24] Two other manuscripts mentioned were those in Cork and Limerick, the former being an incomplete biography by Mary Teresa Wildridge, and the latter a sketch by an anonymous "Sister in Limerick." Convent chronicles there state that Mother Vincent Hartnett, while assisting Mother Elizabeth Moore in Limerick, obtained information from Mothers Mary Anne Doyle, Xavier Warde, and Elizabeth Moore in order to supplement her own personal knowledge of the foundress. The Ennis Manuscript, an incomplete biography of Catherine McAuley in beautiful script, is so close in content and mode of expression to the published Hartnett book that it seems to be either her original account or an early copy of it. Her *Life of Reverend Mother Catherine McAuley* was published while Vincent Hartnett was the superior of the Immaculate Conception convent in Roscommon. The publication date of 1864 was twenty years after Vincent had begun to collect her data and about ten years since she had authored her Limerick Manuscript.[25] The impetus for the 1866 published life and tribute may very well have arrived in Roscommon in the same envelopes as the questions and queries from Mother Warde in New Hampshire, through her secretary Mary Austin Carroll.

Besides the loving tribute by Mother Vincent Hartnett, Austin listed several other published biographies, the earliest being that in the March 1847 *Dublin Review*. On occasion, this article has been attributed to Dean Dominick Murphy of Cork, possibly because he had written a biographical article on Nano Nagle and later published his research on other foundresses. Mary Austin knew Dean Murphy well, was familiar with his research, had heard his lectures, but certainly, had never heard him say that he had written the 1847 article.[26] On the other hand, Mother Mary Clare Moore knew Dean Miles Gaffney quite well, had assisted in his work on the Mercy Rule, and had mentioned in the Bermondsey records that Gaffney had authored Catherine's biography.[27] Yet further and more authoritative testimony to Gaffney's authorship came from the expert editor of *The Irish Monthly*, Matthew Russell, SJ. A specialist for many years in literary detective work, he regularly published the names of anonymous and pseudonymous authors which he had personally ferreted out. In 1881 Russell stated in his regular "Notes on Books," that Dean Gaffney of Maynooth wrote "the graceful memoir of his friend" Catherine McAuley in the 1847 *Dublin Review*.[28] Since any reference bears extra weight when it comes from such a knowledgeable source, Austin was certainly in good company when she said that Gaffney authored the 1847 biographical tribute.

However, the internal evidence as furnished by the humility of Gaffney himself, is really the best reason for re-stating that he authored the article in question. Dean Gaffney regularly told the Mercies in retreat lectures not to speak of themselves at all, neither in praise nor dispraise; and this advice Gaffney sedulously followed himself in the tribute. While other biographies of Catherine name Gaffney as the one who aided Catherine with the Rule, the article says an anonymous "competent authority" helped her. Others list Gaffney among those who assisted at the deathbed of the foundress; the article omits his name. Others quote the words of the dying Catherine to Father Gaffney; the article gives the words as addressed to those present.[29] Adding to this internal evidence that of the numerous similarities in both phraseology and subject matter as found in both the article and newspaper reports of Gaffney sermons at Mercy Profession liturgies gives further credence to the Gaffney authorship. Many of the celebrated speakers for the reception and profession ceremonies cited the medieval Order of Mercy which ransomed captives as a forerunner of Catherine's Institute. It was only Gaffney who always made the point, as the *Dublin Review* article does also, of attributing the origin of the earlier order to the same compassionate charity which inspired Catherine McAuley. Others referred to Mother McAuley as the "amiable lady foundress;" the article speaks of "her expansive heart." Others said that she helped the "poor, sick and ignorant;" the article and the Gaffney sermons expand that to "visiting the sick poor, instructing the needy children, and relieving the destitute female servants." This accumulation of internal evidence, especially the evident humility of Father Gaffney, has in effect, signed Gaffney's name to the anonymous tribute.[30]

Just as it was a slow procedure for this writer to check on the accuracy of Mary Austin in the one small matter of the identity of an author, so it was an exceedingly slow process for Austin to secure primary source material such as the Mercy manuscripts and the Gaffney article. Each had to be copied by hand in the days before photocopiers, and the nuns were short of time. The additional difficulties of Austin's research become even clearer when one considers that it occupied the bits and pieces of time before and after teaching, visiting the sick, playing "the melodeon, etc." There were two other considerations furthermore, for the Mercies of the 1850s did not want their names in print any more than Gaffney did; and these sources so reluctant of publicity were an ocean away. Austin's persuasive powers relied heavily upon the promise of anonymity. Her letters were incessant; her pleas persistent, and her thanks given quickly.

> Won't you put down every single thing, no matter how small, which you remember of Mother Foundress and the early days of your Institute. . . . I am longing for your next.

> Now let me thank you for the New Zealand letters. They are most edifying . . . and I got a new effusion of zeal.

> Thanks for your letter and reminiscences of our Holy Foundress. . . . That was the most precious package ever I received. I anxiously await its continuation. . . . Please don't keep me waiting too long for the rest. I was never more anxious for anything, and that is saying a great deal.[31]

In the final analysis, however, it was probably Mary Austin's loving warmth and unwavering reverence for Catherine McAuley that procured for her the information she sought, that allowed her appeals to bridge at one and the same time both the Atlantic and an ocean of natural reserve. Austin Carroll's own fascination with Catherine McAuley and her certainty of the sanctity of the foundress seemed to have been the deciding factors in the gradual transformation of complete strangers into friends. Mercies serving half a world away or in another area of the United States became careful correspondents, forwarders of information, sharers of mutually interesting material, and, eventually, faithful friends. This is the process which began in Manchester and prospered during Austin's five-year assignment there.[32] By the time that Xavier Warde needed her elsewhere, Austin had made substantial progress with the writing of the biography and was able to complete it in St. Louis, Missouri. Prior to that, however, there was travel and travail, for the United States was split in two by the fratricidal struggle of the Civil War.

From her peaceful pinnacle in the Northeast Mary Austin witnessed through the eyes of her Mercy correspondents the conflict spreading across the un-united states. Although their stories were primarily of the efforts of the various Mercy motherhouses in behalf of the sick and wounded soldiers of both armies, New Hampshire was far removed from the scenes which called for these services. In the Manchester area itself Austin noted that the "patriotic solicitors" seemed to concentrate their efforts upon the enlistment of the youths from the Irish families. Other than their distress over the boys going off to the fray, the Manchester Mercies did not seem to be emotionally involved at the beginning of the turmoil, probably because they were so far away from any actual violence or fighting. Unfortunately, the absence of any extant manuscripts or correspondence at this moment when these Irish sisters were suddenly thrust into one side or the other of this fratricidal war makes it impossible to know their personal feelings about it. Correspondence that has been preserved does not discuss the pros and cons of the philosophies or take stances about the opposing factions. Instead, the letters show that the Sisters of Mercy, with their innate mercy and compassion, gave their care unstintedly to the wounded warriors of both sides.

Later, as the young men of the Manchester area returned injured or crippled, Mary Austin noted that the New Hampshire sisters faced then, and only then, the reality of the horrors resulting from the strife. Many of their boys, she related, who "came back to school bereft of a leg or arm, and unable for the hard work of the factories, tried to fit themselves for such lighter occupations as their maimed condition could undertake."[33] But long before any injured soldiers returned to their families, Austin began receiving news of the Mercy wartime activities along with the data concerning Catherine McAuley. Many of the letters in the spring of 1861 described the nursing care and the involvement of the Mercies, but more of the correspondence was less heartening as it told poignant tales of violent death and senseless destruction. These wartime missives, especially those from the South, etched deep scars on Austin's heart, impressions never to be obliterated. Repeatedly, her later writings reveal her depth of compassion for the ill-treated people of the suffering South. Prior to her reception of news from the Mercies serving in the Confederacy, however, Austin Carroll left no expression of opinion about the sectional conflict other than her opposition to the practice of slavery in any shape or form. Although she later found fault with the way in which slavery was abolished, she thought it had to be abolished "at any cost."[34]

Quite naturally, each group of Sisters of Mercy saw the war, from its own perspective, but that view did not affect the services given by the sisters. As events happened in the turmoil of the war, Mercies who were Union sympathizers ran a hospital which changed hands as the battle lines shifted to become a Confederate facility. At the same time, in Washington, D.C., a group of sisters sympathetic to the South staffed a Union hospital, while some Northern Mercies had gone to the South just as the war opened.[35] As Union boats began securing Southern ports on the Mississippi River in the late summer of 1861, the Baltimore Mercies became anxious about the safety of their companions who had recently been sent to a mission in Mississippi. Just six months prior to Fort Sumter the Sisters had left Baltimore to establish a Mercy motherhouse in Vicksburg, a foundation sent only after lengthy negotiations on the part of the Most Rev. William Henry Elder, the determined Bishop of Natchez.[36] Mother Xavier Warde in Manchester, however, had no reluctance about subdividing her forces, and prepared for another foundation as though the war did not endanger Philadelphia. Possibly, the principals involved in this new venture thought, as many Americans did at the time, that the "rebellion" was not going to last any time at all and, certainly, would never get so close to Washington, D.C. Also, the transportation available in 1861 probably made the City of Brotherly Love seem to be a greater distance from the capital than it was in reality.

Present as preparations were made for the Philadelphia house, Mary Austin quite casually mentioned several unusual points about the formation of this new community. For more than a year Xavier Warde had been pleading for professed sisters from England and Ireland, and five sisters had come over from Ireland and two more were overdue from England. Though this process was Xavier's normal pattern for acquiring qualified sisters quickly, the intensity of the effort over such a long period was unusual. Even stranger was the statement that these new acquisitions had come "to aid Mother Warde at the Central House and in the foundations."[37] The expression seems to imply that, prior to the year of canvassing for sisters with particular qualifications, Xavier Warde had decided to establish some type of central novitiate which could prepare young sisters for the Mercy apostolate of teaching. Xavier had arranged to bring over two specially experienced sisters, one who had been serving as mistress of novices and another who had been awarded a Certificate of Merit by Her Majesty's Council on Education. There were several others, but either the mistress, Mary Patricia Waldron, or the master teacher, Mary Gertrude Ledwith, would certainly have been appropriate personnel for a central Mercy novitiate. Austin Carroll was also a certified teacher from the National Teacher Training Program in Ireland, and the reader will recall that her first assignment in the United States was that of teaching educational methods to the young sisters in Providence. Thus, a Mercy normal in Manchester would simply have been an extension of Xavier's earlier practice in Rhode Island.[38]

The new factor in 1861 was the idea of centralization, and Bishop Michael O'Connor, Xavier's mentor since he brought her to America in 1843, might have furnished the incentive to centralize. He had urged Xavier to have regular meetings with the other Mercy superiors in America in order to foster unity and to adopt a common Book of Customs in 1855, and to discuss differences centering on pension schools and other works in 1856. By 1858, Xavier's bishop-friend warned her strongly of the harm resulting from sending unprepared sisters out on foundations as teachers, about appointing too few sisters to new establishments or keeping too few at home to carry out the assigned works, and cautioned her against so rushing the extension of the Mercy Institute as to harm it.[39] Apparently, this sharp admonition was the catalyst which caused the plan of a central institution for training young Mercies and the search for the personnel needed. It seems that the delayed arrival of the superior-delegate necessitated some change of plans, mayhap some shifting of location so that the mistress-delegate could serve also as superior. In any case, Xavier sent her mistress of novices, Mary Patricia Waldron, to Philadelphia on August 21[40] with four professed sisters and four candidates, and Mary Austin was in the crowd wishing them farewell and God speed. Xavier herself visited the mother-houses in New York and Pennsylvania, possibly in an attempt to win their cooperation with the plans for the central house.[41]

All the dashing about, like all the preliminary search for personnel, was brought to nought, however, for Bishop James Wood of Philadelphia was adamant in his opposition to any connection of the new motherhouse in his diocese with that in any other. So, Michael O'Connor's agitation for some type of union or federation would rest for the present, but would arise again after the Civil War.[42] While the conflict raged, however, several events caught the attention of Austin Carroll and seemed to exert an influence which was to last throughout her life. For instance, her Chicago correspondents related details of their situation in Jefferson City, Missouri, where a slave-owning family gave them hospitality throughout the time that they nursed in the military hospital there. As the opposing forces overran the area, their hosts and other Southerners fled to safety. To the complete astonishment of the Mercies, natives of either Ireland or the North, all the slaves continued to care for their owner's homes as though the families were still present. Even though many Union sympathizers urged them to leave, the blacks refused to abandon "their families" and remained faithful to the trust which had been given them. Mary Austin, like many another who abominated slavery, found such a tale almost incredible.[43]

Similar reports found their way into letters sent to Austin, strongly influencing her to become less skeptical. The trustworthiness of the slaves struck the sensitive chords of loyalty in Austin's own heart, and she resolved to do everything in her power to help the blacks once the war was over. Austin and her Mercy friends were not the only ones astounded by the loyalty of the slaves, for several New England journalists remarked on the same phenomenon. Nichols wrote that "the great mass of Southern negroes are with their masters . . . and have dug trenches, brought intelligence to their friends, and deceived the invaders."[44] After the war Brownson added,

> The relation between the former slaveholder and his slaves . . . was much more affectionate and less galling to the slave than that which obtains between the . . . overbearing Northern employer and his hired workmen. The slave felt that he belonged to his master's family, and identified himself with its fortunes. He felt himself far superior to a hired man.[45]

However others were affected by these reports and comments, compassionate Austin Carroll was permanently scored. Throughout her life in the South, she managed to fulfill her resolve to aid and assist the blacks. This she did primarily by offering educational opportunities, even when she had to establish the schools herself.

Another way in which the war affected Mary Austin was to extend her outpouring of sympathy, which had early been given to the fighting men, to the beleaguered people of the South. As she read in her letters of the tribulations of the families down in St. Augustine, Florida, her heart bled for these people caught between the opposing forces in 1862. The Mercy school was not yet two years old when the spring semester was suddenly interrupted on March 10 by the invasion of Yankee soldiers.[46] And when some mothers packed a few necessities and fled to safety with their children, the sisters thought they had panicked needlessly. The Mercies changed their minds, however, when the families that had remained were forced out of their homes and compelled to leave the city and most of their belongings. The sisters closed the school for lack of pupils and sent the novices to their homes for lack of food. Florida witnessed the burning and looting of rectories and churches and the theft of sacred vessels.[47] Such desecration of buildings and materials dedicated to God was one of the major factors in the winning of Austin's heart for the Southerners.

In view of the violence in Florida, Bishop Augustin Verot decided that the lives of the sisters depended upon their transfer to Georgia. All horses having been seized by the soldiers, mule carts transported the bishop and seven Mercies as they left their lovely new convent August 17 for a three-week journey by dump-cart, a stagecoach which crashed, a springless wagon, and railcars to reach Columbus on the Chatahoochie River. Some twenty years later Austin Carroll wrote a rollicking twelve-page account of their adventure.[48] In his biography of Bishop Verot, Michael Gannon telescoped the hilarious saga into six pages, explaining that he considered it such a "classic misadventure" that it deserved retelling.[49] The availability of the more recent, though shorter, version obviates the necessity of any detail here, and it certainly reinforces previous statements about the strength of Austin's sense of humor. The Mercies found a great scarcity of food and clothing in Columbus, Georgia, and though it caused no laughter at the time, it was all fodder for fun a generation later. Their "tea" was made of "dried blackberry leaves," for example, and their "coffee" was a brew using "parched corn." But even these drastic shortages might have seemed like luxuries to the Mississippi Mercies, who had to fashion "shoes" of old rags and an occasional rabbit skin, and whose very home had been taken over by the siege-winning military and turned into their commissary in Vicksburg. After the looting and firing of Jackson, where the church and school were burned also, the Sisters of Mercy moved with the doctors and the wounded from Canton to Lauderdale Springs, then over to Alabama, where some of the sisters would be on nursing duty at Shelby Springs until the last battle had been fought.[50]

In New England, meanwhile, Austin Carroll's special talents for history and literature had been channeled into what was to be her lifelong service to the Sisters of Mercy all over the world as biographer, annalist, and historian. By sending out the appeals for data concerning the foundress of the Mercy Institute and receiving information from the very Sisters who had worked with Catherine McAuley and known her personally, Austin began forging links of Mercy unity. This was no bond of government, of course, but a singleness of spirit and purpose. Facts and feelings about Catherine began arriving from many quarters during the war so that the strength of this chain of correspondence was to be tested through the next several years both by the harrowing fire of the sectional conflict and by Austin's assignment and transfer to other areas. While in Manchester, however, the news which Austin received was both bad and good. The bad news frequently arrived in the envelopes from Mercies who sent reports of death and suffering in their strife-torn area. These personal views were often more devastating than the items in the newspapers, like the tragic numbers of soldiers who gave their lives or limbs. What matter that they wore blue or gray, the fact that thousands died while as many others were permanently maimed appalled Austin. Such statistics probably increased her fears about the safety of her brother, the fun-loving favorite Willie, serving with the troops in India.

Austin might have felt it unjust, in a way, that so many were suffering and dying while the environs in which she worked were so tranquil and enjoyable. Thirty years later she still recalled the fun that she and her Mercy friends had singing, playing the piano, writing verses, and the extracurricular activities with her "devoted fellow soldier," Mary Gonzaga O'Brien.[51] She had many an exultant moment, also, as the mail arrived with a copy of another of Catherine's letters or more of the reminiscences of the early days of the Mercy Institute. These memories often proved highly enlightening, for some of the sisters had taken notes as Catherine gave the daily lecture, an explanation of the Rule, or occasionally, retreat talk. On the whole Austin found her correspondents exceedingly generous about sending her information. Here or there, of course, no answer was ever forthcoming from certain convents. And just as Austin reveled in the successes of her research, so did Xavier Warde become excited with the prospect of sending out another foundation. In 1863, she promised Bishop James O'Gorman, the Vicar Apostolic of Nebraska, a group of Mercy teachers. This second motherhouse Xavier established from Manchester during Austin's assignment there was thus destined for the largely unsettled Territory of Nebraska.[52]

Encapsulating the tangible growth in the tiny frontier town entitled Omaha City, the annual *Catholic Directory* listed the advance as follows: 1856—"A Church" under construction and "soon to be supplied with a priest," 1857—Omaha City had one of the "three churches building," 1858—Omaha City "attended from St. John's, Doniphan, Kansas Territory," 1860—Bishop O'Gorman reported, "as yet no religious institutions in the Territory." If the Civil War had not stifled the *Directory* for two years, the bishop could have stated in 1862 that he was canvassing the convents in the Northeast for a group of religious teachers.[53] Then "in the summer of 1863," after writing Xavier Warde "for over a year . . . his request was granted" provisionally.[54] Mother Xavier promised a colony once a convent had been completed.[55] That point in time would not arrive until the middle of 1864; and as far as safety was concerned, was too close to the unresolved turmoil of the war to allow travel without grave danger. It was not too soon to advertise, however, and the *Directory* did: 1864—"A convent, nearly finished, will be ready by the first of May . . . a school for females, boarders, and externs," 1865—"The Sisters of Mercy have commenced their school for girls," some of whom might board with the sisters and others could be day scholars, the "externs" who would live at home.[56] Thus, all was being readied out in the far reaches beyond the Midwest in the Nebraska Territory.

The financial accounts in Manchester bear proof that preparations were underway in the spring of 1864. In April, for instance, there was an expenditure of $5.50 for "materials for Fair at Omaha City," and for that travel necessity, "straw bonnets for the Sisters," $17.00 was spent. Possibly, Mary Austin and the other designated travelers were having their shoes resoled, retipped, or reinforced in some other way because there were three separate entries of "boots for Sisters" to total $14.25. Finally, there was the payment "to P. Donahoe for printing copies of the Rule" for $17.00. Obviously, all of the necessities were being gathered together over a period of months.[57] In the West preparations had taken years as poor Bishop O'Gorman struggled along on the minimal donations from his sparse flock, a few collection tours to other dioceses, and the financial allotments of the European mission societies.[58] None of the bishops along the American frontier could have progressed as they did without the generous aid which arrived periodically from the Propagation of the Faith of Lyons or Paris, the Leopoldine Society of Vienna, and the Ludwig Missionsverein of Munich. With their help Bishop O'Gorman had purchased property and built the first school and convent, the latter due for completion in May. As so often happens with construction, the new convent was a bit behind schedule even though the sisters were expected in June, 1864. In July, however, Xavier Warde wrote that she planned to have the Mercies there by the first of September.[59]

As in the Philadelphia foundation, the superior-designate was one of the sisters that Xavier had brought over from St. Joseph's in Ballinrobe. Omaha City was to have Sister Mary Ignatius Lynch, a native of Galway, who was professed before Archbishop John McHale. This event, like her family background, evidently lent an éclat to her reputation, which seemed to have been given an exaggerated weight at the time. Chosen by Xavier to accompany her was an Irish crew: Austin from Clonmel, novice Regina Crane from Newtonbarry, Joseph Jennings from Dublin, and Anne Fahey of Partry, thus representing a cross section from Wexford and Tipperary in the East and South, the capital in the center, over to the West, in Galway and Mayo. The other two sisters, Augustine Meagher and Francis O'Hanlon, although entering the Manchester convent from New York, could also have been natives of Ireland.[60] The Mercies in New York quietly performed a service as tremendous as the city itself for the Mercy mother-houses in the interior of the country. The New York community had established sodalities which offered religious, educational, and social benefits for the girls and women who joined. An unexpected outgrowth was the fact that the sisters noticed many girls who were attracted to religious life. When superiors came East seeking candidates, there were often several young women awaiting just such an opportunity to serve God and His people as religious.[61]

Possibly, this was the process by which the Misses O'Hanlon and Meagher reached Manchester, or the pathway by which the latter's sister, Margaret, and Elizabeth Fahy reached Nebraska shortly after the founding group. Whatever the procedure, these reinforcements raised the count to nine. It was Xavier and the original crew of seven, however, who set out "on July 27." Austin also said that they stopped overnight at Albany and Syracuse and mentioned "the heat and dust which made traveling anything but pleasant." All of this implies they went by stagecoach rather than by railcar, and since the expenses of the trip were being defrayed by Sister Anne Fahy, cost was certainly a factor in choosing their transportation. With the five stopovers in New York state Austin noted that "the sisters everywhere treated them with the greatest cordiality." Rochester and Buffalo provided hospitality also for the annual retreat, each taking four of the travelers.[62] During retreat Manchester frantically recalled Xavier because her assistant, Philomena Edwards, was mortally ill. Xavier wrote Bishop O'Gorman from Rochester of her change of plans, expressing her concern for the seven for Omaha because "the distance is so far and the weather so warm."[63] Evident once again was the fact that the Northeast was so undisturbed by the violence of war that Xavier seemed to be unconscious of it elsewhere. She worried about the heat of late summer rather than the red-hot turmoil, actually warfare, through which the sisters would have to pass in order to reach the Territory of Nebraska.

Prior to that section of their journey, however, the Mercies had a peaceful and entertaining trip through Indiana. Mary Austin described their visit to "Notre Dame du Lac at South Bend," where the president himself, Rev. Edward Sorin, had given them the grand tour of the campus. Thereafter, the Mercies were "most hospitably entertained . . . by the holy and accomplished Mother Angela Gillespie" of the French Marianites of Holy Cross.[64] Early the next day the missionary group was on its way to the motherhouse of the Sisters of Mercy in Chicago, where they had requested hospitality for about a week until their Bishop came for them. Austin explained why the six days turned into six weeks. "Railroad bridges had been burned, tracks torn up, carriages fired into, trains delayed for weeks, food not to be had . . . and their friends advised the sisters not to proceed."[65]

The decision was really up to O'Gorman, who was still trying to have the convent completed, as to how soon he could arrange to transfer the Mercies to Omaha without risking their lives. In the meantime Austin presented an enthusiastic picture of her participation in the regular wartime works of the Chicago community. She accompanied the sisters to Camp Douglas to visit the sick among the Union soldiers and to see the Confederates imprisoned in Chicago after the fall of Fort Donelson. Austin's generous assistance that September initiated friendships with Sisters Mary Francis de Sales Mulholland, and Genevieve Granger, both of whom Austin met again as they all continued down the broad pathway of Mercy service. But the immediate trip was once again at hand as O'Gorman sent Rev. James M. Ryan to escort the Omaha missionaries through the "disturbed areas of irregular warfare,"[66] termed guerrilla tactics. The grateful travelers bid adieu to their generous sisters and, with courage and carpetbags,

> left Chicago at 10 p.m., October 11, 1864. . . . Guerrillas carried on irregular warfare in several places. . . . Military companies had disbanded, and tramps . . . surrounded railway depots. . . . After meeting with various accidents, the party reached St. Joseph, Missouri, about midnight. Here they were led to a wild-looking barn, styled by courtesy, the Waverly Hotel.[67]

Austin Carroll continued with a vivid description of the economical plan whereby the owner's family and servants gave up their beds upon the arrival of guests. Thus, the sisters were ushered into rooms with the just-vacated beds still warm and too dirty to permit the Mercies to sleep in them. Early the next morning an immigrant train arrived with a motley crowd of "sick, hungry, and weary" families from various countries. As there seemed to be "the wailings of hundreds of babies" in the polyglot chaos, the sisters amused toddlers and quieted infants while mothers tried to serve sparse rations to the older youngsters. The pastor of St. Joseph's, later the archbishop of Dubuque, Rev. John Hennessy,

> who knew something about the quarters they were in . . . conducted them to the Convent of the Sacred Heart. The sisters received them with much kindness, and never did convent look more like heaven to them. . . . October 13, the steamer arrived to take them to Omaha. . . . The landscape as seen from the boat was wild and bleak looking . . . the prairie flowers coarse and scentless.[68]

Evidently, the sisters were feeling a bit of homesickness for the Northeast as the *Montana* took a whole week to reach Omaha. When the steamer slowed to a stop in the Missouri and dropped anchor off the river bank of the young town, it was October 21, 1864. Bishop O'Gorman welcomed them, explaining that his vicariate would grow up with this frontier town, "which had a great destiny."

There were many hands to load the sisters' trunks and bags onto the horse-drawn omnibus which took them to see the bishop's church and his poor little rectory, then up to their grand new home "high on a bluff above the river." Not only was there wide open space all about it, but the three-story convent was a "spacious brick house . . . a mansion," Mary Austin termed it, in which the sole furniture was a pianoforte and a stove. The bishop had ordered the necessary furnishings earlier, but the same conditions which delayed the sisters had probably stalled the furniture shipments. After close to three months on the road since their farewells in Manchester, these Sisters of Mercy were happy to see a convent building — empty or not. Classrooms were to be on the second floor, and on the third,

> their sleeping apartments were arranged like a Trappist dormitory, in compartments, each having room for only a small bed . . . partitions about seven feet high . . . like a huge stable. . . . The situation was altogether so ridiculous that they laughed themselves to sleep.[69]

The next morning the sisters "arose betimes" and set out for the tiny church, in reality, the bishop's "little wooden cathedral." The community historian related that the Order of Mercy was established in Omaha with words of thanksgiving, and certainly, that was not just a *Deo Gratias* the evening before. At their first Mass in Nebraska these Mercies just as surely sought God's grace and strength for their work in this frontier town with the "great destiny."[70]

In the light of early morning the sisters could compare the reality of their new town, Omaha City, with an enthusiastic description by the press:

> Its streets are grand and spacious, opening out eastward into space, bright, broad and luminous. . . . The plan of the town is splendid, being raised far above the river plain, and losing itself miles away to the north in the . . . gently sloping hills covered with brushweed. . . . The chapel is small, but clean and neat.[71]

Practical matters occupied their attention as they walked back home on the broad lanes, "the streets of the future," as breakfast called for ingenuity. Two Mercies trudged "across the prairie to a sort of farmhouse to buy milk." Another pair of the nuns borrowed some tin cups; several more found a boy to go for bread and another willing to gather kindling for the kitchen stove. That first meal was served Japanese fashion as the sisters "sat on the floor about the stove, and stirred their coffee with chopsticks picked up under the carpenter's shed." All the buying and borrowing by the Mercies alerted their kind neighbors to the extent of their needs. So, word was passed, and "a wealthy lady supplied some of the more pressing wants," with others aiding as they could.[72] Meanwhile the Sisters readied a room to serve as their chapel; and according to the paper, all the bustling about was appropriate for "the whole of the townspeople are as busy as bees, building, trading, grading, etc. . . . Pretty Gothic cottage houses with thin lofty gables are numerous. . . . Small beginnings characterize the town."[73]

Like the town, the sisters made a small beginning also, with Ignatius Lynch as the music teacher and Austin Carroll as the faculty of St. Mary's Academy. That left several sisters for Holy Angels School at Eighth and Howard, plus two lay sisters to assist with the cooking and housekeeping. The local papers welcomed the Mercies, praised the usefulness of "a Female College," and encouraged the citizens to send their daughters and "to induce your friends to send theirs."[74] The lack of furniture must have delayed the opening of the academy. Even before the desks arrived, however, registration might have begun, for the sisters had long been expected. Louise Burkley and Mary O'Brien were the earliest students to register, with Mary Wareham, Annie Murphy, and Charlotte O'Connor soon joining the roll for "the high or first class."[75] Similar numbers might very well have comprised the middle or second level and the minim or primary group. Twelve or fifteen pupils would have made a good crowd for this school opening in the middle of a semester, especially as a photograph taken four years later showed only twenty-six girls.[76] Austin said that she was the first teacher at St. Mary's and "a splendid school it was."[77] In every school in which she had taught, Austin had turned the teacher-student relationship into a mutually pleasant experience, and St. Mary's was no exception.

Bishop O'Gorman noted that the sisters were "much liked by the people" in those early days. Austin seconded this, mentioning her enjoyable associations "with both children and people."[78] The bishop and Austin shared similar views on crosses and trials, also: "As trials go before virtues," he said, "so difficulties go before every work intended to give glory to God." Austin added that the sisters did not expect that

> the universal popularity which they first enjoyed . . . could last forever. The cross must come in many forms . . . for their house was to have exceptional success, and no Convent of Mercy ever flourished save beneath the blessed shadow of the cross.[79]

Whether or not it was in order to "have exceptional success," the community had to face several types of problems, and one of these was economic. Letters to the Leopoldine Society explained that nuns could hardly make a living in Omaha, as Catholics were too few and too poor. Account books illustrate how frugally the Mercies lived, with the largest expenditures made for the wood which gave them warmth.[80]

In spite of the bills for fuel, that first winter brought into the convent a biting cold that would not be dispersed until the first superior withdrew from the community. Possibly, it was exaggerating the importance of heritage and assignment which made it difficult for her to interact with either the American families or her own Irish sisters. Whatever the case, she managed to alienate both the generous Omaha families and also the members of the community able to further its success.[81] As the appointed assistant to the superior, Mary Austin felt it her duty to protest to Mary Ignatius concerning several problems, the neglect of several aspects of the Rule among others. When questioned by Bishop O'Gorman, Austin was just as open and honest in her replies to him as her Ecclesiastical Superior. Later she said, "I know what my candor cost me."[82] Unable to influence the decisions of Ignatius, and possibly fearing scandal, the bishop did not force the issues, but let action await the arrival of his successor. In his *History of the Catholic Church in Nebraska*, Henry W. Casper, SJ, made a carefully detailed study of the problem of the sisters with Ignatius Lynch. His work makes repetition of that material unnecessary and, also, gives exceptional weight to his conclusions as those of both a trained observer and an impartial witness. Father decided that,

As a result of twelve years of her government, the unrefuted good and gain accomplished by most of those under her was to a large extent nullified by the dissatisfaction Mother Ignatius caused within her community and the bad rapport without.[83]

Pertinent to this work, also, is the historian's carefully weighed conclusion about Mary Austin Carroll, who tried to remedy the situation on behalf of the community. "Looking back in retrospect" long years after Austin completed forty years as a successful administrator of the numerous Mercy convents and institutions across the Southern states, Father Casper stated that "one can deplore the circumstances that this remarkable woman was never destined to take the helm of the expanding operations generously undertaken in Omaha by the Sisters of Mercy."[84] In that pioneer group of Mercies, Casper considered Austin the one "temperamentally best suited to direct the foundation."[85] He also noted that Austin left Omaha "ostensibly" to continue writing the biography of Catherine McAuley. The connotations of that "ostensibly" were accurate, for Austin wished to leave no negative impressions about the fine sisters with whom she worked in Nebraska. Although Austin stated the positive reason of completing the biography, her letters demonstrate that she made the negative reasons clear to Bishop O'Gorman and the archbishop of St. Louis, Peter Richard Kenrick,[86] who gave permission for her transfer to the St. Louis Convent of Mercy.

Austin's sympathy for the oppressed in Nebraska, as in each locale in which she served, inspired her devotion to the prison apostolate. In Omaha she gathered periodicals and newspapers from the townsfolk in order to have reading material to bring to jail each Sunday. Convent funds were so scarce that first year in the West that she was probably unable to purchase the traditional gifts of tobacco and soap for the inmates. Regardless of the funding, however, in each jail she visited in the United States Austin Carroll managed to begin the formation of libraries. She urged the prisoners who could read to do so in order that they could emerge better informed than when they were arrested. Austin was just as consistent about establishing other types of libraries, like those in the schools, sodalities or Sunday classes, and even parish "circulating libraries." Funding for the various collections differed as tuition covered the first, membership dues took care of the second, and the ways and means of financing the third varied with the parish.

In that year in Omaha Austin Carroll inaugurated not only book collections of all kinds and systematic prison visitation, but she also added her own touch to the final exhibition or closing entertainment. Such annual productions generally consisted of recitations and songs interspersed by piano selections. Austin's presence brought the additional dimension of drama, if not an entire play, a few dramatic scenes. These histrionics were usually historical and centered about one of the royal ladies like Marie Antoinette, Mary Queen of Scots, one of the Tudor sisters, or Katherine of Aragon. These were the ladies with the titular roles when Austin later published her series of school plays.[87] Because the tragic Marie Antoinette was the heroine in the dramatic scenes presented at the closing of the first scholastic session, Austin Carroll's imprint was clearly present in the event at St. Mary's Academy. The press stated that the drama was so "masterfully executed by the pupils" that it even surpassed the expectations of the appreciative audience.[88] Probably, the author of the drama and the elocution coach, Austin herself, was one of the sisters receiving the compliments of the proud and delighted parents that summer evening.

Prior to the happy conclusion of the grand exhibition, Mary Austin might have begun the paperwork connected with a transfer. Since she hoped to be settled for the fall semester and the mails were terribly slow, her first letters could have gone out early, perhaps in the spring, as one account says.[89] The ecclesiastical permit Austin sought, in a way like the visa of the foreign traveler, finally arrived and Austin, with permission to go to St. Louis, bade her friends goodby. Throughout her life Austin was blessed with an exceptionally large number of friends and admirers. This is not to say that she was a paragon of perfection, for like any strong character, she made enemies here and there along life's way. More often than not it happened, as it did with Ignatius Lynch, because Mary Austin seemed to have an inability to overlook the mistreatment of others on one hand, while on the other, she was impelled by her courageous forthrightness to protest the injustice. As she pursued this course, however, Austin Carroll's intensity, persistence, and candor often angered those who were pricked by the points she made.

Yet, Mary Austin Carroll had a natural charm that attracted people of all classes — jailers and journalists, not just pupils and parents; sinners and socialites as well as women and writers; printers and publishers and not just sisters and shopkeepers; and newsboys and the neighbors as well as legions of priests and prelates. Austin's numerous friends came to know her not only as a woman unafraid to state the unpopular truth, especially when she spoke in behalf of others; but also as the religious sister whose gentle ways and tactful approach could adeptly soften the hardest of hearts. Austin's compassion was so quick and deep that it drove her to heroic efforts to alleviate the pain and suffering of others. Upon occasion, others have also demonstrated just such an extraordinary depth of caring. In great disasters hundreds of people from all walks of life usually put forth heroic efforts on behalf of others, and many governments and religious communities have certainly had leaders of this special caliber. In the Mercy Institute, for example, quite a few of Austin's friends and correspondents were, like herself, exceptionally fine leaders.

In this instance, Austin's resilient spirit refused to allow a failure to prevent her prompt and wholehearted involvement again as soon as the next appeal for help arrived. She often said, "I don't like giving up unless it is impossible to proceed."[90] Here the impossibility was clear, but she wondered why she had not been able to find a successful way to solve the problems. Her attempts had only worsened the situation in the frontier community. Thus it was in 1865, as the Omaha sisters waved to the travelers who had just boarded the sturdy river packet.[91] It was their farewell view of Mary Austin Carroll, her face sad, her small frame erect, but wrapped as always in her cloak of compassion. Her trunk was light, but her heart was heavy. Although she hated failure of any kind, she still carried with her an expectancy of better times ahead and her treasured McAuley manuscript.

5 PRISONERS & PUBLICATION
Saint Louis
1865–1869

raveling down the Missouri River was far easier in 1865, according to Mary Austin Carroll, than was the frightening trip upstream the year before. In fact, it was probably difficult for Austin to realize that almost an entire year had elapsed since the terrifying journey through guerrilla-infested territory in 1864. Some of that area had been cleared, however, as the torturous conflict limped along to its conclusion. Austin could not help thinking about the most recent bits and pieces of news which had come to her from her Mercy correspondents. Of course, she never received the sisters' letters until long after the events had been related in the papers from an entirely different perspective. The Mercies had written recently of the emaciated Confederate soldiers making their way home from the disbanded field hospitals, men who believed so firmly in their cause that they had sacrificed both their health and their possessions for it. Whether or not the sisters agreed with the Southern cause, they felt that the condition of the men was heartrending. Furthermore, the sisters knew what the men would find at the end of their belabored trek—their homes and crops burned, their farm animals gone, neighboring stores, towns, and even churches looted and torched.[1]

The people throughout the South, and the sisters with them, were living on cornbread and some kind of peas or beans, with the occasional luxury of a cup of parched corn "coffee." Some of the sisters spoke of a near famine and a period of several years with neither tea nor coffee. Clothing was as scarce as food, and the Mercies were overjoyed to locate even the flimsiest white muslin, which they managed to dye a brownish black and use for veils and aprons which hid their "holey habits." Since Confederate money was almost worthless, prices were exorbitant, with calico selling for $40 a yard and thread, $20 a spool.[2] In the spring one of the sisters had written of the last day in Charleston before the city fell to the enemy. Since the convent orphan asylum had already been shelled, prominent Southerners fleeing the city had begged the sisters to utilize their homes as convent, asylum, or school. It was impossible, the Mercies felt, ever to forget the despair of the people as they saw the inevitable end of both the conflict and their city rapidly approaching. Sister thought that she would remember forever that night filled with howls and "triumphant shouts as the Yankees" occupied Charleston.[3]

News from Georgia was even worse, for there the Union forces were despoiling the Catholic cemetery. The Sisters of Mercy, like many of the families still in Savannah, had the herculean task of transferring the remains of their loved ones from the St. Vincent de Paul or Cathedral Cemetery. The Mercies and their helpers managed to beat the Union shovels to the bodies of two bishops and several priests and sisters. As the decrepit pine coffins were temporarily reinterred in the convent yard, Bishop Verot protested to the authorities, not only about the occupation of the church grounds, but especially concerning the desecration of the cemetery and the bodies which had rested there.[4] What really amazed the sisters was the evident conviction of the Union officers that the Confederate soldiers were coming after them to avenge the Union swath of devastating arson and awesome desolation. The Georgians wondered how any sensible person could actually believe that there was still a strong Southern Army with sufficient food and ammunition to threaten anyone. That the Union vandals feared reprisal was quite understandable, however; for they had appropriated any valuables they could carry, torched homes, broken the furniture not burned, and taken the food from the homeless. Such were the injustices that led many foreign-born Americans, like Tipperary's Mary Austin Carroll, to sympathize with the ravaged South and its suffering people. "Apart from politics," Austin wrote, "the sympathy of the sisters belongs to the vanquished and unfortunate."[5]

Irish sisters like Mary Austin were not the only Southern sympathizers, for all of the foreign-born bishops in the South spoke out in behalf of their people. Bishop Auguste Marie Martin of Natchitoches, Louisiana, a native of St. Malo in Brittany, appealed to the Propagation of the Faith; while Verot, a native of LePuy in Haute-Loire, wrote Martin J. Spalding that his people had to have aid soon or "die of hunger." Both Bishop Verot and Bishop John Quinlan of Mobile, a native of Cloyne in County Cork, worried about their orphans. The former said that the Mercies and their forty girls were on the verge of starvation. The archbishop of New Orleans, Jean Marie Odin who was a native of Ambierle in the Loire, explained that even the country areas had an absolute scarcity of food because of the soldiers' appropriation of farm horses and mules. The Louisiana plantations were "wildernesses . . . and the desolation both horrible and universal."[6] Graphically describing the situation, Bishop Verot said that there was no money at all in the South, only worthless Confederate paper; and that from the people had been stolen their cotton and other crops down to "their last grain of corn." With all these urgent appeals, help began to arrive as Spalding and other Bishops asked their people for help. The Vatican contributed $1000 in equal amounts to the North and the South, and the Propagation of the Faith sent donations, also.[7]

Correspondence completed, Mary Austin probably turned her thoughts away from the South and toward the Mercy community in St. Louis. Although she did not know these sisters personally, Austin easily recalled Mother Agnes O'Connor of the New York City motherhouse from which St. Louis had been established. Austin remembered how much, as a novice in 1854, she and the others in Cork had enjoyed hearing of the many works of mercy which flourished in the great port. Austin especially relished the account of Agnes fashioning a trumpet from a sheet of music and calling out, "Who's for New York?" to her Dublin community.[8] Of the numerous volunteers, seven were allowed to take ship for America. Upon their arrival, one of the welcomers announced that seven hundred sisters would be needed to keep pace with the immigrants needing help. As it did not take the Mercies long to agree with this assessment, they begged five more helpers from Dublin in as many years. One of the additional sisters arriving in 1851, the twelfth Mercy to come over from the Baggot Street motherhouse, in fact, was the exceedingly delicate novice Mary de Pazzi Bentley, later the superior in St. Louis. If de Pazzi had not left for Missouri in 1856 just a few months before Austin Carroll's arrival in America, the two might have met before Austin started for Providence.[9]

In Rhode Island Mary Austin learned how Agnes O'Connor had lent musicians to Xavier Warde for the earliest reception and profession ceremonies in New England.[10] The principal vocalist was Elizabeth Seton's daughter Kitty, Sister Mary Catherine, "whose voice is of the highest note and cultivation," said Mother Agnes. She considered Kitty's entrance into the Mercy community "a singular favor from Providence."[11] Named for the Mercy foundress when she received the habit, Mary Catherine Seton shared with Austin Carroll both a deep interest in the prison apostolate and a special loving veneration for another Kitty, the saintly Catherine McAuley. Certainly, the spirit of Mother McAuley was rife in this lending of voices, sharing of interests, and donating of personnel. Just as Dublin had been generous with New York, Agnes O'Connor responded in turn to a plea for sisters for a Mercy foundation in Brooklyn in 1855, and another for St. Louis in the following year. The annual *Catholic Directory* announced these in the issue following each departure: in 1856, "Last September, six professed sisters were sent . . . to the city of Brooklyn," and in 1857, "Last

June, five professed sisters were sent . . . to establish a foundation of their order in the city of St. Louis."[12]

The convent chronicles identify these five professed missionaries leaving for Missouri as Mother de Pazzi Bentley, superior of the group composed of two choir sisters, Mary Jerome Shubirck and Mary Aloysius Comerford, and two lay sisters, Liguori Galbraith and Joseph Byrne. Although the New York archives list only these five as leaving for St. Louis,[13] several accounts state that a sixth sister made the June 1856 trip to the city on the Mississippi River.[14] Quite possibly, there was a candidate in the missionary party, for the Irish-born Mary O'Farrell entered the Mercy community right after the sisters arrived in St. Louis. Perhaps, she had accompanied them from New York as a postulant and been counted as one of the religious. She was received into the community by Mother de Pazzi as Sister Francis, and like Sisters Liguori and Joseph, had been in St. Louis almost ten years by the time that Austin arrived. Sisters Jerome Shubrick and Aloysius Comerford had both returned by then to the New York community. So too, had Elizabeth Callanan, who had earlier assisted for a time in Rochester and it was not many months after her recall from Rochester that Agnes O'Connor sent Elizabeth to St. Louis. Arriving there on September 5, 1858, Elizabeth Callanan aided Mother de Pazzi for two years before returning to her New York motherhouse.[15]

Among the ten sisters sent by Mother Agnes during the pioneer years to assist the Missouri foundation, two missioned in 1858 were postulant Anna Walker and the newly-received novice Mary Grant. Unlike the short-term helpers, this pair was to work for a full decade in St. Louis before leaving to establish foundations elsewhere, Catherine Grant being assigned to New Orleans and Ignatius Walker going to Louisville.[16] These new motherhouses were still four years in the future, however, when on September 5, 1865, Mary Austin Carroll saw the river packet edging its way carefully past a dozen boats until it located a vacant slip on the busy waterfront. Mary Austin received a warm welcome from the Sisters of Mercy, partly because another sister was surely welcome, since so much of their New York help had been temporary.[17] There would be other reasons for cordiality, however, as soon as the sisters had a chance to work with this Irish nun that Xavier Warde had described as "both educated and accomplished" as well as one "of our very best teachers."[18] Austin had requested time to complete her biography of Catherine McAuley, and Sisters of Mercy the world over should appreciate the insight shown by de Pazzi Bentley in her acquiescence to this request. Certainly, it was Mother de Pazzi's realization of the value of Austin Carroll's life of the Mercy foundress that led to the completion of the manuscript during Austin's first year in St. Louis and its publication a year later. That was 1866, the tenth year in which the Sisters of Mercy had served the people of St. Louis.

During this decade the work of the Mercies had so expanded that their convent at Tenth and Morgan Streets soon proved too small for their needs. Hence the superior, having surveyed the area in 1860, decided that they should move and called the sisters to beseech St. Joseph for the means to do so. Then, with perfect timing as an answer to their prayer, Archbishop Kenrick offered the sisters a new location on the corner of Morgan and Twenty-second. This lot held ample space for the construction of a convent and school as well as accommodations for a House of Mercy for working-girls. "The joy and worry attached to the erection of the new building," related the Mercy historian, "were the special lot of Mother Mary de Pazzi Bentley."[19] The efficiency of this superior is demonstrated by the fact that the sisters were able to get into the new building in just over a year, with the transfer accomplished on July 16, 1861. Because of the turmoil of the war, construction on the east wing was simply postponed until the return of peace allowed the completion of the original plans in their entirety.

As the country moved closer to actual combat, Mother de Pazzi thought it appropriate to offer to the local officials the services of the Sisters of Mercy as nurses if that were agreeable to Archbishop Kenrick. He answered that their "services might be needed," but he thought it "more advisable to await an invitation than to anticipate the necessity by offering them."[20] Thus it was that the Mercies were constrained to limit their work during the course of the Civil War to the confines of the city itself. That was no small matter, however, for the wounded continued to overflow from the four city hospitals until 25,000 soldiers had been assigned to a makeshift tent hospital established at the Fair Grounds campsite. There the Sisters of Mercy visited daily as they tried to console and instruct the poor sick and suffering men. This work was nothing new for the nuns, for ever since their establishment in St. Louis, they had given time and attention to the visitation of those imprisoned by society in the local jail or by sickness in their homes. Austin had previously seen the same type of emphasis on these works of mercy in Cork, Dublin, and New York. Now in St. Louis Austin would restrict her apostolic work to prison visitation until her biography of Catherine McAuley was forwarded to the publisher in New York.

Before the manuscript could be placed in the hands of the type-setters, Mary Austin had several trouble spots which called for careful study. Looking into just one of these makes the type of problem that beset her more understandable. Austin's primary sources were the Mercy manuscripts from Derry, Bermondsey, and Dublin; "several incidents of the early life of the Foundress" related by Mother Xavier and her collection of Catherine's letters; and finally, several memoirs written for Austin by Catherine

McAuley's personal acquaintances among the early sisters.[21] These eyewitness accounts gave a reliable picture of Catherine during the time in which she established the Mercy Institute, but problems arose about Catherine's early life and the date of her birth. Her brother stated that her birthday was September 29, 1787, and that she was fifty-four when she died in 1841. Hence, on the strength of the brother's testimony, 1787 was the date used by the sisters for obituaries, official convent records, and for later inquirers such as Mary Austin Carroll. Yet the birth date was listed as September 17, 1778, in an 1847 article about Catherine McAuley.[22] Austin commented in her preface in Catherine's biography,

> The first account of her was published in the *Dublin Review*, by her friend, Very Reverend Miletius Gaffney, Dean of Maynooth. . . . Where he and other historians disagree, we follow him in preference to any other, because as her spiritual director, he had abundant opportunities of acquiring accurate information.[23]

In this instance which concerned a family celebration like a birthday party, Mary Austin considered Catherine McAuley's brother James a more reliable source than Gaffney, a friend made only after Catherine no longer advertised each passing year. Austin probably saw in 1864 that Mother Vincent Hartnett's life of the foundress had combined the Gaffney year, 1778, with the day of the month cited by Catherine's brother.[24] Perhaps September 29, 1778, was the correct combination of day and year, but to this day, documentation of that is yet to be found. During the massive research efforts of John MacErlean, SJ, legal papers were unearthed which established 1787 as erroneous because of the death of Catherine's father in 1783.[25] Knowing Austin's determination and thoroughness makes it easy for one to believe that, had she not been 5000 miles away from Dublin sources, she might have cajoled authorities there into allowing her to research the records needed. Until after she had become an established author, however, nineteenth-century bureaucrats would probably have refused to open their files to a woman or a nun. Suppositions aside, Austin was so aware of the likelihood of erroneous data that she appealed in her preface for notification of errors.

> If notwithstanding all our efforts to verify each circumstance connected with Catherine McAuley, any inaccuracies be found in this work, they may be easily rectified in a future edition, as the brother of the Foundress and several of her early associates are still living; and should they detect any error, . . . they have only to communicate with us.[26]

Mary Austin would have been delighted to have heard from Catherine McAuley's brother or close relatives. But even though she received a good bit of comment from other sources, she had to wait fifteen years to hear from a cousin. Literary columns of newspapers and magazines carried a tremendous number of positive reviews as well as a few negative ones. For the most part the latter came from Mercy convents whose members felt that the life was far too revealing. The published reviews gave quite a bit of space to the biographee, Catherine McAuley herself, and that delighted Austin. On the whole the American press was quite pleased with the author's humor, honesty, and frankness in her portrayal of Catherine as a real person and not just some plaster statue. John Francis Maguire, in his *The Irish in America*, thought that the biography had such "a vivacity and freshness of style" that it would be read with "both pleasure and profit."[27] Others spoke of the work as "popularized" or as told with "sallies of quiet humor, anecdotes, and details" which gave it "the same type of merit" as Boswell's life of Dr. Johnson. More than one Catholic paper pointed out that this life would furnish for curious Protestants an accurate and interesting view of life in a convent, an account much more entertaining than Maria Monk's tales and one more likely to help them understand why women freely chose this lifestyle.[28]

In Ireland a typical reaction to the new life of Catherine McAuley was that expressed in *The Irish Monthly* by Matthew Russell, SJ:

> It is so lively in style and full of such graphic and interesting details as to be one of the most entertaining pieces of biography we are acquainted with. Our readers will not be the less disposed to become its readers if we add that there are sundry expressions and particulars in this American life which would hardly pass a revising board committee of Irish nuns sitting in solemn conclave.[29]

And the editor was correct in his second statement, because many of the Irish Sisters of Mercy in various parts of the world thought "the American author," as they called her, had spoken too openly about the problems that confronted their foundress. Mercies who knew that Mary Austin was a compatriot felt that "she had in no small degree imbibed the undisguised spirit of the New World's Catholic authors."[30] One incident which bothered a number of readers was the occasion on which Catherine McAuley drew forth a violently angry reaction on the part of her Protestant brother-in-law by informing him that his wife, shortly before her death, had renewed her Catholic faith and died as a member of the Church. Fearing this uncharacteristic violence, Catherine fled down the military Road to Abbeyville House, the family home of Sir James William Cusack, MD, who was an old family friend.[31] Even though the early manuscripts mention the incident, Austin might have shown more prudence by reserving it to such private accounts and the Hartnett biography. That was not the author's way, however, and indignant denials came to Austin indirectly from several sources and connections. In spite of this, corroboration of the incident found its way into print when a niece of the Cusacks, Margaret Anna Cusack, later a religious foundress herself, mentioned in her autobiography that her uncle, Surgeon Cusack, and his wife had given shelter to Catherine McAuley until the contrite offender appeared to seek her pardon and ask her to return to his children.[32] Possibly, Austin felt that Catherine's example of forgiveness and reconciliation was too beautiful a lesson to lose by omitting the earlier part of the unusual event.

On the other hand, Mary Austin was quick to retract a financial reference to an uncle of Catherine's because it offended one of his descendants.[33] At the same time, Austin explained to a friend that quite often "the passages that gave umbrage to some are those which gave the greatest delight to others."[34] By then the author had received directly contrary reactions for identical selections and had come to terms with the critics by balancing the positive and negative opinions. What really gave her pleasure was to hear that readers personally admired Catherine McAuley and her Mercy Institute. For instance, Orestes Brownson, nineteenth-century convert apologist and editor of his philosophical *Quarterly Review*, gave a ten-page tribute to the foundress after reading Austin Carroll's work.

> The *Life of Mother Catherine McAuley* before us makes us feel more deeply than ever, that the ways of God are not man's ways, and . . . what a noble and pure-minded and simple-hearted woman, working in the way Catherine McAuley worked, accomplishes for the glory of God and the spiritual and temporal good of men. . . . We are charmed with her character and with this *Life* of her, . . . destined to do great good . . . judging from the effect its perusal has had on our mind and heart.[35]

As to the author herself, Brownson thought that Mary Austin wrote "with modesty and humility," as well as "with rare ability," and in his opinion, "in the spirit" of the Mercy foundress. Brownson specifically noticed Catherine's approach to the evil of poverty, a point that had caught Austin's attention also.

> Catherine McAuley did not undertake to remove poverty by making the poor rich; . . . her great study was to put the poor . . . in the way of earning their own living, . . . besides the inestimable benefit of acquiring industrious habits and the sense of independence and proper self-esteem.[36]

This aspect of Catherine's vision, the concern for assisting the poor to advance on their own talents, was evident to Austin from her earliest days in the Cork community. With such background and philosophy, Austin was fortunate to have chosen St. Louis where Mercy priorities were so definitely for the poor. Even the announcement in the *New York Freeman's Journal* about the Mercy foundation starting for St. Louis mentioned this purpose. "On the feast of the Nativity of St. John the Baptist, six Sisters of Mercy left the Convent of St. Catherine in this city, to establish a house of their order in St. Louis . . . to minister to the poor according to the spirit of their Rule."[37]

The reporter then extended good wishes to the people of the new location in what was the approved journalistic style of the period.

> We congratulate the Catholics of St. Louis on their good fortune in obtaining a Convent of Mercy in their large and flourishing metropolis. Among their many Convents and Colleges they will now have an order of religious specially devoted to the sick and the poor.[38]

The news item illustrates what the public knew of the work being done by the Mercy community of Mother Agnes O'Connor in New York, and the emphasis placed on social work there was to be expected for several reasons. First, the New York foundation had been established directly from Catherine McAuley's original Dublin motherhouse. Even though there were schools attached to the Baggot Street Convent, heavy emphasis was placed upon the relief and assistance afforded to the poor through the visitation of the sick and the refuge for young women in the House of Mercy. Secondly, these particular works of Mercy were the great need of a busy port in any country, and the same pattern of service was established in turn in New York City and St. Louis. Further, although she did not know it as yet, Mary Austin was to bring it down to the crescent port of New Orleans in just a few more years. In a way, one might see the type of service as a combination of need on the one hand and, on the other, as links in the chain of Mercy genealogy.

There was an entirely different kind of need in the inland towns, such as Carlow in Ireland or Manchester in America. Since many young girls left such areas to find work elsewhere, early instruction was a fundamental necessity. When the Sisters of Mercy were invited to such locations, it was primarily because a school needed staffing. Hence, the main focus of attention was on education, usually in both a free school for the poor and a pension school or academy where tuition was a requisite. In 1856, just over from Cork where there were schools for the poor, for the deaf, and both pension and industrial schools, Mary Austin Carroll had seen no problem about the academies which Mother Xavier Warde established in each of the convents she founded. Since it was Catherine McAuley herself who had opened pension schools in Cork, Carlow, and Charleville, Austin wondered how any Sister of Mercy could oppose the actions of her foundress. In the spring of 1856 Xavier Warde had visited Agnes O'Connor in New York for a fortnight, during which time the two superiors had come to a better understanding about the pension and boarding schools.[39] Later Xavier explained that she had quoted "the very words of our Holy Foundress" on the subject, thereby tantalizing any reader who would wish to know exactly what that wording happened to be.[40]

From her experience in Cork's pension school "in which all accomplishments were taught," Mary Austin realized that such academies could be a source of candidates well-prepared for the work of the Mercy Institute.[41] But newly arrived Austin of the 1850s, who referred to the worry about the select boarding schools as "foolish scruples,"[42] certainly did not have as full an understanding of the finances involved in providing social services as she did ten years and five assignments later in the city of St. Louis. By then she had noted that the funding of the early days in Cork was similar to the generous support for the poor provided by Archbishop John Hughes in New York. The great success of the Sisters of Mercy in both ports was due in large measure to the solid backing or patronage of the respective prelates. Upon her arrival in America Mother Agnes O'Connor had assured her Dublin sisters on this point, "Do not feel any anxiety about our success; it is enough for us . . . to succeed in every thing" to have the bishop as our sponsor. She also described the influence of the popular archbishop over his flock, whom Mother Agnes thought were "nearly all Irish."[43] In the Cork novitiate Austin had heard of the services and successes in New York — of the hundreds of starving immigrants who arrived daily during Ireland's famine years, of the hundred or more young women placed in situations each month by the Mercies, and the House of Mercy provided by Archbishop Hughes so that more girls could be trained to hold the kind of jobs that the sisters could locate for them. On a smaller scale, of course, this was the same work being done by the Sisters of Mercy in St. Louis.

Together with her Mercy companions, Mary Austin had experienced less fortunate situations in several American towns where the funding needed was not as available as in Cork and New York City. Experience proved to her that the willing efforts of the sisters could give consolation in such towns, but little real aid to the poor when financial support was lacking. The tuition from a pension school in those places provided both the frugal living expenses of the teachers and the means to help the most destitute. These inland towns did not have the immigrant influx of the ports although they all had their share of the poor. In such places the select school actually became what Mother Xavier Warde termed "the sustainment of the community,"[44] and need of a different kind was the key to the work of the sisters. Then too, the locations from which the Mercy missionaries proceeded were almost as important as those to which they journeyed. Manchester in the 1850s was comparable to quiet little Carlow and its branch in neighboring Naas, just to the east of the rolling checkerboard of farms and meadows edged by the country lanes of Xavier Warde's childhood. This area so beautifully fringed by the heathery Wicklow Mountains had many similarities with Manchester in the foothills of the dramatic White Mountains and just northeast of the Berkshires. According to her recent biography, Xavier Warde felt that in Manchester she "had come home — home to Carlow."[45] One who knew her as well as Austin might have added, home to her academy and to an endless succession of catechumens, converts, and convents, for these were her specialties throughout her religious life.

In St. Louis Mary Austin learned that the Sisters of Mercy in New York City had been invited to the Midwest by Rev. Arnold Damen, SJ, who wished to establish an industrial school for girls in St. Francis Xavier Parish. Mother de Pazzi and her sisters chose to make the long journey for the sake of the afflicted poor. Just one month before their arrival in St. Louis, Father Damen's project was explained by the renowned Indian missionary and fellow Hollander, Pierre Jean de Smet, SJ.

> Just now Father Damen is contemplating the erection of an industrial school under the care of the Sisters of Mercy, as an offset to schools of their kind among the Protestants. . . . He has been engaged in this venture scarcely two months and already the subscriptions amount to more than $16,000. With $4,000, which he expects to obtain before long, the school will be founded, and two hundred children at least will be saved from the hands of the sectaries.[46]

De Smet was right, for before long the Mercies arrived and over two hundred girls were soon enrolled. Just a year later the Sisters of Mercy became the afflicted poor themselves because Father Damen, characterized as "a zealous worker, ardent and courageous by nature . . . and gifted with uncommon eloquence," was assigned to Chicago.[47]

Archbishop Kenrick assisted the sisters and gave them a lot on which to build at Morgan and Twenty-second Streets. As a result of this transfer in 1861, the Mercies ceased staffing the industrial school in St. Francis Xavier Parish in order to teach at the new location. That decision resulted in a real financial crisis for the sisters because they lost the generous support given by the Jesuits while the Sisters of Mercy taught in their parish.[48] The archbishop suggested that, in the absence of any other revenue, opening a pay school seemed to be a necessity, and he explained:

> Almost everywhere in this country where endowments are rare, candidates for the religious life almost without dowry, and public charity not always an available source, experience has shown that the pension [or tuition] school is a necessary adjunct to religious institutes.[49]

So, acting on the suggestion of Archbishop Kenrick the following year, Mother de Pazzi Bentley established "a select school . . . until means should be provided." This was no meaningless condition to de Pazzi, as she was completely opposed to pension schools. Her convictions were so strong on this point that a few years later she endeavored to get Rome to modify the Mercy rule and mandate the exclusion of all the select or pension schools sponsored by Sisters of Mercy.[50]

Although Mary Austin was not inclined to establish academies herself, she believed that they were often necessary for the survival of a particular community. She was also aware that Catherine McAuley had not only established pension schools in Cork and other towns but that she had also opened one at Baggot Street itself.[51] Therefore, Austin said that she could never censure any of Catherine's followers for doing likewise, adding in the same letter, that she could not understand any Sister of Mercy trying to cancel out any practice of the foundress.[52] Austin's own personal application of Catherine's ideal was that the apostolates of the Sisters of Mercy should be primarily for the poor, but not exclusively so. The width of Austin's views embraced all God's children. When she directed the work of the New Orleans community a bit later, she gathered the children of both the poor and the middle class into the parish schools, as one of the priests explained:

> All Catholic children are admitted to all classes without distinction — the rich and the poor are invited to partake of the same advantages — the rich of course are in duty bound to contribute towards the support of the schools; otherwise, they could not be sustained.[53]

The variations in Mercy opinions about pension schools have been so belabored here because the pension school itself, a little further down Mary Austin's road of Mercy service, became part of a *cause célèbre* as one item on a list of complaints sent to Rome about the lively Irish nun. That event was still years in the future, however, when Austin taught in the basement of St. Joseph's Convent of Mercy on the corner of Morgan and Twenty-second Streets. One of Austin's letters gave her opinions about including practical work in the school day.

With us, children of every class *learn to work.* . . . We believe it of the greatest importance to bring up our children to industrious habits, especially in a country like this, where reverses are so common. . . . The public common schools never teach manual work of any kind — hence their pupils grow up with a sort of contempt for it, and in the case of family reverses, find it difficult to hit upon any honest way of earning a livelihood. They are willing to take professions, but dislike . . . trades.[54]

Creative herself, Austin especially appreciated that the young girls learned drawing and fancy stitchery as well as plain sewing.

More memorable within the community than her teaching skill, according to Mercy history in St. Louis, was Mary Austin's prison apostolate. To see how highly this type of visitation was regarded by Austin is easy, for she gave the lion's share of space to that aspect of the various works of mercy fostered by the St. Louis community. First of the Mercies engaged in this work at the St. Louis municipal jail was Sister Mary Jerome Shubrick, who was remarkable "through her whole religious life . . . for devotion to visiting and instructing prisoners," according to Austin, who knew sister quite well some years later.[55] Serving with the prison work later was Sister Mary Elizabeth Callanan, related Austin, who met Elizabeth in Rochester before she came down to Missouri. Following these two sisters was Austin, who like Jerome Shubrick was loyal to the prison apostolate as long as she lived, and like Elizabeth Callanan was completely devoted to the work, even continuing her regular weekly visitations when serving as superior in New Orleans.[56] As her partner on the regular visitation treks in St. Louis, Austin Carroll took young Sister Magdalene de Pazzi McDermott. Sister quickly caught the enthusiasm of her mentor, but in all too short a time, she also caught the cholera. After sister's death in the epidemic of 1866, Austin related that the young Mercy had made an offering of her life to God for the spread of the faith, and concluded, "It would seem as if God accepted the sacrifice."[57] Austin's aim was to help those in jail or the prison camps learn of their merciful and loving God. Through the years many did, and of one of these Austin commented: "God has "chosen souls' in the most unlikely places."[58]

The apostolate of visiting both the wounded and the imprisoned became vastly enlarged with the fighting and capturing enemy prisoners in the area. Both the soldiers and their captured troops needed instruction in their faith, messages sent to their families, encouragement under trying circumstances, and, now and again, some food tidbits or goodies from their loved ones. The sisters in St. Louis had done this for several years before Mary Austin's arrival, but she enjoyed having the opportunity of participating. She mentioned later visits to Confederate prisoners in the McDowall

College and the non-military Southern sympathizers in the Gratiot Street prison. Mary Austin also made the rounds in the Work House prison, the Camp Grounds, the Military Hospital, and several others in St. Louis.[59] This time of violence across the nation brought large numbers back to the faith of their childhood. Some of the wounded found the period of recovery from devastating injuries to be a time for offering gratitude to God for their survival. Others of the soldiers had never before seen religious emissaries such as these nuns who did them kindnesses and introduced them to their God, bringing the good news of salvation to all who wished to hear it. Austin, very much impressed by their sincerity, never tired of relating tales of these war-time visitations and the countless conversions that she had seen occur.[60]

Austin Carroll was certainly not alone in taking note of the phenomenon; Church leaders commented upon the remarkable renewal of faith during the conflict. In correspondence with France, the archbishop of New Orleans, Most Rev. Jean Marie Odin, CM, wrote that the sisters had charge of nearly all the military hospitals and that numerous conversions, especially at the hour of death, occurred regularly among the soldiers of all faiths. The American press was generous with its coverage of all news concerning the conflict, and this was true of announcements that the war was really over. Finally, the President declared "the insurrection at an end" in April of 1866.[61] Journalists were quite fluent in their praise and appreciation of the services of the various sisterhoods in behalf of the wounded soldiers, for Austin received notices of that type from far and near. Not many papers could equal the flowery style of the item below, and readers who find Austin's period prose too fancy might be startled by this florid newspaper piece. The reported speech accompanied a monetary gift to replace the orphanage roof destroyed during the shelling of Charleston several years earlier.

> When the ploughshares of war had marked your streets with its red furrows, these good women moved by day and night amid the nameless horrors of your prisons and hospitals, bearing food for the famishing body, and words of comfort and of healing for the stricken soul. To the Sisters of Mercy it mattered not whether the sufferers were cloven down beneath the banner of bars . . . or upholding the starry symbol of our country's sovereignty; but saw in them all only the human, and made them all one under the banner of the cross! They shrank not from the path of duty during the four year's seige of this devoted city. The shot and shell of the besieger spared not the roof that sheltered these apostles of humanity. . . . Yet, when many of the brave soldiers of that besieging army fell into your hands, these Sisters of Mercy were the first to minister to their wants.[62]

Mary Austin certainly was happy that the Mercies and their orphans were once again to have a roof over their heads, but she must have been absolutely delighted that the war was finally over. The religious who had been serving in the infirmaries and hospitals lost no time getting back to their ordinary work in the schools and other institutions. Here and there new apostolates began, as sisters established asylums for the widows and orphans of the fallen warriors. So much publicity had been given to the work of the sisterhoods during the war that even some of the Protestants looked to the organization of such congregations for help with their own work. One Episcopal prelate addressed his fellow ministers in New York City, and according to this Bishop Simpson,

> The Catholic Church, by her Sisters of Mercy and Charity, recognized the employment of the female in the great work of . . . Christianizing the population. . . . Much as there was error in the Catholic Church [sic], . . . he believed that the women of the Church were doing more to give it influence and power [sic] than all the men combined.[63]

With her reverence for the priesthood as a class set apart for God's work, Austin would not have agreed to the final words, but she must have been delighted to see the sisters receive the public recognition.

Often declaring that women and their accomplishments deserved much more recognition, Austin Carroll made this point forcibly in her second published work. This was the translation from the French of a life of Margaret Mary Alacoque, a book which seems to have been completed much earlier but not printed until 1867. To this biography by Father Charles Daniel, SJ, Austin added a forty-four page introduction, an exceptionally lengthy one even for the nineteenth century.[64] This foreword gave quite a bit of space to women, for Austin explained: "God has often selected women for His greatest enterprises." Although she admired the humility of Margaret Mary, Austin's praise was showered upon the livelier gifts of other religious ladies, like the intellectual depth of Teresa of Avila, the energy of Jane Frances de Chantal, the enthusiasm of Catherine of Siena, and the affectionate heart and burning zeal of Catherine McAuley. Austin applauded Charles Daniel's use of the annals of the Visitation nuns, stating that convent chronicles are rich mines in which authors could locate veins of historical value in the interesting and detailed source material. After mentioning several memorable incidents from the records of religious women, Austin concluded that the chronicles showed not only gentleness and holiness associated with the nuns, but also that they had courage enough to face death calmly. Austin gave as an example the cloistered Carmelites of Paris,

who sang as they moved toward the guillotine, the chorus becoming succes-
sively "a quintette, a quartette, a trio, a duet, and at last a solo."[65]

Any reader who explored convent archives, Mary Austin believed,
would be most agreeably surprised at the lovely courtesy and charming
friendships pictured therein. "Sisters do not divest themselves of their
human affections," she added, "they just regulate them." She wished to
make it clear that a religious vocation was not a negative thing[66] and made
reference to an English minister who wanted Protestant sisters. Like the
American Episcopalian, this man admired the work of the sisters on the
Crimean battlefield, where the duties required not only love and patience,
but also "energy, foresight, economy, and the habit of working in concert
and subordination." The minister assumed that all these qualities were the
result of "the severe and methodical training of the Mercy novitiates."
Austin wished him to understand that a sister needed Catherine McAuley's
spirit, her love of God and her zeal for His people. Otherwise, "all the
discipline of the Prussian army would not avail. . . . All the heroism Protestants seek . . . comes from the fire that Christ came on earth to kindle, as
Catherine McAuley often said."[67] Unless a religious vocation was based on
such positive reasons, Austin felt that it would not have the strength to
overcome obstacles raised by the heart's affections. For this aspect of convent life she quoted the Mercy foundress on the pain of religious friends
who are parted by their assignments.[68]

This kind of heartache was that which Mary Austin knew well from
personal experience because she had repeatedly had to leave close friends
behind as she was sent down the road of Mercy service to her next appointment. Although she did not know it yet in 1867, Austin was to face that
same pain again in 1869. For even as the reviews of *Margaret Mary*
appeared in the press, the Redemptorist priests from New Orleans were
searching for sisters to staff their parish schools. During the year and a half
in which St. Louis refused the invitation Austin found that,[69] the numerous
sales of her biography of Catherine McAuley encouraged publishers to print
her translations of the French works of Charles Daniel, SJ, and Jean Bap-
tiste Saint-Jure, SJ. Translations such as *Margaret Mary* had been initiated
long years before as "fillers for odd moments of time between other duties."
For over ten years they had progressed steadily, but the St. Jure works were
not yet complete in 1867 when arrangements for their publication were
discussed. There would be six volumes in the entire series eventually, and
the entire project took much longer than anticipated.[70] The final volumes
were published only after Austin was already down in New Orleans, for the
books were published sporadically as she had time to complete the
translations.

One might wonder if the material produced by the literary critics and book reviewers had any influence on Mary Austin. Even though there were occasional barbs about "a female writer," most of the critics were quite complimentary. Those who pleased Austin found some resemblance between the biographer and the biographee. One such stated "that a woman alone — and that woman a good and holy one, whose heart was in the great work of the foundress of her Order — could have done justice to the beautiful character" of the illustrious Catherine McAuley.[71] That type of remark certainly pleased Austin Carroll, who had been seeking Catherine's spirit for sixteen years. The statement or one like it in 1869 might have caused her to analyze her years of Mercy service up to that point. If she did that, she would have noted a nice round dozen, twelve years, with the two Warde sisters. Austin's first three years in the Mercy Institute were under the tutelage of the gentle and generous Josephine Warde in St. Maries of the Isle in Cork. The ensuing nine years Austin spent serving wherever and however the zealous Xavier Warde assiduously assigned her in New England and New York and Nebraska. Then followed her transfer to St. Louis in the very heart of the country in 1865. Four years later in 1869, more than half her lifespan was still ahead of her, for she had forty full years left. During each and every one of these two score years Mary Austin Carroll was to give her loving concern and compassionate care to the people of God in New Orleans, Belize and along the Gulf Coast from southwest Louisiana to Apalachee Bay in Florida.

6 MOLLIE ABLE & MARY AUSTIN
River & Riverfront
1869–1870

Of all the early American cities which had invited Catherine McAuley's sisters to establish Convents of Mercy within their boundaries, New Orleans was certainly the site which persevered through the longest waiting period. Almost twenty years elapsed between the first invitation proffered and the eventual arrival of the Sisters of Mercy. Mary Austin Carroll recalled in the *Annals* how Rev. John Flanagan of St. Patrick Parish in New Orleans, had applied in person to several Irish motherhouses before reaching St. Maries of the Isle in Cork. There he addressed the entire community, for he was anxious "to plead the cause of his distant parish . . . and lay its wants before them . . . with all the eloquence that proceeds from genuine feeling." As had happened in other Irish convents, Mercy volunteers were willing to brave the perils of yellow fever, but Bishop Delaney "would not allow them to go to a city which had the name of being the most unhealthy spot on earth."[1] Although this Irish trip in the early 1850s proved to be a failure as to locating Sisters of Mercy, John Flanagan did not give up easily. Bishop Andrew Byrne of Little Rock wrote Archbishop Antoine Blanc of New Orleans in 1857, that he thought there was the possibility of obtaining Sisters of Mercy from the foundations already established in this country. At that time, the archbishop was interested in locating the sisters for both St. Patrick and St. John the Baptist Parishes.[2]

Evidently, Bishop Byrne was overly optimistic, however, because his efforts to obtain some Mercies from the Northeast were in vain. In 1860, Rev. Jeremiah Moynihan, the pastor of St. John the Baptist, made a trip to Ireland, where he hoped to gather Catherine McAuley's followers for his parish school and that of St. Patrick's. There his friend, John Flanagan, already had a building for a convent just awaiting the arrival of the sisters. In June Father Moynihan sent home the news that, once again, it was "impossible to get" the Sisters of Mercy. He added, however, that since their "primary object is the visitation of the poor and sick, and education is only secondary with them," he was delighted to have found instead the Dominican nuns from Cabra near Dublin.[3] Thus was postponed the arrival of the Sisters of Mercy in New Orleans once again. Yet, the city was an area which Father Moynihan's letter referred to as a field ripe for the harvesting of a "most luxuriant and abundant crop."

By the middle of the 1860s, several priests of the Congregation of the Most Holy Redeemer were looking for Sisters of Mercy to staff their school in New Orleans. It was 1866 when Redemptorists William Meredith and Henry Giesen applied to the Sisters of Mercy in Vicksburg.[4] These sisters, devastated by the war, were still too small a community to subdivide just then. With a view to building their numerical strength so that they could serve in New Orleans, Father Meredith encouraged a number of zealous young women from the city to enter the Mississippi community.[5] That process proved too slow for the other priests, however, and in 1868 their quest for Mercies turned northward to St. Louis. Mother de Pazzi Bentley, then reigning in her twelfth year as superior, thought it premature to release her sisters for a foundation elsewhere. This view was not shared by her successor, Mother Mary Ignatius Walker, or by Archbishop Kenrick, who had recently been in New Orleans where he had seen a trio of schools in the three Redemptorist parishes. The German school was staffed by the School Sisters of Notre Dame, and the French and the Irish schools, the latter for all the English-speaking, were seeking Mercy staffs. The archbishop described the fine prospects for "the contemplated establishment, praised the generosity of the New Orleans people, and expressed astonishment at the number of churches and schools" they had erected in the tri-parish area.[6]

With this kind of episcopal encouragement, the St. Louis community "began seriously to entertain the project." Reverend Joseph Helmpraecht, CSSR, offered generous terms and promised that the Redemptorists would rent a house for the sisters until the parishioners could complete the erection of a convent for them. When Mother Ignatius Walker said that only a few sisters could be spared, the New Orleans rector declared that there were many young ladies in the parish just "awaiting their arrival to join them, and a novitiate could be opened at an early date."[7] Negotiations progressed so smoothly that Austin wrote a friend on January 9, that the first foundation from the St. Louis motherhouse was to be sent forth before too long.[8] One of the prerequisites of a Mercy foundation was the written consent of the bishop in whose diocese the new establishment was to be located. Most Rev. Jean Marie Odin, CM, the Archbishop of New Orleans, wrote Mother Ignatius Walker to express his satisfaction with the project under consideration and to extend his own cordial invitation to the sisters. In conclusion, he said: "I most cheerfully authorize you to establish a house of the Sisters of Mercy in the Diocese, and . . . you will find here a vast field for your charitable works."[9] Although the latter was dated the fifth of February, it could have reached the sisters by the second week of the month. And Austin identified February as a time of prayer and consultation as Mother Ignatius carefully selected the group of sisters for the new foundation.

Mary Austin later shared her feelings concerning this period of prayerful decision-making. Although she felt a strong inclination to volunteer, almost as though she were specially called to serve in the South, Austin decided to practice "holy indifference." When the superior interviewed her, therefore, Austin replied, "I am ready to go or to stay."[10] Yet, she always recalled how disappointed she was when her name was not on the early tentative list. She also remembered her distress at the opposition "within the house and outside of it" toward sending sisters to a city "where they would be likely to be swept away by yellow fever." Certain sisters judged that it would be far better to send the sisters to a safer area, for there were applications from the healthy towns of Chillicothe, Dubuque, and Louisville. After their appeal to Archbishop Kenrick, however, "the well-meaning parties inimical to the good work" decided to leave matters to the superior. In Lent a letter from New Orleans reminded Mother Ignatius that a sister capable of teaching in the French language was needed for the parochial school of Notre Dame de Bon Secours, popularly known as the French School. And it was probably to this reminder that Austin owed her inclusion on the final list of the personnel who were to establish the new foundation.[11] Whatever the reason, Austin left it on record that she was delighted with the new arrangement and the opportunity to join the previously selected band of missionaries for New Orleans.

A native of Booterstown, County Dublin, forty year old Sister Mary Catherine Grant, was appointed superior of the foundation. Mary Catherine had begun her religious life in New York City, where two of her sisters were also Sisters of Mercy. She had then spent ten years in St. Louis, the last as mistress of novices. Catherine's health had always been quite delicate, but the *Annals* relate that her doctor "was very sanguine as to the beneficial effect the genial climate of the South" would have upon her weak lungs.[12] Besides Catherine Grant and Austin Carroll from Ireland, the third in the trio of professed choir sisters, intended to be the mainstays of the new motherhouse, was an American, Mary Xavier McDermott. A native of Madonersville, Monroe County in Illinois, Xavier was the younger sister of Austin's assistant in the prison visitation, the late Magdalene de Pazzi McDermott. Just as this deceased sister was a martyr to her apostolate, having caught cholera from one of the poor families she attended, so her sister, Xavier, was destined to contract yellow fever from the sick she nursed in a New Orleans epidemic. But that was in the future when in 1869 Austin described her young friend as lively, zealous, and a fine little teacher.[13]

The eldest of the six sisters forming the foundation community was Sister Francis O'Farrell, who had already served ten years as a lay sister in St. Louis. A native of Ireland, Sister Francis had had contact with the New York City Mercies before she journeyed to St. Louis and entered the Mercy foundation there. In New Orleans Sister Francis was going to give faithful help with the many practicalities of housekeeping and with the care of Catherine Grant, whose health was to worsen rapidly in the New Orleans heat and humidity. Like most motherhouses, the new establishment looked to the future by including in the original group several young women still in their novitiate program. In this instance, one was a senior novice close to the completion of her studies, and the other was a new candidate just beginning her spiritual formation. Novice Mary Camillus Lucas, having already part of her novitiate in St. Louis under the direction of Mary Catherine Grant, was to be the first of Catherine McAuley's followers to profess her vows in New Orleans.[14] Candidate Eliza Shields, a twenty year old Irish colleen who joined the Mercies just in time to make the roster for the new venture, was to be the first novice accepted into the Mercy community in the Crescent City. One year after her reception as a novice, this youngest sister in the original group for New Orleans was destined to be the first Mercy to die there—a victim of virulent yellow fever when she was scarcely in her twenties.[15]

In the early months of 1869 the plans for establishing a new motherhouse, especially deciding its location, had caused some differences of opinion; but by March all were of one accord and "anxious to fulfill the will of God at any cost." Rev. Michael Corbett, SJ, the confessor of the Sisters of Mercy in St. Louis, praised these good dispositions, but solemnly added the warning: "You will have many tribulations, but do not look for them until they come. You will do much good and convert many souls. Never draw back." Shortly thereafter, a second serious message came from another priest friend, Rev. James Archer, who told the missionaries that he knew of cases where certain ecclesiastics did not treat religious as they should.[16] In response, the sisters hoped that history would not repeat itself in their regard. The two similar and rather solemn warnings might have caused the sisters to worry, but consolation came when Archbishop Kenrick visited the Convent of Mercy for an encouraging farewell. He was convinced that the missionaries "would do a world of good in New Orleans." Austin and her sisters found him not only unusually genial and fatherly, but also "impressive and affectionate as he imparted his solemn benediction and wished them every spiritual and temporal blessing."[17]

Arrangements had been made to leave on the evening of March 17, on the packet entitled *Mollie Able.* St. Patrick's Day dawned as a fine one for the departure services and ceremonies. First, in the chapel there was community Mass and union in the Eucharist; and later, the Hibernian Procession arrived before the convent to receive flowers from the orphans.[18] At the time of this occurrence, certainly, neither the brave and brawny Hibernians nor the admiring Mercy missionaries appreciated how marvelously appropriate this St. Patrick's Day parade was as a foreshadowing fete for these sisters headed for the Irish Channel in New Orleans. For within the area of the Channel, St. Patrick is annually hailed in one of the most flamboyant and enthusiastic celebrations to be held anywhere in the world. Early in the day there is always Mass in Patrick's honor, to be sure, but then the feast continues with the kind of party the Carnival City loves to host. In and about the floats with "throws" as big as cabbages, dancing bands and costumed marchers strut before the eager crowds of Irish, Irish-American, and Irish-for-the-day, with many a refreshing pause for beer served as green as the Emerald Isle itself.

But in St. Louis in 1869, that Wednesday March 17 brought another sort of joy, for the travelers learned that their departure was postponed for a day or two. *Mollie Able* had reached the St. Louis wharf on time but, as so often happens with ladies, she was not ready to leave on schedule. The sisters were delighted to have time and opportunity to visit some of the other religious in the city, as Mary Austin said, "to gain experience by inspecting the good works carried on."[19] *Mollie's* departure was announced for Friday March 19, the feast of St. Joseph, himself an experienced traveler. It is only fair to *Mollie* to explain that her delay was required to make some essential repairs necessitated by an accident, for she was considered quite dependable. For instance, for this trip up to St. Louis, she had left the levee in New Orleans on March 9, in rains heavy enough to dock all but two other river boats. The gentlemen of the press toasted her that very day.

The large and fleet passenger steamer, *Mollie Able*, is a permanent fixture in the trade, and deserves all the encouragement our shippers can give, as she is in every manner of speaking well worthy of it. Her accommodations and fare to travelers are first class in every particular. This, combined with clever and attentive officers, ought to ensure an overflowing trip.[20]

Before the trip began on Friday evening there were other overflowings as the community farewells were said. Mary Austin explained how sad the leave-taking was as the "tears flowed plentifully and promises of frequent correspondence" were mutually pledged.[21] Thus had gone the sorrowful, yet courageous, farewells down the years as the torch was passed to younger hands for the next lap of the run. Mother Agnes O'Connor had received her torch in Dublin in 1846 as she left for New York, and then handed it on to Mother de Pazzi Bentley in 1856 as she set out for St. Louis. Now in 1869 de Pazzi's successor, Mother Ignatius Walker, was passing the flame to Catherine Grant, who could have had a premonition that her lungs already nurtured her mortal illness. If such forewarnings worried her, she had the consolation of knowing that she had an exceptionally capable assistant in Austin Carroll.

Many of Mary Austin's friends were in the crowd which gathered before the convent at departure time to wish the sisters a safe and pleasant trip. Present with gratitude in hand were the poor, school children and their parents, friends, and even a few released prisoners. Surprised at the size of the group, Austin and her companions were deeply touched by the display of affection. Mothers Ignatius and de Pazzi accompanied the travelers down to *Mollie's* wharf and saw them settled aboard the packet. Austin found "the parting with the Mothers very affecting"[22] as they exchanged prayerful good wishes and promises of faithful correspondence. The contemporary convent records support this picture of rapport, relating that the foundation was established "under the happiest of auspices."[23] The local press as well as the *Boston Pilot* and the *Western Watchman* wished the Sisters of Mercy all the best in their new venture, and considering the fine Mercy schools across the country, "their usual amount of success."[24]

With this encouraging send-off *Mollie Able* began the voyage of some 1,275 miles down the Mississippi River, the winding multi-lane waterway that was the nation's busiest traffic artery in 1869. Even before the engineers had sufficient pressure in the boilers to start the engines, the sisters assembled for evening prayers in one of the state-rooms. Accustomed to the small cubicle allotted to each in the convent dormitory, the religious found that one compact state-room quite amply housed a pair of nuns. They must have been crowded, however, when all six gathered together for their prayers. Austin was delighted when the sisters decided to be up "at day-break"[25] so as to have office and meditation on deck before most of the passengers would be up and about. Previously on the Missouri River, Austin had found that praying on deck early was a delightful experience, and on this trip *Mollie's* deck at dawn became an open-air chapel, a spot where Austin felt especially close to her God. She arrived in time to catch the sunrise and see the mists vanish as the sun swept away the haze. Then the sisters chanted *Matins* softly, alternating verses in bell tones and a foggier echo, but ever mindful of sleeping passengers. Following their Latin chant, the Mercies had a period of contemplation, silent except for *Mollie's* murmuring and the wash of the water against the hull. Mary Austin thought it a lovely way to start the day.

Meals aboard the steamboat followed a rather late schedule for the early-rising sisters, as breakfast was served from eight to ten, dinner at three, and supper at seven. But the hour mattered little once the sisters learned that they could have Lenten fare at their table. *Mollie Able's* captain, John Leavenworth, had not only agreed to that request, but also made a generous cost reduction for the religious. He assured the Mercies of his packet's safety, explaining that *Mollie* was a strong young vessel, as she had been built just five years earlier and could carry 873 tons.[26] That first night as Mary Austin fell asleep to *Mollie's* gentle rocking and the muffled hum of her engines, she envisioned the packet moving downstream at a great rate. One can appreciate her surprise the next morning to find St. Louis still in view in the distance. The captain explained that shortly after his passengers had taken their repose, so had *Mollie* — on a sandbar. In working the boat free, the first mate's leg was badly crushed, and two of the Mercies managed to stop the bleeding. When the doctor arrived, he decided on immediate transfer to the hospital for removal of the leg. The sisters had given care and consolation to the young mate, who dreaded the amputation; they promised to continue their prayers for him. Later Austin learned through correspondence that the mate completed in the hospital the instructions begun by the Mercies on the boat and was baptized before his death just one month after the accident had occurred.[27]

Although the first Mercy service given on the boat was nursing care, the sisters spent most of each day involved in education of one kind or another. Much of it was catechetical instruction, as the sisters regularly taught some of the cabin boys who had asked for it as well as the black child whom they prepared to receive the sacraments. A surprising kind of instruction was the teaching of Catholic hymns to the Protestant passengers. The only Catholic in the Ladies' Cabin was the nurse for the captain's family, but there had been a good bit of informal inquiry as conversation either on religious questions or about the Mercy mission to New Orleans from the gracious Protestant ladies. On Palm Sunday the ladies wanted to have a musical commemoration of the day and appealed to the Mercies, whom they had heard chanting the psalms of *Matins*. The sisters willingly shared the Latin words of the hymns in their office books, while Mary Austin, an enthusiastic pianist, rehearsed the impromptu choir. With a little practice the ladies were able to join the sisters in such hymns as "the *Tantum Ergo*, the *Stabat Mater, Vesper* psalms, and other grand chorals." These selections, Austin noted, were "as easy as effective" and had all "the charm of novelty for the performers."[28]

Certainly it was a new and unusual event for *Mollie's* regular patrons to see a rather petite nun leading the singing as she played the pianoforte in *Mollie's* grand Salon, which approximated the size and grandeur of the

ballroom of a fine hotel. Mary Austin enjoyed any musicale because of her
delight in lovely voices and the joy she found in a group singing as one. This
event had the additional aspect of an ecumenical union and also a bit of
private amusement for the pianist. Her keen sense of the ridiculous quietly
savored the humor in the incongruous situation, the fashionably dressed
Americans of various Protestant denominations joining several Irish Mercies in their flowing robes to sing Marian hymns. So successful was the
Latin choir, incongruities aside, that the passengers petitioned for a second
session. During the ensuing week, in fact, the chorale of sacred music was
performed several times. Perhaps the encores were requested simply for the
social aspect, the enjoyment of singing together. Or, possibly, they served as
an appropriate way to commemorate the significance of Holy Week. With
this special season in mind, the Sisters of Mercy watched for opportunities
to get ashore and locate a church. In several towns, like Cairo, the sisters
were able to visit several religious institutions — the church, the school, and
the hospital. But only in Memphis did the hour of *Mollie's* stopover coin-
cide with that of the Eucharistic sacrifice. The sisters appreciated the sacred
liturgy more than usual that day at the Dominican Church of St. Peter's, as
this was their first chance to assist at Mass since they had left St. Louis.[29]

Wednesday, March 24, happened to be the day of this special liturgy as
well as the mid-point in their journey. The ten-day trip seemed to be just full
of surprises, and Mary Austin could recall years later how startled she was
"that the sisters were shown the greatest deference by persons who had
never before met religious."[30] One might hazard the guess, even though
contemporary evidence is lacking one way or the other, that the openness of
Austin to her fellow travelers might have been just as much of a shock or
surprise to the non-Catholic ladies aboard. In fact, Austin's friendliness
could be shocking to some of her own sisters, as was her geniality with
Mollie's Protestant passengers. However, the greatest moment of astonishment for both the Mercies and others aboard the packet was probably one
experienced at Cape Girardeau. Having noticed the unusual sight of sisters
on *Mollie's* deck, as their voluminous habits were hard to miss, a crowd of
rivermen at the landing uncovered their heads and saluted the nuns, several
calling out their thanks in a totally unexpected show of gratitude. Nor was
that a unique experience, for here or there along the river, boatmen and
stevedores repeated similar tributes, standing at attention or hailing the
sisters as their nurses during the late war.[31] The Mercies were deeply
touched, as they received grateful recognition in this symbolic way for all
the religious congregations which had staffed military hospitals on battle-
fields, on riverboats like *Mollie*, or in the camps for the prisoners of war.

This appreciation of the work of all the sisters was a warm human gift,
but Austin had found another human gift, a bouquet of children who

warmed the cockles of her heart. As they journeyed down the Mississippi together, the youngsters on the boat became her friends and admirers. There were the children of Captain Leavenworth, Grace and Mark, and also the captain's nieces, Esther and Fanny Pepper.[32] Mary Austin thoroughly enjoyed children and found no exception in these, whom she taught for a while each day. For both the pupils and the teacher the time spent in study seemed to be a rewarding experience, a time for fun and mutual education. Austin not only related fascinating tales connected with the history of the great river, but she also encouraged the children to share with her information about the packets and the places *Mollie* passed along the way. The Mercy nun, historian and author, understood how to catch attention with her stories about the titles of the river, thus introducing the explorers, colonies, and countries involved.[33] Austin's stories came down the centuries as the name of the river changed from the Father of the Waters or the *Messachebe* of the Indians to the Spaniards' River of the Holy Spirit in the 1500s. Then followed the French explorers' names, such as the River of the Immaculate Conception, Pere Marquette's title and her own favorite, and the Rivière la Grande and Colber in the 1600s, and the Rivière St. Louis in the 1700s. Finally, she had other stories of the time that the French government in New Orleans sent Pierre Laclède and René Chouteau to establish a trading post farther up the river. Laclède's chosen site became in turn a tiny village, a frontier town, and eventually, an enterprising city – all dedicated to St. Louis. Austin's historical lore never lasted too long, and often, led her listeners into curiosity about the next day's subject.

With the children Mary Austin was in a learning process herself, becoming more Americanized all the time. The graciousness of the Protestants aboard had been a real surprise for her, a great contrast to the anti-Catholic zealots she had met upon her arrival in New England. The non-Catholic children imparted trivial bits of Americana concerning the vessels and villages they passed. The youngsters were quite knowledgeable about the river and its surroundings because the Leavenworth family had pursued maritime interests for several generations, and at the time, were running a string of packets.[34] The girls admired *Mollie's* beauty, especially the unusual dome over her pilothouse. Mark was proud of her speed among the side-wheelers, particularly of the fact that she had set a record for speed in 1865. The youngsters were alert to point out various types of watercraft, as *Mollie* frequently passed steamers with paddle wheels at the stern or sidewheelers like herself, towboats with several barges of produce, woodboats ferrying cordwood out to customers.[35] The children knew all about "wooding the boat" from the piles of cordwood along the banks and had heard that all the passengers once helped in order to speed the chore. The only "broad-horns" or flatboats they saw seemed to be in use as bulwarks or wharfs as they lined the banks near town landings. Grace had heard that some of the low-lying towns were under water for a part of each year, but all the children could recognize the towns perched on bluffs above the highwater level of the annual flood season.

Such a city was Vicksburg, as it was established high on the Third Chickasaw Bluff, and proved to be one of the high points of the trip for the sisters in more ways than one. The day before *Mollie* reached Vicksburg happened to be Holy Thursday, and Mary Austin succumbed to a real loneliness. She longed to receive her Lord in the Eucharist on His special day, but it was in vain that she and the other sisters watched for any sign of a church or chapel. Finally, Austin consoled herself by recalling the beauty of the churches and convent chapels she had known and then by imagining the loveliness of Mercy "chapels all over the world on this day of love."[36] Surprisingly, Good Friday turned into a day of good cheer and sisterly love according to Catherine McAuley's own heart. The missionaries had written the Mississippi Mercies of their coming a week earlier, as they hoped to meet their prospective neighbors. The Vicksburg sisters, "on the lookout for the *Mollie Able* since daybreak," were at the landing, waiting "with carriages to take the whole party to the convent. They visited the church on the way. Though Good Friday is rather an unusual day for visiting, everything was in readiness for the guests, and the sisters gave them a warm reception."[37] Traditional Southern hospitality, here dressed in Catherine McAuley's ideals and Mercy habit, escorted the travelers back to their steamer in a few hours. But brief as the visit had been, it left the New Orleans bound sisters physically replenished, psychologically reinvigorated, and spiritually revitalized.

It is well that they were refreshed for Holy Saturday marked their ninth day on the river, and the sisters were most anxious to reach their destination before Easter morning. Captain Leavenworth really expected to be in the city before nightfall that Saturday, but *Mollie*, like Robert Burns, knew what could happen to the well laid plans of mice and men. After having behaved so well ever since that first night on the bar near St. Louis, *Mollie* had a relapse near Helena. In spite of the best efforts, according to Mary Austin, *Mollie* dove into every bar they had to pass and pugnaciously "got into difficulty with every snag."[38] Even through the afternoon *Mollie* dallied under the influence of her irresistible urge and sidled up to many a bar. Finally, Sunday saw her reformation, and she sailed soberly downstream. The sisters would later share their laughter at recreation over *Mollie's* erratic behavior, but not on Easter Sunday when time was of the essence. The sisters scanned the banks that morning for signs of "the Southern metropolis, hoping that they might have the coveted privilege of hearing Mass."[39] Eventually as noon approached, the Mercies struggled within themselves to accept the fact that on this Easter Sunday they would not arrive in time for the beautiful liturgy of the risen Christ.

The faint echoes of distant church bells tantalized the sisters as the packet steamed past the verdant farms of the German Coast. Although this section of Louisiana was completely level, the scene held the interest of the viewers not only for the unusual architecture of the plantations but also for its fresh greenery. The latter was in great contrast to the wintry grays and the monotonous browns of the past week. Exceptionally busy with her note-taking on this tenth day of the Mississippi Odyssey, Mary Austin waxed poetic over the rows of cotton almost in bloom, the waving fields of rice, and, what she believed, were "seas of green sugar cane." More easily recognized were "the orange trees starred with cream-white blossoms, . . . magnolias with dark, glossy leaves and enormous buds, . . . and broad, low, airy planters' residences."[40] She bemoaned the sight of deserted overgrown plantations and "many a lonely chimney standing like a grim sentinel over blackened ruins." Even these desolate and somber views were muted by the gorgeous Easter skies, which also softened the tones of the rich delta panorama. Occasionally she spotted some bright spring flowers along with the roses everywhere. Here or there a gaudy garden marched in an Easter parade from the dwelling place right up to the levee, each stem flaunting its bonnet of violet, gold, or fuchsia blooms. Austin accepted these lovely landscapes as Easter gifts, bounty from God's munificence. She might have arranged the delta scenes near the glorious sunrises and sunsets of the past week in the art gallery of her memory. There she could enjoy them any foggy day and share them with others at community recreation, or some thirty years later in her Mercy *Annals*.

As *Mollie* neared New Orleans Mary Austin's mood of reverie was replaced by activity as an effusion of farewells and showers of gratitude descended upon her. The children found the thought of leaving the sisters a heartbreaking one. Mark was stoic, the little girls cried, and Grace clung to Austin, declaring that she would never be parted from the Mercies. Consolation and parting gifts helped to dry the tears, and Austin's fondness for children and their reciprocal affection had already been demonstrated in each school to which she had been assigned. Two other points seemed to have been, to a certain extent, after-effects of her time with the children. Within a short time she would publish several more collections of short tales for youngsters; and the interest of some of the adults, who regularly managed to be on deck within earshot for the history session, might have encouraged Austin to appeal to this interest in history in articles for periodicals. The second group of young people taught were a number of the black cabin boys who received religious instruction. The boys came with thanks for the sisters and left with rosaries for themselves and souvenirs for the rest of *Mollie's* crew. This teaching of the blacks on the packet was probably the first such opportunity for Mary Austin, but it was just the preface of her lifelong effort to provide educational opportunities for Southern blacks.[41]

The parting from their fellow travelers in the Ladies' Cabin was so affectionate that it belied the fact that these Protestants had known the sisters for such a short time. The ladies had been edified and impressed by all the Mercies, but especially by the Mercy musician who assisted them to form their choir. The graciousness of these fine people could have influenced Austin to continue her natural openness in any future association with non-Catholics. The encouragement might have served as the weight needed to balance the scales, this positive reaction on one side and the discomfort of Catherine Grant on the other. The river voyage was obviously difficult for the latter as those stirring breezes, which the others found refreshing, probably chilled her to the bone. Even the swirling river, which entertained the rest with its endless parade of rivercraft from the dilapidated shanty-boat to the palatial steamer, must have aggravated her condition with its mist and fog. Certainly, singing in the chorus or engaging in prolonged conversation was more than her delicate lungs could endure. For Captain Leavenworth, however, Catherine and the other sisters had offerings of prayers and gifts. Several spiritual volumes which Austin had translated from the French were presented in appreciation for his many kindnesses, especially his efforts to satisfy their request for simple Lenten fare. The captain himself was grateful on two counts — pleased like any proud father that his children, captivated by Austin, had behaved so well, and happy that his friend, the injured first mate, had been the recipient of the nursing care of these Sisters of Mercy.[42]

While mutual thanks were being exchanged, *Mollie* ably made her way past hundreds of commercial vessels, first the bayou stern-wheelers, then the trans-oceanic screw steamers and multi-masted sailing ships, and finally the coastal and river steamers near Canal Street.[43] There, after a bit of nudging, *Mollie* wedged herself between two companions at the Gravier Street wharf right at 2 p.m. Even for these sisters acquainted with the ports of Dublin and New York, there was immense novelty on the New Orleans levee, where the daily scene had been described as one of constant activity. "Sailors, river-men, merchants, shipping-clerks, foreigners of all nationalities, travelers, priests, monks and nuns are constantly passing and repassing, forming a panorama which for variety and life has probably not its equal on this continent."[44] But that was the typical workday and quite different from a rainy Easter Sunday like that of March 28, 1869. Yet *Mollie* was not the only steamer discharging passengers; and several packets, evidently loaded the day before as there were no roustabouts in sight, were preparing to embark later that evening. Although a messenger had been dispatched to the Redemptorist rectory the moment *Mollie* was moored, it was after three in the afternoon before the priests were able to procure carriages on that rainy holiday.[45]

The sisters were worried about getting all their boxes and bags and bundles through the rain and across the wide levee, but when their transportation arrived, the Irish Mercies witnessed Southern chivalry in action. Regardless of the rain and their Easter best, several gentlemen and officers insisted on transferring for the nuns all their odds and ends of luggage.[46] The sisters were most grateful for this charitable assistance, which was in reality a foreshadowing of future events. With the arrival of the two Redemptorists, Rector Henry Giesen and Rev. William Meredith, the sisters received a blessing, a cordial welcome, and were escorted to the two carriages. The drive was shorter than the travelers expected it to be, as they had understood that they were to be out in a suburb called Lafayette. This faubourg, which had recently become a part of the city itself,[47] was not far from the Gravier Street wharf where *Mollie* berthed. The conveyances, heavy with luggage, turned from Canal Street and moved rapidly up Magazine through torrential rains to Jackson Avenue. There a corner building (x on plan 1), earlier an apothecary shop with family living quarters above, was ready to serve as a temporary convent. After a luncheon served by two parishioners,[48] the sisters were given a tour of the pharmacy-convent. They had just learned how to eat a banana and were now surprised at the sight of bobbinet mosquito bars draped over each bed. The ladies laughed, remarking that the Mercies would soon learn how important the netting was for a good night's sleep. The sisters were agreeably surprised that the house was so aptly arranged because, Mary Austin noted in the *Annals*, "everything was far better than they had been led to expect."[49]

Before the priests left, they introduced two "intending postulants," Mathilde Gourrier and Mary Lewis. Mary, though a native of Wales, had lived in New Orleans for the past dozen years. Barely nineteen that Easter Sunday, she was planning to delay her entrance into the novitiate until she was twenty-one. Ready to join the sisters shortly, however, was the second visitor, Mademoiselle Marie Mathilde Gourrier from the town of Plaquemine in Iberville. Mathilde was destined to be the first Louisiana Creole to profess for life the religious vows of the Sisters of Mercy in the New Orleans community. Just seven years younger than Mary Austin, this lovely Mathilde was the first of many Southerners who were attracted to Austin and whose acquaintance grew into a strong and affectionate friendship.[50] Although neither of the interested young women had ever seen Catherine McAuley's followers before that Easter day, the two made a wonderfully encouraging welcoming committee. Archbishop Odin sent word that he would visit the convent the following Thursday to complete the formalities of the canonical installation of the Mercy Congregation in the Archdiocese of New Orleans. On that occasion the archbishop was delighted to learn that Mathilde, the daughter of his late friend, Doctor André Gourrier "who had travelled with him through the missions of Texas," was to become a member of the community.[51]

Austin found Archbishop Odin to be especially cordial in his welcome as he stated that he "had been long anxious" to have the Sisters of Mercy serving in the archdiocese. He confirmed the St. Louis appointments of Mary Catherine Grant as superior and Mary Austin Carroll as assistant. The archbishop explained that, since he could not give the community his personal attention, he would assign Henry Giesen as their ecclesiastical superior for "he knew that the Redemptorist priests would represent him kindly."[52] Where there were just a few religious congregations of women, the bishop himself could be their director, but New Orleans, even prior to the arrival of the Sisters of Mercy, had some twenty religious orders or congregations. These were listed in the *Catholic Directory* as follows:

> the Ursuline Nuns, Religious of the Sacred Heart, Daughters of Charity from Emmitsburgh [sic], Congregation of Mount Carmel, Sisters of the Holy Family, Congregation of the Holy Cross, Congregation of Notre Dame, Religious of St. Joseph, of the Good Shepherd, of the Order of St. Dominic, the Little Sisters of the Poor, and the Oblate Sisters of Providence.[53]

The people of the Crescent City were also served by eight orders of religious men who were considered self-sufficient by the Church and in need of no Ordinary-appointed ecclesiastical superior.

With the blessing of Archbishop Odin that first Thursday in April and his encouragement to pursue their "charitable works" in what he termed "the vast field" of the old Catholic city, the Sisters of Mercy began their visitation in the homes of the sick poor that very afternoon.[54] Within a few weeks Mary Austin had met with local officials to make arrangements for the sisters to visit the penal institutions and hospitals on a regular basis. Not only did these gentlemen promptly affirm all requests, but they also explained that the sisters could ride free of charge on the city horsecars. As to the city's Charity Hospital, the Sisters of Mercy were free to visit at any time since it was staffed by the Sisters of Charity.[55] All told, conditions were so favorable that the sisters decided not to delay their Mercy Home, but immediately to rent a home (y on plan 1) that could serve as a temporary shelter for young women newly arrived in the city or temporarily without a job. And though the priests had doubted the feasibility of a chapel in the pharmacy-convent, the archbishop graciously agreed that the Mercies could arrange a chapel and harbor Christ in the Blessed Sacrament under their roof. Mary Austin expressed surprise that so many of the local clergy called to welcome them, and a number of these priests donated articles needed for the Eucharistic liturgy. Mathilde Gourrier and other generous ladies provided vases, carpets, silk, and decorative items and, before the first Mass in the convent in April 6, "the chapel was declared elegant."[56]

Also on the sixth, several of the Redemptorist fathers met with the sisters to decide which of the parish schools the sisters should staff immediately. Father Meredith was anxious to have the Sisters of Mercy replace the lay teachers in St. Alphonsus Girls' School (a on plan 1). Because of the few teachers among the Mercies missioned to New Orleans, however, the rector thought it more practical to have the sisters begin their educational work with the French School (F on plan 1) that bore one of the favorite titles of the French and French Canadians for Our Lady, Notre Dame de Bon Secours.[57] Only two Mercy teachers would be required for the girls of the French School, as the lay teachers would continue with the boys' classes. Austin related that she and the other Mercy teachers listened to the discussion, ready for whatever might be agreed upon by the rector and the directors of the two schools. All the participants of this educational conference hoped for an influx either of candidates or temporary reinforcements, so that the New Orleans community would have enough sisters in September to staff the girls' classes of both St. Alphonsus and Notre Dame de Bon Secours.[58] The immediate question was settled by the decision of the German Redemptorists—the Irish sisters were to teach in the French School as their first assignment in the Irish Channel. The sisters, delighted to have definite appointments, began their educational work in the South on the following Monday, April 12, 1869.

Mary Austin related how much she enjoyed hearing the Redemptorists explain the origins of this unusual triple parish within a single geographical area. This district adjacent to the riverfront sheltered so many Irish workers and their families that it had become known as the Irish Channel. Because the section also housed numerous German immigrants, Bishop Antoine Blanc, later archbishop, who had no German priests in the early 1840s, invited a visiting Redemptorist, Peter Chakert, to help the German immigrants to organize for religious services. This priest was collecting in New Orleans, a city celebrated at the time as much for its affluence as for its generosity, for he sought funds for his destitute German mission in Pittsburgh. As the bishop had requested, Father Chakert called the Germans together and celebrated Mass in Kaiser's hall. Before the missionary left with his largesse from the Crescent City Catholics, the bishop had bought a lot (G-1 on plan 1) for a church on Josephine Street between Constance and Laurel.[59] Rev. Joseph Kundeck, another German priest in the city temporarily, built the small frame church for which Vicar General Etienne Rousselon had laid the cornerstone on January 14, 1844. Unaware that there had been a church staffed by the Capuchins on the German Coast in the early 1720s, Kundeck described the building to the Leopoldine Society as the first German church in Louisiana and said that Bishop Blanc had dedicated it to "the Assumption of the Blessed Virgin."[60]

Having returned to New Orleans in late 1847, Peter Chakert, CSSR, was installed as the pastor "of the Catholics of all nations resident in the City of Lafayette." The following year the Redemptorist pastor, having decided that the diversity of nationalities required several churches, bought lots (I-1 on plan 1) on St. Andrew Street, just opposite the church (G-1 on plan 1) on Josephine, in order to build a church for the English-speaking parishioners. The foundations of this first small St. Alphonsus Church were dug in January 1850. Thereafter, the Irish and Irish-American congregation constructed their frame church with such rapidity that it was ready for an April dedication by the renowned Irish "Apostle of Temperance," Theobald Mathew. Mary Austin was delighted to learn that this priest, whom she had known in Cork, had brought his crusade to the Irish Channel in New Orleans. Upon the completion of that first church, Father P. McGrane and his flock demonstrated the kind of thrifty wisdom so often born of necessity. In this instance, they killed two birds with one cornerstone by using the same structure as a church on Sunday and as a school Monday through Friday. At this point, an enthusiastic young Redemptorist, John Duffy, arrived and began to stir the waters of the Irish Channel.[61]

Father Duffy had reached the city in July of 1851, had the little church enlarged in September, planned in October to build a parish school, and in November invited Archbishop Blanc to bless the renovated church. That was just the beginning, for Father Duffy really whirled the waters as the suburb, the City of Lafayette, became a part of the city of New Orleans.[62] That 1852, Father Duffy collected the funds needed for the construction of the school building, bought lots (a on plan 1) for it on the river side of Constance Street, and laid the cornerstone for the brick building. Completed in June of 1853 and opened the following August 26, this "permanent school house" was to prove no more lasting than the renovated church, which was once again too small for its burgeoning congregation.[63]

Mary Austin had tremendous admiration for the tirelessness of the zealous Irish pastor, John Duffy. In 1853 four lots (I-2 on plan 1) were purchased for an extensive brick church on the lake side of Constance Street, in 1854 the plans were drawn for the immense structure destined to be St. Alphonsus Church, and in 1855 the cornerstone was laid by Archbishop Blanc. For the next three years the bricks were laid at a record-breaking pace. "Even women lent their aid, carrying the bricks in their aprons from Jackson Avenue, since the deep mud permitted no traffic on Constance Street . . . which was yet unpaved."[64] On April 25, 1858, the magnificent new St. Alphonsus, complete and free of debt, was consecrated by the archbishop and three bishops in the presence of numerous clergy and religious and amid throngs of admiring Irish, French, and Germans. It was to this huge edifice, which Father Duffy Considered "the most beautiful church in the United States," that the Sisters of Mercy were walking daily in 1869 in order to assist at the Eucharistic Liturgy.[65]

As Austin and the other sisters exclaimed over the accomplishments of their compatriots, the Redemptorist priests hastened to make it clear that the Irish were certainly not the only builders in the area during those pioneer years. The Germans of St. Mary's Assumption laid the cornerstone for their brick church (G-2 on plan 1) immediately after the consecration of St. Alphonsus Church, and the French parishioners, who had set their cornerstone (F on plan 1) in place on the Fourth of July a year earlier, expected to dedicate their own church to Our Lady before 1858 was over. While the Irish hodmen hefted bricks in the 1850s, so had the other nationalities. The Germans had constructed a school (d on plan 1) in 1853, an orphanage (e on plan 1) in 1854, a cemetery in 1855, and had begun the new St. Mary's Assumption in 1858.[66] National pride was a wonderful incentive to speed the construction crews, especially those involved in the seemingly competitive German and Irish building booms.

The Civil War was soon to halt construction, but prior to the conflict the Irish managed to raise one more building. The second St. Alphonsus School (b on plan 1) was located on the uptown side of St. Andrew between Magazine and Constance, where the lengthy three-story building included a great hall on the top floor. This new school, in which the Mercies were one day to teach, was completed at the close of 1860 and blessed in January of 1861, just before Louisiana passed its Act of Secession. In spite of turmoil and martial law, the large structure attracted so many new pupils that an overflow had to be relegated to the earlier "permanent schoolhouse." Also in the years just before the war, the French congregation developed in patterns similar to those of the other two parishes. Organized by Redemptorist Michael Girard in 1856, the French purchased lots (F on plan 1) on Jackson Avenue in 1857 and began construction just four days later. Although suffering from the tragic loss of Father Girard in the yellow fever epidemic of 1858, the French completed their church as the year ended. On January 6, 1859, the lovely little church with the graceful steeple was dedicated as Notre Dame de Bon Secours.[67] Like the larger congregations, the French also established their school shortly thereafter, and it was to these classrooms next to the church that Mary Austin and her partner proceeded in April.[68]

Since half the classes were taught in French, Mary Austin instructed one group in French in the morning and the other in the afternoon. Welcome relief arrived the following September, however, in the person of Sister Mathilde Gourrier, the French-speaking young lady who became their first Louisiana postulant.[69] She learned that the French School accepted not only the bilingual Creoles, but also such English-speaking pupils as wished to acquire a fluency in French. This variation was indicated in the register by such names as Buisson, Castellanos, Conway, deRussy, Freret, LaBarre, McKenna, Masson, Parra, Ryan, and Sougeron. Austin described the pupils of the French School as "docile and affectionate, and so grateful for the least kindness"[70] that she found it a real pleasure to teach them. Evidently, the children let it be known how much they enjoyed classes with their new teachers, because the enrollment had doubled, increasing from thirty-two to sixty-five, long before the semester ended on July 29. That teaching conditions were not always ideal, however, is apparent from a June item in the *New Orleans Times*.[71] A teacher complained about the frequency of the arrival of droves of cattle at the Jackson ferry landing. The educator bemoaned the loud cries of the herders and the mooing of the cows as they moved along Jackson Avenue as their regular route toward the slaughterhouses. The writer, Mary Austin perhaps, was distressed because the noisy disturbances interfered with both the attention and the educational progress of the pupils.

Regardless of the lowing of the cattle, these early months in the Crescent City witnessed just a few minor inconveniences. As to those crosses and trials foretold by their St. Louis friends, though true predictions all, their occurrence was simply delayed. Also slow to appear were the candidates supposedly planning to enter soon after the arrival of the sisters. Among the callers at the convent were young ladies who talked of becoming nuns, but "few went beyond the parlor" in those early months. At length, the superior arranged to borrow several teachers for September.[72] Once that problem was solved, everything else looked rosy. Austin had not seen so many lovely gardens and orchards since her two years in the Flower City, Rochester. She was fascinated by the profusion of orange trees in the area later termed the Garden District. She commented that "multitudes of flowers" were sent to the Sisters, along with "bunches of the choicest blossoms to give out their fragrance" in the tiny Mercy chapel. As roses bloomed in almost every yard, Austin called New Orleans a city of roses. To this Mercy who had found the ice and snow of New England and Nebraska almost devastating, the climate of the Crescent City was no problem. "The sunshine was beautiful," she wrote, "and the weather propitious."[73] In an interview many years later she recalled,

I used to look from my little window in the apothecary shop and catch of a morning the fresh, sweet scent of the orange blossoms filling the air. . . . We had a mocking-bird in our window, and the singing of the beautiful songster and the sight of the orange trees in full bloom are truly pleasant memories.[74]

As some of the factors which contributed to the special quality of her first year in New Orleans, Austin enumerated the following in the *Annals*: the enthusiastic welcome and affectionate acceptance of the sisters by the parishioners, the exceptionally favorable opportunities for the visitation of the sick and the imprisoned, the generosity of the New Orleans people as shown by their willingness to help the sisters gather food and clothing for the sick and the destitute, and by the fact that the sisters were "blessed by so many incidents calculated to draw out one's better qualities and bring one closer to God." Austin's enthusiasm was boundless as she continued: "Never since the days of the holy Foundress herself" had the Sisters of Mercy been so advantageously situated; "their virtues were magnified, their shortcomings overlooked." Except for poor Catherine Grant, whose lung disease seemed to be worsening, the sisters were "full of health and happiness, and busy all day long." Referring to this timespan some thirty years later as "an oasis in the desert of life," Mary Austin reminisced: "Never were we more busy, . . . but our good works appealed to all hearts." Not only were "the skies bright and the breezes refreshing," but for that period at least, there was not even a cloud in the sky.[75]

7 IRISH CHANNEL CONVENT
New Orleans
1871–1874

Mary Austin seemed to have fallen in love with the area as soon as she arrived in New Orleans. Thereafter she lost no opportunity in letting it be known that "Among the fairest and most favored portions of the earth . . . none is more charming than Louisiana."[1] Even though it was a lovely 70° in March 1869 when the sisters arrived in New Orleans,[2] the Irish Mercies were surprised at the mild temperatures as the months passed. Earlier they had been informed that the New Orleans summers were so unbearably hot that all who could afford to do so left for cooler climes in June. As she visited the homes of the sick poor in July and August, however, Austin experienced several ways in which the heat was alleviated. Besides the river breeze which generally stirred the air in the Irish Channel, regular and frequent showers kept down both the temperature and the dust of the unpaved streets. After having experienced a half dozen semi-tropical summers, Austin was still enthusiastic about the glories of the area,

> fair flowers and delicious fruits . . . every day in the year; green fields of rustling cane; the mocking-bird making music in the glades; the breeze laden with the odours of jasmine and magnolia; cotton scattered in the sun-lit fields like a miraculous snowfall; parterres gaudy with colour and radiant with dewdrops, aglow with the beauties of paradise.[3]

Since she wrote the above selection as a preface for an article about yellow fever, Mary Austin knew quite well that she was not already in paradise and that there were a number of clouds on the horizon. Perhaps, she even surmised that one of them represented yellow fever. Before that cloud made its appearance, however, one of the earlier problems was the shortage of personnel. Even with the arrival of the four Sisters of Mercy from New York on June 10, 1869,[4] the community had difficulty the fol-

111

lowing September staffing the girls' classes of both Notre Dame de Bon
Secours and St. Alphonsus. For one reason or another local candidates were
slow to make a commitment of Mercy service in 1869, and the sisters were
probably being unrealistic in the expectation of immediate recruits. Like
children at the shore, just dipping one toe into the water and then jumping
back before the advancing waves could cover their feet, several of the
aspiring ladies showed a sincere interest by their inquiries in the parlor of
the apothecary shop convent, but wavered when it was time to test the
waters of religious life. Also, the lengthy hesitancy of the St. Louis Mercies
themselves before sending the foundation to the South caused some of the
young women to tire of the waiting and to venture elsewhere. Mother de
Sales Browne of the Vicksburg Mercy community, the fortunate recipient of
a number of candidates from the New Orleans area, wrote her bishop,
William Henry Elder, that "six of our Sisters passed here on their way to
New Orleans."[5] Then she generously added that she hoped that God would
"bless their mission though we will lose subjects by it."

In New Orleans the Sisters of Mercy decided to have a public ceremony
of reception in the French Church on Jackson Avenue for their lovely
Creole postulant, Mathilde Gourrier. Mary Austin knew that there would
be much publicity for this first Louisiana candidate, a member of a prominent family. The Notre Dame de Bon Secours Church was crowded that
February 24, 1870, not only with four of Mathilde's brothers and their
families, but with other relatives, friends, and for special éclat, some of the
first families of the state. There were also the wide-eyed school girls and a
number of those hesitant aspirants. Naturally, local papers gave generous
coverage to the special event:

> The young lady . . . very handsomely dressed as a bride in white moiré
> antique . . . made a profession of her desire to enter the novitiate. . . . The
> church, exquisitely decorated with palms, ferns, and flowers, was
> crowded, many desiring to witness a scene so interesting from a religious
> point of view, some from mere curiosity on account of the novelty to them,
> and others from personal interest in the welfare of the young lady who was
> about to take so decided a step in life.[6]

With all the pageantry that the people of the Carnival City loved, the
bride was preceded up the aisle by several preschool angels and eight schoolgirl bridesmaids. The ten priests assisting in the sanctuary certainly lent an
aura of special solemnity, and according to the press, the sermon was "an
appropriate, eloquent, touching, and beautiful oratorical effort."[7] Mary
Austin and the other sisters certainly recognized that it was the grace of God
which called young women to a life of religious service. From the days of

Catherine McAuley at Baggot Street, however, her followers had repeatedly experienced the advantages of favorable publicity. Just as Dublin and New York acquired additional candidates by such public receptions and professions, so did New Orleans. There the Mercy community received an influx of fourteen aspirants before the year ended, as each month witnessed the arrival of another candidate or two. And except for two who remained for just a brief trial, these 1870 postulants were the early mainstays of the New Orleans community. Several had been lay teachers in one or the other of the Redemptorist schools before the arrival of the sisters, and these were a tremendous asset to the young community.[8]

Their arrival effectively dispersed the storm clouds of insufficient personnel, and did so just in time to clear the skies for the black clouds of fever and death. Late summer in the South was the opening of the annual fever season, and Mary Austin listened carefully for the distinctive symptoms while natives discussed illnesses which they expressively called undulating, breakbone, and vomito fevers. Assuming that the references were to malaria, dengue and yellow fever, respectively, Mary Austin was anxious to learn the distinguishing signs and the best method of nursing each. The press often allotted space to various medical opinions, and in May of 1870, conjectured as to whether or not yellow fever was already in the city. The Mercies in the Irish Channel felt completely safe both because they were far from the site of the fever, and because as yet, they had had no experience with a virulent epidemic. In mid-June the sisters heard of the death of Archbishop Odin, the saintly prelate who had invited them to his city. News of his death in Ambierle, France, on May 25, 1870, finally reached America almost a month later, and his co-adjutor, Bishop Napoleon Joseph Perché,[9] became the next Archbishop of New Orleans. As Bishop-elect Perché's consecration was being announced for May 1 in the local papers, one suggested that this ceremony might be an appropriate time to remove the episcopal residence to a more central location in the city. Though it had mentioned a site such as St. Patrick's parish, the suggestion went unchallenged and ignored.[10]

A cloud which appeared upon the horizon just then for the Mercies, also concerned St. Patrick's. Both Father Flanagan, pastor there, and Bishop Auguste Martin of Natchitoches in central Louisiana were desperate for teachers. It was painful, especially to Mary Austin, to have to tell these kind friends that there were no sisters available for a few more years. The passage of time, even as it lightened the burden of available personnel, increased the weight of several other problems. Mother Catherine Grant's tuberculosis, already advanced when she arrived in New Orleans, had not improved in the mild Southern climate as her St. Louis physician had hoped it would. Instead, her health deteriorated rapidly. At the same time

Catherine Grant became so dissatisfied with Redemptorist interference in community affairs that she considered transferring to St. Patrick's. Convent records first mention this development in August of 1870, when Catherine asked the opinion of the professed sisters of the original community. All said much the same as Mary Xavier McDermott, "As they had come here only in obedience to their superiors," they did not intend leaving unless they were appointed to do so.[11] Catherine evidently dropped the question at that time, but the cloud hovered overhead.

Mary Austin recorded that the whole community was tremendously busy in August and September readying the new convent (C on plan 2) nearing completion on St. Andrew Street. Bishop Auguste Martin had laid the cornerstone the year before, and the construction had progressed as rapidly as the collection of funds. Father William Meredith said that all the St. Alphonsus parishioners were willing to contribute for a convent for the Sisters of Mercy. The people knew that the funds were carefully budgeted. For instance, to add the wings (A & B on plan 2) for the girls' school, the old "permanent school" (a on plan 1) was demolished and its bricks, lumber, window frames and other millwork — all utilized in the "new school." The opening of school had to be delayed three weeks while the workmen completed the building; and it was September 22, 1870, when the sisters moved their boxes and bundles from the drugstore on Jackson Avenue (x on plan 1) down the two and a half blocks to 1017 St. Andrew Street.[12] Mary Austin and her companions in the movers' brigade shared many a laugh through the years over the memory of their parade composed of children pulling wagons, boys trundling wheelbarrows, and Mercies lugging valises. They certainly presented an unusual spectacle as their cortège moved along the banquettes in front of the busy Magazine Street shops.

Settling in at the new convent had to be accomplished most hurriedly as the grand dedication was to be held on Mercy Day, two days after the sisters had brought trunks and luggage over. The ceremony was to include an open house for the parishioners, many of whom had contributed generously. Motivation varied, of course, but nationalistic competition was still part and parcel of any parish expansion program in the Irish Channel. Without a doubt, some of the donors wanted the girls of St. Alphonsus Parish to have as fine a school as the girls of the German parish, St. Mary's Assumption. Saturday, September 24, dawned beautiful enough to forget ulterior motives, a day weather-perfect for the usual procession of all the societies of the three Redemptorists parishes. Leading them were the priests, and following them were the school children who were curious to see the inner sanctum of the convent. Once the solemn blessing was imparted by Archbishop Perché in the presence of thirty-six priests and numerous friends, there followed a gala open house, guided tours, and a reception for the dignitaries.[13] As a result of several tremendously hectic weeks of preparation by the sisters, each and every aspect of the ceremony was declared to be eminently successful.

One future candidate among the throngs visiting the new structure exclaimed to the rector that the sisters would never be able to fill the forty bedrooms. Father Giesen answered, "So many will join this Institute that the sisters will be able to spread from this convent to many parts of the South."[14] He continued to explain that the superior would send sisters out annually to the surrounding towns and villages. This exciting and prophetic vision of Mercy service might have aided that aspirant to toss aside her hesitation and proceed with definite plans to enter the community. In any case, she joined the Mercy novitiate shortly, and Father's words made such an indelible impression that she could quote them verbatim twenty years later, long after his prophecies had been fulfilled. Mary Austin was jubilant about all of these events, but even more so about the new classes in the school. She had opened two secondary classes, St. Alphonsus High School for girls, on September 23, 1870. Although only a Junior High for the first two years until the addition of two more classes, the event was significant as it was the first time that classes on a secondary level were introduced into any of the Redemptorist schools in the three parishes.[15]

Less than a month after the new schools were in operation, the New Orleans sisters received a completely unexpected offer of help from four Sisters of Mercy in Ireland. It seems that they had decided that they would like to devote the rest of their religious lives to missionary work somewhere in America.[16] Sisters Mary Aloysius Oliver, Ignatius Gayner, Margaret Hessian, and Joseph Stapleton had been professed in the Convent of the Immaculate Conception in the town of Clifden on the beautiful coast of County Galway. The Mercies in New Orleans quickly accepted this surprising offer of assistance as a grand bonanza. The community also recognized the fact that their temporary helpers from New York City were to return to their motherhouse at the end of the school session. In a way, the Irish missionaries were to be an exchange for the earlier help. The sisters in New Orleans understood that the Clifden Mercies wished to join their community on a permanent basis, but the four missionaries sought work where no other religious served. Thus, the Irish Mercies remained in the city only three months before moving on to Natchitoches, where Bishop Martin desperately needed religious teachers.[17]

For the moment the young Mercy community, blissfully ignorant of the fever clouds overhead, seemed to be enjoying prosperity of every kind. In spite of the sporadic cases of yellow fever in pockets in and about the city during the summer, the Fourth District was not seriously affected until October.[18] Even then, Mary Austin related, the sisters did not know that only the "acclimated" were safe near fever victims. Natives who left the city each summer were not acclimated, but those who remained in town for several successive summers acquired a certain amount of immunity, one which only the most virulent of epidemics seemed to penetrate. Perhaps the mosquitoes themselves, with their stinging inoculations, built up a gradual immunity in their victims. The cause of yellow fever was an unknown factor, but it was common knowledge that a summer of frequent torrential rains preceded fever in the fall. In September of 1870, natives were speaking of a miasma, of fever in the air. Several types of fever had been rampant in August, yellow fever dominated in September, and by October the Irish Channel had such a malignant type of yellow fever that a third of the victims were unable to recover.[19]

The Sisters of Mercy, like the Daughters of Charity, did marvelous service in nursing the sick, but two unacclimated Mercies caught the disease in late October, and two more were afflicted with it in early November. Mary Austin feared that she had brought the fever into the convent as she was one of the first to fall ill. The community doctor insisted on calling in two Creole nurses, and it is to their experience and proficiency that the community attributed the recovery of Mary Austin and one of the other sisters. Claiming that she had a less virulent strain of fever than the others, Austin made light of her bout with Yellow Jack and averred that it was the skill of the nurses that secured her recovery. Less fortunate was the youngest of the founding group, Sister Benedicta Shields, who died on November 4, still a novice and barely twenty-one.[20] First to be received into the community in New Orleans and first to die there, she was carried to the cemetery and laid in a borrowed tomb. Less than a week after that Mercy funeral, there was another, the second being for Mary Xavier McDermott.[21] In her death the community lost an exceptionally devout follower of Catherine McAuley, while Mary Austin lost her dearest friend in New Orleans. It was especially fitting that this beloved sister of hers, Austin wrote, "passed to God whom she loved so well . . . on the same day of November, and even on the same hour as the venerated Foundress"[22] — about eight in the evening of November 11. Thus it was yellow fever that sent two of the New Orleans sisters to join the growing Mercy community already with God.

"This is your life, joys and sorrows mingled," Catherine McAuley had reminded her sisters.[23] Because Mary Austin had already experienced so much joy in New Orleans, she was not at all surprised to find that the hour of sorrow had come. The sudden void left by the death of her beloved friend would gradually heal with time, but the memories of this friend were fresh and detailed twenty-five years later in Mary Austin's published tribute. the pain of loss may also have been assuaged by an ever-growing circle of friends, for Austin had the special gift of attracting people both to the gospel message and to a sharing of her personal friendship. Although time could soothe the pain of loss, it was unable to change Catherine Grant's health or her desire to transfer to St. Patrick's parish. Late in 1870, she seems to have promised Father Flanagan that he would have Sisters of Mercy for the parish school by the following fall semester because early in 1871, Father Flanagan held a series of events to raise the funds needed to establish a school for the girls of the parish. The publicity connected with the fund-raisers in April included the information that St. Patrick's Parochial School for Girls was to be conducted by the Sisters of Mercy.[24]

Also in April, the Mercies on St. Andrew Street received word that the Irish missionaries were on their way to America via Limerick to make retreat and via Liverpool "to take ship."[25] Mary Austin and the other sisters were as excited as Catherine Grant over the prospect of help from Ireland. The four Sisters of Mercy, expecting to see Indians, reached New Orleans in mid-May with their hope of converting the savages and of working where other religious were not available. The Crescent City was as short of Indians as it was full of various orders and congregations of religious, and counting the recent influx of candidates, the Mercy community in New Orleans was much larger than they had expected. Perhaps because the newcomers were disappointed and shared the dissatisfaction of the superior, their presence seemed to strengthen her plan to leave the Redemptorist parish. With this resolve in mind, Catherine Grant and an Irish missionary went to Archbishop Perché on August 19, 1871, with two petitions.[26] The four Clifden sisters wished to establish a foundation in the Diocese of Natchitoches, where Bishop Martin was pleading for sisters, and Catherine Grant herself desired to transfer to St. Patrick's parish, where Father Flanagan was readying a convent and school for September. The kindly archbishop agreed to the requests provided the Ecclesiastical Director, Father Giesen, could staff his own schools as well as the new foundations.

Mary Austin made no direct reference to this subdividing of the community in the published *Annals*, but her indirect allusions show that she found it to be a most painful time. In October Catherine Grant, accompanied by one choir sister, newly-professed Camillus Lucas, and several Irish postulants transferred to St. Patrick's Convent of Mercy, where the sisters opened a select school and replaced the lay teachers in the girls' classes of the parochial school.[27] The greatest deterrent to the success of this venture was the failing health of both pastor John Flanagan who had worked so long to obtain Mercies for his schools, and of Catherine Grant who was anxious to assist Father with his plans. Because both the pastor and the superior had severe congestion of the lungs, their doctors prescribed the standard palliative of the day, "change of air." Father Flanagan had traveled to Canada in the fall of 1871, but survived the trip by only six months. Having learned of Catherine Grant's need for a trip, Mary Austin mortgaged the House of Mercy (J on plan 2) as it was the only Mercy property in the city at the time. Austin wanted Catherine to use the funds to obtain treatment at a special tuberculosis sanatorium, but Catherine would not even go to one of the Mercy hospitals. Instead, she requested Mother de Sales Browne of Vicksburg to give her hospitality while she "recruited her health."[28]

Thus, shortly before Father Flanagan's death on April 14, 1872, Catherine Grant had gone upriver to Vicksburg, where the city high on the Third Chickasaw Bluff presented the most picturesque view between Memphis and New Orleans. No matter how cool and stirring the breezes at St. Catherine's Convent of Mercy in Vicksburg, they were certainly too little too late for an advanced case of tuberculosis. Mother Mary Catherine died at the Vicksburg convent on May 23, 1872.[29] Though aware of the seriousness of Catherine Grant's condition at the time that she arranged for the mortgage, Mary Austin was surprised at the rapidity with which Catherine had succumbed. Austin had a series of Masses celebrated for Catherine Grant and offered to her successor, Mary Camillus Lucas, her assistance in any way needed. The young community at St. Patrick's decided to continue there for another year or two, and it was just two years thereafter that Camillus Lucas arranged to transfer her little community to Indianola on the Texas Gulf Coast.[30] From that spot, like the flourishing mustard seed, the small group in due time was to spread the works of mercy across the plains of Texas.

The Natchitoches foundation in Northcentral Louisiana was just about as temporary as the establishment in St. Patrick's parish for several of the same reasons. The Mercy missionaries from County Galway, like Catherine Grant's group, suffered from a shortage of personnel and candidates, and after the death of their sponsor, the gentle Bishop Auguste Martin, a complete lack of funds. Hence, these Irish missionaries also transferred elsewhere.[31] In fulfillment of their pre-New Orleans plans for teaching native Americans, the sisters later worked, some in the Indian mission of Oregon in the Northwest and others in the Southwest mission schools in New Mexico and Arizona. Before leaving Louisiana to serve farther afield, both of these short-lived foundations allowed their sisters who preferred working in the Louisiana area to join the New Orleans Mercies on St. Andrew Street. These transfers were still several years into the future, however, in the fall of 1871, when Catherine Grant chose to leave St. Alphonsus parish. Because of this departure, coupled with the deaths of her two companions in the yellow fever epidemic, Mary Austin Carroll suddenly found herself in a unique position. She was the one experienced Sister of Mercy with a group of fifteen young sisters,[32] eight of them novices, but all of them in various stages of the Mercy novitiate program. Perhaps these young women were also unique, because several of them had already acquired teacher certification, while others were well on their way toward their Normal School accreditation.

Thus, the girls of St. Alphonsus and Notre Dame de Bon Secours were able to continue classes without interruption, in large measure because of the quality and education of these apprentice Mercies. Archbishop Perché dealt with the unusual situation in his own way, and since it was based upon his experience as director and/or chaplain of religious women for thirty years, Mary Austin assumed that his arrangements were as correct canonically as they were practical in the circumstances. The archbishop would not even consider naming a superior until a number of the novices had completed their novitiate and professed their vows. Instead, Perché declared Mary Austin to be the mistress of novices until the above conditions had been fulfilled. Midway during her two-year term as novice mistress, Austin asked the archbishop to allow an escalation of his earlier timetable so that she and the first newly-professed sisters could form a Chapter and select their officials. At once gentle and steadfast, Perché refused the request and restated his original plan that delayed until 1874 the organization and canonical erection of the community.[33] The decision affected neither the rapidity with which the membership increased nor the constancy of the zeal and enthusiasm of this mistress of novices, who never seemed to realize that there might be a relationship between her enthusiasm and the phenomenal increase of applicants to the Mercy community.

Mary Austin's sensitive compassion for people, coupled with her quick and effective response to these needs, certainly seemed contagious. The spark that lit the fire of emulation repeatedly fell upon the young women with whom Austin had been working, either as associates in the schools or as assistants in one of the many projects that called in lay helpers. Austin herself attributed the large influx of aspirants, in part to the generous nature of the New Orleans people and, more weightily, to "service unto death," as she termed it.[34] "Scarcely a month elapses without bringing a candidate," Austin wrote, adding that when any of the sisters died of yellow fever, "God speedily filled the places of the departed." By 1874, the eight novices of 1871 had expanded into a novitiate of twenty-seven, missing a total of thirty only because three had died. Austin counted these deaths as the grains of wheat that must die and fall into the ground before the Gospel harvest can be gathered. The seed of the yellow fever martyrs had fallen into the fertile delta soil, and charitable witnesses saw the personification of Christ's message of "no greater love" in these Mercies dying in the attempt to save others. In Austin's opinion, it was the dedication of those who lived through the fever epidemics unscathed as well as the charity of the sisters who died that inspired so many to join the ranks of the Sisters of Mercy.

Catherine McAuley's words, "We were joined so fast it was a matter of general wonder,"[35] could have been echoed by Austin Carroll. Whatever their motivation, the candidates came in droves, as Austin wrote a friend,

> We get all the postulants we can take, and of the best class. Our Sisters are nearly all natives of Louisiana, and have the advantage therefore of being acclimated. . . . We are twenty-six Sisters . . . and get on very well, thank God. I have never had serious fault to find with any of my Sisters, and they bear my faults very sweetly.[36]

Catherine McAuley had thought the first recruits on each foundation were especially important, for she wrote, "Great caution is necessary selecting persons to commence an institution."[37] Mother Austin, also, the early sisters related, always made a careful study of a prospective aspirant and scrutinized sharply the reasons for the application. "A good will is the chief thing I look for . . . I am cautious enough about admitting young ladies, but once in, I don't know how to send one away."[38] Actually, she did it very tactfully and gently, usually managing to have the candidate herself decide to leave. Many staunch friends of the Mercy community were ladies who treasured happy memories of their brief novitiate experience and of the kindness of Mother Austin as their mistress of novices.

One such candidate, Sister Lizzie, happened to be a recent graduate of the parish school. After several weeks of rising at dawn and keeping busy all day with unaccustomed tasks, Lizzie was "all tuckered out." The next morning at five, instead of bounding out of bed at the first sound of the rising bell, Lizzie rolled over and took a nice long sleep. One of her companions related the sequel.

> After breakfast as Mother Austin walked into the dormitory, our friend was still under the covers. Hearing footsteps she peeped out and said sweetly, "Good morning, Mother." "Good morning, my dear," answered Mother Austin with even greater sweetness than the little postulant.[39]

And to the surprise of those novices who had been in the novitiate long enough to have merited some reprimands, that was it — no more. Mother Austin gave the teenager a few more weeks and another late sleep before she helped her recognize that she was not yet ready for the rigors of the Mercy horarium. Mother suggested that she might like to return in a few years, and then bid her a fond adieu. Five years later Lizzie returned, completed a successful novitiate, and professed her vows. The novices wondered if Mother had the gift of prophecy. Perhaps it was just the keenness of Austin's observation as she studied the character of her charges, for the young lie-abed was later to be a leader in the Mercy community.

"I have the name of being very strict myself,"[40] Mother Austin wrote a friend, and to a certain extent, according to several memoirs, her novices agreed.

> God help you if you walked too heavily or banged your window shutters and disturbed your neighbors. How could you be so thoughtless if every action was done for the honor and glory of God. . . . Mother's great love and devotion for our holy foundress made a lasting impression on us, as she mentioned Mother McAuley daily in her lectures, particularly her love of the poor. . . . Mother Austin demanded the strictest observance of the Rule of Silence from the attic to the basement, but her inspiring daily instructions stressed the perfection Mother McAuley desired for each of her Sisters, or offering every deed of the day to God in thanksgiving for His graces and for His honor and glory. . . . Mother's expounding of the Holy Rule was so clear and convincing, and so filled with loving persuasion that you felt impelled to rise at once and put the advice into action. . . . Mother exacted strict enforcement of the Rule, but her enforcement was tempered with kindness. We knew that she wanted each of us to spend our life in the friendship of Christ, and we loved her for her concern. . . . Mother had such a way of inspiring the Sisters that they could do anything assigned. She filled them with self-confidence by reminding them that they could do anything with God's grace of Obedience — and to their surprise they accomplished even the most difficult tasks with success. . . . We had Silence like the Trappists, but that helped us walk hand in hand with Christ.[41]

For the members of this noviceship, there was no doubt that Mother Austin was the captain at the helm, or that for each member of the crew, there was the highest of expectations. Yet, when one of her Mercy correspondents wrote that it was difficult for any novice to succeed in a certain motherhouse, Mother Austin replied that though strict herself, she thought it "better to lighten the sweet yoke than to make it too heavy."[42] Announcing that she had twenty-six sisters and seldom lost one who had completed her candidacy, she continued,

> Indeed I find no fault of any consequence in those who come — if we want wholly faultless people, we should advertise for angels. . . . I find beginners who have the most exterior faults have also the most generosity, most capability to acquire virtue, etc., when one had a little patience with them.[43]

Judging by the outstanding caliber of these first Louisiana Mercies, many of them Creole ladies unused to much physical exertion, Mother Austin did a marvelous job, as they learned from her not just a passion for helping the poor and a fascination with the ideals of Catherine McAuley, but also the ability to live with Christ as a close and loving friend.[44]

Mother Austin patterned the New Orleans novitiate after her own formation period twenty years earlier in St. Maries of the Isle in Cork, where Mother Josephine Warde had introduced her to Catherine McAuley as to an affectionate companion. Austin had not only appreciated the virtue of the foundress but also the magnificence of her plans and aims for her Institute of Mercy. As Austin continued to gather more first-hand information on the life and character of Catherine from Josephine Warde's sister, Mother Xavier, and from many of the other early companions of the foundress, she became convinced of the sanctity of Catherine McAuley. And before she had been ten years in the community, she was writing to both Irish and English motherhouses that it would not be difficult to open the Cause for the canonization of the foundress.[45] These efforts of the 1860s were unsuccessful, even though periodically renewed, because the sisters thought that any such attempt was premature, it being then only twenty-five years after Catherine McAuley's death. So, for a time Mother Austin postponed further efforts, but decided that everyone who read the New Orleans newspapers would periodically find information available concerning the zeal and sanctity of Catherine McAuley. Austin tried to publicize every jot and iota that she could learn of the foundress and the works of her Mercy Institute; for Austin felt that once people got to know Catherine, they would appreciate her exceptional holiness, love her gentle compassion, and call for her canonization by popular acclaim.

An abundance of material, usually several columns in length, found its way into one or the other of the local[46] papers for each of Catherine McAuley's special dates — birth, profession, death, feast of Our Lady of Mercy. If there was no time to compose an article, Mother Austin selected an appropriate section from her *Life of Catherine McAuley*, and editors graciously printed enough to fill several columns. Austin lost no opportunity to report local events such as receptions and professions of her sisters, and the school plays, exhibitions, and graduations. Even this type of news item included some tribute to the foundress, whose newspaper blitz, like her biography earlier, had a silver lining.[47] Though the rate of pay for free-lance writers was none too large, Mother Austin accumulated a tidy sum by the sheer bulk of those lengthy columns. That sum, plus the royalties coming in regularly from her books, enabled Austin to finance the social works undertaken at this period. By far the best fund-raiser was her biography of the foundress, which was in its second edition and its fourth printing by 1874.[48]

This book sold well because it appealed to both lay people and religious, and certainly it was appropriate that the foundress, through her story, helped to feed the orphans and the babies in the crèche or day-nursery. One of the book's reviewers had even hoped that it would "raise a sum for the present Works of Mercy somewhat similar to the fortune that the heiress of Coolock House had invested."[49]

Although Mother Austin's translations from spiritual works did not have such general appeal as the biography, her Saint Jure series translated from the French sold well to religious communities on both sides of the Atlantic.[50] Like such early Mercies as Sisters Mary Anne Doyle and Vincent Deasy who were trained by Catherine McAuley herself, Austin Carroll had always used the spare moments between other assignments to translate devotional works[51] from the French and Spanish, primarily in order to provide spiritual reading in English for her own sisters. As she expressed it in the first Saint Jure preface, her hope was to further "enkindle the love of Jesus Christ in the hearts of the readers."[52] For this same end and for the religious who could not secure a priest to give the retreat lectures, Mother Austin compiled a small retreat manual.[53] Reviewers of the translations became progressively more favorable with regard to her translating. One critic had even faulted the quality of *Margaret Mary*,[54] her first work, which seems to have been translated during her novitiate. Most reviews concentrated on the valuable material of the second translation rather than on the translator's style.[55] For the third and subsequent translations, however, reviewers became quite complimentary about the quality and grace of the translation itself. According to a wide diversity of reviewers, Mother Austin's fluency improved with each new work.

During this decade Mother Austin also authored a different type of book, as she wrote four collections of stories for children. She had accepted the challenge from youthful readers to produce stories of realistic youngsters who were lively enough to enjoy some fun and mischief, or who were quite naughty until, through some series of persons or events, they were convinced to change their actions. The pupils in Mother Austin's classes, like the youngsters on the *Mollie Able*, when urged to read religious stories, had complained that the pious tales available were dull and boring and filled with prudes and prigs. The school children wanted adventures peopled with some young villains, but Mother Austin protested that she had "never known a bad child, just some who could be troublesome at times."[56] Yet, in order to keep her students reading, she decided to try her hand with some capricious youngsters in lively stories that could also carry the positive message of God's love. One preface reminded her readers that when Christ said "Let the children come to me," He had called all of them, the bad as well as the good. He makes no exception. Probably there were naughty children in the crowd around Christ. . . . If all had been well behaved, I think the apostles would not have wanted to drive them away . . . but whatever kind they were, Christ blessed everyone of them.[57]

Entitled *Happy Hours of Childhood, Angel Dreams, Glimpses of Pleasant Homes*, and *By the Seaside*,[58] the collections went through several printings. Judging by that fact, children must have found the religious messages positive enough to be palatable and the young protagonists more enjoyable than their earlier counterparts.

Reviewers found these children's stories "full of boyish fun and beautiful parental love," were imaginative and "captivated the fancy," that they "amused as well as instructed," and that for the tales set in Ireland there was the enrichment "of memories fair as its sunrise and greenly fresh as its fields."[59] Orestes Brownson thanked Austin Carroll "in the name of boyhood" for two unusual features—one being the presentation of girls who were, on occasion, far from saintly and the other, the portrayal of boys with character who could act upon religious principle.[60] Brownson especially liked the story of one such lad who was transformed from a spoiled brat into a manly youth through his enforced labor as a deckhand aboard a commercial fishing boat. Although Austin Carroll's character study was published thirty years before *Captains Courageous*, the latter is oddly similar though lengthened considerably with details of seafaring life. The *Catholic World* stated that Austin's stories joined the fascination of a lively plot with spiritual teaching,[61] thus noting the very combination which the author had striven to accomplish. Perhaps her collections of tales full of sprightly youngsters served as a bridge between the earlier moralistic stories and those without any moralizing which were soon to follow. Austin Carroll's mischievous protagonists preceded Tom Sawyer, Becky Thatcher, and Huckleberry Finn by less than a decade.

Ever since her arrival in the United States in 1856, Austin had tried to encourage the formation of libraries because she considered the availability and use of books essential to true education. At times her hopes had been thwarted by a lack of means or of the approval of those in authority. Once she was the one in charge, libraries were to flourish everywhere. She found the means to establish a library and then increase it annually in each school her sisters staffed just as she found the energy to strive continuously to get her students interested in reading. There were books for the orphans, the sodalists, the House of Mercy girls, and even collections in prison. Books were also made available to the students in the evening classes. These sessions Mother Austin began scheduling several days a week in 1873, so that the working girls could continue their education. One of the first activities of the Children of Mary in the Sodality of Our Lady was the purchasing of books to establish their library. In several American cities Mother Austin knew that the Sisters of Mercy had established the first local sodality. While organizing the Children of Mary in 1872, Mother Austin learned that it was 142 years since the Ursulines had formed the first Sodality in New Orleans. Shortly thereafter Mother Austin heard the interesting fact that during the past century the Ursuline Nuns had owned the site of the Mercy convent on St. Andrew Street.[62]

As Mother Austin was making arrangements to purchase a house and lot adjacent to the convent, she saw that the land had once been within the Faubourg Nuns. Later she questioned the Reverend William S. Murphy, SJ, who "gave her a graphic sketch of the rise and progress of the Crescent City."[63] The elderly Jesuit related that some hundred years ago the area had been the vegetable garden for the Ursulines. As the city began to spill over its boundaries, however, the nuns followed the pattern set by the neighboring plantation owners and had their farm subdivided into blocks and sold. The three streets surveyed through their property were named for three of the Ursuline administrators — Mère St. Félicité, Mère St. Marie, and for St. Andrew Street, Mère St. André.[64] With the two neighboring suburbs, Faubourgs Panis and Livaudais, Austin learned, the area was incorporated as the City of Lafayette[65] just about the time that she was born. Twenty years thereafter Lafayette merged with New Orleans and the city boundary moved from Felicity to Toledano Street. During her term with the novices Mother Austin witnessed the further expansion of the city, as it included the suburbs of Jefferson City, Burtheville, Greenville, and Carrollton. Father Murphy, an Irish Jesuit from Cork, enjoyed the extent to which this bright Irish Mercy from Clonmel was interested in the Catholic origins of the city. For her part, Mother Austin appreciated being able to exchange news of their mutual friends in Cork and basked in the delight of sharing friendship with this scholarly nephew of the late Bishop John Murphy of Cork.[66]

Another Irish priest, shortly after their arrival in New Orleans, had told these Sisters of Mercy from St. Louis that they were not the first of Catherine McAuley's daughters to come into the city. Father John Flanagan had explained that Bishop Andrew Byrne of Little Rock obtained a Mercy contingent from Naas.[67] The bishop and his "excellent colony of Sisters of Mercy"[68] left Ireland in November of 1850, and it was seven weeks later that the New Orleans *Daily Delta* announced that the sturdy *John O'Toole* arrived from Dublin on January 23, 1851.[69] Mother Austin noted that the date was exactly one month before her sixteenth birthday when the Naas sisters of Mercy disembarked in New Orleans. The bishop obtained hospitality with the Ursulines for the four professed sisters and the six candidates. Besides attending to business for his diocese, Bishop Byrne took the sisters to meet families and interview prospective pupils in the American sector and suburbs. Among the daughters of his many Irish and Irish American friends, he was able to garner some pupils for his Mercy school, one young lady being Margaret Fitzpatrick.[70] She was to be the first from New Orleans to become a follower of Catherine McAuley, for she was later to join the Mercy community in Little Rock. On February 2, the bishop and his Irish sisters embarked on the *Pontiac*. Almost three months after they had bid their friends in County Kildare farewell, the sisters from Naas landed at Little Rock on February 6, 1851. Mother Austin was as fascinated to hear the details of the brief stopover in New Orleans as she was surprised to learn that the Arkansas sisters had preceded the St. Louis group to the Crescent City by almost twenty years. Later she would get in touch with them, collect a regular ship's log on their transatlantic journey, and publish it in the *Annals*. For the moment, however, she appreciated the fact that there were Mercies in Arkansas.

Much closer as neighbors were the Sisters of Mercy in Mississippi, and not just because they were nearer geographically. Transportation was the important factor as both Vicksburg and New Orleans fronted on the nation's nineteenth-century superhighway, the Mississippi River. The Vicksburg sisters had entertained the Mercy travelers from the *Mollie Able* on the memorable day in 1869 when they shared Lenten fare. The following year the Mississippi sisters began to serve in Pass Christian on the Gulf Coast,[71] and the New Orleans sisters were able to return some hospitality as the Vicksburg teachers passed through the city. Packets steamed upriver regularly and daily, but sisters going to the Pass often had to wait a day or so at the convent on St. Andrew Street before a passenger boat was ready to cross Lakes Pontchartrain and Borgne to reach the Gulf Coast. Thus the two groups became fast friends, and with these Mississippi sisters the late superior had found her change of air. Since the convent at Pass Christian was vacant during the month that her sisters were in Vicksburg, Mother de Sales Browne offered Mother Austin its use as a resting place where any delicate sisters might recuperate.[72] Mother Austin divided her community into fourths and sent each group over to the Pass for a week. The New Orleans sisters were to enjoy the memories of that joyful experience for many a year. Mothers de Sales and Austin consoled each other on the losses of their sisters to yellow fever, and parts of such letters found their way into the *Annals*,[73] bur most of their correspondence is no longer extant. This is also true of Austin's letters to other Mercy friends, whose only correspondence preserved is that contained in the *Annals of the Sisters of Mercy*.

One letter of Mother Austin's, carefully preserved in Rome, was sent to Pope Pius IX.[74] Written in 1872 during the Piedmontese encroachment upon the papal territory, the letter in diplomatic French pledges the daily prayers of the devoted Sisters of Mercy in New Orleans. For herself "and the young women that God has confided to her care" Mother Austin requested the Apostolic Benediction, declaring that it would "encourage me in the battle of life." The gracious letter accompanied five of her works[75] and as many volumes of translations, which Mother Austin sent the Pope as "a testimony of my respect and a measure of my filial love." In keeping with her esteem for the pontiff and her boundless admiration of the Mercy foundress, Mother Austin had a copy of the *Life of Catherine McAuley* especially bound in white moiré silk and lettered in gold. This volume, as permanent as her letter to the Pope, is preserved at the Vatican. Pope Pius IX sent Mother Austin Carroll a silver crucifix and his blessing "in his own handwriting."[76] The *Morning Star* reported that the books were presented to the Holy Father by the rector of the American College, Dr. Francis Chatard, and that the Pope "acknowledge in his letter the eminent services to Catholic literature of the authoress."[77] The 1873 news item continued, perhaps with a bit of exaggeration stemming from local pride, "This is the only instance, we think, in which the Pope has given so high a mark of distinction to any lady in America."

Mother Austin Carroll must have been one of the born letter-writers, for her correspondence was as varied as it was massive. Requests for favors were complimentary and gently persuasive; business matters were handled with polite brevity; and her fluent outpourings to friends were marked by varying degrees of affection. Friends in need knew where to turn. There were funds for Vincent McGirr and Genevieve Granger after the Great Fire in Chicago, and Teresa Maher in Cincinnati sent her gratitude for Austin's prayers and encouragement.[78] Mercies in Dublin, Birr, Limerick, and Bermondsey heard that many distinguished priests were impressed with the extraordinary holiness of the Mercy foundress and urged "having her proposed for canonization," or that the New Orleans sisters had a life-size portrait of Catherine McAuley recently enshrined in the convent. Mercy news was regularly exchanged with Passage West and Cork through Mother Josephine Warde and Austin's sisters, Mary Mercy and Dominica Carroll, with Xavier Warde in Manchester, Elizabeth Strange of Pittsburg, and with her most affectionate friend from their childhood in Clonmel, Juliana Purcell of Providence. With these and many other Mercy friends, Mother Austin's letters forged a chain of Mercy sharing from coast to coast, as notes were posted to New Orleans from Manchester, Providence, Worcester, Hartford, New York City, Philadelphia, Pittsburg, Rochester, Buffalo, Cincinnati, Louisville, St. Louis, Vicksburg, Chicago, Davenport, and San Francisco.[79] In another year or so, Austin Carroll would use her Mercy network to gather the data for the *Annals of the Sisters of Mercy*.

Apart from her Mercy exchanges, Mother Austin's letters more often than not put her in touch with editors, publishers, and writers. Letters handled her business with Patrick O'Shea, the Sadliers, John G. Shea, M. H. Phelan, James McMaster, Lawrence Kehoe, Orestes Brownson, and John Francis Maguire, to name a few. In his *Irish in America* Maguire published some of Austin Carroll's views on education.[80] Brownson, who did not care for many women authors, published a fine tribute to Austin's work.[81] McMaster learned that, rather than the public collections as the press stated, it was Mother Austin who was supporting the wife of the late Captain Fry.[82] This lady was just one of the many widows aided regularly during the economic rape of Louisiana in the period so inaccurately termed reconstruction. Mother Austin's unbiased friend from Belgium described the ruin.

> Ladies and gentlemen ask for bread — 50,000 real estate holders have to pay $2500 per capita. . . . The misery is appalling — properties are for sale, over 12,000 for unpaid taxes. . . . Here in the city the custom officers and carpet baggers and scalawag officers bid for the amount of taxes due — and after all, they pay over this amount with the money stolen from the treasury of the people.[83]

To relieve the destitute Mother Austin bought huge quantities of bread from her friend Margaret Haughery, who had just enlarged her bakery on Commerce between Poydras and Lafayette. Yet when Margaret heard that the bread was for the poor — both the *nouveau indigent* who had lost their homes and the poor families in the Channel, she sold the loaves for cost or less. These generous Irish women shared a deep compassion for the people suffering under the vindictive system which the press dubbed the "party of theft."[84] Mother Austin had a real anger, also, over the greed of the corrupt adventurers and the injustice of having them kept in office through the power of federal bayonets.

While working in the Northeast, Austin Carroll had become largely Americanized, but these injustices now transformed her into a whole-hearted Southerner. "The distress especially among people who were once well off is awful,"[85] she wrote, and added that she used most of her funds for food for the needy, "We do not reserve anything from them . . . for money at my touch melts." Nor did she hesitate to buy fresh vegetables for her community so that her sisters could maintain their health. Later they could recall that she kept a good table and preferred paying for plenty of well-cooked wholesome meals rather than for a lot of medicines."[86] She knew the value of relaxation for her busy sisters, also, and in the evening they enjoyed an hour of spirited fun. Often Mother Austin played the piano to accompany lovely Irish lyrics or some lively tunes for jigs and clogs.[87] Although most of the sisters were natives of the Irish Channel rather than of the old sod itself, these Irish Americans had preserved both their heritage and their dances. Letters, too, were sometimes a part of this recreation hour, usually before one of the sisters in a branch convent was to celebrate her feastday. Each sister would write a personal note so that, even with several greetings on a page, the addressee would receive a nice bundle of correspondence for her feast. Any traveler headed to one of the branches usually carried a packet of notes for the sisters there, also, as Austin was convinced that communication led to unity.[88]

Now and again during the hour of relaxation, Austin had one of the sisters read aloud from a letter of Mercy progress afar, perhaps from Blackrock or Bermondsey across the Atlantic, or from Brisbane or Ballarat across the Pacific, or from one of their own branches along the Gulf Coast. Thus the New Orleans community came to know of their sisters half a world away. There was lots of talking and laughing about events close to home for Austin was witty and encouraged the sisters to remember amusing classroom incidents to relate at recreation. She herself could tell a funny tale with enough verve to send them into gales of laughter.[89] Others soon learned to entertain as they shared daily events. Yet, with all their merriment each evening, these earliest New Orleans Mercies gave testimony that Mother Austin's "first concern was always for their spiritual welfare."[90] Once she read that a British journal, after extolling all the various works and ministries of the Sisters of Mercy, praised their "unflagging spirit and energy."[91] Mother Austin explained to her sisters that Catherine McAuley's followers must be energized and vitalized by her zealous spirit, one which Austin identified as "the spirit of the Heart of Jesus."[92]

Austin Carroll herself had a loving personal devotion to the Sacred Heart of Jesus and to His mother as the Immaculate Virgin.[93] Without foisting her own devotions on the other sisters, Austin took care to see that the special prayers to the Sacred Heart of Jesus and Our Lady of Mercy were observed as specified in the Mercy Rule. As it happened, the two particular devotions of Austin's received prominence in the archdiocese of New Orleans shortly after Archbishop Perché was consecrated. He dedicated his See to the Immaculate Virgin of Lourdes on December 8, 1873, and to the Sacred Heart of Jesus on June 14, 1874.[94] Later, Austin was to recall that this double consecration concerning her favorite devotions caused her to feel as if a definite seal of approval had been stamped upon her ministry in the old Catholic city.

8

INCREASE & EXPANSION
The Gulf Coast
1875–1878

J
ust as the husbandman nurtures his young tree by setting its roots into soil which has been filled with nutrients, so had Mother Austin Carroll striven to establish in the Irish Channel in new Orleans a community rooted firmly in the nourishing spirit of the foundress of the Mercy Institute. Catherine McAuley's aims, ideals, and virtues were the sources of enrichment which, as Gospel values, Mother Austin combined with God's word and the traditional nineteenth-century devotions to nourish and inspire her young sisters. Judging by the results, the recipe must have been a successful one. "We get all the postulants we can take . . . of the best class . . . nearly all native of Louisiana,"[1] she wrote a friend. Although the two-year term during which she had served as the mistress of novices was a short period in which to send roots deep enough to fashion a truly sturdy tree, Mother Austin's foundation in the Crescent City was able to send out two Mercy groups, each to staff several schools as the community spent its fourth year together.[2]

The seven novices who formed the New Orleans community with Mother Austin in 1871 all successfully completed their novitiate, professed their religious vows, and with Austin Carroll, formed the sturdy foundation of the Louisiana motherhouse. Archbishop Perché, familiar with canonical regulations for Roman Congregations, considered the young community a new foundation for several reasons. Catherine Grant had left the Redemptorist Parish not for a branch, but for another foundation, and two of the other three sisters in the founding group from St. Louis died of yellow fever. Thus, Mary Austin Carroll was the lone professed Mercy with a band of Louisiana novices, the eight forming the second New Orleans foundation. The episcopal procedures seemed to be both correct and appropriate, for Mary Austin had served as assistant superior to Catherine Grant for three years, then as novice mistress in 1872 and 1873. "Postulants crowded

131

in" during this period.[3] The sisters increased annually from eight to fifteen, to twenty, and to twenty-six by the octave of the Ascension in 1874. Archbishop Perché had appointed this day as the date Austin Carroll was to begin her term as the first canonical superior of this young community.[4] The enthusiasm and vitality of the group was already expanding the Mercy apostolates in the Irish Channel.

The work which had made the most obvious strides forward, perhaps, was the assistance provided for unskilled working women. The House of Mercy was one of Mother Austin's favorite works because it enabled women and girls to utilize their own abilities and talents to better their situations. Established in 1869 in the compact building adjacent to the apothecary-shop convent at Jackson and Magazine Streets, the Mercy Home flourished from the start. In 1870, the young women moved with the sisters into one section of the large new convent at 1017 St. Andrew Street. There the Mercies shared their shelter with the girls just as had been done in the first House of Mercy on Baggot Street in Dublin and in St. Catherine's Convent of Mercy on Houston and Mulberry Streets in New York City a decade later.[5] One floor of the four-story Mercy Convent in St. Alphonsus Parish housed the girls for almost a year. Then Mother Austin was able to finance other quarters in 1871, when she purchased a frame dwelling (J on plan 2) to serve as the House of Mercy. Although this two-story house faced Constance Street, the back of the lot adjoined the parish property on which the convent stood. Within two years the home was far too small for the number applying, and Mother Austin worked to procure the substantial brick residence (K on plan 2) on the Magazine Street side of the convent.[6]

During the drive for funds for these larger quarters a news article, probably the result of an interview with Mother Austin Carroll, explained the threefold object of the House of Mercy.

> *First*, to receive from shipboard immigrant females and prepare them for new duties by teaching cooking, washing, ironing, etc., and finding respectable situations for them. *Secondly*, to protect any females of undoubted good character who chance to be out of place [work], or supply board or lodging to those who cannot get it where they work. *Thirdly*, to furnish medical assistance, medicines, and accommodations, if needed, to the sick of the same class.[7]

As this ministry for working women and girls was a unique service at the time in the New Orleans area, it seemed to appeal to the members of the press. Another article reported that the Sisters of Mercy saw a need for this type of housing and went right out to buy a dozen simple camp beds, "the crown jewels of the benefaction."[8] The enthusiastic reporter continued,

"While legislators have discussed the ways and means without results, these unobtrusive religious ladies, without flourish of trumpets or drums, or caucuses of investigation or reform, have made the necessary provisions."

"With the audacity which characterizes Charity, this institution has begun operations without an exchequer and no patron but Providence," noted another reporter.[9] Mother Austin agreed in a letter to a friend, Bishop William Henry Elder of Natchez, "God has always helped us and sent us means enough to keep our institutions going — blessings for which we are not grateful enough, but we must improve."[10] Then she confided further, "How they are to be supported never troubles me," because she had already experienced "the unexcelled generosity" of the people of New Orleans. In a later letter she wrote that, especially in regard to the Church, these Southerners were "the most generous people I ever met."[11] Her judgment was an echo of that of the Norman survey in 1845, for after his compilation of local charitable organizations, he added,

> There is probably no city in the United States that has so many benevolent institutions as New Orleans in proportion to its populace. Certainly, it has not an equal in those voluntary contributions, which are sometimes required to answer the immediate calls of distress.[12]

Mother Austin Carroll's research made it clear to her that local charity was not anything new. More than a century earlier than the Norman survey, local benefactors were bestowing endowments upon the colonial city. The first gift of service was that of the Ursulines who nursed in the Maison de Charité de Saint Jean, the legacy of Jean Louis in the 1730s. After the destruction of this St. John's Hospital in a 1779 storm, Don Andres Almonester y Roxas erected the Hospital Royale San Carlos. Mother Austin hailed him as "the most liberal philanthropist America had yet seen" because of his many gifts to the French town under Spanish rule.[13] Early in the American era the Creoles, Americans, and immigrants each formed benevolent groups. Prominent among the earliest of these were the Female Charity Society and the Hibernian Society. During the next decade these were followed by the Young Men's Howard Association and *Les Dames de la Providence*. By the 1840s, the cosmopolitan city had numerous charitable associations organized along national lines, and Mother Austin was delighted to see how many Irish groups had given good service. Among them were the Shamrock Benevolent Society, St. Michael's Benevolent Association, and St. Joseph's Charitable Society of St. Patrick's Parish.[14]

Mother Austin herself witnessed the activities of several of these groups, along with others such as the Society of St. Vincent de Paul in several parishes. Members of this organization fostered special projects like assisting the prison chaplains and the Sisters of Mercy in their work with the imprisoned. Then there were the tremendous benefices of Austin's friend Margaret Haughery in behalf of the orphans of the city. Repeatedly, Mother Austin depended upon the generosity of the Crescent City. In order to purchase a dwelling to serve as the House of Mercy, for instance, Mother Austin borrowed the sum needed from several friends who asked no interest and allowed her to repay the loan gradually while she met payments of a thousand dollars a year on the real estate.[15] The bulk of this amount Mother Austin obtained by sponsoring an annual "charity lecture." With a popular topic, a prominent speaker, and several thousand tickets sold in advance for fifty cents apiece, this type of fund-raiser was quite effective financially. It was also as popular a social event in the Irish Channel in New Orleans as similar charity sermons were in Dublin, where several institutions were supported in large measure by the annual sermon.[16] St. Alphonsus Church, besides being such a handsome structure, seated an extensive attendance, as did St. Alphonsus Hall when the audience heard a layman give the lecture. Even so, many of the kind ticket-buyers probably considered their purchase simply a donation for the worthy cause.

Most generous in the early 1870s among the local orators who bespoke Mother Austin's projects for harboring the harborless were the Redemptorist priests, especially John B. Duffy, Henry Giesen, and Ferreol Girardey. Several priests from away and a few prominent laymen, usually relatives of the sisters, like John G. Devereux, also contributed their talent as speakers. Reverend Michael O'Connor, SJ, the former bishop of Pittsburgh who brought the Irish Sisters of Mercy to the United States and who had lectured in St. Louis for the Mercies there, lent his assistance to Mother Austin in the spring of 1872.[17] In her invitation to his brother, Reverend James O'Connor, who was her friend and advisor for long years before he became a bishop, Mother Austin mentioned details which led to the success of the lecture series.

> I had what I hoped was an inspiration some time ago to ask you to come down here this winter and give a Lecture for the Charities under our care. . . . We have a Lecture every year for our House of Mercy, as it is not yet half paid for. . . . Of course, we would be only too glad to defray all traveling expenses, etc. We are all praying that you may be able to gratify us. Any time in February or March would be suitable. We would like to have about two months notice of the date, [and] subject, because we generally sell most of the tickets before the Lecture. I hope you will be able to oblige us in this, for I should dearly like to see you again, and to consult you on various subjects. . . . To be perfectly candid with you, much as I would like to have you give it this year, I would like much better to have an opportunity of renewing my acquaintance with you.[18]

In this letter Mother Austin was referring to the second Mercy Home at 1021 St. Andrew Street, where the second story originally provided the only dormitory space. However, Mother Austin found a contractor who raised the roof and constructed dormer windows, thus adding a third story and doubling the space for sleeping accommodations. The industrial school was located on the first floor, and the trades and skills taught there were an integral part of the success of the House of Mercy even though classes were attended largely by non-residents. After just two years in the small house on Constance Street, statistics revealed that the girls and women placed in situations after receiving training numbered more than 600, of whom only 240 had resided in the Mercy Home. Numbers increased dramatically, almost fourfold, after the transfer of the facilities to larger quarters. Thereafter, while the training in kitchen and laundry work in preparation for jobs in hotel and household service continued on a limited scale, the emphasis shifted to needlework. Later there were to be other trades, also, for the years saw an ever-changing list of skills taught. It was through her employment bureau that Mother Austin kept her finger on the pulse of the city's needs and repeatedly adapted the curriculum to meet the job openings of the time.[19]

Probably, it was only in this last point and in the connection of the Industrial School with the House of Mercy that the New Orleans institution differed from those in other cities. Sisters of Mercy in their Mercy Homes everywhere made religious instruction available, encouraged reception of the sacraments, and offered young women opportunities for renewed spiritual growth. Nor was Mother Austin alone in inviting the girls to Sunday sessions as was done in Manchester, and she followed the lead of New York City Mercies by establishing sodalities and circulating libraries for the girls and encouraging them to return often to see the sisters.[20] Mother Austin's advertisements noted that work ordered at the House of Mercy was "executed with neatness, dispatch, and on the most reasonable terms," that the seamstresses were prepared to assist "milliners and couturiers," that orders were being received "for ornamental needlework, Church vestments, banners, artificial flowers, etc.,"[21] and that the additional items listed would not delay the articles so frequently ordered, like dresses, personal garments, shirts and shrouds. And to the great surprise of Mother Austin and her young crew, the sewing director reported that the "dead habit" or shroud was the item most often ordered. These had been made originally in order to give them to destitute families when one of their number succumbed to the annual fevers.[22] Later, however, orders began to come in from other families who not only liked the appearance of the Mercy shroud, but also seemed to find it especially appropriate that the Sisters of Mercy, who had earlier assisted the patient to wrap himself in God's merciful love, might also provide a "Mercy shroud" with which to wrap the corpse.

Although Mother Austin and her sisters did often assist as death closed the eyes of one of the elderly sick whom they visited regularly, the sisters also spent themselves in caring for the very young. Besides the girls in the parish schools of Notre Dame de Bon Secours and St. Alphonsus, the Mercies were concerned about a group of pre-schoolers. As soon as the former Mercy Home on Constance Street was vacated by the transfer of the working women to the larger building, Mother Austin established a Crèche there in order to help some of the mothers in single-parent families.[23] After acquiring additional skills in the industrial school, some of these mothers obtained much better jobs while their pre-school children resided in the Crèche. Mother Austin explained this institution as "a nursery . . . in which a number of small children are received and cared for during the day while their mothers earn their subsistence."[24] The Crèche filled a real need at a time when so many wives had husbands crippled in the recent war or had lost them to yellow fever. From the day that the Crèche opened its doors to the babies it was a popular institution and, unlike the House of Mercy, had no need of ads. For a time the little girls orphaned in the fever epidemics lived on the second floor of the Crèche, but these children, after sparking another work of mercy, were transferred to the three-story Mercy Home so that the Crèche could expand to the entire building.[25] With day nurseries so common today, it might be difficult to realize that this Crèche of Austin Carroll's was a unique institution in New Orleans at the time.

Before an orphanage was planned, however, Mother Austin decided that the increased numbers in the Mercy community of New Orleans made it feasible to accept several of the requests for the services of the sisters both as teachers and as visitors of the sick. A number of pastors had been asking for these dual services for their parishes. First of these offers to be accepted was a parish on the Gulf Coast, where Mother Austin initiated the application because she had a double purpose in mind.[26] Besides staffing the parish school in a small town, she wished to establish a safe refuge during yellow-fever season for her newly arrived candidates.[27] Natives had convinced Mother Austin that any person who spent several successive summers in New Orleans acquired an immunity to the annual local fevers. And conversely, those who left for several months of vacation often forfeited much of the resistance which they had possessed earlier.[28] Hindsight suggests the probability that the mosquitoes, while they slaked their thirst, gave their victims minimal doses of fever germs as a series of stinging inoculations. If so, the frequent vaccinations assisted the victims to acquire a certain amount of resistance which the booster shots of later summers could raise to an almost total immunity. This information helped Mother Austin, ever watchful of the health of the young sisters as she was; for she insisted that, before they began nursing yellow-fever patients, newcomers must become "acclimated." Her practice raised the Mercy survival rate considerably, and so did the branch convent to be established shortly on the Mississippi Gulf Coast.

In 1874, Mother Austin consulted Archbishop Perché about the dual project, especially since the small town considered was Biloxi in the Natchez Diocese. She never planned any new work, however, without consulting the gracious archbishop. Endorsing her idea heartily, he assured her that his neighbor in Natchez, Bishop William Henry Elder, would be delighted to have another group of religious teachers in his missionary diocese. Mother Austin's letter to Bishop Elder brought the expected response. Not only would he be happy to have her staff "a parochial school on the Gulf Coast,"[29] but he mentioned as likely sites, Biloxi, Ocean Springs, and Pascagoula, with the suggestion that she "visit the places and see how much encouragement they can give." The prelate blessed her efforts and offered any further approbation that she needed. Mother Austin followed the bishop's advice in order to ascertain the best location for this first branch convent from New Orleans.[30] The sisters' early visits to the Gulf Coast were usually made by boat, often in one of the schooners moored at the head of the New Basin Canal.

Their route lay directly across Lakes Pontchartrain and Borgne, through the Rigolets Pass and the Mississippi Sound, and into the Gulf of Mexico. From the deck Mother Austin described the "admiral views:" Waveland with its humble cottages, "the magnificent oaks and magnolias of the Bay" or Bay St. Louis, "the summer retreat of many of the old French families" from New Orleans and the site of the boarding school of the Sisters of St. Joseph, then "the white villas of the Pass . . . the forest stretching to the water's edge . . . a broad ribbon of silver sand separating the woods and the Gulf . . . the villas like white patches among the green trees festooned with the gray moss,"[31] and the Convent of Mercy with its pink walls shining through the oaks and elms and hickories of Pass Christian. This lovely convent was the one to which Mother Mary de Sales Browne had generously invited Mother Austin and her sisters for the month of August one sultry summer. Later, when the Vicksburg sisters wished to withdraw from the school at the Pass, Reverend Francis Xavier Leray of Vicksburg "strove earnestly to make" Mother Austin change her plans and take over that branch convent.[32] By that time however, the pastor in Biloxi, Rev. Peter Chevalier, had already written Bishop Elder that "I have done all I could to induce the sisters to come to Biloxi for we need a school, and I was not able to keep up a school any longer. . . . There is a great deal of good to be done here."[33]

Mother Austin Carroll agreed heartily with that last sentence. "Most of the whites were Catholics," she wrote, "and the many Catholics among the blacks telegraphed their religion to the Sisters by making the sign of the cross."[34] With a population of approximately 2,000 at the time, Biloxi was "the largest and prettiest town . . . between New Orleans and Mobile." In mid-August Mother Austin sent Bishop Elder the details of the Biloxi educational program she had planned. The parochial school was to have "a good plain education for boys and girls,"[35] and the poor would be taught along with those who could pay monthly fees ranging from a dollar downward to twenty-five cents, or two bits as the natives termed it. Mother Austin expected to open religion classes for the blacks immediately, and later, establish a school for them. For the summer months, Mother Austin planned to inaugurate special tutoring programs for the wealthy summer visitors. The children could make intellectual progress, either through remedial or enrichment studies, without inconvenience to the vacationing family. Since the tutoring was to be at the best of prices, the summer program would indirectly assist with the financing of the regular sessions for the local children who were poor.[36] Further, for the July and August pupils, this loving superior planned to bring the Biloxi staff to New Orleans and send each of the city teachers over to assist with the tutoring program and to enjoy several weeks on the Gulf Coast.

Bishop Elder answered on the feast of Our Lady's birth, appropriately because the Biloxi parish was named for the Nativity of the Blessed Virgin Mary. He was pleased especially with Mother Austin's concern for the poor, but told her that she could have "a select school" also.[37] Except for the summer program and other tutoring or music lessons, she preferred to teach together the children of differing financial backgrounds. However, the Sisters of Mercy complied with the contemporary custom across the deep South of maintaining separate classes, even in different buildings in many parishes, for the boys and girls. As 1874 came to a close Mother Austin found an old inn and, undaunted by its need for renovation, decided that the land alone made it a bargain.[38] The *Annals* relate that she

> purchased for a thousand dollars, a very dilapidated hotel, between the church and the beach, only a few minutes' walk from either. It was prettily situated and quite surrounded with orange trees. Several thousand dollars were expended in enlarging and repairing it, and by March, 1875, when the Sisters took possession, the ruined hotel had become one of the prettiest villas on the coast, and was named Maris Stella.[39]

Thus under the banner of Our Lady Star of the Sea, Mother Austin's plans gathered the children of the village fishermen and the middle class families, the blacks, and the wealthy summer visitors who doubled or trebled the town's size during vacation, for her radiant energy could project to the people of the entire financial spectrum.

Although preparations had begun earlier in Biloxi, the staffing of St. Patrick's Girls' School in New Orleans' early Irish Channel occurred before the Gulf Coast branch convent was ready. Archbishop Perché himself requested Mother Austin in 1874 to assign a few Mercies to replace the small community transferring out of the archdiocese, and Mother Austin was happy to have an opportunity to oblige the pious prelate, even though the sisters were to teach for almost nothing as very few of the children could afford tuition.[40] In fact, the departing religious had placed their teachers in "a select school" and the parish had hired a lay teacher for the parish girls. With thirty-one sisters in the community and the two Redemptorist schools needing only nine teachers, Mother Austin could easily have maintained both of the girls' schools in St. Patrick's parish. She chose not to continue the "select school," however, for she believed it to be more beneficial educationally as well as more democratic to teach the children of various social classes together. Early in 1875, the Christian Brothers gave up St. Mary's College, their boys' school in St. Patrick parish,[41] and the Mercies were then asked to staff a parochial school for the boys also. This arrangement calling for six teachers to commute daily via the horsecars to the St. Patrick schools was a temporary measure,[42] an expression of gratitude to the parish which had waited twenty years for the services of the Irish Sisters of Mercy. However, the work was undertaken primarily at the personal request of Archbishop Perché and as a favor to him.

One of Mother Austin Carroll's characteristics was a strong and lasting sense of gratitude for favors, especially those done for the Institute of Mercy. In New Orleans she looked to several others, besides the gentle archbishop, as benefactors of the Mercy community. This is clear from her letter to Father James O'Connor after the death of his Jesuit brother Michael, the retired bishop of Pittsburg. "The good Bishop . . . visited us several times, and showed the greatest interest in our establishment. His visits were delightful and most edifying to us, and I believe a precious recreation to him."[43] She was distressed to hear of his death so soon afterward, for she considered the retired bishop a Mercy benefactor for several reasons. As a young priest at the Irish College in Rome, he had translated the Mercy Rule into Italian prior to its approval. As a young bishop in 1843, he had brought to his new diocese in western Pennsylvania a group of Sisters of Mercy from Carlow led by the regal Frances Xavier Warde in the ship so appropriately named *Queen of the West*. An oft-neglected point of history, however, is the fact that the *Queen* did not lead, but followed eighteen months later in the frothy wake of *Sir Walter Raleigh*, the knightly escort of Mother Mary Frances Creedon and her companions from the first Convent of Mercy in Dublin to the first on the shores of America.[44] This pioneer group of Catherine McAuley's leaders crossed the Atlantic and established her Institute in Newfoundland in 1842, although the harbinger role of Frances Creedon has seldom been heralded since the publication of Austin Carroll's *Annals*.[45]

As faithful to her sense of gratitude as to that of history, Mother Austin extended her sympathy to Father James O'Connor by listing the masses and prayers that she and her community had offered for his brother whom she considered both a personal friend and a community benefactor "to whom we owe eternal gratitude."[46] She requested and received a small photograph after the death of Michael O'Connor, but wished to commission a portrait in early 1874. She explained, "I have just got a life-size oil painting of Mother McAuley done which is greatly admired" and it would be fitting to have a "companion picture of Bishop O'Connor." If Father O'Connor could have one done by a Philadelphia artist, she "would take it as a great favor. We are not rich, but we would go to any expense to procure this." In June she sent the dimensions of the McAuley painting so that the O'Connor portrait might be similar.[47] Then, thinking of the annual bout with the fall fevers, she added "If you let me know the probable expense, I'll remit in any way you direct, so that if I die of yellow fever in autumn there will be no mistake about the payment." This offer must have been declined, for the completed painting arrived as a gift and drew great reviews. The sisters were delighted and said that "the likeness was perfect." The sender would be in their prayers, for thanks were certainly not enough for "the magnificent present." The late bishop would always be remembered, for "his honored name stands at the head of the List of our Deceased Benefactors in America. His lineaments . . . will now become familiar to all future generations of our Sisters."[48]

Mother Austin was happy that so many of the Redemptorist priests recognized the picture immediately, but the priest who admired the bishop most deeply and had looked forward with eager anticipation to the completion of the painting had gone to God before its arrival. Father John B. Duffy had known both Michael and James O'Connor in Pennsylvania and had studied with the latter in Philadelphia. It was his death on September 8, 1874, that brought deep grief to Mother Austin and her community. He had proved himself one of their staunchest friends during the early days in the Redemptorist parishes. He not only supported her efforts to teach the poor along with those who could pay tuition, but also saw to it that the salary for which the Sisters contracted before they left St. Louis was paid regularly and did all he could to aid the sisters with their works of mercy.[49] "Among the losses which the New Orleans sisterhood had to sustain," Mother Austin

Carroll wrote, "the death of Father Duffy was among the greatest."[50] She had found in him a counsellor, especially for business concerning St. Alphonsus School, which Father Duffy had nurtured for years. He followed Father Giesen as the second ecclesiastical director and gave "the Mother Superior every possible aid in the formation of her large and rapidly increasing community," related the *Annals*.[51] "So good a Father, and so true and constant a friend, deserves more than a passing notice in these pages," was the introduction to a lengthy and loving tribute to this zealous man of God, recollections Mother Austin published two decades later.

Shortly after Father Duffy's death, however, Mother Austin arranged a collection of the numerous obituary tributes in the local papers, added her own detailed account of his virtues and accomplishments, and had the collection published as a memento for his numerous friends and parishioners.[52] Her obituary tribute, in keeping with the encomiums customary in Gaelic eulogies, was fulsome praise at its fullest and second in that respect only to the superlative obituary eulogy written lovingly with hyperbole and superlatives for the late bishop, Michael O'Connor, SJ.[53] Death also took away another episcopal friend in 1874, the Most Reverend David W. Bacon, Bishop of Portland, Maine, whom she knew as a kind and fatherly prelate during her years of service in Manchester, N.H.[54] Among the Sisters of Mercy, Mother Austin mourned the death of one of her correspondents in England, Mother Clare Moore of Bermondsey, a loss which called for another superb tribute in February of 1875.[55] Closer to home that year was the death of Mother Austin's spiritual advisor, Reverend William Stack Murphy, SJ.[56] This elderly priest had been appointed one of the confessors for the Mercy community upon their arrival in the city in 1869. From the beginning Father Murphy "showed the greatest possible interest in the new establishment; partly, he said, because of its utility to the people of the city, and partly because many of his relatives were Sisters of Mercy."[57]

Mother Austin also knew that Father Murphy's "cousin, Bishop [John] Murphy [of Cork], had been a personal friend of the venerated Catherine McAuley," and that alone was enough to assure him a special place in her heart. But there were other reasons, also, why Mother Austin was attracted to Father Murphy as a friend. She mentioned several in the *Annals*,[58] her "edification at his example, . . . her instruction through his counsels" for he gave the sisters a monthly "lecture on some point of religious life," and especially, her enjoyment in sharing news or their mutual acquaintants and family connections in the Counties of Waterford and Cork. She also noted that many New Orleaneans found him to be "a skillful director . . . especially adapted to persons of higher gifts of intellect." During the fall of 1875, Mother Austin's account book lists several expenditures for "medicated flannel for Father Murphy," as she tried to ease the discomfort of the

final illness of "this distinguished man . . . kind and gentle and genial."[59]
Upon his death in October, she once again published a beautiful tribute to a
friend, this one containing more biographical material than the others.
Included was Father Murphy's remark, "I like to aid Religious because they
can influence so many. Whatever good is done to them reflects itself on a
multitude."[60] Applied to the Convent of Mercy and its vivacious and compassionate leader, the words could hardly have been more applicable, for
even before his death, Austin Carroll was planning for further expansion to
reach more of God's children.

Late in 1874, with plans for the branch convent at Biloxi well on the
way to completion, Austin discussed the necessity of an asylum for the
orphans of St. Alphonsus parish with its pastor, Father Girardey.[61] In spite
of the financial difficulties of the times, she thought that an orphanage
could be successfully built as a memorial to Father Duffy because the
parishioners had experienced his concern for their welfare and witnessed for
so long his zealous service. The asylum was a real need, especially for the
orphan boys of the parish. The Conferences of St. Vincent de Paul of the
various city parishes maintained St. Vincent's Home for Boys,[62] but the St.
Alphonsus Conference could not keep up with the number of orphans and
was monthly increasing its indebtedness. Several parish boys had even
found refuge in non-Catholic asylums. "Fathoming this intolerable situation," reported one of the local papers, "the zealous Redemptorist, Very
Reverend Ferreol Girardey, after a conference with the gifted Mother Austin . . . started the work of preparing a Home. . . . Moved by tender charity,
Mother Austin previous to this time had thrown open the portals of the
convent of Mercy, and sheltered" all the orphan girls of the parish from
what the press termed "the bitter blasts of the cruel world."[63] These little
girls had been moved from the convent into the Crèche, and later over-
flowed into the House of Mercy. With these needs in mind, Mother Austin
offered to take charge of all the orphans, boys and girls, if the Redemptorists and their parishioners could establish an asylum and provide a portion
of the annual support.

Delighted with both Mother Austin's offer and her idea of erecting the
asylum as a monument to Father Duffy, Father Girardey set out to obtain
all the necessary approvals. One after the other, the pastor cleared each
hurdle as he won the consent of the Redemptorist Provincial, Father
Helmpraecht, who had earlier arranged for the Mercy foundation from St.
Louis; of the New Orleans Rector, Father Maximus Leimgruber;[64] and of
Archbishop Perché, who admired Mother Austin's initiative. He also won
the cooperation of the leading men of the parish, particularly the members
of the Conference of St. Vincent de Paul, who were relieved to learn that
the new institution would absorb the parish boys and their debt from St.

Vincent's Home. The original plans were to build St. Alphonsus Asylum and a church at Eighth and Chestnut Streets, but the Redemptorist superior in Rome vetoed erecting a fourth church in the single geographic area already supporting three national churches and directed that the new orphanage be located on Redemptorist property at Washington and St. Patrick Streets.[65] This commodious square was described in 1875, as an excellent location in "the suburbs of the Garden District," abounding with fresh breezes and bracing country air, yet "within convenient distance of the markets and [street] cars."[66] Just as the German orphans had always been supported in part by the revenue from St. Joseph Cemetery, so did early plans for the new orphanage call for partial support from the revenue of a projected cemetery in the Carrollton section.

When the original plans were changed by the authorities in Rome, a number of loud repercussions occurred locally.[67] Once again, as had often happened earlier in the Redemptorist district, Nationalism reared its ugly head and roared a challenge to all in the volatile Irish Channel. Certain Germans felt that an Irish asylum located next to the German cemetery was an encroachment on their turf and bragged that they intended to sell the land. Certain Irishmen thundered threats to anyone who dared to sell the square facing St. Patrick Street and "for sure, asthore," Irish sod. Perhaps it was the luck of the Irish, that the bayonets were in the hands of the troops keeping Grant's usurpers in office and not in the possession of either the Irish or the Germans. Both national groups made their points with sharpened pens instead, as this typical inflammatory item demonstrates.

> There is but one objection to the success of the undertaking. . . . The sect of Infidels, Atheists, etc., may get possession . . . and sell our Asylum to divide the proceeds among themselves. . . . It will be the cause of chasing away the good Sisters because these scrupulous gentlemen always get up a vast indignation among themselves, and resolve the poor nuns into public enemies before they steal their property.[68]

Thus did the overly-ardent advocates of the Asylum try to involve the sisters in their nationalistic fray.

In spite of the opposition, but more slowly than if they had been unopposed, Father Girardey and Mother Austin moved ahead with the realization of their plans. On August 9, 1875, the ground was broken by Father Girardey[69] and his assistant, Reverend Benedict Neithart, who addressed the large crowd of parishioners a month later when the cornerstone was laid on September 19. The following spring Mother Austin had the school children present a musical performance as a benefit for the orphans.[70] As the entertainment did well financially, she had the troupe present several other musical and dramatic programs on behalf of the orphans. Other contributions from Mother Austin at this time probably included some of the conciliatory articles that appeared in the local press. Such items stressed the work of Father Duffy and the other Redemptorists, one mentioning that the priests and their generous parishioners had built three churches, six schools, two convents, and were erecting their second asylum. After a tour of St. Alphonsus institutions, a member of the press corps gave a report.

> We visited the classrooms . . . passed from room to room through the spacious halls . . . the House of Mercy . . . the Industrial School . . . the Orphan Asylum [in the Crèche at the time]. The Sisters also visit the inmates of the jail and other penal institutions on Sundays and the sick poor always. . . . Father Giesen told me that the Reverend Mother in the short space of four or five years organized and put in full and successful working order all these noble Catholic Institutions.[71]

Through the decades many newspaper articles had related the work of the priests, as did this one: "Some years ago a few Fathers of the Congregation of the Most Holy Redeemer, after great exertion . . . in the midst of a sparsely settled neighborhood" began their German church. "Gradually there arose another for the American and Irish population, then a school, "afterwards another church for the French and other schools, "then large brick buildings arose . . . the desert bloomed like a garden . . . a magnificent church with its cross-crowned turrets penetrates the skies," then another and another, all three great "ornaments to the city."[72] After the arrival of the Sisters of Mercy in New Orleans, journalists seemed to transfer their gracious coverage to the Sisters, especially to their leader, Mother Austin Carroll. Appended to a report of one profession ceremony, for instance, was the note, "The talented and accomplished Lady Superior has received from His Holiness, Pope Pius IX, a most precious souvenir . . . a silver Crucifix."[73] Attached to another news item was a reference to Mother Austin as "most gracious and gifted . . . no less distinguished by her prudence and administrative ability than for her accomplishments, for to her facile pen Catholic literature is deeply indebted." Annual commencement news always contained generous accolades by the presiding priest for the ability and qualifications of their parish teachers, noting on one occasion that "school authorities in some places have given several public schools to the Sisters of Mercy."[74]

More than in any other way, favorable publicity came with the publication of each new work from Mother Austin's pen. Critical reviews[75] referred to her as "pious and gifted," "of rare ability," "prolific talent," "with a graceful wit," "modesty and humility," "a lively and piquant style," and as wisely as correctly noted by John Francis Maguire,[76] "a good and holy woman whose heart is in the great work of the Mercy foundress." Mother Austin must have grown used to this type of comment long before June of 1876, when the *Catholic Record* carried a ten-page article on the "Irish Service to Education, Science, and Literature."[77] Close to thirty Irish compatriots were singled out for honor, twenty-six men and two ladies. The latter were Mrs. James Sadlier, neé Mary Ann Madden of Caven, and Mother Austin Carroll, née Margaret Anne Carroll of Tipperary. Within a few weeks of the tribute from Philadelphia, she received more accolades in the *Western Watchman* and the *Connecticut Catholic*.[78] In spite of these items from the Northeast and the Midwest, her own favorite piece would have been that in a local paper which praised the work of her community, noting that the sisters, besides staffing "the enormous schools of the Redemptorist Fathers . . . their own night schools and industrial schools,"[79] also serve the poor in several ways as they "carry on a cooking establishment" to serve soup or stew and bread to the destitute, "go about their quarter of the city hunting up the poor who are too infirm to come to them, and their visits are like those of the angels." At that time of conflict this type of praise was probably noisome ad nauseam to the Germans, while the Irish, the French, and the Americans welcomed such items, considering them appropriate recognition for exceptionally devoted service. The reporter concluded his article with the remark, "wherever anything in the way of charity or piety or mercy can be done, these indefatigable Sisters are to be found on the picket line."[80]

The 1876 "picket line" gave no image of a line of protestors, but the war definition—a line of scouts who preceded and cleared the way for the rest of the troops. Undoubtedly, the Sisters of Mercy were on the front line that September 10 in 1876, when St. Alphonsus Asylum was blessed, formally dedicated, and opened its doors to fifty of the orphan girls from the Crèche, the parish orphans from St. Vincent's Home for Boys, and the Mercies who were to care for the children. These sisters had been in the line of action since the end of August as they prepared the new building for occupation. During the opening ceremony the parishioners were reminded that the asylum had a "meagre supply of furniture and other articles of prime necessity," that there was immediate need for such items as "bedding, bolts of cotton, flannel, and jeans, with sewing machines to make clothes for the children."[81] Since Father Duffy's monument was not wholly furnished on the day of dedication, it was suggested that his friends in commercial enterprises donate some "articles of stock—hardware, drygoods, provisions, shoes, feed, etc.," so that the new asylum could be a fitting monument to Father Duffy and the kind of home that he would have wished for the needy orphans. This was the aim which propelled Mother Austin and Father Girardey forward in the realization of their plans. Although both had tried to calm the turbulent waters, these leaders in convent and parish were destined to bear the brunt of the German-Irish brouhaha.[82]

Possibly because Mother Austin had been supporting so many of the parish orphans all along, certain parish authorities thought that she should continue to do so. One is reminded of Catherine McAuley caught in the Kingston imbroglio because she made a partial payment to a contractor anxious to receive some of the money due him from the pastor.[83] Mother Austin, too, in her charity had sponsored benefits during the erection of the asylum in order to assist with the furnishings, and thereafter found herself expected to provide everything but the building itself. Two months after the orphanage opened, Mother Austin was still arranging events to raise money to buy bedding. She had a concert in early December with more than a hundred pupils and orphans presenting a musical concert which, in spite of the bitterly cold weather and the bitter German opposition, succeeded well enough to furnish warm blankets before Christmas.[84] Unfortunately, the Irish parish was unable to take responsibility even for furnishing the kitchen with provisions or providing chapel necessities because of the regulations of the German authorities. Although Mother Austin stated emphatically that the Mercy Institute was not a mendicant order, she felt even more strongly that the orphans should not be neglected. Hence, it became a common sight to see two Sisters of Mercy direct their sturdy horse to pull their black-covered cart next to the French Market stalls so that the nuns could ask for gifts of vegetables and fruit for their little charges.[85] Soon a lengthy list of grocers and butchers became regular donors, never refusing to share their produce with God's little ones.

Years later the early struggles were briefly alluded to by such generalities as, "A good deal of opposition to the [asylum] undertaking was raised, much of it sad to say, by the very persons who were expected to approve and help the work in hand."[86] Even so, Father Girardey and Mother Austin patiently bore "the opposition usually met in carrying out good works." The reporter continued with a belief common in nineteenth-century Catholic circles, especially in Irish-American thinking with reference to difficulties, "We need not be astonished at this, for good and holy works always meet with opposition, and the greater the opposition, the greater the proof of the goodness of the work."[87] Although Mother Austin may not have agreed with the final premise, she certainly believed the first. Hence, she accepted the hostility both as proof that the work was a worthy one and because of her love of her Lord. Yet, just as she was surprised by the vehemence of the opposition to the orphanage,[88] she would later be astounded to feel the continuing effects of the German antagonism. Establishing the Irish asylum had somehow engendered an ill will; later reinforced, this ill wind expanded into a storm that blew forcibly enough to reach all the way to Rome.

Prior to that storm, however, there were a few dark clouds on the horizon along with further community expansion. That, too, was to become a cloud, but the first problem concerned salaries. In St. Louis in 1869, the Redemptorist and Mercy superiors had established a contract for a generous $45 monthly teacher's salary. This had been honored by Fathers Giesen, Duffy, and Girardey.[89] After Father Duffy's death, Father Leimgruber, as rector, reduced the Mercy salaries to $35. Times were hard as people were wrung dry in the wringer of Reconstruction, and Mother Austin accepted the change without a word, as she knew that many of the parish families could not afford to pay full tuition. Both Fathers Girardey and Duffy had agreed with her that these poor children attend gratis and learn along with those who could pay. Two years later the rector again cut the salaries, this time to $30, and once more Mother Austin, less easily than the first time, accepted the reduction even though this occurred right after the fracas over the asylum termed the "Irish Revolt" by the Germans. Several months later Mother Austin received word from the Redemptorist Provincial, Rev. Nicholas Jaeckel, that he wanted the sisters to teach for no salary at all — just for what they could collect from the poor children and the proceeds of an annual entertainment.[90] Not only did Mother Austin know that these two sources together would yield only half the contracted $30 a month per teacher, but she was also aware that the proceeds of one entertainment could not possibly support both the orphans and the sisters.

Therefore, Austin Carroll protested this move in a clear and positive fashion, one which in an old-world German view, was too bold and lacking in respect for a priest who was also the provincial superior. Mother Austin told him that "the capacity to improve or build up is a rare gift . . . as nothing is easier to some than to injure or destroy. . . . One of the Fathers is always dissatisfied or embarrassing in some way or other."[91] Each priest might be a self-constituted superior of some other community if he wished, but not of the Sisters of Mercy. If no contract can be kept, what guarantee did she have that her sisters would be able to subsist? The provincial spoke of the "general ruin" by the radicals and peelers of "oppressed Louisiana," where he must "prepare for the worst" until a change of administration occurred in Washington, D.C.[92] He thought it a "still rarer gift" to preserve what has already been built. As to the complaints, "it is simply the duty of the Fathers to call your attention to whatever they consider amiss . . . and it is the duty of the Sisters to obey, as this is the natural order of things, the Fathers, not the Sisters, being Pastors." Concerning a guarantee, he added that "as long as the Sisters remain fervent Religious, docile and obedient children, so long will the Fathers stand by them."[93] At forty-two years of age, Mother Austin could hardly have been considered a child, and docility to the officious complainers would never be her claim to virtue. It was her firm belief that she owed obedience to the one ecclesiastical superior appointed by the archbishop, usually one of the school prefects, like Fathers Duffy, Girardey, or Faivre, with whom she cooperated with never a sign of a problem.

These priests who worked closely with Austin admired her as an exceptionally energetic and zealous religious woman. In this crisis they knew she was worried not about her own welfare, but for her young sisters and the destitute who depended upon her for help. Mother Austin felt it essential for a community with the Mercy schedule of monastic prayer and their assignments of teaching or other work plus the visitation of the sick to have a sufficient amount of nourishing food, allowed nothing fancy but insisted on meals that were nutritious.[94] Having followed her conscience by protesting an action which she and her council saw as an unjust decree, she would now try to manage finances according to the edict of the German provincial.[95] Mother Austin did not seem to realize at the time that her remonstrance in behalf of those for whose health she was responsible was to double or triple the ill will already engendered among the German priests. Perhaps, this was because she did not really have any dealings with them. She worked in close unity with the prefects of the parish schools of St. Alphonsus and Notre Dame de Bon Secours, but these Redemptorists were most often French, Belgian, or American men who seemed to have no difficulty working in harmony with Mother Austin Carroll. Their parishioners called her Ireland's gift to the Irish Channel.

Because she had experienced interference in community affairs during the tenure of Catherine Grant, Mother Austin concluded upon becoming superior that it was wiser to consult the archbishop himself on important business, as he had no inclination to usurp the responsibilities of the mother superior.[96] Hence, she checked with Archbishop Perché before she acted on the requests of several neighboring bishops for sisters to staff their schools. Although she had received invitations before the completion of the asylum, she had delayed any serious consideration about establishing new branches because finding funds for the orphans took so much of her time. And she wrote a friend of other delaying reasons, "The Bishop of Mobile has asked a colony of us, and I have to go see the place offered," but quarantine curtailed travel and, lest she be detained there, she was "afraid to stir till all danger is over. He is very anxious to be supplied by us, as most of our Sisters are thoroughly acclimated, and all Southern cities on the river or sea are as liable to yellow fever as New Orleans, some more so."[97] The size of the community was a consideration too, for she added, "We have not a sufficient number who have finished the four and a half years novitiate." In the New Orleans noviceship at the time, the young women performed the works of mercy except during their first year as novices. After profession, they continued to attend spiritual lectures for an additional two years in order to further their growth as religious. That letter was dated 1876, however, and a year later in September of 1877, eleven more young Mercies had completed this period of training.[98]

In Pensacola two other religious congregations, the Sisters of Holy Cross and the Sisters of the Third Order of St. Dominic along with the Sisters of St. Joseph in Warrington, had each served a short time in the diocese, but had withdrawn after yellow fever ravaged their communities.[99] Because of this triple tragedy, Bishop Quinlan wished Mother Austin to see the locale before making any commitment either to Pensacola or the Navy Yard near Warrington. He had invited her to the latter, also, but she delayed considering it until she had more sisters available. Viewing both places was the object when she and a companion left New Orleans on the *Amite*, sailing from the New Basin canal late in June.[100] Mother Austin enjoyed seeing the boats spread their sails and be whisked away by the wind, symbolic in a way of her own drive to make progress quickly. Yet, as much as she loved to race along with the speed of the breeze, she knew from experience that rough weather meant that the canvas must be hauled in until the storm was spent. And if the sails must be furled for a time in salaryless New Orleans, she would find other areas where the canvas could again be spread like wings and fly before God's gales. The trip called to mind the missionary priest and skipper, Symphonian Guinand, who ministered to the Gulf Coast from Pensacola to Pass Christian in the 1830s sailing to each village in turn.[101]

The *Amite* did not drop anchor in every town as Guinand had, and from a distance Mother Austin tried to catch sight of "the Biloxi Sisters on the wharf that extended several hundred feet into the sea from Maris Stella Convent." They were too far away, of course, but the following day she "caught her first glimpse of the Land of the Flowers through the haze of a June sunrise."[102] Mother Austin might have recalled a similar sky seen at dawn from the deck of the *Mollie Able*, as she watched "a red, round sun coming slowly out of the water" and noted that "a raw breeze attended the unfolding of the morning."[103] The captain steered through the Snapper-Banks, past the ruins of Fort McRee, the barracks of Fort Barrancas, and came to the Navy Yard. There the "splendid brick and stone houses . . . were in fine contrast with the shingle-roofed cottages of the outlying villages of Wolsey and Warrington."[104] The Sisters spotted the gulls and frigate birds above the boats and were amazed at the width of the bay, "spacious enough to hold the navies of the world," bragged the natives. The Pensacola harbor looked its brightest as some one hundred fifty vessels from various countries, although at anchor, had their festive colors flying. Mother Austin commented that she "stepped ashore to the music of the noonday Angelus."[105]

Rev. James A. Bergrath, the pastor hopeful of their assistance, welcomed them cordially. After lunch he escorted them to see his little church, rebuilt since the war as it, like most of the town, "had been fired," during the enemy occupation of the area.[106] He then took the sisters to visit the frame convent, unoccupied since the Dominicans had returned to Tampa, and to inspect the two schools, one for the girls and another for the boys, as was the custom in New Orleans also. Assuming that the Mercies wished to establish an academy as the other sisters had done, the pastor said that he had no objection to that, but was hoping to have the sisters teach his black school. Mother Austin promised to staff the parish school for girls which she would later extend to secondary level, another for the boys, and the school for the blacks, but declined the privilege of the private school.[107] Father Bergrath was delighted with her plans, but explained that the town had a large mulatto population which refused to send their children to a school for blacks. From her work with the mulattoes who belonged to a sodality in the Notre Dame de Bon Secours parish in New Orleans, Mother Austin was familiar with their desire to preserve their special language and culture.[108] That knowledge, plus her inability to accept a lack of educational facilities for any group, led her to bow to their desire for a separate school for the mulattoes. The pastor could hardly believe either his good fortune or that it had arisen so rapidly, but he promised to alert the parents of all three groups that schools were to open in September.

Business completed, Mother Austin had time to admire the lovely "old town slumbering besides its beautiful bay . . . the snow white sand blinding in the summer sun . . . the clumps of fan-shaped palmetto and the scraggy cypress."[109] She was fascinated with the quiet in this port, because it was such a contrast to the clatter on the cobblestone streets of the New Orleans riverfront. Here the "deep sand of the roadways muffled the sound of every vehicle" and only the darting lizards enlivened the plank walks.[110] Mother Austin noted that the heat, "tempered by the brisk sea breezes," lessened as she reached the sloping hill above the town. There she explored the ruins of an ancient Spanish fortress, dedicated like the parish to St. Michael, and according to local tradition, the site whereon the first Mass was celebrated in Western Florida over 200 years earlier. When she turned from the ruin to face the water and the truly magnificent view, her favorite line from Faber came to mind, "There's a wideness in God's mercy like the wideness of the sea."[111] Many years later she could still recall the scene, "the limitless sweep of water beyond the bay, the deep blue sea and the deep blue sky, divided by the sandy slopes of Santa Rosa . . . a sand key to the gulf . . . the whole shimmering in the noonday sun."[112]

Back home in her Irish Channel convent, Mother Austin said that she had "met hundreds of Catholic children coming out of a monster public school — how the sight pained me!"[113] Since Austin judged all public schools by those of Know Nothing times, she added, "I promised God to do my share in mending the matter." By August all was in readiness as she wrote a friend, "We open a house in Florida early next month," and like Biloxi it was "to remain a branch of this establishment by agreement of all concerned."[114] Bishop Quinlan knew that the Catholics among the 7,000 people in Pensacola could maintain a small branch convent although they would not have been able to finance, build, and then fill a motherhouse and novitiate. Mother Austin rejoiced that for this convent, unlike that in Biloxi, she did not need to purchase the land and the residence, for "His Lordship had made the house, ground, etc., over to us, on always keeping the parochial schools of the place."[115] Even though the other orders had been chased away by Yellow Jack, Mother Austin was hopeful that her acclimated community could withstand the annual fevers and banish them from the branch. "This will be the sixth establishment I shall have to superintend, but I shall send seven of our very best there, and hope from it more consolation than anxiety."[116] Reverend Frederick Faivre, the Redemptorist prefect of Notre Dame de Bon Secours and a good friend of Mother Austin, escorted the missionaries on their journey to Pensacola and "helped them establish" the new branch called Las Mercedes. His assistance was probably needed in establishing the St. Joseph Select School for the mulatto pupils, as he was used to dealing with the mulatto section of his French congregation. After several days of readying convent and classrooms, the Sisters of Mercy opened the school doors on September 8, 1877, to 300 children, "mostly white, but with a fair proportion of black and brown."[117]

Two weeks later Mother Austin was forwarding the good news, "Our new house in Pensacola surpasses our most sanguine expectations as to the number of pupils, etc. Two hospitals await us, but we cannot undertake them yet. I beg that you will pray for this branch, so much for the good of Religion depends upon its success."[118] That was not her only plea for prayerful remembrances, as her letters regularly begged prayers for each new project. In this instance, news had gone to Ireland in August with the request, "Pray that God may bless the good work."[119] Six months earlier friends had also been told of another mission under consideration, as Austin wrote Elder, "We have just had an application for Sisters for St. Thomas Island, W.I., for schools and hospital. Pray that God may direct us — I am inclined to comply as we are about the only convent that can supply acclimated Sisters."[120] To another bishop-friend, she said that she had learned that the island "is a delightful place, but yellow fever never leaves it. . . . Pray that god may direct us."[121] In June before she visited Florida to assess the mission, Mother Austin mentioned in another letter "the house that we are about to establish at St. Thomas."[122] Although correspondence implied that a decision had already been reached to take the foreign mission, something about the arrangements for this Redemptorist mission in the West Indies caused Mother Austin and her council to change their minds and cancel their plans. Later Mother Austin wrote, "When V. Rev. Helmpraecht, CSSR, wanted us to settle a branch in St. Thomas, ten or twelve days off, Father Giesen urged us to do so. And with the leave of the archbishop, I would have obliged him had the conditions offered been suitable."[123] Unfortunately, especially since the negative decision became another source of anger to the German priests, the archives contain no record of the conditions deemed unfavorable at the time.

So much was positive about the projects of the thriving Mercy motherhouse in New Orleans that not much attention was paid to the negative after-effects of the decision to decline the St. Thomas mission. Mother Austin was already involved in the next business on the agenda. That happened to be, in later 1877, the schools in St. Patrick parish which had been staffed as a favor to Archbishop Perché. In order to satisfy pressing diocesan debt at that time, his finance committee decided that, having already delayed the sale for a year, they had to sell the two buildings which had been housing the parochial schools.[124] Since St. Patrick's schools could not reopen after the Christmas holidays, it became possible in January 1878 for Mother Austin to grant Bishop Quinlan's request that she accept the mission in Warrington and the adjacent United States naval base. Several weeks were consumed in notifying the authorities concerned and arranging details.[125] Mother Austin had already met the young Irish pastor, Rev. William Lane, on her trip to see the available facilities in Pensacola and Warrington the previous summer. In late January five sisters left New Orleans for the small town next to the Navy Yard on Pensacola Bay. Their convent, St. Joseph-by-the-Sea, was the one in which Sisters of St. Joseph had served until five of their community succumbed to yellow fever. The schools for boys and girls, dedicated like the parish to St. John the Evangelist, were quickly organized and classes began on February 2, 1878. Contacting the Negro families and coaxing them to give their children this educational opportunity took a little longer, but St. Joseph School for blacks opened with more than fifty pupils two weeks later.[126] Possibly Mother Austin Carroll had set some type of record by establishing two branch convents and staffing seven schools in less than six months.

There were other numbers in the lists of convent expenditures of that first decade in New Orleans which present some revealing data about

Mother Austin Carroll. With money so short, on what was it spent besides the Mercy Homes, the Orphanage, and the Crèche? Among expenses within the convent, various aids for the spiritual welfare of the sisters weighed most heavily in the balancing of the books. Of course there were the usual annual Mercy retreats, eight days in August, three days at the end of the year, and a monthly Sunday of recollection. For this last there were purchases of retreat meditations for each individual sister along with numerous spiritual books for the convent libraries, but "retreat masters" were invited to give the spiritual lectures[127] or conferences for the longer retreats. Every possible accouterment was procured to make the chapel a fitting site for Christ and the daily liturgies, and to facilitate the affective devotion of the sisters. The improvements in the chapel, though made gradually and only as they became financially feasible, included beautifully embroidered altar linens, hand-painted tabernacle curtains and vestments, chaste liturgical vessels, imported statues, two rows of monastic choirstalls the length of the nave, pews for the visitors who crowded into profession ceremonies, even plasterwork to improve acoustics and painting to transform the deeply arched ceiling into a work of art. Just outside the chapel was a life-sized portrait of Catherine McAuley. Last, although acquired among the first of the furnishings, an intricate and very fine little pipe organ.[128]

Herself a gifted organist and lover of liturgical music, Mother Austin trained the sisters to sing beautifully, and a portion of the recreation hour was sometimes devoted to a songfest featuring all manner of tunes from the comic to the sacred.[129] She frequently accompanied the sisters on the piano or organ, and they claimed she was unexcelled as an accompanist. There was no shortage of musicians, however, for in the early years Austin had brought in professional musicians and artists of several types so that her teachers could acquire the proficiency they needed in order to teach several instruments or singing, as well as sketching, making wax flowers, painting and such other arts then in fashion.[130] To each branch convent Mother Austin sent a small organ or melodeon, and like the library collection, it was always in the vanguard of the supplies. Music dealers on Canal Street must have found in Mother Austin one of their steadiest customers because she often needed sheet music or hymnbooks, and she purchased a melodeon annually from Grunewald's for many years. Besides sending the small organs to the convents in Biloxi, Pensacola, and Warrington, and to St. Alphonsus Asylum, she felt that the imprisoned unfortunates should have music to enhance their liturgical celebrations. Hence, melodeons were bought in turn for the Orleans Parish Prison, the New Orleans City Jail, and the Boys' House of Refuge as well as for the young street waifs at the Newsboys' Home. There were also pianos for each convent, of course; for once the cost of the instrument was cleared, music lessons were a steady source of sustenance in each and every branch, no matter how small the village.[131]

Judging from the financial records, the physical welfare of the sisters came second only to the spiritual. Little was spent on medicine for the community, however, although much went for medical supplies for the sick poor. These remedies were carried in special "sick-call baskets," next to the bread, soup or stew, and small packets of tea and grits or rice and sugar. The dry packs varied with the quantities on hand, but there was always something to take along with prayer leaflets and books, and a crucifix to bless the sick.[132] Mother Austin made her purchases wholesale, as tea was bought by the chest, sugar by the sack, butter by the firkin, and bread in huge quantities from Margaret Haughery to insure a supply for the poor. Memoirs of the sisters recall that Mother Austin believed in "having a good table" and that she preferred paying for food rather than for medicine.[133] Just as there were several lovely oratories in the motherhouse for personal devotions to the Sacred Heart and Mary Immaculate, there were individual opportunities for five or six days of summer sun on the Gulf Coast. Even the trip was an adventure, for the sisters caught the streetcars to travel beyond the Vieux Carré. There at Elysian Fields they took a little train which traversed the tracks that formed a perfectly straight line from the Mississippi River to Lake Pontchartrain. Perhaps they enjoyed the happiness of the gods' Elysium with their anticipation of the fun to come. During their fifteen-minute-or-so ride through the picturesque cypress swamp, the sisters enjoyed seeing the cardinals darting like bright flames in and about the Spanish moss, ever unhindered by the abundance of its streamers. Once at the lake, the sisters walked out to the end of a lengthy pier to board the coast steamer which allowed them reduced fares. The high point of the trip was always the lovely ride across Lake Pontchartrain and along the coast to Biloxi and Maris Stella Convent.[134]

Mother Austin regularly sent over a few of the more delicate orphans along with her teachers each week, the latter in rotation to help with the summer classes and tutoring as well as to enjoy the sandy shore and the salty water. "The gulf shore style of dipping" had great advantages over surf-bathing, explained Mother Austin, for "when you plunge into the waves from the ladder of the bath-house, you are completely shaded by the planks"[135] of the pier, the dressing rooms, and the porch. Entering the water thus also provided the bathers with a bit of privacy, because the bath-house was constructed at the end of a several-hundred-foot "wharf or bridge, four or five feet wide, built on cypress posts" high above the water. The pier, house, and "railed platform" made such a shady spot for the dip that sun hats, according to Mother Austin, "were a superfluity in the bathing costume."[136] One must wonder in vain just what these nineteenth-century nuns wore in the waters of the Gulf as they went "for a dip" in the semi-privacy of the shadows of the pier structures. Of course, the important point to note is not what they wore, but that Mother Austin did not think it unseemly for her well-covered sisters to take a discreet dip at the end of the pier. Certainly there were a few extra expenses that first summer, for Maris Stella Convent purchased crab nets for $4, some toweling for $4, six bedsteads at $6 each, and mosquito bars for $9 — minimal costs for maximum recreation in any accounting book.[137]

Most assuredly, these were trivial amounts to the small Mercy from Clonmel who handled money matters like a financial wizard. In just six years as the leader of the community in New Orleans, not only had she purchased ten melodeons and five pianos, but she had also published six books, two of which had over a dozen episcopal approbations. More importantly, she and her ever-growing community had established five convents, nine institutions, thirty-one libraries, bought several pieces of property, and staffed sixteen schools before six years had passed.[138] As far as Mother Austin was concerned these statistics meant little. What really mattered was the fact that more of God's people were being assisted as each new Mercy branch was established. Spectators who witnessed the rapid expansion in this Mercy community, especially the large number of acquisitions in only six years, were impressed even though religious communities had been in action in New Orleans for 150 years. One of those complimentary reporters who seemed to abound in the Irish Channel remarked that the progress of the Mercy motherhouse was a cause of wonder, "Its works have multiplied on every hand, and its ranks have swollen with the constant accessions of young, active, zealous aspirants to the service of God," and all of this "can be attributed to nothing but the special protection of Providence."[139] Venturing another cause, Mother Austin credited the deaths of the eight Mercy yellow-fever martyrs and also the heroism of all the sisters who nursed anyone in need "in fever seasons." Just as the grain of wheat mentioned in the Gospel was alone while alive, but in death yielded much fruit; so did Mother Austin believe that each of the sisters who died had garnered several candidates to continue the works of mercy in her place.[140]

Mother Austin Carroll envisioned each branch convent as a true House of Mercy after Catherine McAuley's own heart, for each was to be a Mercy center from which the poor were to be assisted, the sick were to receive a bit of health care and large doses of compassion and prayer, and prisoners were to be given spiritual instruction. And above all, in times of yellow-fever epidemics when the schools were closed, the townsfolk of every faith or none were to discover that the Sisters of Mercy were experienced nurses who were unafraid to challenge the most virulent fevers. It was extraordinary that this type of nursing was considered simply an ordinary duty in answer to imminent need, but thus it had always been. The early sisters with Catherine McAuley had assisted at the cholera beds in Dublin, those with Agnes O'Connor had nursed the plague in New York City, and those with dePazzi Bentley had braved the smallpox in St. Louis.[141] Hence, nursing the victims of the fever epidemics across the South was just an ordinary work of mercy for the members of Mother Austin's community in new Orleans as it was also for the Mercies in Savannah and Vicksburg.[142] Truly, from the days of their foundress in the Baggot Street House of Mercy, the sisters of Mercy had a heritage of heroism.

In part because of this, Austin Carroll had the firm conviction that each Mercy center would in due time become self-perpetuating as young women would be stirred by the Holy Spirit. "A person expands like a delicate flower to the touch of sympathy, kindness, and affection," Mother Austin said.[143] If girls were touched by the compassion of the sisters, she thought that they would apply as candidates. Far-fetched it may sound, but by 1878 Mother Austin was already witnessing the realization of her hopes in New Orleans. It was not to be too long before each branch convent was to attract several young ladies and a few fine women widowed by the war, then direct them to the Mercy novitiate, from which in four years they could play their part in continuing the cycle of centers. These aspirants from the branches were not in time for the statistics of the first decade, however, for 1878 marked the tenth year since Mother Austin and *Mollie Able* had steamed down the Mississippi River together. In the seven years that Mother Austin had been leading the community, fifty-six women had applied to the noviceship, thirty-five had already been professed, a few had not been received into the community, and fourteen were currently receiving their novitiate training. Already ten sisters had joined the Mercy community in eternity, two having died of tuberculosis and eight while nursing in epidemics.[144] Several of these young Mercies had died in their teens, although the average age of death for the first ten was twenty-one years.

Her sisters related of Austin that she sorrowed, far more than for anything else, over the deaths of loved ones. Some were her Mercy friends abroad or in the Northeast, others her own young sisters in New Orleans.[145] In 1876 and 1877, deaths that brought deep sorrow were those of her dear friend Pauline Maher, like Josephine Warde, an ideal superior in Austin's estimation and "loved and revered as a mother" in Hartford;[146] and Cincinnati's Teresa Maher who was ever grateful for Austin's prayers, sympathy, and support "during her trials."[147] In fever seasons Mother Austin's letters revealed her feelings. "When our Sisters are ill, I cannot leave them day or night. . . . Beseech Our dear Lord to spare the rest . . . but God knows best . . . and many are the conversions we have to record."[148] Later she said, "Although no one with a particle of reason can reasonably complain when

the loved one dies happily, still it is hard to lose the young and efficient. . . .
God sent us two last week and now has taken one. But Deo Gratias. . . .
Tomorrow the funeral—I would not like to describe how I feel on these
occasions, so sadly frequent—but God's will be done."[149] Mother Austin
often asked her friends to beg God "to send us other fervent souls to replace
those He takes away from us that we may be able to carry on what we have
undertaken for His glory." She tried never to allow her personal grief to
interfere with community affairs. For instance, she had learned just before
Christmas in 1875 of her mother's death in Ireland in the twentieth year
since she had kissed her goodby.[150] Yet she shared the news with just a few
close friends until Christmas was over lest she spoil the day for her sisters.
Austin had a natural effervescence however, and a tremendous fund of faith
in finding peace once she accepted the will of God, a lesson she had learned
from Catherine McAuley.

Repeatedly, Mother Austin declared that she did not have the luxury of
leisure to grieve because of the pressure of community business. "If the day
were thirty-six hours long, I should be able to fill it," Austin told a friend.[151]
Even though she no longer taught in any of the schools in 1878, she supervised five convents, all the institutions, and sixteen schools. Although time
was at a premium, there was always some improvement in progress. Most of
the elementary schools gradually extended their curriculum to secondary
level, and Mother Austin saw that their library collections increased annually, this in a decade or two before many other schools in the area even
established school libraries.[152] With the demise of the radicals when the
federal bayonets were withdrawn from the city in the spring of 1877,
Mother Austin thought that the improved financial climate made the fall of
that year an appropriate time to staff another school. Now with enough
sisters to staff the Notre Dame de Bon Secours boys' school called St.
Aloysius College, the Sisters of Mercy replaced lay teachers in September
1877. She also planned another school for Biloxi, where she intended to
expand the religion classes for the blacks into an elementary program as
soon as she could purchase a suitable house.[153] The Maris Stella sisters were
giving instructions regularly in the Back Bay area near Biloxi so that Bishop
Elder was able to confirm a large number from this isolated section. In the
Irish Channel Mother Austin's various shelters were usually full. The
Crèche always had a crowd of little ones, the parish asylum was housing
close to 200 orphans, the Mercy Home did its part, and some 800 women
had found better jobs through her Mercy employment bureau.

According to the newspaper ads, the night school had recently admitted boys and added classes in bookkeeping, while the industrial school was
offering instruction in "wax work, gold embroidery, banners, flags, and
artificial flowers" in lengthened classes.[154] Already the school had produced

a large share of the banners used in the processions and parades like those of Our Lady in May and of St. Patrick in March. For the latter the Convent of Mercy in the Irish Channel was a designated stop on the parade route so that the bands could serenade "the Irish sisters" while the marchers displayed the magnificent new banners. It mattered not that only six of the forty-nine sisters had been born in Ireland, for many of those from New Orleans were Irish Americans. Mother Austin, like Catherine McAuley, enjoyed the sight of a St. Patrick's Day parade, and on at least one occasion, both the foundress and her biographer Austin Carroll left to posterity a delightful description of such a celebration. Of course, Catherine saw an 1841 parade in Dublin and Austin one in the New Orleans Irish Channel in 1877. Both complimentary accounts praised the great size of the gathering, Catherine estimating that tens of thousands passed before Merrion Square,[155] and Austin listing such groups as the Irish Rifles, the Society of Benevolent Hibernians, the Mitchel Rifles, interspersed with marching bands.[156] Similarities abounded with the clergy in open carriages, the men marching in proud units, and the marshals as outriders on beautiful horses, Catherine gave the hue and kind of each, and the colors of bright flags and banners and picturesque costumes and gaudy regalia.[157] Austin noted the large number of banners made by the Mercy industrial school.

Catherine McAuley in her letter and Austin Carroll in her news item each emphasized a particular point. Catherine stated with both surprise and delight that every man in the Dublin march was a "Teetotaller," and concluded, "It is said there never was such a sight in the world."[158] Although her note was written the year she died, Catherine's enthusiastic description demonstrated not only her delight in fine horses and her pride that the scarfs were made in Ireland, but also her admiration of the sober bearing of the participants. Like Catherine, Austin also enjoyed the sight of beautiful horses, "the supple horsemen . . . lithe and graceful in motion," who rode so "jauntily . . . in their picturesque costumes,"[159] and the stalwart marchers, "broad-shouldered, deep-chester men" with soldierly bearing. However, the main thrust of her lengthy article was that America had benefited in many ways from the arrival on her shores of Irishmen who already possessed "love for freedom and courage to fight for it."[160] She further illustrated America's good fortune by mentioning the strong Irish builders of canals and railroads, the bright Irish politicians and members of the press, as well as the fearless Irish leaders of military companies. "Think of Friday's procession," she concluded.[161] "If there were any defect . . . I could not perceive it. Perhaps there was none." Then, realizing the depth of her loving pride for her native land and her compatriots, she admitted, "Perhaps my eye had not the power to look critically upon such a scene."[162]

Just as Mother Austin was intensely proud of her native land and the accomplishments of her compatriots, so too, did she experience a natural satisfaction in witnessing the recognition of many for the work of Catherine McAuley's Institute of Mercy. And as a proud mother loves to show off her youngsters, so Mother Austin was always happy to have an opportunity to display her talented young sisters. Thus, second only to her joy in offering hospitality to other religious, especially Sisters of Mercy, was her pleasure in having them see her community in action. Her letters often contained invitations such as "take a trip South . . . for the winter"[163] and "benefit your health," or "pay us a visit" during "the lovely spring" or "delightful . . . May and June," and even in July, for "it is scarcely ever as hot as in the North," or "88° — our warmest day yet, and a good breeze," or "not one disagreeably warm day, and always cool nights." From 1870, the Vicksburg sisters visited regularly as they journeyed to and from Pass Christian, but other Mercies began to arrive by 1875, visiting Mother Austin when they came to the city on business or to get transportation for a farther destination.[164] Mother de Sales Browne of Mississippi had accompanied Mother Clare McMahon of Nashville for a visit that year and came down before going to Chicago on another occasion. Mother Austin hosted numerous others like "the French sisters from [Brownsville] Texas" on their way home to get candidates, or the German sisters from Alton on a begging tour, and more from as far away as "Canada and the West Indies,"[165] who wished to share in the proverbial New Orleans generosity.

Some of Mother Austin's Mercy correspondents-turned-friends began to arrive also, as did Mother Augustine McKenna of New York City, who spent the coldest part of two consecutive winters in the South.[166] Though this "change of air" ordered by the doctor was too late to cure the bronchial infection, the mutual friendship thrived. Just so did that of Mother Jerome Shubrick, who found a haven with Mother Austin between her assignment in Worcester, Massachusetts, and her foundation in Carrollton, Missouri.[167] The latter was in the diocese of Mother Austin's friend, Bishop John Joseph Hogan of Kansas City, Missouri. During the course of her stay, Mother Jerome was helpful in the prison apostolate and trained several new members for her community. Another Mercy friend, who had seen the New Orleans Mercy community and institutions, referred to them as Austin's Eden. If the Irish Channel convent were an Eden, then nationalism was the serpent poised and ready to spout poison in the near future. After complimenting the Mercy center, the press declared it most unusual "that a young plant should strike root so vigorously and unfold its growth so rapidly and luxuriously."[168] Mother Austin's concern was that the roots of her young tree gain enough depth in solid spirituality to maintain the healthy growth of the trunk and all its branches. As to serpents, she never gave them a thought.

9 YELLOW FEVER & GOLDEN JUBILEE
The Deep South
1878–1881

lthough she might not have noticed any serpent in the grass early in 1878, Mother Austin Carroll, ever taking the large view, did see clouds on the horizon as she completed her ninth year in the Irish Channel. Having finished her fourth year as superior, but her sixth year as leader of the Mercy community, Mother Austin asked Archbishop Perché to rescind his earlier decision that 1874–1880 was her appointed term in office.[1] He refused, explaining that after yellow fever took her two companions, he did not consider the handful of novices and postulants a canonical community. Mother Austin then requested Ferreol Girardey, prefect of St. Alphonsus and ecclesiastical director of the Sisters of Mercy, to ask Perché to allow an election. In his usual graceful French, the archbishop repeated that she was to remain in office until the specified date in 1880.[2] He enclosed his most cordial blessing for her and all the sisters. Mother Austin decided to seek advice once again from James O'Connor, for she believed him to be, after the death of his brother Michael, the American prelate most knowledgeable about the Mercy rule. As a young priest James had served as chaplain, friend, and advisor to several communities of Sisters of Mercy, and would continue to advise many through correspondence from Omaha as long as he lived.[3] Mother Austin, who by 1878 had been consulting him for over a dozen years, wrote that she worried "lest my staying over the ordinary time [as superior] even under peculiar circumstances may give bad example."[4]

"What would you advise me to do? Before God, I'd rather be a simple Sister, and I love all the duties and can do them as well as ever I could. The Sisters would keep me in office forever if they could."[5] She continued with the fact that she had not been feeling too well and "that I had best devote

161

the rest of my days to my own poor soul." Bishop O'Connor might have asked about Perché's wording because her next note enclosed the letter from the archbishop to Girardey so that O'Connor could check to see if it "admits of an appeal."[6] She weighs the archbishop's fifty years of experience as director for several Roman Congregations of religious women and fears that "it would be great presumption . . . to question his orders on ground of equity, for Monseigneur is universally admitted to be a most learned and holy Prelate." If she were again to apply for a change in his decision, perhaps she should give other reasons like ill health or dislike of office in order to avoid offending. If he allowed an election, "I should certainly be elected, and re-elected in three years most probably — then I should not be eligible, but the present arrangement adds two years to my cross." Then she tried to view the problem from another angle, "Still as God knows this would not be my choice, I suppose it is best to submit. . . . Though very firm exteriorly I am seldom without scruple about my actions. Pray that God may enlighten me to do right by all — that is my highest ambition."[7] Whatever the advice, she accepted the judgment of Perché with no further remonstrance. A light breeze had whisked that cloud from view, if only for the moment.

Mother Austin often touched on other points of community business in her correspondence with James O'Connor. For instance, she related that she used the Baggot Street *Customs* as a guide when arranging "the *Customs* of this house and its branches . . . as near as possible to the original practice."[8] Certain variations were absolutely a necessity. "As I understand the Spirit and scope of our Order, I think 'essentials' should be unchangeable and nonessentials regulated according to the circumstances of the place." If the New Orleans horarium were identical with that of the North, she "would have a hospital instead of a convent before many weeks."[9] Because her sisters were so near the Tropics, necessary changes had been made in the weight of clothing, type of food, and distribution of time. During the summer months, for instance, the sisters visited the sick in the Irish Channel from five to seven in the evening when, though the day was still bright, the air had cooled down considerably. This "arrangement displaced several exercises, which are always anticipated or postponed."[10] Mother Austin wanted the *Customs* to be specific enough that the sisters could "know *exactly* what they have to do, and that Superiors cannot make changes at will," for her Dublin correspondent had explained that only a Chapter assembly could change the *Customs*. As for herself, she hoped during her term in office "with the consent of all concerned, to make things as secure as possible . . . that all may go on as satisfactorily hereafter as now." She concluded proudly, "We have a most fervent community, Thank God."[11]

Mother Austin had also discussed with James O'Connor points concerning the Mercy Institute in the United States. When he suggested that the Sisters of Mercy in America ask Rome for a Cardinal Protector, she responded, "I'd willingly unite with any house disposed to make the application. Such protection is necessary. As my experience goes, there is more mischief done by small weak heads . . . than by bad men."[12] A year later she prodded, "Nothing yet about the Cardinal Protector, I suppose,"[13] and she wondered if the idea had been dropped when she heard that Rome had acted for the benefit of the Mercies in Pennsylvania. Although she knew from her correspondents that two other Mercy groups had also appealed to Rome on certain cases, she thought that "for the most part we are entirely on our own resources."[14] She had learned of the dissolution of several small Mercy groups when some of the disbanded Sisters applied for admission in New Orleans.[15] Hence, she felt that, at least in the South where convents were isolated, small groups could last only as branches supported by a strong motherhouse. "Let other regions do as they please,"[16] and as they both knew of one community which was trying to have restrictions placed on all the others, she added, "I don't interfere in any way with others."[17] Even so, Mother Austin declared less than fifty years after the death of the Mercy foundress, "I feel the whole Order will one day be turned into a Generalate, with provinces, etc., . . . a change which must come gradually and sweetly."[18] In Angers, she related, Perché had assisted the "Good Shepherd community which once had the same form [of government] as ours" to establish a generalate. Whenever the Mercy Institute did likewise, she hoped to have "a Southern Province ready to affiliate."[19]

Although many of Mother Austin's consultations dealt with the future well-being of the sisters, she also asked O'Connor's opinion about current concerns. This was especially true when some practice, branch houses, for instance, was not in the original Mercy Rule. Because several Irish mother-houses had staffed workhouse hospitals in other dioceses, she knew that her branches on the Gulf Coast were not unique in the Institute. This question was put to O'Connor as "the Prelate in America who has given most attention to our Order and acquired most experience in directing it,"[20] as she sought his thoughts on the best method of holding annual visitation in these branches. At first she had called the sisters to New Orleans, but wondered if it might be just as correct to ask Bishops Elder and Quinlan to visit the branch convents in their dioceses. Or perhaps, Perché could deputize the same priest who visited the New Orleans motherhouse to visit the branches, for the archbishop never visited in person all the convents in the Archdiocese. She felt confident that the Bishops of Natchez and Mobile would gladly make visitation as they were both pleased with the work of the New Orleans sisters. She states clearly that she seeks advice before she talks to her sisters because "whatever I propose will be acceded to by all . . . and I wish to do not only what is right but what is best."[21] As always, her letter concluded with a request for prayers, her procedure being to read, consult, pray, and then make her own decision based on the input of those consulted.

The original Mercy *Rule*, an 1863 copy printed in Dublin in both Latin and English, was the source which guided Mother Austin at all times.[22] When making decisions on matters beyond the scope of the Rule, one of her primary sources besides her invaluable experience with Josephine and Xavier Warde, was the book of *Customs* from Baggot Street. Her copy was an 1869 edition, evidently a reprint of the practices agreed upon by the superiors in Ireland in the summer of 1847.[23] In Limerick there was an 1864 meeting attended by three other original houses and a dozen additional convents. The results were published in two collections of expository material on the Mercy Rule and aimed at uniformity in customs.[24] Like many of the superiors who declined to attend the meeting, Mother Austin believed that the early *Customs* was sufficient and that the foundress did not intend her convents to be identical. In a letter which enclosed the Dublin horarium, Catherine McAuley stated, "The distribution of time is considered in our observances, not in our Rule, and therefore subject to any alteration that place or circumstances might require."[25] It was Mother Austin's belief that the foundress demonstrated her genius by giving the Rule such wonderful simplicity that it was adaptable to the needs of the Church in all parts of the world. She also credited this adaptability with the rapid growth and spread of the works of mercy from the Irish Channel to the Gulf Coast.[26]

Even though Mother Austin had copies of the *Guides* for reference, she rejected certain ideas, like manifestation of conscience to superiors, as more customary for religious of the previous century and foreign to Catherine McAuley's Institute as they were not a part of the original *Rule*.

> Although there are saints and many saintly person of a different opinion, I fancy that to make a law compelling manifestation of conscience was silly from the beginning. In certain cases it might be recommended — some people *must* throw off their troubles as some constitutions must throw off the bile. But to *force* people to put such confidence in other people argues an ignorance of human nature.[27]

Thus from early 1870s, Mother Austin made sure that her sisters knew that they need not manifest their consciences to superiors. A second related point about which she also felt strongly was that a religious woman should not have to give up her right to select a confessor and spiritual director when she became a religious. Hence, she took every opportunity to ask her friends in the hierarchy to urge Rome to allow more latitude in the canonical regulations. She returned to the topic periodically even though she found that priests were supersensitive about the matter, and "I have made enemies by telling my mind about this."[28] In 1884 she replied to one of her episcopal correspondents, "You ask me if there is anything I wish to say about Convents previous to the Baltimore Council."[29] She then suggested that religious women have greater freedom of choice by selecting one from a list of approved confessors. Her two decades of lobbying may or may not have helped her ideas become reality, but on December 17, 1890, Rome issued a decree giving greater freedom of conscience to religious men and women on both issues.[30]

Mother Austin had another idea that leaned toward the twentieth century, and there was no delay before she put it into operation. During her early years in New Orleans there resided in the House of Mercy some fine lay women whose services she began to call upon to bolster her forces. The ladies were out of work; the sisters needed assistance; thus, it was mutually beneficial. Because of their special caliber, she decided to accept them as lay affiliates, at least for a time. She had a real shortage of personnel because she was trying to nurture her novitiate flock to spiritual maturity before involving them too heavily in the works of mercy. The half-dozen ladies in question continued to live in the House of Mercy for several months as a trial before a more permanent arrangement was undertaken to work in close association with the Sisters of Mercy.[31] After several months, if the affiliation was still mutually desirable, the ladies were received as full-fledged lay Mercy affiliates, even acquiring a religious name and dress similar to that of the sisters. The six who thus joined their talents with those of the sisters, though none too young, were in good health and literally doubled the number available to visit the sick and to care for the orphans and the babies in the Crèche.[32] They assisted at the Eucharistic liturgy with the sisters, but not at their office and prayers, and professed no vows. After the mid-1870s when candidates swarmed into the community, the acceptance of lay affiliates ceased. Two of these lay auxiliaries gave temporary service for about six years, but the others continued for long years, two serving the social ministries well into the twentieth century.[33]

As innovative as Austin Carroll was in some ways, in others she followed closely the traditions set by Catherine McAuley. Both Catherine and Austin accepted as lay sisters the pious and zealous poor women whose circumstances had prevented extensive schooling. The lay sisters in New Orleans loved to relate that Mother Austin insisted that they were absolutely essential to the progress of the order and that by their fervor they could call forth God's blessings upon the entire community. She made them feel so confident that they could succeed with the help of God and the special grace of obedience that they often surprised themselves at their ability to accomplish difficult tasks and charges.[34] Mother Austin appointed them not just to housework and the purchasing and preparation of food, but also to the management of the dispensary, the almonry, the industrial school, the Crèche, the store for schoolbooks and supplies, and the commercial laundry which supported the House of Mercy.[35] Although the lay sisters wore white aprons in the convent as part of their habit, the lay sisters as well as the lay affiliates dressed "without any remarkable difference," as the Rule prescribed, from the habit of the choir sisters when on visitation of the sick. These nineteenth-century Mercies added to their voluminous habits and lengthy veils when out in public an extra face veil which covered head to hip. Thus, who was to know that Mother Austin's partner on Monday was a fifty-year old Mercy affiliate whose belt was a cord and tassel, or that her companion on Thursday was a teenage novice who exchanged her white veil for a black one to venture out and who cinched her habit with a leather cincture?[36]

At the same time that the veils obscured individual distinctions and hid the wearers' faces, they proclaimed to all the witnesses that two Mercy nuns were once again bringing a basketful of God's mercy and their own compassion to His sick and needy. Mother Austin had experienced the necessity of disguising herself in secular garb when traveling from one convent to another in the Northeast. In the Irish Channel she enjoyed telling her young sisters how, after the sisters nursed the soldiers of both sides during the Civil War, the religious dress won more respect than any other attire.[37] That was certainly true in New Orleans where everyone seemed aware that the Sisters of Mercy took their vows for the glory of God and the service of His people, thus combining "the recollection of the Carmelite and the active zeal of the Sister of Charity."[38] When reporting on Mercy profession ceremonies for the local newspapers, Mother Austin frequently explained the dual aims of the Mercy Institute. "The Sisters make perpetual vows, observe choir, spend hours daily in their spiritual exercises, and nearly a month of every year in retreat," because the first purpose of the order was "the sanctification of its members."[39] As the second aim was "the amelioration of society," she explained that the Mercies added to their vows of poverty, chastity, and obedience, "a fourth vow of service to the poor, sick, and ignorant."[40] Though young women taking their vows were to start each day in the chapel, return at noon and "for evening prayer and vesper hymns before going to a silent cell," during the day they were to go not only into the classrooms, but also "into the homes of the poor, into the wards of the hospitals . . . and into the prison cells."[41]

Undoubtedly, Mother Austin's pen was often used to make known the work of the Sisters of Mercy and call forth contributions for the maintenance of their institutions. Yet, that same pen sometimes became a powerful weapon fighting to win some benefit for a needy group on the fringe of society. The young vagrants, black for the most part, at the Boys' House of Refuge felt its power more than once, though they were probably unaware of the reasons underlying improvements in their educational situation. Mother Austin made the most dramatic use of the power of the press, however, in behalf of the women in Orleans Parish Prison. Throughout her first ten years of service to the prisoners in the dingy brick pile at Orleans and Marais near the Treme Market, she had talked the officials into improving the arrangements in the women's section on numerous occasions. In her articles about the jail and prison apostolate, Austin made a point of testifying to the cooperative attitude of the prison officials. For instance, when the state prisoners were transferred to the penitentiary near Baton Rouge, the usual crowded conditions were relieved considerably, and the warden was able to allocate a room to serve permanently as the chapel. The sisters were grateful for this improvement as the altar and the organ would no longer have to be shifted about from week to week. Then when the city building next to the prison became vacant, the warden agreed to Mother Austin's often-reiterated request for separate quarters for the women. Delighted about the new arrangement, Mother Austin immediately asked that matrons rather than male deputies be appointed for the women's building. She had won so many other concessions for the women that she felt confident that matrons would not be long in coming.[42]

On this point, however, the mellifluous tongue of this Carroll from the honeyed leas of Clonmel failed to soften the hearts of the political officials. So Mother Austin decided to make points with her pen, and articles appeared in the local papers praising the work and the improvements of the warden and his deputies, but also relating that prisons all over the country were using female deputies in their women's departments. Should Louisiana be the only exception to the modernization? Under the state "constitution the Criminal Sheriff is authorized to appoint as many deputy sheriffs as may be necessary to assist him" in the proper discharge of his duties.[43] Because hiring matrons would be something new for the sheriff, she suggested that the City Council take the initiative and instruct him to do so. There were other pieces calling the matter to the attention of the mayor and his council. After about four weeks of items about the vexing problem, Mother Austin learned that the absence of matrons was being blamed on the lack of funds. She took counsel with her sisters and decided to call the bluff of the city officials, as she knew that guards would be paid more generously than matrons. So she published this statement in the newspaper: "If the city cannot afford to pay two ladies . . . to act as matrons of the prison, the Superioress of St. Alphonsus Convent of Mercy will give two or four Sisters, without pay, to manage the female section of the prison."[44] The article continued with assurances to the sheriff that the presence of the sisters would not interfere with the work of the warden and his deputies. With that notice she won the day, for the officials, evidently preferring not to chance having that feisty nun constantly looking over their shoulders, quickly found the funds for the matrons' salaries. Once again the power of the press and her adept pen had been employed by the determined Irish Mercy to effect a bit of social reform.

Strangely enough, it was publicity about the prison apostolate that brought the assistance of the Sisters of Mercy to a number of poor fellows in other areas of Louisiana. Mother Austin related that from the jail "in his native parish, Calcasieu . . . a condemned man telegraphed for the Sisters of Mercy to instruct him" and help him get ready to die.[45] "I could not refuse such a request," she wrote, "and sent the sisters, though it would be easier to go to New York—so difficult of access are these remote places."[46] That first call to a scaffold outside the city arrived in 1877, but pleas of the same nature later came from the state penitentiary near Baton Rouge whenever the sentence of death was pronounced. Each time, two sisters went up the Mississippi River about five days before the execution date in order to bring the condemned prisoner religious instruction, preparation for the sacraments, and prayers to follow him beyond the gallows to plead for mercy. "Although most people smiled at the idea of reforming prisoners," Mother Austin said, "there is no doubt that many solid conversions have taken place here."[47] "God has chosen souls in the most unlikely places."[48] She recalled cases like the wild young murderer to whom she taught drawing to calm him down, and then was able to instruct him in the faith and prepare him to face death. "He became as gentle as a child . . . most edifying," yet he was "one of the wildest and most reckless . . . brought to repentance by prayers, patience, instructions, and above all, the grace of God."[49]

Mother Austin attributed to God's grace, also, the fact that she was able to work so wholeheartedly in the prison apostolate because, as a young girl, she disliked even to hear about violence and death. At that time she never could have imagined that her compassionate zeal as a nun would lead her to befriend the imprisoned, even the confessed murderers.[50] Invited to witness an execution, she answered that "she would not be present for the world, unless the poor boy expressly desired it, in which case I would willingly mount the scaffold with him. Yet, I would rather suffer the death myself than see it inflicted on any one."[51] Her pleasure was in bringing souls back to God. One reporter seems to have caught her spirit as he described "the dingy jail with row after row of small grated windows where sunlight tries in vain to penetrate . . . but within, the bright light of charity sheds its rays, the criminal's soul is awakened by the sweet voice of a Sister of Mercy who, little by little . . . leads the poor wretch to trust in a loving Savior's mercy."[52] Though she worked very hard with the condemned men, Mother Austin's greatest efforts were probably spent striving for the reformation of the women. She often spoke of her wish to "establish a home for discharged female prisoners, wherein their reformation, begun in prison, could be completed and suitable employment provided for them."[53] She hoped to finance this project once all the needs of the asylum had been met, but finding funds for the orphans postponed indefinitely her dreams for this halfway house. "Such a refuge is a crying need in our city," she said, revealing that she had adopted New Orleans as her own.[54]

If that ownership were not mutual beyond the Irish Channel before 1878, it was to be so thereafter, for Mother Austin Carroll and her sisters were to work during the yellow fever epidemic from one end of the city to the other as they assisted at sickbeds from Carrollton six miles above their convent in the Channel down to Jackson Barracks five miles below it. Before that trial by fiery fever began, however, that year and the preceding one had been a wonderful time for Mother Austin, her literary productions, and the expansion of the Mercy Institute. Much of the local growth has already been noted, but Mother Austin also became involved in a movement to incorporate into Catherine McAuley's Institute of Mercy a group of sisters in North Carolina. The incident began with the bishop of Richmond, James Gibbons, who was in New Orleans to visit relatives. On these periodic visits Mother Austin managed to have the bishop officiate occasionally at a profession ceremony, as he did on February 3, 1877.[55] She told a friend that on this occasion the bishop "asked me about affiliating Bishop England's Sisters of Mercy to us. I made the conditions as easy as possible — a nominal novitiate — no change of any kind that would be noticed by outsiders — no expense."[56] She also wrote to Dublin to consult the original motherhouse about the conditions necessary for the aggregation into the Mercy Institute of these diocesan religious.[57]

Mother Austin knew that the congregation of the Sisters of Our Lady of Mercy had been established in 1829 by John England, the first Bishop of Charleston. Although the sisters in North Carolina had been performing the works of mercy for over thirty years as diocesan religious by the 1870s, they desired to have papal approval. Bishop Gibbons was evidently planning to send several sisters to New Orleans so that they could, with Mother Austin's help, familiarize themselves with the McAuley Rule and customs. On their return to Wilmington in North Carolina, they could teach the rest of the community the new Rule. Delighted to be assisting with this extension of Catherine's Institute, Mother Austin wrote, "I dare say we shall have some of these good Sisters here soon."[58] Just then Gibbons was raised several steps up the hierarchial ladder, however, and the plans for the Sisters of Our Lady of Mercy slipped between the rungs. First, he was nominated the coadjutor of Archbishop James Bayley of Baltimore, and within a few months automatically succeeded to the See upon the death of the archbishop. Mother Austin was disappointed that the Wilmington sisters were not to join the Mercy Institute, but in a way this early plan was a harbinger of future events. Later, she was to give the same type of assistance to the Savannah community of Bishop England's sisters in 1893, the same year that the Wilmington Mercies adopted the McAuley habit.[59] In deference to the wishes of their bishop, these sisters delayed longer before adopting the Rule of the Institute of Mercy, in 1912 completing the unification of the Belmont Mercy congregation of Bishop England with that of Catherine McAuley.

Evidence that Mother Austin had a special knack for explaining the Rule and its obligations and privileges came from every quarter. Her listeners among the New Orleans community were to reiterate for years to come how greatly they were inspired and how much their zeal was heightened by her words during lectures on the Rule and the aims of the foundress.[60] Bishop England's sisters evidently found her presentations of explanatory material tremendously helpful, for one of the sisters wrote to a distant Mercy that Mother Austin "had opened the way for us. . . . We reverence her as a dear, good Mother, who by her broad-minded liberality and consideration made the transition as easy as possible."[61] Mother Austin liked to share good news concerning Mercies with her correspondents, and told Mother Baptist Russell in San Francisco about the Savannah aggregation. Mother Baptist then sent some pictures of Catherine McAuley to Mother Austin to give to the affiliates, who seemed to be overwhelmed that strangers had sent "the kind and generous recognition of us as Members of your great Community" and noted that it was Mother Austin's charity which had "influenced you all favorably toward us."[62] Bringing Mercies together always gave Mother Austin special joy, and she was delighted to be causing the Sisters of Mercy on the West Coast to join hands with those on the Atlantic seaboard. To bring Sisters of Mercy closer and help them to know their foundress and one another better was one of the aims behind several of Mother Austin's literary projects in 1877 and 1878.

Mother Austin searched for some time before she located a copy of the *Sayings of the Foundress*, edited by Mother Mary Clare Moore.[63] Because the book was out of print and no longer available, Mother Austin decided to republish the original in the United States.[64] Her compact reprint sold for less than a dollar. She wanted to keep the price reasonable enough to be able to give the book away in quantities on the occasion of the approaching fiftieth anniversary of the Institute. She planned to give copies on the golden jubilee to all the children the Mercies taught, all the families they visited, and to all in their institutions. Mother Austin thought that everyone the sisters served should know some of the beautiful words of their foundress. She also notified the Mercies in this country and her friends abroad that copies were once again available, and "our foundress's instructions . . . should be most useful to us."[65] Primarily, of course, she wanted each of her own sisters to have a copy, as she wrote a friend, "We read the book twice a year for lecture . . . some Sisters make a meditation from it, and all take a sentence a day to reflect on . . ."[66] Mother Austin believed that Catherine's *Sayings* were so helpful to the sisters that she compiled a companion volume in 1878.[67] Both small books had several more printings, apparently the usual procedure for Mother Austin's works as they were progressively sought by sisters farther afield. By 1878, for instance, her *Life of Catherine McAuley* had seen its fifth reissue;[68] her translation of St. Jure's *Love of Jesus Christ* and her *Spiritual Retreat* were in their third printing; and her biography of *St. Alphonsus* and her prayerbook-like *Commandments and Sacraments* were in their second printing, as were her three small collections of stories for children.[69]

Too recent as yet to be reprinted were her 1877 biography of *Clement Hofbauer*, which carried the imprimatur of the first American cardinal, his Eminence John Cardinal McCloskey, and her 1878 translation of St. Jure's *L'Homme Spirituel*.[70] She never referred to this book except by its French title, but she never gave any reason for her preference for the French. Though the publishers' commissions were beginning to help considerably in financing the various works of mercy, Austin's most important literary work of this period was conceived as a private publication for the sisters of Catherine McAuley's Institute of Mercy, and therefore, not likely to bring much of a commission. But financial gain had nothing to do with it. Mother Austin Carroll, at her creative best, decided that the most valuable gift she could present to the Sisters of Mercy for their golden anniversary was a series of Mercy *Annals*. She hoped that they would "preserve much that would otherwise be forgotten, and be of great use . . . in many ways."[71] One of these was the unity of the sisters, for she said, "I intend to touch, incidentally, on every point about which there has been difference of opinion—the more I study the more I find out that ignorance is the root of most of these differences."[72] Her letters had often mentioned her desire to find stories of the early Mercies and carried remarks such as, "We are reading now for evening lecture the lives of the first Mothers of the Visitation. How often I wish we had the lives of our own early members. When I think of all the holy Sisters I knew, I think it a pity that we have to look so much to others for examples for our Novices."[73]

As Mother Austin Carroll gave the details of her projected *Leaves from the Annals of the Sisters of Mercy*, she noted, "from the title no connected history could be expected."[74] At this date she intended to publish "it in three parts: Ireland—England and the Colonies—America . . . it cannot be all out before three years."[75] One might wonder whether or not the project would have been started had she known that it was to demand her time and effort sporadically for more than a dozen years. Probably, the most difficult task was getting the sisters everywhere to outline or summarize the stories of their motherhouses. She wrote to all the foundations of the Institute asking that they would furnish her with "particulars of their foundations, the deaths of their sisters, and whatever should edify and enliven the work."[76] As the correspondence progressed, plans were modified so that the work was to be for general reading. The Limerick chronicles explain that, "At first, though pleasure was universal at having her undertake the arduous task, the tendency seemed to be brief and cautious,"[77] trying to omit what might not be understood by seculars. To collect her information Mother Austin had to coax and cajole, praise the correspondent's ability, and promise not to mention her name. Here and there she found annalists who sent her fine resumés, but they were the favored few, for many were content to forward newspaper clippings of jubilee or school events.[78]

"I have called the work 'Leaves,' which gives me a margin to leave out what I please," Mother Austin commented, adding, "This could not be done in History."[79] Possibly because she had received complaints about some facts in the life of the foundress, Austin decided in this work to use only the information sent her. "My plan is to ask information from all houses—of those who do not give it, I can say nothing but tell the fact of their foundation and the house from which they affiliated."[80] She repeatedly asked for data, however, and commented on the excuses of those in default. Jot it down in any fashion, "Your secretary need not mind mistakes of any kind as I should correct all—all I want are the items, anecdotes, and incidents, etc. . . . I'll put it into my best style."[81] As to the sisters not having time,

> No one could give the excuse of want of leisure more truly than I, yet . . . I deem it my duty to devote that gift of God to my Order—this is why I snatch the time to write. . . . This is very important for the whole Order and some ready writer should be spared to do it. . . . My young community and our six houses absorb all my time. Even when writing a book, I rarely get two hours a day free, and have to work a little at night too.[82]

The chronicler in Limerick wrote of Mother Austin, "Hers was a mind that knew how to get on with little and expect more; and so amidst the cares of office she had progressed far with the work when fearful yellow fever broke out . . . and of course, all then had to be suspended."[83]

By 1878, yellow fever had become simply an annual unpleasant visitor to Mother Austin even though she had heard of the earlier terrible visitations, like that in 1853 when the death toll soared to 8,000, or to 4,000 in 1858, or to over 3,000 in 1867, shortly before her arrival in New Orleans.[84] Since then, her own experience was gained in the annual fever seasons between the limited epidemics of 1871, 1873, and 1875, each of which included the area near the wharves of the Irish Channel riverfront. In each case Mother Austin and her sisters knew many of the sick personally, witnessed the destitution of the laborers and their families during the quarantine, and suffered the devastating loss of a few of her sisters.[85] Thus she equated these small epidemics with the great ones of the past and was taken completely by surprise by the massiveness of the 1878 attack. It was "entirely unexpected," she related.

> The summer was warm, but New Orleans knows nothing of the dreadful heat waves that scorch the northern cities. Heat is comparatively easily borne here. Dwellings are constructed with a view to ward off its most troublesome effects. Low, deep houses, surrounded by spacious verandahs, shaded by clusters of trees impervious to the sun but not to the breeze, are pleasant noon-tide retreats. And beneath the towering pecan, or the graceful sycamore, or the struggling fig tree dark with heavy foliage, trifling is the inconvenience felt at any time from the rays of an almost vertical sun.[86]

One needs to be on the street unsheltered by the trees, "to feel the broiling, sweltering, maddening heat, which produces the sugar cane and cotton."[87] An exceptional heat alternated with torrential rain in 1878, so that the older people were saying by midsummer that it was already damp enough to be "yellow fever weather." When she wrote a friend in July, it was hot enough for Mother Austin to mention the warmth, the presence of "a little yellow fever,"[88] and her worry that Irish candidates might arrive during the fever. For the first time since she was in New Orleans, she had asked her sister Katy, who was Mother Mary Mercy and Mistress of Novices in Passage West, to select some prospective postulants for her because of the recent rapid expansion along the Gulf Coast. She had already sent word to delay the passage lest the Irish candidates succumb in the epidemic upon their arrival, but feared that her message might not be in time to effect the change of plans.[89] By August she could say, "I believe the courage and devotedness of the Sisters have done much to allay the insane panic which took hold of the poor people in the beginning of the calamity."[90] Unlike the small towns from which the frightened fled, New Orleans had numerous beneficial groups besides the clergy and the religious who helped the fever victims. News came that the Irish candidates were safely detained, but Mother Austin begged her friends for prayers that "God will leave us intact this year. We have already lost such valuable Sisters."[91] Although none of her sisters had caught yellow fever before August 15, several local priests and religious had already found the fever to be fatal. "Our whole time is occupied with the fever-stricken, visiting them, preparing medicine, nourishment, etc., instructing them for the Sacraments. . . . Thank God we are able to do some good, that is the only thing worth living for."[92]

Until mid-August, Mother Austin did not think the fever was too dangerous, because ninety percent of their patients were recovering. The secret of the Mercies' successful nursing was just what they had learned from experienced Creoles. Though the doctors made heroic efforts to reach as many as possible, most of the poor never called a doctor. Following the pattern of the Creole nurses, the sisters gave no food for the first four or five days, but administered a mild laxative and lots of hot tea, made with either orange leaves or watermelon seeds, to cause profuse perspiration. They covered the patient well, but threw open the shutters and windows and drew back the curtains so that the fresh air could rid the room of the miasma. "Yellow fever does not keep the interested parties long in suspense,"[93] Austin said, as three or four days sufficed to break the fever. If it was down by the fifth day, the patient usually recovered. "Convalescence is the most dangerous period—nourishment must be given by the drop or crumb—excess is sure to prove fatal."[94] Rest was most important as nourishment was increased very gradually, milk toast alternating with thin broth for about five days, then adding grits or gruel. "The least imprudence . . . eating or drinking a little too much . . . may result in death, and for several weeks after recovery, danger of relapse lingers about the convalescent."[95] As August waned the fever became more virulent, blanketed the South, attacked the acclimated, and the New Orleans Mercies, like those in Vicksburg, began to fall victim to the malignant fever.

On August 17, "We lost our darling Sister . . . despite the best medical advice, nursing, frequent prayer, Our Lord took her."[96] This first Mercy victim of the 1878 new Orleans epidemic was a twenty-five year old Louisiana native, and according to Mother Austin, almost perfect. "It may sound like exaggeration . . . yet I never saw a fault in her. . . . She was certainly the best prepared to go . . . but her death was a terrible shock to me . . . God wanted her . . . He knows best . . . God's will be done. Thank God the others . . . [are] out of danger today."[97] Judging by her own patients, Austin thought the worst was over, "The fever is abating, thank God . . . I hope that God will spare the rest."[98] She was dead wrong on both counts and might have realized it when she heard from the neighboring Mercies that Vicksburg was deserted "with not a human being to be seen in the streets save the sisters or some member of the benevolent societies hurrying on their mission of mercy."[99] Mother de Sales Browne thought the fever "the worst character I have ever seen, whole families swept away," and two of her sisters with them in early September. "We found a dead body in every house on the levee . . . and the Sisters from our other houses have come here to help."[100] Mother Austin also had called her experienced nurses from the Gulf Coast and sent her unacclimated as replacements. The city schools were closed of course, and many of the nuns were helping the sick. Mother Austin and her forty sisters were "working with unflagging energy" all day among the stricken,[101] and "in the evening some went in a barouche to the worst districts, carrying with them everything necessary to treat the disease, especially in its early stages. For the doctors could not reach them all; and the Sisters, from long experience, knew what to do."[102] Mother Austin was convinced that the Mercies saved many lives on these evening visits.

By September most of the country had heard of the terrible plight of the stricken areas across the South, and bishops began taking special collections to send aid. The convent finances had dwindled drastically as there was no income from teaching, and Mother Austin began writing her friends for help to feed the orphans and the destitute. She feared that "a famine would follow the pestilence. So far we have been able to relieve the distress we have met with—God grant that we may never have to refuse the poor," but already she was buying food and medicine on credit.[103] "The quarantine has destroyed almost all business—stoppage of trains, boats, etc., has thrown thousands out of work, all whose daily bread depends on labor."[104] The Mercies in Biloxi and Pensacola had their pupils give entertainments to help feed the orphans; the fire companies of Pensacola and Brewton, Alabama, sent funds, as did the businessmen of Biloxi and Pensacola. All this helped, but it was primarily due to the friends and correspondents of Mother Austin Carroll that the New Orleans Mercies were enabled to continue their assistance to the sick poor. Donations came directly from Mothers Baptist Russell in San Francisco, who knew what an epidemic did to a city, and Josephine Warde of Cork, "who consoled and encouraged . . . and assisted them most generously."[105] Liberal gifts were also forthcoming from several houses in the Northeast and from Austin's episcopal friends, Bishops O'Connor in Omaha, Hogan in St. Joseph, Missouri, Gibbons in Baltimore, and, perhaps at the request of Elizabeth Strange, Bishop Tuigg in Pittsburgh.[106]

Yet all these sources added together might not have equaled the quantities gathered by Mothers Augustine McKenna and Elizabeth Callahan of New York and Jerome Shubrick of Worcester, Massachusetts. In both places the power of the press made the difference, for Austin's letters describing the horrors of the epidemic were published in newspapers, and many pursestrings were loosened by the realistic descriptions. Jerome Shubrick had the help of the mayor and the people of Worcester, the Jesuit faculty and students of Holy Cross College, and John Boyle O'Reilly of the

Boston Pilot. The paper carried letters, the editor's personal appeal, and names of donors from September to December.[107] In New York the same help was garnered through James McMaster of the *Freeman's Journal*, who printed letters, made an appeal in his own name, and gave frequent updates on new cases and the deaths in Mother Austin's community and institutions. One letter told of the fever spreading at the asylum because "the Sisters have taken little ones from the beds in which one or both parents lay dead . . . the terrible mortality among the soldiers and their wives [at the barracks]. We have taken all their orphans so far."[108] She explained that she had "promised Our Lord that no orphan would be rejected by us. This promise involves a great deal, but I know God will provide for these helpless babies."[109]

When John Pierpont Morgan signed a check for a thousand dollars, one wonders just which words were the precipitating agent.[110] Was it the frankness about how the sisters were catching the yellow fever themselves at the bedside of the dying, where "inhaling the fumes of the black vomit once or twice is not much; but when this happens frequently, like produces like. . . . Four of them took the disease from coffining bodies that no one else would touch."[111] Then Austin concluded, "If our friends in New York knew exactly how things are, I am sure that some streams of their charity would flow to us. I know you will explain our case as opportunity offers, and get all the prayers you can."[112] The accompanying note asked that contributions be sent to the Mercies either at 35 East Houston or Eighty-First and Madison, so that they could be transmitted at once. The thousand-dollar check must have seemed a heaven-sent gift to Mother Austin. Her note of gratitude mentioned that they were correctly addressed as Catholic Sisters of Mercy, "but we have never been accused of pausing to inquire as to the creed of those whom we can benefit by our ministrations."[113] Her prayer was that God would "return your charity a thousand fold . . . and that you may be saved from ever witnessing the appalling scenes that hourly harrow our souls."[114] Mother Austin had confided to one of her correspondents in August, after the death of her first sister, that she had "made a vow to take every child orphaned in this epidemic if God would spare the rest of the Sisters."[115] She loved them more than ever as she witnessed their "perfect selfless devotion . . . with the sick morning, noon and night . . . yet had not heard one complain that she was tired."[116]

Ever mindful of the Mercy foundress, Mother Austin placed a letter of Catherine McAuley under the head of a novice dying of yellow fever. The young Sister recovered, and posthaste, Austin sent the news of the miraculous recovery to Ireland, and the incident refreshed her as a breath of Ireland's air in the midst of the epidemic's miasma. In early October, yellow fever broke out in Biloxi, where Mother Austin had assigned her unacclimated sisters. Immediately, she sent out sisters who had had yellow fever to "replace the unacclimated and do all they can for the fever-stricken."[117] If the young sisters were to get sick "better here then there," she said, as she could nurse them in the city. Those going to Biloxi "are perfect nurses, and know as much about the disease now as most doctors."[118] Mother Austin herself was convinced that the disease was "not contagious, but under particular conditions indigenous in certain areas."[119] In the convent many sisters never caught it from the others, and in the orphanage, while every child brought in during the epidemic was a victim, the orphans in the asylum prior to the epidemic, with only several exceptions, did not succumb to the fever. And of all the little children brought in with yellow fever, only one died. Each of the other tiny victims was gradually nursed back to health, a fact which Mother Austin pointed out, illustrates "what care and good nursing will effect."[120] She was not alone in this recognition, for by the middle of October, papers all over the country were giving accolades to the courageous men and women, especially the large groups of religious in New Orleans, who were nursing the victims.[121]

Two more of the Mercies nursing in New Orleans were soon to become victims. Shortly after Mother Austin bemoaned, "the poor Sisters in Vicksburg have sent four to heaven," she had "eight down, but all are out of danger but two."[122] Then suddenly, that pair was gone, "two of the loveliest, most zealous and useful Sisters we ever had. In their case the disease was of the most virulent type." The best physicians and nurses could give little relief, and "the loss has been a dreadful blow to us, but we must say 'Welcome' to God's holy will."[123] In writing to the home of one of the young martyrs, Mother Austin said that sister "led among us the life of a saint and died the death of one. In a short time she fulfilled a long space, and our good God called her to Himself . . . because her beautiful soul was not unfit to deck His paradise."[124] The second young sister lasted just a few hours after her companion, both dead at twenty-three and bringing fresh vows to the Lord. Mother Austin spoke of her grief at the sight of "those two fair young creatures lying side by side in the chapel . . . the first double funeral we ever had. Our tomb is more than full now — one of the last lies in that of the German Sisters . . . till we can enlarge ours."[125] Then, thinking of the work still before them, she asks for prayers for several intentions, "that God may send us some good subjects for those He has seen fit to take from us" and that a frost will appear "soon, please God, but until it does come, no one knows who will be next."[126]

After the double funeral Mother Austin noted that the tally among her sisters was twenty sick, eleven recuperating, three dead, and "only ten to go out among the plague-stricken in the city" as some had gone to help in Biloxi.[127] There the fever did not seem as virulent although there were about a hundred cases, including two priests. "Scarcely a household in New

Orleans was unvisited by the Destroying Angel, who has not yet sheathed his sword," and each Louisiana native among the Mercies "had death to mourn in her family."[128] A pall overshadowed the entire city, wrapped in its grief, silent in mourning. Mother Austin found the gloom oppressive, for "not a bell rang . . . not a note of music—the very song birds have deserted us. Not a conversation of which sorrow, anguish, and death do not form the burden."[129] Death and dying occupied everyone. Funerals grew smaller, mourners scarcer, presenting cavalcades of death "like shadowy spectres."[130] Fumigation crews were overworked, as were the noisy carts collecting corpses for city burial; and the busiest sites in town were the cemeteries where family tombs were opened repeatedly for another coffin. Mother Austin, turning her thoughts from graves to gratitude, was pleased that so many of their patients were recovering.[131] She was thankful to God for the continued convalescence of her sisters and for the babies taken from their mothers' cold arms by the Mercies and brought home to their own warm hearts. She even tried to be appreciative that God had promoted one tiny orphan and "three of our dearest members to His own bright mansions, but this last lay entirely in the superior regions of the soul," for she could not speak of their loss without tears.[132] "Our time and strength and means were joyfully offered, and we thought that God would ask no more of us."[133] She accepted God's will repeatedly, but found that it did not lessen the anguish.

Brighter skies finally appeared as November approached and the thermometer dropped a little, "but no security till after a good heavy frost."[134] Austin told a correspondent that "the cool weather of the past few days has abated the pestilence"[135] causing a reduction in the official statistics, "today's report: 42 dead and 114 new cases,"[136] four of her sisters among the latter. With the others improving rapidly and the attack on the latest four less malignant, Mother Austin began to count the blessings of the last three months. Most consoling was that God knew it all, even how often they "coffined a putrid corpse that no other hands would touch."[137] Alms had arrived in time to enable her to replenish the supplies in the soup kitchen and pharmacy, to sustain countless destitute families and numerous orphans, and to pay some of their patient creditors. In assigning monetary aid, Mother Austin gave to those who were not being reached by the public relief agencies, like the Howard or Catholic Relief Societies. Primarily, she assisted those too devastated to know where to turn, and "respectable people who would rather die than make their wants known in any public way."[138] She confided that more than once she had "gone out with a hundred dollars and come in without one, and I don't think I gave fifty cents not absolutely needed."[139] She and her sisters were familiar with the most destitute areas of the Irish Channel, of course; but during the course of the epidemic they had been directed to many a lovely home only to find victims and survivors on the verge of starvation, or to the more modest abode of an elderly widow who was quietly trying to barter family heirlooms for food.[140] To these and countless others, charity was literally personified by the compassion of Mother Austin Carroll.

In all parts of the country the press was highly appreciative of the heroic service of the priests and religious, ever more so as their death count rose to ninety-eight with "three seminarians, six brothers, thirty priests, and fifty-nine sisters."[141] A Methodist minister declared, "Too much cannot be said of priests and nuns who have gone into the very jaws of death."[142] And a columnist pointed out that "In justice, it should be remembered that for a century before we heard of a Howard or Nightingale or Fry, the Sisters of Charity and Mercy were known in the prisons and hospitals of both hemispheres."[143] But for her part, Mother Austin praised the laity. If she were to make a list of the heroes of the epidemic, "the physicians would rank high . . . but heroism was not confined to any class. The lowly who had only time to give, gave it."[144] Working people gave their modest best, and the rich donated generously of their abundance. "Ladies, fair of face and regal in form, sought the fetid atmosphere of death and bent over the suffering victims with maternal love."[145] On the other hand, she wrote "That priests should administer the sacraments at the risk of their lives is nothing new. That Sisters of Mercy should serve the stricken till they themselves fall, is doing nothing more than is appointed them. . . . God who gives the vocation . . . gives the grace to fulfill all its requirements."[146] For herself, she was happy to have done her part "to relieve the sick, to soothe the agonies of the dying, and to assume the responsibilities of the dead when neither relative nor friend was nigh." Yet, she was insistent that it was "nothing more than is our duty."[147]

One article interesting enough for Mother Austin to clip and save was by Lillie Devereux, a member of the New York Press corps. Without detracting in any way from the efforts of men who worked in the fever districts, the author gave an accolade to the heroic women of all classes who had done the same. Mothers and wives "stood unflinchingly nursing their sick, although death himself stood beside them ready to demand their lives."[148] Nuns "of gentle lineage and delicate rearing sought out the infected cities . . . ventured into squalid homes and endured privations . . . wherever their ministrations might bring alleviation."[149] Finally, she brought to the attention of the public certain "ladies of the evening," the Memphis prostitutes who transformed their houses of business into hospitals for the homeless, the transients, and the riverboatmen, and then, "heedless of their own fate, went into the pit of death to nurse others back to health."[150] In conclusion, she said that the epidemic proved again what history had already recorded, that women—"saints and sinners, gentle and simple, in all ranks

of life . . . have shown the highest qualities of courage and self-sacrifice,"
yet not one deemed fit to vote.

> When women . . . athirst for knowledge, ask admission to our colleges; or
> when longing for freedom, they ask for the right of representation, they
> are met with sneers or reminded of their mental and physical weakness. In
> the face of such a record of woman's courage as this fearful ordeal of fever
> has shown, is it too much to demand that those who have shared man's
> labor and transcended his loyalty shall be his equal in liberty?[151]

Perhaps it was the approach of the above article which first caught her
attention, but Mother Austin Carroll had always been interested in any
proponent of higher education for women. For years she had been teaching
that there was no limit to what women could accomplish even when
deprived of the opportunity for university education. Once given better
opportunities to develop their God-given capabilities and talents, Mother
Austin felt that women would excel in many fields. She took every opportunity to point out instances in which women had succeeded in traditional
male roles, such as her mention of "the learned gentlewomen who lectured
on civil and canon law at the University of Bologna . . . long before
woman's rights . . . and a female professor of anatomy and surgery . . .
became an issue."[152] This remark came later, but Austin's books of 1866 and
1867 began with the ways in which women excelled, and one of her plans for
the future was to establish a Catholic college for women.[153] For the
moment, however, the pressing duty was to fulfill their commitments and
find enough teachers to staff the schools. With a number of her sisters just
recuperating as the quarantine lifted, substitutions had to be arranged and
the Mercies nursing on the Coast recalled. Even so, each school would be
short a teacher for a time, but there were also fewer children; for just as
many of their convalescent pupils were among the 13,000 fever cases, so
others were among the 4,000 who had died.[154] December of 1878, exceptionally busy as it was, marked the passage of twenty-five years since Margaret
Anne Carroll had arrived at the Mercy novitiate in the beautiful convent in
Cork to begin a thorough preparation under Mother Josephine Warde for
her subsequent career as one of Catherine McAuley's most devoted
followers.[155]

In honor of the occasion of her "half jubilee" on the feast of Mary
Immaculate and as a gift to the members of the Institute of Mercy, Mother
Austin compiled her collection of Catherine's *Sayings*, which she considered
a continuation of those compiled by Mother Clare Moore of Bermondsey.[156]
It delighted Austin that Archbishop Perché had referred to the foundress as
"saintly" in his approbation of her *Sayings*. Perché had noted also, in praise

of the zeal he had long witnessed in Austin, that "the new collection has been gathered by pious hands."[157] In announcing her anniversary to her spiritual director, she added "I ought to be a saint by this [time], and yet have scarcely begun."[158] Her rather humble assessment differed from that of others who found Austin Carroll to be an extraordinarily zealous religious woman. She had written Bishop Elder earlier, "We shall not take one cent from you towards the purchase of a place for the school for Colored children."[159] If he remembered the sisters at Mass, "We shall be more than repaid for the little charity we prepare to do . . . in gratitude to God for many favors received."[160] Thus almost a decade before the town opened a public school for blacks, she planned hers for September, although the epidemic delayed it for several months. "God has blessed us so wonderfully," she told Elder. "You must let us put a little monument in Biloxi to testify our gratitude."[161] All was finally arranged and St. Joseph's Colored School opened its doors on Monday, January 6, 1879.[162]

St. Joseph's was not the only community project put on hold by Yellow Jack, for the Irish candidates had been told to await word that New Orleans was "safe" before they "took ship for the American missions." Although six sisters had been professed that year prior to the advent of the fever, there were four more novices ready to take their vows and several postulants to be received before the year came to an end. It was for this ceremony that Mother Austin wrote an exceptionally detailed article on the Mercy Institute, explaining the combination of the active and contemplative aspects of religious life in the Mercy Rule. It was as though she feared that people, having seen the constant service of the Mercies during the lengthy epidemic, might forget that they were also essentially women of prayer. Mother Austin pictured Mercy religious not as haters of this world, but as lovers who relinquished its vanities and retained its sorrow and suffering because they had found a greater love in Christ.[163] In taking the four vows of poverty, chastity, obedience, and service, their aim was both their own sanctification and the amelioration of the ills of society, thus aiming at what is now termed systemic change. Austin mentioned the youth, the fecundity, and the rapid spread of the Institute established in 1831, and gave statistics like "355 Mercy convents in the world, of which 121 were in Ireland and 108 in the United States.[164] She spoke of Catherine McAuley, the holy foundress who "was not content just to give her gold but gave herself also with all her . . . intelligence, her beauty and grace, to the service of God and His creatures."[165] In concluding, she said that although "the fever of the summer carried off three gentle Sisters . . . heroic souls, already three other brave hearts have filled up the broken line; and the work, even the names of the dead, are taken up by the living."[166]

The press ceased its daily set of statistics on fever cases and deaths and,

like Mother Austin, turned to regular business and events, some of them
forever timely and others quite new. In the latter class were the items
concerning an amusing new invention termed a phonograph, the growing
fad for the peculiar velocipede called a bicycle, and the frequent ads which
proclaimed that the instrument known as a telephone was not a toy at all,
but could prove quite helpful to a doctor or priest, and in an apothecary
shop or hospital. Besides such items about new machines, there were the
events which seem to occur in cycles even into modern times. Quotations
from European papers declared that "Russia . . . now knocks at the back
door of Afghanistan . . . an insidious approach . . . and she must not be
allowed to get in by intrigue and chicanery."[167] As to the local economy, "the
city groans under the weight of debts . . . dishonestly piled upon it,"[168] yet
especially onerous were the licenses placed upon each business, a "barba-
rous system of taxation . . . in its effects destructive of prosperity," and the
proposed cure, "to cut down expenses inexorably: diminish the police force,
curtail the number of teachers, extinguish half the gas lights, and check
street improvements."[169] Private letters spoke more frankly of the cause of
the situation, which was due not just to the quarantine which aggravated
matters already bad, but mainly to the recent carpetbagger government
which placed both the state and the city

> on the verge of bankruptcy. Millions of dollars were spent . . . without
> benefitting anyone except those who . . . filled their own purses; and our
> laws are so nicely framed that the perpetrators cannot even be brought to
> trial. On the contrary, hundreds of innocent men are seized by apparent
> legal process and brought here for trial before judges and juries packed for
> the purpose of condemning them, whilst their families will be reduced to
> want and starvation.[170]

Nor was the archdiocese much better off. Mother Austin confided to a
friend that the archbishop had gone to Europe seeking help, to France for
money and to Rome for an auxiliary to help reduce the debt. "His troubles
always increase, and he says he is unable to cope with the difficulties . . . I
feel sorry for him—he has always been most courteous and obliging to
us."[171] The elderly archbishop had been just as kind to many others and
quietly assisted many a parish near bankruptcy or, like Mother Austin,
many a family on the brink of starvation. With conditions as they were, and
no salary being paid the teachers in the Redemptorist schools, Mother
Austin turned to raffles. For the most part, the relatives of the sisters
donated the objects to be raffled, anything from a silver watch or gold
thimble, or an antique brooch or lavaliere, to a magnificent horse from the
Gourrier plantation.[172] Mother Austin commented to Mother Teresa Maher

of Cincinnati, "How our Sisters across the Atlantic would feel if they were depending on what we call chance for their support! No doubt it cramps our exertions a little; but I think we can accomplish even more for the glory of God than they."[173] At this point it was fortunate that Mother Austin was always able to borrow money without interest from one of her friends as she needed to do so in order to purchase the property for the black school in Biloxi. Her name was enough to guarantee the investment, for as she put it, "It is a saying here that whatever I undertake prospers."[174]

Rightfully so, for her projects had all been successful, and borrowed money always repaid right on time. In New Orleans she had organized several different works for the benefit of the blacks because she had resolved during the late war to assist them in any way possible. At Notre Dame de Bon Secours she aided the Holy Family Sodality for the mulattoes and blacks, annually prepared their children for the reception of the sacraments just as she and sisters did for the blacks in the Boys' House of Refuge, and when the Notre Dame pastor, Nicholas Berchem, planned to open a school for the black parish children, Mother Austin assisted him with the raffle to finance the venture.[175] Unfortunately, the school was burned down one week after it opened in the Irish Channel because both the German and Irish neighbors were adamantly opposed to it.[176] Repetitions of arson on two other occasions closed the school permanently. Austin's efforts for the blacks were more successful. When Monseignor Herbert Vaughan, who was to become the Bishop of Salford within several months of his visit to New Orleans, collected for his missionary college in 1872, he told Mother Austin that he hoped to send sisters over to teach the blacks. She promised to assist by sheltering the sisters until they could obtain a convent of their own, and for her help he sent her the *London Tablet* gratis for a number of years.[177] When the next emissary from Mill Hill, Canon Peter L. Benoit, came to the city three years later, Mother Austin helped him also with introductions to generous donors. He commented upon her extraordinary "anxiety for the welfare of the Negroes," and was even more surprised to learn as they visited the children in the St. Alphonsus classrooms, that even the smallest Irish American grew up with a heritage which included a "hatred of England" as intense as a love of Ireland.[178]

Before he left by riverboat with a gift from Mother Austin of one of her books, Benoit noted in his diary, "I said Mass at the convent for Mother Austin's intentions as my thanks for all her kindness to our work" for the benefit of the blacks.[179] He also jotted down several points which he found "striking with regard to the inhabitants" of this city he had thought was French, but which proved to be cosmopolitan with almost everyone able to speak English. In the Channel he noticed the nationalism, as "the German sees his children discarding their Mother-tongue. . . . Redemptorists are alarmed at this, feeling that the loss of the German tongue may be followed by a loss of Faith."[180] He was as astounded as to "the great number of Irish and the great impetus the Irish have given to Religion" as to their feeling against England, "more intense than it is in Ireland itself." From the archbishop he learned that the Negroes were taken care of in all the French parishes, "where they occupy pews in one of the aisles . . . and are quite satisfied with their position."[181] Benoit also noted conditions which were greatly affecting the work of the Church. When stated by the natives these conditions found no belief in the North. But Benoit noted that the diocese and "this famous city" were in financial trouble in large measure because of "the present gigantic swindling" which has thrown into poverty the natives who had so generously supported the Church in the past.[182] Mother Austin found that the situation called for creativity and cooperation in the cause of charity. She had always tried to awaken in the students in the schools and the working girls in their sodalities a real concern for the less fortunate, especially the orphans.

Thus Mother Austin simply reached out further in this time of economic depression, and involved charitable lay people as auxiliaries. Each Christmas season was a time of special sharing in which she involved the families of the school children and a special group of parish ladies, who according to one of the memoirs, were formed into a charitable association. These "deserving ladies . . . who were proud to contribute in no small measure and with amazing success to the annual Christmas assistance to the poor," were certainly not rich and some had large families.[183] Annually they loaned every classroom a large wash basket so that each child could bring as a birthday gift to the Infant Christ some "little article . . . handkerchief, bar of soap, stockings, pair of socks, box of candy." Many of the children gave several times, one of the memoirs recorded, but for those too poor to drop anything in "the basket of treasures, we prudently reported that to one of our personal friends or assisting ladies," who donated dolls and other gifts. These were then slipped secretly to the poor to be placed in the basket, and "to save them from humiliation, we made them promise to keep what we gave them a profound secret."[184] Knowledgeable from their visits to the sick poor, the sisters gave in the names of the families in greatest need, with the number of children and their ages. Then Mother Austin and the sisters worked for two weeks setting up the baskets, three or four from each of the classroom hampers, with appropriate gifts for the family members. At the last moment, with the help of the ladies and the generosity of grocers and butchers, a good supply of foodstuff was added.[185]

According to one of the young Mercy participants in the annual event, the sisters "on Christmas eve, two to a basket, navigated all over the city, armed with the names and addresses of the destitute families. . . . Only the mercy of God,"[186] declared one tiny nun, "preserved our arms from being broken, for those baskets were heavily loaded. No rich man could enjoy a better dinner on Christmas, thank God, and they had provision enough for a week. Many of them received us with tears trickling down their faces." Like Catherine McAuley placing her House of Mercy "in the vicinity of the wealthy" to remind them to give alms, so Mother Austin worked to bring the needs of the destitute to the attention of those who were fortunate.[187] As Josephine Warde organized the "Young Economists" in Cork "to make warm clothing for poor little ones," so Mother Austin involved the pupils in all of her schools, even when they were far from wealthy, to assist the needy.[188] At the same time that she worked as if everything depended upon her exertions, she was giving herself over to a whole-hearted dependence upon Divine Providence. In fact, her deep trust in the goodness of God seemed so imprudent now and again that it frightened her sisters. But she would say, "If God helped us through all our other undertakings, He will not desert us now."[189] Her reliance on God's love and mercy showed forth especially when she took in more orphans than the sisters believed that they could shelter and feed. Once she explained her feelings on this point.

> Like most of my countrypeople I do the thing first, and reflect after—but in this matter no one could make me believe that I am wrong. . . . If I should find a hundred orphans who had no other way of being brought up Catholics, I should take them at once and trust to God. He is bound to help me, for the work is one of incessant labor and anxiety, and is undertaken solely for His sake. If I opened a dancing school or a saloon, I could not look for help from Him, but He must help what is done only for His honor. . . . People tell me differently—I listen, but follow the instincts of my faith all the same.[190]

In spite of the last statement, Mother Austin occasionally asked her advisor and confidant, Bishop James O'Connor, for his advice on a personal matter and then followed it. The year she celebrated the twenty-fifth anniversary of her reception into the Mercy community, such a point occurred as she had decided to change her lifestyle if necessary in order to advance in holiness.

> When I reflect in particular on what I ought to avoid in order to become more holy, it seems to me that if I resolved never again to write or rather to publish anything, my progress in virtue would be much more rapid. I have collected matter for a work I thought of bringing out, and I have translated from the Spanish Louis of Grenada's Treatise on the Passion, or a good deal of it. I say to myself: Let me publish these, and I shall write no more. But again, why should I not burn these, and have done with writing? . . .

On one hand, I fear that writing is a hindrance to perfection to my case. On the other, I sometimes think I do some good by writing. People read my books who might not read other good books, and hundreds of people who know me in this city, for instance, will buy a book because it is written by me, and so the circulation of good books is promoted — a great thing these times.[191]

Mother Austin then suggests various ways in which writing might hinder her advancement towards holiness. She might be tempted "to be proud of the little talent I have . . . or my peace of mind might be ruffled when a work of mine is not well received."[192] She even wonders "if I might . . . do my duties better if my whole mind were concentrated on them," and she allows herself to read secular works because of her writing also.

Yet in conscience, I cannot say that I neglect the duties of my office, only that they might be better done if I applied wholly to them. I sometimes think writing or translating a good book is one of the ways in which I can fulfill my vow to instruct the ignorant. Now, what am I to do? My tastes and inclinations lean to literature, and to write sometimes seems almost a necessity for me. But I could give up all that if I thought God required it. And though I try to write only for a high motive, yet if I knew it to be more pleasing to God that I should not write at all, I would do the more pleasing thing. And indeed nearly all I have written has been done in compliance with the request of persons whom I could not well refuse.[193]

Then she closed with the declaration that until she hears from him, she will be praying daily to the Holy Spirit and concluded with the promise, "I shall with God's help follow your advice."[194] Almost immediately a positive answer was on its way back to New Orleans, and the material that she had already collected for the *Annals* was saved from a fiery sacrifice. She thanked him graciously and mentioned how limited her hours for writing were, but "I will try to make the best of them."[195]

Her immediate project was to return to the collection of information from Ireland for the first volume of the *Annals*, the work which had been postponed by the epidemic and would have been thrust aside if her director had thought it best for her spiritual growth. Fortunately for the Mercy Institute, his decision was favorable toward her continued literary work. The Limerick chronicles described her renewed efforts to coax her reluctant Irish correspondents to send more data:

Mother M. Austin Carroll resumed her pen . . . made application again earnestly "for profuse descriptive information both serious and entertaining." The result of this second appeal may be found in the book itself — though in it cannot be discovered the remodeling needed from the gifted pen; nor the research which in so many cases gives "Religious, historic, or amusing records of sites" now occupied by Convents of Mercy in the dear Old Island of Saints. Yet all that must have taxed well her already filled time.[196]

That last point was certainly true, for the three years after the quarantine of 1878 were exceptionally busy for Mother Austin for several reasons. Primarily, she wished to move ahead with the endeavors planned prior to the epidemic even though the general economy at the time was in a real depression. "I have an awful fear of debt," she said, "especially now when there is so much scandal flying about in connection with debts of persons who should set the brightest example of honesty."[197] In spite of her fear, the depression caused her to carry a debit column close to $5,000, until the sale of the first volume of the Mercy *Annals* wiped out the whole debt.[198]

Although that period was a poor one financially, it was especially rich in vocations, and Mother Austin felt that the three sisters lost to yellow fever were calling down God's blessings in the wealth of new members. By the end of 1881, the third year after the epidemic, the community had increased from forty-seven to sixty-eight. Of course, the new members, like the four candidates from Ireland, were still in the process of their novitiate training. The number of babies in the crèche also increased after the fever decimation. Hence, when a brick home (L on plan 2) adjacent to the House of Mercy (K on plan 2) became available, Mother Austin saw it as an opportunity to obtain larger quarters for the crèche, which was drastically over-crowded. Mother Austin and the sisters managed the purchase by selling property that belonged to one of the sisters. This sale brought in almost enough to buy the lot facing St. Mary Street and abutting the Mercy property at 1021 St. Andrew Street. The remainder of the cost was obtained by selling the former crèche building to a buyer who would remove it from the site.[199] Thus for the third time, Mother Austin managed to enlarge the playground for the school children when she purchased property. Spurred by the opportunity in 1879, Mother Austin acquired the larger crèche rather suddenly, but several other projects completed that year had begun prior to the epidemic. Such were the Lourdes Oratory dedicated to Mary Immaculate and erected in the convent, St. Joseph's School for the blacks in Biloxi, as already mentioned, and a chapel established at the Boys' House of Refuge where the number of weekly religion classes was doubled.[200]

Completed that year also was Mother Austin's translation from the Spanish of Luis of Granada's meditations on the passion of Christ.[201] Among her works it was one of her favorites, in large measure because of the sensitive treatment of the passion. Like Catherine McAuley, Mother Austin had deep devotion to Christ in His sufferings. Also, she especially liked the clarity of the treatise on meditative prayer. "I will be so glad to have a reliable book of this kind for beginners," who she found often had "trouble in making meditation."[202] To the translation she appended the method of assisting at Mass in honor of the passion, and the Way of the Cross, both from the *Little Companion of the Sisters of Mercy.*[203] Like her life of *Clement Hofbauer*, these meditations carried the imprimatur of Cardinal McCloskey and, like all her works published in his lifetime, the approbation of Archbishop Perché. That year Mother Austin wrote an article for a San Francisco publication printed in behalf of the street waifs there.[204] Probably, this article was done as a favor for Mother Baptist Russell, who shared with Mother Austin mutual friendship and involvement with the problems of large ports such as epidemics and street youngsters.

One last piece of literary business in 1879 was Mother Austin's trip to see her publishers in New York, Lawrence Kehoe of the Catholic Publication Society and Patrick O'Shea. With convent finances so low, Austin wished to arrange to receive her annual percentages more quickly.[205] Austin Carroll might also have planned to make preliminary arrangements for the publication of the Mercy *Annals*, at that time projected as a series of three volumes. While this was a possibility, it was definite that Mother Austin contacted a number of Mercy motherhouses along the way to urge them to work on the historical accounts of their foundations for the Mercy *Annals*. Since she traveled on a railroad pass, it cost nothing but the effort to write ahead for hospitality, to stop a day or two at each major Mercy convent along the train route. Thus Mother Austin could encourage the sisters who were already compiling data, and coax the others to begin. Mother Austin had been so successful in accomplishing her research through correspondence that modern writers have assumed that Austin traveled to Ireland and England prior to 1866 to gather materials for the biography of the Mercy foundress and that she went abroad later to get information for the *Annals*.[206] That fanciful assumption is false. The reality is that she kept busy with her assignments on the American missions and relegated her writing to odd times. Fortunately, she was extraordinarily persuasive in her appeals for data, and counted among her friends and confidants many a Mercy correspondent whom she had never met in person.[207] Hence, she rejoiced that since she had to attend to business in New York in 1879, she could arrange at the same time to meet some of these Mercy friends. At the same time she could visit their schools and institutions to gather new ideas.

All along the route mutual joy erupted as Mother Austin met face to face with her pen friends—in Cincinnati, M. Baptist Kane; at St. Xavier's near Pittsburgh, M. Elizabeth Strange; and in Worcester, M. Jerome Shubrick. Here and there Austin also renewed old acquaintances—in Philadelphia, M. Patricia Waldron who had worked with her in Manchester; in New

York, M. Augustine McKenna, who had visited New Orleans to recuperate; in Brooklyn, her advisor Bishop James O'Connor, also in town on business; in Providence, her school chum M. Juliana Purcell; in Manchester, M. Gonzaga O'Brien who was her companion in such activities as sodality, library, and choir; and of course, M. Xavier Warde, upon whom age had taken its toll in mind and body.[208] "I found her much impaired in every way," Austin said, but the years had brought a new dimension, too.[209] As she found Mother Xavier "more gentle and kind in manner than ever I had seen her, and really careful of her Sisters," showing in her final years some of the gentleness that Austin had loved in Josephine Warde. Then too, the more experienced she herself became, the better Austin could appreciate Xavier's firmness.

One might wonder what the sisters had to say of their visitor from New Orleans. However, only Cincinnati and Worcester gave details of the visit of Austin and her young companion, Mary Antonia McKinley. The Worcester chronicles noted that "Reverend M. Austin of New Orleans . . . charmed and edified the Sisters during her brief stay."[210] The chronicler in Cincinnati wrote that Mother Austin, who had "long been expected . . . entertained the community with amusing stories of the times and doings in their Southern home." She "paid a flying visit to St. Edward's . . . St. Patrick's," and two hospitals.[211] Then before she left, the sisters from St. Patrick's came up to spend the evening with the visitors. The supreme compliment of these sisters was their claim that "the genial holy Mother" reminded them of their "dear departed Reverend Mother Teresa."[212] Unfortunately, no annals recorded Austin's Manchester visit twenty-three years after she was first assigned to New England. For her part, Mother Austin referred in letters to her "delightful visit" with Mary Gonzaga O'Brien, "faithful ally . . . going after the backsliders,"[213] Father MacDonald, "the holiest priest I ever knew," and, of course, with Mother Xavier Warde, whose condition was distressing.[214] "I was truly pained to see her so delicate," have been praying for her, "did not think she'd live a month," and wondered if she would even be able to relate her memoirs.[215] Based on her brief visit, Mother Austin thought the finest schools were those of Patricia Waldron and Elizabeth Strange at St. Xavier's, and that the best south of those were her own in New Orleans. With the exception of Latrobe and Philadelphia, she found the schools "very close," and judged her own better "as to furnishing, ventilation, etc.[216] But our doors and windows are open almost every day, and we don't require fire twenty times a year." She thought that Mercy schools in general were just about "equal to those of other religious."[217]

After the quick trip, which Mother Austin always called "her tour," she dashed home to the Irish Channel to seek ways to improve her schools further. She must have been spurred on by exceptionally fine Mercy schools, as she said later, "I have a sort of ambition to have things which are done for God, done with the utmost perfection. Hence I give the closest attention to schools, and do not want to be surpassed by any—that is, when I hear others are better . . . I exert myself to equal or surpass them."[218] Thus, summer classes for the teachers and improvements in both quantity and quality were regular and constant in the schools already staffed by Mother Austin's community. Just prior to her trip she had staffed special evening religion classes at the Newsboys Home. The members of the St. Vincent de Paul Society had asked Mother Austin, whose charity for the street waifs was already legendary, to prepare the newsboys for the sacraments in regular classes as she did at the Boys' House of Refuge. These gentlemen, who had established the boys in a building next to the newspaper, willingly financed a closed carriage two evenings a week to transport the sisters so that they need not be on the street late.[219] With the inauguration of the Home and the catechism classes, Austin donated an organ, taught the boys hymns, and played each Sunday for their Mass. After the fine reception of one semester, Mother Austin expanded the educational opportunities for the newsboys by adding basic classes in the three Rs, as the archbishop thought the work was worthwhile enough to permit the Mercies to be out several evenings a week.[220]

Perché was also happy that Mother Austin could answer affirmatively when invited in 1880 to staff the schools of St. Michael Parish. Reverend Thomas Heslin, pastor of the Irish Channel parish, told Austin Carroll that he was most anxious to have the Sisters of Mercy staff his two schools, but because he was still paying the indebtedness on the parish buildings, he could not purchase a convent.[221] Mother Austin believed that her teachers could commute for a few years until the community could afford to purchase a residence near the schools on Annunciation Square. To assist the sisters with funds, the pastor assigned to them the salaried positions of parish organist and choir director, and agreed that Austin could establish a circulating library.[222] Mother Austin not only loved to encourage reading and spread good books, but she also liked the opportunity the library gave the sisters to meet and become more friendly with the individuals who did not have children in school at the time. The more friends the sisters could make in the parish the better, because Austin intended to establish a school for blacks later. The building might not be safe from the arsonists' torches, however, until the convent was nearby, for Mother Austin felt confident that neither the German nor the Irish neighbors in the Channel would set a fire that might endanger the sisters. For the time being, she bowed to what Catherine McAuley called "the particular ideas and feelings" of a place.[223] Three years later, and two days after the convent was established, Mother Austin opened her school for the blacks without any type of problem.

"Money at my touch melts either in charity or in making improvements," said Mother Austin Carroll, and the latter were in large number in the Irish Channel motherhouse in the years just before and after 1880.[224] The large convent in St. Alphonsus Parish had been promised to the sisters before they left St. Louis, planned by one of the Redemptorists, and funded by the parishioners, who donated generously to defray the cost of school and convent. Redemptorist Henry Giesen, their ecclesiastical superior, said that he did not put the convent in the name of the sisters lest it became entangled in diocesan debt, but that it was their home.[225] With absolute trust in the statement of their appointed superior, Mother Austin spent substantial amounts in making improvements just as if the sisters possessed the deeds. Earlier, Austin had financed the landscaping of the yards, walks, and gardens, the installing of gutters on each of the buildings, and the fencing of all the properties, the asylum alone costing $4,000. She had a second cistern constructed in the convent to hold 22,000 gallons, for which she had pipes installed to carry water to each of the four floors. At the back of the convent she had a gallery erected along the entire length of the building and had benches set up in its shade. From the convent to the out buildings she had a covered walk erected, shielded both walk and building with lattice-work arbors, and had the area beneath the porch and all the walks paved. Turning her attention again to the interior, she had some repairs and plastering done in both convent and the school, and decorated all the halls with Biblical quotations, lovely in artistic calligraphy and the delicate water colors of the sisters.[226]

These religious decorations were greatly admired by visitors, especially the Sisters of Mercy who came to New Orleans. Mother Augustine McKenna remained a guest for several months in 1878, Sister Juliana Purcell in 1880, and Mother Jerome Shubrick in the winter months of 1880–1881.[227] Mothers Augustine and Jerome were down South in Mid-winter, the former to recruit her health; both had nothing but praise for all the works of mercy they saw. Juliana Purcell came down during vacation, as she sought the editing and assistance of Austin in order to publish her retreat meditations. It was a joyful time for these old friends; and upon her return home Juliana wrote, "Never have I met a sweeter set of Sisters . . . in the pleasantest visit I ever made. Your unparalleled generosity can never be repaid, but I will ask God to assume the debt and repay you in graces."[228] She dedicated her book to Austin, "whose tried and true friendship has, from early childhood, blessed and brightened my life."[229] Along with editing Juliana's manuscript, Austin also prepared two school plays for the printer, one of them *Marie Antoinette*, which her students had staged so often.[230] Primarily, however, Austin's limited time for literature was spent editing and expanding notes for the *Annals*, or else readying two special books for the approaching

Mercy anniversary. These were a French translation of the Mercy Rule and an American reprint of the Kinsale meditations honoring Our Lady of Mercy.[231] Yet, all of the others were as nothing when compared to the compilation of the *Annals*.

Many of the convents abroad, in spite of Mother Austin's urgent letters, were as miserly with information as they were slow in getting it to her. Several houses sent data too late for the first volume, so that Austin worked some of their material into the second volume as the preface to their mission to Australia.[232] Editing and compiling, however, were far down Austin's priority list of activities, for in 1880 she began preparations for a branch convent in St. Martinville in the heart of French Louisiana. Arrangements begun in the fall were completed early in 1881, thus making this "the jubilee branch" of the New Orleans Mercies.[233] A newspaper announcement of the new mission mentioned the "cordial sanction" of Archbishop Perché, the donation by the pastor, Reverend Ange Marie Félix Jan, of a "suitable house," and the fact that "the same prolific" Mercy community was soon to have a second branch at Jeanerette.[234] Mother Austin explained to a friend in early January 1880, "We are to open a Convent in St. Martinsville in March and one in Jeannerette a little later. Both towns are in the beautiful [Bayou] Teche country immortalized by Longfellow and containing a large proportion of Acadiens."[235] Seeking a superior made Austin recall Catherine McAuley's comment, "Feet and hands are numerous enough but the heads are nearly gone," at least "among those we can spare from this house," appended Austin. Her letter also mentioned that everyone spoke French in Evangeline's town, St. Martinville, but that there were more English-speaking in the village of Jeanerette, where "the pastor [John D. Flanagan] is an Irishman."[236]

As to New Orleans, "Even in our French schools it is all but impossible to get the children to speak French," Mother Austin said, "I often think it is a pity to have churches for nationalities who will all soon speak only English."[237] Once again, she was suffering from the effects of German antipathy. Yet her letters do not reveal that she considered it unjust that each German teacher was receiving a thirty-five-dollar salary at the same time that the German priests were telling her there was no money to pay their Mercy teachers any salary at all. She may have referred to this indirectly when she wrote, "Things that seem dishonest to me are done without scruple."[238] Mother Austin answered the problem in two ways. First, every Sunday "We have Mass said in our Chapel for the Clergy . . . I never let a word be said against them, but I cannot close my eyes to facts."[239] Secondly, she protested the injustice of the situation to those who arranged it.[240] Her letters were not only in vain, but complaints about her "scathing epistles" were sent to the new episcopal ally of the Germans, the coadjutor, Bishop

Francois Xavier Leray.[241] Having just been appointed Administrator of Temporal affairs in the archdiocese so that he could settle its indebtedness and avoid bankruptcy, Leray was quick to lend an ear and immediate credence to these German complaints.[242] The same priests certainly had not brought their protests about Mother Austin's "bold letters" and branch houses to Perché, because he had given his blessing to each branch convent, agreeing with Bishops Elder and Quinlan that in the small Gulf Coast towns the convents could not survive at the time as independent motherhouses.

For several reasons it was unfortunate that Archbishop Perché was in France in 1880 trying to raise money. The Mercy election was scheduled for that summer and Austin Carroll heard indirectly that several German Redemptorists, angry about the branch convents, wished to have her out of the parish. Had she seen the letters between Leray and the German rector, Benedict Neithart, she would have had proof that the rumors were perfectly true.[243] Neithart insisted on examining the Mercy Rule to see if Mother Austin could be elected after an appointment of six years, even though this matter was within the province of their ecclesiastical superior, Ferreol Girardey, CSSR. As prefect of the schools, this American priest knew the Mercy teachers well and esteemed Mother Austin as a friend and as a religious. Austin termed Neithart's attempt to change the structure of their community "unjust interference" in convent affairs; he claimed that "her Reverence" had not treated him with the special respect due the rector. However, like the unfriendly witness in court, Neithart's report to Leray bore the additional weight of antipathy when it stated that, according to the Rule, "Mother Austin may be elected Superior once or twice yet."[244] He thought it better not to forbid her election, as he told Leray, "In my humble opinion . . . we could not prevent her being elected, and then it would be a greater triumph her her." He then bestowed the reluctant praise that she followed her Rule "pretty well . . . whatever her adversaries may say to the contrary." Austin told a friend that they were doing well and "thank God, never without our share of the cross, and from unexpected sources."[245]

Austin also regretted the absence of Perché, without mentioning that she needed his support against the false accusations of the clique. "To those who work for God and try to do a little good, this [absence of the arch-bishop] is disheartening. But since God sees all and has patience with all, we must strive to do likewise."[246] Although Leray accepted all he heard as true and asked for no corroboration or denial of the accusations from the sisters, Mother Austin had her assistant send copies of documents pertaining to either the election or the branches to the chancery.[247] Possibly, the German priests had expected Austin Carroll to leave the parish in the face of their opposition as Catherine Grant had done earlier. Instead, Austin told Neithart that she intended "to remain . . . whether as superior or subject," which fact, like the rest of the German machinations, became a permanent record in the history of the local church when the Germans shared their aims and ends with their episcopal ally, Leray.[248] The Germans also involved Bishop Quinlan in their conflict because he objected to their trying to close his branch convents from which the Mercies staffed seven of his poor parochial schools, three of them black. Neithart thought it essential that Leray cut off these branches from New Orleans and portrayed himself as Leray's defender against such "enemies" as Archbishop Perché, Bishop Quinlan," other high dignitaries," and "her Reverence," Mother Austin Carroll.[249]

If she had known, Austin would have been pleased to find herself in such good company. All of this German interference must have come as an unpleasant surprise for her, however, because she had taken care to deal directly with Archbishop Perché on all important matters precisely in order to avoid this type of situation. Although she steered clear of several German priests, Austin had been working closely and in harmony for a decade with the Redemptorists who supervised the parish schools, Fathers Faivre and Berchem of Notre Dame de Bon Secours, and Fathers Meredith, Duffy, and Girardey of St. Alphonsus.[250] The German priests, on the other hand, were involved in St. Mary's Assumption Parish, the German schools and asylum and the direction of the German sisters. They really did not have any official connection with the Sisters of Mercy, yet they knew that the tuition collected by the Mercies from their pupils was never sufficient because the sisters allowed the poorest children to attend without payment. That financial matter, the branch houses, and the fact that Mother Austin had dared to protest the cancellation of the salaries of the Mercy teachers, seemed to have been the prime causes of contention. Incidentally, the sisters were still struggling along without regular salaries and managing to survive with the help sent from the branches plus a number of raffles. Nationalism was a part of the problem, also, though Neithart wrote Leray that Austin was the "most clever female" he had ever known, for "she can talk and write and carry her point like no other woman."[251] Neithart himself was said to have the orator's "gift of winning hearts," and he certainly coaxed Leray, a native of France, to the anti-Irish side very quickly. However, Neithart considered Austin the politician, claiming he had yet "to meet the first Irish priest or bishop whom she had not won over."[252] Besides possessing the tremendous reverence of the Irish for each "priest of God," Austin Carroll had just as deep an affection for her compatriots as for her native land. Even though Austin was most gracious to the clergy in general, that was hardly a factor in the large number of priests, including a number of Redemptorists, who were her lifelong friends.[253]

Because they had worked closely with Mother Austin and had come to know her special enthusiasm and zeal, Redemptorists Meredith, Duffy, Girardey, and Faivre had each grown from associates to personal friends. It was precisely because they were so well acquainted with Austin and her sisters that their opinions differed from that of the Germans. Father Girardey probably knew Austin and her community better than any of the other parish priests, as he had been named several times by Archbishop Perché to make the annual visitation, had often served as community confessor, and had dealt with the teachers as prefect of the schools.[254] He testified to Mother Austin that in her appointment of six years prior to the first election and

> in establishing branch houses, you have in all things been guided by the direction of your ecclesiastical superiors, and have conformed to the customs of the Sisters of Mercy in other parts of the world. You have never undertaken anything of importance without properly consulting according to the directions of the Rules, and you have ever suffered yourself to be guided and directed in all matters of importance by your ecclesiastical superiors. This I know![255]

Girardey also thought that her accusers must be "shamefully prejudiced," for in his opinion as prefect of the parish schools, "No one can justly accuse you of doing any injustice to St. Alphonsus Schools."[256] Then he concluded with the fact that he had been working with Mother Austin and her sisters for a decade and "never had any difficulty . . . probably because" he had done his duty "without interfering with what did not concern me."[257] The sisters evidently agreed with Father Girardey because, in the election that August, they unanimously voted Mother Austin their superior.[258]

Relieved that the interference of the clique in their community government had been overcome, Mother Austin concerned herself with the approaching golden anniversary of the Institute of Mercy and the preservation of the spirit of the foundress in her deep-South community. Constantly on the alert for more material on Catherine McAuley, Austin sought a copy of the Coleridge tribute to the Mercy foundress in one of her letters,[259] mentioned her desire to maintain Catherine McAuley's spirit in another,[260] and worked her new data about the foundress into the *Annals* which were to come off the presses in time for the jubilee on December 12, 1881.[261] Of herself and her sisters, Mother Austin confided to a friend, "We apply ourselves most earnestly" during the annual retreat;

"all about me are happy and contented";[262] and added with pride, "We have a most fervent community, thank God."[263] Yet her letters frequently closed with the request, "Pray for my flock that they may never lose their fervor."[264] With one exception the works of these Mercies were appreciated. Only from two or three German priests came harsh words about these Irish Sisters. A Methodist minister, in New Orleans three dozen years, paid tribute to that which he witnessed.

> Never till I went to Louisiana did I behold the living and most perfect exemplification of a Christian's spirit exhibited in the conduct and benefactions of those denominated Sisters. . . . They feed the hungry and clothe the naked. . . . Calm and gentle as angels they stay at their posts amid the most frightful epidemics. . . . These angels are to be seen in all our hospitals . . . and in other places where their services are required, irrespective of the distinction of name, religion, party, clime, or nation.[265]

During her first decade in New Orleans Mother Austin thus found that the same works of mercy somehow called forth from different sources both praise and blame. Brushing aside reactions to both, she managed to forge ahead, wrapped as she was in the protective cloak of her intense desire to follow Catherine McAuley's ideals and shielded by her escutcheon emblazoned, like her ring, with "Ad majorem Dei gloriam." Although Austin reminded her young sisters so often that their intention should always be to work for the glory of God that they grew tired of hearing her motto, she could also make them laugh by calling them to chapel with "all hands on their knees."[266] Mother Austin's sorrows, as they were apparent to her community, came not from the complaints of the faultfinding clique, but primarily from the loss of her sisters. The rapidly deteriorating health of several caused her to say, "We try not to take consumptives but they get in, and we find it out only when we cannot have the heart to send them out."[267] One of Austin's first New Orleans sisters died unexpectedly in the spring of 1880,[268] and shortly thereafter Austin received word of the death of her beloved first superior, Mother Josephine Warde in Cork. Austin's sister there, Mary Dominica Carroll, wrote that Josephine "was the soul of honor and the living copy of our holy Rule. . . . Her meekness, patience, and mercy were inexhaustible."[269] Austin's own tribute to Josephine Warde was a loving twelve-page memoir published in the first volume of the Mercy *Annals*.[270]

Mother Austin left just such a permanent record, also, of the great contributions of another of Catherine McAuley's early companions, Sister

Clare Augustine Moore, who died in 1880. Clare Augustine completed not only magnificent works of illumination, but like her sister Mother Clare Moore of Bermondsey, wrote an excellent historical manuscript concerning the early days of the Mercy Institute.[271] When Mary Dominica's letter told of twelve coffins in the Mercy vault at Cork in 1880, Mother Austin realized that New Orleans lost more Mercies in twelve years than Cork had in forty.[272] Already fifteen sisters who had served in the Irish Channel had joined the "Mercy community in heaven," the high total being due primarily to yellow fever, though several sisters had died of consumption.[273] Austin commented with the words of Catherine McAuley as she often did, "Thus we may say as did our holy Foundress, 'the tomb is never closed in our regard.' "[274] Austin made certain that the deceased sisters had their share of remembrances in the hundred Masses for the approaching fiftieth anniversary. She also took steps to "mark with new benedictions the Golden Jubilee of the Mercy Institute" by obtaining indulgences for each visit made to each of the convent oratories, one dedicated to the Sacred Heart and the other to Mary Immaculate."[275] Of course, marking the day of Catherine McAuley's profession on December 12 was the anniversary celebration of a solemn high Mass in St. Alphonsus Church. Present were "about fifty priests, representing all the orders and churches in the city . . . and some 3,000 persons, including pupils, orphans, and friends assembled to do honor to the ilustrious . . . saint-like Catherine McAuley."[276]

Mother Austin Carroll explained that the "spirit of the festival was one of thanksgiving, for God had wonderfully preserved and blessed the Institute that 'rose out of nothing,' as the Foundress had said fifty years before."[277] Besides the spiritual aspect of the day, Austin thought that Catherine McAuley would like the poor to enjoy some of the celebration. Hence she arranged the following: "fifty poor women partook of a substantial breakfast, and thrice fifty poor children were regaled in a similar manner in the school-rooms, relief was sent to fifty poor families, fifty books were added to the children's library." Nor did Austin forget the newsboys, as "twice fifty small gentlemen of the press, after piously assisting at Benediction in the convent chapel, adjourned to a large school-room where they ate to their hearts' content."[278] In Austin's judgment, all this was as the Foundress would have wished. One section of the jubilee celebration was a year late, as Austin was unable to locate in time *Cottage Controversy*, Catherine McAuley's publication of a catechetical story.[279] In 1881, Austin Carroll herself celebrated her half-jubilee, as the twenty-fifth anniversary was termed. After giving such a wealth of services to others through the years since her profession, Austin revealed her feelings about the Mercy Institute. The years have not been without trials and crosses. Yet I thank God daily, even hourly, for the establishment of that Order which has been home to me, and the only one in which I could live, much as I esteem all others. And despite a spot here and a wrinkle there, it is to me a mother—I can name nothing holier—something which the hand of God has touched and blessed, in whose bosom I regard it as a blessed privilege to live and a still more blessed one to die. Pray that the latter privilege may be mine.[280]

10 ANTAGONISM, BRANCHES, COMPLAINTS
The Irish Channel
1881–1886

Mother Austin Carroll could have been a passenger on a Ferris wheel during the 1880s, for all the ups and downs of that period. If 1881 carried her to the top of the cycle, the following year kept her there. Possibly, the lengthy celebration bolstered her natural endurance and enabled her better to withstand the approaching hardships. In July 1881, she had rather quietly observed the twenty-fifth anniversary of her religious vows, primarily as a spiritual commemoration. The celebration was quiet only in the sense of being for the community only, for the jubilee Mass was ablaze with alleluias, lights, and the glorious music that Mother Austin dearly loved. The chapel was exceptionally beautiful, dressed as it was in many of the jubilee gifts the sisters had prepared for Mother Austin. They knew how much she appreciated embroidered altar linens, rich vestments, and fine vessels for use in the liturgy.[1] She was delighted with their thoughtfulness, as her one request earlier had been for a grand feast for those waifs and newsboys the sisters were teaching in the evening several times a week. One is reminded of that true daughter of a saintly mother, Sister Catherine Seton of New York, who on her anniversary, had asked for gifts of clothing for the destitute.[2] Both petitions were granted, of course, and the poor in New York got their outfits just as the newsies in New Orleans ate to their hearts' content. The boys had written, probably with the help of one of the reporters, a clever address for the jubilarian, and this oration did not neglect to express their gratitude for the spiritual and educational benefits and opportunities Mother Austin had worked to procure for them.[3]

"When we are men, our lives will praise and bless you louder than any tongue can do," promised the orator, and the other boys seconded the words with their loudest cheers.[4] Touched by their sincerity, Mother Austin treasured their witty tribute and mentioned it more often in her letters than the more usual musical entertainment of the children or the play performed by the novices. It seems that Mother Austin had kept her jubilee private lest it encroach on the public celebration to be held five months later to commemorate both the fiftieth anniversary of Catherine McAuley's profession and the inauguration of the Institute of Mercy. Not only was the golden jubilee celebration in New Orleans a grand success, but for months afterward, Austin received letters and clippings which described special jubilee events in Mercy convents all over the world. The *New Zealand Times* reported a reception in Ponsonby and a school drama in Wellington. Australian papers carried news of Perth and Melbourne,[5] and Austin received data from Vincent Whitty near Brisbane and Evangelista Fitzpatrick in Adelaide. News items arrived from both Ireland and England, also, as Austin learned of a hospital in Dublin, a chapel in Bermondsey, and that "the room in which the foundress had died" was being dedicated in Baggot Street.[6] From Clifden Teresa White and from Birmingham Juliana Hardman, superiors appointed by Catherine McAuley, sent Austin their news, as did Margaret Mary Byrne, Catherine McAuley's young cousin in Bermondsey. All the news was being forwarded as grist to be ground and refined by Austin Carroll for the Mercy *Annals*.[7]

Several other Mercies who had been personal acquaintances of the foundress also corresponded with Mother Austin from across the Atlantic. Mother Aloysius O'Connell of Sunderland wrote of planting a tree as a long-lived symbol of the Institute. From Liverpool came the sad news of two who had been Catherine McAuley's novices and whose memories Austin had begun to gather while receiving hospitality as she awaited the day to take ship for America in 1856. Liguori Gibson had died a few months before the jubilee and Aloysius Consitt a few months afterward.[8] Mother Austin's American correspondents sent news of the ceremonies, poetry, pageants presented, and often, the text of the jubilee sermon. By many accounts there were dozens of grand orators to sing the praise of the saintly Mercy foundress on her anniversary, and from Canada to Florida the data arrived.[9] The *Terra Nova Advocate* emphasized the fact that the Sisters of Mercy in Newfoundland who arrived with Mother Francis Creedon were the first to reach the American continent, a fact which often needs clarification even a century later. By the golden jubilee the Newfoundland Mercies were thriving with a half dozen convents and institutions in several dioceses. The *Connecticut Catholic* listed the foundations sent forth from the Hartford diocese as those in Rochester, Nashville, and that in Macon, which had transferred from Columbus, and earlier, from St. Augustine, Florida.[10]

Arriving in Mother Austin's mailbox that year was a veritable plethora of jubilee material in praise of the Mercy foundress, Our Lady of Mercy, or the members of the Institute. As 1882 wore on, Austin managed to have the local papers reprint items like the sermon of Rev. Nicholas Walsh, SJ, at Baggot Street, and some of the poetry of Dr. Patrick Murry and Mary Alphonsus, among others.[11] From California came data from Austin's dear friend, Baptist Russell, and poetry from Harriet Skidmore; from Pennsylvania, data from Elizabeth Strange and a poem from Eleanor Donnelly; and from Cincinnati, data from Baptist Kane and Susan Elder's poetry.[12] In all of these items, plus the plays and pageants that schools presented in every clime, Mother Austin took great pleasure, not in a triumphal way so much as with delight that Catherine McAuley was becoming better known. Only after people learned of her sanctity would they ask for Catherine's intercession, and not until then, would the miracles begin to appear. Perennial hope led Austin to look forward to the day that the holiness of Catherine McAuley would be recognized officially. In fact, Austin's aim in writing the biography of the foundress and one of her purposes in compiling the Mercy *Annals* was her desire to bring before the public Catherine McAuley, her virtue, and her works. Austin had no idea that the *Annals* were to be responsible, also, for contributing to a stronger sense of unity in Sisters of Mercy around the globe.

Several of the Mercy chroniclers in Ireland mentioned the "large share the *Leaves from the Annals* . . . had in heightening . . . the interest felt by seculars" in the Mercy anniversary.[13] The *Annals* "came from the press only a couple of weeks before [Dec. 12] and gave great impetus to Catholic writers and filled their Journals."[14] The Limerick chronicler thought that the *Annals* "embodied again the life and spirit of Mother C. McAuley, with the devotedness and progress of her spiritual children in the Institute."[15] Although many of the Irish Mercies found in the *Annals* "much that stimulates to great sacrifice," they also found the author "too frank about adverse circumstances."[16] Because of this openness the sisters often thought that Austin Carroll was an American. One chronicler knew better, and wrote of Austin, "Though Irish, she has in no small degree imbibed the undisguised spirit of the New World's Catholic Authors."[17] Yet, the *Annals* were well received by both religious and laity in spite of Austin's tendency to be frank. Perhaps it was this honesty, as well as the peep behind convent walls that made the book so appealing to the laity. Earlier, Austin had said that the chronicles of religious were "a mine which the Catholic writer might explore to advantage," because "many a dusty folio of monastic chronicles . . . contains gems too long hidden."[18] She felt that readers would find such material both interesting and instructive. Her aim was to provide an "addition to that very small stack of pious books which are edifying to all without being tedious to any."[19]

In the annals of any religious congregation, Mother Austin knew that readers would discover unexpected features and mentioned that she herself had found, "When occasion requires, a patient endurance, a noble bravery, an invincible energy, an unconquerable activity, which go far to prove that the term "weaker sex' is a definition that has nothing to do with the soul."[20] Reviewers were generally quite complimentary, an English journal finding her style "racy of the old soil, and her selection of anecdotes very happy."[21] In Dublin *The Irish Monthly* noted that "there are a few traces of American freedom and frank personality; but it is hard to be bent on being always safe and proper without being also dull. Our Irish Nun is anything but dull."[22] Literary reviews in the United States were quite positive, one stating, "Perhaps the most important book of the season in its special department is Mother Austin Carroll's *Leaves from the Annals of the Sisters of Mercy*."[23] Austin probably preferred the critic who held that "The most indifferent reader would be delighted and the most spiritual would be profited by its perusal,"[24] for she hoped to make "a religious book as interesting as a romance." She often commented, "There are Catholic books enough, but they're mostly uninteresting and our youth will not read them."[25] Austin's friend, Bishop John Hogan of Kansas City, Missouri, said that she wrote "with warmth and tenderness . . . and with a modest and delicate pen . . . of the religious character of the women of Ireland who . . . shrink from no sacrifice in serving God and enlightening the poor." He liked the *Leaves*, thought them "charming and not likely to fade."[26]

Mother Austin and the New Orleans community, like others around the world, founded a branch during the Mercy jubilee year. This branch established in Southwest Louisiana, as previously mentioned, was special for several reasons. As it was in the heart of the Acadian area, everyone spoke French at that time; and the pastor, no English. Hence, the Irish sisters had the jolly task of learning to confess their sins in French. Another distinction was the generosity of the pastor, Père Ange Marie Félix Jan, who gave the sisters the deeds for a small pink house as a mark of his appreciation for their willingness to teach all the children of the town, girls and boys, black and white.[27] In 1882, Mother Austin bought more property to double the size of the Mercy facility, for the pupils of all the schools had increased. Of the Catholic schools for blacks across the South in the 1880s, Mother Austin thought that the Mercy-staffed black school in St. Martinville was second only to that in Pensacola. The jubilee branch was certainly unique in the transportation needed to reach it, for the sisters took the ferry to Morgan's Landing, the train from Algiers at noon to reach at midnight New Iberia, where the Mount Carmel sisters offered hospitality for the rest of the night, then a boatride up the Bayou Teche to Evangeline's remote village.[28] But the finest distinction of this pink convent on the slope next the bayou was the fact that a lovely young woman awaited the arrival of the sisters so that she could apply as a candidate, and within a month she was welcomed into the novitiate.[29]

Mother Austin was truly astounded at the beauty of the St. Martinville area and delighted with such an auspicious beginning as the arrival of a candidate upon the opening of the Acadian branch. Austin was never to forget the bayou trip from New Iberia, passing the old drawbridge and "gliding beneath the hoary trees garlanded with wreaths of gray moss" northward to St. Martinville.[30] When writing of the Bayou Teche, "the jewel of the environs," she waxed poetic.

> Its meandering course lies through . . . the fertile fields of St. Martin. Its banks are studded with substantial plantation residences . . . yet for long stretches its solitude is as unbroken as when Père Félician and Evangeline navigated its sluggish waters. It is spanned by arches of cypress and live oak, whose dark, massive foliage, heavily draped with Spanish moss, gives the whole a melancholy yet most poetic aspect. There is little underbrush between the heavy trunks, and one will frequently catch the delicious vistas of the bright green and golden yellow of cultivated fields beyond. The immortal oaks which sheltered the Indians and waved their branches to welcome the sad exiles of Acadie, lean lovingly over the bayou and embrace each other in the skies. At times, one seems to be in a gorgeous cathedral whose roof is interminable, and so closely are the leafy branches above interlocked, that in the blazing noon of a semitropical region a dim, religious light is enjoyed by the peaceful travellers below. The whispering winds that rustle through the leaves . . . the spirited rehearsals of choirs of mockingbirds . . . make this region of sunshine and shadow, of delicate fancy and elysian beauty, "glorious beyond the muse's painting."[31]

Perhaps it was too much for the muse, but Mother Austin found the words for three articles for periodicals, two on the entrancing area, and one a history of the Church in St. Martinville from its inception in colonial times down to the 1880s, when she wrote as well an entire chapter in the *Annals*.[32]

Evidently, the experience of enjoying such unusual scenery and learning the early Catholic history of this Acadian section of Louisiana, was the catalyst which precipitated Mother Austin into writing a series of descriptive articles on St. Martinville and the Gulf Coast towns where the other Mercy branches were located. She felt that articles about these Catholic areas would be interesting enough to be accepted by the editor of one of the Catholic periodicals.[33] Payment for an article would be quicker than waiting for the publishers' percentages, and convent funds were still tight, as the Mercies were teaching without any regular salary from St. Alphonsus Parish. Except for their little raffles and the minimal amounts of tuition collected, the sisters at the motherhouse depended upon the financial assistance sent from the branch convents and payments received for Mother Austin's publications. By this time, fortunately, the sale of Austin's prayerbooks and biographies brought in substantial help.[34] In addition to the articles on the bayou and Gulf Coast towns, Austin wrote one in the series on yellow fever. Besides information on the epidemic disease and its treatment, she made the point that, for many, the fever was a great blessing. The epidemic was "a last grace to many a prodigal . . . strengthened and ennobled the fervent," awakened in others a stronger dependence on God, and "opened heaven for many of the stricken."[35] Austin also noted that the epidemic had helped considerably in narrowing the breach torn open by the war between the blue and the grey, as it inspired "a splendid generosity in the victors, and a noble gratitude in the vanquished. . . . It has knit together the once sundered peoples of the North and South."[36]

Probably Mother Austin was overly optimistic, as she always had that propensity, but the thought was certainly the wish of her heart. That loving heart had been given early in her youth in a special way to Christ through devotion to His Sacred Heart, and it was her delight to learn as a Mercy novice that she shared this devotion with Catherine McAuley. Before Austin came to New Orleans, she had written the history of the spread of this devotion across Ireland as the preface to her translation of the life of Margaret Mary Alacoque.[37] Shortly after Austin's arrival in New Orleans, she established a small room at the top of the stairs as an oratory in honor of the Sacred Heart of Jesus. As funds became available, the plain little room was gradually decorated beautifully and transformed as the walls were papered, stained glass inserted in the window, and the small statue replaced by a life-sized one. The Sacred Heart Oratory had become "a thing of beauty," and to Austin Carroll, "a joy forever." From 1881 on, visitors to the oratory were able to receive special spiritual benefits,[38] and in 1882, Mother Austin established the Association of the Sacred Heart of Jesus in order to promote devotion among the members by maintaining perpetual daily prayers and an eternal flame in the oratory.[39] Members had their names carefully inscribed in the Registry, received a share in the monthly Mass for their intentions, and a perpetual remembrance after death. This New Orleans Association was patterned on that in Oscott in England, where the Mercies at Maryvale fostered devotion to the Sacred Heart. News of their perpetual lamp must have reached Austin Carroll in 1882.[40]

Other news from across the ocean that year brought the long-awaited copies of the catechetical story published by Catherine McAuley. Mother Austin explained in a letter, "Thanks to dear S. M. Elizabeth Strange I learned that Mother McAuley published a little book called *Cottage Controversy* — I sent for it in all directions and succeeded in getting it."[41]

Austin's extant letters do not specify where she found the copies after two years of writing to England and Ireland trying to locate them. Mother Austin forwarded at least six copies to friends along with her plans, "I mean to get it brought out handsomely and give it away by the hundreds among our pupils, prisoners, newsboys, etc. It contains such simple explanations of the points that bother so many of the poor and uneducated."[42] Thus it was that these precious first editions were sent in late spring and early summer of 1882 to Cincinnati, Omaha, Manchester, and Marysville, California, as well as to Archbishop Perché and Father Girardey in New Orleans. Austin's correspondents heard the praises of the McAuley work, "There's more in it than in a dozen ordinary instruction books . . . and the style is so attractive that one must read it to the end."[43] Austin asked her bishop-friends for approbations, for "it really deserves them," and she wished to use their recommendations as the preface for her reprint.[44] From extant correspondence it is impossible to know how many of Austin's other friends received first editions of *Cottage Controversy*. How rewarding it would be for a Mercy bibliophile to locate one of those copies published by the foundress about forty-five years before Austin Carroll's 1883 reprint.[45]

Because Mother Austin intended to distribute the small booklet in large quantities, she had her publisher bind hundreds of copies in paper covers so that she could afford to give plenty away. Austin thought also of the poor, for she had already had a large percentage of the Mercy *Annals* published in paperback so that they would be inexpensive as well as light enough for the sick to handle.[46] Besides getting *Cottage Controversy* reprinted, Austin edited *Mary Queen of Scots*, a school play, and wrote another called *The Tudor Sisters*.[47] Neither of these, or her article on Lady Jane Gray,[48] took very long, for Austin's literary time was needed for editing the material coming in for the second volume of the Mercy *Annals* concerning England, the Colonies, and the work of the sisters in the Crimean War in the Near East. Then, busy as she was with her community and the publications, Mother Austin took the time to encourage a young New Orleans author. Mother Austin had received *Madame Delphine* from George Cable, so sent him her thanks, "Your works are charming—perfect in their kind. . . . I do not like a few passages which seem disrespectful to my Faith, but then you have not the happiness of being a Catholic—yet."[49] Austin said that she recognized in his writing "that rarest of God's gifts, genius," and mentioned her happiness that slavery was "abolished at any cost" and her sorrow that Cable called the killer in his book an Irish boy. Even so, "nothing of the kind gave me greater pleasure since I revelled in Scott, oh, so many years ago." Her closing blessing read, "May God give you grace to use your great gifts for His glory and the good of souls—the only objects really worth striving for, as we all find out sooner or later."[50]

Then in August of 1882, Mother Austin and her sisters had another "season of anguish," as yellow fever became epidemic in Pensacola. The unacclimated sisters were recalled immediately and experienced nurses, enough to double the forces in Pensacola and Warrington, went to the stricken city. In a controversial decision, made with the consent of the bishop, Austin allowed the sisters to nurse in the hospital in shifts around the clock.[51] Thus, many of the poor who had no other help and would have succumbed at night, were able to recover. "All the poor women of the unfortunate class who died, first made their peace with God," wrote Austin to a friend, and "men who swore they believed in no God were so touched by the Sisters' devotion that they asked for Baptism."[52] The local papers were generous with their praise, quoting the doctors, the people, the firemen, the Board of Health. For instance, Dr. Edward Jones who worked in the hospital with the sisters, said "Pensacola's benediction rests on each of these good women's heads. They are braver in pestilence than was Achilles in war."[53] Mother Austin preferred to read an item that called the sisters "true daughters of Mother McAuley" as they gave "aid to the plague-stricken," not only helping to nurse the sick but "relieving generously the wants of the destitute."[54] In a letter to Xavier Warde, Austin counted 2300 cases and about 300 deaths, "an immense number for so small a place," but she believed that the "awful sickness was the road to heaven for many a soul." Her tributes were always for her sisters, who worked "uncomplainingly and cheerfully, seeing Christ in the wretched outcasts, who looked upon us as angels."[55]

At the height of the epidemic, while the Warrington sisters were nursing in Pensacola, a fire destroyed some forty buildings in the United States Naval Yard. A personal letter from the scene read, "What a loss for those devoted Sisters of Mercy. The church, convent, adjoining school buildings, and many houses were destroyed in the middle of the night. It is a great loss to Mother Austin."[56] It was, and even Austin's optimistic temperament became depressed, for a month later she wrote to Xavier, "We have cross upon cross there, and I was often tempted to withdraw the Sisters, but it would be such a blow to Religion that I couldn't do it."[57] The Warrington letter detailed the losses, "The schools were new, and many improvements about the convent had recently been made. I have not heard that anything was saved. The sisters are especially grieved on account of the chapel, where there was a beautiful altar, with pictures, chalice, etc."[58] But Austin told Mother Xavier that despite the crosses, she would not withdraw because "the Sisters are so much beloved and respected that they do a world of good in the prison, hospital, schools, instruction of adults and converts. We have there [Pensacola] the finest Colored Schools in the South."[59] After the mention of any cross, Austin usually added, like the Mercy foundress,

"Thank God." Austin also had absolute faith in Catherine McAuley's often quoted, "Without the cross, the real crown cannot come."[60] Perhaps the crown built on the crosses arrived a few years later in company with the sixth candidate to be accepted from Florida.

One cross which Austin did not reveal to her correspondents was a far greater loss than that of the chapel or chalice. When one of the sisters withdrew that fall, Mother Austin seems to have been devastated.[61] Although this sister so suddenly gone was the only one who had made a novitiate directed by Austin Carroll to fall by the wayside, Austin was profoundly affected in a reaction typical of the period. Perhaps her spirit was assuaged a bit when an official in Pensacola published a tribute declaring that "the self-abnegation of the community," their devoted service, "and tenderness in nursing entitle your Order to be pre-eminently nominated 'the Angels of Mercy.' "[62] Consolation also came when the only sister to be stricken down by the fever made a complete recovery. Upon her return to New Orleans, Mother Austin wrote that "'the dreadful days are over for the present, and for a long time, I hope."[63] It was to be just one year. Then the town of Brewton in southern Alabama, which like Pensacola, had sent generous donations to the Mercies for the fever victims when New Orleans was crushed under the heel of Yellow Jack in 1878, petitioned Mother Austin to send some of her nurses to help them. Their earlier generosity had been bread cast upon the waters, and in 1883 it returned to them a hundred-fold. Sisters of Mercy went to the aid of the Brewton people during the worst of their epidemic.[64] Such scenes were to be repeated several times more after Austin brought her sisters down to the tropics in Central America.

The saga of Mother Austin's mission to Belize had already begun before yellow fever struck Pensacola, for several Jesuit missionaries had come to New Orleans to ask the Sisters of Mercy to establish a mission branch in Belize. There they had a school for the boys, but needed religious sisters to teach the girls. The description by Reverend Henry Gillet, SJ, "of the needs of the place was such as to awaken in most of the Sisters a great zeal" to serve there as teachers of the girls.[65] Bishop Leray, upon learning of the tentative plans for the Mercy branch there, sent for Mother Austin and refused to allow sisters to go to Belize unless their every connection with the New Orleans community was to be severed in another year or so, and he did not want any funding to go forth from the archdiocese.[66] Such conditions made the Mercy mission, even as a foundation, absolutely impossible because of the impoverished condition of the people who were native to the area. The Mercy chronicles noted that "had Archbishop Perché been home, there would have been no difficulty."[67] Mother Austin notified the Jesuits that she had to decline the Belize mission under the conditions set by Leray.

Austin Carroll, with the welfare of her sisters at heart, was convinced that a Mercy convent in Belize could succeed only as a branch for several reasons. First, the sisters would periodically need to be transferred to other branches, for outsiders found the climate in British Honduras exceptionally debilitating; secondly, the British Colony would probably need some time before it began to furnish vocations to a religious community from among the students taught there by the Mercies; and lastly, though quite important as practicalities go, the motherhouse would need to furnish the finances to maintain the poor mission until such time as it could become self-supporting.[68]

Determined not to lose these prospective teachers for the Belize girls, Father Di Pietro went to Rome, and among other things, consulted Propaganda Fide about the mission.[69] From abroad he wrote Mother Austin that a branch mission was agreeable to "the Cardinal of Propaganda" and he hoped that she would be ready to go to Belize in early December.[70] Until Archbishop Perché returned and gave his consent, however, Mother Austin would not think of leaving for the tropics. Then Perché arrived, gave his approval to the branch in Belize just as he had previously consented to each of the other Mercy branches from New Orleans, and finally, blessed the sisters before their departure. Mother Austin and her six companions were accompanied to the boat by two carriages of sisters, who made the departure of the missionaries a true *bon voyage.* Wrapped in the protective cloak of the archbishop's permission and the blessing of the Roman authorities, Austin Carroll took ship with her young Mercies and headed for the small British Colony south of Mexico.[71] Earlier, Mother Teresa Maher had written Mother Austin, "What prudence and grace we Superiors need that the good work may not suffer from our impetuosity or our carelessness."[72] Perhaps Austin recalled the thought during the rough voyage across the Gulf of Mexico, and wondered if she had been careful enough about the arrangements for this branch in Central America. She had waited several years before thinking seriously about the mission, decided only after Rome had spoken, and then delayed further until she could learn the mind of the archbishop. Possibly, after all that prudent caution, she felt no worry at all and sailed as smoothly ahead as their steamer did once it began to flank the Yucatan Peninsula.

Mother Austin Carroll had sent to the local Catholic paper a news article which was published the day she left for British Honduras. Besides enumerating the missionaries and asking the readers for their prayers for the success of the Mercy mission, the item carried several salient points.

Seven Sisters of Mercy, five to remain, will leave today, January 14th, for Belize. . . . By special arrangement with the Holy See, the Belize House will remain attached to the Mother House in New Orleans. . . . His Eminence Cardinal Simeoni has congratulated His Grace Monsignor Perché, on supplying this distant mission, and His Holiness Pope Leo XIII has sent a special blessing to the zealous Sisters who have volunteered to go forth to establish the first Convent of their Institution between the Tropics.[73]

Even though Mother Austin thought it prudent to mention the special arrangement with Propaganda Fide, she knew that she was taking a risk by accepting this mission to Spanish America.[74] As it happened, it was the only Mercy convent in Central or South America in the 1880s, for the Mercies had left Argentina for Australia in 1880.[75] Evidently, when Austin balanced the needs of the girls in Belize for a Catholic education against the anger and further antagonism of the coadjutor Leray, the weighty needs of Belize took precedence with Austin even though she expected to pay a penalty later when Leray succeeded to the See of New Orleans. Yet, she never could have dreamed the risk was to be so great and the cost so high, even though her eyes were not closed when she acted. She saw clearly, without reading the correspondence that was proof of it, that the German clique opposed to Mercy branches had found an auxiliary tool which they manipulated quite skillfully.

In British Honduras, Mother Austin's skills and thoughts turned from the Germans to the Spanish and Indians and Caribs, for she was busy establishing on a firm footing the convent, schools, and works of mercy of this mission branch. Like Catherine McAuley, Austin Carroll saw that visitation of the sick began immediately in each new branch, and Belize was no exception. The Mercies arrived on January 20, and within that first week had staffed the Spanish school, later called Holy Redeemer, and the English school, named St. Catherine's in honor of the foundress.[76] Besides opening the schools and visiting the sick in their homes that first week, Mother Austin also began the visitation of the prison, barracks, and hospital.[77] In the homes the sisters were startled to see on the family altar a little statue of Christ or Mary adorned in rich clothing. Mary was most often dressed like Our Lady of Guadalupe, though they also saw her dressed in the Mercy habit. Even stranger was the appearance of Christ wearing the garments of a great Indian chief, with lots of beads and long black hair adorned with a magnificent feathered headdress. These natives certainly knew that their Savior had become one of them.[78]

Mother Austin located a fine site on Dean Street which she was soon to purchase for St. Catherine's convent and school. The lot fronting on the bay contained two homes, one to serve temporarily as the convent and the other as the school. The sale would not take place until Austin could return home and find the $4,000 needed.[79] She followed the custom of the Mercy foundress by remaining a week or so in each new branch in order to assist the new superior in making the initial arrangements and she was in Belize close to three weeks.[80] Also following Catherine McAuley, Austin generously gave of her best for the superior of each branch. In this case, Evangelist Kearney, who had served for a time as mistress of novices, was the choice and she was given a small but capable community. Before one year in Belize was completed, however, she received three more teachers, and another four in the next two years as the community grew to a dozen in order to staff the elementary school for boys and extend St. Catherine's to secondary level.[81] As Austin and her lay sister companion left them on February 6, 1883, the hearts of those original five were sore, for the chronicler wrote, "How our hearts ached when we said goodby to dear Reverend Mother."[82] For her part, Mother Austin said that she would send more desks and school supplies immediately and promised to see that the missionaries received news from home on the weekly mailboat. As a missionary away from home thirty years herself, Austin was well aware of the joy brought by letters from family and friends. From the day she opened her first branch in Biloxi eight years before, Mother Austin had encouraged the sisters to write regularly, especially for the feasts of the sisters and all the days of special community celebration in memory of Catherine McAuley.

As proof that letters from New Orleans and the other branches arrived regularly is the abundance of news from the other convents entered into the Belize chronicles. But such news events were not the only items sent to the mission branch, for their chronicles also reveal their joy at an occasional treat of sweets from New Orleans and the "loving letters received from our dearest Reverend Mother."[83] Naturally, there were disappointments recorded too, as expected sisters missed the boat or the large crate in which the sisters hoped to find decorations for the chapel contained, "to our great disappointment," nothing "but books for the library."[84] Yet, spiritual reading for the sisters and literature and pleasure reading for the students were an essential part of establishing each school or institution for Mother Austin. Certain that she did not live by bread alone, she tried to convince others of that fact by making books and libraries available to them. Since writing was also a real part of her life, she probably, while sailing home, made notes for the lengthy article on Belize that was destined to be in her series of "Southern Sketches," or the other article which was to become part of the Mercy *Annals*.[85] Using her time wisely was an art in which Mother Austin had few equals. Her letters reveal that she made a practice of writing the basis of an article as she went to or from the various branches. Once home, she could revise and polish it, then have one of her sisters recopy it neatly for the editor or publisher.

Upon her return to the New Orleans motherhouse, Mother Austin sent some books not only to Belize but to South Bend, where the Notre Dame library collection had burned the previous year. She was thinking of more than replacing books, however, for she wrote, "I am sending to the 'Lemonier Library' several copies of works written or translated by me, in order that we may have a share in the Perpetual Mass, etc., which is mentioned in the *Ave Maria*."[86] Such an opportunity to aid a library and gain prayers at the same time was irresistible to Mother Austin. Even in her bestowing of gifts, Austin thought of prayers and books. Repeatedly, some poor priest on a collection tour visited the convent in an old worn cassock, only to leave with Mass stipends, one of her books, and perhaps, a new cassock. And for the crowning of Xavier Warde on her golden jubilee, Austin decided to send fifty copies of the *Annals* which described Xavier's profession on January 24, 1833. She wrote the jubilarian that the books were to be given the sick or the poor "so that they may have the pleasure of reading on your account and thus be the more obliged to pray for you."[87] Austin added, "If there is anything else you desire me to do, I shall deem it a favor to comply." But Austin's presence, requested by Xavier who even offered to pay transportation, was unavailable because Austin had previously committed herself to establish the Sisters of Mercy in Belize. However, Austin arranged that the Mercies in New Orleans and all the branches have Masses and prayers in honor of the jubilarian and that the Southern sisters celebrate a *Te Deum* day with the Manchester sisters by enjoying the proverbial recreation at breakfast of the Mercy "first class feast."[88]

In the spring of 1883, Austin proofread the final pages of the second volume of the Mercy *Annals*, as the work was scheduled for publication in the summer. Proofs completed, she confided to a friend that she found the second volume superior to the first.[89] The literary critics and reviewers were soon to agree with her, noting especially the material on the Mercies nursing in the Crimea. Again, the reviewers were overwhelmingly positive, though the *London Tablet* found fault with the verses she had quoted in an appendix. Austin believed that the *Tablet's* editor, like Bishop James O'Connor, thought that any poetry written by nuns was poor. Just as Austin laughed at this prejudice, she joked about the review, "It must be a splendid book that hasn't a fault till the appendix, and that had to be found in a quotation."[90] On occasion, Austin could decide that a paper was not worth its price because it seldom said anything good about her books. More generally, however, she took the critics in stride and advised her correspondents to do the same with, "We must let people talk according to their tastes," or "Journals may say what they like," or even that "the book which will please all has yet to be written."[91] Mother Austin tended to ignore the reviews, both complimentary and less favorable, of periodicals which she considered "of small literary repute." Yet she treasured the critiques of certain individuals, usually authors or editors like John Boyle O'Reilly, Reverend James Corcoran, Katherine E. Conway, James McMaster, and Rev. Matthew Russell, SJ.[92]

Austin Carroll's letters show that she frequently encouraged her Mercy correspondents to give their opinions about her works with a request such as "the more candid you are regarding my books, the more I am obliged to you."[93] She invited and treasured critiques from friends like bishop James O'Connor and Father Ferreol Girardey, and Sisters Mary Juliana Purcell, Augustine McKenna, Catherine Maher, and her unnamed chronicler in Limerick. "Indeed, no hesitation was required," wrote this Limerick Mercy, "in any representation made to the courteous, warm-hearted good Religious who . . . while possessed of talents of a high order, possessed likewise the humility and good sense which give real value to her writing."[94] Although Austin did not see that compliment, she often took a friend's opinion with a grain of salt. Bishops Elder and James O'Connor both criticized *Clement Hofbauer* for her, and she wrote the latter that "Bishop Elder made me laugh . . . thinks that one passage endorses Communism!"[95] O'Connor wondered if Austin in another passage was censuring her sisters for establishing select schools. Austin answered that she "never established academies" herself and thought that the Sisters of Mercy "ought to be employed chiefly for the poor."[96] Yet, as long as the majority of the sisters worked in the parish schools or in other ways with the needy, she saw no reason why a few sisters should not be occupied in teaching those who could afford the best, especially since that was the practice of the foundress in both Cork and Carlow. She intended the paragraph in question simply as a reminder to all religious orders that there was a tendency to part from some of the ideals of the founder.

Suddenly one summer day, nationalism was again in action, and Mother Austin might have recalled her words on Clement Hofbauer's community. "Perhaps no congregation has suffered so much on the score of nationality, or had its effects so cramped from the same ignoble cause," she had written, "and there is certainly none whose founder and distinguished members have fought more strenuously against this uncatholic and irreligious spirit."[97] Such was not the case with the German trio who opposed her, for Austin learned from Rev. Gustave Rouxel, the Vicar General, that the German priests had a number of complaints about her and the Mercy community sent, not across the street to the Mercy community or to the archbishop of New Orleans, but to Rome through German channels.[98] Cardinal Simeoni had assigned Rouxel to investigate the matter[99] even though "*L'umile Oratore*" of the German clique's petition had proposed that their auxiliary, Leray, be given the power "to depose Mother Austin Carroll and send her to a branch" as the "only means" of solving the problems.[100] As in

1880, the complainers claimed that Austin was elected repeatedly from 1871 onward, that she broke her Rule by establishing branches, some even in other dioceses and foreign countries, and that she often transferred teachers from Redemptorist institutions to the branches so that their asylum and schools were "greatly neglected."[101] The first claim had been declared false before the Mercy election in 1880 by the Redemptorist rector, Benedict Neithart, who said that, according to the Rule, Austin could "be elected once or twice yet." He added that she observed her Rule well, whatever "Father Giesen and her other adversaries may say to the contrary."[102]

Rouxel's careful checking revealed that each branch had been established with the approval of the archbishop at the request of the other bishops concerned, and with the additional approbation of Rome for the Belize house. Also, each branch had been requested for a small town or village unable to support a motherhouse and novitiate, but with the understanding that the convent could become independent whenever that was agreeable to all parties concerned.[103] According to the testimony of the school prefects the third claim was also incorrect, for each prefect often spoke publicly of the successful progress of the students and the fine work of the teachers.[104] Community records listed many teachers never changed from the parish, including the principals of both schools, who had been serving since 1871. Austin sent news of the complaints to Father Girardey, who had long served as prefect, and often as the appointed confessor or spiritual director of the Mercies. Austin asked him to comment upon the items that he found to be false, and he wrote, "Either your accusers are woefully ignorant or shamefully prejudiced," and sent his "candid testimony."[105] He knew that the election scheduled for 1883 was to be the second held and that Austin was eligible to serve as superior for a second three-year term. He was aware that each branch was established only after obtaining full ecclesiastical approbation to answer a real need in some small town. He considered the occasional changes of teachers insignificant, saying "No one can *justly* accuse you of doing any injustice to St. Alphonsus schools and asylum."[106]

Without a doubt, Mother Austin found the accusers unjust. She also considered the German petition an attempt to control Mercy elections, and hence, unwarranted interference in Mercy government. Earlier, in answer to their German parishioners who wanted a voice in the selection of their pastor, the Redemptorist provincial George Ruland, wrote the archbishop that he "indignantly rejected such an impudent demand at once, by telling them, we were not accustomed to let anybody meddle with the governing of our Congregation; that was our affair; and there should be no other Superior" than the one the Redemptorists selected.[107] Had Mother Austin seen that letter, she certainly would have been in full agreement with those statements and Ruland's conclusion, that it was his "duty to defend and preserve our independence against intruders."[108] But now that the shoe was on the other foot, Austin was condemned by the double standard of the clique for doing exactly what their own men considered an essential policy. Although Rouxel had received only three complaints from Rome, he must have heard long lists from the Germans, for he appointed a special visitor for the Mercies.[109] In a quirk of fate, the Germans happened to complain about several points completely opposite to Austin's habitual actions. Sure proof that the clique did not even know this lady they wished to depose, for instance, was their claim that she allowed no Visitations. Yet the ecclesiastical superior of the Mercy community attested, "Far from trying to prevent Visitation from taking place, you have always reminded the archbishop . . . and accepted the Visitor he appointed—myself for several years."[110]

The clique evidently had no knowledge of how often Austin urged the teaching of rich and poor alike in the parish schools, and hence, clearly erred in claiming that she founded branches in order to establish academies. Also unaware of Austin's breadth of vision about the need of religious to select a confessor, the clique claimed that her sisters were restricted in this matter. An astounded Mercy confessor said, "I have never known a Convent where the Sisters were allowed greater freedom in the choice of confessors."[111] In fact, had the Germans known how Austin found opportunities to invite the extraordinary confessor to the convent, the complainers probably would have carried tales to Rome about that. Yet, here and there, a complaint had some truth, such as one that noted that the entire original community at the asylum was no longer there after eight years. That was true, for two sisters had been changed and three others assigned to care for the children, but an extra pair of hands was certainly not to the detriment of the children. The clique noted that Austin reserved her "honeyed words and polished manners" for others, but called them "Dutch" instead of "Deutsch," and she probably did.[112] They thought that she called their German-American Redemptorists Germans to insult them. Yet, judging by how pleased any Irish-American in the channel was to be called Irish, Austin would hardly have thought it an insult to refer to German-Americans as German. The clique had meddled, interfered, and caused enough problems to have led some personalities to retaliate with sneaky annoyances. But such pettiness would certainly have been uncharacteristic on Austin's part and completely foreign to her frank and open nature.

No matter how tiresome and trivial the charges, the clique clacked on. They accused Mother Austin of taking too many candidates not able to teach and of treating the young sisters with rigor. The visitor learned what these sisters, though prejudiced in favor of their Reverend Mother, had to say about the complaints. They all believed Austin to be an exceptional leader, "very exemplary" in her religious life and also a "richly endowed," and "intelligent woman."[113] They saw no problem about candidates because some entered for the visitation of the sick and the prison apostolate and not to be teachers. Not one sister denied that Mother Austin was strict about the observance of the Rule, for she had high standards for followers of Catherine McAuley. As to a strict novitiate, they thought it better that a novice understand what was expected of her as a religious before she took her vows.[114] Some also noted that Mother Austin had the mistress run a tighter noviceship since a defection the previous year, the only one in New Orleans in fifteen years. Yet they did have some complaints and worries about Mother Austin, for these Louisiana ladies were eminently conservative by heritage and *changer* was a wicked word. On occasion, therefore, they found their Irish leader was too broadminded. For instance, she did not arrange enough separation between the boys and the girls in small parish schools. She even allowed one orphan family of four to remain together in one room so that the two older girls could take care of their little brothers. Several of the sisters worried about the safety of attractive young sisters attending the jails, even though they served as partners for the older Mercies, usually widows, who were in charge of the three prison apostolates.[115]

Other worries of some of the community concerned the number of branches, for they feared that once the present superiors died, it might be difficult to find enough good superiors to replace them. Then there were several sisters dying slowly of "lung disease," whom Austin wanted kept away from the young sisters. Some thought this too hard on the sick. Lastly, nearly all noticed that Mother Austin enjoyed close friendship with certain sisters closer to her age than others, and that her lack of "good rapport" with the German Redemptorists was "much to be regretted."[116] Rouxel reported to Rome that he and the visitor believed that "there were few convents where a better spirit reigned . . . that Mother Austin seems determined to obey all that is required of her."[117] The vicar then pinpointed quite accurately the cause of the trouble when he said, "the great difficulty comes from the Reverend Father Giesen . . . and several of the Fathers who do not agree with her."[118] This last clause was an understatement of classic proportions. Rouxel rightly believed that temperament, personality, and nationality all were a part of the problem on both sides. He had judged Austin to be overly protective of the sisters' rights of self-government, and a "little haughty" in the face of the German attempts to interfere in Mercy internal affairs. The Redemptorists, "believing that they are in the right, exaggerate their office to intervene in the [Mercy] community,"[119] as they had previously done when Catherine Grant was superior. Rouxel could not foresee peace, however, because the Germans "do not want Mother Austin as Superior," and she requests in the name of the community "that the spiritual direction be given to the Jesuits."[120]

The 1880s and the decade that followed formed a period of great turmoil in the Church in this country because of nationalistic antagonisms. At the time therefore, there was nothing unique about the Irish and the Germans having another fray, especially in the Irish Channel. The only unusual facet of this gem of an impasse was that the force opposing a powerful German congregation with great experience in these battles was neither a bishop nor a priest, but a rather small Irish nun who seemed to carry all the courage of her Tipperary forebears within her staunch Carroll frame. Earlier, her sisters had pictured Austin Carroll as in a Southern Eden unaware of the wily serpent of nationalism. When the snake in the grass raised its ugly head in 1880, Austin believed that the investigation had scotched the creature.[121] But three years later, she suddenly found it slithering about stronger than ever. The clique wanted the Mercy convent within their parish separated from all their branches and isolated from the rest of the community so that they could be directed by the pastor and work only within the parish limits. In order to maintain the integrity of their Rome-approved Rule as well as the structure of motherhouse and branches, Austin thought it essential that the sisters prevent the interference of the German clique in their internal government. Austin probably had no adequate understanding, however, of the hugh German organization ready to support the clique in their complaints. The German priests had been busier than Mother Austin realized in organizing their complaints and petitions.[122] Rev. Peter Matthias Abbelen, the chaplain at the Milwaukee motherhouse of the German sisters and friend of the German fathers, had visited the Redemptorist rectory in New Orleans in January and that in St. Louis a little later, the same route from Giesen to Jaeckel traversed by the complaints before they left for Rome.

Mother Austin Carroll, too, was busy about many projects in 1883, for until the year was half over, she knew nothing of the kettle of complaints being carefully brewed by a creative chef. She had conferred several times with her advisors about changing the focus of the House of Mercy since immigration had dwindled. She now envisioned as the greater need a residence for working women and girls. Quick as she was to spot the signs of the times, Mother Austin took time before she acted to consult her council of discreets and to determine if the new plan was in the spirit of the foundress.[123] Austin was consulting the archbishop, also, for the Belize sisters were to be free simultaneously with the other teachers only during Christmas vacation. So she and the sisters asked Perché to transfer the date of the election from August to December.[124] He saw no problem and thought it wise to select a date that would not interfere with the school calendar. In

January Mother Austin invited Leray to officiate at a Mercy profession, probably hoping that he would become less antagonistic toward the community. But in April, as harbinger for the Germans, he wrote Rome to herald the coming complaints. Mother Austin regularly invited visiting prelates and priests through St. Alphonsus School, and local papers often mentioned the visitors' compliments. Typical were those of early 1883, when Austin gave the tour to Francis Janssens of Natchez in January, to Ignatio Montes de Oca from Mexico in February, to Edward FitzGerald of Little Rock and William Elder of Cincinnati in March, and to Archbishop Perché in May.[125]

Certainly apparent to the visitors was Mother Austin's pride and joy in the advancement of the pupils and the fine work of her teachers. If she suffered any fault in connection with these classes, it was perhaps too great a pride in the accomplishments of her community, not any neglect. Austin's letters repeatedly mention this parish school as the "finest south of New York" or Baltimore or Philadelphia or Cincinnati[126] and that vacation was her busiest season because "most of the Sisters are here, and I have to direct their studies."[127] Several of the bishops who visited the school had come to the city in March at the death of Bishop John Quinlan. Mother Austin considered it a privilege to have assisted at St. Theresa's rectory, reciting for the dying bishop the familiar prayers said by his mother in Ireland.[128] Quinlan had brought the Mercies to his diocese of Mobile in 1877, and grateful that they were to teach the children of every shade, had given them the Pensacola convent. In New Orleans the sisters had been saving for three years in order to finance the purchase of a residence near St. Michael's parish schools. The Mercy commuters were hoping that the house could be theirs that fall. Mother Austin was to celebrate the thirtieth anniversary of her entrance into the convent of Mercy in Cork. When the sisters questioned her about preferred gifts, she answered, "Every blessing I can desire in my state, God has given me." Yet she would appreciate some of the chapel furnishings soon to be needed for the branch convent in St. Michael's Parish.[129]

In fact, a season of jubilees had occurred after Mother Austin noted the 155th anniversary of the arrival of the Ursulines on August 6, 1727.[130] This date designated, in the area now covered by the United States, New Orleans as the first site and city to have religious sisters staffing their Catholic school and nuns nursing in their hospital. Austin included such information in her article about the Ursulines in the series, "Southern Sketches." Next to that century-and-a-half of service, Austin realized how dwarfed was her own thirty-year record, as were the thirty years since the profession in Arkansas of Mary Aloysius Fitzpatrick, the first New Orleanian to take the religious vows of the Mercy Institute.[131] So, too, were the

forty years since Mother Frances Creedon received the vows of Mary
Joseph Nugent on March 24, 1843, in Newfoundland, in the first of
Catherine McAuley's Mercy convents in America and, fittingly, one which
came from the cradle of the Mercy Institute in Dublin.[132] That February of
1883 marked the first anniversary of the death of Austin Carroll's generous
friend, Margaret Haughery, who showed extraordinary charity towards the
orphans of New Orleans. In tribute to her friend Austin Carroll wrote,
"Unfettered by religious vows, her life was a daily sacrifice on the altar of
charity."[133] Mother Austin knew how generous Margaret had been in her
small bills for the large quantities of bread the Mercies distributed to the
sick poor. Nor had Margaret forgotten in her will the orphans tended by the
Mercies. Austin's final compliment in the graceful memoir was the suggestion that the memory of Margaret Gaffney Haughery "be kept forever with
that of Catherine Mcauley and Nano Nagle."[134]

Like her holy foundress, Mother Austin made light of her problems to
others, mentioning only to several correspondents her need for their prayers
along with their recollections for the *Annals*.[135] For helpful statements she
turned to only two priests, Ferreol Girardey, CSSR, and Salvatore Di Pietro, SJ. The former was the recent school prefect who understood the
nationalistic situation in the parish, and the latter was the vicar apostolic of
Belize, upon whose word of Rome's approval she took her sisters to open
the mission branch. Girardey immediately sent Austin his testimony to be
used as needed,[136] and the vicar said he would write to Rome. Di Pietro went
straight to the top, writing directly to Pope Leo XIII to explain that it was
"absurd and impossible" for the German priests to insist that the Belize
convent immediately be "separated and form an independent motherhouse."[137] Not only did he speak of the zeal shown by the sisters in teaching
the girls and assisting the poor sick, but more importantly for Austin, he
pointed out the specific passages of the Mercy Rule followed in establishing
the mission branch. Finally, he requested and the Pope granted, that the
Belize community was "to remain affiliated to the New Orleans motherhouse until they are able to form a good novitiate."[138] Before this good news
filtered back to Belize and then up to New Orleans, Austin asked a favor of
Bishop James O'Connor who had been for years both spiritual director and
practical advisor. Would he give her a character reference, "let Cardinal
Simeoni know, should opportunity offer, that I am a person whose word
may be relied on."[139]

To Mother Austin it seemed a small favor, for all the bishops concerned with the branch convents "agree the houses should remain attached
to this," and the vicar, Gustave Rouxel, and the Visitor, Theobald Butler,
SJ, "see things as I do."[140] Convinced that her cause was right, Austin said,
"In case I do write to Rome, I want the cardinal to understand he may rely

on my word." When O'Connor's negative reply arrived, she tried again, "Pardon me, my Lord, if I differ."[141] Then referring to her previous confidential mention of a number of scandals in the area involving several members of the clergy, she added,

> You could help the matter by writing to C. Simeoni to *verify* what I have said about small weak houses, and the necessity for centralization in many parts, especially the South. Let other regions do as they please—I have to mind my flock, and I want to be sustained by Rome as far as the houses founded by me are concerned—I don't interfere in any way with others. As the Sisters have all been trained and professed by me, they are one with me in this, as are all who have our interest at heart. I feel the whole Order will one day be turned into a Generalate with provinces. . . . What I desire is for future stability, not for my own convenience. A word from you as to my reliability and as to the necessity that exists for the arrangement I mention, would help the cause.[142]

Mother Austin felt that to leave the sisters in the branches without the protection of the motherhouse "would be a crime." If Rome says cut off the branches, "I should obey, but all the sisters would return here, as they have a right to do."[143]

While Rome pondered the case, Austin took steps to avoid more local complaints by having both Perché and Rouxel sign written permission for the shift of the election date to near Christmas.[144] "I hope with God's grace our troubles are over for the present, but there's nothing like having decisions in writing."[145] As to herself, "I school myself to holy indifference, at least so far as being anxious only to do God's will as it shall be manifested in this matter." Austin mentioned that part of the difficulty stemmed from "the perpetual feud between the Archb. and the Coadj. If the Archb. gives leave for a thing, the Coadj. will say it is wrong, and vice versa."[146] Belize had been one illustration of this point, St. Michael's Convent was the second. Community finances allowed Mother Austin to purchase the house next to St. Michael's School on October 4, 1883, and the next day the local papers carried the real estate transaction of the $9,500 double house adjacent to the church and school. The sisters moved in that Saturday, and before the day was over Rev. Thomas Heslin, the pastor who later became the Bishop of Natchez, had blessed the convent and placed the Blessed Sacrament in their little chapel. Though rather plain, the two-story house on the corner of Race and Chippewa was sturdy, and Mother Austin thought that its location doubled its value. On Sunday Father Heslin "gave them a puff," as the chronicler put it, by announcing to the parishioners that the long-awaited convent was a reality and that the "pious and zealous"

Sisters of Mercy were in the parish. Everything, like the garden, was coming up roses.[147]

Then out of the blue on Monday, Mother Austin related to her advisor, "We were no sooner in the new convent than Bishop Leray . . . said he wished us to close it," because "he was the Administrator of Temporalities, and the house had been bought without his sanction."[148] When she referred the matter to Perché who had given permission for the house, he told her to continue the branch.[149] Trying to make assurance doubly sure, she consulted Archbishop Elder, Vicar Rouxel, and Visitor Butler as to whether she should listen to the archbishop or the bishop.[150] All indicated the former, and it was at this point that she followed Bishop O'Connor's advice and wrote to Bishop Kirby of the Irish College in Rome. In case Leray wrote to Simeoni about the convent, she wanted the true facts known, but "should his Lordship [Leray] become archbishop, we are ready to obey him, and though he has not been kind or fatherly to us, we would obey his Lordship now, were it possible to obey two masters."[151] Then Austin gave a succinct bit of background to Kirby.

> I am thirty years in Religion, fifteen in New Orleans, and never till this season have I written to Rome. . . . By the singular assistance of God, I have established eight Convents, every one of which gives gratuitous teaching to all the poor of its vicinity, black and white, without expense to the Church or State. And we do not owe a single dollar. Much of the expense is met by my own literary profits, for I have published many books, all of which have been successful in a pecuniary way. We instruct in all the institutions in the city, and are, thank God, the means of drawing hundreds to the Faith. We nurse in all the epidemics, and strive to do as much for their souls as for their bodies. . . . All this will show your Lordship how little we deserve the persecution which Bishop Leray and one or two German Redemptorists have been waging against us. I know God will not suffer their efforts to hurt us, but my director informs me I am bound in conscience to lay this matter before Rome, and I take the liberty of doing so through your Lordship.[152]

Archbishop Perché had consented to the convent in St. Michael's Parish three years earlier, and authorized Mother Austin to continue the branch because it had been "paid for without either expenses to the diocese or collections made in the diocese" and, therefore, did not concern Leray.[153] The latter did not agree and sent his unsealed messages for Mother Austin to Giesen, who reported back to Leray, snickering over Austin's reaction to receiving open letters through German channels and gloating over what he considered excessive payment for an old house not sturdy enough to last long.[154] Time has proven Austin's judgement more accurate than Giesen's, as more than a century later, the house still serves as a convent. Earlier Perché had warned Austin to be extremely careful when dealing with Leray, for he had publicly "proclaimed himself her enemy."[155] When Leray's second open letter arrived, Mother Austin threw caution to the winds, however; for she not only enclosed a copy of Perchés authorization and announced that she had been directed to proceed as the archbishop decided; but she also answered the accusations point by point.[156] He complained of branches beyond the diocese, yet he himself had tried to get her to take the Pass Christian schools in the Natchez diocese when other sisters did not want to keep them. In the same way Giesen had urged her to take the mission in St. Thomas Island, and in fact, only after she refused that mission 2,000 miles off did he begin his relentless persecution. Leray complained of her being in office too long at twelve years, yet as director of the Mississippi Mercies, he kept Mother de Sales as the superior for eighteen years.

Mother Austin demonstrated the similar inconsistency of Leray regarding sisters and property, for he had earlier lent money to other Mercies so that they could purchase real estate. In fact twenty years later he was still charging annual interest for the favor. Finally, she explained that she did not go to him for advice because, when she did so earlier, he revealed to others what she had confided to him. And since Leray had accused her of being underhanded, she replied,

> Crookedness is too foreign to my principles . . . Instead of adopting crooked ways . . . I have always gone to the fountain head, His Grace. . . . Everything during my administration has been done with the permission and blessing of those I was bound to obey, else God would not have blessed us as wonderfully as He has. . . . Those who know me best say I am too straightforward for my own good. . . . If you continue to persecute us, God grant that we may be as gold tried in the furnace. . . . I have now opened my whole heart to you, and told you frankly why I cannot come to you as to a gentle Father, with my doubts, difficulties, and sorrows. Alas, Bishop, if you knew all I have to wear and disturb me, the ceaseless toil of mind and body under which God alone can sustain me, you would not seek so earnestly to embarrass my administration, and even my conscience. . . . Asking your blessing, and your forgiveness if you are angry that I have told painful things to yourself direct, I am, Monseigneur, with an easier mind like one who has made a good confession.[157]

Austin's friends were right; her letter had been too straightforward for her own good and did not advance her cause with Leray. Her mind was at peace, however, and she told a friend that "It is good to be opposed in this way, for it makes us humble and circumspect, and gives us a purity of intention we could not otherwise have."[158] Since Mother Austin felt that she and her sisters needed additional graces to sustain them, her every letter begged for extra "prayers that we may always do God's will in these difficulties."[159] Every cross was AMDG for Mother Austin just as each joy was for the greater glory of god.[160] Austin did take the time that fall to request of the neighboring dioceses some factual statement as to the origin and current need of her Mercies in their schools. Yet, her time was primarily given to others. This was the period in 1883 when Brewton in Alabama suffered the scourge of yellow fever, which involved three of her best nurses for a month and herself for a shorter period. Also that fall, a pitiful case came to the attention of Mother Austin. An elderly couple, once in comfortable circumstances, had become destitute, and their recent attempt to auction their paintings had failed. A group of charitable ladies decided to give a tombola to raffle the art, but appealed to Mother Austin for some immediate relief for the family. Mother Austin and her companion visited the home with a packet of food and found that the man of the house was the great historian of Louisiana, Charles Gayarré. Austin wanted to help with the raffle tickets, but Leray had forbidden raffles except for his debt. So Austin decided to appeal to her friends across the continent, and many were generous, none more so than Mother Baptist Russell in San Francisco.[161]

Charles Gayarré also wrote his friends, and in this particular instance, confided to his dear fellow-author, L'Abbbé Adrien Rouquette in Lacombe, both the news of the raffle and his certainty that it would fail, as well as the fact that it had led to one of the most memorable hours of his life.[162] As Gayarré told it, the heart-warming incident was none other than the first visit of Mother Austin with her gifts of compassion and encouragement. He was pleased that she took fifty tickets for the raffle immediately, but what touched him was her appreciation of the depth of his research and his wealth of historical knowledge. Gayarré was completely surprised to find that "this superior woman" had a thorough knowledge of his four-volume history of the colony and State of Louisiana.[163] Within a few days Mother Austin returned to show Gayarré his name in a *Dublin Review* as she tried to break through his discouragement with the knowledge that he was known abroad. Again she brought him copies of the two volumes of her Mercy *Annals* as a gift and let him know that she was concerned about his spiritual welfare. Gayarré was overwhelmed by Austin's sensitivity to his humiliating circumstances and related to Rouquette that this "exceedingly polished authoress" was distressed that he should be so neglected by the public.[164] After several more visits from "L'Ange Austin," Gayarré returned to the practice of his Faith and was writing articles for periodicals again, for Austin had promised to assist by dealing with the *Catholic World* and the *American Catholic Quarterly Review*. When Austin Carroll edited and praised his "Women of Louisiana," Gayarré said it was his "heart which held the pen."[165]

Once again, like hundreds of times before and after, it was Mother Austin's heart-felt concern that led her to become a friend in need. Yet on this occasion, it so happened that a poverty-stricken gentleman in his eightieth year was an author and historian whose correspondence documented for posterity his memorable meetings with "L'Ange Austin." For the remainder of his life, Austin was to share with Gayarré her friendship, her interest in Louisiana history, and her assistance with editors of Catholic periodicals. This instance of Austin's charity and compassionate help is especially enlightening, as it occurred in the midst of the German machinations against her as the clique continued to send accusations to Rome. Instead of sitting at home worrying about her case in Rome, Austin did not count the cost in time or effort in order to aid the destitute couple. Even as Mother Austin found the time to assist these new friends, she did not neglect her old ones. Before Xavier Warde's feast on December 3, Austin's letter read, "If I wrote as often as I think of you, the letters would have to remain unread, for never could you . . . find the time to get through them."[166] On December 12, not long before the community election, Mother Austin requested a special blessing from Rome for her seventy-eight sisters and eight houses.[167] Perhaps Austin had thought that her term in office was to be concluded at the Chapter of Elections. Not so, for her sisters for a second time voted for Austin Carroll to lead them forward in the footsteps of Catherine McAuley. Even though Vicar Rouxel was present for the election, Mother Austin later had the Chapter Book taken over to the archbishop so that Perché could add his signature of approbation.[168]

In her Christmas greetings, Austin Carroll asked her friends to pray "that I may to the utmost of my ability promote the greater glory of God," or that she might "in all things do the holy will of god and be enlightened to show it to others."[169] She was soon to have great need of these graces, for Archbishop Perché died after Christmas, and the reins automatically fell into the hands of Leray. Mother Austin had visited Perché on December 26, 1883, the day before he died. She mourned this prelate "who was so kind that everyone loved him."[170] As the New Year was ushered in Austin was uneasy at the long silence of Rome, but was lulled into a false security as Leray was "being very civil."[171] In February the papal blessing arrived to Austin's delight, and later that month news came from Rome indirectly through Bishop Edward FitzGerald, "Please tell the sisters that they must look sharply, as . . . the Redemptorists are very strong."[172] All he could learn about the case was that matters were to remain "in *status quo* until the new Bishop can be consulted." The handwriting going on the wall seemed to be in German script. The complaints were highly organized and arranged to claim that the sisters broke their Rule. For instance, the Germans claimed that they gave the Sisters of Mercy a convent in New Orleans for the teachers of the parish schools, but that Mother Austin had turned it into an academy and sent teachers away to academies in other places, thus breaking the Rule which said to teach the poor.[173] Once again the same false accusations, or embroidered variations of the earlier ones, had been made. "When first these accusations were brought against us," Austin wrote her director, "I demanded a Visitation . . . and though it proved every charge false, as the Vicar told me, yet our enemies return to the same charge."[174]

Rome has a "singular way of doing business," Mother Austin continued, for "it seems to me that when one or two Redemptorists complain of what we have done in other dioceses that Rome would simply tell them to mind their own business, since it is certain that we never would have placed houses in other dioceses without the concurrence of the Bishops concerned."[175] Austin reminded Bishop O'Connor that she has never opened any academy, even though one black school in Florida is called select. In New Orleans the Mercies teach 1200 children, of whom not 200 can pay, that all their schools have about 3,000 pupils, but the only students set apart anywhere are the thirty-seven in the English school in Belize, where there are 300 in the Spanish schools. Enclosed with her letter, Austin sent her director a copy of the statement from Rev. C. T. O'Callaghan, the administrator of the diocese of Mobile. He stated that in the Mercy schools "the children of the poor are received without money and without price, and are placed on the same footing with the children of the rich without a shadow of distinction."[176] The report mentioned the black schools and that the Sisters of Mercy were "the only community in the diocese that is doing anything toward the Christian education of the Colored race."[177] Inexplicably, no statement was forthcoming from Bishop Janssens of Natchez. Austin's letters to friends mention that "We have our share of the cross here, Thank God, but so many blessings that we will not repine,"[178] or that her community of eighty-three was "flourishing, though never without our share of the cross, Thank God."[179]

Two of the blessings had been appointments, that of a bishop for the See of Mobile, Dominic Manucy from Brownsville,[180] and that of Father William Meredith as prefect of the parish schools, a position he had held when Mother Austin arrived in 1869 with two other professed sisters, both dead since 1872. That had been a dozen years earlier, but after little more than a year in New Orleans, Father Meredith also went to God. That was March, and in May he was followed by another of Austin's friends, Rev. Jeremiah Moynihan of Sts. Peter and Paul.[181] Within the year death had also taken Mothers Vincent Haire of Brooklyn and Augustine McKenna of New York, an especially close friend of Austin's. Then news came of the death of Mother Juliana Hardman, whom the foundress had appointed the superior in Birmingham, England.[182] Word from Manchester was sad, also, for Gonzaga O'Brien kept urging Austin to come for a farewell visit as Xavier Warde was failing fast. "How I would like to be with you . . . but duty keeps me here," Austin replied; "I often tell the Sisters I can scarcely keep myself from running to see you."[183] Possibly, Mother Austin felt that Leray would have refused consent as his reply to each request for Mercy teachers was negative. Nevertheless, it gave Mother Austin pleasure to know that these bishops and priests who had visited the St. Alphonsus classes wanted her teachers to staff their schools. Since actions speak louder than words, Austin saw each request as further vindication of her teachers. For, had the German accusations been true, not one of these clerics would have wanted her sisters for their schools.

Determined to move forward only as Leray allowed, Mother Austin gave the same reply to each request, "After you have the written consent of Leray, we can begin to consider staffing your schools."[184] Applications went to Leray from both within and beyond the archdiocese, from Jeanerette and Loreauville on the Bayou Teche and Sacred Heart on Canal Street, from Stann Creek near Belize, and from St. Paul's in Birmingham and St. Joseph's in Mobile, with Bishop Manucy urging the last.[185] Leray heard from Simeoni, too, just as Rouxel had the previous year, but with the additional concern that the requirements of both the Redemptorists and the Jesuit mission be satisfied.[186] Simeoni mentioned Austin Carroll only as the subject of the complaints and did not even refer to Rouxel's investigation. Unlike Rouxel, Leray investigated nothing, but gave universal endorsement to the clique's complaints with "I believe everything against Mother Austin to be true."[187] In 1880 the clique called the first Mercy election the third, but now termed the second election, that of 1883, the third.[188] If Leray had checked the records, he could have learned the truth. Instead, he declared that the election was obtained "by irregular means and little conscience," and demanded that it "be declared null by Rome." Besides enclosing the clique's rehash of earlier complaints, Leray said Austin acted in opposition to his authority, explaining neither that when he was only the administrator of temporalities, she had the approval of the archbishop in buying St. Michael's Convent and the approbation of both Perché and Propaganda Fide before she went to Belize.[189]

Many of Leray's misconceptions could have been corrected had he been willing to make inquiries, check the Mercy documents, or hear both sides in any way. Without any investigation, however, his condemnations were based on the mistaken information and false accusations of the clique. And, in the *modus operandi* of this trio, these accusations were sent to Rome in great secrecy, as were the newly expanded versions of the complaints from the clique.[190] Thus, Mother Austin knew of no movement in the case. Then in the summer of 1884, the tide seemed to turn on several shores. The ebb and flow on the American shore might have followed the movement in Rome, where action had eventually occurred. Propaganda Fide turned the case over to an experienced consultor, Cardinal Dominic Gregory Bartolini, SOC, who divided the material into two cases, the first being that of Leray against the Belize convent as a branch of New Orleans. This Cistercian Abbot, who served as a cardinal prefect in the Roman Curia, was impressed by the lengthy testimony of Di Pietro, the zeal of Austin Carroll and her sisters for the people of the mission, and the fact that his own thorough study of the Mercy Rule revealed nothing to forbid branches.[191] Mother Austin had noted in her testimony that when Rome confirmed the Rule in 1841, the foundress had already established two branches, which would have been accepted in the confirmation. Austin's frank, straightforward manner of answering brought favorable comment from this consultor. Then Cardinal Bartolini, giving five separate reasons for his decision in this first case, recommended that the Belize convent remain affiliated with the New Orleans motherhouse until Propaganda Fide decreed otherwise.

His Eminence saw the second case as that of two or three Redemptorists against Austin Carroll, rather than the whole community on either side. He noted two other points: the close connection between Leray's case and that of the Redemptorists and the fact that the complaints began only after Austin Carroll refused to take their mission on St. Thomas Island. The cardinal consultor praised the fine investigation and visitation of Rouxel and Butler, was impressed by the testimony of the school prefects as it contradicted the claims of the clique, and again noticed Austin's direct and thorough answers, her clarity, and her openness to appeal to all the bishops in whose dioceses her branch convents were located.[192] Substantiating evidence for Austin's explanations had come from the Administrator of Mobile, the vicar general of New Orleans, and the vicar apostolic of Belize.[193] In Bartolini's opinion, the second case was not one of real merit and true doubts that called for a decision from Rome, but rather a disagreement of personality. Further, as had already been discovered by Rouxel and Butler, some of the Redemptorists' accusations were "less than true, some less than exact, and some exaggerated." With this knowledge, and that Austin Carroll was "ready to obey all that is asked of her," Bartolini suggested that Rouxel be appointed the official "to resolve peacefully the question at issue."[194]

As had been known to happen in administrative bodies closer than the Roman Curia, there seemed to have been a leak; and Cardinal Bartolini's recommendations flowed out of Rome and across the ocean, case one reaching Di Pietro on the coast of Central America and case two following the waves across the Gulf of Mexico and into the See of New Orleans.[195] Later the first decision reached Austin, but such smooth sailing was not to be the course of the second case. In the pursuit of diplomacy Propaganda was apparently attempting to satisfy two strong orders of religious men with their solutions to the cases. The Jesuits in Belize had been pleased with the first suggestion, and a resolution which would pacify the Redemptorists was sought for the second. One must appreciate the dilemma as the Cardinals set aside the consultor's recommendation. Not only had they been bombarded for months by the German clique's lists of ever-increasing complaints for which Leray gave universal endorsement, but they might have been enduring also the pressures of diplomatic harassment from the powerful coalition of Church and German officials in Rome. Further, the prefect had written Leray and received in return the demand that the last Mercy election be declared null.[196] All of this considered, it was fortunate that Austin Carroll did not learn of Bartolini's suggestions, for the knowledge would certainly have heightened the pain inflicted later by injustice for the one who expected justice even while "ready to obey all that is asked of her."

Whatever the catalyst precipitating the sudden reaction, both Leray and the clique made sudden changes. Leray withdrew his previous negative reply and allowed Mother Austin to establish a branch convent in Mobile at the request of Bishop Manucy and Rev. Joseph Winklereid, SJ.[197] Leray's plan was that in two years the branch become an independent motherhouse, a plan he wanted Rome to enforce. However, Bishop Manucy said a foundation was impossible at the time, and Austin intended to recall her sisters if the branch was cut off prematurely.[198] On August 30, 1884, the Sisters of Mercy arrived in Mobile to staff the schools of St. Joseph's parish. Mother Austin bought several properties, one for the Mobile convent and another for a later secondary school for girls.[199] Like Leray, the Redemptorists also made sudden changes at that time, including the appointment of Rev. William Loewekamp as provincial superior to replace Nicholas Jaeckel and the reassignment of Father Girardey to the Irish Channel parish. Further, Loewekamp agreed to a new contract to be signed before a notary by himself and Mother Austin Carroll, whereby the parish teachers were to receive a regular monthly salary of $35.[200] Another, even more-pleasing agreement followed the pattern of the great early Redemptorist, Bernard Hafkenscheid, who had declared that "the spiritual direction of religious is entirely forbidden to our Fathers by our holy Constitutions." Perhaps Loewekamp subscribed to this interpretation also, for he said that neither Geisen nor the other priests were to be ecclesiastical superiors of the Sisters of Mercy.[201]

Although the contract did not include the sisters who cared for the orphans, that mattered not. The Mercies had always served without salaries at the asylum and were to do so as long as the asylum stood, for Mother Austin considered this apostolate a labor of love.[202] Because of her concern for her sisters, it was certainly a relief for Mother Austin to receive once again a monthly income for her parish teachers. If she learned of any reason for the sudden change of policy, after seven years of Jaeckel's abrogation of the 1869 contract with Provincial Helmpraecht, she did not record it. Amidst the rejoicing over the new arrangements, news of Xavier Warde's worsening health that September was a prelude to the telegram which later arrived to announce her death in Manchester.[203] Although Gonzaga O'Brien had been writing for two years of the increasing weakness of "Reverend Mother," as she and Austin often referred to Xavier, Austin called the telegram a thunderbolt. Then Austin wrote that she was arranging for masses in her nine convents, where Xavier had been in the sisters' prayers for some time, and promised to play the organ herself for the Gregorian Requiem to be chanted in the New Orleans motherhouse. "You more than anyone else require a word of comfort," Austin told her friend Gonzaga, but there is "only One who can really console you, and to Him I commit your bruised and bereaved heart."[204] Austin felt that Gonzaga was dearest to Xavier at this time, herself second. "As you know, she loved me better than anyone now living except yourself, and was anxious to communicate to me all she knew" of the spread of the Mercy Institute.[205]

"With all proper permission," Austin hoped her friend would "send me all her papers, letters, etc."[206] Austin Carroll planned to go through them "to classify, arrange all, make extracts as I need," just as she had done with the papers of the late Bishop Michael O'Connor, before she returned them to his brother.[207] Always the historian, Austin was anxious that details of Mercy origins in the Northeast not be lost. Austin never failed to compliment Reverend Mother Warde in the *Annals*, as Mother Frances in Ireland and as Mother Xavier in the United States, and gave several chapters of tribute in the *Annals* besides a lovely obituary in the newspaper.[208] Only in her confidential correspondence with her spiritual director did Austin let it be known that she did not consider Reverend Mother Xavier Warde quite up to others among Catherine McAuley's early followers.[209] Mother Austin's opinion was based neither upon that of the foundress' early companions nor upon some imaginary lack of understanding, but upon Austin's personal experience while serving under Reverend Mother Warde in Providence, Hartford, and Manchester. Possibly, Austin had been so overwhelmed by the virtues of Josephine Warde in 1856, that she was disappointed to find Xavier unlike her sister. "Perhaps no two sisters were ever so dissimilar in mind, manner, taste, and even in person," Austin stated in the *Annals*.[210] Praising in Josephine the traits and virtues many of which were not mentioned in connection with her younger sister, Austin noted particularly patience, kindness, and an affectionate disposition, meekness, sympathy, and a healthy recognition of the joys of friendship, gentleness, prudence, and a warm motherly manner, and as an administrator, a keen appreciation of the ability of her sisters and the discrimination with which to employ each in the most fitting position.[211]

Austin Carroll aimed not just at the virtues of Josephine, but at those of her ideal, her revered Catherine McAuley. "In governing it was quite perceptible," according to one of Austin's successors as community leader, that Austin "took our saintly Foundress for her Model."[212] Certainly, Austin fell short in many ways, as she was the first to point out, often asking prayers that she might increase in virtue. On one occasion when a reader/ editor wrote that her secretary had sent the wrong bundle of proofs, Austin replied, "I have no secretary, never had . . . all mistakes are mine."[213] Even so, Austin was particularly successful, as was Josephine, in her appreciation of ability and her wise choice of superiors. Xavier Warde had teased Austin about spreading AMDG across the entire southern coast, but Austin claimed that her ideals really were being extended by her able young superiors. As Austin had done earlier for Pope Pius IX, she again sent a collection of her books to the Vatican, this time to Pope Leo XIII, requesting his blessing for her community.[214] To Austin's great joy, 1885 opened with the news that the papal benediction had been sent. The Pope thanked Austin Carroll with a beautiful benediction for herself, her sisters, "and all her works — benevolent, literary, and spiritual."[215] Besides her work on the *Annals*, Austin's main literary thrust in 1883 had been sending out her reprint of Catherine McAuley's *Cottage Controversy*, as she wanted all the Mercies to know of this fine catechetical work. Mother Austin also continued her "Southern Sketches" through 1884, her own contributions readied in advance for the final volume of the Mercy *Annals*.[216]

During this period when the cross "made itself a local habitation among them,"[217] Austin seemed to give special emphasis to the spiritual, for she prepared her personal retreat notes for publication as *Lectures Delivered at a Spiritual Retreat*, as well as her translation of Ribadeneira's *Principles of Government of St. Ignatius*.[218] Thus, as so often happened, Austin's editing and translating united the literary and the spiritual work which Leo XIII had just blessed. As to Mother Austin's benevolent work, much of it was as quietly accomplished as her assistance for Charles Gayarré and his wife. Yet such help often became known, partly since it was incessant, but also because recipients from all walks of life spread word abroad about the charity of "L'Ange Austin." Other benevolent works, however, like Austin's efforts to provide educational opportunities for poor young boys, drew more attention. In this area where culture preferred religious congregations of men to educate the boys, the New Orleans Sisters of Mercy were teaching boys in all the parochial schools they staffed except St. Alphonsus. But teaching in the parish schools did not raise as many eyebrows as the work with the delinquent boys in the House of Correction and with the waifs in the Newsboys' Home. The latter gained prominence because of the publicity given it by the Society of St. Vincent de Paul which started the work and by the newsmen who befriended the little fellows. One reporter noted that Austin's "kind heart always leans toward those whom the world usually overlooks," and that she believed in boys, even though they "are prone to look upon refining influences as beneath their dignity."[219] Austin had the knack of turning the energy of mischief-makers "into a truer, nobler channel."

Another news item mentioned that the same Sisters of Mercy who prepared "the graceful concert given by the innocent school girls" one evening had been at the prison the previous week "directing the prayers and inspiring with true contrition . . . the doomed men who faced death upon the gallows."[220] The reporter thought that few realized "how varied and arduous" were the works in "'the broad field" of the local Sisters of Mercy. His surprise would have been greater had he known that the same broad-minded nun who had inaugurated the prison work and the newsboys' school, had more books on display at the 1884–1885 Cotton Centennial Exposition than any other authoress in Louisiana.[221] In the literary exhibit from each of the states, Mother Austin Carroll shared the honors with Louisa Alcott and Harriest Beecher Stowe, among others. As the Exposition grounds on the site of the old Foucher plantation could be easily reached by the streetcars, Austin had her local teachers accompany their pupils and made sure that the children saw the displays from the Mercy schools in the Education Hall. Convinced that the scientific and educational exhibits presented a mini-normal course, Austin arranged for the Mercies from outside New Orleans to attend as well. The appearance of the long-robed sisters at the exposition made a stir until they were joined by the nuns from other congregations. William T. Francis, who was arranging for the piano much of the music that the fair's Mexican Band played, composed "Convent Chimes," which, the cover sheet proclaimed, was "respectfully dedicated to Mother Superior of the Convent of Mercy, New Orleans."[222]

In spite of her concern over Rome's long-delayed decision, Mother Austin found the spring of 1885 a "delightful season." The award committee from the "Woman's Department of the World's Exposition" bestowed upon Mother Austin Carroll their first-place ribbon for the publications she displayed during the Exposition.[223] Austin was impressed with the fact that not one of the members from the national committee was of the Catholic religion.[224] How different from her anti-Catholic experiences in New England three decades earlier was the ecumenism of the Crescent City, where a priest might speak in behalf of a civic group and a minister had recently given a lecture for a charity sponsored by a Catholic group. That bright spring the World's Fair had brought to New Orleans numerous clerical visitors as well as such recent scientific advances as electricity,[225] so that Austin thought the world, one site in Rome excepted, seemed to be moving faster. Gone were the trains of a decade earlier which could take five hours to get from Pensacola to Mobile.[226] Since the railroads of the 1880s had gained the "lightning speed of thirty miles an hour," the New Orleans Mercies were "taking the cars," rather than the coastal steamers to reach their Gulf Coast branches.[227] New York and Chicago had a long-distance telephone connection, and Austin wondered if Rome might one day have a phone line to America. Even though she took the time to make several visits to the exhibits of the World's Centennial Exposition, Mother Austin was especially busy that spring with construction ready to start in one branch and already in progress in another. In St. Martinville, property had been purchased, and with some assistance from the Society of St. Joseph of Mill Hill, England, a new building was to be erected for the black school.[228]

A convent was under construction in Belize, where work was never rapid. Father Di Pietro was pleased that several more sisters were to staff the government school for boys if Rome decided that the branch could continue. Sir Roger Goldsworthy, the governor of British Honduras, lent encouragement with the promise of assistance to the schools, and the natives of Stann Creek clamored for a Mercy mission there.[229] Closer to home there were always improvements in progress, like decorative painting in the chapel and the oratories, repairs on one of the cisterns and the back gallery, new books for the library, and, with concern for rising prices, bargains from the Hy Reis Bakery. Austin's breadth of vision reached with little effort both bread and back gallery, and from Bayou Teche to Belize, just as her zeal prompted every form of charity to the needy both within and beyond New Orleans. Her hospitality to Mercies who sought either shelter or literary help was legendary. Sister Mary Juliana Purcell had come south in 1880 for editorial assistance with her book of meditations, and Mother Mary Jerome Shubrick in 1881 for a temporary respite before starting a new foundation in Missouri.[230] Besides such guests, Austin Carroll and her sisters gave permanent haven to ten Sisters of Mercy whose communities collapsed. For instance, when Leray as Bishop of Natchitoches, closed two destitute foundations during his brief tenure in the Red River diocese, some of the Sisters moved to the Midwest and others found refuge with Mother Austin as they preferred to remain in Louisiana. Such was the case, also, for several Mercies from the foundation on the move in western Missouri and eastern Texas.[231]

The zeal of fifty-year-old Austin Carroll and her creative methods of carrying out the ideals of Catherine McAuley were still contagious in 1885. Forty young women had entered the Mercy novitiate in the Irish Channel between 1881 and 1885. In the latter year Bishop Eugene O'Connell, who was visiting from Grass Valley, California, officiated at the reception of a group of postulants. Recuperating from an injured leg, O'Connell was delayed in the city a month. After visiting the Mercies at the motherhouse and the branches, he wrote Rome of the beautiful spirit of the community.[232] In the meantime, Mother Austin was contemplating plans for future projects in what she called her "corner of the Lord's vineyard."[233] One idea considered since 1882 was the establishment of a home for working women which would give them quarters better than their dingy boarding houses or the fine homes sponsored by the Protestants. Mother Austin wished to provide, with minimal board and regulation, a fine Catholic environment where the women could entertain friends. It was to differ vastly from the dormitory type of Mercy Home used for a dwindling number of immigrants. Another idea just forming in 1885 was the founding of a Catholic college for women. Perhaps, this idea arrived along with the news of Radcliff and Bryn Mawr in the Northeast. As Austin pondered its feasibility, she decided that the largely Catholic city of New Orleans was the ideal site for such a venture. Yet neither plan could be started, she explained to Bishop O'Connor, until she could "receive written authority to use for our support the fees paid" by those who would live in one or attend the other.[234]

Early that year Austin Carroll and her Assistant Superior, Mother Mary Teresa Gourrier, had considered going to Rome with Bishop James O'Connor. A mutual friend, Mother Mary Patricia Waldron of Philadelphia, told the bishop how agreeable the trip would be, for "Mother Austin has a fund of pleasant wit."[235] However, when Mother Austin asked Leray if he would advise her to make the trip to attend to business about her books, he said, "No, if you went you'd never come back."[236] At this, Austin told O'Connor, "I took a fit of laughing," for she knew that Leray frequently spoke "*of* me as if he wouldn't be sorry if I were out of his way." Disappointed, Austin continued, "It is a good act of mortification for me to lose this opportunity of going," yet recalled that "Archbishop Perché trusted me entirely. . . . I could have gone to Rome every year with his consent. . . . But mortification is specially suited to this holy season [Lent], so I will say *Deo Gratias*."[237] She was also thankful that Belize seemed safe as a branch, for Father Di Pietro had told her "that he had the victory in Rome, but I was never officially notified." Mother Austin then listed the points which she hoped Bishop O'Connor might be able to obtain for her. First, she believed, along with a number of other religious superiors in the area at the time,[238] that it was essential for the welfare of her sisters that the branch convents in small places "remain united to our . . . Central house unless a majority of the Sisters and the Bishops concerned" agree to establishing a branch as a foundation. Second, for her women's college she wanted "written authorization" to charge tuition for teaching the "higher branches . . . always bearing in mind and practice that . . . the poor are our chief charges and that a majority of our Sisters be engaged with them."[239]

The third point Austin requested was "authorization for opening a department in the House of Mercy in which young [working] women . . . may pay for board, etc."[240] One might wonder why Austin Carroll needed Rome's permission to accept tuition or board, when Mercies were already doing so in academies all over America and in a number of schools and teacher-training institutions in England and Ireland. Austin Carroll knew that Bishop Michael O'Connor had asked and received for the Sisters of Mercy in the United States this very permission from Propaganda Fide some thirty years earlier, for in 1881 she had published that fact in the *Annals*.[241] "The verbal and tacit permission for these things in the forty-one years of our Order's existence in America is enough for our consciences," she told James O'Connor.[242] "Yet were I to open such a House [of Mercy] as the circumstances of this city require," or establish a women's college requiring tuition, "the two Germans would report us to Rome as breaking our Rules." Catherine McAuley "put a select school in almost every place where she opened a convent," Austin recalled, "and she ordered a boarding school in Carlow."[243] Austin Carroll certainly appreciated the irony of the situation, because most Mercy communities in America staffed academies in order to maintain financial solvency. Yet, Austin's personal preference for teaching the poor was so strong that she chose not to establish private schools. Yet, if she now answered the needs of the times with her projected residence and college, an endless stream of accusations would flow to Rome. She told James O'Connor, "Our Foundress, a woman of wonderful sanctity and common sense, always did what the circumstances of each place required. . . . We ought to have the freedom to do the spiritual good . . . which Providence puts in our way."[244]

Before O'Connor left for Rome, Mother Austin wrote to wish him *bon voyage*, to let him know that she would keep "a lamp burning before the Sacred Heart" for a safe trip, and to make it perfectly clear that she did not wish to impose her requests upon any other Mercy community.[245] Her triennial was to end in December 1886, and "were it God's will, I'd like our part of the business settled while I am in office. . . . We form a kind of Southern province now and all goes well."[246] Those famous last words were to be contradicted within the month by the actions of Leray. The jolt came while Mother Austin was in St. Martinville, where she had gone for the annual school entertainments and to arrange for the erection of the new black school.[247] On Saturday, May 16, Austin received a note from Leray which had been mailed to the motherhouse in New Orleans and then forwarded to St. Martinville. With sublime faith in the postal service, Leray mailed it Thursday, expected Austin to receive it Friday, and told her to have the sisters assembled for elections the following day, May 16. Had Austin been in New Orleans, the overnight notice would have made it impossible to have present any but the sisters in New Orleans, thus according to the Mercy Rule, illegally excluding the sisters in the other branch convents. Yet, Leray's note said that the election was to be "according to the Constitutions of your Order." Austin immediately notified the branches that, if Leray held the election without them, they should protest the violation of the Constitution and of their individual right to participate in the election of their own superior.[248]

Mother Austin's answer to Leray's note stressed the lack of justice in his demand and quoted the Constitution, which stated that "the Superior, when elected or re-elected, shall govern three years."[249] Thus, she noted that her triennial was to last another eighteen months. After mentioning the impossibility of assembling the sisters in the motherhouse on overnight notice and the difficulty of calling the teachers from their classrooms before the session ended, she added, "Why summon them at all if the previous election be set aside? . . . If the former election be a farce, what is the use of another?"[250] Austin reminded Leray that he had changed the election date in 1880. "If you as co-adjutor [in 1880] had the power," certainly Perché as archbishop could transfer the date in 1883, a fact which had angered Leray. "Though as a private person," said Austin,

> I should covet persecution, of which I have had my share and from those who should assist and encourage me, yet in my public capacity, whoever makes an accusation against me will be invited to prove it. Every act of my administration will bear the closest investigation. Your Grace, who holds the place of our Father, friend, and the Guardian of our rights, should in common justice, find out the calumniator and punish him.[251]

Mother Austin concluded with the news that she would return Monday to the motherhouse, where she would await further explanation.

Leray let her wait for a week before he answered; in the meantime he spread the news gleefully to his German clique. Mother Austin wrote O'Connor in Rome, asking him to learn if there were any new accusations there, as the Redemptorist provincial had told her that he had dropped the Giesen complaints of the year before. Although Loewekamp did not mention that he had learned that Rome had found the charges false or faulty, he told Austin Carroll that Giesen should have taken his complaints across the street to her rather than across the ocean to Rome. If there were some new round of charges, Austin wondered what they could be. She questioned, too, if Leray could really put her out of office without giving her any reason.[252] Then Leray replied, answering her last question, for he said that it was Propaganda which had ordered a new election because of the complaints and "difficulties" concerning her community. Then came the statement which struck Austin as a thunderbolt: "In regard to you personally the sacred Congregation has decided that you cannot be permitted to complete the three years for which you were elected in 1883."[253] Earlier, Austin had told James O'Connor, "Our Lord Jesus Christ knows that I would joyfully give my life for the honor of His Church."[254] Suddenly, the time had come to give not just her life, but her reputation. Once Rome had spoken, however, Austin Carroll acquiesced completely from the depths of her great love for Christ. Immediately after reading Leray's message, she sent her *fiat*, fluently extravagant as it poured from a heart bursting with emotion.

> Not an army of ten thousand soldiers could force me to remain in office one moment after what Yr. Grace states of Propaganda. In justice, if any justice is to be meted me, originals or copies should be shown me. But . . . Rome did the same in the case of St. Alphonsus and other holy persons with whom I am unworthy to be associated, so powerful is calumny for evil. But the day of the calumniators will come. There are no "difficulties" existing in any of our communities. Our Sisters are devoted, laborious, and zealous. Perfect union and charity reign among them, thank God. . . . As I am no longer Superior . . . please direct all further communications to the Assistant, Mother Mary Philomène Butler. . . . I shall turn all over to her immediately, arrange business matters, and notify the Sisters as soon as possible.[255]

The signature, "Mary Teresa Austin Carroll, late Superior Sisters of Mercy, New Orleans, etc.," wore the emphasis of double underlining. Austin told O'Connor that the sisters had already written very strongly to Leray, as "American Sisters are not going to be deprived of their rights" and "American converts are awfully scandalized at what Leray says is the action of Rome.[256] I try to calm them," but they all know that Leray "closed two houses of our Order in his late diocese and put the Sisters out without a place to go" until Austin took them in and asked her sisters to give them a permanent home.[257]

Mother Austin's letter to Bishop Kirby was even more frank, as she explained that she "was utterly in the dark as to what can be charged against us that would cause Propaganda" to set aside both superior and lawful election.[258] She mentioned that the Americans "found this particularly hard, but we who are of Irish birth know how to handle the cross." She asked several favors: "please pray that the trials we have may be borne AMDG," ask for an investigation, "ascertain what I have done . . . and what is the exact punishment meted out to me."[259] She gave a brief account of their works of mercy in the schools and institutions, for the poor, the imprisoned, the sick, and concluded, "Our whole lives are devoted to spreading the Faith."[260] Austin then gave a resumé of their trials. Although "no complaints of any kind have ever been made against us to our faces," two Germans sent charges to Rome; she asked for an investigation; Simeoni appointed Rouxel, who made a thorough one, found the complaints faulty and false, reported such to Rome; and Simeoni "wrote me a reassuring letter. We thought all was over." Now, "I, after my life-long devotion to Rome and the church, am singled out by name . . . as one unfit to finish the triennial."[261] She assumed it was more calumny from the clique. Even so, she could not understand how she could be condemned unheard,

> without a word of explanation or a hint of the crime, whatever it may be that is laid to our charge. True, no document from Rome has been shown us. . . . We must only pray the Sacred Heart to give us patience. . . . I have been in religion since 1853, and should therefore have the virtue to bear this heavy cross. Pray that I may. I shall do my best, with God's help.[262]

"For anything you wish to know of me," Mother Austin told Bishop Kirby, "I refer Your Lordship" to Archbishop Gibbons, Bishops Hogan, O'Connor, Manucy, and O'Connell, and to priests who served as community confessors for many years: Fathers Girardey, CSSR, Hubert, SJ, and Butler, SJ.[263] Yet her staunchest admirers and defenders were her sisters. From the branches they wrote Leray to question an election called in the middle of a term and to protest the attempt to have an election without them. They upheld Mother Austin and her administration, each branch noting special points to praise. "We have the best of mothers and we mean to keep her if we can. But if Rome refuses, we shall be obedient children of the Church."[264] "But for her administration, we might be scattered like the poor Sisters in your late diocese . . . for our trials have been many and grievous, but her prudence and charity brought us safely through it all."[265] Leray was reminded that he knew "the havoc F. Giesen caused among the religious in Shreveport," and we know what he did here. "Under Mother Austin, by God's special help, the house rose from the ashes — debts of $15,000 were paid, credit re-established, etc."[266] "Ungrateful indeed, should we be, did we forget the Mother that built up our community when, through the machinations of one man, it was almost destroyed."[267] "Mother Austin received us all into religion, instructed and professed us, and her gentle but firm rule has brought our large and efficient community to its present high prosperity."[268] "Were she out of office, we would love her as dearly and obey her as cheerfully. If people have said otherwise to Your Grace or to Rome, they have slandered us."[269]

In these letters of protest, several pointed remarks were made to Leray, one by a sister who had been converted to Catholicism,

> I am astonished that Your Grace should allow anyone to calumniate our Mother at Rome or elsewhere. I don't know another in America, man or woman, who has done so much for Religion as she, and I assure you, if a woman of her grand abilities devoted herself to Religion in the Protestant Church, such a one would receive different treatment from the Protestant prelates."[270]

The group letters continued. "As to branches outside the diocese, if this was right at the Pass when Your Grace was the first to propose them to our community, they cannot be wrong in other instances."[271] "If your predecessor had not the power to grant us a dispensation, as Your Grace has said, how can we apply to you? Your Grace blames us for obeying Abp. Perché, and your successor may blame us for obeying you."[272] "What security have we if one prelate disowns the actions of another? And what if the views of Your Grace's successor be entirely different from yours?"[273] "We do not covet the fate of the poor Sisters at Natchitoches, seven of whom were rec'd by our charitable Superior. Abp. Perché, who understood religious life so well and had our interests so much at heart, said such would be our fate if ever we separated from the Mother House."[274] "We intend to petition Rome for leave to elect our Superior again when her term expires."[275]

The petition was no idle threat, for after several weeks of prayer and meetings the sisters wrote their petition to Pope Leo XIII, begging that Mother Austin Carroll be "eligible for election as Mother Superior" in each successive election because her "whole life has been devoted to the sick, the poor, the plague-stricken, the orphan, and the instruction of the ignorant by tongue and pen."[276] Mother Philomène noted that Leray was aware that the sisters were sending the petition "and has said nothing to us against it."[277] The sisters sent copies of their request to Cardinal Simeoni and to Bishops Kirby and Leray. Mother Philomène also wrote to Bishop Kirby, asking him to urge the granting of the petition as

> a grateful mark of recognition of the great service our beloved Mother has rendered the Holy Catholic Church, in illustration . . . of which she has published some thirty works. . . . But her writings are the least of her works. For the thirty-two years of her religious life, she has devoted her best energies to the spread of our holy religion, especially in providing education for the poorest and most abandoned classes. . . . You will understand, my Lord, how strange it will seem to Americans accustomed

to "fair play" that . . . [anyone] would condemn unheard the Mother and Foundress of our eight convents. . . . Thank God she has virtue enough to bear this mean attack of cowardly men . . . and to turn to her spiritual profit the persecutions that assail her. But it is for us, her spiritual children, . . . to demand that justice, which we have heard Rome always shows to the weak and the persecuted. Therefore, we beg Your Lordship to aid us in freeing . . . the foundress of our Order in the South from the slanders that have found their way to Rome.[278]

Mother Philomène referred Kirby "for the truth of our presentation" to Archbishop Gibbons or to any of the clergy in any of the places where they have established convents.

Mail was so slow in crossing the ocean that it was two months before Austin Carroll finally saw the directions Rome had sent Leray in May.[279] Bishop Kirby, proving himself a great friend, sent the information to her even before she saw Simeoni's letter. No wonder Leray had not shown it sooner, for Austin had won nearly all the different points, although she had lost a big one. Leray could not act unilaterally to cut off the branch convents, either that of St. Michael's Parish or those beyond the diocese. All must agree before Leray could separate branches from the motherhouse. The safety of the Belize convent was locked in, for Leray could not change its status to that of independent foundation without the consent of Propaganda itself.[280] Austin's request for an investigation was also granted, and the false charges were not even mentioned. The cardinals had tried to balance the scales. On one was this rather slight nun carrying the weight of the years and her voluminous Mercy habit, and on the other scale was Leray bearing the huge weight of his office. At this point, the scales might have balanced quite evenly. Then the weight of Di Pietro and the Jesuit community joined Austin's scale for the issue of the branches, particularly that of Belize, and their side became the heavy weight.[281] But when the decision concerned Austin as superior, Leray was joined by the stalwart Jaeckel, the 300-pound Giesen, and the power of the Redemptorists and the political presence of the Germans in Rome. Quite naturally, the scale jerked up and flipped Austin out. At the time unfortunately, the Sisters of Mercy had no Cardinal Protector in Rome, and Bishop Kirby had been asked to help only after the balancing of the scales had been accomplished.[282]

Keen and clear, Austin's insight led her to notice the balancing and to tell James O'Connor, "Having given me so much, something must be done to me, no doubt to satisfy the opposition."[283] But what caused the wise report of the astute Cardinal Bartolini to be cast aside for a new decision? Evidently, the cardinals accepted the word of Leray, the unhappy little man they had appointed to succeed Perché, but were now wishing would resign, as Denis O'Connell told Gibbons.[284] Leray backed the complaints of the German clique so firmly that, without investigating a single charge, he had written Simeoni that every accusation was true.[285] Concerning the Mercy election, for instance, the cardinals had all the evidence and declared it to be proper and legal, hence, the charge to the contrary to be false.[286] Since the same was true for most of the complaints, the cardinals must have discarded Leray's substantiation of false accusations. Actually then, it was Leray's second personal charge against Mother Austin Carroll upon which the cardinals based their negative judgment. This, according to Leray, was that Austin "disobeyed ecclesiastical authority."[287] Leray neglected to state that he referred to Austin's establishment of the branches in Belize and St. Michael's Parish in 1883, when Perché not Leray, was the local "ecclesiastical authority."[288] Because Simeoni had had to admonish Leray in this period when he opposed whatever Perché approved, Leray's acknowledgement either of the year or of the specific events would have provided the cardinals with truth in the case.[289]

Leray had also worked to keep the truth from Austin by refusing to show "Rome's orders." Only two months later, when Austin saw Simeoni's directions, did she learn that except for the extraordinary election, Rome had upheld her understanding of Mercy government, and also that Leray had been told "to ascertain which month would be convenient" for a new election.[290] The sisters chose August, and the Belize sisters sent precedent-setting written ballots. Since Austin Carroll could not be named superior in this election, the sisters chose the assistant as superior and named Mother Austin her assistant.[291] It took five minutes. "To keep myself out of mischief" after the voting, Austin told O'Connor, "I went to play 'Ave Maris Stella,' etc., hoping Leray would be gone before the music ceased."[292] But he waited to condemn, saying that Austin was not legally in office since 1883, and that Perché "had done extremely wrong in giving the decisions he gave."[293] The new superior, Mother Philomène, went up to explain to Leray, and then the bursar went, "but he wouldn't listen. Then," Austin related,

At last I went up and he heard me, but wouldn't give in. I said I couldn't allow Archbishop Perché to be so spoken of in our chapel, that he had always been a Father and a friend to us, that he was a gentleman and a scholar, thoroughly versed in everything relating to religious life. "Now," said I, "if such a man gave us wrong decisions, what guarantee have we that Your Grace will give us the right ones?" It would take a volume to describe the scene—all the Sisters were crying and sobbing. His Grace abused them roundly, not a kind word or even a courteous word. Yet they had done all that Rome had asked.[294]

Although Mother Austin did not believe that Leray's post-election claims were correct, she was angry that he had so disturbed the peace of the sisters by impugning the validity of their vows during the 1883–1885 period, as well as such other official acts as her disbursement of funds and establishment of new houses. While Austin consulted O'Connor[295] and the Sisters wrote Kirby,[296] Leray and his big friend broadcast to everyone the news of the Mercy Chapter of Elections and his own claims. This was hardly the intention of Propaganda, especially since Leray's words contradicted both the Bartolini and the later Franzelin conclusion.[297] Although this unwarranted publicity was probably one of the most difficult and unjust aspects of the whole proceeding, it continued for four months. The reverend visitors appointed for the investigation requested by Austin and called by Propaganda were Fathers Philippe de Carrière, SJ, and Jean Baptist Bogaerts. These priests chosen to please both sides, one being a Jesuit and the other a German, agreed with the earlier investigations concerning the elections. Like Neithart in 1880[298] and Butler and Rouxel in 1883,[299] the visitors said that Perché followed the Mercy Rule in appointing Austin Carroll superior 1874–1880, that there were proper canonical elections for three years each in 1880 and 1883, and that Austin's legitimate term should end in 1886.[300] Certainly, it would have been reassuring to Mother Austin to have heard this conclusion, but the visitors had to report to Rome, the final decision to be later.

The visitors heard the "unanimous testimony of the sisters that their Rule is observed, obedience practiced, and that unity and charity dwell among them."[301] But the two priests heard much more from many others, priests, members of the Society of St. Vincent de Paul, and even Redemptorists. For instance, the report stated that

> the Jesuit Fathers in particular have known these Sisters since they first were established in New Orleans and have been greatly aided by them in several of their works of zeal. We know positively that the Jesuits unanimously state: "We cannot adequately praise the spirit of piety, zeal, and compassion which animates them. In this city these Sisters undertake works of zeal which no other religious could or would attempt. Their eminent virtues, especially their admirable charity, have won for them a universal influence — not only among Catholics, but even among Protestants and unbelievers."[302]

In reading letters addressed to Mother Austin from "outstanding bishops and pious and wise Redemptorists," the visitors saw "sympathy, spiritual advice, and testimony in her behalf."[303] The report said that "sympathy from eminent friends was not enough," for the accusations against her and her sisters were "so deplorable" that one might think them "deliberate lies or abuse," for here their wonderful works of mercy are seen by *"tout le monde."* The visitors thought it "evident that the great spiritual good which they have accomplished has aroused jealousy and enmity toward them" on the part of their accusers.[304]

Mother Austin found it exceedingly painful to have Leray raise "a serious question about the validity of vows during the period of litigation" and to see their Rome-confirmed Rule cast aside by "the special election which negated their Constitution."[305] The visitors thought that Propaganda should "reassure the Sisters" about their vows, especially since the "investigation has compromised them in the eyes of the public," giving rise to "harmful suspicions," which are reinforced by their bishop who speaks "most unfavorably of them."[306] The visitors found the sisters hurt and discouraged because "of the extraordinary way" Propaganda has acted toward them. They fear that there are "powerful and influential enemies in Rome who blacken their reputation," and are even more afraid that the German clique's "spirit of prejudice and opposition here turned against them their own bishop . . . whose words are not carefully weighed, are repeated in public, and are commented upon to his own disadvantage and to the detriment of the Sisters' interests and reputation."[307] Referring to the complaints, the two visitors said,

> If any real wrongs ever did exist, they should have been made known to the Sisters, in conformity with Canon Law, before denouncing them to Propaganda. . . . Since the complaints were not even communicated to them before being sent to Rome, the Sisters were not treated with justice because they were deprived of their right to defend themselves before being sentenced.[308]

As to Mother Austin Carroll, the special visitors discovered that "the Sisters are singularly devoted to her . . . and praise her qualities of mind and heart, and her generosity and kindness to the Sisters."[309] In fact, the two priests concluded that the sisters were actually at fault because "they nearly idolize" Mother Austin. Basing their belief on her exceptional zeal and natural talent, the majority of the sisters thought that only she could successfully govern their large community. Thus, they did not have the highest motive for religious obedience. The report noted that although there was "obvious accord between Mother Austin and Mother Philomène," the sisters were "saddened by Mother Austin's sudden and unjust replacement," and felt that the denigration of Austin's name by public denunciation was despicable and inexcusable.[310] For remarks of this nature, however, the two Old World visitors said that the sisters, especially Mother Austin, had spoken out too forcefully by word and letter against the vindictive actions of the local "ecclesiastical authority." In true nineteenth-century form and regardless of mutual antagonism, the two priests called for more "suffering in silence" and a sharper practice of "humility, docility, and respect for the Ordinary."[311] In fact the whole report was heavily weighted with reference to respect, possibly because it was Leray's main complaint,and probably because of Leray's demand that he receive a copy of this report to Propaganda Fide.[312]

Although the visitors complied, they protested that the demand "hindered the freedom of communication" which they needed.[313] The report concluded with a request and a summation, the former an appeal to Simeoni "to render full justice to the Sisters" and to send them in reparation, "since truth and justice have been so lacking in their respect," a testimonial that could be shown to friends and enemies alike.[314] The visitors closed with

> Since God endows His prelates with the authority necessary for the edification and not the destruction of His children, especially His religious communities, we are hopeful that Propaganda will console these Sisters of Mercy in the tribulation which they are presently experiencing . . . and that the Church will continue to love them and protect them against false accusations and the devilish evil of ruthless enemies.[315]

Although the sisters did not know that Leray had access to the report, they immediately felt an aftershock as Leray removed their Jesuit confessor. From the time they arrived in New Orleans, one of the two confessors of the Sisters of Mercy had always been one of the Jesuit priests, but Leray had substituted the man who had repeatedly sent complaints to Rome.[316] Yet the protest of the new superior could not get Leray to change his assignment. Though difficult, as one of the sisters wrote, Mother Austin was trying "to bear all in silence, trusting that God will defend us when He sees fit."[317]

With a view to pleasing both sides, the two visitors did believe, and so recommended, that maintaining the *status quo* in the Mercy community for one three-year term would not only provide an opportunity for "a harmonius and stable calm," but would also be a period of propitiation wherein the sisters could "perfect the motives of their religious obedience" and Mother Austin could acquire the spirit of "docility which she is greatly lacking."[318] Leray had claimed that the sisters "showed a disposition to resist" his orders, but the investigation showed that the only time this occurred was when the orders opposed their Constitution. Even then, however, as soon as the Mercies learned that the special election was a direction from Rome, they accepted the decision. As to the overly-frank letters written before that,[319] the visitors said, "It seems to us that one must treat with

National Model School, Clonmel

The West Gate of the ancient walled Clonmel

St. Maries of the Isle, Cork

St. Alphonsus Convent, New Orleans

Mercy-staffed black school, Birmingham, Ala.

Mercy High School, St. Martinville, La.

Mother F. Xavier Warde,
Manchester, N.H.

Rev. Michael O'Connor, S.J,
retired bishop

Mother Gonzaga O'Brien,
Manchester

Rev. William McDonald,
Manchester

Bishop David Bacon,
Portland Me.

Mother Patricia Waldron,
Philadelphia

Austin Carroll's friends from the Northeast

St. Katharine's College, New Orleans

Mercy Convent and school, Belize, Central America

Group from the Newsboys' School, New Orleans

Rev. John Duffy, CSSR,
New Orleans

Mother Philomene Butler,
New Orleans

Archbishop N. J. Perche,
New Orleans

Mathilde Gourrier,
first Mercy from La.

Rev. Ferreol Girardey,
CSSR, New Orleans

Mother Borgia Walsh,
New Orleans

Several Southern friends of Austin Carroll

Austin Carroll's Creche, New Orleans

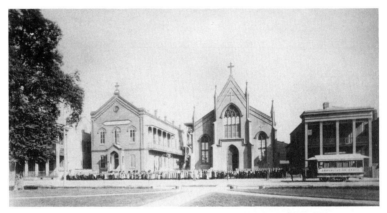

St. Michael Convent, School, and Church, New Orleans

Tomb of Mercy yellow-fever martyrs, New Orleans

**Bishop Thomas Heslin,
Natchez**

**Bishop James O'Connor,
Omaha**

**Mother de Sales Ihmsen,
Loretto, Pa.**

**Mother Baptist Russell,
San Francisco**

**Mother Genevieve Granger,
Chicago**

**Bishop Thomas Becker,
Savannah**

A few of Austin Carroll's scattered friends

Girls near St. Katharine's College, New Orleans

Coolock House near Dublin in the 1890s

Austin Carroll's grave (large cross), Mobile

Convent of Our Lady of Mercy,
St. Alphonsus,

New Orleans, Dec 2 1881.

Monseigneur:

Your Grace's humble children, the Sisters of Mercy, beg that you will graciously bestow forty Days' Indulgence for every visit made by the Sisters or others to their Oratory of Our Lady of Lourdes, and to their Oratory of the Sacred Heart, in St. Alphonsus' Convent of Mercy.

This will mark with new benedictions the golden Jubilee of our Institute

With profound respect

Yr. Grace's humble Child in +
Sister M. T. Austin Carroll.
M. Superior

Most Rev. Archb. Perché

granted according to the aforesaid petition.
New Orleans, December 3rd 1881.
+ N. J. Perché, Archbishop of New Orleans

Letter of Mother Austin Carroll

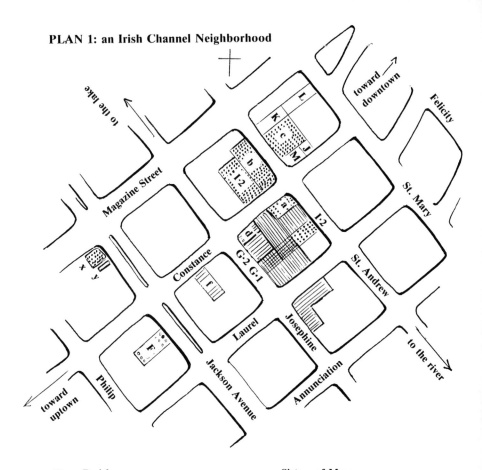

PLAN 1: an Irish Channel Neighborhood

Three Parishes

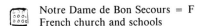 Notre Dame de Bon Secours = F
French church and schools

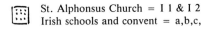 St. Alphonsus Church = I 1 & I 2
Irish schools and convent = a,b,c,

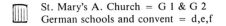 St. Mary's A. Church = G 1 & G 2
German schools and convent = d,e,f

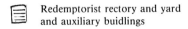 Redemptorist rectory and yard
and auxiliary buidlings

z = downtown lake corner
w = uptown river corner

Sisters of Mercy

x = pharmacy rented for a
convent
y = house rented for a Mercy
Home

J = frame house bought for Mercy
Home, orphan girls, and then
a day-care center

K = brick home was industrial
school, Mercy Home, then
home for elderly

L = building erected for creche,
laundry to support Mercy
Home, later housed elderly

M = St. Katharine's College, served
as the novitiate, then Mercy
Normal

PLAN 2: MERCY SQUARE

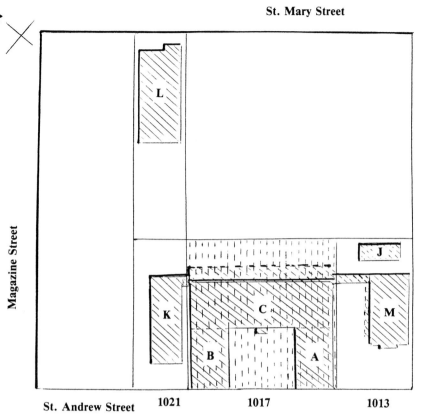

St. Mary Street

Magazine Street

Constance Street

St. Andrew Street   1021   1017   1013

Key

property purchased by
Mother Austin Carroll

locations of buildings
erected or renovated

property purchased by
St. Alphonsus Parish

Parish buildings

A = Junior Girls' Hall
B = Senior Girls' Hall
C = Convent of Mercy

Sisters of Mercy

J = frame house used for Mercy
Home, orphan girls, and day-
care center

K = brick dwelling used for Mercy
Home for working women,
then home for elderly women

L = building erected for creche,
Mercy Home and a laundry
for the support of the poor,
and later, a home for elderly
women

M = building erected as St.
Katharine College for
Women, then served as the
novitiate, and later as Mercy
Normal College

Mother Austin Carroll

some indulgence these noble-hearted women devoted to their Church, thinking themselves unjustly persecuted by their bishop, have forgotten themselves to the point of raising their voices too high in the complaints made to him."[320] Possibly, Mother Austin revealed her hurt to the visitors as she did to Bishop Kirby, when she wrote

> True I felt and feel keenly the action of Propaganda to me. Had I been a thief or a drunkard, no worse could be done . . . I happening unfortunately to be very well-known. Still I say *Deo gratias* for every pain and humiliation caused to me and to those who love me. And I am more resigned than anyone else concerned that Rome has thought well to reward my life-long services to Rome and Religion by so public . . . a penance. . . . But I thank God, and the authors of it all the same.[321]

By September the sisters learned that Archbishop Gibbons had been named Apostolic Commissioner to settle several controversies and check on the reduction of the archdiocesan debt. Prior to his November visit, Gibbons asked Janssens for pertinent information.[322] After warning Gibbons that he did "not know much of the affairs in New Orleans, and what I know may be only one-sided," Janssens proceeded to demonstrate the wisdom of his introductory statement, for he referred to the first Mercy superior in New Orleans, evidently under the impression that this was Mother Austin.[323] Actually, the bishop was trying to assist Gibbons, but his misinformation certainly did not help Austin Carroll, as she knew nothing of it, and therefore, had no chance to correct the error. Just then, however, Bishop Kirby was working in her behalf in Rome, for in October he wrote Mother Austin that he had related to Leo XIII in a papal audience

> what a countrywoman of mine had done in New Orleans, of your eight convents, eighty-six nuns, and useful and edifying books. His Holiness was pleased to listen to all with deep interest and evident pleasure and in the end charged me to send you his apostolic benediction for yourself, for all your houses, Sisters, schools, etc., and he added of his own accord, for your Father in Ireland, *al suo padre* — I had been speaking of him to His Holiness. And this benefit sent to you with all the affection of the paternal heart of the Vicar of Christ, is to be for you, Dearest Child, a secure pledge of the final grand and consoling benediction which through Christ's mercy you are to receive one day from your heavenly Spouse.'[324]

Perhaps Kirby was forewarning Mother Austin that consolation was to be found only in eternity, for November was to bring *déjà vu* to the New Orleans Mercies in the visit from Gibbons, for he was simply going to repeat the March directions from Rome. Since propaganda did not "deem it opportune to consider the validity of the Mercy election" in 1883, Gibbons was to resolve the differences with the two Germans and Leray and to see whether Mother Austin should complete her term until 1886.[325] Besides the data from Rome, Gibbons received from the Germans all the old false and faulty Giesen complaints, which Loewekamp told the sisters had been dropped.[326] The clique added two new ones also, that since the parish was now giving fifty dollars annually for each parish orphan housed in the asylum, they did not want the sisters to have any type of raffle or money-raising activity in the parish. Evidently, they thought that the sisters should be able to keep the children warm, fed, clothed and in shoes for thirteen cents a day! Probably, this caused the complaint that Austin did not manage her finances prudently. Gibbons was surprised to learn that there was no debt on any of the Mercy institutions.[327] He heard, too, of the sisters consorting with the ruffians who sold newspapers. The sisters said that they would stop teaching the newsboys until they received written permission from Leray or Rome, but Gibbons told them to continue the work after he saw that they were transported in closed carriages so as not to be out on the public street.[328] And the Jesuit chaplain not only told Gibbons of the tremendous improvement in the boys, but also took him to see the boys busy with their studies.

Gibbons also heard from the archbishop, who felt that Simeoni treated him unjustly. "If one half of what is said of his mismanagement of the ninety millions of Propaganda property is true," said Leray, how can he complain about the pace at which the diocesan debt is being reduced.[329] Leray's complaints about the sisters were those he had sent to Rome, with the additional accusation that they were not obeying Rome. Hence, Gibbons had each sister declare that she accepted the directions from Simeoni, even though they had held their election as Rome demanded months earlier.[330] In every way Gibbons accepted the word of the unhappy prelate, for he had certainly heard nothing of the favorable proceedings of Franzelin and the wise decisions of Bartolini.[331] And though it would seem logical that he base his decision on the exoneration of the sisters in the recent deCarrière/Bogaerts findings since it had been a part of this "apostolic process," there is no evidence that Gibbons even saw that report.[332] It would hardly have had the time necessary to get to Simeoni and back to Gibbons, and it seems most unlikely that Leray would have shown it to Gibbons since he fared so poorly in it. And the Sisters of Mercy, after having been found guilty of defending themselves with too much ardor by the last two visitors, may have not said enough to Gibbons. He did compliment the community on "the good dispositions they manifested," but declared that the decisions of Propaganda were to be enforced.[333] For months Mother Austin's letters had been beseiging her friends with the same request, "Pray that we bear up patiently to the end. We need all the prayers we can get in this conjuncture."[334]

When Mother Austin thanked Bishop Kirby for his helpful letters, she related that Gibbons, in his visitation, had "found everything satisfactory" and told the sisters that he would send a "most favorable" report to Rome.[335] Gibbons' letters to Simeoni relate that the main causes of Mercy conflict with the German priests had been removed by the signing of a legal contract, that Austin had "subjected herself laudably to the decree of Propaganda," and that "all the Sisters, without exception," also submitted to the directions from Rome.[336] Simeoni must have assumed that the Apostolic Commissioner accomplished these events, for Gibbons never mentioned that the contract had been signed the previous year nor that Austin Carroll and the sisters had bowed to the direction to have a new election the previous summer, in fact, as soon as they learned it came from Rome. In her letter accepting the decrees, one of the sisters explained to Gibbons, "While our beloved Foundress [Mother Austin] is dearer to me than any one else, I and all here submitted to the decrees of Rome when we heard them last July."[337] Then speaking of Austin, she added,

> Every act of hers has my fullest concurrence. She has always taught us by word and example to submit unreservedly to those who have a right to our obedience. Had it been otherwise, her administration would not have been so fruitful in good and so singularly blessed by God, for this dear Mother often said that it is only the obedient who can count their victories in religion.[338]

Having taken care to explain to Simeoni what a difficult task he had with this case and that his negotiations were not easily brought to a satisfactory end, Gibbons closed with, "Nevertheless, I trust that a stable peace has been established and that all concerned will scrupulously observe the decrees . . . which I again promulgated."[339] Since neither the summary nor the long report sent to Simeoni could be considered that "most favorable report," which Gibbons had told the Mercies he would send to Rome, his personal opinion might have been similar to that of Leray as expressed by Gibbons' Roman agent, Denis O'Connell. From the cathedral rectory in Baltimore, O'Connell wrote Kirby at the Irish College in Rome, "I drop you a line to put you on your guard against the wiles of a woman that [sic] is calculated to entrap unsuspecting victims in her meshes. I mean Mother Austin of New Orleans La."[340] O'Connell had never met Austin Carroll and, certainly, did not know her. Fortunately, Bishop Kirby did. But since Gibbons' secretary in New Orleans had been Placide Chapelle, and not Denis O'Connell, one might have reason to wonder why O'Connell had even heard of Mother Austin. His note said that "she has been fighting for years with the archbishop and has of late gotten herself in conflict with Propaganda."[341] As Mother Austin's agent in Rome since 1880, Bishop Kirby was fully aware of the problems Leray caused Austin while she heeded Archbishop Perché, rather than Bishop Leray. The latter seemed to wish to direct the Mercy community, even though he was in the See simply to reduce the diocesan debt. Could it be possible that O'Connell actually believed that an appeal to a court, even that of Propaganda, was equivalent to conflict with the judge?

In any case, he did state, "She is unfair toward her Archbishop and makes it very annoying for him by the opposition of moral power she elicits."[342] Certainly, there was no love lost between Leray and Austin, but as each of the visitors except Gibbons knew from experience, it was Leray and not Austin who publicized the problems. Several of those appointed visitors had noted how gravely Leray hurt himself by speaking against such zealous religious as Austin Carroll and her Mercies.[343] O'Connell wrote that Austin "is unable to rest easy under her defeat. She wishes to triumph; — a very bad spirit."[344] In her letters to Kirby, Mother Austin spoke more freely than to anyone else. Revealing how deeply hurt she was that Rome had "acted so strangely towards me," she yet added her compliance. "I am quite resigned. . . . Pray that I may never again be Superior . . . that I may never hold any office which might have come to me unlawfully. May God grant we may be left in peace for the future."[345] O'Connell's letter concluded, "I thought I would drop you a line since I know that she corresponds with you and since I thought you ought to know the facts."[346] Could O'Connell have feared that a successful appeal to Kirby by Austin might brew enough of a gale to send Baltimore's rumored red hat swirling afar like a frisbee whipped away in the wind? Austin Carroll had kept no secrets from Gibbons as visitor, including her correspondence with Kirby. O'Connell was not so open, however; for he added a postscript to his letter, "Unless you deem it necessary, you need say nothing of your information to Mother Austin."[347] Later that year as Abbelen and the Germanizers worked for special favors from Rome in just such secrecy as that of O'Connell, Gibbons and the American bishops made a great protest about this manner of acting.[348]

Even in the mild New Orleans winter of 1886, Mother Austin found the winds harsh. Although she had hidden her discouragement from her sisters, Austin revealed it in her correspondence with Bishop Kirby, who, though half a world away, had become a close friend. She related how the "annoyances arising from the complaints to Rome have set us back ten years and injured us every way," for candidates steered clear of the community "spoken of unfavorably" and publicly with extraordinary spite.[349] Several of the appointed visitors had referred to "the devilish evil of their ruthless enemies."[350] Austin continued, "We were almost disheartened. Many a time I wished myself in my dear Convent at home, as it seemed that in this disturbed bankrupt diocese no one could live in peace."[351] Yet Leray, explaining to Gibbons how none of his problems originated from his own actions, enumerated the causes of conflicts. As he went down the list, he stated, "The affair of the Sisters of Mercy originated from the redemptorists."[352] Leray, whom Gibbons had nominated for episcopal office, thanked Gibbons for exonerating his every action. "The rectitude of your judgement has sustained me in all those cases."[353] Austin Carroll's consolation and sustenance were found in her deep love for her divine Lord and in the support of her sisters. As Austin expressed it, "Our whole community is a unit in the Sacred Heart, thank God," and Mother Philomène, "who is one with me in everything, couldn't be kinder."[354] For her part, Mother Philomène found that Austin "was as obedient and docile to me as the youngest novice."[355] Together these two awaited Rome's reply to their question, sent the past August, as to the validity of the sisters' vows during the partial term of Austin Carroll.[356]

At this point Austin was still hoping to receive a positive answer. Meanwhile, she was asking all her friends to pray "that I may be thankful for the sufferings and humiliations that come to me, no matter from what source, and use them all AMDG"—for the greater glory of her God.[357] Her motto kept cropping up, as it did in a letter to Kirby in this period of discouragement. "It is hard to legislate for so many houses, schools, etc. and procure everything for soul and body for so many . . . without a word of encouragement from those over us, and threatened with Rome, as if we would not rather lose our lives than disobey Rome—as if our whole lives were not devoted to the promulgation of the true religion, AMDG, and the corporal works of mercy."[358] Although Austin had received no financial aid of any kind for her institutions during the reign of Archbishop Perché, she had found in the gentle prelate a generous appreciation for her compassionate spirit and an encouraging gratitude for her energetic zeal. This spirit had died with him, however, and throughout Leray's term, turmoil reigned supreme. More trouble was yet to come as he threatened Belize by refusing to allow sisters to be missioned there.[359] The reply from Rome arrived at the end of January. Even though the consultors had stated that Austin's term was valid, this knowledge and the consolation it would have brought were still withheld. Instead, conditional sanation was asked of the Pope "if any defect crept into those professions."[360] Then, in spite of the fact that Leray had pronounced publicly for months that the vows in question were illicit, the Mercy superiors were mandated to silence on the question.

As the case was closed, Austin thanked Bishop Kirby for his "extraordinary kindness" in standing beside her through it all, and once again opened her heart to her friend.

> I had fondly hoped that Rome would say: "You were lawfully in office, but we thought well to remove you." . . . I feel more keenly on the subject today, if possible, than I did when it happened. Perhaps time may heal the wound, and in any case it is foolish to complain. The authorities can do as they please—we must submit. . . . It seems to me that I have not been justly dealt with, but I will bear all for God's sake. . . . Our adversaries were powerful, and we were in no wise a match for them. . . . I am resigned, and I try not to allow my mind to be embittered at what has been done to me, which I embrace as my portion of the cross. . . . Heretofore, it was universally admitted and acted upon that our Constitutions allowed the first Superior of every foundation one appointment and two elections. . . . That I should take a position to which I had no right, is something like an indelible disgrace to me, and little less than a scandal to the hundreds who know me as having established so many houses for the propagation of Catholic principles. . . . Feeling so strongly on this point, [I know] your lordship will understand how the last letter from Rome pained me. . . . Pray that god will give me perfect resignation. But I don't want to alter things. I would rather bear the cross than have it removed, even if I could, and I know I could not. . . . I hope that at last we shall now be left in peace. May we go on spreading the Faith in silence and obscurity, so that Rome may never have to write to us or of us. . . . I have always desired to serve the Holy Church in the past, and I have done it to the best of my ability. The same with God's help, and more, if possible, I shall do in the future.[361]

11 ORPHANS, ANNALS, FRIENDS
At Home & Afar
1887–1890

By the latter half of the 1880's, everyone knew of Mother Austin Carroll's long love affair with the Crescent City. Perhaps the mutual affection had blossomed so fully because of the characteristics shared by the pair. Though no longer young, both New Orleans and Mother Austin had unusually charming ways. Tinged with a strange mystique, they both had a European ambience as well as a hint of mystery, the city in the shadow of centuries, the sister veiled by her religious life. Though neither possessed classic beauty, both attracted followers readily, in part, because both had consumed a recipe which combined heavy portions of charity and compassion with the unlikely mixture of religious devotion and natural *joie de vivre*. Through the years both the city and the sister had shared their relish of joyful celebration, prodigal hospitality, and Creole seasoning. Both enjoyed children and books, beauty and friends, and even cemeteries on Sundays. In what other city on a Sunday could so many families be found in the local cemeteries visiting with cousins and kin on the wrought iron benches next to the family tomb? And where else could most of the nuns from the Mercy convent be found on a Sunday morning in one of four institutions giving religious instruction to either newsboys or prisoners?

That a few might have considered the Crescent City and the Irish sister a strange pair should come as no surprise. Many others, however, called them not only unusual but also serene and optimistic—the city "easygoing," the sister hopeful and a lover of peace, unless attacked, of course, as any proper Gael could understand. Bright and buoyant even then, Austin Carroll was as full of *bon mot* and apt retort as she was of mother wit and genuine humor. Through the decades however, the sister, like the city, had on occasion acted in a way that caused criticism and controversy. Yet both had demonstrated common sense and courage under censure as they forth-

249

rightly faced their critics. A friend once told the beleagured nun, "Censure is the tax which the eminent must pay to the world." In good times and in bad, however, the old city and the elderly Mercy displayed a certain poise and pride in their identity. Sham was no part of either the *grande dame* that was the Crescent City or the great-hearted Irish woman whom God had chosen as His own. By the 1880's, though a New Orleanian by adoption and affection, Mother Austin was at all times tremendously proud to be one of the Carroll sept, that pious, keen, and generous clan from the golden Vale of Tipperary and Clonmel on the banks of the River Suir.

This pride of Mother Austin had not allowed her to share her Roman problems and personal hurt with her numerous correspondents. Had Austin been a complainer whining about injustice in every letter, her biography would certainly have been written long ago. Only recent research in Roman archives, however, revealed the events and ordeal related in the previous chapter because Austin gave full documentation only to the few prelates who tried to assist her case in Rome. Her extant letters to those bishops indicate that she shared the full depth of her pain and disappointment with Bishop Kirby alone.[1] Letters to friends, unlike those to her advisors and one or two confidants, regularly contained happier news or lesser problems.[2] As a result of Austin's optimistic attitude, later accounts of Mercy foundations usually depicted that in New Orleans as having had no problems or only those caused by yellow fever. One survey stated that during their six decades in New Orleans, the Mercy community "had suffered none of the hardships of poverty and other vexations incident to the beginnings of new founda-tions."[3] The author did add that the community was "not without other trials, but God blessed their labors with signal success." The chronicles in a Mercy convent in Ireland read in a similar strain. "Ere long Mother Austin was placed at the head of her present establishment to plant the seeds of mercy beneath the sun of its nearly tropical climate where each seems to have taken root and flourished wonderfully, AMDG." The writer then related the story of the New Orleans epidemics and the deaths of several of the Mercy nurses.[4]

Although the record referred to the efforts of the sisters to assist the fever victims, the passage in nineteenth-century imagery applied more aptly, perhaps, to the problems of Mother Austin Carroll and her sisters while they suffered the effects of the German persecution.

> Hitherto the trials of the community had been those only of "uphill work" experienced usually on new foundations — difficult and oft-recurring no doubt, yet never assuming the appearance of a heavy cross. Now, however, things were changed, and the Crucified with His own blessed hand marked out that by which they should prove themselves His true followers . . . and

[their actions] showed how faithfully and courageously they followed Him on His blood stained road of Calvary.[5]

Determined to put the painful events of 1885 behind her, Mother Austin turned again to the third volume of the Mercy *Annals* as the new year opened. This American section had been started earlier, but worry about the Roman case and the two buildings under construction in Belize and on the Teche had halted the literary work. The *Annals* were especially involving to Mother Austin as she found in them an opportunity to illustrate further the guiding inspiration that the Sisters of Mercy had received from their foundress.[6] In the opinion of the Limerick Mercies who had known Catherine McAuley personally, Mother Austin succeeded, for their chronicles stated that the *Annals* not only portrayed the progress of the Mercy Institute but they also "embodied again the life and spirit of Mother M. C. McAuley."[7]

Before delving too deeply into the *Annals*, however, Mother Austin had to catch up with her correspondence. Her congratulations went to several of her episcopal friends who had moved up another step on the hierarchial stairway. In October 1885, the bishop of Dibona, James O'Connor, became the bishop of Omaha as his vicariate was promoted to the status of a diocese.[8] Later, her Roman agent and friend, Bishop Kirby of the Irish College, became the archbishop of Ephesus. By late January she sent her congratulations and admired his new patron as especially appropriate.[9] She had copious thanks for him, also, for the Apostolic Benediction which he had procured from the Pope for her father, along with that previously mentioned for herself, the sisters, the pupils and institutions.[10] After this blessing arrived, the Mercies repeatedly tried to get Leray to specify who was to extend the blessing to all the designated recipients.[11] In spite of the requests from the various convents, Leray *déjà en colère*, deigned no answer. Mother Austin had no such delay before forwarding the Pope's blessing to her father in Clonmel.

> The Pope has sent you his Apostolic Benediction! This will be the best birthday present you could receive. I am more glad for you than for myself. It happened this way. Writing to Right Rev. Dr. Kirby . . . Rector of the Irish College in Rome, who is in his 82nd year, I mentioned you and that you were in your 89th, and if you lived till Nov. 10, you would enter the nineties. He told all to the Holy Father, who immediately sent you his Apostolic Benediction. He could not do more if you were an Emperor. How good God is to us![12]

Mother Austin enclosed a copy of her letter from Kirby, which included the remark, "As I am from Waterford, fellow diocesan . . . of your admirable father tell him that I calculate on an occasional memento in his holy prayers for my poor soul."[13]

Mother Austin herself had recently received pleas for prayers for a young bishop-elect when the Sisters of Mercy in New Hampshire learned of the appointment of Denis Bradley as the first bishop of Manchester. Austin thought it must be gratifying for the town "to have a son of their own for first Bishop."[14] Then her thoughts turned to a woman as she added, "I hope his mother is still living to share the delight of all who know him. But small indeed must their delight be in comparison to hers."[15] Then Austin swapped recollections with Gonzaga O'Brien and recalled that Denis Bradley was among the pupils when she taught the boys in the Park Street School. She remembered his membership in the sodality and in the group of boys who vied to work the bellows, or "pump the pianner" as they put it, when she played the organ. Gonzaga was reminded that Austin was "her aide-de-camp," for you "always had me by your side in those happy days."[16] When Mary Gonzaga urged her friend to attend the consecration of their bishop, Mother Austin answered,

> Your last letter made me laugh plenty. Just think of my going to the consecration of a Prelate who never invited me! How could I face the angelic young Bishop and say: "Monsignor, I have come from New Orleans to Manchester for your consecration." No doubt he would be too gracious to say: "You might have waited until I invited you," but he could scarcely help thinking that I was anxious for an excuse to travel.[17]

"Did duty permit," added Austin, she would have been delighted "to steal from incessant work a week or two" to visit her old friends.[18]

Mother Austin did manage to steal enough time from her busy schedule to visit via postal service with her friends in other areas, especially the early Mercies who had been acquainted with the foundress personally. Since more of these sisters joined Catherine McAuley in eternity each year, Austin treasured increasingly those who remained. In Ireland the lone surviving superior appointed by Mother McAuley was Teresa White, whose fiftieth anniversary celebration Austin announced in New Orleans in December 1885. Several decades earlier, in one of the appeals for funds to feed the destitute in famine-ridden Connemara, Teresa White had addressed Archbishop Antoine Blanc as "Dr. Anthony White." Possibly, he enjoyed this translation of his name and replied in·kind to Therese Blanc.[19] Another name change was that employed by Anastasia Beckett of Birr, the town adjacent to the turf of the ancient clan O'Carroll. Mother Anastasia wrote "Austin O'Carroll," to the hearty delight of Austin.[20] Her correspondent in London was Catherine McAuley's cousin, Margaret Mary Byrn, whose sister Camillus Byrn had died in Baltimore in 1885. In the same year both Ursula Frayne and Evangelista Fitzpatrick had died in Australia, though Vincent Whitty was still serving in Queensland.[21] Vincent's letters on the death of the foundress gave the details of how, shortly before her death, Catherine McAuley's thoughts concerned the consolation of her sisters. Vincent related that Reverend Mother, as she called the foundress, said, "Will you tell the sisters to get a good cup of tea. I think the community room would be a good place—when I am gone—and to comfort one another, but God will comfort them."[22] Austin enriched Mercy heritage by relating the incident of Catherine's concern and originating what was to become that popular phrase in Mercy tradition, "a comfortable cup of tea."[23]

Austin's own concern for the sisters was revealed in some of her letters to Catherine Maher of Carlow.[24] One of the stranded Mercy missionaries to whom Austin gave permanent hospitality was Mary Agnes Greene, who as the first candidate in Carlow received the postulant cap from the foundress herself. Agnes Greene became one of the founding Mercies in both Naas and Little Rock, Arkansas.[25] Later Agnes went to aid a small missionary group of Mercies in eastern Texas and applied to Austin Carroll when the mission failed.[26] Catherine Maher must have been happy to hear of Austin's generous reception in New Orleans of Agnes when she was a frail elderly nun and of her golden jubilee in 1889. Austin also shared her concern with Catherine Maher for another religious, Francis Clare Cusack, who was soon to found the Sisters of St. Joseph of Peace.[27] Austin's interest was aroused when Cusack, in Kenmare at the time, showed great concern for the poor and followed the McAuley idea of training women so that they could earn a decent living. Like Austin, Cusack wrote extensively in the field of religious biography, and after her social efforts made the news, for the newspapers as well. Austin felt that the controversial articles were a mistake however. From her experience establishing black schools, Austin knew that gentle persuasion was much more effective than condemnations. No matter how well deserved, the latter caused antagonisms likely to snuff out the light of the project.[28] Austin was distressed to see the cause of the poor hurt and feared that Cusack's tactics would boomerang.

After Cusack's rejection at Knock, Austin's sympathy turned to Cusack herself. And the success of the new order in Nottingham, England, and then in Jersey City in this country cheered Austin. When later opposition caused Cusack suffering, Austin wrote her friend James O'Connor about Cusack, "I feel truly sorry for her. And if I could, I'd go at once and bring her here and take care of her while she lives. I feel sure we could manage her with kindness. I'm told she is near seventy . . . and that her health is broken."[29] Regardless of Austin's charitable intentions, she was no longer superior, and therefore, unable to rescue Cusack. Because Cusack was a convert, Austin thought that religious life might have been especially hard for her. Recalling her own problems, Austin said, "God knows what her difficulties were."[30] Austin assumed that some of Cusack's trouble in America had arisen because she was searching for suitable locations for new foundations. Judging by her own standards, Austin wrote, "I have always said we should be sought, not offer ourselves for foundations."[31] Then, mentioning the scarcity of good superiors, Austin paid tribute to Cusack's gifts. "We have nine houses—nine heads in ninety-nine women is a large proportion—and it means eighteen, for we should be able to change our locals . . . How this good lady could manufacture religious and Superiors I know not, and I have a little experience."[32]

After Francis Clare Cusack published her autobiography, *Nun of Kenmare*,[33] Austin mentioned that she received from Chicago "a lengthy review . . . which shows it can harm only herself, poor misguided creature."[34] From the review Austin judged that Cusack had not "been generously treated."[35] Her curiosity piqued and her sympathy reinforced, Austin sent for the autobiography. None of Austin's extant letters give her reaction to seeing the corroboration of the incident in which the Mercy foundress sought refuge in the Cusack home. However, there were a number of other comments on the book in Austin's correspondence:

> There is an immensity of truth mingled with her peevishness. She says bishops and priests persecuted all foundresses. Ah, but the genuine kind stood the persecution. . . . I feel more pity for her than I can express, and I wish I could serve her . . . I could write a far more spicy book if I gave one side of my experiences, a side I keep in abeyance or try to forget. . . . One paper has reviewed her book against her. Another sent the book to me to review. I did so in one third of a column, most kindly and gently, remarked that the book gave evidence of mental deterioration, was contradictory of her other works, but we had no feelings save compassion and sympathy for one whose life was so full of sorrow, and felt sure that in calmer moments she would regret, etc.[36]

Possibly, O'Connor thought that Cusack was looked upon too favorably by Austin, for she answered him that the person judged by the clergy of New Orleans to be overrated was not Cusack, but Gibbons. After having seen the results of the Gibbons decisions in the various local cases as 1885 came to a close, local clergyman were referring to the Apostolic Commissioner as "a born politician."[37] Nor were they alone in this opinion, for in 1886, when Gibbons had been a cardinal for only six months, Bishop Keane thought it was necessary to warn his friend Gibbons that "an impression has taken shape in Rome to the effect that Your Eminence is changeable in view, weak and vacillating in purpose, anxious to conciliate both parties on nearly every question."[38] Keane hoped that Gibbons would begin to show "such singleness, consistency, firmness, nobleness, in every word and act" as to regain his former reputation.[39] At the time several episcopal parties had nominated a preferred candidate as auxiliary to the ailing Leray, who seemed to be deteriorating rapidly. Gibbons had first nominated Chapelle,[40] but then switched to the platform of Janssens, who was not popular in New Orleans. His nationality did not appeal to the French clergy,[41] while others thought him arrogant because he seemed to assume that his post at Natchez was a prelude to that in New Orleans.[42] Even the press was guessing at the man to be named for the archdiocese. Austin explained to O'Connor that the "secular papers here are very nice to Catholics — some send me their articles on Church matters to see if they are correct, etc. Of course, I make them right, and can do some good that way."[43]

The press, especially the Catholic press, received attention from Mother Austin in the latter half of the 1880s, for her study of the Ursulines in New Orleans was published in booklet form in 1886.[44] That was the same year that Mother Austin wrote three articles on education. The first of these was an essay which Austin entered in the competition sponsored by the Louisiana Educational Society, which sought "to induce more careful thinking on public education and obtain the most practical thought" on the subject.[45] Austin Carroll's essay was selected as one to be read before the society, "composed of Jews and other non-Catholics." As Austin related to Kirby when she sent him a copy, the essay was written "in response to a request from the chief literary society here. . . . The secretary, a Rabbi, came here to ask leave to publish it at the expense of the society."[46] Since Austin Carroll felt that she should "publish under Catholic aegis," the *Catholic World* printed the essay entitled "What Is True Education?" in the summer of 1886.[47] The other two articles of Mother Austin were historical studies which delved into the type of education available in Louisiana during the French and Spanish colonial periods. The resulting research was published in the *American Catholic Quarterly Review*, one article in 1886 and the other the following year.[48] These two studies might have been the key which opened the doors of the Louisiana Historical Association to Austin Carroll, for the group presented to her a perpetual honorary membership.

Another notable work based on her research into local Catholic history was Austin's "Church of the Attakapas, 1750–1889," a study of the Catholic parish in the Acadian village of St. Martinville. Not only the story of the parish, this presented the interesting tale of Père Jan, who had left his beloved France at the time of the French Revolution.[49] Mother Austin's other articles in the 1880s also concerned people primarily, for she wrote of

Mother Evangelista Fitzpatrick and her sisters during their "Twenty-Four Years in Buenos Ayres" and of Mother Francis Mulholland in her "Western Heroine."[50] These articles stemmed from Austin's concentration on the American *Annals* as they covered material to be located there. After several years of trying, Austin was able to coax Gonzaga O'Brien to send some of Reverend Mother Xavier Warde's papers and correspondence. They evidently arrived wrapped in warnings from Gonzaga about using them with great discretion, for Austin answered, "Those suggestions of yours are thankfully accepted and will prove useful. At the same time we must not forget that no one ever wrote so as to please every one."[51] Gonzaga also learned a fact which Austin had experienced, that the sections which some might think inappropriate were often the passages which others found exceptionally enjoyable. Then revealing the great extent to which she had become Americanized, Austin told Gonzaga that while some preferred her English volume to the Irish one, she wanted her to "pray that the American may be the best of all."[52]

This Americanization never for a moment caused Austin to forget her beloved Ireland, but she did take pleasure in reminiscing with Gonzaga about their "early days" in Manchester.[53] After going over some of their "happy young days" in one letter, Austin wrote, "Only 'twould keep us too long out of heaven, I'd like to go over them again."[54] Time had melted the ice and snow of her earlier memories, just as it had mellowed her recollections of Mother Xavier Warde. Early letters of Xavier led Austin to the conclusion that Mother Warde was more holy and zealous than she had thought.[55] More than a year before she received the Warde papers, Austin had asked for Xavier's picture and Gonzaga had obliged.[56] Austin had the photograph enlarged enough to frame a lifesized portrait just as she had done earlier with Michael O'Connor's photo. Austin also had copies made so that the branch convents could share in displaying these portraits along with that of Catherine McAuley. In fact, Austin Carroll hoped that the process for the canonization of the saintly Mercy foundress would soon begin. Twenty years earlier when Austin tried to stir up enthusiasm in Ireland and England for Catherine's canonization, others thought it too soon. Now in the 1880s, Austin decided to broach the subject to Rome, for she asked Archbishop Kirby why the Pope "never canonized a native of Ireland?"[57] She explained that she had expected to find "Nano Nagle, Catherine McAuley, Mary Aikenhead . . . on the Church's altars long ago. We Irish are often reproached that we have no saints in modern times." As far as she could see, Austin added, "The Irish are the best Catholics in the world" and there "would be no Catholic Church in American without them." And yet, "Just think—none of them canonized."[58]

Of course, Americanized or not, Mother Austin was always prejudiced in favor of her homeland and its people. Mother Austin had witnessed the wonderful growth of the Church in many places besides the Irish Channel in New Orleans and felt that this growth was due in large measure to the generosity and piety of her countrymen. In many of the areas in which she had taught, they had sparked rapid expansion in both church and school buildings. Austin's second message for Kirby was the less pleasant fact that Leray was forbidding the acceptance of any Mercy candidate unless the superior signed an agreement that the sister would not be sent to Belize.[59] Austin feared that "even after Rome had spoken," Leray could do away with the branches he opposed as "he could kill them by forbidding subjects to be sent to them." Her sisters felt that they had no earthly recourse, but she reminded them that "the miserable man who wears the mitre" was not stronger than God, "and in Him we trust."[60] As this letter left New Orleans for Rome, it crossed the path of one sent by Monsignor Caprara requesting Father Butler of the Jesuit College to thank Leray for his cooperation. In fact, Butler was to thank each member of the Commission for the Apostolic Process, which "had been examined and declared *all right* as to *substance*" [sic].[61] Hence, Rome liked the substance of the Bogaerts/de Carrière report which had favored truth and asked that, in justice, amends should be made to the Sisters for the lack of honesty in the accusations against them.[62] However, the latter request was evidently not within the *substance* of the report. It was well that Austin had asked Kirby to pray "that God may give us patience under these painful circumstances."[63]

Besides the uneasiness which Leray's actions fostered, Mother Austin had a double share of personal sorrow that year for God took to himself her father and older sister. Blessed with a long and exceptionally devout life, William Carroll survived his wife by a dozen years and enjoyed good health until his final illness. Because Katy had written several weeks earlier from her convent near Cork that their father was seriously ill, Austin had time to gather numerous prayers for him, and that was a consolation for her.[64] Another was hearing of his delight upon receiving the papal blessing several months earlier, as Mary, with whom their father lived in Clonmel, forwarded such news to Katy in County Cork, who relayed it to Austin. But the best of consolations for Austin was her knowledge of his piety and his lifelong charity. Even though his death gave a great wrench to her heart, she had to appreciate the blessing of his ninety years, the brevity of his last illness, and his devout life. Katy related that the inhabitants of Clonmel considered him a saint. Earlier, Austin herself had told a correspondent that she felt that the many blessings of her community in New Orleans had been gained by the prayers of her father and her older sister in Ireland.[65] The latter was that confidant and friend, her sister Katy, who sent the details of their dad's final days. She wrote that, regardless of the cold, he walked to church daily at five in the morning. No matter that he would wait in church two hours before that first Mass, for he was happy to be in the presence of the Lord. During the week on his deathbed, Mass was said in his room several times as the priests assisted in his desire to prepare for eternity. Katy concluded, "We have a saint in heaven. May we not be unworthy of such a father. . . . The greater part of his life was spent in prayer, and in prayer he died. Good-bye, I shall write more later."[66]

Yet, when Katy closed that letter with her love, she signed her name for the last time. In fact, while Austin read Katy's consoling description of her father's death, Katy had already joined him in eternity. One week after Austin received Katy's last letter, she heard "the saddest news that ever came to me."[67] From the Convent of Mercy in Passage West, where Katy had been serving as the mistress of novices, the superior wrote Austin, whom she had known in the novitiate in Cork, "The news I have to convey will crush your affectionate loving heart."[68] She described Katy as our most efficient, and better still, our most holy, charitable, and edifying member, who has, thank God, implanted her sweet spices in her community." Sister told of Katy's sudden illness in school on a Tuesday with "some heart trouble," a ruptured aneurysm, "that took our darling from us so suddenly" on Wednesday. Sister considered Katy to be "the most perfect creature" she never knew, "a pearl among women . . . God comfort you and us—no one else can."[69] Mother Austin shared her grief with a friend.

> My Sister whom I loved so deeply, who was everything to me—consoler, advisor, sympathizing friend to whom I could tell all my troubles and difficulties, always sure of her assistance and her prayers—gone almost suddenly. . . . Her death has been a terrible blow to me. . . . She transacted business for me, sent me subjects, was at our service in every way. I leaned on her so much[70]

that her death left a void. While the abruptness dealt a terrible shock to Austin, it was not yet "the bitter in the cup."

Mother Austin's sisters made every effort to console her in this time of sorrow, just as they had tried to erase the hurt Austin experienced during the false accusations, the apostolic visitations, and the public humiliations. The community, especially the older sisters who had borne the heat of the day with Mother Austin, suffered in sympathy with her. They tried in little ways to ease their mother's pain. Mother Philomène as superior worked closely with Mother Austin and utilized Austin's talents. Making use of each available opportunity, Philomène gave Austin assignments that denoted special honor, like reading the annual consecration to Mary on the feast of Our Lady of Mercy. Regularly, Philomène had Austin make the rough draft in answer to important letters, as much to profit by Austin's literary talent as to prove that she was not assistant in title only.[71] Government of convent communities at that time was not of the style advocated in Vatican II. In her experience of religious life, Austin had seen certain superiors rule alone. During her own term, however, Mother Austin had relied heavily on her council, called the Discreets, and in important matters, included as councilors the superiors in all of the branch convents. Mother Philomène's style was different. She was inclined to check first with her assistant, Austin Carroll, and then discuss her decision with the Discreets before giving it to the other sisters.[72] Possibly it was this shift in style of government, as well as the efforts of the older half of the community to assuage the pain of their former leader, that upset three of the sisters.

On the other hand, perhaps it was just one of the results stemming from the efforts of the originator of all those complaints from the German clique. Henry Giesen was still unreconciled to the influence of Mother Austin among the sisters whom she had guided in their religious formation and inspired to actions of extraordinary zeal by her personal example through a dozen years. Had Austin Carroll had no influence upon her sisters, that would have been exceedingly strange. Yet, Giesen's enmity caused the sisters to live in uneasy expectation of another round of complaints to Rome. Although several appointed visitors had recommended that Giesen be assigned elsewhere, his superiors allowed him to remain in New Orleans. Hence, in any business with the German priests, Mother Austin distanced herself so that Mother Philomène and one of the other councilors could be as conciliatory as humanly possible.[73] This compliant approach won them little, however, for the sisters were notified by the Redemptorist provincial that he was reducing the teachers" salaries from $35 to $25 per month and imposing an annual rent of $400 for the use of the convent.[74] When he added that the rent could be halved if the motherhouse was removed and the rest of the rent absolved if the novitiate was transferred, the sisters saw that the demand was simply leverage to attain a specific end. the provincial explained that the salary reduction was to be made because the Mercies taught the poor children gratis and "the schools did not pay well and were a drain on the parish."[75]

Since the superior, like Austin and the other councilors, felt that the demand for rent was unjust, Mother Philomène visited the German provincial on his next trip to New Orleans. He was under the erroneous impression that the convent had been erected just for the six parish teachers in 1869. Philomène explained that the motherhouse and novitiate had been promised the Mercies before they left St. Louis, that all arrangements made by the bishops of St. Louis and New Orleans had been accepted by the Redemptorists. All was done "according to the Constitutions of the Order of Mercy.

Otherwise, the Sisters of Mercy would not have come here."[76] Mary Joseph Devereux, Philomène's partner, related that in 1870, she had asked the rector how far she would need to go to enter the Mercy novitiate. In answer he took her to see the convent under construction and pointed out the section which was to house the novices. When he announced that there were rooms for forty nuns, she remarked that they might never be filled, but he projected that the motherhouse would soon overflow and send sisters across the South.[77] Though surprised at this information, the provincial protested that the sisters were not investing their resources in the parish, but were allowing the branches to siphon their funds. Philomène contradicted that idea. Not only had the Mercy community spent over $5,000 for repairs and improvements on the convent building, but they had also expended $50,000 more in the purchase and renovation of property adjacent to the convent. Further, much of the funding for these improvements came from the branches, as did most of the community resources during the years when the parish paid no regular salaries.[78]

Finally, the sisters pointed out that from the branches came candidates who were especially welcome, since the influx of candidates from the parish had slackened considerably because of the negative attitude of several of the German priests.[79] Were it not just speculation, one might wonder if the attempt to remove the motherhouse from the parish stemmed from the assumption that Austin Carroll was to become superior in the next Mercy election. Conjectures aside, the provincial agreed to drop the demand for rent, but maintained the reduction in salaries, which were later lowered to $20.[80] With such a reduction in funds, the sisters found it necessary to cut back on both the quantity and quality of food and clothing. Older sisters, having lived through the depressed periods following yellow-fever quarantines which halted all business and salaries, paid little attention to the shortages. They just tightened their cinctures and carried on as usual. Having been professed only five years, the unhappy trio had not experienced the frugal early days or the hardship in the wake of each epidemic. Because of the current inconveniences, however, they saw fit to complain endlessly, blame Austin for their discomfort, and claim that it was her fault that there was trouble with the German priests. The memoirs note that the leader had felt aggrieved ever since her term as a novice was extended. Novice Mécontente, blinded by what her pride considered an affront, lost the benefit of the further guidance prior to the time that she was to take her religious vows.[81]

Since Mother Austin and her sisters considered true dedication essential for spiritual and natural fulfillment as a religious, this six-month delay was not an uncommon procedure. Whenever there was doubt about the maturity, the understanding, or the zeal and spirituality of a candidate, the extra period was assigned. Most of the novices who had this slightly extended novitiate period profited by the additional instruction to become fine religious.[82] Unfortunately, the aggrieved novice hid her displeasure until after her profession. Only several years later did it become apparent to the sisters that Mécontente believed that the council, particularly Mother Austin, had wronged her by delaying her profession. In a way, she was obsessed with the conviction that a grievous mistake had been made in her regard. Through the years the other sisters agreed that an error had been made — not in the delay, however, but in the final acceptance. But in the late 1880s, Mécontente had just chosen two lieutenants among the younger sisters and her discontent was surfacing through their voices. One had labored to enlarge the trio and the other, evidently selected for the purpose, carried complaints to a neighboring prelate whom she knew.[83] Mécontente worked so quietly that, before the sisters were aware of it, she had cultivated a half dozen followers and formed a clique. This was a new experience for the community, for during the German problems earlier when Mécontente was a novice, Mother Austin had received nothing but encouragement from her sisters. Their union was so strong that Austin had described their community as a "unit in the Sacred Heart of Jesus."[84]

While the sisters spent long hours in their diverse works of mercy, the unhappy trio decided that, primarily because of Mother Austin, the schedule was too lengthy, the work too difficult, and the food too poor and spare. One memoir states with heavy sarcasm that, "in the wisdom of the trio," Mother Austin was too old, too strict, and overly zealous about too many works of mercy.[85] While others looked forward to the next election so that they might elect Austin Carroll again, the trio worked against that end. They had no knowledge of the close cooperation between Philomène and Austin in the government of the community, so fell into false assumptions which they spread as fact. For instance, they assumed that Philomène never changed Austin's rough drafts of letters and that Austin sought special honors and assignments. They were wrong on both counts, for Philomène declared that Austin was "as obedient as a novice."[86] Once rumors surfaced, Austin refused all further honors, but Philomène and the council insisted that Austin continue in the position to which she had been elected. Although the community leaders had no knowledge at this point of either the source of the rumors or the number of the disaffected, just the realization that there was a clique angered and saddened the sisters and was bitterly painful to Austin. The knowledge that a lack of unity had crept into the community was the bitter draught in Mother Austin's cup.

After just five years of profession, Mécontente sought a superior who would lighten her work, shorten her schedule, and provide better fare. Perhaps one might begin to wonder what had happened to Austin's ability to study the character of candidates. Once before Mother Austin had erred in the case of Sister Rose, the young woman who had left the community. Of all the Sisters who had been novices under the direction of Austin Carroll, Rose was the only one who ever renounced her commitment. In the case of Mécontente, the novice director, the council, and Mother Austin were all misled even though all three judged that further preparation was necessary for the novice.[87] At that time Austin was not directing the novitiate herself, although she had done so from 1871 until 1880. During that nine year period, Mother Austin not only instructed and guided all the early members of the New Orleans community, but she also developed the leaders who were to continue her work long after she had gone. Several of these sisters, like Mothers Mary Philomène Butler, Aloysius Cook, and Antonia McKinley, served alternately as superior of the New Orleans Mercies well past the nineteenth century. Other leaders, who had been formed in spirituality while Mother Austin directed the postulants and novices, were repeatedly chosen as local superiors or as members of the council. Among them were Sisters Mary Clare Fitzpatrick, Evangelist Kearney, Inez Jones, Mercy Wiendahl, Liguori Duncan, and Dolores Generally.[88]

These few names surface as does the tip of the iceberg, for there were far too many others to list. However, it is impossible, when naming the leaders Mother Austin developed, not to mention three whose service and edifying lives were shortened by early death. These exceptionally zealous women were Sisters Mary Teresa Gourrier, Xavier Durand, and Margaret Mary Killelea.[89] Early death was also an important factor in the life of Mother Austin's dearest friend, Kate Imhoff Walsh. Kate herself did not die young, but had to face the sudden loss of husband and children because of yellow fever and other illnesses. Mother Austin's warm heart sent her to pay a visit of condolence to this perfect stranger. Already stricken by the loss of her husband and two children at the time, Kate Walsh received an extraordinarily comforting visit from the compassionate nun. Mother Austin continued to visit Kate as illnesses took her remaining little ones. Gradually, as Kate and Austin became fast friends, the widow became deeply interested in the works of mercy that Austin described with such enthusiasm. Before too long, Kate decided to join the Mercy community in order to assist with these works for others. Named Mary Borgia, she remained one of Mother Austin's closest friends, and within a few years grew to be, like Austin, a great-hearted, compassionate leader.[90] As to their success for the Mercy community, Mary Borgia's terms as superior some years later were second only to those of her mentor and friend, Austin Carroll. If any proof be needed that Austin Carroll was an accurate judge of character, in spite of two errors in ninety-one sisters, evidence is supplied in abundance not only by her choice of superiors, but also by the caliber of the leaders she bequeathed as her legacy to the New Orleans community.

Just as Austin Carroll had a singularly sharp eye for the characteristics essential in community leaders, so too was her perception keen concerning the talents and gifts of individual sisters. Austin considered this necessary for the sister's successful fulfillment and for the community to benefit from her giftedness. Thus, bowing to individuality was as important to Austin as community adaptability. After studying the peculiarities and customs of a new location, Austin noted what was required and found the best means of meeting those needs. Rather than pushing for uniformity in the branches, she confided to a friend, "We suit ourselves to the places where we live and that is the secret of our great success here, T.G."[91] Austin also observed an adaptability to changing needs and praised the manner in which Clement Hofbauer "read the signs of the times," to quote her 1877 phrase.[92] She herself tried to follow that practice by revising apostolates to keep them current. Yet, as modern as Mother Austin was in that respect, her view of opposition was truly that of the nineteenth century. Her bishop in Cork had told the sisters, "Your work is so manifestly the work of God that we must expect various contradictions as a matter of course."[93] Austin agreed and noted that Catherine McAuley had received similar episcopal advice. She was to be ready for conflict, for "every good work was, like the divine Author of our religion, a sign to be contradicted."[94] This was deep conviction with Mother Austin Carroll.

Writing in the twentieth century, Martindale stated that, regardless of time or place, religious foundresses had to suffer similar trials "from outside (jealousies; fears that they want to monopolize), and from within (clashes of temperament, personal ambitions, formation of cliques . . .)"[95] The author thought it "was amazing how far such human frailties may go even among good people."[96] Austin accepted the clique as one of the signs that the works of mercy being done were truly God's own. Austin had written of a superior whom she particularly admired, "Everywhere she met the trials and contradictions that await noble women, but the cross was never too heavy for her generous soul."[97] The words could have described Austin herself, for her thoughts and efforts were so concerned with the needs of others that she had no time available for brooding about the clique. Her letters regularly revealed her primary interest at the moment, as she begged her friends for prayers for such varied requests as these—for the orphan boy who seriously injured his foot when he stepped on a rake, for the conversion of two sinners, for the funds needed to build a larger crèche, for the opportunity to open a branch and two schools in a second Acadian town, for the commutation of the death penalty imposed on a young murderer who was terrified at the thought of being hanged, that her plans to establish a Catholic college for women might materialize, that her latest book "will be AMDG in every respect," for God's blessing on the minister who helped with funds for the prison chapel.[98]

Austin found an odd contrast in the fact that the work of the Sisters of Mercy in Ireland, was, on occasion, hampered by the government sponsorship of Protestant institutions. Yet in largely Catholic New Orleans, ministers were often cooperative in civic endeavors, like the chapel in the prison, while opposition was left to several German clergymen.[99] Austin's ecumenicalism shocked them in this instance. After noting in one of her letters that St. Catherine of Siena reproached certain "vicious churchmen," Austin added, "Would that we had her for a week!"[100] Yet there was good news also, for 1887 saw the transfer of the instigator of the German complaints and the assignment as rector of the kindly Frederick Faivre, CSSR, Mother Austin's friend who had previously served as prefect of Notre Dame de Bon Secours. The new bishop of Mobile, the zealous young Jeremiah O'Sullivan, besought Leray to allow the Mercies to establish a branch and staff the schools of Birmingham.[101] Although unable to obtain Leray's consent, O'Sullivan welcomed Austin's help in gathering funds for a priest for the Mobile diocese, much of which was still missionary territory at the time.[102] Austin made two trips on behalf of others, as she journeyed to Baltimore in 1884 with a sister whose brother was dying there, and then attended to business in Washington, D.C., on behalf of the orphans from Jackson Barracks, whose father had died of yellow fever while serving in the army. Two years later Mother Austin accompanied one of the sisters and her younger brother to a novitiate north of St. Louis where he was to attend the seminary. Austin called this young orphan "who was with us eight years . . . one of the best boys I ever met and, by far, the cleverest."[103]

On the occasion of each trip, Austin Carroll visited her friends so that she could see their institutions before she wrote their section of the *Annals*. From St. Louis she visited Pittsburgh and Loretto, and then Chicago where Austin expected "to see my sick old friend, Mother Vincent McGirr, but to my intense disappointment, she was in Davenport. So Mother Genevieve [Granger] whisked me off there, and I had a few hours with Mother Vincent — Sisters doing splendidly there, a most holy charitable community."[104] The Davenport Mercies were not alone in receiving Austin's compliments, for no matter which houses she visited, Austin wrote that she was "delighted and edified with every institution and the Sisters all over."[105] In fact, a constant source of joy to Mother Austin was the ongoing spread of Catherine McAuley's Institute of Mercy. The two Catholic newspapers in New Orleans frequently carried items Austin had received about new Mercy foundations or new developments in the older houses. On one occasion however, an episcopal friend asked about a group of Mercies who transferred frequently from place to place. "A few bands of that kind have done incalculable evil to our Order in this country," Austin answered.[106] She believed that each foundation should depend upon the invitation of a bishop who wanted it for his diocese and the consent of the bishop whose See the founding group was leaving. These were just her personal views, Austin explained, "but I must give your Lordship my candid opinion."[107] Although she did not wish to interfere in any way, Austin thought it wrong to encourage such houses formed by the discontented at variance with authority.

In another instance, she received a letter highly critical of religious women in general and several Sisters of Mercy in particular. The bishop's letter must have been quite strong because her answer was anything but calm. From her own experience, she had found that trouble often resulted from "an incorrect idea of the power of the Ecclesiastical Superior."[108] Then she asked, "Why do Bishops receive Sisters who go about the country without leave or authority? Each community should be responsible for its own professed, nor should Ecclesiastical Superiors connive at or order the sending of troublesome people to new places."[109] Common sense told her that "if they will not do at home, they will hardly do elsewhere, and after a fair and merciful trial [period]," should not be allowed to take their vows. "Instead, Bishops allow them to be invested with authority and sent where they ruin religion and their order. . . . A house founded that way cannot succeed."[110] Austin noted that the vast majority of convents and "all we have in the South," Vicksburg, Macon, Little Rock and New Orleans, "do immense good . . . and certainly trouble no one but the devil."[111] As to temporalities, "I admit most of us are not very bright, but we do not owe a dollar," and many "never go beyond their resources." As to housekeeping, the houses she had seen "were in fine order, well kept, and the food all it should be." She could not say "whether they all make ends meet . . . or if there has been mismanagement.[112]

Her love for the Mercy Institute caused Austin to become defensive.

> If there has been mismanagement, it has nearly always come of our delicacy of conscience or an incorrect idea of the power of the Eccl. Sup. over these affairs. . . . Certainly it is hard that priests should talk as you describe, considering the example and the treatment many of them give Religious. . . . But everything of this kind is the subject of grief to me. . . . No human being knows better than Your Lordship how much of the blame of the shortcomings we all dislike is to be attributed to causes outside of the Sisters.[113]

Suddenly she realized that the fervor with which she had been writing might offend. "Excuse my warmth," she said, but "it really does seem to me that you are a little severe."[114] At the end of the letter, Austin appended another apology, "Forgive me this." But her friend was highly offended for she continued to apologize when she answered his next letter. "Certainly none can doubt your affection for the Order . . . for indeed, it is akin to the love God bears us . . . always trying to correct and encourage us and make us worthy of His love."[115] After apologizing again, Austin spoke for her hopes for her sisters.

> I am quite apt to overlook the faults of people who are indifferent to me, but faults in those I love have a serious aspect in my eyes. My own community wears a gracious and edifying appearance to outsiders in general, but it never half satisfies me, my love for my Sisters and my Order being so intense that the very best of the good to be attained in this world of imperfection seems too little. . . . If I cared less about them I should see fewer of their shortcomings.[116]

While discussing the necessity of her sisters" careful training for teaching and other duties, Austin remarked, "my vigilance is incessant, and yet I cannot always get things done with the perfection which it is my ambition to make our normal way of doing such portions of God's work as are committed to us."[117] Sisters who had been Austin's novices found no problem with this striving for excellence. In fact, most of the sisters found Austin's daily explanations of the Rule and the ideals of the Mercy foundress inspiring. Thus, when a priest scheduled to preach the annual retreat withdrew his commitment suddenly, the sisters were delighted that Austin Carroll gave the lectures herself. Afterwards, so many of the sisters wanted copies of her notes that Austin published the retreat.[118] That same year Mother Austin offered helpful advice to Mother deSales Ihmsen of Loretto, Pennsylvania. DeSales was considering a transfer to a mission on Trinidad, just off the coast of Venezuela. Before deSales made a final decision, Austin suggested that she or several of her sisters visit Belize, see their convent and schools, and experience the climate.[119] Austin explained that a mission branch necessitated financial support from the mainland. Belize, for instance, was unable to pay for the new convent and school that had been erected. Hence, the cost for the new buildings came almost completely from the New Orleans motherhouse.[120] Austin had been invited to staff all the schools and hospitals in Spanish Honduras, but declined because the political climate was too unstable for the safety of her sisters, even if it had been possible financially.[121]

Throughout 1886 and the following year, rumors were rampant as to the name of an auxiliary for Leray, whose health was deteriorating rapidly.[122] The sisters must have felt as if the storm cloud of their uneasiness was shifting a bit when, in the summer of 1887, Leray left New Orleans for France. Several months later Leray left France for eternity on the eve of the feast of Our Lady of Mercy, the special patron and protector of Catherine McAuley's Institute of Mercy. The black cloud that had been hanging over the Sisters of Mercy suddenly lifted and the sky seemed to brighten. Again the plethora of rumors arose, having shifted from the name of an auxiliary to that of an archbishop. Since the city was no longer a French enclave, Mother Austin hoped that the next prelate would be a native of either Ireland or the United States.[123] Since most local projects had come to a halt during Leray's tenure, many pastors and religious congregations reactivated their earlier plans, in a way, to make hay while the sun shone. With the consent of the administrator, Vicar Rouxel, the Sisters of Mercy also reopened several projects. These moved forward rapidly under the guidance of Mothers Philomène and Austin Carroll. Two lots on the corner of Constance and St. Andrew Streets, adjacent both to the convent and the first Mercy Home, were secured as the site for the college.[124] The small house on the lot was sold and rolled across the street. the architect's plans for the new building were already complete, and the contractor was soon making great headway with the construction.[125]

Mother Austin and her sisters also decided that, after the college was completed, they would raze the small crèche facing St. Mary street and erect a much larger building that could house a substantial crèche and laundry on the first floor and an expansion of the Mercy Home on the upper floors.[126] Austin assumed that this second project would be another year in process. Likewise underway were the plans to enlarge the black school in Biloxi. Mother Austin had been faithful to her 1863 decision to do all that she possibly could for the educational advancement of the blacks. She told a friend that, "including our Belize schools, we teach over 600 colored children."[127] Although she had established eight schools for "the colored races,"[128] Austin wished to do "a good deal more. Pray the good God to send us means and subjects for this, AMDG. . . . You know that I am [committed] heart and soul . . . to do directly and indirectly all I can without coming in collision, etc."[129] Racial conflict, the "coming in collision, etc." had caused loss of students and financial support when other sisters opened black schools in both Florida and Louisiana.[130] Lest all her efforts for black education fail, Austin realized the necessity of treading lightly around sensitivities. So with blarney and blessings, her silver tongue won white support for her black schools. This feat was as unusual as her use of music to coax regular attendance from black youngsters unaccustomed to school discipline.[131] Using songs ranging from the sacred to the comic, Austin had her teachers insert music breaks between the classes in religion and other fundamentals. As the pupils quickly excelled in rhythm and harmony, this success spread to other classes and school became fun.

Rhythm, harmony, and humor were to be found also in the Mercy classrooms and motherhouse near the college site. The senior girls were basking in good cheer because they were to enjoy the privilege of finishing their final semester in the new building. Harmonious excitement filled the air in the convent as happy anticipation rose as fast as the brick walls of the handsome structure. In the ordinary rhythm of Mercy triennials, the 1888 election was scheduled for the coming summer. Before late spring the college was roofed, rooms ceiled, galleries finished, and the building accepted.[132] Dedicated to the Mercy foundress, St. Katharine's College opened its doors in preview to the seniors in April, May, and June. Austin Carroll planned to build the four-year curriculum gradually by adding another level annually for three more years. Publicity invited any woman who wished to take higher studies after her graduation from high school either for a full literary course or for more practical courses for teachers and women who wished to prepare for the business world. Many electives were available in music, art, education and stenography.[133] The state of Louisiana presented to the Sisters of Mercy the charter of St. Katharine's College empowering them to bestow diplomas. Degrees were to come only after the full curriculum was in progress in the 1891–1892 session. According to the prospectus, the aim of the college was the formation of "the highest type of womanhood," who qualified in "all the virtues, studies, and accomplishments necessary to grace their homes."[134]

Austin Carroll had little respect for finishing schools where too much emphasis was given to the arts and stylish crafts.[135] Instead she presented a solid secondary program so that the girls could become proficient in mathematics, composition, history, physiology, and science as well as the languages and arts which dominated some academies.[136] Yet, she believed that artistic accomplishments were appropriate as long as they did not encroach upon the essentials. For instance, she hired an expert "for everything new in calisthenics," as she told a friend, "and don't be disedified, dancing."[137] In Austin's opinion, lighter courses needed to be available as electives lest, to find them elsewhere, the student desert the Catholic school. Thus, she had numerous options available in music, art, as well as dancing. Artistically inclined herself, Austin tried to give each sister an opportunity of developing her special talent. In the summer, therefore, Austin regularly hired artists, dramatic elocutionists, and musicians to instruct her teachers until many of them became highly qualified organists, vocalists, painters, or calligraphers who replaced the hired experts and taught the other sisters.[138] Her plans for the college were to follow similar lines, first hiring professors through whom her sisters could gradually qualify and then later replace.

Austin looked forward to a time when all the professors would be Sisters of Mercy or other women.

In her *In Many Lands*, Austin gave particular praise to the University of Bologna, which dated from the twelfth century, because it introduced women lecturers.[139] Austin stated that "the platform from which learned gentlewomen lectured on civil, and even canon, law and the chairs they held long before women's rights became an issue show that there is nothing new under the sun."[140] Austin's breadth of vision bridged six centuries in this instance to shine the light of history upon the abilities of women. In more recent history Austin had witnessed many young women widowed by the Civil War or plunged instantaneously from the level of affluence to that of destitution by the Reconstruction. No matter how handy they had been with wax flowers or the pianoforte, most were as desolate as they were unprepared to become the breadwinners for their families. Hence, Austin wanted to encourage young women to add to a liberal arts program enough courses of a practical nature to ensure themselves a successful career if ever one were needed.[141] Austin Carroll planned no watered-down program, however, since she believed that only a strong curriculum tested mental ability adequately. Her broad aim was that St. Katharine's College would assist women to understand that they should place no prejudicial limits of any kind upon their intelligence or their capability to accomplish whatever they wished to do.[142] Mother Austin was so involved with the wide horizons of her hopes and the narrow lines of specific courses and so delighted that another of her ideals was about to be realized that she failed to see the elongated shadows upon the college wall.

Shadows aside for the moment, Mother Austin's collection of clippings indicate her interest in the advancement of women into various fields of endeavor. One unidentified cutting held this anonymous bit of rhyme.

> Honor the famous women; each artist, singer, writer,
>   And all who lift from women the old barbaric ban.
> Welcome the glad new era when all comers shall invite her,
>   And every portal open to her the same as to a man.[143]

As Austin prepared to open the portals of "higher studies" to women in New Orleans, she learned of the death of a brilliant Mercy friend. "I do not know in the world or in the cloister a more thorough scholar or a more accomplished woman," wrote Austin when she was notified of the sudden death from pneumonia of her "oldest and dearest friend, Mother M. Juliana Purcell," on Ash Wednesday in 1888.[144] Juliana was "a great loss to Religion and Education. . . . All her beautiful gifts with a still more beautiful heart" had been devoted to God since her youth in Clonmel. This childhood chum was "almost the last of my early friends,"[145] said Austin, recalling Juliana's spiritual and mental talents. "She was exceedingly clever," wrote Austin, "and clever people are not admired by those who think we should all be like pebbles. I like strong individualities, and I think it a pity to deprive them of the benefits of religion [in religious life] or religion of their services by the narrowness too often shown by clergy and other superiors."[146]

Just such narrowmindedness in three German priests formed a rather shadowy force to work against Austin's rapidly rising college for women even as she worked out the curriculum. Certainly neither Austin or Philomène, who had worked so assiduously to maintain peace with the German clique, was seeking further opposition. Yet in spite of Philomène's efforts, her term in office had seen the attempted imposition of rent, the demand for the removal of the novitiate, and the nullification of the salary contract which Austin had negotiated.[147] After Mother Austin announced the establishment of the first Catholic College for women on February 15, 1888, Mother Philomène was sent letter after letter from the German superior in St. Louis.[148] He demanded complete details about the college even though Austin and Philomène explained that the college was financed "at our sole expense."[149] Since the site chosen was within the parish bounds, the Germans assumed that it was within their purview.

This repeated interference in community affairs and projects makes it seem as if the old-world German clerics believed themselves to be parochial princes reigning with "the divine right" of kaisers over the parish that was their empire. Perhaps this attitude had been encouraged by the German ascendancy in Rome in the 1880s, a fact which was obvious not only to the bishops of other nationalities in the United States at that time, but which is revealed with historical accuracy in the many relevant series of episcopal correspondence from the United States to Roman agents.[150] After Abbelen's petition for German privileges was discovered, one bishop felt that the difficulty was not really over, for the "snake was just scotched, not killed." Several bishops were convinced that a direct German channel existed that brought German wishes directly to the ear of Propaganda Fide. Blame was bandied about as surmises shifted from certain cardinals to German diplomats to several professors in the Roman colleges. American bishops, angered by this foreign control of the Church in the United States, felt that the Germans in America would never yield as long as they were supported by the power of the German cardinals. That the Germans had the inside track seemed evident because they repeatedly won episcopal appointments even when the German nomination was listed third. Some bishops attributed Rome's skipping over the first two men named to the fact that the Germans were "so aggressive and systematic in their underhand work."[151]

Of course the Germans had no monopoly on underhand work, as it could be found in every secret camp, such as the unhappy clique within the Mercy community. Even as plans were laid in the spring to have all the sisters present for the retreat prior to the election scheduled for August 7, 1988, the clique secretly sent complaints to the neighboring bishop in Mississippi.[152] Rumor had so often mentioned the name of Bishop Janssens of Natchez as a possible successor to Leray that a large percentage of the archdiocesan priests, seeking to avoid his selection, petitioned to have the Bishop of Natchitoches, Antoine Durier, transferred to New Orleans.[153] Not long after the petition, the appointment of Janssens was leaked to the press, some papers naming Gibbons as their source.[154] Assuming that Gibbons was right, both Rouxel, administrator in New Orleans, and Loewekamp, the German provincial in St. Louis, contacted Janssens about the Mercy election. The latter wanted Rouxel to postpone the election or refuse to accept the nomination of Austin Carroll.[155] Rouxel wrote Janssens that three years earlier Gibbons, to settle the differences between the Germans and Austin, had "appointed Philomène Superior, thereby giving full satisfaction [sic] to the Redemptorists. Now the coming election gives much fear to the Reverend fathers because they are almost sure Mother Austin will be elected and past troubles renewed."[156] Thus does the documentation of the German interference in Mercy community affairs prove its occurrence.

Rouxel had decided to bow to the German pressure and postpone the election, but when he so notified Mother Philomène, the sisters were already in retreat at the motherhouse. Philomène explained that deferring the election for a month would not only cause distressing financial problems because of double transportation for more than sixty sisters, but also that the election date and been specified during the canonical process. Further, that process was called to solve problems caused primarily because an earlier election had been changed by Archbishop Perché. And how could they, in justice, close their Belize schools for two weeks and the other branches for two days to allow the sisters to return to the motherhouse?[157] Mothers Philomène and Austin then sent Janssens these reasons, welcomed him as their spiritual father, and prayed that he would find the Sisters of Mercy "in the future, as in the past, doing all we can in your diocese for God and souls."[158] Janssens postponed the election, however, evidently preferring to appease the Germans.[159] Perhaps he thought that the Mercy pecuniary loss would be an insignificant amount from the coffers that had always provided for the black school in his diocese without any help from himself. His predicament of having to deal with problems even before he is officially named for the archdiocese should gain him some commiseration, as should the fact that many of the priests had already indicated, if not their dislike for him, at least their preference for another. If he were to grant the request of the Mercies, he would lose the potential for support from the powerful German order.[160] In such circumstances, his decision against the sisters was certainly the lesser part of valor.

A second point that Janssens settled before he became archbishop was the establishment of the Mercy branch in Jeanerette. In 1881 Mother Austin had been requested by the pastor, John D. Flanagan, to send Mercies to establish parish schools.[161] Austin thought they could do so in a few years. But only after the death of Perché were there enough sisters available to open the branch, and Leray refused permission. In fact, invitations to open convents and staff schools were refused annually during Leray's reign. In 1888, the permission depended upon another, and the second Acadian town obtained its Convent of Mercy[162] and the sisters opened a secondary school for girls and two elementary schools.[163] Yet Mother Austin felt sad that money was not available to open a school for the blacks in Jeanerette.[164] Austin had just completed the financing of the college, and the work on the new créche facing St. Mary Street had already begun.[165] In any case, the three new schools in Jeanerette were thriving long before the election.

It was unfortunate that the election, which could easily have been held immediately after the August retreat, was postponed three different times by Janssens.[166] The triple delay must have been due to the pressure from the German provincial who had written again and again, repeating his theme that Mother Austin should be prevented from becoming superior.[167] Perhaps Janssens agreed with Loewekamp, as he had in 1885, when Gibbons wrote for information about the conflict of the Germans with Austin Carroll. At that time Janssens had immediately assumed that Austin and not the Germans had caused the problems, then proffered the suggestion that Austin should not be allowed to remain in New Orleans.[168] Evidently, that was still his opinion, because he would strive to bring about that effect before too long. However, that was not until after the election, one held without a quorum present. Partially responsible for that insufficient number were the triple postponement and the trip for an election that was cancelled. When the date set by the bishop finally arrived, many of the sisters did not. Of course, the novices did not vote, and as Philomène had told Janssens earlier,[169] the date made it impossible for the Belize sisters to attend, just as it did for several sisters in each branch. Even so, there should have been more than a third of the ninety members present. Although the Belize votes had been sent weeks before, there is no record that they were tallied. That fact and the limited number present gave neither Austin nor Philomène a clear majority.[170] Thus the stage was set for the bishop to select a superior.

According to the Mercy constitution, a canonical appointment by the presiding prelate was in order after three votes without a majority. In this instance the key to the deadlock was probably in the hands of the clique.

Janssens appointed as superior Mary Joseph Devereux, younger and less experienced than either of her predecessors.[171] Up to this point the procedure had been according to the Mercy Rule, but Janssens then proceeded to negate the Rome-approved Rule by depriving the sisters of their right to elect any other officials. He wanted one sister to have absolute power and appointed Joseph to be bursar and mistress of novices as well as superior. Perhaps he assumed that Austin would be without influence if there were no council of advisors or other officials. Later that evening, however, the sisters met and elected Austin Carroll as Joseph's assistant. They wanted to choose other officials also, but Joseph was afraid to contradict the bishop in any way, even when he went counter to the Rule.[172] Thus the day of the election was a preview of the next three years. Mother Joseph made a gracious Sister of Mercy, tall and regal, pious and pleasant, and as Janssens must have learned, pliable. For several years she had been bursar. Yet she worried excessively about finances, never having acquired either Mother Austin's trust in Divine Providence or Mother Philomène's comprehension of Austin's wizardry with finances.

During Mother Joseph's term, the style of governing changed again as it had with each of the previous superiors in New Orleans. Catherine Grant had originally depended too much upon the ecclesiastical superior. When she realized that she could not prevent his interference in community affairs, she left his jurisdiction by starting another foundation. Even though Austin Carroll was on the best of terms with the priests who served as the prefects of schools, she avoided interference by requesting permissions from the archbishop. This evidently angered the former director and certainly was one of the underlying causes of her trouble with the German clique.[173] Within the community, Austin's early friends and advisors were Teresa Gourrier, the novice nearest to Austin's age, and Philomène Butler, an experienced certified teacher who was five years younger than Teresa. When Archbishop Perché decreed the canonical establishment of this community in 1874, Teresa was assistant and Philomène bursar. After the establishment of the branch convents, Austin appointed in her place as principals, Teresa for Notre Dame de Bon Secours and Philomène for the girls" school of St. Alphonsus. Community government continued under the guidance of Austin and her two principals until 1880, when a council of advisors was formed. This group met with Austin and the other officials at regular intervals to discuss old business and new ideas and suggestions.[174]

Community records reveal that these sisters not only approved of each new plan that Mother Austin suggested, but also cooperated zealously to turn each idea into a successful reality. Their consistent reaction of hearty enthusiasm must have lulled Austin into accepting their unanimous agreement as the ordinary or expected response.[175] Probably she should have pressured her sisters to give negative reactions also, or to show creativity by originating their own ideas. She and her council had been able to appoint fine superiors for all the branch convents, and Austin's successors came from among the councilors. Yet in the position of the superior who governed the motherhouse community and those branches, each felt the need to lean heavily upon another. For instance, Philomène depended so much upon the judgment of Austin Carroll that the clique arose during that term. Some of the councilors thought that the dissatisfied were lazy, for they complained about the extra works of Mercy among the sick and imprisoned. Because their resentment was concentrated upon Austin, not the council, and their complaints paralleled those of the German clique, others believed that the two cliques were connected.[176] Be that as it may, the link uncovered later was that to Janssens, who had so readily accepted the discontented grumbling of the trio as general truth. In any case, the prejudice thus engendered, reinforced as it was by the demands of the German provincial, boded ill for Austin Carroll.

Although Austin did not know the reason for the prejudice of Janssens, she felt its effects as soon as he visited the motherhouse to preside at the oft-postponed election. Without quoting his remarks specifically, she later wrote him, "I do find it strange that Your Grace seems always ready to believe anything against me and never inquire of me if these things are so. Plotters, persons utterly unreliable, have been able to prejudice Your Grace and cause you to write and speak to me in a manner to which I have not been accustomed."[177] Regardless of what he said about Austin to the sisters, they knew her for what she was and elected her the assistant to Joseph as soon as he had left. When he heard of that election, he again nullified the Mercy Rule by cancelling the choice of the community.[178] As Joseph relayed the message to Austin, "even though the community elected her to office," she must not fulfill its duties as these were "His Grace's orders."[179] Later Austin explained to Janssens, "I never complained, which perhaps was wrong. But I love peace."[180] Austin's silent reaction, rather than a loud and clear protest, tends to catch one by surprise. Yet, Austin might have been in a state of shock resulting from the sudden and unexpected attack from Janssens. Throughout the interim when the archdiocese awaited the appointment of the next prelate, however, Austin had frequently asked her friends and correspondents to pray that there would be peace with the next bishop.[181] The seven years of Leray's antagonism, followed by the resurgence of complaints from the Germans in 1887 and 1888, had apparently caused Austin to long for a return to the fine and harmonious relationships which marked the reigns of Archbishop Odin and Perché.

Any number of other considerations, of course, might have contributed to Austin's motivation in this instance. Possibly, feeling that harmony

was essential to get the college established, Austin decided to sacrifice herself in its behalf. If so, her efforts were in vain, for word soon came that
Janssens wanted her out of the motherhouse lest Joseph depend upon her.
In gigantic understatement, Austin later wrote the bishop, "Some might
think that my years and services to religion in the New Orleans diocese
deserved a different recognition."[182] But bowing to his authority, she
offered to stay in another convent. "I should have been marked to do so had
I not offered," she explained to Bishop O'Connor six months later.[183]
Although she had frequently written him concerning the *Annals* during
these months, her hurt had evidently been too deep to mention sooner.[184]
Leaving the motherhouse was the cancellation of her dream for a woman's
college, and seeing it changed into a secondary school was certainly bitter in
her cup. Finally she was able to share her feelings with O'Connor and the
news that she was in charge of the orphanage.

> I am quite contented here, busy enough, doat on the children, etc., have
> the sick and ailing of all the houses here, as it is almost in the country. I felt
> deeply leaving the convent where I had spent twenty happy fruitful years.
> But it was a terrible sacrifice to offer to God, and I hope it will not hinder
> my sanctification. This is entirely *entre nous*. You are the only one to
> whom I have mentioned it. . . . Thanks for your prayers — continue them
> for me. I never forget you. I read the chapter on the cross often.[185]

Almost a decade earlier, when Austin Carroll selected her letterhead,
she chose one in which the cross was the focal point. Furled gracefully
about the cross in the design was a banner emblazoned with the word
"mercy."[186] How often in the troubled times must Austin have pondered
Catherine McAuley's thought, "without the Cross the real Crown cannot
come."[187] In the months just before and after her election to the cancelled
position of assistant, Austin often saw the letterhead cross while she clari-
fied details for the *Annals*. She must have appreciated its appropriateness
even as she filled her letters with questions. Was the birthplace in Cork or
Queenstown? What date of March was Ash Wednesday in 1851? Pray that
the circulation may be good and the book AMDG. Could you return the
proofs in five days?[188] Then Austin received questions from Little Rock,
where Bishop Edward Fitzgerald thought she was unduly glorifying his
predecessor, Bishop Byrne. Having arrived amid the devastation left by the
war, Fitzgerald could not picture antebellum prosperity and implied that
Austin stretched the truth when she quoted statistics from the pertinent
Catholic Directories. She answered that she hated lies, "as one often does
who has suffered from the untruths of others."[189] Since she would "never be
the medium of publishing a falsehood," she asked the bishop to edit the

section on Arkansas. But she retained events related by the Mercies who witnessed them. She also held her ground that eight priests had served with Byrne, and named those living so the bishop could check for himself.[190]

This re-editing by Fitzgerald delayed the American *Annals* for some months, but Austin preferred a delay to inaccuracy. Besides, she had another literary project already underway since the beginning of the year. At that time, looking forward to the completion of the college building, she moved ahead with a school paper to be edited by the seniors soon to be moved into the college classrooms. This paper, entitled *The Young Collegian*, represented all the schools across the South staffed by the Sisters of Mercy from the New Orleans motherhouse.[191] Each of the schools contributed new items and essays as well as the business ads which financed the monthly paper. The editors of the *Collegian* in 1887–1888 were the talented young women who, Austin hoped, would become the first students enrolled in the college.[192] After Mother Joseph's appointment, Austin saw her plans for the women's college dropped and the building used for high school classes. Several of the better students remained that next year for postgraduate courses and edited the paper for a second year. Publications from other schools commented upon the *Collegian's* exceptionally lively style as well as the unusual aspect of one paper serving so many schools.[193] Having begun the project primarily to foster a greater interest in writing and literature, Austin was delighted when the English teachers credited the paper with having "given a great impetus to the study of composition."[194] Austin supervised the *Collegian* for three semesters before giving the sponsorship to Philomène Butler.

Transferring responsibility was one of Austin's goals during her three years at the asylum. At that time, incidentally, "asylum" did not carry the unpleasant connotations with which it was later burdened, but was synonymous with haven or sanctuary. Austin worked to make it also a home and wished to gain time for this aim by transferring some of her responsibilities. Also she wished to place the social and educational ministries of the community in qualified hands. Mother Joseph seemed completely occupied trying to complete and finance the crèche, a project handled so easily by her two predecessors. Earlier Austin had appointed Philomène, who was a fine educator, to supervise the Mercy-staffed schools in the city. Now Austin added the responsibility, formerly hers, for the schools served by the branch convents. Philomène, like Austin, recognized the leadership potential of young Sister Borgia Walsh, who was assisting Austin to mother the orphans. During this period Austin gradually passed on to Borgia the chief responsibility, herself becoming the assistant, for the newsboys and the prison ministry. She knew that Borgia was to make a compassionate successor in both ministries. Mothers Philomène and Austin, after establishing the

Jeanerette convent in a temporary house in 1888, transferred the sisters to a better location in early 1889.[195] In October 1889, Rev. Joseph Gerlach, SJ, asked the Sisters of Mercy to staff St. Philip's School, which was to be opened the following month in Immaculate Conception parish.[196] To Austin's joy, the sisters accepted, and classes began in November 1889. Austin enjoyed the sight of the Mercies shepherding ranks of pupils across the broad thoroughfares to reach the Jesuit church for services, as startled Canal Street shoppers stared in amazement.

During the years when she served as superior of the Mercy community, Austin often referred to herself as a prisoner of her office or position. Before each election, in fact, she would ask friends to pray that all would be AMDG and that she could accept God's will if elected. She even confided that she "looked forward to a release from office as to a long holiday."[197] Her days with the orphans turned out to be the holiday, as she indulged herself with more visitation of the sick and imprisoned. Her special compassion poured out upon the elderly poor, like the Gayarrés who had formerly been in comfortable circumstances. Austin's joy was immeasurable when Gayarré told her that her charity and consideration, greater than any he had encountered in his eighty-odd years, had so touched his heart that his faith in God and Church had returned.[198] While at the asylum, Austin wrote to editors of several Catholic journals in behalf of the elderly historian, and he deeply appreciated her efforts for his manuscripts.[199] She considered his articles "really splendid." Giving so much of her time to the orphans and visitation allowed Austin little time for literary work. Even so, she managed to pay tribute to a friend, Mother Francis Mulholland, whom she met in Chicago when the guerilla fighting impeded their progress westward to Omaha.[200] Austin also completed the history of the ancient parish of St. Martinville.[201] Then, the third volume of the *Annals*, though delayed for six months until the Arkansas section was satisfactory to the prelate there, arrived from the publisher in May 1889.[202]

A year after Janssens had established Joseph as sole ruler, he allowed the sisters to elect their officials and nominally recognized Austin's office. Although the council was allowed to meet, the bishop did not want Austin to reside in the motherhouse.[203] Joseph was so used to acting only upon the direction of the bishop that the new arrangement was not easy for the council. Angry about the pretense that she was serving the community as the assistant and that Joseph continued to let the Rule and customs slip into oblivion both within the convent and in dealing with Janssens, Austin was in tremendous distress about the situation.[204] Certainly this was one of the factors in Austin's decision to make her long-considered visit to see Mother Baptist Russell and her institutions in San Francisco.[205] Austin sought Joseph's permission, explaining that she could pay her way by writing articles along the way. Joseph sent Austin to ask Janssens, who to the surprise of the superior, gave consent.[206] Austin Carroll immediately made arrangements to serve as special correspondent for several newspapers, thus easily covering travel expenses for herself and her companion. Perhaps to make assurance doubly sure, Austin arranged to become duenna for several recent graduates of St. Katherine's. Their families were happy to have Austin chaperon their daughters; and the girls, besides enjoying their trip, helped Austin by recopying her rough drafts for the newspapers.[207]

Although Baptist Russell and Austin Carroll had become friends many years earlier through their correspondence, they had never met. As they shared mutual problems, sound advice, and similar favors through the years, their friendship blossomed to form a bridge reaching from the Pacific Coast to the Gulf of Mexico. Austin was now preparing to cross that span to California. Her motivation was not the fact that Baptist had been such a steady customer who regularly purchased Austin's books hot from the presses, nor was it that Baptist, like her brother Matthew Russell, SJ, encouraged Austin to continue the lengthy task of recording the annals of the various Mercy communities.[208] Austin's sincere admiration and deep friendship rested upon what she characterized as Baptist's "inexhaustible charity and compassion for those who needed help and sympathy."[209] Certainly, Austin's visit to such a friend could not have been more timely. Explaining that she was to go "by the new Southern road, "Austin said that would "be much cheaper than to go and come by a Northerly route."[210] In order to gather material for future periodical articles, Austin planned to see some of the California missions on her way to San Francisco and the Mormon settlement on Salt Lake after she left. Together, these sites were to furnish the data and inspiration for a half dozen articles which were to see publication on both sides of the Atlantic.[211] Also to be published in the *Irish Monthly* later was the beautiful life of Sister Mary Joanna Reddan,[212] one of the founding group who had brought to the West Coast her letter from Catherine McAuley. It was incorporated into the *Annals*, of course, though the heart of the material lay amid the works inaugurated by Mother Baptist in the great city dedicated to St. Francis.[213]

The Mercy chronicles in the San Francisco motherhouse relate that on July 25, 1889, Archbishop Alemany gave Baptist Russell permission "to accompany the New Orleans sisters anywhere they may wish to go throughout the State."[214] Therefore, several days before she was to leave, Austin was accompanied by Baptist to Sacramento and Grass Valley. The two weeks with Baptist marked a period which Austin was to cherish among her fondest memories. Along with them was stored the happiness brought by a return visit to New Orleans, for the following year Baptist Russell also crossed that bridge of friendship to give Austin the joy of entertaining her at the asylum.[215] Austin took the greatest delight in showing Baptist their varied works and institutions, especially the orphans and the newsboys. Though Austin could be justly proud, since she had established eight of their nine convents, she seemed more pleased that her community was so happy with Baptist Russell. Austin commented that her friend made a delightful addition to their recreation period because she was full of anecdotes and a wonderful *raconteuse*.[216] But this enjoyable visit was still a year away, as the California sisters witnessed the affectionate parting of these two extraordinary religious women. Followers of Catherine McAuley, yet leaders of others, these Mercy foundresses of the West and the South answered the needs of society's unfortunate in vastly different cities. Though half a continent apart, they had no problem finding unity amid the diversity of their ministries, for they were driven by the same love of God. Each spread His mercy and had the common sense to accommodate the works of mercy to the needs of her area.

Anxious to see her friend Bishop James O'Connor, Austin had chosen to return via Omaha. Although the bishop, like Baptist Russell, was a correspondent of many years, Austin had met him in the Northeast thirty years earlier and once again in 1879. In fact, half of the incentive for this lengthy journey came from Austin's wish to see O'Connor once more.[217] Salt Lake City was the only stop hastily arranged after Austin noted how near the railroad line passed. With the assistance of John Fitzpatrick, the brother of one of the New Orleans sisters, the young ladies were toured about the Mormon capital and vicinity while Austin managed to obtain several interviews.[218] Then the party "caught the cars," as Austin termed the train, and headed for Omaha at the same speed which was to take Nellie Bly around the world in seventy-two days before the year was over.[219] As the cars sped eastward Austin might have recalled the many favors of Michael and James O'Connor for the Sisters of Mercy, the reasons for which she dedicated the third volume of the *Annals* to them.[220] Although it was true that James, not wishing to become involved, had refused to write a statement in her behalf when the Germans sent complaints to Rome, she had accepted the refusal philosophically.

"Our friends are not always brave enough to espouse the weaker side," she had commented, but she never doubted his friendship.[221] Writing about him to Bishop O'Sullivan, Austin explained that O'Connor always trusted her completely in spite of the accusations sent to Rome. Perhaps she did not realize that, since she had so often consulted O'Connor about community affairs, her letters to him contained every fact which Leray later refused to believe.[222] Austin found O'Connor's insight keen and his advice sound, "His bright eye seemed to read one's soul, and his counsel stood me in good stead when I sadly needed it." She recalled his efforts in the 1860s to assist her brother Patrick,[223] in the 1870s his financial aid during the fever epidemics,[224] and in the 1880s his editing of her *Annals*. From long experience she could say, "He would go to any trouble for me or those dear to me."[225]

In her generous tribute in the *Annals*, Austin praised James O'Connor, noting especially the strength of his commitment to his friends.

> Those who had the good fortune to meet Bishop O'Connor socially will long remember his sweet courtesy and gracious humility. As a friend, he was unique. Not a summer friendship was his. If he loved you in prosperity, he loved you still more in adversity. *Semper fidelis*, he would deem it a pleasure to take any amount of trouble for a friend, but indeed, he would not refuse a stranger. He was the Good Samaritan to all whose woes he could reach; his purse, his time, his influence, were at the disposal of all. He never refused help to the poor . . . destitute friends who had known better days, and literary personages overtaken by poverty.[226]

Austin's anticipation like her memories, ran high as they reached Omaha. There the travelers received the gracious hospitality of the Sisters of Mercy for several days, and Austin enjoyed her conferences *vis-à-vis* her spiritual director.[227] Saddened to see that his health had deteriorated, Austin suggested he try a trip to the South during the coming winter. She thought that the moderate climate would benefit him. He was excited about the plans of Kate Drexel, whom he had been advising for some time. She had already been generous to his Indian missions, and he hoped to improve enough to attend her reception in the Mercy novitiate in Pittsburgh. After her vows, Miss Drexel was to establish a religious congregation dedicated to aiding the American Indians and Negroes.[228]

Evidently O'Connor had told Austin of this new order the previous May when Kate Drexel entered the Mercy novitiate in Pittsburgh, for Austin replied in June that she was "deeply interested in Miss Drexel's work — more in the Negro than in the Indian."[229] As to candidates for the work, Austin added that she wished she "could get some subjects of the genuine kind for Miss Drexel."[230] Austin promised to remember the new order in her prayers and "place it high in my intentions, for the project is surely AMDG."[231] As to Kate Drexel herself, Austin thought that the wealth of the lady made her sacrifice the greater, and in these days of worship of the golden calf, it is a grand act of faith for such a woman to enter religion."[232] During the Omaha visit, Austin must have talked so much about the plight of the blacks who lacked schools across the South that O'Connor asked her to gather some statistics for him. She wrote the bishop of Mobile that O'Connor wanted data on the Negro Catholics as he had "the direction of Kate Drexel, now a postulant in the Convent of Mercy," and she intended "to devote her fortune to the Indian and Colored races."[233] By the time that

O'Sullivan sent his plans for black parishes and schools in Alabama, O'Connor was "critically ill" and had to miss Kate's reception. Finally, O'Connor's doctor sent him by boat to winter in the South. Stating that O'Connor had left for New Orleans on November 26, Austin suggested that O'Sullivan plan to see him and present his needs for the blacks. After requesting his prayers for her sick friend O'Connor, Austin explained to O'Sullivan that "few combine so much learning with such deep humility, so much zeal with a charm of manner which puts every one who approaches him at ease."[234]

Sharing her concern for O'Connor's health, Austin wrote that "he would be a heavy loss to the Church. . . . The progress of religion in his diocese has been marvelous and he is revered and beloved by priests and people in an uncommon degree. To myself personally he would be a serious loss."[235] Turning her attention to the plans of Bishop O'Sullivan, Austin revealed her own feelings about the blacks.

> As for your projects regarding the Colored race, it is unnecessary for me to say how deeply I sympathize with them and how anxious I am for their success. Were all concerned satisfied, I would gladly labor in that field myself and train others for the same, though I dislike exclusiveness and would not wish to see a branch of our Order devoted *solely* to the Colored race, but I should have no objection to have it devoted *chiefly* to the amelioration of their condition.[236]

From her years in black education, Austin had learned that most blacks preferred "what they share with whites. A convent teaching both, though separately, would be more pleasing to them than one teaching blacks only."[237] She had found that past experience caused blacks to believe that whatever "is solely for them is inferior."[238] Austin felt strongly that anyone who wished to teach the blacks should first get to know them so that the school could succeed. "To know the Colored thoroughly you should live some time in the South and investigate the subject." She thought this lack of knowledge was a flaw in the plan of Bishop, later Cardinal, Herbert Vaughan.[239]

The blacks really did have a special niche in Austin's heart, and once she said, "If God rewards us according to our desires and intentions for the colored, I hope to get a good place in heaven."[240] Before her trip West, she told the Josephite priests how her efforts to establish a black school in the neighborhood of the orphanage had failed because the pastor was not interested and the bishop forbade it. Instead, she had quietly inaugurated at the asylum religious instruction for the blacks. Then "a Protestant Colored School opened, and to my grief, it is full of children who should be Catholic."[241] Her letters to the priests from Mill Hill usually enclosed her respects for Bishop Vaughan, whom she had aided in 1872. As Austin sent the 1889 statistics to O'Connor, she reminded him of the long years of work for the blacks by her community. "You say the new Order would do for the blacks what we do for the whites. Well, Sisters of Mercy in the South have always taught the blacks, visited them when ill or in prison."[242] Not only did she visit the blacks in prison weekly, but she was one of the first to be concerned about black education. "I caused all attention to be shown them when there was little talk about their wants and no encouragement from the clergy. I have always been particularly devoted to them, but I don't like exclusiveness."[243] Austin also hated pretense, and she noticed that the publicity about the Drexel fortune available for the new order seemed to inspire several bishops with a sudden concern for blacks. Among those dashing up to Kate for funds was Janssens, who had started an Indian parish in Mississippi, but had never given Austin the least encouragement or financial assistance for the black school in Biloxi.[244]

Evidently, Austin foresaw that communities like her own which had struggled alone for years to finance their black schools would receive no help from a new religious congregation.[245] She questioned O'Connor about his decision to have Kate Drexel found a new order after she completed her Mercy novitiate. Could not Kate work for the Indians and the blacks as a Sister of Mercy?[246] Austin thought this a better method because Kate could begin her work immediately with numerous Mercy co-workers, and there would be no period of delay such as that necessary in a new congregation while the candidates were in their novitiate training. Hoping for an arrangement that could quickly bring financial help to open black schools, Austin pictured Kate "in the principal house in the south" spreading the schools with largesse and speed.[247] Of course, O'Connor looked to the permanence of Kate's plans, while Austin hoped to have Kate near enough to see both the progress already made and the current needs of the black schools staffed by the Sisters of Mercy from New Orleans.[248] Austin convinced herself that had O'Connor lived a little longer, he would have had Kate organize her benefactions through the Mercy institute, which Austin called "the Order of his predilection." In the *Annals* Austin said that she had come to this conclusion from her "conversations [with O'Connor] held during the last months of his life."[249] Austin Carroll had many opportunities to talk with James O'Connor before his death because in 1889 his doctor ordered him to winter in the South.

It was November 1889, when Austin learned that her friend was finally coming to New Orleans. His doctor had wisely insisted that O'Connor travel by water as the least fatiguing means of transportation. No matter how happy she was at this news that she was to see her friend again, Austin worried that he was still too sick to make the trip.[250]

While the bishop and his secretary, Rev. A. M. Colaneri, journeyed down the Mississippi, Austin used the time to see that several types of lodging would be available for O'Connor's consideration. Not sure whether he would prefer to stay at Hotel Dieu or the rectory in St. Michael parish, Austin hoped that he might choose to recuperate in a comfortable room in St. Alphonsus Asylum.[251] Although he did so decide, his plans allowed him only several weeks in New Orleans before continuing along the Gulf Coast. In the Mercy *Annals* published six years after his visit to the city, Austin recalled that he "praised the children and seemed charmed with the flowers they gathered for him."[252] He enjoyed walking in the sunny gardens and said that "the sight of flowers blooming in the open air in December made him feel as if he could get new life in our southern climate."[253] Perhaps he should have remained longer in the suburb of the Garden District where he was apparently improving. With Kate Drexel's projects in mind, however, the bishop insisted on traveling on to gain further knowledge of the blacks in the Southern dioceses. Thus, in the second week in December he went to Pass Christian, where Austin tried to arrange for him to meet Bishops Heslin of Natchez and O'Sullivan of Mobile, both of whom were struggling financially as they tried to provide facilities for the blacks.[254]

Austin accompanied O'Connor and Colaneri to Pass Christian to introduce the two neighboring bishops,[255] both of whom were her friends, Heslin for twenty years in New Orleans, particularly in the second decade when sisters staffed his parish schools. As he himself had a keen interest in Catholic education, Heslin appreciated Austin's efforts to provide excellence in parochial schools with well-trained teachers.[256] Having come South only after his appointment to the diocese of Mobile in 1885, O'Sullivan had known Austin for a shorter time. Yet he already had a deep admiration for her zeal for souls and her work in behalf of educational opportunities for the blacks. After the brief stop at the Pass, O'Connor moved ahead to Mobile, where "the Sisters of Mercy showed him every attention and courtesy."[257] Delighted to hear from them that he had improved, Austin wrote on December 21, "Thanks be to God for that good news. It gives me the best tidings Christmas could bring me."[258] Much of her news was lighthearted. He is in the prayers of the sisters, Doctor Brickell inquires about him regularly, and the Jesuits heard from Springhill that he is better. The Indians near Bayou St. John are receiving religious instructions regularly and his lamp is kept burning in the Sacred Heart oratory. Austin closed with "I am only sorry that I am not on the spot to see the improvement myself—it would be such a pleasure to me."[259]

The joyful news was short-lived, for two days later Austin wrote

O'Connor, "A few lines today give me the sad news that you have had another back-set. I am really grieved for you."[260] She enclosed several dietetic remedies from New Orleans doctors and one from a Creole nurse. Although he could not expect "to get well rapidly," he must not get discouraged as improvement would come in time. She tried to raise his spirits with the cheery news that "ever so many letters" had been forwarded to him, the sick orphan he had seen was recovering "with God's help," and all united with her in wishing him "a holy and happy Christmas."[261] Austin's Mercy correspondent in Mobile must have reported that the bishop was depressed, for she told him that he should not worry about the opinions of those who differed with his ideas for Kate Drexel's order. "You said I ought to know your Philadelphia friends, and indeed I'll be glad to know them. But how is it to be managed? I am grateful to them for their kindness to you and for the good they do in the Church."[262] As she closed, Austin tried again to cheer him. "This long letter is to cure you if you feel lonely Christmas day—and that is why it is written."[263] Colaneri wrote shortly to let her know that the attack had abated, but the bishop wished to see her once more. When she went to Mobile at the end of the year, she found him hopeless of recovery and speaking of death. "How different life seems when one is about to leave it!"[264] She asked, "Would you wish to begin again?" When he acquiesced, she asked, "Without the knowledge you now have?" Reflecting that he might not do as well, he said, "It is better to finish now, if it be God's will."[265] Austin hated to leave. No matter how reluctant she felt, however, Austin had to obey Mother Joseph's call to return.

Certainly, Austin realized that she would never see James O'Connor again, that this farewell was forever. Perhaps this realization was mutual, for after she left, the bishop wrote Kate Drexel that he was depressed and felt "crushed and forsaken. Faith alone sustains me. Pray that its support not be withdrawn."[266] To complete his tour of the dioceses across the South, he and Colaneri went to St. Augustine to see Bishop John Moore. Austin's letters reminded her friend "not to worry about *anything*" and not to tire himself with correspondence "until writing becomes a pleasure."[267] Father Colaneri let her know that O'Connor was growing weaker. She hid her grief and sent cheery news. She had a lamp burning for him, "try to keep up your spirits," take care of yourself, "the salt water will, please God, have a fine effect."[268] She had written to the Omaha sisters as he wished, "you have all our prayers—no need to tell you that. And indeed the Sisters are wonderfully good."[269] Father John O'Shanahan, SJ, a good friend of Austin's, planned to stop to see O'Connor, and Austin relayed the news, adding "See how God sends you friends,"[270] and He was to send two more. As the bishop was no better by the end of January, Mother

Sebastian Gillespie, Mercy superior in Pittsburgh, and Novice Katharine Drexel went to Florida to bring the bishop to Mercy Hospital in Pittsburgh. In April, O'Connor returned to his diocese to die. Bishop John Hogan, a friend of both O'Connor and Austin, wrote her in May that James "was emaciated to the last degree, but brighter in mind than ever, and going home like a Saint."[271] Austin was notified when his death came on May 27. Later in the day she wrote O'Sullivan, "My best friend on earth . . . died this morning at 11:20 – R.I.P."[272] A part of Austin Carroll had died with him.

12 OLD AGE & NEW WORKS
Alabama & Florida
1890–1909

P rior to the final illness of her friend in Omaha, Austin Carroll had obtained the permissions necessary to make a trip to Ireland in the summer and fall of 1890. From her recent experience as she went West, Austin realized that she could readily cover her expenses by serving as a special correspondent for several newspapers during the course of her journey. Hence, she repeated that process and financed her voyage across the ocean.[1] As it was the thirty-fifth year since she had crossed the Atlantic, Austin certainly must have looked forward to seeing her family and friends again. Such a reunion was not the motive which impelled her to make the lengthy trip, however, as Austin was returning to Ireland and England specifically to check on the accuracy of her *Life of Catherine McAuley* and the *Annals*.[2] The letters of the foundress and the early manuscripts, which Austin had used twenty-four years earlier as her primary sources for Catherine's biography and the first part of the *Annals*, had been copied from the originals in longhand and forwarded to her. Without photostatic machines there was the chance that inaccuracies had crept into the copies. When Austin heard indirectly in the late 1880s that a member of the family was claiming to have found several serious errors in the biography, she decided that she should check the original documents. Perhaps William Montgomery McAuley, the youngest nephew of the foundress, was the one in error; but Austin thought it essential to determine the accuracy of the biography. There must be no fallacy in the material concerning one who, in Austin's opinion, would be canonized in the near future.[3]

By 1890, eight reissues of Austin's *Life of Catherine McAuley*, most of them the second edition, had been released by the publisher.[4] Austin wondered why it had taken so long for this rumor of error to have reached her. Distance was partially responsible because this nephew Willie, whom the family thought to be dead, had settled in Australia.[5] While rearing his large family there, Willie saw the biography of his aunt. He tried to contact his cousin, Sister Camillus Byrn, but she had left Dublin with a foundation to America. She had already served in New York City, Providence, and New Haven when his letter found her in Baltimore in 1884.[6] Camillus answered Willie's questions and then forwarded his letter to her sister, Sister Margaret Byrn in London, lest "the Writer of the Annals . . . should ask to see it."[7] Thus it was from Margaret that Willie's complaints were relayed to Austin Carroll. As the records of burials in Dublin were to prove, Willie had erroneous dates for the deaths of his two brothers and was unaware that the eldest, James, had previously sold the estate from which Willie hoped to receive a substantial return.[8] Quite justly, and like Twain's Huck Finn, Willie found the report of his death greatly exaggerated. As time proved, however, most of his other complaints were based on a mixture of mistaken information and the natural inaccuracy of Willie's memory as a pre-school child. Yet his complaints were fortunate because they revealed the tremendous concern of Austin for complete accuracy. Even so, she was quick to admit that the perfect book is yet to be written.[9]

This was not the first occasion on which a complaint had reached Austin Carroll indirectly from a relative of Catherine McAuley. Catherine's cousin, the eldest Byrn daughter, as was mentioned above, complained in the 1860s that both Hartnett and Carroll had erred in their mention of the financial reverses of her grandfather.[10] This Byrn cousin, whom Willie called Kate, also denied the antagonism between her father and grandfather. In answer to Kate's protest, Austin had her publisher delete the several offensive sentences even though the financial ruin was a matter of public record.[11] Austin Carroll had no desire to offend the family connections and dropped these facts because they were not really needed to portray Catherine's character. On the other hand, Austin refused to omit an incident she thought essential in illustrating the gentle, forgiving spirit of the Mercy foundress.[12] Thus Austin retained the eventful evening when Catherine fled to the Cusack home to escape the violent anger of Willie's father. Naturally, Willie could not believe that his loving father could lose his temper because this father so doted on his youngest son that he allowed him to skip school whenever he wished.[13] Catherine's flight became public knowledge in 1889, however, when a member of the Cusack family included the incident in a published biography.[14] Willie's complaints centered on dates and minor details concerning himself and his brothers and sisters. Willie noted, for instance, that his sister Mary was already consumptive when eleven, several years earlier than Austin had stated; that the family property was in County Longford, not Louth; and that one of his aunts was Eleanor, not Frances as the biography had stated. Although Willie was confused about the dates he listed, his letter is noteworthy for the detailed information he gave about himself and his feelings.[15]

Details of another kind kept Austin busy that spring. Besides writing for hospitality to the convents in England and Ireland where she hoped to check her data and sources,[16] Austin was still trying to assist the elderly Gayarré couple whom she visited regularly. When Judge Gayarré, as she always called him, sent her his article entitled "Women of Louisiana" for editing, she returned it quickly with her sincere and generous praise.[17] Gayarré related to a friend that her encouragement enabled him to overcome his depression and again write for publication.[18] Austin understood from her own experience as a writer that encouragement was essential even to the authors she considered "men of genius." Earlier she had offered her congratulations to Charles Dickens and George Washington Cable, among others. Her communication to the latter was quoted above, but her letter to Dickens has not survived. However, one of the sisters kept a copy of his reply which thanked Austin for her praise, her interest in his work, and explained that he was unable to include the city on his [second] tour to this country.[19] The memoirs of several sisters noted that Austin especially admired the way that Dickens used the medium of the press for good by shining the light of public scrutiny upon certain types of institutions which sorely needed reform.[20] Another writer who worked to remedy the social order was Frederick Ozanam of France. Some of his writings were given to Austin by William Blair Lancaster. As a student at the Sorbonne, he had been greatly influenced by Ozanam and brought to New Orleans the rules for Ozanam's Society of St. Vincent de Paul. Austin Carroll was so taken by Ozanam's concern for the poor that she enclosed excerpts of his writings in letters to her friends.[21]

Just as Austin had a deep admiration for this French gentleman who established groups to work for the poor, so she had for the men of New Orleans who gave their time as his followers. Lancaster, like many of the leading citizens in the city who belonged to the Vincentian conferences in the various parishes, was exceptionally generous in his religious efforts for others. He and other Vincentians regularly supported the work of Austin and the Mercies in the prisons and the Newsboys' Home.[22] Just as William Castell attended gratis to Austin Carroll's legal business,[23] so Lancaster was a steady benefactor in every drive for funds for the newsboys or the orphans under the care of the sisters, and he once donated property in Mandeville, as he specified, to establish a home where the sisters could get a rest in the summer.[24] Another of Austin's generous friends was Thomas Rapier, whose support was largely responsible for the success of the Newsboys' Home. Active through both his newspaper coverage of and publicity for the work and his own kind influence as an officer in the St. Vincent de Paul Society,

Rapier was of double assistance to the young newsies.[25] In 1890, the old home on Bank Alley was replaced by the more serviceable building on Baronne near Perdido Street. In this home the Sisters of Mercy were entrusted with its management, primarily because of the dedication of Mothers Austin and Philomène.[26] According to Rev. Albert Biever, SJ, who served for a time as the newsboys' chaplain, "The management of the Home passed into the hands of the gentle, black-robed Sisters of Mercy, who for many years exercised such marvelous influence over motley crowds of ungovernable urchins."[27]

Just as she thoroughly enjoyed the newsies or the young gentlemen of the press, as she liked to call them, so did Austin seem to have a marked rapport with reporters, editors, and publishers. Locally, these gentlemen consistently accepted her items for their papers.[28] Yet these members of the local press corps were not her only friends in the profession. For quite a number of editors of Catholic papers and periodicals Austin had the special admiration she reserved for compatriots who had had to leave their beloved Ireland. The gifted pens of many of those had secured the positions with Catholic publishers in America. For a time Abram J. Ryan, the poet of the Confederacy, edited the *New Orleans Morning Star*, and farther afield were Thomas D'Arcy McGee and Richard Dalton Williams. James McMaster of the *New York Freeman's Journal*, Charles O'Malley of the *Catholic Record* and later the *Chicago Sun*, and James A. Corcoran of the *American Catholic Quarterly Review* were as quick to use Austin's contributions as were John Francis Maguire of the *Catholic Examiner* of Cork and Matthew Russell, SJ, of *The Irish Monthly* of Dublin. When William J. Fitzpatrick was gathering data for his life of Thomas Burke, OP, Austin Carroll served as his U.S. collector and forwarder of any papers concerning the American Tour.[29] Denis and James Sadlier published Austin's most frequently reissued work, *Catherine McAuley*. Lawrence Kehoe of the Catholic Publication Society published more than a dozen of Austin's books. She admired Kehoe's dedication to excellence, calling him "perfect in his field," but pestered him for her "percentages."[30] O'Shea's Catholic Publishing House printed as many of Austin's titles as Kehoe did, Patrick O'Shea publishing several as multi-volume sets.

Notwithstanding all the above friends in writing and publishing, the warmest of these relationships were to be found in the offices of the *Boston Pilot* with Patrick Donahoe, John Boyle O'Reilly, and Katherine E. Conway. Though Donahoe was not as close to Austin as the other two, he had correspondence with her, asking in 1889 to include an excerpt from her forthcoming *Annals* as "the most realistic piece of writing" he had seen in a long time.[31] Before she came to know O'Reilly personally, Austin admired his staunch Irish patriotism. Later his compassion and unasked assistance during the horrors of the fever epidemic of 1878 earned Austin's deepest gratitude and led to real friendship. Later she gave O'Reilly an antique miniature of Count Alexander O'Reilly, one which she especially treasured because Gayarré had given it to her.[32] Austin gave this unusual gift because of the O'Reilly family connection, as she generally presented benefactors with one of her own books. Katherine Conway did the same for Austin, sending a copy of each book she published to her friend in New Orleans.[33] Austin must have returned the favor for she thought highly of this talented young woman who was succeeding in a man's world. Besides Katherine Conway, Austin had as her friend another woman author and editor, Kate Madeleine Barry. Katherine, who could claim Austin's longer and closer friendship, and Kate, whom Austin seems to have met through Kehoe's company, shared with Austin their hopes for greater justice for women in salaries and opportunities in the business world, especially in their chosen literary field.

Perhaps Katherine and Kate should have come to New Orleans where Eliza Holbrook Nicholson, succeeding as the first woman publisher of such a major daily paper as the *New Orleans Picayune*, was sending a sharp young reporter, Martha Smallwood Field, on assignments to Washington, DC, and other locations.[34] In Chicago she was to cover the World's Fair in 1892, the same year that Katherine Conway was urging that Austin Carroll be selected as one of the speakers during the approaching Catholic Columbian Conference.[35] That same year Kate was expressing regret that Austin was going to delay the publication of her fourth volume of the Mercy *Annals*,[36] and it would be interesting to know to what extent Kate's decision to write about the Mercy Foundress was influenced by her friend Austin.[37] These incidents needed to await Austin's return to Ireland however. In 1890, the year of the long-awaited trip, both Lawrence Kehoe and John Boyle O'Reilly died.[38] Austin's notes of sympathy to their families do not seem to have survived, but another letter of condolence did.[39] Still extant and addressed to Sister Veronica Nelligan, one of the lay sisters, this letter illustrates Austin's concern for the suffering which the sad news of her sister's death had brought to Veronica. Austin enclosed details of the funeral arrangements and the plans of the family for her sister's children, several too young to realize that they had lost their mother. The extant letter also demonstrates Veronica's affection for Austin. After Veronica's death fifty years later, Austin's beautiful words of condolence were found as carefully preserved as the document she signed when she took her religious vows.[40]

Austin Carroll was held in almost as much affection by some of her long-time correspondents in England and Ireland. These sisters loved Austin for her devotion to Catherine McAuley and must have looked forward to meeting her in person. Here and there along the way, however, Austin was to arrive only to learn that her elderly correspondent who had known the Mercy foundress personally, had already joined Catherine in eternity. On such occasions Austin must have certainly berated herself for having delayed so long to make this trip. Those early days of June in 1890 must have dragged for Austin as she had to wait until the tenth for her partner, Sister Mary Borgia Walsh, to complete the school session. Bright and early on June 11, they enjoyed a jolly send-off as they started for New York.[41] That spring Austin had found that her funds would cover a quick trip to Rome before her tour of the early convents in Ireland and England. Both Bishop James O'Connor and Mother Baptist Russell had strongly urged that she go to Rome,[42] and Austin herself thought her "future work would be the better for the opening one's mind gets in Rome, and therefore most useful to the Church."[43] As the special correspondent, her articles on the Italian situation would be most welcome. In the interval since she had crossed the ocean, the month of passage in 1856 had been cut in half by 1890, when the voyage averaged two weeks. As on her earlier crossing, Austin did not leave the name of the ship unless she returned on the same vessel, for she mentioned seeing her nieces as she left Ireland on the *Gallia*.[44]

Austin's detailed series of articles giving literary and historical information concerning the locations she visited were later published in her book entitled, rather obviously, *In Many Lands*.[45] Since this work was addressed to the general reader, especially the actual or armchair traveler, Austin did not include her itinerary to the convents of Mercy. This ocean voyage must have been a great improvement over Austin's 1856 trip, for she was surprised at the smooth way in which the ship cut the waves and found that she could banish seasickness by remaining on deck as much as possible.[46] Their vessel reached Liverpool in two weeks and docked at the Mersey quays. Austin's plan was to go from Liverpool to Dover, seeing several English convents along the way, then take the ferry to Calais and entrain for a rapid trip to Rome and back to England. There she had arranged to visit convents in the London area and then move northward, stopping briefly at the principal convents in England and Scotland. Austin had discovered that the shortest and cheapest route across the Irish Sea ran between Stranraer, south of Glasgow, and Larne, north of Belfast. From the latter city, Austin intended to move southward, seeing the Sisters of Mercy she passed, as she advanced to Dublin. From there she made several loops westward and just south of the capital, and finally, went to the southern Counties where she could visit with family and friends. Austin and Borgia were scheduled to embark in Cobh for their return voyage to America.[47]

Austin Carroll had planned her entire tour with an extremely stringent timetable because there were so many convents she wished to visit, most for an hour or two, and some for an overnight stay. Here or there, however, Austin allowed several days for a motherhouse like Liverpool with a half dozen branch convents. Austin recalled her visit to the Mount Vernon Street Mercies in 1856 and the deceased Mothers Liguori Gibson and Aloysius Consitt. The sisters, as Austin and Borgia were to find all along the way, were most gracious and hospitable and accompanied the visitors to see their institutions.[48] At each city Austin intended to visit a number of churches and historic sites because her aim as special correspondent was to present a travelogue giving special attention to the religious and historic, the points often neglected in many travel guides. Shrewsbury, according to Austin, "all but enraptured" the visitors.[49] The town was picturesque enough to merit the longest of Austin's articles about the cities she visited.[50] Their "considerate hostess" was Sister Stanislaus Ward.[51] Two years earlier she had sent a letter, previously endorsed by six bishops, to the English and Scotch convents urging "a combination of the different Convents of Mercy" to form a generalate.[52] Stanislaus was thinking of the special advantages of a consolidation which would foster a strong central novitiate and greater mobility of the available Mercy personnel, but like the suggestions of Michael O'Connor in America decades earlier, the time was not yet ripe. Although her plan was rejected by some and ignored by others, Stanislaus sent a copy to New Orleans as she knew that Austin was interested in anything concerning the Mercy Institute.[53]

The itinerary called for several days at the next stop because Birmingham had neighboring sites to be visited and a prelate to be interviewed. The Mercy convent in Birmingham was precious to Austin because Catherine McAuley herself had founded this second house in England. Her presence was especially strong here, also, for it was only six years since the death of Mother Juliana Hardman, the superior whom Catherine had appointed.[54] Austin saw the branch in Harborne and the foundations in Wolverhampton and Maryvale, this last being the site of the first chapel in England to be dedicated to the Sacred Heart of Jesus.[55] There in the old college of Oscott, the Mercies maintained the perpetual lamp in honor of the Sacred Heart,[56] and perhaps they also gave Austin the idea for the perpetual lamp or eternal flame which she established in New Orleans.[57] For literary associations, Austin made a rapid trip to Coventry, where Mother Elizabeth Watkins was translating a series of meditations,[58] and dashed over to Stratford-on-Avon. Yet as much as Austin admired Shakespeare and revered the chapel of the Sacred Heart, none of these locations were as important to her as the Handsworth convent in Birmingham, where Catherine McAuley had resided for a month in 1841. The foundress had called the chapel exquisite and felt surrounded by Mercy.[59] She wrote that "the ceiling of the choir is blue and gold with the word Mercy in every type and character all over it."[60]

Austin Carroll evidently felt surrounded by Mercy also, for she spoke of "the proverbial excessive kindness and hospitality" of the English sisters. They were surprised to learn that Austin had met Newman thirty-six years earlier, when he was the rector of the Catholic University in Ireland.[61] The sisters doubted an interview would be possible as the cardinal was feeble, in his ninetieth year, and had been ill since May. Austin sent word to the Oratory that she had a message from Newman's old friend, the late James O'Connor, but that she could give the information to one of his priests if necessary. "But as soon as he heard the name of Bishop O'Connor," Newman sent for the "American sisters."[62] Austin saw the emaciated cardinal, assisted by the infirmarian and framed in the window near his tribune. With the light filtering down upon him. Austin related that this prelate who had turned the Oxford movement into the Second Spring

> looked like an apparition from another world . . . his wondrous voice clear and resonant, and his intonation perfect. When he recalled his obligations to Bishop O'Connor — who had been his tutor in Rome — and spoke of their happy times at the Propaganda, and his keen sense of sorrow for his death, his beautiful voice trembled with emotion, and his eyes were suffused with tears. . . . The Cardinal eulogized O'Connor's zeal and labors, and asked many questions about the Church on the other side of the Atlantic. He expressed much love for America, and blessed his visitors several times.[63]

Austin knew that she would never forget this solemn interview.

This meeting with the saintly cardinal served as a preview of her meeting with Archbishop Tobias Kirby, the friend in Rome whom she had yet to meet in person. Like Newman, Kirby was not a young man, having already served as rector of the Irish Pontifical College for over forty years. Austin spoke of the journey to Rome as a flying trip, not referring to aerial flight, of course, but indicating that it was to be rapid and direct. She did have several stops planned along the way, however, as she and Mary Borgia went by rail to Dover, where they took the steamer to Calais. As she habitually found the most reasonable mode of transportation, Austin noted that "many travel third class because there is no fourth."[64] While the Sisters made their way to the car marked "Dames Seules," they were amused to hear a native comment that "Americans and fools travel first class."[65] Austin had planned to stop in Paris long enough to explore "the sublime Notre Dame" and the treasures of the Louvre, to visit a few churches, the Bois de Boulogne and the champs Elysées, and to admire the "grandeur of the capital."[66] Yet there was certainly not enough time to meander down the narrow twisted streets of the old city. Later, as the cars made their scheduled delays at Dijon, Macon, and Chambéry, Austin found some of the quaint old France that she had missed in Paris.[67] Entering from Savoie in the lower Alps, the train passed through Turin, then turned south to the seashore. Two coastal cities and another were to furnish material for Austin's articles, "Genova la Superba," "Pisa and Its Four Fabrics," and "Firenze la Bella."[68]

In Genoa Austin saw the font at which Columbus was baptized, the chapel that housed the remains of Catherine of Genoa, the ancient palazzo in which Daniel O'Connell died, and churches "glittering with gold and frescoes and mosaics like rainbows in stone."[69] Down the coast in Pisa, Austin noted especially the peaceful Campo Santo, the lovely Baptistry, the amazing leaning tower, and the "gorgeously beautiful Cathedral . . . one of the grandest edifices on earth."[70] Austin promised that those "who have the courage and the nerve" to climb to the top of the Leaning Tower will be rewarded with "one of the loveliest views in the world."[71] Then Austin and Borgia went inland to "a grander city." There they had arranged to remain a few days with the English Nursing Sisters on Via del Campucchio. Wondering if the sister who greeted them spoke English, Austin asked, " 'Are you English, Sister?' 'No, my dear,' she replied, 'I am not English, I'm Irish.' " Of course, they all had a good laugh.[72] Even though Austin had known that she would find the Florentine cathedral magnificent, the flawless facade burst upon her "as a vision of beauty and radiance."[73] She considered this Santa Maria del Fiore, with its variegated marble shining in the sun to be "both a poem and a prayer," and she judged that "among poems in stone, this is surely the epic of the world."[74] She also found that this Duomo was not a museum, but a house of prayer surrounded and frequented by its people. The sisters saw peddlers calling their wares, girls selling flowers, boys tugging donkeys, and children playing in its shade. "Occasionally they wandered into its cool depths . . . and some dropped on their knees to say a prayer before a favorite shrine."[75] They were at home in their Father's house.

Austin and her friend admired the delicate tracery of the Campanile, studied the bronze doors of the Baptistry of St. John, and tried to find St. Philip Neri's home. But on the site where he had lived as the boy "Pippi Buono," a church had been erected. They located the deMedici monuments by Michelangelo and found them in great contrast to the artist's own memorial.[76] Even so, Florence was not as kind to other native geniuses and Austin's ready compassion went out to them. The sisters found the home of Dante, whose works were censured and who was expelled from the city he loved. They paced the square in which Savanarola preached his fiery calls for reform in high places and then was burned in the fiery pile lit by his enemies. Sobering thought continued as the two Mercies located the tower from which the skies were studied by Galileo, whose scientific research was condemned.[77] Whether the field were literature, religion, or science, great men suffered because lesser minds and spirits were incapable of understanding the value of their work. For these who were treated so unjustly in centuries past, Austin might have felt a kinship. If so, she did not mention it, but explored as much of the beautiful city as she could manage. Only the Arno River disappointed her, for she thought it as muddy as the Mississippi.[78]

Then the devout travelers caught the cars for the long-awaited visit to Rome. There the now intrepid climbers intended to go to the top of St. Peter's dome. Though the feat was not accomplished immediately, they did complete the difficult curving route within the dome of the basilica. Austin found the view from the top of the dome to be "unsurpassed . . . but the ascent fatiguing to people accustomed to the charming flats of the Gulf States."[79] The Mercies had arranged for rooms with the Nursing Sisters as they had in Florence, and the convent of the Piccola Compagnia di Maria was on Via Sforza.[80] Just one block from St. Mary Major and two from the church of St. Pudentiana with its painting of Our Lady of Mercy, was the convent from which they spent a fruitful ten or twelve days drinking in the spiritual and the beautiful, the literary and the historic sights and sounds of Rome and Vatican City. Austin commented that there was "a church for every day of the year" and that "every day is a festival in one of them."[81] Sister Mary Borgia enjoyed watching Austin as she reveled in the marvelous sculptures, murals, and mosaics. She also teased Austin because she spent so much of her time seeking out relics. Austin believed that one of the principal reasons for any Christian to go to Rome, was to return home with some relics. "Rome is rich in treasures of art," she declared, "but incomparably richer in heavenly treasures."[82]

Thus regardless of the extent to which Austin's artistic appetite feasted on the magnificence of the churches and basilicas, her heart was captured by the sites which had been hallowed by saints through the centuries. Accordingly, she revered the place of Peter's imprisonment, the area of death for thousands of martyrs, and their tombs deep in the catacombs. She was filled with awe at the Scala Santa, its chapel of precious remnants, and the relics from Jerusalem in Santa Croce. Near the Gesu, she walked the same halls as had Ignatius of Loyola and Francis Borgia and their followers to sainthood.[83] Even in Rome Austin revealed her perennial interest in books and libraries. Although she did not mention seeing her own works there, she greatly admired the manuscripts and rare books in the Vatican library. She mentioned having located libraries like those next to the Minerva, the Barbarini, the Corsini, St. Augustine's, that of the Pontifical Irish College, and those of all the other seminaries and universities. She concluded that "every chiesa, collegio, and palazzo has its library."[84] In St.

Agatha's Austin felt a surge of patriotic pride at the sight of the tribute to Daniel O'Connell and the mural monument which enshrines his heart. The inscription in the marble read, "Erected by Charles Bianconi, the faithful friend of the immortal Liberator and of Ireland, the country of his adoption."[85] Austin felt both happy and proud to have met O'Connell and to have known Charley Bian, as they called him in Clonmel.

The meeting with another Irishman, her dear friend through correspondence, was the high point of the Roman visit for Austin. This gentleman was Tobias Kirby, the archbishop of Ephesus and the rector of the Irish College. He gave the sisters a guided tour in and about Tivoli, where he and the seminarians enjoyed a respite from the heat and study of Rome during the late summer. Several years earlier when Austin needed a friend in Rome, Kirby had given her staunch support, and she would never forget it. Now that he had met Austin in person, "nothing could exceed his kindness."[86] Among her dearest memories of her days in Italy, Austin was later to write, were "those connected with the venerable, white-haired Rector, a gentleman of the old school," who had "led a life of goodness and sanctity for nearly a century."[87] Austin explained that it was

> during this delightful visit that the kind Archbishop informed her that the Holy Father had selected, blessed, and indulgenced a picture of Our lady of Mercy to be the proper emblem of the whole Order of Mercy. Like most, if not all, miraculous pictures, it is not exactly handsome, though very striking. . . . Engravings of it were sent by most Reverend Dr. Kirby to the writer, and an oil painting of the same, which adorns a shrine in the chapel of the Mercy Convent in New Orleans.[88]

To her great joy, Austin was to witness the installation of this striking painting in another month, because her visit to the Dublin motherhouse on Baggot Street coincided with the ceremony on the feast of Our Lady of Mercy.[89] That date was still a month away as Austin saw that her time allotment for Rome had been exhausted. If she went to the Alban Hills to see Castel Gandolfo, she did not record it. Because she had already received a personal blessing from the pope through the kindness of Dr. Kirby, Austin probably skipped that excursion. As she and Borgia left Rome "on a bright summer evening," Austin did record that she and her companion were "full of memories that will be a joy to us while life lasts."[90] Their train sped back to Calais through Rheims, a more northerly route through France than they had taken on their way to Rome. After the ferry across the Channel, they reached London quickly, and went to the Bermondsey section, where Catherine McAuley had established her first English foundation. In this Mercy community was the cousin of the foundress, Sister Margaret Byrn, a correspondent of Austin for almost a decade. Among the archival treasures there were several letters in Catherine's own hand,[91] as well as her explanation of the dual spirit of the Mercy Institute with its mutually dependent aims of prayerlife and ministry.[92] One of the primary sources which Austin had come to examine was the convent chronicle, for the opening gave a brief history of the Institute and its foundress as recorded, apparently, from the recollections of Mother Clare Moore.[93] Also in the archives was a scrapbook which contained several clippings from New Orleans, one being the lovely obituary tribute which Austin had composed upon Clare Moore's death.[94]

Following the pattern of the numerous foundations of Catherine McAuley, Clare Moore had established eleven independent houses.[95] Bermondsey was soon to have as its twelfth, one "in the colonies," for the sisters were finalizing arrangements to establish a Mercy foundation in Kingston, Jamaica.[96] Probably, Austin described her own convent in the Tropics and gave some practical tips about the supplies and clothing necessitated by the climate in the West Indies. Although she must have been fascinated with the McAuley relics in Bermondsey, Austin knew it was time to transfer to St. Edward's convent in northwest London.[97] Like Birmingham and Liverpool, this convent on Blandford Square had been established from the Dublin motherhouse, and through the years Austin had corresponded with several Mercies there. These sisters were soon escorting their visitors to the other Mercy institutions in and about London, Reverend Mother herself accompanying them to the Crispin Street Night Refuge.[98] At St. John's and St. Elizabeth's Hospital, so long managed by Sister Gonzaga Barrie, Austin was delighted to see bookcases in the wards of the Hospital for Incurables and here and there a patient reading. For ten or twelve days she enjoyed the hospitality of the London sisters while she checked on the accuracy of the information in the *Annals* and sought any new data or relics of Catherine McAuley.[99]

During this time in London Austin and Borgia had also managed to visit several more famous museums and galleries and admire the monuments or homes of literary figures like Dickens. Above all, however, Austin was delighted to be able to revere the sites glorified by martyrs like Thomas à Becket, John Fischer, and Thomas More.[100] As a fitting close to her eventful London stay, Austin succeeded in arranging an interview with Cardinal Henry Edward Manning. Although he had the reputation of being rather cold, Austin found him "quite affable and pleasant," and not nearly "so ghastly in appearance as some of his portraits indicate." He received the Sisters of Mercy in his sitting room, like his home, "very plainly furnished."[101] Deeply impressed with his poverty, Austin learned that he had no cathedral, as his priorities were assisting the poor and establishing Catholic schools. She reported that he asked her a good many questions about America and that he "possessed that unaffected simplicity of air and mien, which is often associated with high gifts and a kingly nature." Yet he

> identified himself with the laboring classes and the poor, and was conspicuous for his love of them. He did all he could for them, and was a total abstainer for their sake. He spoke much to the writer of his obligations to the Irish Bishops for lending him priests, and expatiated with admiration on the immense number of vocations to the priesthood and the religious life in Ireland.[102]

This interview must have intensified Austin's pride in Ireland, if that were possible, and increased her anticipation of the approaching visit to relatives and friends. Before she was to see her family in Clonmel, however, she would meet numerous Mercy friends whom she knew through correspondence. At the next stop, Derby, she was to greet some of these. Following the route mapped out months earlier, Austin and Borgia moved northward through the park-like midland counties. Then the lovely English hills appeared and the sisters left the cars in Derby. The Sisters of Mercy there, some from the area of Cork and Kinsale, showed the visitors through their schools, "the spacious Gothic church, and the handsome Mercy convent."[103] Then Austin hurried on to York, where she wished to see two "superlatives," one being the Yorkminster Cathedral with its magnificent stained glass and the largest window in England. The second site was that of the oldest convent in the country, Mary Ward's group established in the early 1600s and located on the ancient thoroughfare of Mickel Bar. Here the community persevered in spite of persecution, eventually to become the Institute of Mary or the Loretto Sisters. Austin held this group in the highest admiration for their bravery and determination, some of their early superiors accepting prison terms rather than agree to close their schools for girls.[104] Austin certainly enjoyed the beauty of the cathedral and the history in York's narrow streets, but her memories were to center on the courageous nuns of the Bar convent.

The brief stop in York was followed by another in the brighter city of Durham, where Austin wanted to visit the cathedral, and the attraction was more than beauty. Still "Margaret the historian," she wanted to venerate the resting place of St. Bede, the "Venerable Father of English history." She thought that this jewel of a cathedral had a fitting setting in this city of greenery, water, and spires.[105] As it had been founded from Cork, the Convent of Mercy in Sunderland had a special interest for Austin Carroll. She knew of the literary work of the founding superior, Mary Vincent Deasy. Her successor, Mary Aloysius O'Connell, also professed in Cork, had continued as Austin's correspondent, and the sisters gave the visitors an especially warm welcome.[106] These Sunderland nuns even accompanied their guests to the convents in the area. At Newcastle-upon-Tyne, for instance, the chronicler commented that the "four Sisters from Sunderland, who introduced with them two Sisters of Mercy from America" visited in August, but stayed less than two hours as the guests "insisted on preceding to Edinborough."[107] And so it was. Austin's itinerary called her to rush off to Scotland, make a quick stop with the Sisters of Mercy in Edinburgh and Glasgow, then dash westward to the coast to take the ferry at Stranraer. While the sturdy ship plied the waves, Austin shared with Borgia the fact that both the lovely lowlands they saw first and the rugged highlands on the west had awakened memories of Sir Walter Scott's works. Four decades earlier one of her passions as a youngster, Austin related, had been the reading and reveling in Scott's novels.[108]

As Scotland grew fainter in the haze and Ireland's hills loomed closer, the two Mercies were recalling the numerous sisters they had become acquainted with even before they reached Ireland. All had been strangers to Borgia, but Austin was enjoying in one convent after another the pleasure of meeting face to face with her correspondents of many years. While she was having this satisfactory experience, what did others say of her? Like customs and chronicles, reactions differed as widely as the houses she visited, and in a convent where ministry allowed little time for a chronicler's pen, one of the lacunae and Austin's visit often occurred simultaneously. Aside from such misfortunes, archives yielded rich details. Some sisters had expected to see their visitors in the bonnet and cloak like theirs and such as Austin had used in New England three decades earlier to disguise the fact that "the walking nuns" were religious sisters. Concern about the absence of cloaks was noted in these houses. However, many others, like Bermondsey several decades earlier, had laid aside special "outdoor clothing" as no longer needed, and their habits were alike. A surprising number of English convents were staffed by Irish sisters. In other houses English reserve found the guests "true Americans," or lacking "in reserve," or "not at all bashful." More communities found the visitors "lively," or "charming," or "marvelous travelers to get about so rapidly." Yet this brevity caused offense in several instances when an expected visit of several days was only a two-hour stay.[109] The intrepid travelers found little variation in hospitality, as they noted a most generous welcome in every convent.

Reactions in the Irish convents were to vary in much the same manner, if looking ahead for a moment can be countenanced. The sisters found that Austin did not act like a famous author, but was friendly, full of anecdotes, and a grand conversationalist. The visitors were both "frank in manner" and had the openness of Americans; and judging by her books, one community thought that Austin was a "native of the New World." Except for Austin's eyes, one chronicler wrote, "nothing about her look . . . indicated the fine intellectual powers hidden within." She did not question much, but "had a mind which took in a great deal, and a memory capable of hoarding it up till needed." The Irish sisters noticed that Austin "showed much sympathy" for one in sorrow and that her "heart was large and generous." Austin's interest in everything concerning Catherine McAuley, especially her canonization, was surprising to some. Talking with those who had seen the foundress gave Austin the greatest delight, and nothing so disappointed her as learning that a dear correspondent who had promised to relate everything she knew about Mother McAuley had just suffered a stroke and could no longer say a word, or that the eyes of one who had seen the foundress were already closed in death. Such news devastated Austin, and the sisters saw her crying. It struck the sisters everywhere that Austin was filled with gratitude at the graciousness of her reception.[110]

Besides these recorded points from the chronicles, here and there precious memories were retained in the minds and hearts of sister witnesses. An alert senior sister in Belfast treasured one such event. In her request for hospitality, Austin must have mentioned that she looked forward to the opportunity of trying on the precious ring of Catherine McAuley. Possibly, she also explained that she had the same motto as the one in the ring, Ad majorem Dei Gloriam. Thus, before Austin's arrival there was serious consideration and discussion about granting this favor. Suppose Austin's intense admiration of the foundress caused her to try to keep the ring. What could they do if, after she slipped it on, Austin refused to remove the ring from her finger. The community prayed about their decision, then decided to be risk takers, and to have faith in this sister with the extraordinary love of Mother McAuley. Upon arrival from the busy port of Larne where the ferry docked, Austin had the great privilege of placing the ring of the saintly foundress upon her finger for a few moments. Of course, she then removed it as the sisters would not think of parting with it, but the fact that they allowed her to try it on made her visit to this Belfast Convent of Mercy a memorable occasion. The feeling was mutual, as the young sisters were so impressed by the fear of losing the ring to the house, Austin's reverence for it, and her desire for relics of the Mercy foundress that they preserved the incident in their memories for the next fifty years.[111] Austin Carroll was to treasure the memory as long as she lived.

Actually there were to be other special moments, also, before the visit to Ireland had been completed. From Belfast Austin journeyed to Derry to see the early manuscript by Sister Mary Ann Doyle;[112] to Armagh to interview Archbishop Michael Logue;[113] to Downpatrick to visit the graves of Ireland's great saints, Patrick, Brigid, and Columba;[114] and to Newry, where she hoped to see several friends. One of these was the Bishop of Dromore, John Pius Leahy, OP, whom she had known and admired in Cork.[115] The other was the superior, Mary Emmanuel Russell, a sister of the late Mary Aquin and of Mother Baptist in California, all three, Austin's friends.[116] Among the convent treasures at the time in Newry was a set of vestments which fascinated Austin and Borgia because they had "belonged to Archbishop John Carroll of Baltimore."[117] In Dundalk and Drogheda Austin found Mercy Motherhouses and learned that for the martyred archbishop, Oliver Plunkett, memories were abundant in the former and relics in the latter. The scene of the Battle of the Boyne on the river's banks was the site which captured her attention, and the battle itself was the subject of one of her longest pieces.[118] Evidently written with both heart and heat, the article noted that the defeated James II was an advocate of "liberty of conscience," one of her own causes. She felt that James deserved some measure of honor for having advocated "a great principle" as much as a century and a half ahead of his time.[119] Then in what Austin considered "an incredibly short time," the train carried them through the beautiful country which lies along the northern approaches to the city of Dublin.[120]

In both beauty and hospitality, Dublin was to fulfill Austin's highest hopes. Before she left New Orleans, Austin had written a friend that "Sisters of Mercy feel obligated to me and would do for me what they would do for no one else, on account of my having written the *Annals*, the *Life* of the Foundress, etc."[121] That certainly sounds exaggerated, but from all reports Austin seems to have been right on target with her assessment. Austin had been given such a warm welcome everywhere that she believed that she was already receiving her hundredfold. Her companion Borgia decided that Austin was being justly rewarded for her own generous hospitality all through the years. In the above letter Austin had also said, "The Superior of the Parent House, Baggot Street, Dublin, offered to do anything for me."[122] Actions soon proved these words true. As befitted the prolific motherhouse with more than thirty branches and foundations, St. Catherine's Convent of Mercy in Dublin gave Austin a grateful and gracious welcome. She felt the presence of the saintly foundress not only in the room in which she died and in the cemetery on the grounds, but also in the chapel, on the stairs, and in every nook and cranny of this first House of Mercy. More importantly, of course, Austin experienced in the community the loving spirit of Catherine McAuley herself. Austin was able to read the correspondence of Clare Moore and her sister, Clare Augustine Moore, as well as the latter's manuscript.[123] Austin was watching for sections possibly omitted when a copy had been made for her many years before.

Austin was delighted to see that Clare Moore's collection of the *Sayings of Our Revered Foundress* had been republished in Dublin because the first edition from London in 1868, as well as her American reprint ten years later, were both exhausted.[124] Austin, too should have been exhausted by this time as she had been involved in her research or travel for close to two months. Along the way, furthermore, she was taking notes and recording her impressions for future articles for newspapers and periodicals. In spite of the fatigue which she must have felt, Austin continued her hectic pace in Dublin. At the convent she relaxed by enjoying the magnificent illumination and painting of Clare Augustine Moore.[125] Austin managed to get out to Coolock House in the suburbs and in the city to locate several other sites associated with Catherine McAuley. She visited the Presentation Convent at George's Hill, and on the way home suffered a fall which seriously injured her right arm. Taken to Mater Misericordia for medical treatment, Austin had to remain there for a short time and was then detained in Dublin to continue medical treatment.[126] Although the injury was serious enough to delay her, it did not cancel Austin's plans entirely. While still hampered by the arm, for instance, she went to All Hallows in Drumcondra as a favor for two friends, Bishop Thomas Heslin of Natchez and Bishop Jeremiah O'Sullivan of Mobile.[127]

Since Alabama and Mississippi were truly missionary territory, except for the Gulf Coast, the Bishops were anxious to obtain some Irish seminarians. Their dioceses, like that of New Orleans, were not furnishing native priests as yet, and they hoped that Austin Carroll might secure commitments from several Irish students.[128] By making several short trips and returning after each for treatment, Austin intended to accomplish her aims, like talking with the elderly Mercies who had known the foundress and having a nice visit with her family and friends in Clonmel. She started the first cycle of towns with expectations of handling Catherine McAuley's letters, and she did just that in Tullamore.[129] She went to Birr and visited with Mother Anastasia Beckett,[130] to Roscrea to chat with cousins,[131] and to Naas with news of Agnes Greene.[132] The second cycle was by train south to Wexford for news of Mother Ignatius Walsh,[133] to Waterford to see the sisters and some family connections,[134] and to Clonmel for the long anticipated family reunion. She greeted brothers and sisters and in-laws as well as nieces and nephews of all ages. It was an extraordinary occasion, and Austin would never forget it.[135] Austin showed Borgia the remnants of old walls and the ancient once-Catholic St. Mary's Church, where, Austin related, the Church had "an organ of wonderful power and sweetness, on which we played an *Ave Maria*, begging Our Lady to intercede that it may yet be restored to its rightful owners."[136] In her articles Austin proudly mentioned that Clonmel was served by six religious orders, one the Sisters of Mercy, and revealed how much she was charmed by the beauty and the history of the Golden Vale.[137]

Although she found it hard to leave Clonmel, Austin was anxious to reach Carlow to chat with a beloved correspondent, Mother Catherine Maher. Earlier, Austin had written that she would be in Carlow for several days to hear all that Catherine could relate about the foundress.[138] It was not to be, as Catherine had suffered a stroke and could not say a word.[139] Austin was devastated. She saw her friend when she arrived on September 21, and had an appointment at St. Patrick's College on the 22nd, but expected to return quickly. Plans had gone awry, however, and the president, with whom Austin had the appointment, was not available. While confusion caused lengthy delays, one of the priests gave the visitors a tour of the cathedral, Braganza, and the college.[140] Finally Austin saw the rector, who told her that there were no men available. Austin's time had vanished. She had to leave Carlow on the following day in order to be present for a special event in Baggot Street. The hasty departure, especially in order to get to another convent, seemed to give offense, as had previously happened in England. Even with all the rush the characteristically compassionate Austin tried to console one of the sisters who had just suffered a tragic death in the family. It is no wonder that the chronicler saw Austin crying before she left.[141] She had just consoled a sister in deep personal grief and she herself had certainly sustained a hard blow in finding her friend silenced by paralysis. The college had been the third strike, and for the moment, she was down and out. Before the feast of Our Lady of Mercy on the morrow, she would be able to regain, if not her normal vivacity, at least serenity.

Once in Dublin, Austin sent the report of her failure to the two bishops.

> I have seen the authorities of Carlow and All Hallows. They tell me every man they have is engaged. They could however get you some, but not for three years. If you were on the spot, I think some in Maynooth would volunteer for you. There are 500 students there, almost all for Ireland. Archbishop Dunn of Brisbane has been searching for priests and sisters since July and has secured a good many. Nothing like being on the spot.[142]

On September 24, 1890, Austin and Borgia were on the spot in Baggot Street to participate in the "grand *Te Deum*" and witness the dedication and "unveiling of the special painting of the picture of Our Lady of Mercy which Our Holy Father sent from Rome."[143] This was the copy about which Kirby had told Austin in Rome, when he then surprised her with the news that a copy was already being made for New Orleans. The previous evening she had received a package of relics from Kirby and the promise of more engravings of Our Lady of Mercy as the patroness of the Mercy order. He hoped that they would spread devotion to Mary, but had them made specifically to record the above fact.[144] Austin had found the dedication ceremony especially impressive because "150 ladies . . . at the [Teacher] Training College were present." As it was similar to the St. Katharine's College which she had envisioned for New Orleans, Austin was interested in curriculum, professors, financing, and management. She wrote home that, through their graduates, "the Sisters *leaven* the whole country, and even the colonies."[145]

Austin would have enjoyed staying longer to learn more about the college, but when the feast of Our Lady of Mercy was over, so was her visit. The lovely ceremony, plus Dr. Kirby's great gift of relics, must have eased the crushing disappointment of arriving in Carlow too late to do a thing for her friend or to hear a single memory of the foundress. Filled with gratitude, Austin thanked these sisters at "the fountainhead" for their generous hospitality and medical care, made her affectionate farewells, then took the train to Galway. Had time been available, Austin would have stopped in Lissoy near Lough Ree not only to see the home of Oliver Goldsmith, but that of the Edgeworths in neighboring Mostrim, as Austin greatly admired the naturalness of Marie Edgeworth's writing.[146] These stops, like many others, Austin cancelled after her injury.[147] In that group seem to have been Roscommon, established by Mother Vincent Hartnett;[148] Westport, where Mother Paula Cullen was a faithful correspondent;[149] Clifden, where her dear friend Teresa White had died just two years earlier;[150] and Tuam, where the convent nestled in the shadow of the great cathedral. Austin did not skip Galway or Limerick however. In the latter, she was enthralled with all the relics and mementos of Catherine McAuley, and parted with the hope that she might return for another day or two.[151] On her way to Cork, Austin went through Tralee because of its associations with Daniel O'Connell;[152] Killarney, as it was "the gem of Kerry";[153] and Kinsale, where the chronicler noted that Austin had "paid a flying visit," remaining only a few hours, but unable to bypass the former home of Baptist Russell.[154]

Finally the travelers reached Cork and "one of the grandest convents in Ireland,"[155] where Austin and her sister Johanna, Sister Mary Dominica, had a great reunion. Just seeing Johanna in the Mercy habit was a treat as Austin had last seen her as a teenager. A religious for thirty-four years now, Johanna had entered the community about six months after Austin had been sent to America. Together they prayed at the tomb of their beloved Mother Josephine Warde, and then went to St. Joseph Convent of Mercy in Passage West to visit the sisters and pray at the grave of their beloved Katy. St. Joseph's gave them an exceptionally warm and affectionate welcome.[156] The sisters shared many reminiscences of Katy, whom they called Mother of Mercy and considered their own community saint. Memories of her novitiate days were revived in Austin as she had known the superiors in both

Passage West and Cork as well as many of the other sisters in the 1850s.[157] Southern Ireland did not have the high death rate that yellow fever had established in the New Orleans community, and Austin noted that deSales Lane, who had entered in the 1830s, had just died.[158] Mary Francis Meade, who had tried to help the American Indians in 1856, was looking forward to her golden jubilee in a few more years. Besides renewing old acquaintances, Austin had two short trips planned, one to the third Mercy convent established by the foundress, Charleville.[159] There the sisters had been most helpful when Austin sought data on the service of the Irish Mercies in the Crimean War and were delighted with her visit.

On her way back to Cork after that flying visit to Charleville, Austin probably made brief stops at several Mercy convents along the way. A second one-day trip eastward to Midleton, Youghal, and Cappoquin could have been cancelled because time was fast disappearing.[160] As it did, Austin impressed upon Johanna what a fine liaison service she had rendered throughout the summer by forwarding letters to the next convent on the list. Thus it was that Austin heard the distressing news of the typhoid fever and later the death of Sister Margaret Mary Killelea.[161] The loss of any gifted and capable young teacher would have been a hard blow, but this one was special. Even as she lived and taught with them, her companions considered her a saint.[162] Like their sisters at home, Austin and Borgia were convinced that their community had lost one who had attained sanctity by the perfect observance of the Mercy Rule. Calling Sister Margaret Mary "our best and brightest," Austin was deeply touched by her death.[163] Then in Cork, there was another, but Austin counted herself fortunate to have had the opportunity of seeing once again an old friend as she assisted at the deathbed of Bishop John Pius Leahy, OP.[164] The two happy deaths made their parting a little sadder, perhaps, but good cheer arrived with Austin's sister Mary from Clonmel and her three daughters, May, Clare, and Margaret Mary Byrne.[165] With affectionate and grateful farewells for Johanna and her sisters, the travelers left Cork accompanied by Mary and the girls.

All six went aboard ship at Cobh, the sisters on the liner *Gallia*, Mary and the children on a coastal steamer. Several years later Austin could still recall what a picture they had made "sitting on the bench of the little steamer when our big ship, the Gallia, was moving off."[166] As so often happens, the voyage home seemed much shorter than that leaving New York for Liverpool. Yet the crossing provided time for correspondence as well as for expanding the notes which were to furnish the base on which to build her numerous articles in newspapers, journals, and, later, a book.[167] In describing the new places she had seen, Austin frequently made comparisons that bore the accent of her three dozen years in America. The great natural wonders of the Old World, in Austin's opinion, had few surprises for anyone who has seen North America.[168] Her interest lay principally in the grand records of achievement to be seen in art and buildings from the past. For instance, she was tremendously impressed, even awed, by the magnificent cathedrals which, "though ablaze with the richest materials known to man, had no debts."[169] Thinking it foolish to call this period of great sculpture, mosaic, and architecture "the Dark Ages," she said it "was truly the Age of Faith."[170] Austin's thoughts run through her notes, and when Cardinal Newman's interview is in part the eulogy of Bishop James O'Connor, one knows she is the questioner.[171] Her feelings were also clear when, as a self-styled "exile from America," she took offense at a slur against Americans.[172] Now and again, she reacted with phrases such as "the Southern people feel," or as a "Louisiana Creole would say," thus marking her location. Austin's pronouns indicated her involvement also, as "Our Southern cities, with their wide thoroughfares and perennial greenery, are perhaps the brightest commercial marts in the world."[173]

Yet, as soon as Ireland is mentioned, there is no doubt that this Southerner by adoption is first and foremost, a native of Ireland. Proud of the charity of her people, she listed with delight the numerous institutions for the poor, like the homes for elderly widows, night refuges for the homeless, and hospices for the dying. She believed that those dating from the 1870s were among the first hospices in the world.[174] For the care of young children, she noted that day nurseries were, "happily, quite common now."[175] National pride might have been most noticeable when Austin described her compatriots at home and abroad, and though she said little of convents and nuns in her published articles, her letters reveal that convents, especially those in Ireland,

> were grand in every way, and they are, thank God, in perfect religious discipline . . . They are the homes of tens of thousands of poor children who are brought up in the love of God and spread the true religion wherever they go. Here in America they are often genuine apostles, and lead saintly lives, sometimes in spite of much bad example from laity and clergy. They are thoroughly imbued with Catholic principles, and thank God, few fall away.[176]

Also aware of the numerous Irish religious sisters serving in many communities in America, Austin wished to bring home some candidates on her return.[177] Even though no postulants had joined the New Orleans community since Mother Joseph had been given charge, she refused the suggestion.[178] Funding was such a great worry with her that, possibly, she feared the cost of transportation for any needy candidates.

For two years Austin had worried about the ability of the sisters to continue their many ministries with such rapidly diminishing numbers. Not only had there been no candidates, but at the same time there had been a loss of ten sisters, most from the novitiate,[179] but two for eternity besides Margaret Mary Killelea, whom Austin "had known and loved since infancy."[180] This trio was safe with God, and Austin placed the rest of the community in the hands of Divine Providence. While honoring Joseph's directions, Austin's heart ached when she saw the fine young Irish women, some recent graduates of the Mercy schools, yet was unable to accept those who wished to return with her. Austin accepted Joseph's decision, however, just as she had decided that only God Himself could relieve the community from the episcopal interference in internal government that was contrary to their Rome-approved Rule. During her trip, Austin had enjoyed being able to lay aside these worries almost as much as learning that the manuscripts which she had originally used for the life of the foundress were accurate and the life correct in essentials. While writing aboard ship of this research, her Mercy friends, and the scenes of the summer, Austin noted that all was still AMDG. "We willingly return to our ordinary haunts, to our prescribed routine of life, to the common daily duties of the career in which God wishes us to work out our salvation."[181]

Even the ordinary haunts could become a bit unusual however when left to the creative spirit of Mother Austin Carroll. She had decided before her trip, for instance, that the best way to ensure the privacy of the orphans was to take a job with the United States government as "census enumerator" for the asylum. Her application was accepted, and the plan proved as successful as she had hoped.[182] Upon her return from Ireland one of the first envelopes she opened was that from the Department of the Interior, which contained a check for $4.49 for her services in the recent census.[183] Other letters were to keep her busy those first few weeks after her return because a number of the convents she visited had ordered copies of some of her books. Thus a lot of the correspondence concerned orders or payment to her two publishers on behalf of the convents in Ireland and England.[184] To the motherhouses in the United States Austin sent copies of the small engraving of Our Lady of Mercy which Kirby had given her and, evidently, news of the large painting in Dublin and that in process for New Orleans. Of course, Kirby was soon deluged with orders for steel engravings and requests for other copies of the famous painting.[185] Austin's copy reached New York on March 9,[186] and arrived in New Orleans on March 23, 1891, with Kirby's note, "A little present from Our Lady of Mercy to our dear Sisters in New Orleans."[187] Within twelve months Archbishop Kirby managed to have Roman art students complete enough copies for many of the motherhouses in the United States. Thus did Our Lady of Mercy as pictured in St. Pudentiana Church in Rome become familiar to Mercies throughout the nation because of the graciousness of Kirby and the time, interest, and correspondence of Austin Carroll.

While Austin was away, there had been other correspondence that was to start, domino fashion, a series of decisions which were to have a profound effect upon Austin's situation. The Religious of the Sacred Heart had been writing Bishop O'Sullivan about giving up their academy in Selma, Alabama. Although the convent and school were nicely situated, this "arch Protestant" town in central Alabama had so few Catholic families that there were not enough pupils to finance the school.[188] Having delayed their withdrawal for a year to enable the bishop to contact their superiors in France, the nuns finally received his consent to leave the mission.[189] The efforts of the pastor, Rev. John O'Shanahan, SJ, immediately concentrated on obtaining other religious teachers for the Selma schools. He asked Janssens, with O'Sullivan's approval, to allow the Sisters of Mercy from New Orleans to staff the schools.[190] Janssens refused unless the Mercy branch convents in Alabama and Florida were to be divided from the Louisiana motherhouse and allowed to form their own novitiate as a separate community[191] Janssens had previously urged this "total separation" upon O'Sullivan, but the bishop of Mobile, like the Sisters of Mercy, believed that his poor missionary diocese had neither the means to support a novitiate nor the large Catholic population needed to supply candidates.[192] Knowing that he could not help subsidize the project, O'Sullivan thought it would be imprudent for the sisters to accept a large financial burden. He hoped to delay the separation until the diocese had overcome its debts.[193] He also thought that the Mercies could get to Selma, for he told O'Shanahan, "If you keep knocking, the archbishop will grant your request."[194]

Although this episcopal correspondence continued for months, the Sisters of Mercy were not participants. Until the summer months, in fact, they may not even have been aware of the subject of the dialogue.[195] Oblivious to its effects, Austin had thrown herself enthusiastically into her ministries with the orphans, the newsboys, and the prisoners. Always on the alert for a special treat for the orphans, she accepted free tickets for a Sunday matinee in one of the theaters. The orphans, accompanied by two of the sisters, thoroughly enjoyed the entertainment. Then Janssens wrote that he had "forbidden all entertainments for churches on Sundays," and considered that the orphans and the sisters had given bad example.[196] Austin must have been quite surprised at this somber view of Sunday, one that she had noted abroad in Protestant or Jansenistic areas as being in great contrast to the relaxed atmosphere of the typical New Orleans Sunday.[197] After assisting at Mass, many families in this largely Catholic city observed Sunday with the confidence that God enjoyed seeing His people relaxing after they had celebrated His day with morning Mass. *En masse*, families took the trains to

Milneburg or Spanish Fort, or caught the cars to City Park for picnics, sports, and enjoying the band. Dressed in Sunday best, others raced their handsome pacers along the Shell Road to West End or made the promenade on Esplanade or that city square called Lee Circle. Notwithstanding all these activities, the popularity of balls and theaters and the racing of boats and horses, Austin believed New Orleanians to be truly religious. Not only did they support a hundred or so churches, but they were most earnest in worship and astonishingly generous in their charity.[198]

The same affective natures that could respond so readily to an appeal for funds, however, could occasionally turn to the violence of a duel or an act or retaliation. In the spring of 1891, she was once in close proximity to the latter.[199] After a series of violent crimes rocked the city just before 1890, the New Orleans superintendent of police began investigating the activities of a mafia-like gang of Sicilians. Suddenly, the investigator was shot to death, and about twenty Italians were imprisoned as the murderers. They were tried, but because of a lack of evidence, acquitted. During their months in jail, Mother Austin had come to know them. She was giving religious instruction to them on her visit of March, 14, 1891,[200] when suddenly there was a great noise and shouting outside the main gates of the jail as a mob, infuriated by the acquittal, began battering down the gates with the intention of lynching the Sicilians. As the mob seemed about to gain entrance, Austin had the jailer release the Italians in a quick action that saved half the men, who managed to escape or hide before the mob broke in.[201] When the sisters tried to leave the prison, they were locked in a cell, "under arrest for my pains" to save the men, as Austin put it.[202] One of the sisters explained the situation at the convent.

> Imagine the consternation of the Sisters at home as the hours passed on, for she was never absent from any [spiritual] exercise, and they did not know where to look for her. But she was busy with her pen while in jail, as she had great influence with the officials of the City, pleading for the [released] men, not thinking of herself or her companion. . . . Our dear Lord never failed her. Late in the day she was at home adoring her hidden God. . . . The men were set free through her influence.[203]

In a letter to Rome which gave her account of the infamous day, Austin did not give too many details, but did say that she had tried to save the poor fellows from "the massacre that disgraced this city ten days ago."[204] Austin related that she had been visiting the New Orleans prisoners for close to twenty-four years

> and often meet Italians there . . . but I do not think all of the eleven men murdered in the prison last Saturday week were guilty — indeed it is not

certain that any of them were. I knew them all, RIP. While in prison they came regularly to Mass every Sunday. . . . An Irish Jesuit is chaplain. We play the organ and conduct the choir.[205]

Since the Sicilians were immigrants and still citizens of Italy, the United States apologized to Italy, and Austin's letters to local officials probably had no real influence in the failure to retake the men released. Austin did not mention to Kirby that she regularly published in one of the local papers before an execution that "the Sisters of Mercy earnestly desire a substitute of life imprisonment for the death penalty."[206] The letter to Kirby must have reached Rome just before May, as it contained a request for prayers for Austin's special intentions "which are all AMDG. I beg prayers particularly just now that God may give us light to know His will and grace to do it in this juncture."[207] The wording of this request seems to indicate that Austin had finally been apprised of the Janssens-O'Sullivan discussions about allowing the Sisters of Mercy from New Orleans to staff the Selma academy, formerly that of the Sacred Heart nuns.

By May, Janssens had told both Joseph and Austin that he was definitely going ahead with his plans to divide the New Orleans community into two groups. He wished to do it immediately if O'Sullivan would agree to it; if not, he intended to work through the authority of Rome to accomplish it "as soon as possible."[208] Hearing this, O'Sullivan asked Joseph for a copy of the 1886 ruling that, as Gibbons had told him, said the branches were to remain in *status quo* until the two bishops concerned agreed to change this arrangement.[209] Unfortunately, Gibbons had given his verdict verbally to the sisters also. Janssens was refusing to allow the New Orleans sisters to bear any expense for a motherhouse and novitiate in the diocese of Mobile.[210] For her part, Joseph said that no sisters serving in the diocese of Mobile could take their doweries with them, a point often allowed when a new motherhouse was established.[211] Thus, in every way, Joseph seemed to be working heart and soul to the advantage of the New Orleans community, which was already well established with newly built institutions in the midst of a numerous Catholic population.[212] O'Sullivan told Janssens, "The separation may promote the interests of religion in the archdiocese, but it will in my judgment, be hurtful to the same interests in Alabama and West Florida."[213] Although he had reduced the debt of the diocese, O'Sullivan was still financially pressed. Hence, his frustration at Janssens' insistence caused him to write that the diocese of Mobile, "not having a sufficient number of Catholics to make a decent parish, is a diocese only by a fiction of law, and a diocese we live upon, not the charity of our more favored neighbors."[214]

Finally, O'Sullivan wrote Janssens, "In view of your urgent desire that the Sisters of Mercy in Mobile be separated from the parent community in

New Orleans, I have concluded to accept the inevitable and to consent to the separation on the following conditions."[215] He then listed the four points of his capitulation terms: if the project fail within three years, the parent house will again accept the sisters and staff the Mercy schools in the diocese of Mobile; the parent house must furnish the same number of sisters for the branches plus three for Selma; Mercy property in the Mobile diocese was to be transferred to the foundation; and any sister who wished to exchange communities after two years could do so.[216] Janssens accepted immediately, and O'Sullivan went to see Mother Austin. He knew how much she was against separation, as she had always enumerated "the advantages of affiliation with a numerous and vigorous community."[217] So difficult was it going to be for the new venture to succeed, however, that the bishop thought that Austin was the only one who could give it a real chance of success. For several months Austin's prayer had been "for light to know God's will and the grace to do it."[218] Her answer reached Janssens the following day, "I can only say *Ecce ancilla Domini*, especially as all has come about without any action of mine. I will, therefore, undertake what Your Grace and the Bishop of Mobile ask, trusting that God . . . may aid me to labor efficaciously for His glory in this new field."[219]

As Austin wrote Mother Joseph, her attitude shows clearly, "It is my desire that the friendliest relations exist and be maintained between the two communities, and that all may be AMDG."[220] After their annual retreat, the sisters had to signify their preference for one diocese or the other, a painful decision for all. Catherine McAuley had written her friend Mary Teresa White, that "separations in religion are bitter sorrows."[221] No matter what their choice, most sisters were to lose some of their companions to the other diocese. Knowing that they could change their minds after two years did lighten the weight of the decision somewhat, but the burden was especially heavy for Mother Austin. As she explained to her friend Archbishop Kirby, she was "greatly attached to New Orleans" after close to twenty-four years there.[222] Yet, because both bishops had asked her to take charge, she felt obliged to go on the new mission. While New Orleans houses were fully established with institutions in the best order, almost "everything here has to be created."[223] Austin's requests, besides "begging for prayers for us and our works," were for the special blessings and spiritual favors which Kirby had previously obtained for the New Orleans sisters.[224] She also priced a painting of Our Lady of Mercy, "for when we become a little better off pecuniarily, we shall want one."[225] Austin Carroll, at fifty-six, had accepted the challenge of the missionary diocese, and the last of the eighteen sisters for the Mobile diocese left New Orleans as September opened. The formal establishment of the motherhouse in Selma was September 3, 1891.[226]

Because money was so short at the time, Austin Carroll asked Mother

Collins to allow her to purchase the property in Selma over a period of years. Sister and her community graciously agreed to this arrangement. Thus it was 1893, before the deeds for the Selma convent changed hands.[227] Payments could be gathered slowly, but an increase in personnel was more urgent. Bishop O'Sullivan had been trying to get additional sisters for the past several years, but Joseph would not increase the number of teachers. Now he encouraged Austin to begin an effort to get extra sisters quickly, if necessary, by borrowing a few nuns. As he put it, "Beg your friends everywhere to send or loan you some."[228] Austin sent letters in several directions, and by November could tell a friend[229] that they had eight postulants with three more on the way. "We need all we can get. The Bishop wants us to establish schools in many places."[230] Before long her letters brought in more. Father Slattery wrote of two candidates who wanted to teach only in black schools. "Mercy cannot be exclusive," Austin said, "Miss Drexel's Order might suit them."[231] One third of their pupils were in the black schools, but Austin needed teachers available for any of the schools. Father Russell, SJ, was to send a candidate who was "an expert on the type writer."[232] But many others who were being recommended were too old, had proved unsuitable in another order, or were incapable of performing the works of mercy. To her sister Mary, Mrs. Charles Byrne, Austin asked, "Do you know any nice girls that would like to join us out here? If so, tell me about them, and ask them to send me their pictures."[233]

Although much of her time that fall was occupied in trying to locate suitable candidates, Mother Austin had numerous other concerns. Like beginnings in Buffalo, Omaha, and other foundations, Selma was exceedingly primitive. Austin did not want to make other debts beyond that for the convent building and school necessities.[234] Chairs were carried from chapel to dining room to parlor as occasion required. Vegetable or fruit crates served adequately as night stands and clothes presses.[235] Only after other debts had been cleared several years later was real furniture acquired. Four sisters in Austin's community had spent two decades in the convent, long enough to have experienced the poverty of early days in New Orleans, and two nuns with ten years in the Mercy community had lived through yellow-fever days and the destitution caused by quarantine. Selma did not worry them. The dozen younger sisters, six years in the convent, had seen little real poverty and found their new situation trying. Urging them to embrace the hardships for the sake of souls, Austin told them about the Russian prince, Dimitrius Augustine Gallitzen, who gave up his position and heritage for priestly service in western Pennsylvania. "If the Prince had contented himself with a life of ease and pleasure, we should never have heard of him." Because in Loretto he preached, worked, and died for the sake of others, "he is glorified on earth . . . almost a place of pilgrimage."[236] Most of the dozen young sisters accepted the hardships and shortages in stride; but later, after the three-year period specified at the division, three returned to the more comfortable quarters of the New Orleans community.[237]

But that was in the future in 1891, when the need for funds in this new Mercy province was severe and Austin Carroll found the time to complete several more articles. The *American Catholic Quarterly Review* carried her work three times in 1890 and 1891.[238] Father Russell did even better in *The Irish Monthly*, carrying three in the same period plus three more in 1892.[239] Each contribution did its part to replenish the bread box. When Austin was coaxed in late 1891 to write a paper for the National Convention of the Apostolate of the Press, however, the motivation was not the honorarium but zeal for souls. This gathering of prominent Catholics from all parts of the country was called to improve the use of Catholic print in the missionary campaign among non-Catholics.[240] Since Austin was far too busy in January 1892 to attend the convention herself, the Rev. Walter Elliott read her paper, which dealt in part with the many ways in which she fostered Catholic reading through literature in school and circulating libraries.[241] Primarily however, Austin treated the use of Catholic newspapers and periodicals in the prison ministry. Beginning with practical points, like the necessity of marking books not only on the inside but also on "the compressed edges of the leaves" in bold print, lest the books get carried away, "sold or pawned for a trifle, . . . and be recognized on second-hand book-stalls."[242] The paper warmed the hearts of the listeners with examples of the way in which Catholic reading materials often led prisoners to request religious instructions. Her paper, judged "beautiful" by Katherine Conway, closed with the plea that Catholic papers and magazines be saved everywhere for distribution in public hospitals and prisons.[243]

Only the intensity of her zeal for souls could have impelled Austin to accept the commission to prepare a paper for a national convention when she had so little time. This same burning zeal was also the stimulus which was to send Austin to Ireland for candidates in the summer of 1892. Early that year the small Selma noviceship had seen progress as two novices professed their religious vows and three of the five postulants were received as Mercy novices.[244] In a way, the novitiate was thus readied for new recruits, but the diocese of Mobile was not yet prepared to furnish them. One graduate in Mobile had planned to join the Sisters of Mercy, but her father strenuously opposed his daughter's wishes.[245] Examining and obtaining prospective candidates by correspondence had already proven that business depending upon the speed of the postal service for every step of a complicated procedure was a tortuous one. Thus, Austin concluded that their only hope for community expansion in the near future was to go to Ireland. As she explained to Bishop O'Sullivan, she intended to coax some of her friends among the Irish Mercies to act as her recruiting agents for the next few years in order to replenish the Alabama novitiate regularly.[246] Although Austin assumed that one or two postulants might be able to return with her immediately, her primary aim was "to insure a supply" for years to come. She expected to establish a permanent method of locating pious, capable, and steady young women who desired to serve God in an American missionary diocese. Austin thought that she might be able to locate and "put at schools" a few girls and "engage" a few students at teacher-training institutions.[247]

Once school closed, Austin appointed Sister Clare Fitzpatrick the mistress of novices in Selma, arranged for vacations in the other convents, and left with young Sister Caroline Macready as her companion.[248] The trip was a grand rush from start to finish with Austin popping in and out of motherhouses so rapidly that few recorded her visit. In each convent where she stopped, Austin made certain that her friend and agent knew the kind of candidate she was seeking. Each young woman needed to be determined to serve God faithfully and to be capable of performing the works of mercy. It was important that the girl consider carefully and weigh the matter well before making her decision. Here or there, Austin met girls who had already told the sisters that they were thinking of "going out" to enter the convent in America. Austin seems to have found these girls too immature, not yet finished with their schooling, or something similar. One chronicler noted what several might have thought, that Austin Carroll "was most exact about those she selected."[249] She had told O'Sullivan, "I am sure you would not like us to take any one below par."[250] Austin firmly believed that it was better for the prospective candidates to delay any decision until they were absolutely fixed in their commitment. "Then, if they decided on going out, to go *resolved* to be *good* and *faithful*."[251] Moving rapidly to a convent or two a day, Austin encircled Ireland if one judges by the cities, towns, and villages from which candidates journeyed to Alabama. Only in Dublin, Limerick, Kinsale, and Cork was there a record of her visit.[252]

Besides all the stops to see about candidates, Austin made others in order to arrange interviews which were to reimburse her for transportation expenses.[253] Cardinal Newman had died shortly after she had seen him several years earlier, and Cardinal Manning had died that year. However, she had no problem interviewing Herbert Vaughan, the archbishop of Westminster, who was to be named cardinal within the year.[254] When he saw her in the same room in which she had seen Manning in 1890, Vaughan recalled her help in 1872. Then she interviewed his brother, Father John Vaughan, who had served for a time in Australia when his brother Roger was the archbishop of Sydney. Austin had previously had correspondence with Charles Russell, the attorney general and soon to be the first Catholic lord

chief justice in Great Britain since the Reformation, and planned to schedule an interview.[255] Whether she succeeded at that time is uncertain, but she
had a fine one with his brother, Matthew Russell, SJ, the experienced
Dublin editor of *The Irish Monthly*. Like his sisters, Mothers Baptist in San
Francisco and Emmanuel in Newry, he assisted Austin in her quest for
candidates.[256] Austin was able to interview a number of Irish bishops, from
Cardinal Michael Logue, archbishop of Armagh, southward. The Catholic
papers of the United States seemed to find news from Ireland always popular with their Irish-American readers, and Austin's pen had an additional
flair for any topic concerning her beloved native land.[257]

Interviews, a quick family visit, and candidate arrangements completed, Austin returned with two postulants. One was a young woman from
Maryborough in Queen's County and the other came from a bit to the
southeast in County Tipperary.[258] Even with her highly optimistic disposition, Austin probably had little realization that these candidates were just
Ireland's opening trickle of help which was to expand until it became a
strong and steady stream. Following the first postulants in rapid succession
were two girls from Fermanagh, an experienced music teacher from Dublin,
a novice from Newry, two young women from Ardee and two from Dundalk, a novice from Sussex and one from Dunmore.[259] Except for three
novices and one professed sister, all the others from Ireland and England
were candidates. They came from Counties Clare, Louth, Meath, Tipperary, Cork, Dublin, Antrim, Waterford, Tyrone, and Lancashire; or left
homes in Limerick, Sligo, Dublin, Wexford, Cork, Ardee, Liverpool, Dundalk, and other towns.[260] Most of the postulants arrived while Mother
Austin was superior, 1891–1900, and tapered off after the turn of the century as Alabama slowly began to furnish candidates. Of course, there was
novitiate training before the young sisters were ready for a full schedule on
the missions. Yet the total number of sisters professed rose from 15 in 1892
to 24 in 1895, 51 in 1900, and 72 in 1903. There were some losses also, as
several did not complete the novitiate; three returned to New Orleans, and
by 1900, seven had gone to God.[261] In this period few candidates had come
from America, several from the diocese, and two from as far away as
Michigan. This community was as Irish as Catherine McAuley herself.[262]

Although she had already passed the average 1890 lifespan as she
approached her sixth decade, Austin Carroll still embraced life enthusiastically. Her affectionate reception in Ireland had been both heart-warming
and encouraging; and before the year ended, eleven postulants had joined
the novitiate in Selma. Bishop O'Sullivan's plea for aid had won favor also,
as Katherine Drexel had promised to send a donation to assist with a church
building for "St. Joseph's Colored Mission" in Pensacola.[263] Both Austin
and the bishop were delighted. She was finding it refreshing to work once

again with a prelate who was as open to her zealous efforts as he was pious and zealous himself. Like her friend Bishop Heslin in Natchez, O'Sullivan had Austin act as his agent in 1890 in order to obtain some seminarians for the diocese.[264] This mission was a failure, probably because the time was not yet ripe for the rector of any seminary to deal with a nun as the representative of a bishop. Although O'Sullivan admired Austin's accomplishments over the years, especially in behalf of blacks, he thought that she was inclined to move forward too rapidly and to accept too many responsibilities. He thought it impossible in 1892, for instance, for Austin to go to Savannah to assist the sisters in their transfer from Bishop England's rule to that of Catherine McAuley.[265] Bishop Thomas Becker then interceded because he had already given the Georgia sisters the new Mercy Rule. He said that the sisters needed Austin's help with the practical customs and the spirit "of the Madame McAuley" Mercies.[266] Austin's joy at the large Georgia addition to the Mercy Institute was mentioned above when she was first asked to assist another group make the same transfer.[267] With O'Sullivan's consent in 1893, since she was acting "for the glory of God," Austin managed to give a month.[268] She agreed with Becker that the Georgia sisters already had "a spirit of kindliness and gentleness."[269]

Judging by Austin's schedule in the fall of 1892, it is no wonder that the bishop worried that she was trying to do too much. Besides handling the business and correspondence which had accumulated while she was in Ireland, she was writing the paper for the Apostolate of the Press convention, planned the ceremony to receive several novices in October, was repeatedly asked to help in Savannah by both the sisters and the bishop there,[270] was herself urging O'Sullivan to improve the dilapidated convent in Pensacola,[271] and had been invited in December both to open a school in Huntsville and to prepare a paper for another national convention, the Columbian Catholic Congress to be held in Chicago.[272] But Austin Carroll seemed to take it all in stride. The Georgia sisters had been impressed with "her broad-minded liberality and consideration" in their transition.[273] Her only worry seemed to be the declining health of several of her older sisters. This was a factor in her attraction to Huntsville in the hills of northern Alabama, which because of its "fine and healthy location,"[274] might help the delicate to recoup their strength. Not too far from Huntsville, however, were Anniston and Birmingham, both of which had asked for sisters as early as 1884 and 1885.[275] O'Sullivan also noted, most practically, that Huntsville had too few Catholics "to support a convent, no matter how small."[276] As she hoped soon to accomplish the recovery of her ailing sisters, Austin told the bishop that she considered "time more precious than money." Yet, in spite of the large influx of young sisters, Austin agonized as she watched three of her experienced sisters, weakened by continued ill health, succumb. One died in 1895 and two in 1896.[277]

With Huntsville canceled, Austin asked about buying Quinlan's old camp across Mobile Bay, so that her sisters could take turns getting some sun and sand, as others did earlier in Biloxi. O'Sullivan graciously answered that, if he did not use the house himself, he would lend it to the sisters.[278] Since none of the memoirs mention this camp, the plan must have fallen through. A few years later when Austin could manage the financing, she purchased a residence in St. James Parish in Mississippi City. It was a lovely spot at the corner of Teagarden Road and the beach.[279] This became the convent for sickly sisters who could teach a small class, and the site served admirably from its opening in July 1898 until the church no longer had a resident pastor.[280] Austin's friend, Bishop Heslin, was delighted to have Catholic education available, especially as the sisters opened both black and white schools. When the pastor, the Rev. L. A. Dutto, died in 1902, the sisters were recalled to Mobile because, according to the memoirs, Mother Austin never assigned her sisters where they could not enjoy the privilege of daily Mass.[281] But prior to the small convent on Teagarden Road, there was other expansion considered and discussed by O'Sullivan and Austin, the latter ready to move ahead and the former preferring to delay a bit longer.[282] Finally in 1895, the bishop agreed to the transfer of the novitiate from Selma to Mobile, where there was enough room for the ever-growing novitiate. In the See city, besides St. Joseph School which the Mercies had staffed since 1884, Austin opened elementary and secondary classes, the latter called Mercy High. The following year Austin also inaugurated private lessons in several languages and a kindergarten for youngsters.[283]

From 1895 on, during Mother Austin's term in office, the annual expansion was steady. Before noting the various branch convents opened and schools staffed, there were other activities to be indicated. In 1893, Katherine Conway was urging W. J. Onahan, "get a gifted and broad-minded nun to write your paper on the Work of Women in the Church." I beg to suggest Rev. Mother Austin Carroll . . . a great friend of mine . . . her name and influence would be most valuable."[284] Onahan wanted to put the eight women speakers on one day, and this distressed Conway, who related how the Catholic Press convention had interspersed papers of men and women with great success. Since Onahan did not change the program, Conway dropped out, refusing to be a party when "the sharpest line possible is drawn between men and women in the intellectual order."[285] Austin had already declined the honor of the invitation because "the more direct duties of my position leave me no time."[286] Although she was not in Chicago to speak, her name or work was before the throng from all over the country in more than one paper. She was announced as one of a dozen outstanding

Catholic women authors in America.[287] In spite of the fact that Austin had not allowed her name to be placed on the title page of a single one of her books, her literary efforts were being recognized in this gathering of prominent Catholics. Speeches were reported verbatim in the Chicago papers, of course, and Austin must have read the clippings sent by her Chicago friends. If so, she saw the description of her work as a Sister of Mercy with long fluttering veil, hovering over the sick and the needy like an angel of hope and peace.[288]

Certainly, Austin's long Mercy veil fluttered in the coastal breezes as she walked along the shaded streets of Selma and Mobile on her regular visits to the sick. Some of the older sisters in the 1960s could recall their excitement when Austin visited some member of the family who was ill.[289] In Mobile Austin arranged with the St. Vincent de Paul Society to furnish a carriage on a regularly monthly basis so that she could visit the County Poor Farm some miles out of town.[290] Hope in God's mercy and love were her watchwords whether visiting or writing, and she always had a large correspondence. Most of her letter ministry remains in the mind of the God she loved. Once again, however, Charles Gayarré proved the exception, as there are not only copies of some of his correspondence, but also lists of the names and dates of his correspondents and their letters.[291] Austin even wrote to Janssens in behalf of the elderly gentleman, discouraged and despondent over his financial situation, as he grew closer to death.[292] Of course, there were letters to the many Mercies in Louisiana who found occasions to send some homemade candy or cookies and a loving message to their "beloved Mother Foundress." When Agnes Greene was anointed, Austin went over for a last visit at Agnes' request, and she attended the funeral of her friend, Frederick Faivre, CSSR.[293] A happier visit was that when Austin brought Mother Genevieve Prendergast, the Mercy superior of the Savannah and Atlanta sisters, to witness a reception ceremony in Selma and then to see the Mercy institutions in New Orleans which Alabama and Florida did not possess.[294]

Since the diocese of Mobile had an adequate number of charitable institutions, Austin's effort in both Alabama and western Florida was primarily in the visitation of the sick and the imprisoned and in the field of education. For the period of Reconstruction in the South and thereafter to the twentieth century, Austin Carroll placed an extraordinary emphasis on black education.[295] Perhaps it followed from the fact that she appreciated the plan of Catherine McAuley to teach women to raise their economic standard of living through the use of their own talents. Following that plan, Austin's efforts for the blacks actually began twenty years before those of Katherine Drexel. At the time that Janssens pressured O'Sullivan to agree to the division of the Louisiana Mercies in 1891,[296] about a fourth of the pupils taught by the New Orleans Sisters of Mercy were black, while in the diocese of Mobile the black pupils were almost a third of those taught by Austin and her sisters.[297] The percentages were gradually to drop in the Crescent City as several of the black schools were closed, but as Austin continued to open several more black schools, statistics there continued to rise as long as she was leading the community. In the expansion of 1896, for instance, she opened a branch convent in Birmingham, staffed Our Lady of Sorrows School, and established a black school. In 1897, the Warrington schools were reopened when the shipyard did, and the Mercies again staffed St. John the Evangelist and, after Austin made extensive repairs, St. Joseph's Colored School.[298] Besides establishing St. James Convent on Teagarden Road in July 1898 and starting on September 5, a school for the whites and another for the blacks, Austin and her sisters accepted the invitation of the Rev. M. F. Filan, the pastor of St. Mary's in Mobile, to staff the parish schools.[299]

Also during the 1898–1899 school year, Austin assisted the Savannah community by lending two teachers to their Atlanta school.[300] In the course of the first semester, she went to Anniston to see the facilities that were mentioned as opportune for a convent and school. Investigation proved otherwise, however, and Austin did not staff the Anniston schools. Quite naturally, the priest was unhappy with her negative decision, but Austin had, on more than a few occasions, caused the same reaction by demanding adequate quarters for a convent and decent classrooms.[301] In one place, she herself paid the water bill for the school so that children and teachers would not go all day without a sip of water. Indoor bathrooms were few and far between at the time.[302] As Austin worked hard to get proper facilities, some of the pastors thought her far too particular.[303] In 1899, Austin investigated the facilities at Bessemer and Appalachicola, found them both adequate, and planned to open a branch and staff the schools of one or the other the following September. Instead of selecting only one of the two, Austin decided that the Sisters of Mercy could take both at once. Thus on the same day in 1900, the Mercies opened two more branches and staffed St. Aloysius in Bessemer and St. Patrick in Appalchicola, the convent in the latter being dedicated to Our Lady Star of the Sea.[304] These were Austin's final two community decisions in the diocese when she served as superior. While her expansion of educational facilities moved ahead, it obviously depended upon a increase of religious teachers.

Solving that need for an entire decade by making one trip to Ireland, Austin's friends there created a golden treasury of candidates for the diocese of Mobile. Had Austin taken the time to tally the numbers as her superiorship came to a close in 1900, she would have listed the following as her work of nine years: 33 schools, nine of them secondary, many of them for black children; 42 libraries in convents and schools; five convents owned and four maintained.[305] More startling statistics were based on Austin's introduction in less than a decade of 78 religious candidates, 83 counting those soon to arrive.[306] In the nine years from 1892 to 1901, the Mobile community became almost as large as that of New Orleans because Austin received an average of more than nine postulants annually during her term as superior.[307] That was high even for Austin who, while she was superior in New Orleans had an annual average of 7.9, or almost eight candidates. New Orleans numbers had dropped because of Joseph Devereux's disastrous 0.3, a more normal average being the 4.2 of Philomeme Butler.[308] As to schools staffed when Austin was in New Orleans, naturally the count was higher because Austin had been there two dozen years. The totals from the Irish Channel motherhouse were 45 schools, 12 of them secondary, and eight for the blacks. Austin established likewise six convents, not counting the motherhouse, and three institutions.[309] Certainly, Austin's expansion of Mercy personnel, institutions, schools, and branch convents across the South would have been exceptional even for a foundress who was not involved in literary accomplishments and social work.

Almost unbelievable when considered with the above foundations, the numerous publications of Austin Carroll were worthy of note in themselves. Although some had been completed before 1891, Austin managed to finish the remainder of the fourth volume of the *Annals of the Sisters of Mercy* by 1894.[310] In speaking to her reader of the great effort it had taken to gather the material, Austin said, "if they will only do good in proportion, I shall be content."[311] Since the death of Bishop O'Connor, Austin's critical reader and spiritual advisor was Ferreol Girardey, CSSR. This priest who often held positions of leadership in his order had been the staunch defender of Austin when she was falsely accused by several Germans. While these men saw Austin only at a distance, he was the prefect of schools who worked with her and knew her for the zealous and charitable woman she was.[312] It was probably Girardey who suggested that Austin publish a collection of her magazine articles; and thus without much time or effort in 1899, Austin's community had another source of revenue. Except for this *Essays Educational and Historic*,[313] the first decade in the diocese of Mobile saw the production only of the final volume of the *Annals*. As Austin confided to Mary Gonzaga O'Brien in Manchester,

> The series had been a herculean work — I have been collecting for it, writing to all points for the required information, and even traveling to verify matters, etc., for nearly thirty years. The four volumes are the result. May they be AMDG — they have cost me more than anyone can imagine.[314]

Yet Austin seems to have felt that no personal cost was too high for the good that could be accomplished through the Institute of Mercy. Even though busy with the transportation of candidates, their proper formation, and the opening of more schools and branch convents, Austin pushed herself to complete eleven articles for publication.[315] Funds were short, and Austin said the Mercies were not mendicants. Instead, she believed in using natural talents and abilities to earn the money needed for their ministry. Five of the articles concerned locations she had seen in 1890, one was the lecture prepared for the Apostolate of the Press, and five others were based on the *Annals*. Most of the first group were completed prior to the 1891 division because they were published shortly thereafter. When the article was based on a chapter in the *Annals*, Austin usually revised it by rearranging and changing the focus. Two of these selections were tributes requested by friends. Austin wrote the obituary tribute, "Right Rev. Dr. Bacon, Bishop of Portland, Maine, U.S.A.," for Sister Mary Gonzaga O'Brien in Manchester.[316] For Mother Mary Baptist Russell on the West Coast, Austin gave a lovely biographical obituary of Joanna Reddan.[317] This missionary Mercy, who had known Catherine McAuley in Limerick where she had spent thirty years directing a Magdalen Asylum, then entered the Mercy community in Kinsale. From there she volunteered for the San Francisco mission and did great work establishing the home for Magdalens there. Austin's admiration for this zealous sister was amplified because she signed up as a missioner to a foreign land when she was fifty-four years old.[318]

More than a decade older than that, Austin Carroll must have begun to feel her age even though she wrote a Mercy friend, "Of course, I'm growing old, but have not felt it yet. . . . I am well, T.G. — haven't been a day in bed for years."[319] Yet, other details in her letters reveal that daily events and circumstances were a little more difficult. For instance, she found the winter severe "even in these favored regions."[320] More often Austin's comments were "the weather is so hot that many fear the [yellow] fever will return,"[321] or "we have summer in every winter month here."[322] As was her custom, Austin regularly visited the Sisters in the branch convents, but noted in 1895 "the fatigues of travel."[323] Speaking of such a series of visits, she said, "I never was more busy than now, when I ought to be thinking of taking my ease."[324] Yet, judging from the many activities mentioned, taking her ease was not among Austin's priorities. The community had many converts, "T.G., as almost every Sister has some one or more, black or white, to instruct."[325] The sisters nursing the fever victims were often quarantined. She tried to help the soldiers massed in Florida before being sent to Cuba, by "giving them prayer books, etc., and getting them to the sacraments when opportunity offers."[326] Naturally, she and all the sisters were "praying that this miserable War may soon be over. God grant us peace!"[327] That was

1898, but there was ever the visiting of the hospitals and prisons and the sick in their homes, "a duty I was always devoted to."[328] Austin usually closed with the request, "pray that we may have the right spirit and keep it."[329]

Although these details make it seem that Austin had no worry greater than the two-foot long baby alligator discovered in the convent yard in Pensacola, nothing could be further from the truth. In the 1890s she was caught in the middle of a tug of war over the Belize property, and New Orleans Mercies on one side and the pastor in Belize on the other. As superior of the Louisiana community in 1883, Austin had accepted the Honduran mission, bought property, signed the deed, and approved a plan for a simple building.[330] As it happened plans escalated, prices skyrocketed, and the governor's promises to contribute for the school were not honored. In four years Austin sent a total of $7,000, and in the next five years Philomene and Joseph sent $3,000 more.[331] By 1891, however, DiPietro needed further funding and wanted more sisters. When Joseph said no to both requests, DiPietro petitioned Rome to have the mission separated from New Orleans.[332] Janssens and Joseph wanted to give the mission and its debts and demands to another community, but the New Orleans community refused. It was at this point that O'Sullivan, just back from the episcopal consecration of DiPietro in Belize, pressured Austin to assign the property to the new vicar apostolic. The property was still in Austin's name because the community had decided not to establish a corporation in Belize, but to transfer the property by will. Thus, to avoid problems with the English system in the colony of British Honduras, Austin had made a will some years earlier. She told O'Sullivan that she could not transfer the deed until she had the consent of the sisters to whom the property belonged.[333]

According to agreements made in New Orleans in the 1880s three-fourths of the sisters were to consent to changes in property and other important matters. Austin told her bishop that it would violate her conscience to act without the written consent of the New Orleans sisters.[334] Consent from the Louisiana Mercies came in very slowly while Austin was kept under pressure and told that she was to be reported to Propaganda.[335] She appealed to the Apostolic Delegate, while Janssens advised O'Sullivan that a command binding under obedience would not hold in a court of law.[336] O'Sullivan finally decided to let Belize solve problems that were theirs, not his.[337] Both bishops realized that nothing that anyone would say could move Austin Carroll to act in a way she considered contrary to her conscience. Eventually, three-fourths of the sisters in Louisiana did give their consent, and Austin transferred the property.[338] Of course, Austin was made to pay a penalty for heeding her conscience, as there were angry prelates, delayed professions, and confrontations with Janssens and Joseph Devereux.[339] Austin later mused that all concerned had turned their anger on her, DiPietro because she did not give him the property, O'Sullivan because he backed DiPietro, Janssens because he and Joseph wanted to be released from any responsibility for Belize debts, and the many Mercies in New Orleans who had not wanted to give their consent to donate the property.[340] Few seemed to realize that Austin had delayed the transfer long enough for another to replace Joseph, who was sick, and had thus given the community the opportunity to change what many considered to be an unjust decision for both the sisters in Belize and New Orleans.

During the same period of the Belize property problems, another arose with Janssens and the Mercies he supervised, again in behalf of others. As 1894 was the close of the three-year period of trial specified by O'Sullivan in his separation conditions of 1891, two young sisters in Mobile decided to use their option and return to the larger community.[341] Most certainly Austin was disappointed with their choice. They were not only fine young women, but also good teachers and musicians. Unfortunately, Janssens and some of the sisters said that the term was two years, not three, and that it was now too late for the sisters to return.[342] Investigation showed that there had been an error in 1891, with O'Sullivan's conditions listing three years and Janssens' copy two.[343] Austin reminded Janssens that a Sister of Mercy was always welcome in the convent where she took her vows. As she had done so often in behalf of others, Austin gave a magnificent presentation for the two sisters, who had found the Alabama missions too strenuous for their taste.[344] Although Austin would have liked to keep the sisters, she worked hard to win them their right of return. After her research of the Mercy foundress and her Institute for some thirty years, Austin was generally considered an expert on the ideals of the one and the customs of the other, and through the years she had often been consulted by other Sisters of Mercy, their superiors and bishops. Janssens learned that, while in New Orleans, she had not only received sisters from the convents which had closed in St. Patrick's parish and Natchitoches, but also from other foundations that had failed.[345] For sisters who met with such misfortune Austin's charity was boundless.

> Our Annals teem with instances of the fatherly kindness and solicitude of prelates sending out foundations. Such goodness will not cause an apostolic woman to turn back, but it will comfort her in the trials and sorrows of new beginnings, and be a support to her in future contingencies.[346]

Thus read a tiny portion of Austin's lengthy letter to Janssens defending the sisters' return. Yet, instead of accepting the Carroll view, as broad and experienced as it was charitable, Janssens asked the opinion of elderly de

Sales Browne, whom he had known in Vicksburg. Evidently she had little understanding of the way in which Janssens had mandated the 1891 separation, with all the sisters having to select one diocese or the other. Perhaps she believed she had been asked about some religious who had abandoned one community to find another to her liking, as one of her own unhappy sisters had returned to the house of her profession. Yet even this could hardly account for the excessively narrow idea that emerged. Her advice was to receive no sister who had "left the convent . . . by her own free will and choice," as she "forfeits all claim" and is "likely to have a factious spirit."[347] Not realizing that the two sisters had given no disedification in either community, she continued, "It may sound hard, but I sincerely hope you will not receive them as they will most assuredly give trouble."[348] Since Austin and O'Sullivan were ready to appeal to Rome, Janssens and the sisters he governed did later receive the two.[349] And de Sales had been mistaken; until the two died long years afterward, they were a great help to the community.

Death itself was to make this a sorrowful decade for Austin while she also suffered, as a friend put it, because several persons "gave you a good share of your purgatory."[350] Perhaps the years of her deepest grief through the death of friends were 1886–1895. In three consecutive years, as mentioned earlier, Austin lost her sister Katy, Mother Teresa Gourrier, and in 1888, Sister Mary Juliana Purcell. Shortly thereafter followed the illness and death of Bishop James O'Connor in 1890. This was a triple blow to Austin as she lost at once her spiritual director, literary advisor, and critical reader. She often spoke of having treasured O'Connor's advice and friendship for over thirty years. Other deaths that touched Austin's heart deeply were those of the saintly Margaret Mary Killelea and the Redemptorist Frederick Faivre in 1890, and in the next few years several Mercies elsewhere, like Catherine Seton in New York, Vincent Whitty in Australia, and in Missouri Ignatius Walker and Jerome Shubrick.[351] At home, although there was no death in 1891, every sister died a little at the time of the separation. Then within two months in 1895, a trio of deaths brought Austin deep anguish. She grieved for her two dear elderly friends, Archbishop Kirby in Rome and Charles Gayarré in New Orleans, as well as her assistant in Mobile, Mary Clare Fitzpatrick.[352] Death had truly darkened the decade, and Austin noted that "God was more visible in the dark than in the light."[353]

As was her habit, Austin's light and joy were to be found also in the community itself. Writing of the Alabama-Florida community, Austin said with obvious pride. "Although it is I who say it, our Sisters are very nice, good, simple, and industrious."[354] Since she hated laziness, Austin was severe with any young person in either classroom or novitiate who displayed the trait. Her pupils heard that, besides piety and intelligence, they needed industry to succeed in the world. The novices learned that they must use their gifts for God's work as if all depended upon themselves, for it was then that God would assist them. Austin's letters repeatedly contained praise for the community.[355] "I am well pleased with all who have come—not a doubtful one among them, T.G.," she wrote of her postulants.[356] Considering the novices, she noted, "Among the band in retreat for profession, I think I see my successor, and I'd be very glad to give up to her today if it were the thing to do."[357] That time was just a few years away, as the century and her term in office moved together toward conclusion. Her estimate of her sisters as a whole community, "I never saw better or more zealous, T.G.," was followed by the request for prayers that they acquire and keep the spirit of Catherine McAuley.[358] As changes were thrust upon the area in the late 1890's, time might have seemed to increase its speed. Austin mourned the 1896 passing of the zealous Jeremiah O'Sullivan, who "always treated me with respect and confidence."[359] Actually, the bishop often told her to follow her own judgment, as she would do whatever was best for the community.[360]

A year after O'Sullivan's death, New Orleans lost Francis Janssens. Both vacancies were filled fairly quickly, Bishop Placide Chapelle of Santa Fe being transferred to New Orleans and the Rev. Edward P. Allen to Mobile.[361] As so often happened to religious upon the arrival of a new bishop, superiors found that many of the arrangements made according to the wishes of the previous prelate did not suit the new one. All the deeds for property of the community had to be sent to Allen for checking even though Austin said she had an able lawyer in Mr. Glennon.[362] The bishop seemed to think it an offense against poverty that Austin's name appeared on the deeds as the one who had made the purchase in the name of the Sisters of Mercy.[363] Just as O'Sullivan had heard earlier, Allen also received complaints about Mother Austin from two of the pastors, where the sisters had branch convents. Both priests thought she demanded too much in the way of living conditions for the sisters, and one of them believed that she was too strict about the Rule."[364] Austin herself evidently felt the weight of office as a heavier burden by this time for she referred to herself in a letter as "a crowned slave" and told the bishop that she would probably not be in office after the next election.[365] Young himself, he thought it best that she allow the young sisters to take over all the offices. As the "History of the Sisters of Mercy in Mobile" related,

> Although many foundresses continued in office until death, Mother Mary Austin Carroll in a letter dated May 30, 1900, to Bishop Allen stated that she would not leave her name on the slate for the election of Mother Superior that was to take place.[366]

There is no doubt about the fact that she had borne the heat of the day for many a year. At last, her life was to be less pressured, and she would have an opportunity to devote to writing within the framework of a more relaxed schedule. "As life is uncertain," she had said earlier, she planned to complete the *Annals* "and then, laying my pen at the feet of Our Lady of Mercy, devote myself to God unimpeded by the distraction of writing, that I may prepare for the final scene which comes nearer every day."[367] This was not yet the moment, however, as the young community was certainly in need of funds. As soon as her thought turned to correspondence, Austin realized how deeply her heart had already been scored by the departure of her friends as they stepped into eternity ahead of her. Her dear Elizabeth Strange of Pittsburgh had died in 1900, two years after her darling Baptist Russell of San Francisco. Although in need of consolation herself, Austin had sent her condolence to the Russell family in Ireland. Baptist and Austin shared many qualities. Each thought the other a person "of inexhaustible charity and compassion for all those who needed sympathy and help."[368] They knew each other too well to be wrong. Austin estimated that Baptist had performed millions of acts of charity. Yet after Austin's death a decade later, from sites as scattered as St. Maries of the Isle in Cork to the New Orleans daily newspapers, many listed charity as her most characteristic virtue.[369] From New Orleans to Appalachicola Mother Austin was revered during her life as a sympathetic source of help in any emergency.

Austin saw the spirit of the church as the wish that all good gifts be, comparatively, as accessible to God's children as air and water.[370] Typically, Austin put no limits on the gifts or the age, color, or nation of God's children. When problems arose, Austin worked for a solution. . . . It mattered not whether it were a public calamity like a yellow-fever epidemic, newsboys without a bed, or blacks without a school. If it were personal tragedy like the death of a loved one, a relative in prison, or the loss of a job, compassionate listening was just the beginning. If assistance were at all possible, it would be forthcoming from Austin Carroll. She had brought from Clonmel in the southern tip of Tipperary a sharp business sense, a great-hearted generosity, and an extraordinary sensitivity for the plight of the poor. She wrote,

> I have a great taste for improvements, not only because I like to see things looking well, but also because I love to be able to give employment to the poor. It is better than giving charity. . . . We would do more if we could afford it. But we cannot, and I have a hereditary hatred of going into debt beyond our monthly accounts.[371]

In New Orleans, so regularly did funds accrue to Austin that her business acumen became almost as legendary as her multiplicity of charitable projects. These she financed by several methods—some as traditional as bazaars and raffles, others as creative as free-lancing articles in periodicals on both sides of the Atlantic Ocean. In Alabama, with its relatively few Catholics, Austin worked with few funds herself and knew that the new superior, Mary Patricia Ryan, could use financial aid.[372]

Fusing her literary ability and her interest in history had previously brought Austin Carroll recognition in the literary exhibits of several national gatherings or fairs in New Orleans, Chicago, and Atlanta as a "Louisiana Author." Now she would produce three more volumes and nine articles in Alabama. Fascinated with the many facets of the French and Spanish heritage of the Gulf Coast between Louisiana and Florida, Austin was to find material there for most of these last contributions to journals. As one who often had to depend upon the charity of others in order to feed her charges, Austin appreciated the generosity of Don Andres Almonester y Roxas.[373] She treated, also, both Hernando de Soto and Pedro Melendez.[374] With her sense of fairness and justice finely attuned by years of prison work, Austin complimented Alexander O'Reilly, her compatriot who brought law and order to Louisiana.[375] After she read Grace King's history of Louisiana, Austin wrote to say "I entirely dissent from your views . . . of my brilliant countryman, Alexander O'Reilly."[376] She thought him a great governor, "merciful in an extraordinary degree," to quell the rebellion with the deaths of only six leaders. "Had the English come in, they would have slaughtered hundreds to restore order." Austin thought it dishonorable for the six to draw pay from the King of Spain while inciting rebellion against him. She followed the Gayarré history, which "gives quite a different account" from that of King. Austin closed with "I am (despite O'Reilly), Your affectionate and faithful friend."[377]

Although the numbers had been thinned by death, there were other affectionate friends like Katherine Conway, Mrs. Sadlier, and Kate Barry, besides the numerous Mercies. Austin was ever grateful that Catherine McAuley wanted the sisters to write one another as a way "to preserve the spirit of cordial charity, and she herself . . . set the example."[378] Austin took this wish of Catherine's to heart so that her letters became similar to those of early French nuns which were described as "the affectionate throwing of themselves on paper."[379] In her last decade Austin's letters still went afar, to Baptist O'Donnell and Stanislaus Harrington in Buenos Aires, to Dominica Carroll in Cork, to Anastasia Beckett in Birr, and to the many friends in Ireland who sent candidates. For Gonzaga O'Brien in Manchester Austin described the flowers that reminded her of Mother Xavier Warde, "The Carlow garden is like Manchester in several points. How I thought of her that's gone."[380] Or Austin related that Xavier's letters revealed her piety and zeal,[381] or spread the news that "the Cork sisters are lovely. Never could I describe their kindness to me."[382] In answer to a request for a photograph of herself, Austin said the sisters had insisted that she have one done for her silver jubilee. Austin said that she really did not like having portraits of religious until "we have a Sister who is a good photographer," then added, "I have to give example, you know. Besides I'm no beauty, and one's looks do not always improve as one grows old, though it is nice to be venerable and nearer heaven."[383]

More and more, Austin makes references to heaven and eternity. "Old faces are burnished with the light of heaven like ragged hills facing a glorious sunset."[384] To Baptist Crean in Cork Austin wrote, "I'd love to surround myself" with the companions "of my early religious life;"[385] and to another, "Our faces may be wrinkled and our eyes dim, but the kinder we become the more beautiful we are."[386] There were reminiscences to Manchester of singing, playing the piano, and writing poetry "in the happy early days."[387] To Mother Gertrude Bertrand, whom she had never seen, Austin said, "the community in heaven must be very large now. May we meet in it one day."[388] One sister told Austin "I am hungry, as the Spaniards say, for a letter from you,"[389] another, "Your letters are welcome as the flowers in May."[390] Here or there, one of Austin's letters speaks quite frankly to a correspondent. Angry at the refusal of Janssens to allow the return of two young sisters, for instance, Austin said, "Often I think of you and all I have had to suffer from the day Your Grace came to the diocese. And I expected your coming would have brought me such joy. Well, I thank Him who supported me under all AMDG."[391] Much more often, however, Austin enclosed compliments about a mutual friend. Concerning the Redemptorist Ferreol Girardey, Austin wrote, "In many ways he is the best priest I know. . . . Pray God to spare him, for he is one . . . who will serve a friend in trouble,"[392] or "What a friend he has been to me! May the good God reward him."[393] Family letters reveal Austin's warm and affectionate nature as she admits that she thinks of them daily and keeps them in her prayers.

Of course, Austin was not sitting around writing letters all day. She published books, the lengthy *In Many Lands*, in 1904, in 1905 *The Father and the Son, St. Alphonsus and St. Gerard* which was much smaller, and in 1908 *A Catholic History of Alabama and the Floridas*.[394] The last was the first volume of a projected two-volume work and entailed an enormous amount of research. Part of this she was able to do in the various old church parishes in Florida and Alabama and Mississippi, but a large part of the research had to be done in New Orleans. Hence, she was back and forth a number of times, spending several weeks at a time working in the cathedral records and those at the archbishopric. Her preface states that the inspiration for the work came from Bishop Allen, much encouragement from Archbishops Chapelle and Blenk, and Bishops Heslin and Laval. She had special thanks for Fathers Girardey and Chambon, the Visitandines of Mobile and the Ursulines of New Orleans. Austin wanted to mention the courtesy she was shown in all the libraries, especially the Howard. For favors rendered in several areas, Austin enumerated Thomas Fitzwilliam of New Orleans and Mr. Hamilton of Mobile, who lent books. "To John W. Fairfax, we owe many privileges as admission to public records and files of old papers." To Mr. T. P. Thompson "who placed his unique private library at our disposal,"[395] she also wrote, "I often look back at the quiet delightful hours I had there."[396]

The quiet of library research was soon to be dimmed by the publicity surrounding Austin's fiftieth anniversary of religious profession. Some months before the celebration on July 11, 1906, Father Girardey wrote to the Sisters of Mercy reminding them of the great benefits which accrued to the Mercy Institute through Austin's biography of the foundress and the *Annals*. He suggested that their gratitude should be shown with prayers for Austin Carroll on her golden jubilee and thereafter.[397] The Mobile sisters enclosed a printed copy of this note with the lovely invitations sent to numerous Convents of Mercy in the United States and abroad. No expense was being spared for the occasion, and stamps alone must have cost a tidy sum. On July 11, a Pontifical High Mass was celebrated in the cathedral by Bishop Allen, the cathedral and the jubilee cards both bearing dedication to Mary Immaculate. Present were Bishop Heslin, numerous Sisters of Mercy from New Orleans and the whole Gulf Coast, and priests from all across the South.[398] In his homily Father O'Shanahan, SJ, pointed out many ways in which Mother Austin exemplified the work of traditional monasticism as she taught the love of God, educated the people, and encouraged many to strive for sanctity in the religious life. He noted that one could not pry into her spiritual life, "nor can we reveal the crosses and trials, interior and exterior, which unfailingly accompany those who do great things for God's service."[399] This was the theme repeatedly found in the memoirs and recollections of those who knew Austin best. Strangers might vilify her, but those who recognized the intensity of her efforts to follow her foundress, all considered the accusations and humiliations to be the treatment usually meted out to those "especially dear to the heart of God."[400]

Letters filled with congratulations and prayers arrived in great quantities, some even before the day of the jubilee. Needing quite a while to answer all her letters, Austin described the celebration as "beautiful, impressive, and holy," and often added, "What a joy it will be to meet in heaven."[401] Austin certainly looked forward to seeing there the saintly Mercy foundress and all the Mercies with her. Austin's veneration for the

Mercy foundress shone throughout her enthusiastic *Life of Catherine McAuley*, and also through her own. Memoirs recall hearing of the foundress every time Austin gave the daily lecture. Long after Austin's death branch convents continued to celebrate Catherine McAuley's day of reception, profession, feast, birth, death, and the date her Mercy Institute received Rome's approbation and final confirmation.[402] Most mercies throughout the world know of Austin's "anecdotal biography and scenes from the *Annals*"; and according to Catherine's charismatic authority, Mary Joanna Regan, "these are superb revelations of Catherine McAuley, the woman and the superior . . . and contributed to the formation of generations of Sisters of Mercy."[403] For years Sisters of Mercy were nourished on Catherine's spirit during meals in novitiate refectories as they listened to the reading of Austin's biography or her *Annals*. Thus, these books assisted in forming "the identity of the Sisters of Mercy—helping them to keep the same traditions, history, and spirit alive in groups that never saw one another."[404] Earlier Mary Bertrand Degnan, author of *Mercy Unto Thousands*, also paid tribute.

> The heaviest debt of any biographer of Catherine McAuley is to the foresight and indefatigable efforts of Mother Mary Teresa Austin Carroll who assembled data in the years preceding publication of her book in 1866 and continued research over a period of twenty [thirty] years, expanding her account through four volumes of the *Annals*.[405]

Even more importantly, as early as these books of Austin were published, Sisters of Mercy in the convents founded by Catherine McAuley herself or those established by those sisters who knew her personally recognized the value of Austin Carroll's works in preserving the spirit of the foundress they loved so dearly. Sisters who have been involved in community research have a clear understanding of the value of Austin's work, and motherhouses that have published historical accounts or lives of their foundresses know just how much they are indebted to Mother Austin's data. And when Vatican Council II mandated renewal, the Sisters of Mercy turned to Austin Carroll's century-old works as well as to more recent materials as they searched and researched for the marvelous charism of Catherine McAuley. Of course, it runs strong and deep in her letters, items which Austin treasured as the most precious of mementoes. Austin had a life-long collection of letters from the companions of the foundress, as well as from the majority of later foundresses who carried the Mercy Institute around the world. These were more than private mementoes as they were the documents which could shed light upon the zeal and charity of these early Mercy leaders. But unfortunately, Austin Carroll's trunk, stuffed full of the notes and letters of a lifetime, was sacrificed upon the altar of a typical convent *faire le ménage*, clearing an attic because cleanliness is next to Godliness.[406]

Of course, that *ménage* was ten or twelve years into the future in the jubilee year. Austin appreciated all the prayers, as her health was not as good as formerly. She could no longer teach by 1907, and 1908 began to see a series of small strokes. These partially incapacitated her, though she never missed going out to Mass in the parish church, rain or shine.[407] She had two articles in journals in her jubilee year and one each in 1907, 1908, and 1909. Her final book, *A Catholic History of Alabama and the Floridas*,[408] was published in 1908, and was used frequently as a source in *The Catholic Encyclopedia*, edited by Pace, Shahan and others, and the final volume of which came off the Appleton Press in 1914.[409] Her *Annals* were used as source material also, but Austin Carroll's name was not in her books, and beyond the Convents of Mercy and the areas in which she served across the Gulf South, she was an unknown or anonymous historian. She was, in large measure, unknown to her youngest sisters as anyone other than a pious old nun. According to their memoirs, several had not heard except in jubilee sermons or obituary tributes that Austin Carroll had won renown long before she put the Mobile community on its feet. That seems to point to Austin's humility, a quality which is not as frequently mentioned in the memoirs as many of her other virtues.[410] However, her letters show her thanking a friend for a stern reprimand and asking for more whenever they are needed.[411] Among her most worn prayerbooks were the *New Testament* and the *Imitation of Christ*, the latter hardly apt to appeal to one who is proud. As to writing, a letter reveals that she wrote only "what I was asked to do, and I don't know why they have been so well received, for to me they appear beneath criticism."[412]

But criticism had been of all types through the years. The biography of Catherine McAuley, in spite of Austin's tendency to digression, received favorable reviews on both sides of the Atlantic. It was "full of such graphic and interesting details as to be one of the most entertaining pieces of biography we are acquainted with,"[413] according to Ireland, "Of the author of this beautiful volume we dare not speak too warmly, for like all true disciples of the cross, she loves neither praise of men nor flattering public notice."[414] A Southern paper stated, "If New Orleans is proud because a Cable, a Rouquette, a Gayarre live and work within her borders, what homage should she not pay to the quiet lady whose writings are a legacy to the Faith!"[415] Yet one critic noted that "a little more restraint and forebearance toward some who are deemed to have erred in their duty to the Order would have added another grace to the narrative."[416] Austin's first translation fared more poorly than any other, and the praise for her fluency increased with each volume. For that initial translation, however, even though one literary critic thought that "the learned translator has done the work ample justice by the fluent and perfect manner in which she has reproduced it,"[417] another critic thought the translation "bears signs of haste and literary carelessness . . . is verbose, weak, and tiresome."[418] Yet he thanked the translator, "whose efforts toward the formation of Catholic literature . . . will not fail of earning a higher reward than any amount of commendation on our part." Like the biography of the foundress, the *Annals* fared well everywhere, as "The style is so easy, the incidents so varied, the amount of information so extensive and entertaining that we find ourselves as much interested in its pages as reading a novel."[419]

Austin Carroll paid little attention to such reviews, but she would have been delighted to hear comments of Mercy researchers eighty and ninety years later. One stated that "The notes left by Sisters who lived with Mother McAuley are all in the *Life* by Mother Austin Carroll."[420] Another noted that Austin was "as accurate as any historical work of a century ago. . . . Research opens records to which Mother Austin in her day did not have access . . . but the amazing observation is how frequently records disclose how close she was to the truth."[421] Austin loved literary critics who thought that she was the Boswell for Catherine McAuley and her Institute of Mercy or that the author seemed to understand and appreciate the spirit of her saintly foundress. Austin's striving for personal holiness led her to follow closely in the path of Catherine. Sisters who received their training in religious life from Mother Austin shared a wonderful experience, for "her expounding of the Holy Rule and Customs were so replete, so convincing, so filled with loving persuasion that one felt impelled to rise at once and put the advice into action."[422] Although the memoirs vary widely, each makes this particular point, many adding that it was because of Austin's deep reverence for the foundress and her Rule and her profound trust in God that the sisters succeeded in their pursuit of the Mercy ideals.[423]

In her government of the community, noted Mother Borgia Walsh, "it was quite perceptible that Austin took our saintly Foundress for her model, and if she fell short in this, it was due to diversity of character not lack of effort."[424] One might also hazard the guess that any difference lay in part in the local character. Just as the local populace found the great Antoine Blanc too strict a bishop for their liking and burned him in effigy several times, so did ambitious Mécontente urge a few followers to complain of Austin's zealous regime. The later absence of Austin from government soon proved to the trio the value of that which they had lost. Realizing that they had been used, the unfortunate followers parted from their leader and repented their earlier folly. One memoir referred to this as a time when, "after many Palm Sundays, Austin had her Good Friday, sad days of sorrow and humiliation, but humbly accepted the heavy cross awaiting those dear to His

Sacred Heart."[425] Her sisters thought that the heavy cross "brought her very close to God through her profound spirit of resignation to His Holy Will."[426] Another memoir spoke of so many gems of sanctity in the life of Austin that "it is hardly possible to find language that would fittingly pay tribute."[427] During the last year of her life many paid tribute by their visits to Austin as she gradually became more incapacitated. Repeatedly, groups from other houses along the Coast and New Orleans visited her with gifts of love and appreciation.

Austin had wished to give service until death, and she certainly came close to that ideal, for her first volume of the Catholic history was published in 1908 and an article in 1909. In that final year she continued with the second volume until stopped by an incapacitating stroke.[428] Fortunately, Sister Mariana Carroll Clery was assigned to Mobile, where she was a loving aide when tiny strokes began to cause difficulty. By the end of the summer and many visitors, Austin was beginning to feel some paralysis. In an interview with Charles J. O'Malley of the *Chicago New World*, however, her memory was accurate and her mind alert. For a third time she signed a will leaving all future income from her books to her community.[429] In October a severe stroke sent Austin to her bed. Thus imprisoned for close to two months, she had Mariana as a devoted nurse with the aid of Sister Mary who had come from New Orleans to help as long as needed. Earlier Austin had said that being on a bed of sickness was life on the cross and then told her friend, "One thing about sickness, there is no self-will, no one wants to be sick."[430] It was the same letter in which she had asked prayers for a happy death, and certainly that was her prayer on the feasts of All Saints and All Souls. There seemed to have been a second stroke, but Austin could note November 8 as the day of the anointing of the foundress. Her own was not long coming. Catherine McAuley had died on the 11th of the month, and Austin would have loved to go to God on that same date. Probably, Austin wondered once again why she had never been able to rouse the authorities to open the Cause for the canonization of Catherine McAuley.

The foundress had been buried on November 15, and Austin longed to join her on that day. Although the sacramental gifts and graces bolstered her repeatedly, Austin's spirit felt imprisoned in her paralyzed body.[431] The octave of Catherine's burial on the 15th came and went, but Austin remained. The second octave brought the feast of Catherine Laboure, and Mary Immaculate, always Austin's favorite devotion. Mary must have smiled upon Austin's anxiety to reach eternity, for Austin went to God before dawn the next morning, Monday, November 29, 1909.[432] Mothers Philoméne and Borgia had been with her over the weekend, but had returned home Sunday.[433] With eight or ten other sisters from New Orleans, they joined the Mobile community for the pontifical Mass of burial by

Bishop Allen, the eulogy by Father O'Shanahan, and the burial in the Catholic Cemetery of Mobile.[434] Austin's resting place is marked with a marble cross much larger than those of the sisters who surround her, appropriately so, according to the memoirs because, "as gold is tried in the fire, so are acceptable souls in the furnace of tribulations."[435] Even before the eulogy was spoken, the papers of New Orleans and Mobile proclaimed Austin's loss. Their headlines showed that the gentlemen of the press knew Austin well as one abounding in mercy and charity. All began with "Mother Austin Carroll," then "Beloved Sister Dies," "Devoted Her Life to Religious Work . . . Many Mourne Death," "Famous Leader in Mercy Dies," "Called to Her Reward for Charity, Education, Literature."[436] Locally, people remembered Austin primarily as a woman of charity and compassion, then as an educator, and finally as a writer.

As the news was heralded in papers farther away, the emphasis shifted to literature. Obituaries in Boston, New York, St. Louis, and Kansas City spoke of the "Distinguished Nun," "Prolific Writer," quoted O'Malley's interview with the "Most Successful American Catholic Writer," and hailed her as the Mercy foundress of convents all across the Southern United States.[437] These points were true, but her friends knew that they were not the most important; the eulogy tribute was more accurate. O'Shanahan brought out the way she had cut off family ties to devote all her energies and affections to the larger family of the indigent and afflicted. She was "a generous provider for the poor, a gentle consoler to the sick and suffering, a merciful visitant to those in prison, and such a prudent director and advisor to those in trouble that her zeal, her charity, and her teachings converted many souls to God."[438] He mentioned as well her indefatigable work establishing schools and charitable institutions and writing a "small library." He said these were her monuments and that she would live on "in hearts and lives of those she labored for and loved and above all, in the mind of that God whom she so well served." Her efforts were all for the greater honor and glory of God, and listeners should benefit by the lessons Austin's life had taught. "God wishes our character to be as broad as His, and to embrace all within our reach, to be active, energetic, and generous in welldoing, and to be willing to make sacrifices when necessary for the good of others."[439] Only then, said the priest, could they follow as closely as she in the footsteps of Christ.

The tribute mentioned Austin as "a most remarkable woman, with a mind of great strength, a brilliant intellect, stupendous labors; a veritable pioneer, fearless as she was gentle; her charming facility of expression, the loving labor of her pen, and the long list of foundations and institutions." Then the words of a friend came to a close.

Beyond these monuments that stand to her memory . . . and preach of her
wonderful achievements, there are yet millions of monuments in the hearts
of the sad and suffering all over the land, wherever she has rested. For
sorrow drew her as a magnet, and she found it, to comfort and to cheer, in
the most hidden places. We can hardly think of death in such a life. Rather
of rest or going home after a long and laborious journey. So, in your
folded hands, such beautiful, bountiful hands of mercy, we lay this flower
of humble appreciation and this tribute to a truly "valiant woman."[440]

The orator spoke of one he knew quite well, not from one found just in old
letters and documents. Speaking of the works of Austin Carroll always
sounds like exaggeration to persons of another century, and that is understandable. Most certainly, she was a woman who lived in the nineteenth
century, and to paint a portrait of any person it is necessary to consider the
surroundings which shadow the form and delineate the features. An artist
must utilize the light shed upon the subject by her ideals and motivation in
order to capture the facial expression, especially the illumination in the
eyes. Finally, the painter needs to place the picture within the historical
framework of the period, for only under the spotlight of time can one
perceive with true clarity the breadth and depth of such a multi-talented
leader.

Of course there were blemishes on her life as she had her faults in the
natural heritage of human frailty. Certainly, faults have been seen as she
worked among God's people near the waters of the South. For forty years
she served near the Mississippi River levee, on the banks of the bayous in
Acadian Louisiana, and along the sandy shores of the Gulf from Louisiana
through western Florida. Her own tides, like those of the area waters, rose
and fell at the command of forces beyond her own. The area is given to
storms, even hurricanes, and Austin Carroll had her share because her
Gaelic temperament could not stomach "peace at any price." She could carp
at the carpetbaggers, but shower her sympathies upon the disenfranchised
Confederate families. Perhaps she saw similarities between their plight and
that of the evicted people of Ireland. Many of the latter had found refuge in
America, where more than a few earned a place of their own in the country's
press corps. Locally, many a lad from the Irish Channel had rapidly climbed
political or construction ladders to solid success. Austin's friends were
legion in both groups, and editors among them were amazed that her forty
books had financed much of the charitable work of her sisters in the South.
Yet, her life is not the tale of one who spent her days, like the monks of old,
in a musty scriptorium. Nor was she some suffocatingly sweet holycard
saint in faint pastels.

Although Mother Austin Carroll preferred the bright hues and vivid contrasts of Joseph's cloak, she was quick to acknowledge her defects and her many loves. She doted on the smallest and most delicate orphans, and they idolized the jolly nun who played with them and sent them to Biloxi for a swim. She enjoyed the ragged newsboys and street urchins who lived on their wits with a rugged independence and a calling for craps. Yet she got them to school, taught them to study, receive the sacraments, and improve their future. Street smart, they saw both the strict teacher and the motherly heart. In a drive for funds for the works of mercy some seventy years later, donors were told of the benefit to the city of such past works as the guidance that helped the newsies become good citizens and even civic leaders in the community. The columnist also noted that for over a century "the Sisters of Mercy moved quietly about their blessed errands in the grim steel-and-concrete corridors of the Orleans Parish Prison," where Austin had once brought libraries, melodeons, and moral training.[441] There she was firm, but she had a gentle, loving compassion for the elderly, the ill, the poor, and the harried workingwomen. A part of her tremendous ability to attract people to the Gospel message and to service in the Mercy Institute was real affection for prim little school girls and proper young ladies. More importantly, however, her enthusiasm was contagious, her confidence was encouraging, and her community was obviously her pride and joy.

Those Austin attracted, like her achievements, were many; like her failures, those she repelled were few. Among the latter were the chauvinistically inclined. It happened because she was so firmly convinced of the ability of dedicated women in any walk of life. "When occasion requires," as Austin wrote earlier, "they have a patient endurance, a noble bravery, and an invincible energy which go far to prove that the term 'weaker sex' has nothing to do with the soul."[442] She was not seeking equality, for she not only felt strongly about individuality but she also believed that women were often superior to men in particular qualities, like sensitivity, morality, intellectual achievement, and parenting, to name a few. But Austin was termed radical a century ago and failed to win approval for her Catholic college for women, a failure which Austin counted as one of her greatest. That was 1888; yet even in 1906, the local Catholic paper quoted a New York doctor who warned that higher education was dangerous to a woman's health.[443] Fourteen years after Austin's death, however, her friend Borgia Walsh successfully established a college for teachers in St. Katharine's College which Austin had built for the higher education of women thirty-five years earlier.[444] Austin felt that another great failure was her inability to stimulate interest in the canonization of the Mercy foundress. But exactly ten days after Austin died, the Dublin motherhouse sent out letters to Sisters of Mercy around the world asking that all unite in prayer for the beatification of Mother McAuley, then spoke of the result, "The movement on behalf of our beloved Foundress has, T. G., been most enthusiastically taken up by our convents all over the world."[445]

Thus, one of the aims for which Austin had striven during her religious life had begun to fructify only ten days after she had gone to God, and seventy-five years later in the 1980s, her biography of the foundress was to be a major contribution as historical information was assembled for the Cause of Catherine McAuley. Austin Carroll had left this life at the age of seventy-four years, confident of meeting friends in eternity and treasuring special blessings from three popes. Austin had received from Pius X a recent benediction on her golden jubilee, and thirty-five years earlier, a blessing, a crucifix, and an autographed letter from Pius IX, the first pope to have seen the American continent.[446] Through her friend Bishop Kirby, Austin had been favored repeatedly by Leo XIII, whose great gift to many besides Austin was the opening of the Vatican archives.[447] On a number of occasions this pope sent Austin personal messages and, three or four times, apostolic benedictions.[448] Austin was also proud of a blessing of a different kind, the financial success of her publications, a point which gave assistance especially to black schools. Charles O'Malley wrote, "It is doubtful if any Catholic writer in the country has been so successful financially."[449] Another gentleman of the press, who knew Austin during her two dozen years in New Orleans, had higher praise.

> In the passing of Mother Austin Carroll, the Order of Mercy has lost its greatest and most distinguished member with the exception, perhaps, of its noted foundress, Catherine McAuley. Trained in the school of this earnest leader, with the beautiful influence of her life ever reflected before her, Mother Austin fulfilled all demands made upon her as a Sister of Mercy. . . . She loved this sunny clime, and the South may mourne one of its most distinguished, learned, and representative women, and the church one of its noblest daughters.[450]

Of course, he was a friend, one of the hundreds among the benefactors she had met in the Crescent City. Aside from her spiritual life, Austin would have counted her friends as her greatest treasures throughout her years of service. Only her love of God and Mercy dedication had enabled her to cut herself off from friends as she moved forward on appointed assignments. She also made additional friends at every stop, loved each of them, and been invigorated by their letters. In hers she enclosed her heart. Friends found her charitable, warm, energetic, charming, resourceful, hospitable, and spontaneously broad-minded; courageous, dedicated, joyful, generous, witty, forceful, and especially gifted; affectionate, brilliant, devout, logical, persistent, and deeply spiritual. Yet on certain occasions, Austin had been misunderstood, disliked, called too strict, and misrepresented by the malicious. Her friends knew she possessed an unflagging enthusiasm, a love of poverty, a passion for charity, and such a huge capacity for work that "she had raised altars for the honor and glory of God all across the South.[451] Austin's excessive drive and determination made it difficult for some to meet her standards, but "in achievement of purpose, her peer is seldom found."[452] Any community in which she served saw Austin as the personification of charity, the defender of the oppressed, an author who was widely read from her youth yet as approachable and simple as a child, vivacious in personality, strong in character, and keen for justice.

To discountenance the opinions of the best witnesses because they saw virtues and favorable characteristics would not be wise. Might not justice be both keen and honest as found in the judgment of those who knew Austin Carroll personally? Katherine Conway noted that it often happened "in the orders devoted to teaching or works of charity, that . . . a girl of exceptionally brilliant intellect . . . has a convent career more eminent than she had ever attained outside the religious life."[453] Had Margaret Carroll remained in Clonmel, Conway thought, her giftedness and charity might have affected several thousand people, but as a missionary in America, Austin's charity, compassion, and zeal touched hundreds of thousands.

Far from Mobile where Austin breathed her last, several episcopal or convent chronicles noted her death as that of "a great religious," or "an extraordinary woman," or "a remarkable woman and religious."[454] Such tributes as these, plus the numerous letters and memoirs, paint a picture with the light and dark of success and failure. Though limited by the frame of man's nineteenth-century world, the portrait depicts Mother Austin Carroll as extraordinary in talent and compassion, larger than life in courage and character, boundless in energy and zeal for souls, and abounding in mercy.

ABBREVIATIONS

AAB	Archives of the Archdiocese of Baltimore
AAH	Archives of the Archdiocese of Hartford
AAM	Archives of the Archdiocese of Mobile
AANO	Archives of the Archdiocese of New Orleans
AAO	Archives of the Archdiocese of Omaha
ACPF	Archives of the Congregation of Propaganda Fide
	Acta = della Congregazione
	Lettere = Lerrere e Decreti
	SRN = Scritture referite nei congressi, America Centrale
	SOR = Scritture originale referite nelle congregazioni generali
ACUAL	Archives of the Catholic University of America
ADB	Archives of the Diocese of Buffalo
ADJ	Archives of the Diocese of Jackson
ADKC	Archives of the Diocese of Kansas City, Missouri
ADLR	Archives of the Diocese of Little Rock
ADR	Archives of the Diocese of Richmond
ADS	Archives of the Diocese of Savannah
ALSU	Archives of Louisiana State University, Baton Rouge
APIC	Archives of the Pontifical Irish College, Rome
ASM	Archives of the Sisters of Mercy
ASMS	Archives of St. Mary's Seminary, Perryville
ASSJ	Archives of the Society of St. Joseph, Baltimore
ATUL	Archives of Tulane University Library
AUND	Archives of the University of Notre Dame

NOTES — CHAPTER ONE

1. Mary Austin Carroll, *In Many Lands* (N.Y.: P. O'Shea, 1904), 438.

2. Brendan Lehane, *Ireland* (N.Y.: Scribner's, 1973), 198.

3. ASM, New Orleans, collection of Carroll family correspondence and documents, in photocopy except for letters to the author (hereafter cited as Carroll Family Papers).

4. Ibid.

5. R. Brookes, *Universal Gazeteer* 1839 (Philadelphia: J. Marshall, 1839), 130.

6. John Nicholas Murphy, *Terra Incognita or the Convents of the United Kingdom* (Longmans, Green, 1873), 11.

7. Carroll, *Leaves from the Annals of the Sisters of Mercy*, vol. 1 (N.Y.: Catholic Publication Soc, 1881), 93.

8. Ibid., 95.

9. Murphy, *Terra Incognita*, 491.

10. Carroll, *Annals* 1: 96.

11. The Ballynahinch near Cashel should not be confused with any of the other towns with the same name or the spelling Ballinahinch: one to the west, in Connemara; another to the north, up in Down; and a third on the western edge of northern Tipperary, just south of Nenagh.

12. Geoffrey Keating, *History of Ireland*, trans. by John O'Mahony (N.Y.: P. M. Haverty, 1857). Roger Chauvire, *History of Ireland* (London: Devin-Adair, 1961), 96.

13. ASM, N.O., Carroll Family Papers.

14. Mary Bernadette McAtee, "Reminiscences of Mother Austin Carroll," in collection of correspondence, documents, memoirs of contemporaries of Mary Austin Carroll, in photocopy except for letters to the writer and memoirs written at her request (hereafter cited as Austin Carroll Papers).

15. *Register*, St. Patrick's Church, Waterford, documentation obtained through the efforts of Mr. Frank Heylin.

16. ADR, Rev. Patrick Kelly was consecrated for and served from 1820–1823 as the first bishop of Richmond, Va., in the United States. He was then transferred to Ireland to the See of Waterford and Lismore, where he served until his death on October 8, 1829.

17. *Waterford Chronicle*, March 7, 1829, photocopy was obtained from the British Library newspaper collection through the kind assistance of Mrs. Joseph McCarthy, a grandniece of Mother Austin Carroll. The writer would like to acknowledge not only the direct help of Mrs. McCarthy in this research, but also her enthusiastic support and encouragement given over the several years of research and writing.

18. *Baptismal Registers*, Trinity Within, Waterford, use of the records obtained through the kindness of Bp. Michael Russell of Waterford and Lismore, and later, with the assistance of Rev. Nicholas O'Mahony, administrator of the cathedral. The city of Waterford has two

churches dedicated to the Most Holy Trinity, the cathedral being termed "Trinity Within," and the other "Trinity Without," as it was originally on the outer side of the walls of the ancient port.

19. *Baptismal Registers*, Trinity Within, Waterford, Michael James Carroll was baptized on March 29, 1830 by F. Dixon, sponsors being James and   Walsh.

20. *Baptismal Registers*, Trinity Within, Waterford, John Mary Carroll was baptized on Sept. 19, 1831, sponsors being John Brophy and Mary Anna Walsh. Catherine Mary Carroll was baptized on May 22, 1833, and had sponsors Michael Burke and Maria Nagle.

21. *Baptismal Registers*, St. Mary's Parish, Clonmel, the date of birth is listed as part of the entry: Margaret Anne Carroll was born on Feb. 23, and baptized on Feb. 24, 1835.

22. *Baptismal Registers*, St. Mary's Parish, Clonmel, Margaret Anne is the correct sequence of the names.

23. *Baptismal Registers*, St. Mary's Parish, Clonmel, Mary Johanna Carroll had sponsors William Ryan and Ellen Cantwell; William Francis Carroll had sponsors Michael Guiry and Margaret Egan; Mary Carroll had sponsors George Everard and Johanna Ryan; Anne Carroll had sponsors John Cleary and Brigid Egan. Patrick Carroll, the youngest child in the family, could not be located in the records of either St. Mary's or St. Peter and Paul's, the two parishes in Clonmel. The year of his birth is contained in AAO, Carroll to O'Connor, July 31, 1968.

24. Registration Volumes, Registry of Deeds, Dublin, Registers 33–14–46, 42–2–157, 46–7–99, 49–18–128.

25. *New Orleans Daily Picayune*, Nov. 30, 1909; ASM, N.O., Carroll Family Papers.

26. ASM, N.O., Carroll Family Papers.

27. ASM, N.O., Austin Carroll Papers, Purcell to Carroll, n.d.

28. Tipperary Registry of Births and Deaths, Clonmel. Copies of certificates obtained through the assistance of Kevin Fennessey of Lisronagh, grandnephew of Mother Austin Carroll.

29. Carroll, *Glimpses of Pleasant Homes* (N.Y.: Catholic Publication Society, 1869), 49; ASM, N.O., Carroll Family Papers, Patrick crossed the Atlantic in 1868 to seek his fortune amidst the golden opportunities on the western frontier. He visited with Mary Austin Carroll in St. Louis, where she wanted him to accept a position as a teacher in a diocesan seminary. Although she had already obtained the position through the efforts of James O'Connor, Patrick rejected it and crossed the country with an expedition heading for "the Rockies and beyond." His "beyond" became eternity, and the family grieved over another death.

30. Carroll, *Life of Catherine McAuley* (N.Y.: D. & J. Sadlier, 1866), the first of three editions and twelve reissues.

31. AAO, Carroll to O'Connor, July 31, 1868.

32. ASM, N.O., Carroll Family Papers; Keating, *History of Ireland*, 709; William P. Burke, *History of Clonmel* (Waterford: N. Harvey, 1907), 11.

33. ASM, N.O., Carroll Family Papers; A. M. Sullivan, *Crests of Leading Families* (New York: Murphy and McCarthy, 1894), 276.

34. Carroll, *In Many Lands*, 302; ASM, N.O., Carroll Family Papers. William Carroll is listed as eligible to vote as the owner of house and premises in the published rolls of the *Clonmel Advertiser*, October, 1835. The Carroll Flour Shop, several blocks away in Irishtown, must

have been rented as it is not listed with the property. William Carroll is also listed in several issues of *Irish Commercial Directories* as Slater's until 1847, as a "Flour Dealer" until the late 1850s, when he transferred his business to Main Street and expanded to other provisions besides the grain, flour and meal of the first shop. Besides this business, William Carroll had a supervisory position in the local flour mill which prior to the famine years shipped grains extensively. William Carroll had shared provisions so generously during the famine that the family was not as affluent afterward. William Carroll, with his several jobs, was able to provide each of his children with an excellent education and each of his daughters with a substantial dowery.

35. Carroll, Foreword to *History of Blessed Margaret Mary* (N.Y.: P. O'Shea, 1867), 46. (Foreword, 13–56, hereafter cited as Carroll, Foreword.)

36. Ibid; *News Bulletin*, St. Mary's Parish, Irishtown, Clonmel, Dec. 1981; Carroll, *In Many Lands*, 305.

37. Carroll, *In Many Lands*, 208, 301.

38. ASM, N.O., Carroll Family Papers. The location of the Carroll family home and the building which housed the Cannings' School was accomplished with the courteous assistance of Mrs. George O'Brien, grandniece of Mother Austin Carroll. Schools such as the private school of the Cannings were sometimes referred to as "Bishop's" schools because they were originally opened in order to assist Catholics to avoid sending their children to the anti-Catholic national schools such as those of the Charter and the Kildare systems. In the Cannings' School, like others of that type, the parish priests regularly taught the religion classes. When the religious orders later established poor schools for the destitute, parents like the Carrolls who could afford the tuition of the private schools were encouraged to continue to patronize the private institutions.

39. Carroll, *Catherine McAuley*, 187.

40. Carroll, *Pleasant Homes*, 94.

41. Ibid., 209.

42. Ibid., ii.

43. Ibid., 19.

44. ASM, N.O., Austin Carroll Papers, Purcell to Carroll, n.d.

45. *Mobile Daily Register*, July 12, 1906.

46. Carroll, *Catherine McAuley*, 146.

47. Murphy, *Ireland: Industrial, Political, Social* (London: Longmans, Green, 1870), chapters 57–70 cover education in Ireland, in large measure through original documents, reports of investigating committees, etc.

48. Murphy, *Terra Incognita*, 527, 544, chapters 33–37 treat Irish education. Lord Stanley, the Earl of Derby, had set up the National Board of Commissioners for Education with Catholic representation in the person of Archbishop Daniel Murray and a Mr. Blake. Each board member was to have the right of veto to insure fairness in decisions. Many bishops, together with Archbishop Murray, saw it as the first fair government plan because its basis was "association in literary instruction, but separation in religious, with the most scrupulous avoidance of interference with the peculiar tenets of any Christian pupils," as Murphy said on page 523.

Most religious communities involved in teaching in ireland followed the lead of the local bishops. If he were in favor of the Board, their schools were a part of the National system. The Sisters of Mercy, for instance, were happy to have the advantage of the system for their poor students, but did not participate when the diocesan prelate, Abp. McHale for instance, was against participation.

49. ASM, N.O., Carroll Family Papers. *Tipperary Registry* of Marriages, Clonmel, Carroll family documentation obtained through the assistance of Kevin Fennessey and David O'Connor, grandnephews of Mother Austin Carroll. Mary Carroll married Charles Patrick Byrne on September 15, 1869. Their children were Gerald, William, Charles, Mary, Joseph, Clare and Margaret Mary — the nieces and nephews of whom M. Austin was very fond. Three of the children died young — Joseph as an infant, Clare at fourteen, and Charles as a young man. William, who left no children, became the proprietor of the family draper's shop in the heart of Clonmel's business district.

50. ASM, N.O., Carroll Family Papers. Gerald Byrne, M. Austin Carroll's eldest nephew, married Delia Considine and reared three sons just a few doors from the Carroll home in Clonmel. Two of the young men had successful military careers.

51. ASM, N.O., Carroll Family Papers. Mary Byrne, M. Austin's niece who was called Dolly, married Thomas David Fennessey. Their children were Charles, Thomas Austin, Patrick, Brendan, Mary, Kevin, Clare, Eileen, Teresa, Joseph, and Eithne. Two became religious, Thomas Austin, who served as Father Austin, CSSP, on the Trinidad mission until he died in 1981, and Teresa or Terry, who serves as Sister Teresa, FMM, in Madras, India, with the Franciscan Missionaries of Mary. In 1986, the oldest living descendant of William Carroll, M. Austin's father, was Charles Fennessey in Australia, whose son was named Charles Bernard. Kevin Fennessey married Josie Denny and called his son Austin for both the priest uncle and for M. Austin Carroll, the grandaunt nun. Joseph Fennessey, recently deceased, married Kathy Wall and their children were Tom, Brendan, Aidan, and Pamela. Eithne Fennessey married George O'Brien and reared their children just down the street from the Bolton Street home of the Carrolls. The children of Eithne and George O'Brien are Mary Teresa, named for the religious aunt, Anne, now Sister Anne, FMDM, Martin Austin, another namesake of the two religious, Clare who died young, Lucy Assunta, and Michael Gabriel. Several of the children of Tom and Dolly Fennessey died quite young or in infancy. The family data for the others was gathered by Charles and Kevin Fennessey and Eithne O'Brien.

52. ASM, N.O., Carroll Family Papers. M. Austin's youngest niece, Margaret Mary Byrne, married David Francis O'Connor and reared five girls and two boys — Catherine or Kitty, Maura, Eileen, David, Charles, Margaret, and Una. Charles died young, but each of the others married. Kitty married David Cullen and their children were Paul Cullen, SJ, Patricia, Christine, and Loretta. Maura married Francis Burke, and their children were Brigid, Francis, and James. Eileen married William Rowell and reared Sydney, William, Jean, and Bernie. Her youngest, David Francis Austin, died in infancy. David Francis O'Connor, Jr. married Rosaleen Duff, and their family was David Francis who died young, Michael, Mark, Geoffrey, Francis Mary Ann, and Charles. Margaret Mary O'Connor, bearing the first name of her grandaunt, M. Austin Carroll, married Joseph McCarthy and reared a son named Anthony. Una O'Connor married Peter McQuillan and their children were Veronica, Nuala, Anita, Geraldine, and Peter. Information was contributed by several of the above, particularly, Kitty Cullen and Margaret McCarthy, grandnieces of M. Austin Carroll, and by Brigid Burke Cooke and her husband, Damien Cooke.

53. ASM, N.O., Carroll Family Papers. *Tipperary Registry* of Marriages, Clonmel. Anne

Carroll Cleary, or Clery as she spelled it, entered the Mercy community in New Orleans on July 26, 1885, was received on December 21, 1885, and chose to teach in the Mobile Diocese with M. Austin Carroll in 1891. Thus she, with the rest of the Mobile community, transferred to the diocese of Mobile, to serve in Florida and Alabama. Anne's daughter, Mary, who died young, attended school in New Orleans and did exceptionally well in music.

54. ASM, N.O., Carroll Family Papers. Johanna Carroll, Sr. M. Dominica, died on May 12, 1921, at St. Maries of the Isle in Cork. [Maries is pronounced Mary's and is early form of possessive case.] Mary Carroll Byrne died on June 14, 1921, in Clonmel. Anne Carroll Clery, Sister Marianna, died in the Convent of Mercy in Mobile on April 23, 1922, and was buried in the Catholic Cemetery near M. Austin Carroll who had died a dozen years earlier on Nov. 29, 1909.

55. ASM, N.O., Carroll Family Papers, notes of M. Austin Carroll's grandniece, Mary Fennessey. The notes were gathered from her mother and organized for interested Sisters of Mercy in Limerick many years ago.

56. Ibid.; *United States Catholic Miscellany*, May 23, 1846.

57. ASM, Passage West, Co. Cork chronicles; *Boston Pilot*, Feb. 19, 1887.

58. *Mobile Daily Register*, July 12, 1906; ASM, N.O., Carroll Family Papers.

59. ASM, N.O., Austin Carroll Papers, Mercy Carroll to Austin Carroll, Jan. 6, 10, 1887.

60. *Boston Pilot*, Feb. 19, 1887.

61. *The Irish News*, June, 1847.

62. ASM, Carlow, Wexford, Waterford, Cork, Charleville, Limerick, and Birr, named clockwise in the order of their location in the circle about Clonmal. Sir John Forbes, *Memorandums in Ireland* (London: Smith, Elder, 1853).

63. ASM, Cork and Passage West; ASM, N.O., Carroll Family Papers, Katy Carroll entered St. Maries of the Isle on Sept. 23 or 24, 1854, was received into the community on Jan. 25, 1855, and was professed on March 5, 1857. Assigned to Passage West on Aug. 28, 1865, Sr. M. Mercy died there on Jan. 12, 1887. She was Mistress of Novices, and was doubly mourned by her own sisters and also those of St. Maries of the Isle. Obituary is from the *Boston Pilot*, Feb. 19, 1887.

64. ASM, N.O., Austin Carroll Papers. Archives, Dominican Institute for the Deaf, Cabra, Dublin. Through the kindness of Sr. M. Bertranda, OP, the school rolls were checked from 1847 to late 1860, resulting in the conclusion that Johanna Carroll was not registered as a regular student, but simply attended in order to observe the methods of imparting both information and instruction to the hearing impaired.

65. ASM, Cork, Johanna entered St. Maries of the Isle on April 15, 1857, was received into the order on Nov. 12, 1857, and was professed on Nov. 17, 1859. She died on May 12, 1921 after sixty-four years of service to the deaf.

66. ASM, N.O., Carroll Family Papers. Margaret Anne or M. Austin Carroll's family, like that of Nano Nagle, had Browne, Mathew, and Burke cousins and connections. M. Austin herself spoke of some Browne and Carroll family relatives who had come to America several generations earlier. One of the Carroll relatives in her father's generation was Rev. John Carroll who had been ordained in Halifax in 1820 by his maternal uncle, the Most Rev. Edmund Burke, bishop and vicar apostolic of Nova Scotia. This Father John Carroll told M. Austin that he

kept in touch with other family connections on this continent like the descendants of Charles Carroll, "the Signer," and his descendants like Mrs. Emily McTavish of Baltimore. Although attempts to clarify these connections were unsuccessful, portraits of the early Burkes and Carrolls show a strong resemblance to the immediate family of M. Austin Carroll.

67. ASM, N.O., Silver Spring, Md. In clarifying the connection with Nano Nagle, one of the Nagle cousins wrote in 1944 that "Mother Austin [Carroll] and my grandmother [Marguerite Nagle] were first cousins." This same cousin, Genevieve Nagle Herten at the time, explained that each generation of the family had a child named in honor of Nano Nagle and another called Austin in honor of M. Austin Carroll. This custom has continued to the present day, according to F. Russell Herten, so that there are at present in 1986 fourth and fifth generation Austins bearing the name in honor of M. Austin Carroll, who had died before they were born. Marguerite Nagle married J. H. Moore and had four children. Widowed, she came to the U.S. and became a lecturer or note. During her lecture circuits M. Austin attended to the education of her youngest daughter, Clare. ASM, N.O., Austin Carroll Papers.

68. ASM, N.O., Carroll Family Papers. Archives, Religious of the Sacred Heart, Ireland and the United States. Jane Nagle entered Roehampton on July 25, 1865, and made her profession on Aug. 12, 1873. She taught in England and Ireland until 1885, when she crossed the ocean to serve in Argentina and Brazil, where she died Nov. 14, 1931. Data was furnished through the kindness of Mothers Nuala O'Higgins in Ireland and Marie Louise Martinez of the U.S. Archives.

69. *New Orleans Morning Star*, Nov. 7, 1875.

70. ASM, N.O., Carroll Family Papers, M. Austin Carroll's mother and father each spoke of granduncles who served as bishops and priests, and each parent had several uncles in the service of the Church, one of these presiding for a time at the Royal Irish College in Salamanca. Besides the priests and prelates, both sides of the family had numerous cousins and connections who were religious sisters. Mary Austin, on one occasion, mentioned five aunts and several cousins who were Presentation nuns, two who were Religious of the Sacred Heart, and more than eight relatives who were Sisters of Mercy. Besides the grandnieces and nephew already mentioned serving as religious, a cousin of that generation, Sr. M. Aquinata Herten, RDC, now deceased, had served in the U.S. It is as Mrs. Kitty Cullen wrote, "So many family members have brought the torch of Christianity to foreign lands" that it would be impossible to name all of them.

NOTES – CHAPTER TWO

1. *Clonmel Nationalist*, Dec. 18, 1909.

2. Ibid., Aug. 4, 1906.

3. Abp. Daniel Murray, appointed Rev. Myles Gaffney, later the Dean of Maynooth and thereafter a member of the Society of Jesus, to assist Catherine McAuley in her adaptation of the Presentation Rule. More than most others, Gaffney understood Catherine McAuley's aims and ends, and knew that she intended to improve the condition of the poor. As the expert on the Rule of the Mercy Institute, he certainly would have been the logical choice to write a review upon its publication for the literary periodical which published reviews of recently published books. See chap. 2, n. 27, and chap. 4, nn 20–23, and the material to which the notes

refer, for additional reasons why this writer attributes the authorship of the *Dublin Review* article in n. 4 to Gaffney rather than to Dean Dominick Murphy of Cork.

4. [Myles Gaffney], "La Regola e le Costituzioni delle Religiose Nominate Sorelle della Misericordia," *Dublin Review* 22 (March 1847), 18.

5. Carroll, *Pleasant Homes*, 82; Carroll, *Angel Dreams* (N.Y.: Catholic Publication Society, 1868), 78.

6. Leo XIII, "Sapientiae Christianae," in George Shuster, *World's Great Catholic Literature* (N.Y.: Halcyon House, 1947), 258.

7. Carroll, *In Many Lands*, 208.

8. ASM, N.O. Austin Carroll Papers, Purcell to Carroll, n.d.

9. Carroll, *Annals* 3: 433.

10. Friends of the Carroll schoolgirls from the Kelly, Lynch, Nagle, O'Keefe, Reid, and Purcell families became religious sisters. Several members of the Lynch and Purcell families, like the Carrolls, served in different Mercy foundations.

11. ASM, Cork, chronicles.

12. Ibid., Cork records state simply that "Margaret Carroll entered as a postulant in 1853." M. Austin's correspondence repeatedly states the exact date of entrance as Dec. 7, 1853. During her entire life M. Austin Carroll kept this date as a very special one of her consecration to God through service of his people.

13. Mother M. Catherine McAuley to Reverend Gerald Doyle, Sept. 5, 1836. McAuley quotations are taken from Mary Ignatia Neumann, *Letters of Catherine McAuley* (Baltimore: Helican Press, 1969), letters are identified by date in chronological arrangement.

14. Ibid.

15. Ibid.

16. *Boston Pilot*, July 10, 1854; ASM, Cork, Misses Julia Lawler, Agnes Daly, Margaret Murphy, and Margaret Carroll received the names Josephine, Agnes Patricia, and Teresa Austin, respectively.

17. *Cork Examiner*, May 17, 1854, Clergymen present were the Rev. John Browne and T. Scannell of St. Patrick's, A. Maguire of Saints Peter and Paul, D. F. McLeod of the South Capuchin Friary, J. Cummins of South Parish where Dean Dominick Murphy was the Pastor, and J. Parker, who was serving as the Chaplain at the Convent of Mercy. Bishop William Delaney had been a young priest when Catherine McAuley and her Mercies arrived in Cork. The foundress wrote in 1837 to M. dePazzi Delaney that young Father Delaney had the same first name as her father. See Chap. 9, note 63, for Catherine's comments. This letter, recently located by the writer, is not contained in the Neumann collection of letters.

18. ASM, Cork, chronicles, Sept. 24, 1854, feast of Our Lady of Mercy, Catherine Carroll entered as a postulant.

19. McAuley to Delany, Oct. 3, 1837; McAuley to Warde, Sept. 1837, June 16 and May 15, in 1838.

20. Carroll, *Annals* 1: 254-265.

21. Ibid.

22. Ibid., chapters 22–6.

23. Ibid., 225.

24. Mary Ellen Evans, *The Spirit is Mercy* (Westminster, Md.: Newman Press, 1959), 13.

25. ASM, Dublin, Tullamore, Charleville, Carlow, Cork, Limerick, Bermondsey, Galway, Birr, and Birmingham.

26. Ibid.; ASM, N.O., Carroll Family Papers.

27. Carroll, *Annals* 1:480; research data of Sr. M. Dominick Foster, Right Rev. John Pius Leahy, OP, served in Cork until he was appointed bishop of Dromore. Carroll, *Catherine McAuley*, 13, and Foster data, Dean Dominick Murphy was pastor in Cork 1853–1875.

28. ASM, Cork, Mary Teresa Wildridge died Sept. 14, 1848. Timewise, if Dean Murphy was to complete the work thereafter, it could not have been ready for the 1847 *Dublin Review*. Because of the confusion about the author of the 1847 article, this writer made a comparative study of the phraseology and vocabulary in the *Dublin Review* article and the writing style of Dean Murphy in his earlier article on Nano Nagle as well as his later work on Irish foundresses, and also with the Gaffney writing quoted in the Carroll biography of Catherine McAuley and in the reports of his sermons at Mercy profession ceremonies as quoted in *Dublin Register, Boston Pilot*, and *Freeman's Jr.* 1841–1846. Internal evidence showed no similarity with the words and phrasing of Dean Murphy, other than his incorporation of the *Dublin Review* article. Material in his book which is not from the *Dublin Review* article is from the Vincent Hartnett biography of Mother McAuley published one year before his *Irish Nunneries*. On the other hand, the study demonstrated that the Gaffney sermons treated the same material and often used the identical wording of the article, yet were given before the article. Gaffney could have taken parts of the article right from his sermons. See also chap. 2, n. 3 and chp. 4, nn 20, 23. Dominick Murphy, "The Life of Miss Nano Nagle, Foundress of the Presentation Order," *Dublin Review* 15 (Dec. 1843): 363–86; Dominick Murphy, *Sketches of Irish Nunneries* (Dublin: James Duffy, 1865), 114–59.

29. Carroll, *Catherine McAuley*, 14; Carroll, *Annals* 1: 240.

30. Carroll, *Annals* 1: 240; Carroll, *Foreword*.

31. ASM, Cork and Dobbs Ferry (hereafter cited as New York), Sr. Catherine Seton, daughter of Saint Elizabeth Seton, joined the Mercy community in New York City in 1846.

32. Archbishop John Hughes, "Pastoral of 1854," this statement was repeated in 1931 by Cardinal Hayes, archbishop of New York.

33. ASM, Cork, chronicles; Carroll, *Annals* 2: 151.

34. Carroll, *Annals* 2: 216.

35. ASM, Cork, chronicles.

36. ASM, N.O., Austin Carroll Papers, retreat notes; Carroll, *Spiritual Retreat* (N.Y.: Catholic Publication Society Co., 1885); ASM, Cork, chronicles.

37. Carroll, *Annals* 3: 411.

38. McAuley to Warde, June 6, 1840; McAuley to Elizabeth Moore, July 28, 1840.

39. Carroll, *Annals* 3: 411.

40. ASM, N.O. and Cork. When a novice made her vows, she exchanged the white veil of the novice for the black veil of the professed sister. In many communities the young sister continued to receive formation lectures for a certain period, during which she was termed a black novice. The length of this term varied from one community to another, and more recently, was replaced by a period of temporary vows.

41. Carroll, *Annals* 4: 173. This particular quotation, like many another pithy, humorous, or memorably creative selection originating with Mary Austin Carroll, has been repeatedly appropriated by writers who failed to mention M. Austin Carroll as their source.

42. *Irish News*, Oct. 11, 1856.

43. Carroll, *Catherine McAuley*, 41; Carroll, *Annals* 3:48, 57, 149, 330.

44. Edward A. Ryan, SJ, "The Sisters of Mercy: an Important Chapter in Church History," *Theological Studies* 15 (June 1957); 258.

45. *London Tablet*, [Dec., 1881]; this clipping from the Austin Carroll Papers is undated, but internal evidence points to the month and year.

46. McAuley to Walsh, Nov. 6, 1840.

47. Henry James Coleridge, SJ, "The First Sister of Mercy," *The Month* 4 (Feb. 1866): 125. This article was based on Mary Vincent Hartnett, *Life of Rev. Mother Catherine McAuley, Foundress of the Order of Mercy* (Dublin: John F. Fowler, 1864).

48. ASM, Birmingham, Ullathorne to Reverend Mother, Dec. 18, 1888.

49. AANO, Byrne to Blanc, Dec. 3, 1857.

50. History shows that certain bishops believed it to be their prerogative to take over the internal government of religious communities in their dioceses, as did Bp. Verot who served in both Florida and Georgia, and Bp. Timon of Buffalo, among others. These prelates transferred religious from one assignment to another without even consulting the superior whose authority they were nullifying.

51. ADJ, Elder to Cogan, June 20, 1878.

52. Carroll, *Annals* 1–4, passim.

NOTES – CHAPTER THREE

1. ASM, Liverpool; Carroll, *Annals* 2, 449.

2. Carroll, *Annals* 3, chapters 50–1.

3. According to Newmann C. Eberhardt, *Catholic History* 2(London: Herder, 1962) and Peter Condon, *Knownothingism* (N.Y.: Appleton, 1910), the political party began in 1852 when a number of rather small political organizations, all with anti-foreigner themes and titles like the American Republicans or the Sons of America, united and published a ritual which proved them anti-Catholic also. The second article in the ritual, for instance, declared that one of the purposes of the party was the resistance of the "Church of Rome." The aim of the party was political power, but the means chosen to attain that end was violence against Catholics and their churches. Some of those damaged or destroyed in the Northeast were located in Bath, Me.; Chelsea, Dorchester, and Lawrence, Mass.; Manchester, N.H.; Norwalk, Conn.; New-

ark, N.J.; Brooklyn, Palmyra, and Saugerties, N.Y.; Philadelphia, Pa.; and Sidney, Ohio. In Philadelphia and Louisville alone, however, more than a hundred Irish immigrants were burned out or killed.

4. John Lancaster Spalding, *Life of the Most Reverend Martin J. Spaulding* (N.Y.: Catholic Pub. Co., 1873); Condon, *Knownothingism*, 108; Eberhardt, *Catholic History* 2; 575.

5. Carroll, *Annals* 3: 392.

6. *Missouri Leader*, April 11, 1855; Carroll, *Annals* 3: 393, 412.

7. ASM, Providence, and Hartford; Carroll, *Annals* 3: 385.

8. James H. O'Donnell, *History of the Diocese of Hartford* (Boston: Hurd, 1900), 139; Mary Cecelia O'Reilly, *Sisters of Mercy in the Diocese of Hartford* (Hartford: Peck, 1931), 15; Carroll, *Annals* 3: 411.

9. Carroll, *Annals* 3: 392, 411, 428; ASM, Cork, chronicles, Mary Francis Meade celebrated her golden jubilee five months before she died in 1894.

10. ASM, Cincinnati: Delaney to Teresa Maher, Jan. 25, 1858. Bp. Delaney was of the opinion that the missionaries "are liable to recall if the bishop finds a necessity demanding it."

11. ADLR, Carroll to FitzGerald, Nov. 21, 1888; ASM: Providence, Hartford, Rochester, New York, and Omaha.

12. Mary Catherine Morgan, *The Work of the Sisters of Mercy in Providence, R.I., from 1851 to 1893* (Providence: Reid, 1893), 77; Carroll, *Annals* 3: 392–429.

13. Carroll, *Annals* 3: 41; Morgan, *Mercy in Providence*, 85; McAtee, "Reiminiscences," 2.

14. ASM: Providence and Hartford; Carroll, *Annals* 3: 408. Sr. M. Camillus O'Neill died at St. Catherine Convent in Hartford on Nov. 18, 1856.

15. Margaret C. Newton, "Retrospect," 3; Carroll, *Annals* 3: 408.

16. Carroll, *Annals* 4, chap. 58.

17. ASM, Brooklyn and N.Y.; ADB, Timon Diary.

18. McAuley to Teresa White, Aug. 3, 1841.

19. ADB, Timon Diary; Archives, St. Mary's Seminary, Perryville, Timon Papers.

20. Kathleen Healy, *Frances Warde* (N.Y.: Seabury, 1973), 257.

21. Mary Florence Sullivan, *Mercy Comes to Rochester* (Rochester: Sisters of Mercy, 1985), 14.

22. ADB, Timon Diary; Archives, St. Mary's Seminary, Perryville, Timon Papers.

23. John Timon, *Missions in Western New York and Church History of the diocese of Buffalo* (Buffalo: Catholic Sentinel, 1862), 237.

24. ASM, Rochester; Sullivan, *Mercy Rochester*, 16.

25. Carroll, *Annals* 3: 413.

26. Ibid.; Archives, Daughters of Charity, Albany; chronicles checked by Mary Elaine Wheeler, DC, archivist.

27. Carroll, *Annals* 3: 423.

28. Matthew 28: 18–20.

29. Thomas L. Nichols, *Forty Years of American Life*, 2 (New York: Negro University Press Reprint), 123.

30. ADB, Timon Diary; Carroll, *Annals* 3: 414.

31. ASM, Rochester: Catherine McEvoy entered and became the first postulant. Certain accounts of the foundation assume that the schools did not open until the following September. In the Sullivan notes, the *Rochester Union and Advertiser* of June 22 and 29, 1857, show that the academy is already in session during the summer. Also, M. Austin Carroll, who was present as a teacher, states that the schools opened on June 9, 1857.

32. Carroll, *Annals* 3: 413. Subsequent histories referred to are those of Providence: Morgan, *Mercy in Providence*, and Sr. M. Loretto O'Connor, *Mercy Marks the Century* (Providence: Sisters of Mercy, 1951); those of Rochester: Mary Antonia Hyde, *Mercy* (Rochester: G.P. Burns, 1932) and Mary Florence Sullivan, *Mercy to Rochester*; those of Buffalo: Mary Innocentia Fitzgerald, *Sisters of Mercy in the Diocese of Buffalo* (Buffalo: Mt. Mercy, 1942) and Mary Gerald Pierce, *Unto All—His Mercy* (Buffalo: Sisters of Mercy, 1979).

33. *Boston Pilot*, July 4, 1857.

34. ADB, Timon Diary; Carroll, *Annals* 3: 412; Sullivan, *Mercy to Rochester*, 26. Sr. Anastasia Marnell returned to Hartford and served there until her death in 1865.

35. Morgan, *Mercy in Providence*, 16.

36. *Boston Pilot*, July 4, 1857; *Metropolitan Record*, Aug. 13, 1859.

37. Thomas Hughes, S.J., *History of the Society of Jesus in North America—Colonial and Federal, 1645–1773* (London: Longmans, Green, 1917) 338 and maps.

38. Thomas A. Donahue, "Diocese of Buffalo," *Catholic Church in the United States of America* 3 (New York: Catholic Editing Company, 1914), 453.

39. William P. Burke, *Clonmel*, 58–68, martyred priests were Maurice Kenrechtan, Miles McGrath, F. O'Higgins, and William O'Connor.

40. Donahue, "Buffalo," 453; O'Donnell, *Hartford*, 135.

41. Blake McKelvey, *Rochester the Flower City, 1855–1890* (Cambridge: Harvard Univ. Press, 1949), 2.

42. ASM, Rochester, Sullivan notes: candidates were Mary Corbett on June 18, Mary Ann McGarr on Oct. 5, and Ellen Tyrell on Oct. 15—all in 1857. The first profession was that of Sr. Regis Madden on June 24, and the first reception was that of Sr. M. Clare McEvoy on Sept. 8—both in 1857, nd the older novices, Srs. dePazzi Kavanagh and Raymond O'Reilly were affirmed for profession in two months.

43. Carroll, *Annals* 3: 414.

44. Fitzgerald, *Mercy Buffalo*, 33.

45. ADB, Timon Diary; ASM, Rochester.

46. Carroll, *Annals* 4: 173, Michael O'Connor to Warde, Sept. 14, 1858.

47. ADB, Timon Diary; Sr. M. Lawrence Franklin, "Brigidines in America," *Kairos* (March, April, May, 1976); Pater Leo Johnson, "American Odyssey of the Irish Brigidines," *Sale-*

sianum 39 (1944), 61–7. Timon moved the Brigidines out of St. Mary Convent in Rochester six months prior to the arrival of the Mercies and, only after the Religious of the Sacred Heart declined a transfer to the convent in St. Mary Parish did the Bishop look for Sisters of Mercy. The Brigidines were transferred very suddenly also, when they were sent from Buffalo to Medina in order to clear the convent in St. Brigid Parish for the arrival of the Mercies from Rochester.

48. ADB, Timon Diary.

49. Ibid; ASM, New York; Hyde, *Mercy*, 43, the fire destroyed the records on Jan. 2, 1916.

50. ADB, Timony Diary. The Timon Dairy and the Carroll *Annals* are the sole primary sources extant concerning the early days in Buffalo of the Rochester branch convent. Carroll says little, but the diary gives many details. Timon does not gloss over others' failures in his notes, but gives reprimands right and left for each offense or deviation from his plans. Under no condition would he have brooked, without any comment, such major defiance as a refusal of one of the nuns to stay where he assigned her. The writer finds this unsubstantiated assumption erroneous as it negates the Timon Diary.

51. Pierce, *His Mercy*, 21; and Fitzgerald, *Mercy Buffalo*, 35.

52. Carroll, *Annals* 3: 414.

53. Fitzgerald, *Mercy Buffalo*; Pierce, *His Mercy*; and Sullivan, *Mercy to Rochester* treat the union with Batavia and its filiations.

54. ASM, Rochester, Sullivan notes.

55. ADB, Timon Diary; ASM, New York. M. Agnes O'Connor of New York lent the services of M. Elizabeth Callanan reluctantly, and possibly, limited her stay to three months. It was three months to the day of the Buffalo establishment that M. Agnes O'Connor recalled M. Elizabeth Callanan. Even though she had not gone to Buffalo in February, M. Elizabeth seems to have been working in Rochester in May, for she arrived in New York, having been recalled from Rochester, On May 11, 1858.
   ADB, Timon Dairy. Timon noted that he took four sisters, but not the sister from New York, to Buffalo on Feb. 11, 1858. No names are given for the four. Tradition assumes that M. Austin Carroll was the substitute Superior, and news items from Buffalo [see nn. 48, 51] support this tradition. In April Timon refused the profession of a novice, but consented to the reception of a candidate in Buffalo. The *Boston Pilot* names the candidate being received as Mary Ann McGarr. Therefore, Buffalo is staffed by M. Austin, M. A. McGarr, and the unnamed novice, plus one more Mercy. Timon notes a week after the McGarr reception that another candidate [Teresa Tyrell] is received in Rochester. It is both possible and probable that some of the sisters assisted with the ritual and music of both the Buffalo and the Rochester ceremonies. In Buffalo Timon threatens an unnamed novice, perhaps the one whose profession was forbidden. Then Timon mentions bringing Mercies back to Buffalo from Rochester, perhaps after the reception ceremony. Tradition returns M. Austin to Rochester shortly after the McGarr reception in Buffalo — perhaps for the Tyrell reception ceremony, or three weeks later to replace Elizabeth Callanan. No date is given, but judging from the evidence presented in a series of news items [see n. 53] concerning various events in the school and convent in Rochester, it seems almost a certainty that M. Austin was serving in the South Street Convent of Mercy before the end of May in 1858. These points are belabored because Healy's *Frances Warde* made unsubstantiated assumptions concerning M. Austin Carroll and the Buffalo branch convent. Pages 126 and 304 presented conjectures as factual material.

56. Pierce, *His Mercy*, 24; *Buffalo Express*, Feb. 21, 1858.

57. Nichols, *American Life*, 136.

58. *Boston Pilot*, May 1, 1858.

59. *New York Tablet*, April 25, 1858.

60. *Boston Pilot*, May 15, 1858.

61. ADB, Timon Diary; Archives, Perryville, Timon papers. Newspapers: *Boston Pilot*, 1858: May 1, 15, June 19, 26, July 17, Sept. 25, Oct. 2, and 10; *Baltimore Mirror*, 1858: May 29, Sept. 19; Oct. 19; *New York Freeman's Journal*, 1858: May 22, June 27, July 10, Sept. 4, 11, Oct. 9, and Nov. 6.

62. *New York Freeman's Journal*, Sept. 4, 1858; *Boston Pilot*, Oct. 30, 1858.

63. *Catholic Directory*, 1858.

64. ADB, Timon Diary.

65. Mary Jerome McHale, *On the Wing* (N.Y.: Seabury, 1980), 101.

66. M. Austin Carroll spelled the name Hearne. Other sources give variously, Hearn and Heron. Sister M. Baptist Hearn served as superior 1868–1871.

67. McHale, *On the Wing*, 101; Pierce, *His Mercy*, 25.

68. ASM, Manchester and New Orleans. The exact date of M. Austin Carroll's return to M. Xavier Warde is not extant, nor is it clear that she was assigned to Rochester for just two years. Recorded are two facts: in 1859 M. Xavier Warde sent a letter requesting help in Manchester; and M. Austin Carroll answered this call in time to be teaching in Manchester in the fall semester of 1859.

69. *N.Y. Metropolitan Record*, Aug. 13, 1859.

70. ASM, N.O., Austin Carroll Papers. Letters seeking information about Catherine McAuley went out to Ireland in the name of M. Xavier Warde, but penned in the hand of her secretary, M. Austin Carroll. Several of the Irish chronicles referred to the *Life of Catherine McAuley* by M. Austin Carroll as the M. F. Xavier Warde biography.

NOTES – CHAPTER FOUR

1. ADB, Timon Diary.

2. AANO, Byrne to Blanc, Dec. 3, 1857; Carroll, *Annals* 4: 128.

3. *Catholic Directory*, 1858; Carroll, *Annals* 4: 222.

4. Thomas S. Duggan, *Catholic Church in Connecticut* (N.Y.: State History Co., 1930), 622.

5. Carroll, *Annals* 4: 159.

6. ASM, Manchester/Windham, N.H. (hereafter cited as Windham).

7. *N.Y. Freeman's Journal*, Aug. 7, 1858.

8. ASM, Windham; Carroll, *Annals* 4: 167.

9. AAO, Warde to O'Connor, June 13, 1860.

10. Carroll, *Annals* 4, chap. 19–30.

11. N.O. *Morning Star*, Sept. 1885; Carroll, *Annals* 4, chap. 21.

12. Carroll, "A Valiant Soldier of the Cross," *Irish Monthly* 13 (Nov. 1885): 602.

13. C. E. Potter, *History of Manchester* (Manchester: Potter Publishers, 1855), 737.

14. Carroll, *Annals* 4: 169.

15. AAO, Carroll to O'Connor, Warde to O'Connor; ASM, Windham, Carroll to Warde and O'Brien.

16. Nichols, *American Life*, 110.

17. Mary Catherine Garety, *Memoir of Mother Mary Gonzaga O'Brien* (Manchester: Magnificat Press, 1920), 23.

18. ASM, Windham, Carroll to O'Brien, Sept. 14, 1855.

19. Carroll, *Catherine McAuley*. appendix, 473–93.

20. ASM, Carlow, Carroll to Catherine Maher, Sept. 13, 1877.

21. AAO, Carroll to O'Connor, Jan. 10, 1882.

22. Carroll, *Catherine McAuley*, 14; ASM, Silver Spring Md. (earlier housed at Bethesda, Md.), photocopies of the Derry, Dublin, and Bermondsey manuscripts.

23. The Byrn manuscript, like most of Austin Carroll's source materials, is no longer extant, having been burned sometime after her death in Mobile, Ala.

24. ASM, Silver Spring, photocopies of Catherine McAuley's letters and the originals of many; Carroll, *Catherine McAuley*, 14.

25. ASM, Limerick and Ennis; Hartnett, *Mother McAuley*.

26. [Myles Gaffney], *Dublin Review* 22 (March 1847), 1–25; Dominick Murphy, "Life of Miss Nano Nagle," *Dublin Review* 15 (Dec. 1843), 363–86; Dominick Murphy, *Sketches of Irish Nunneries* (Dublin: James Duffy, 1865) contains the author's collection of materials concerning Irish foundresses. The section on Catherine McAuley incorporates both the 1847 *Dublin Review* article in large part and selections from the Vincent Hartnett biography of Catherine McAuley. The Dean explained in his Preface that much of the material had already "been before the public," and that was considered a sufficient acknowledgement at the time for the incorporation of material gathered together from many sources.

27. ASM, Bermondsey, chronicles.

28. Matthew Russell, SJ, *Irish Monthly* 9 (Dec. 1881): 668.

29. [Gaffney], *Dublin Review* 22 (March 1847); Hartnett, *Mother McAuley*, 90; Carroll, *Catherine McAuley*, 436.

30. A comparative study of the internal evidence was made by this researcher to check the work of Dr. Patrick Murray, Dean Dominick Murphy, and Dean Miletius Gaffney (or Myles Gaffney) against the internal evidence in the 1847 article. There were no similarities with the work of either Dr. Murray or Dean Murphy. There were similarities in vocabulary, phraseology and in material covered in the rather limited work of Gaffney that was available. One item is the

letter of his after the death of Catherine McAuley, and there were sections of sermons delivered at reception and profession ceremonies at Tullamore in August of 1836 and at Naas in September of 1841. The sermons had been quoted in Irish papers and reprinted in Catholic papers in the United States. Some of the reprint items were not attributed to a particular source, but the Naas news came from the *Dublin Register* with no date quoted. The *Irish and Catholic Sentinel*, later the *Boston Pilot* and the *New York Freeman's Journal* were generous in their columns of Irish News. The *Boston Pilot* of November 13, 1841 carried part of the Gaffney sermon from the Naas event. The internal evidence agrees strongly with the 1881 conclusion of Matthew Russell that Gaffney was the author of the 1847 article.

31. ASM, Carlow, Carroll to Catherine Maher, April 10, 1878.

32. ASM, Windham and N.O.

33. Carroll, *Annals* 4: 170, 172.

34. ATUL, Cable Papers, Carroll to Cable, Sept. 16, 1882.

35. Carroll, *Annals* 3: 276; *Annals* 4: 82.

36. ADJ, Elder papers; Elder had tried to obtain religious teachers for Vicksburg from the Sisters of Charity of Nazareth, the Sisters of St. Joseph, the Sisters of Mercy in Baltimore, and again from the Sisters of Charity and Mercy. With these attempts unsuccessful, Elder commissioned Reverent Mathurin F. Grignon to try to obtain religious teachers in Ireland. Before he left the United States, however, Father Grignon stopped in Baltimore and Archbishop Francis Patrick Kenrick instructed the Sisters of Mercy there to allow some of their number to make the new foundation in Vicksburg, Mississippi.

37. Carroll, *Annals*, 4: 190.

38. ASM, Merion or Philadelphia (hereafter cited as Merion), New York, and Birmingham, England, Mother M. Patricia Waldron was brought to Manchester to be Mistress of Novices and was accompanied by Sisters Mary deSales Geraghty, Philomena Hughes, both of whom were assigned to Philadelphia with Patricia Waldron, and with Ignatius Lynch and Anne Fahey, who were assigned to Omaha. Sister M. Gertrude Ledwith was invited to Manchester to be assigned as superior inn Philadelphia. Sister Gertrude had received her Certificate of Merit in June, 1855, while serving in Wolverhampton and was accompanied to Manchester by Sister Evangelist Kidgell.

39. AAO, O'Reilly to Michael O'Connor, Nov. 7, 1855; Warde to Michael O'Connor, April 23, 1856; idem to James O'Connor, Oct. 28, 1861; Carroll, *Annals* 4: 173; Michael O'Connor to Warde, Sept. 14, 1858.

40. ASM, Windham, Merion, and N.Y.; Carroll, *Annals* 4: 190.

41. Healy, *Frances Warde*, 288.

42. AAO, Warde to James O'Connor, Oct. 28, 1861; ASM, N.Y. and Cincinnati; Michael O'Connor, SJ to Teresa Maher, Dec. 1, 1870. This letter shows that Michael O'Connor is still urging some type of union or federation on the Sisters of Mercy, just as he had done twenty years earlier. See Carroll, *Annals* 4: 304, where Michael O'Connor's preference for branches rather than foundations as well as his urging of union is mentioned in the *Annals* for the third time.

43. Carroll, *Annals* 3: 177-9.

44. Nichols, *American Life*, 299.

45. *Brownson's Quarterly Review* (July 1873): 405.

46. *Catholic Directory 1860*, ad dated July 30, 1859, "Sisters of Mercy ... to open an academy for young ladies on the first of Sept. next;" *Western Banner*, Oct. 8, 1859.

47. *Compilation of the Records of the Union and Confederate Armies* 1: 356. The orders were given to drive from their homes those who refused to take an oath of allegiance. These wives, mothers, children, and grandparents of soldiers in the Confederate forces felt that they could not take the oath in honesty even though they understood the dire consequences. The church in Fernandina was looted, vestments and chalice stolen in Aug. 1862; the church in Jacksonville was looted and then burned in May 1862.

48. Carroll, *Annals* 4: 334–45.

49. Michael V. Gannon, *Rebel Bishop: the Life and Era of Augustin Verot* (Milwaukee: Bruce, 1964), 66.

50. Carroll, *Annals* 4: 77, 344.

51. ASM, Windham, Carroll to O'Brien, April 2, 1895.

52. Carroll, *Annals* 4: 190.

53. *Catholic Directory*, 1855–1861, 1864–1865; *Catholic Directory 1864*, "The Catholic public have been without their annual ... the last two years."

54. Carroll, *Annals* 4: 190.

55. Henry W. Casper, SJ, *History of the Catholic Church in Nebraska*, vol. 1 1838–1874, vol. 2 1864–1910 (Milwaukee: Bruce, 1960, 1966), 2: 60 (hereafter cited as *History Nebraska* 1 or 2). John Rush corroborates the statement in the *Annals* that M. F. Xavier Warde promised Sisters for the Omaha foundation in 1863, and he gives the additional fact that a "prerequisite" was a convent building.

56. *Catholic Directory*, 1864–1865.

57. ASM, Windham, financial records.

58. Casper, *History Nebraska* 1, Chapters "Manpower and Money" and "Building and Builders" give the financial picture. The writer wishes to express her indebtedness to Father Casper for his wealth of information.

59. AAO, Ryan to O'Gorman, June 3, 1864; Warde to O'Gorman, July 16, 1864.

60. ASM, Windham, Omaha, and N.O.; *Boston Pilot* May 31, 1861; *New York Freeman's Journal*, July 9, 1859; Casper, *History Nebraska* 2: 69–72.

61. ASM, Windham, Omaha, Laredo, and Slaton, Texas.

62. ASM, Windham and Omaha; Carroll, *Annals* 4: 191.

63. AAO, Warde to O'Gorman, Aug. 12, 1864.

64. Carroll, *Annals* 4: 192.

65. Carroll, *Annals* 4: 192, 190–201. Austin Carroll provided a dozen pages dealing with the trip from Manchester to Omaha and the early days of the foundation. Since Austin Carroll was in the group which made this trip, her eyewitness account is of primary value and this writer uses the dates and data as they are found in the Carroll *Annals* whenever they differ from such later Mercy accounts as those of Mary Madeleine O'Flaherty, *Early days of the Mercy order in*

Omaha (Omaha: Srs. of Mercy); *Sisters of Mercy, 1831-1931* (Omaha: Roncka Brothers, 1931); Mary Edmund Croghan, *Sisters of Mercy in Nebraska, 1864-1910* (Washington, D.C.: Catholic University of America Press, 1942); Healy, *Frances Warde*. Although it would seem more logical to have appropriated the chronology of events, Healy and O'Flaherty adopted portions of vivid descriptions from the Carroll *Annals*, but rejected the Carroll time schedule.

66. *St. Louis Democrat* 1864, Aug. 29; Sept. 2; Sept. 5; Sept. 8; and Sept. 13.

67. Carroll, *Annals* 4: 191-2.

68. Ibid., 192-3.

69. Ibid., 194-5.

70. O'Flaherty, *Mercy Order in Omaha*.

71. *St. Louis Guardian*, May 18, 1867.

72. Carroll, *Annals* 4: 195.

73. *St. Louis Guardian*, May 18, 1867.

74. ASM Omaha, *Omaha Nebraskan*, Oct. 24, 1864.

75. Croghan, *Mercy in Nebraska*, 16.

76. Casper, *History Nebraska* 2: 79.

77. AAO, Carroll to O'Connor, Oct. 25, 1876.

78. Ibid.; ASM, Windham, O'Gorman to Warde, Jan. 22, 1865; AAO, Carroll to O'Connor, Oct. 25, 1876. Carroll related that Bishop O'Gorman had told her that her popularity with the students and their parents had caused such jealousy in Ignatius that Austin was slandered. Ill will was engendered strongly enough to cause O'Gorman to permit Austin to transfer to St. Louis. O'Gorman explained to Austin that Ignatius and another sister could not bear that she "should succeed where they failed."

79. ASM, Windham, O'Gorman to Warde, Aug. 26, 1864; Carroll, *Annals* 4: 198. Austin Carroll never lost interest in the Nebraska foundation. She continued for years to correspond with the bishop, pray for the success of the works of the Mercy community, and share the sufferings dealt the sisters by Ignatius.

80. ASM, Omaha; Casper, *History Nebraska* 1: 226.

81. ASM, Windham and Omaha. Ignatius Lynch transferred from Ballinrobe to Manchester to Xavier Warde in 1861; was named superior of the Omaha foundation by Warde in 1864; lived in Omaha 1864-1878; in Yankton, N.D., 1878-1887; outside the community 1887-1898; and in Devil's Lake, N.D., 1898-1919, where she died on July 24, 1919.

82. AAO, Carroll to O'Connor, Oct. 25, 1876; Casper, *History Nebraska* 2: 71-72.

83. Casper, *History Nebraska* 2: 69-72 (subtitles are *The Church on the Northern Plains, 1838-1874*, vol.1, and *The Church on the Fading Frontier*, 1864-1910, vol.2).

84. Ibid., 2: 73.

85. Ibid., 72.

86. ASM, St. Louis and N.O., Austin Carroll Papers.

87. Austin Carroll school dramas: *Marie Antoinette* (N.Y.: Catholic Publication Society Co., 1880); *Mary Beatrice and Her Step-Daughters* (N.Y.: Catholic Publication Society Co., 1881): *The Tudor Sisters* (New Orleans: T. Fitzwilliam, 1883); *Scenes from the Life of Katharine of Aragon* (New Orleans: T. Fitzwilliam, 1885); Carroll edited *Four Days in the Life of Mary Queen of Scots* (New Orleans: T. Fitzwilliam, 1882).

88. ASM, Omaha, *Cincinnati Catholic Telegraph*, n.d.

89. Croghan, *Mercy in Nebraska*, the writer wishes to acknowledge her indebtedness to the collection of data amassed by Mary Edmund Croghan concerning the convent and environs of the Mercies in Omaha. At the same time, the writer agrees with the Casper assessment of the partiality shown. See *History Nebraska* 2: 69, note 27.

90. ASM, Silver Spring, Carroll to Ihmsen, Oct. 31, 1886.

91. ASM, Omaha, St. Louis, and N.O. the exact date when the boat left the wharf in Omaha is not available, but it was Sept. 3, 1865, when the boat reached the landing on the Mississippi River for the city of St. Louis. According to the tradition of the older Mercies, accompanying Austin Carroll and her companion was the Reverend Patrick John Ryan, the Secretary of the Archbishop of St. Louis, the Most Reverend Peter Richard Kenrick. Some records have confused this Father Ryan with the Reverend James M. Ryan who escorted the Sisters of Mercy through Missouri and into Omaha a year earlier.

NOTES—CHAPTER FIVE

1. ASM, Savannah and Vicksburg.

2. Ibid.; Carroll, *Annals* 3: 368. *Santa Rosa News*, June 15, 1863: salt $85 per sack and flour $85 per barrel.

3. ASM, Savannah, and N.O.

4. Ibid.; Gannon, *Rebel Bishop*, chap. 4, "The Living and the Dead." The Bishops were Francis Xavier Gartland, the first Bishop of Savannah, and the Bishop Edward Barron, both martyrs for yellow-fever victims.

5. Carroll, *Annals* 3: 383.

6. *N.Y. Metropolitan Record*, Nov. 19, 1864, Odin to M. J. Spalding, Sept. 7, 1864; Verot to M. J. Spalding, Mar. 15, 1865.

7. ADB, Timon diary mentions the two $500 gifts from the Vatican.

8. Carroll, *Annals* 3: 148-9.

9. ASM, N.Y.; the Sisters of Mercy arrived in New York in 1846; Dublin sent three more sisters on Nov. 14, 1850; and two more on the *Henry Clay* on Nov. 11, 1851—one of these being the delicate novice, Mary dePazzi Bentley.

10. ASM, New York and Providence, Sister Mary Catherine Seton sang in Providence at a reception on Aug. 20, 1851, and at a profession on Aug. 22, 1853.

11. ASM, Dublin, O'Connor to Marmion, Nov. 1846.

12. *Catholic Directory 1856*, 176; ibid., 1857, 194.

13. ASM, N.Y., chronicles.

14. Mary Constance Smith, *A Sheaf of Golden Years* (N.Y.: Benziger Brothers, 1906); Mary Isidore Lennon, *Milestones of Mercy* (Milwaukee: Bruce, 1957).

15. ASM, N.Y. and St. Louis. Mary Farrell entered the Convent of Mercy in St. Louis on July 30, 1856. Returning to New York were Sisters Mary Jerome Shubrick on May 30, 1860; M. Aloysius Comerford on June 26, 1865; and Elizabeth Callanan on Sept. 29, 1860. M. Elizabeth Callanan has been mistakenly listed as having been a founding member of the Mercy community in St. Louis. This can not be correct because she did not leave New York for St. Louis until Sept. 5, 1858, according to the New York chronicles, and she is first listed in the St. Louis annals on Sept. 8, 1858.

16. ASM, New York and St. Louis, Postulant Mary Grant was received as Sr. M. Catherine in New York on Aug. 21, 1857, and sent to Mother dePazzi Bentley five days later. Accompanying her on Aug. 26, was Postulant Anna Walker, who was received in St. Louis as Sr. M. Ignatius in 1858.

17. Sister Mary Austin Carroll arrived at St. Joseph Convent of Mercy in St. Louis on Sept. 5, 1865, and was accepted as a member of the St. Louis community on Oct. 14, 1865.

18. AAO, Warde to O'Gorman, July 16, 1864.

19. Lennon, *Milestones of Mercy*, 19.

20. ASM, St. Louis, P.R. Kenrick to Bentley, Aug. 19, 1861.

21. Carroll, *Catherine McAuley*, 13.

22. ASM, Dublin; Gaffney, *Dublin Review* 22 (March 1847): 2.

23. Carroll, *Catherine McAuley*, 13.

24. Hartnett, *Mother McAuley*, 3.

25. ASM, Dublin.

26. Carroll, *Catherine McAuley*, 13.

27. John Francis Maguire, *The Irish in America* (London: Longmans, Green, 1868), 363.

28. ASM, N.O., Austin Carroll Papers, clippings of newspaper and periodical books reviews, including references to those from the *St. Louis Guardian*, Feb. 2, 1867; the *Catholic World*, March, 1867; and several unidentified clippings.

29. *The Irish Monthly* 9 (Oct. 1881): 668.

30. ASM, Limerick.

31. Carroll, *Catherine McAuley*, 115-9; ASM, Dublin, Derry, and Bermondsey. The anger of William Macauley on the evening in question was aimed first at his eldest daughter Mary Catherine, because of her conversion to Catholicism, the religion of her aunt. Possibly, Catherine McAuley told William of his wife's deathbed conversion as much to distract his anger from his daughter as to support the girl in her decision to follow her mother into the Catholic Church. According to the manuscript accounts by the early companions of the Mercy foundress, when the infuriated father went upstairs to get a weapon, the servants hid the daughter downstairs and helped Catherine to escape. After Catherine fled down the road to find safety with friends, the servants bolted the doors in order to delay the enraged master of the house if he attempted to pursue Catherine. Many minor details differ in the various

accounts, but the fury of the reaction remains the same. Since the incident occurred late in the evening, baby Willie along with the youngest Byrn child, were most likely upstairs being readied for bed. Both denied the event. The eldest Byrn cousin also denied the incident occurred, but she was in Dublin and evidently had not been informed of the matter by the persons concerned. Since this entire incident was contained in the Vincent Hartnett biography of the Mercy foundress in 1864, it is strange that some sisters were upset that Austin Carroll retold the story in 1866.

32. Sr. M. Francis Clare Cusack, *The Nun of Kenmare* (Boston: Ticknow, 1889), 20. Sister Francis Clare, nee Margaret Anna Cusack, spent several years residing with her family in the same large house to which Catherine McAuley fled for shelter. The mansion was Abbeyville, the home of her father's brother, the famous surgeon Sir William Cusack. Hence, it seems highly unlikely that Margaret Anna Cusack would not have had the correct information. According to a recent historical study, the Douglas S. Appleyard *Green Fields Gone Forever* (Dublin: Coolock Select Vestry, 1985), 133, the Cusack family continued until the twentieth century, to reside in the same magnificent Abbeyville House just down the road "past Kinsealy and Watery Lane," not too distant from the home which once was that of William Macauley.

33. Carroll, *Catherine McAuley*, 79, note, "We have learned indirectly that in the first edition of this work, there was some erroneous statement. ... We have suppressed the statements ... but cannot rectify them, because we have received no communication from the gentleman's descendants." Austin gathered data tirelessly for a decade from those who had known Catherine McAuley personally. True, some of the relatives never responded, but Austin had also written to friends and each Sister of Mercy who had known the foundress. Thus Austin had as correspondents numerous individuals, the authors of the early manuscripts among them, who served as her primary sources even though to find them, she had reached across the ocean via the none-to-quick postal service. Those who answered formed a wealth of links in the long chain of research upon which both the life of the Mercy foundress and the later Mercy *Annals* were based.

34. Mother M. T. Austin Carroll to Sister M. Gonzaga O'Brien, Feb. 20, 1886.

35. *Brownson's Quarterly Review*, 1 in series 6 (July 1873): 399–409.

36. Ibid.

37. *New York Freeman's Journal*, July 5, 1856.

38. Ibid.

39. ASM, N.Y.; AAO, Carroll to O'Connor, Aug. 20, 1877.

40. ASM, Windham, Warde to O'Connor, [April] 23, 1856.

41. Carroll to O'Connor, Aug. 20, 1877.

42. Ibid., April 9, 1881.

43. ASM, Dublin, O'Connor to Marmion, April 22, 1846.

44. AAO, Warde to Reverend James O'Connor, [April] 23, 1856.

45. Healy, *Frances Warde*, 274.

46. deSmet, SJ, to Beckx, SJ, May 13, 1856, quoted in Joseph P. Conroy, SJ, *Arnold Damen, SJ*, a *Chapter in the Making of Chicago* (New York: Benziger Brothers, 1930), 47.

47. Ibid., 46.

48. Lennon, *Milestones of Mercy*, 27.

49. ASM, St. Louis, Kenrick to Bentley, May 7, 1860.

50. ASM, St. Louis, Kinsale, N.O.; ACPF, Rome, 1875.

51. ASM, Carlow, Cork, Charleville, Dublin. The Derry Manuscript states that the foundress opened a pension school for young ladies at Baggot Street in the spring of 1830. Because there were only a few pupils, it was closed later the same year.

52. AAO, Carroll to O'Connor, Aug. 20, 1877.

53. AAO, O'Callaghan to Whom It May Concern, Dec. 17, 1883.

54. Carroll to Maguire, June 3, 1867, in John Francis Maguire, *Irish in America* (London: Longmans, Greene, 1868), 363.

55. Carroll, *Annals* 4: 402; ASM, N.Y., St. Louis, and N.O.

56. ASM, N.O., Rochester, St. Louis; Carroll, *Annals* 4: 493.

57. ASM, St. Louis, register; Carroll, *Annals* 4: 496.

58. Carroll, *Catherine McAuley*, 196.

59. Carroll, *Annals* 4, chap. 9, 10, 32, 35.

60. Carroll, *Annals* 3, chap. 26, 38, 46.

61. AUND, Odin to Propagation of the Faith, Feb. 28, 1862; *Boston Pilot*, April 14, 1866.

62. *St. Louis Watchman*, Sept. 4, 1869.

63. ASM, N.O., Austin Carroll Papers, unidentified clipping.

64. Carroll, Foreword, 13–57.

65. Ibid., 13–15, 23.

66. Ibid., 19, 18–20.

67. Ibid., 53–54, 25.

68. Ibid., 54.

69. ASM, St. Louis, Vicksburg, and N.O.; Carroll, *Annals* 4: 356–7.

70. Jean Batiste Saint Jure, SJ, trans by Carroll: *A Treatise on the Knowledge and Love of Our Lord Jesus Christ* 3v (N.Y.: P. O'Shea, 1868, 1869, 1872); *L'Homme Spirituel: or the Spiritual Life Reduced to Its First Principals* (N.Y.: P. O'Shea, 1878); and *The Religious: A Treatise on the Vows and Virtues of the Religious State* (N.Y.: P. O'Shea c 1877). In the 1870s publisher's ads placed at the conclusion of many works as an addenda, the three titles listed above are listed "by the same translater, the author of the *Life of Catherine McAuley.*" Austin Carroll's translation must have been burned in the O'Shea fire which destroyed part of his publishing house. The earliest copy located was copyrighted in 1881 by the Sisters of Mercy in St. Louis. The preface mentions that the manuscript was given to the publisher in 1872, was destroyed in the fire, and had to be redone.

71. Maguire, *Irish in America*, 363.

NOTES — CHAPTER SIX

1. Carroll, *Annals* 4: 356.

2. AANO, Byrne to Blanc, Dec. 3, 1857.

3. AANO, J. Moynihan to Blanc, June 28, 1860. [The sender in Kanturk, Co. Cork, could not have heard that the archbishop had died in New Orleans on June 20.] *Philadelphia Catholic Standard*, Oct. 28, 1860, the buildings purchased for the convent faced Magazine Street between Girod and the site opposite Notre Dame Street, was back to back with St. Patrick's Church, and had a gateway opening into the yard on the downtown side of the church. Rev. John Flanagan had invested some of his own money in the project, but it was to house the Good Shepherd Sisters before it finally became a convent of Mercy in 1871. *New Orleans Daily Picayune*, Aug. 25, 1861, described the convent at the time of the fire.

4. ASM, Vicksburg, St. Louis and New Orleans.

5. ASM, Vicksburg. Candidates from New Orleans were Augustine Assent, Marie Betz, Mary Connaughton, Margaret Harrington, Amelia and Margaret Hoey, Anne Keller, Teresa Kessel, Bridget Murphy, and Amelia and Ameniade Poursine.

6. Carroll, *Annals* 4: 556–7.

7. Carroll, *Annals* 4: 357–8.

8. AAO, Carroll to O'Connor, Jan. 9, 1869.

9. AANO, Odin to Walker, Feb. 5, 1869.

10. Carroll, *Annals* 4: 358; ASM, New Orleans.

11. Ibid., 359.

12. ASM, N.Y., St. Louis, and N.O. Three members of the same family were received into the Mercy community in New York in 1857, Agnes, Mary, and Jane Grant. Agnes was received as Mary Aloysius on Feb. 19, Mary as M. Catherine on Aug. 21, and Jane as M. Ignatius on Dec. 18, 1857. M. Catherine, who was exceedingly delicate, was not professed in New York. She was sent to St. Louis where she was chaptered for profession on June 21, 1859. She was to live barely two years in New Orleans, while both of her sisters would serve for sixty-five years in the Mercy community in New York.

13. ASM, St. Louis and N.O., registers. Bridget McDermott entered in 1862, was received in 1863, was professed in 1865 as M. Magdalene dePazzi, and died of cholera on Aug. 15, 1866. Catherine mcDermott entered in 1864, was received as M. Xavier on Oct. 18, 1864, and professed her vows on Jan. 23, 1867. She was to die of yellow fever in New Orleans on Nov. 11, 1870.

14. ASM, St. Louis and N.O., registers. Mary Farrell or O'Farrell entered as a lay candidate in 1856, was received as Sr. Francis in 1857, and professed her vows Feb. 2, 1859. Margaret Lucas entered in St. Louis in 1866, was received in St. Louis on may 8, 1867 as M. Camillus, and was professed by M. Catherine Grant in New Orleans in Aug., 1869.

15. ASM, N.O. register. Eliza Shields entered as a lay candidate in St. Louis on Mar. 13, 1869, was received as Sister Benedicta in New Orleans on Oct. 19, 1869, and died of yellow fever just a year later, on Nov. 4, 1870.

16. Carroll, *Annals* 4: 359–60.

17. Ibid.

18. Ibid.

19. Ibid.

20. *New Orleans Times*, Mar. 9, 1869.

21. ASM, St. Louis; Carroll, *Annals* 4: 361.

22. Ibid.

23. ASM, St. Louis, chronicles.

24. *Boston Pilot*, April 10, 1869; *Western Watchman*, Mar. 27, 1869.

25. Carroll, *Annals* 4: 361-2; E. W. Gould, *History of River Navigation* (St. Louis: Nixon-Jones, 1889), 542. The distance along the Mississippi River from New Orleans to St. Louis lessened more than fifty miles between 1860 and 1890, as the river channel cut through the oxbows at annual spring overflow season, thus shortening the route at regular intervals and leaving towns and plantations on the shore of a lake instead of the bank of the river.

26. William M. Lytle et al, *Merchant Steam Vessels of the United States, 1790-1868*, N.Y.: Steamship Historical Society, 1975), 147; Nichols, *American Life*, 245.

27. Carroll, *Annals* 4: 362-4.

28. Ibid., 364-5.

29. Ibid., 365.

30. ASM, N.O., Carroll, *Annals* 4: 365.

31. Ibid.

32. Ibid., 364-7.

33. Carroll, *Catholic History of Alabama and the Floridas* (N.Y.: P. J. Kenedy & Sons, 1908.)

34. Carroll, *Annals* 4: 366-7; photograph of the *Mollie Able* in the Historic N.O. Collection.

35. Gould, *River Navigation*, 732-7.

36. Carroll, *Annals* 4:366.

37. ASM, Vicksburg and N.O. The account of the visit in the Carroll *Annals* is heavy with the graciousness of the hospitality in Vicksburg. Mary Aquinas O'Donohue, in *Sisters of Mercy in Texas*, quotes one of the Mississippi Mercies stating that there was not enough food for all because *Mollie Able* had been expected earlier in the day, not at noon. Austin Carroll mentioned no shortages as she is consistent in glossing over any imperfections when she is receiving hospitality.

38. Carroll, *Annals* 4: 366-8.

39. ASM, N.O., Austin Carroll Papers, fragmentary notes made by her on the *Mollie Able*.

40. Carroll, *Annals* 4: 367-8. During the French Colonial period in Louisiana, natives of Germany were settled along the Mississippi River above New Orleans, and because of that settlement the area was entitled *la cote des Allemands*.

41. Carroll, *Annals* 4: 368–9. The bibliography of Mother Austin Carroll's periodical articles lists a number of titles which concern French and Spanish Colonial history, explorers, and leaders.

42. ASM, New Orleans; Carroll, *Annals* 4: 366–9. The books presented to the captain were the first two volumes of St. Jure's *Love of Our Lord Jesus Christ*, which Austin Carroll had translated from the French.

43. William Glazier, *Down the Great River* (Philadelphia: Hubbard, 1887), 421.

44. Nichols, *American Life*, 181–2.

45. Carroll, *Annals* 4: 368–9.

46. Ibid., Captains Able, Badger, and Leavenworth were of special help on the levee.

47. The suburb, according to James A. Renshaw's "Lost City of Lafayette," *Louisiana Historical Quarterly* 2 (Jan. 1919): 47, had been incorporated in 1833 as the City of Lafayette, but became the Fourth District of New Orleans two decades later.

48. Mrs. Horrell and Mrs. Turner were the two ladies who prepared and served the lunch.

49. Carroll, *Annals* 4: 370.

50. ASM, N.O., register. Mary Lewis entered Sept. 18, 1870, was received as Sr. Alphonsine on Mar. 19, 1871, and was professed on Mar. 19, 1873. After sixty years of service she died on Feb. 27, 1930. Mademoiselle Marie Mathilde Gourrier entered on Aug. 24, 1869, was received as Sr. M. Teresa in Notre Dame de Bon Secours Church on Jackson Avenue, professed her vows in the chapel of the convent on St. Andrew Street, served as principal of the French School until her final illness, and died on June 29, 1886. There might be a need to clarify the meaning of "creole," which does not mean a person of mixed race, as a mulatto would be. Marie Mathilde was a creole because she was born in Louisiana, or native-born according to the native understanding as explained in *L'Abeille*, May 19, 1839. Marie Mathilde had paternal ancestry from France and a maternal line that joined Acadian refugees with Spanish officials in Colonial times. Gourrier genealogical data was acquired through correspondence with Mrs. Roland Daigre and Mrs. Sherbourne Anderson, descendants of Marie Mathilde's nine brothers.

51. Marie Mathilde's father, Dr. André Theophile Melchior Gourrier, as a young medical doctor, left France for Louisiana, where he married Marie Mathilde Landry in Ascension Parish (civil parish or county) and later moved to St. James Parish where their daughter was born. From St. James Parish on the German Coast, Dr. Gourrier occasionally accompanied Bp. Odin, the vicar apostolic of Texas, in his missionary journeys across the vast vicariat in order to provide medical care to isolated farm communities and ranches.

52. ASM, N.O., minutes. Abp. Odin "appointed Rev. Henry Giesen, CSSR, Rector of the Redemptorists, as Ecclesiastical Superior of the Sisters of Mercy under His Grace's jurisdiction." At the time it was the custom for each congregation of religious women to have an appointed director. This arrangement could be helpful for the sisters when the priest-director was not only interested in the welfare of the sisters, but also had the ability to remain apart from the internal affairs of the community. Unfortunately, many directors tended to interfere in the acceptance of candidates or the government of the community to the detriment of the peace of the individual sister and of the integrity of the Rule, already approved by Rome.

53. *Catholic Directory 1870*. The congregations and orders have been arranged in the chronological order of their arrival in the diocese. The religious men were listed as follows: the Jesuits,

the Vincentians, "the Salvatorists" or Holy Cross priests and brothers, the Redemptorists, the Brothers of Mary, the Brothers of Christian Schools, and the Brothers of the Sacred Heart.

54. ASM, N.O., the sisters first visited the sick on Thursday, April 1, 1869, the day on which the archbishop gave his formal blessing on the work. The first to be visited were Mrs. Castell, a native of Ireland, and the second, Marie Paul, a black.

55. ASM, N.O. Austin Carroll paid the first Mercy visit to Orleans Parish Prison, the City House of Detention, and the Almshouse on April 24, 1869.

56. Carroll, *Annals* 4: 372.

57. France, Belgium, and Canada have some twenty or so chapels dedicated to Notre Dame de Bon Secours, many of them being ancient shrines of pilgrimage.

58. ASM, N.O.; Carroll, *Annals* 4: 372.

59. Byron J. Krieger, *Seventy-Five Years of Service* (St. Louis: Bechtold, 1923); *One Hundred Years in New Orleans* (New Orleans: Redemptorists, 1944); *The Corner Stone* (New Orleans: St. Alphonsus Parish, 1955).

60. AUND, Kundeck to Midde, 1944; papers of the Leopoldine Society of Vienna.

61. Krieger, *One Hundred Years*, 8, 13, 14.

62. Renshaw, "City of Lafayette," 47-55.

63. *N.O. Morning Star*, Jan. 28, 1883, quoted Ferreol Girardey, CSSR, stating that he was present for the opening day "of St. Alphonsus permanent schoolhouse" on Aug. 26, 1853. Constance Street had been entitled earlier St. Azélie, and later Live Oak.

64. Bp. Blanc had been elevated as the first archbishop of New Orleans in 1850; Krieger, *One Hundred Years*, 10-11.

65. Krieger, *The Corner Stone*, 21-2. Abp. Blanc was assisted by Bishops Elder of Natchez, Odin of Galveston, and Portier of Mobile. ASM, New Orleans.

66. Krieger, *One Hundred Years*, 11-12.

67. Ibid., 17-18, 22; Krieger, *Seventy-Five Years*, 64.

68. Carroll, *Annals* 4: 377.

69. ASM, N.O. Marie Mathilde Gourrier became a postulant on Aug. 24, 1869; was received as Mary Teresa on Feb. 24, 1870; and professed her vows on Feb. 13, 1872.

70. Carroll, *Annals* 4: 377-8, 391.

71. *N.O. Times*, June 18, 1869.

72. ASM, N.O. The helpers were Mary Ignatius Grant, Alphonsus Curry, Mary Massey, and Bridget O'Malley.

73. ASM, N.O. The three sisters from New York City and one from St. Louis arrived in June 1869 to aid the New Orleans community for a year, as described in *Annals* 4: 395. They remained two years, then returned home as a number of efficient members had entered the New Orleans community by that time.

74. Carroll, *Annals* 4: 391-5; *N.O. Daily Picayune*, Nov. 4, 1898.

75. Carroll, *Annals* 4: 392, 395, 391, 392, 394, 393 [in the sequence quoted].

NOTES — CHAPTER SEVEN

1. Carroll, "Cross in the South," *Irish Monthly* 11 (Aug. 1883): 504.

2. *N.O. Crescent*, March 30, 1869, daily weather reports.

3. Carroll, *Irish Monthly* 11: 504. Wealthy families of New Orleans maintained summer homes "across the lake," either on the Gulf Coast or along the north shore of Lake Pontchartrain. The poor did not leave the city, but generally became acclimated to the annual fevers.

4. ASM, N.O., minutes

5. ASM, Vicksburg; ADJ, Browne to Elder, April 1869.

6. *N.O. Morning Star*, March 6, 1870.

7. Ibid.

8. ASM, N.O., register. Among the 1870 postulants were Ellen Butler, who alternated with her friend Austin Carroll as superior for several terms, and Mary Devereux who also served as superior. Many of the others, women of discretion, served for a time on the Mercy governing board, which was officially termed the "council of discreets."

9. French-born Napoleon Joseph Perché, ordained in 1829, came to the United States as a missionary and served first in Kentucky, then transferred to New Orleans to serve with Bishop Antoine Blanc. It was in 1842, as chaplain for the Ursuline nuns, that Perché started the Catholic weekly, *Le Propagateur Catholique*, and used the power of the press to assist Blanc in his opposition to the marguilliers who attempted to usurp Church authority and property. His work continued during the tenure of Abp. Odin, who obtained Perché as his coadjutor in 1870. Fortunately, Perché had been consecrated as Bishop of Abdera on May 1, 1870, twenty-four days prior to the death of Odin.

10. *N.O. Morning Star*, April 10, May 1, 1870.

11. ASM, N.Y., St. Louis, and N.O., chronicles and minutes. Catherine Grant's health had always been delicate — in Ireland, New York, and St. Louis. The climate in New Orleans was difficult for her diseased lungs, and she presented a list of complaints or differences to the archbishop. This list has not been located, but minutes mention interference in community affairs and a complaint about the convent building.

12. ASM, N.O. The community moved into the new convent at 1017 St. Andrew Street on Sept. 22, 1870, and opened the lower elementary classes in the junior hall at 1015 St. Andrew Street on Sept. 23.

13. ASM, N.O. The dedication ceremony was held on Saturday, Sept. 24, for both the convent and the school wings.

14. ASM, N.O. It was Mary Devereux, later Mother Joseph, to whom the rector, Henry Giesen, CSSR, explained his theory about the expansion across the South, as it would grow from the New Orleans motherhouse.

15. ASM, N.O. The sisters established classes on a secondary level, junior high, in several rooms of the senior hall at 1019 St. Andrew Street on Sept. 23, 1870.

16. ASM, Galway, Clifden, and N.O. The four sisters from Clifden had a priest in Ireland contact the N.O. Redemptorists, and it was Giesen who brought the news of this available help to the sisters on Oct. 22, 1870.

17. ASM, N.O. minutes.

18. Carroll, *Annals* 4: 399. C. B. White, *Disinfection in Yellow Fever at New Orleans, 1870–1875* (New Orleans, John W. Madden, 1876), 7–8.

19. J. M. Toner, *Study of Yellow Fever, 1668–1874* (Washington, DC: U. S. Health Dept., 1874), 24.

20. ASM, N.O. register. Candidate Eliza Shields was received as a novice on Oct. 19, 1869, and was buried on Nov. 4, 1870.

21. ASM, N.O., register. Mary Xavier McDermott, received and professed in St. Louis, was the only American in the original group to New Orleans. She died on Nov. 11, and was buried in the same borrowed tomb with Eliza Shields on Nov. 12, 1870. Later, after the Sisters of Mercy had purchased their own tomb, these first two Mercies to die in the city were transferred to the Mercy tomb, which was built to accommodate twelve coffins at a time.

22. Carroll, *Annals* 4: 400–1.

23. McAuley to Warde, May 28, 1841.

24. N.O. *Morning Star*, April 30, 1871. Fr. John Flanagan had purchased a building to serve as a convent some dozen years earlier, when he thought that he would soon have the Sisters of Mercy from Ireland for the parish school. ASM, N.O., chronicles. The convent in St. Patrick's parish sheltered these sisters while their convent was being erected. According to AANO, Rotchford to Odin, Sept. 6, 1861, a fire seriously damaged the convent. By 1871, the building must have needed some renovation because it was five years since the building had been rented by the Sisters of Our Lady of Charity of the Good Shepherd.

25. ASM, Clifden, Limerick, Liverpool. The four Sisters of Mercy left Clifden on Feb. 28, 1871, made a retreat in Limerick during a week in Lent, received the hospitality of the Mercies in Liverpool from April 3 to 13, when they left for "the American missions."

26. ASM, N.O. minutes. The four missionaries reached New Orleans in mid-May, but petitioned the archbishop to allow them to transfer to Natchitoches in August. Bp. Martin had been to the Mercy convent several times seeking some sisters for his diocese, which was desperately in need of religious teachers. John Flanagan of St. Patrick's also kept trying to get several of the Mercy sisters to teach in his parish school. Accompanying the leader of the missionaries to Perché, Catherine Grant presented her list of complaints and requested permission to transfer to St. Patrick's Convent. Aegidius Smulders, CSSR, was the priest dealing with Catherine Grant. He had revised the rules of several congregations, the Third Order of St. Francis and the Oblates of Providence for instance, and wished to make changes in the Mercy Rule, also. At that time, many ecclesiastical directors assumed that the Mercy Institute was not a pontifical order. Mother Catherine Grant asked to be allowed to make a new foundation, not to be in any way under the direction of the Redemptorists.

27. ASM, N.O., manuscript of the writer, "History of the Sisters of Mercy in St. Patrick Parish." Catherine Grant's second foundation was in St. Patrick convent at 139 Magazine street, on Oct. 17, 1871. She was accompanied by newly-professed Mary Camillus Lucas,

novices Vincent Labry and dePazzi Lucas, lay sisters Francis Farrell and Gertrude Deering, and a temporary candidate. Two others were to leave religious life also, and one was to return to St. Andrew Street.

28. ASM, N.O., financial records.

29. ASM, N.O. and Vicksburg. Mother Catherine Grant, ordered by the doctor to find some cooler, drier air, left New Orleans in April of 1872 to visit the Sisters of Mercy in Vicksburg. She lived for only a few weeks, died there on May 23, and was buried there on May 24, 1872.

30. In Dec. 1874, Mary Camillus Lucas, with the consent of the two bishops concerned, transferred the tiny community to Indianola, Texas. She and a novice reached the site on Jan. 6, 1875. According to the thesis of Mary Aquinas O'Donohue and the writer's manuscript, the sisters who left St. Patrick's for Texas were two newly professed, Mary Berchmans Molyneaux and Cecelia Flagherty, and three temporary candidates. Evidently, Francis Farrell or O'Farrell and Emma Shields had withdrawn from St. Patrick's before the community transferred. The sisters transferring to Texas were all young Irish women who had come to the community through the assistance of the New York Mercies. Mary Vincent Labry, the only Louisianian, had returned to St. Andrew Street.

31. ASM, N.O., manuscript of the writer, "History of the Sisters of Mercy in the Diocese of Natchitoches." Mary Ignatius Gaynor and the other three Irish missionaries, after a visit of only several months in New Orleans, left on Oct. 19, 1871, to establish a foundation in the diocese of Bp. Martin, then Natchitoches and later Alexandria. The Mercy missionaries were accompanied by two novices and two postulants who had come from Ireland with them. In 1872, Mary Aloysius and Joseph Stapleton, with two novices, established a second foundation in Alexandria and Pineville, where they remained for a decade. In 1884, the two Irish mission-aries left for the far West, where Aloysius Oliver died in 1910. Joseph Stapleton had answered Austin Carroll's call for help in 1891 and transferred to Mobile, where she died. In 1875 Mary Ignatius Gaynor left Natchitoches with most of the Irish sisters and founded a convent in the diocese of Alton. Prior to this new foundation, she had returned to Ireland for help, and gathered several candidates and from Moate a professed sister, Mary Josephine Brennan. After several short-lived foundations in Illinois and Kentucky, Ignatius Gaynor went to the North-west with half the sisters and Josephine went to the southwest with the rest. Ignatius served in Oregon Indian reservation and then in Kansas, where she died. Margaret Hessian died in western Pennsylvania. Mary Josephine Brennan moved her sisters through New Mexico to Arizona, where they established several hospitals and schools. The four missionaries died in four different locations. In early 1878, all but one of the Louisiana sisters in Natchitoches transferred to the New Orleans community when Leray disbanded the community, and in 1884, several from the disbanded Alexandria community returned to New Orleans also.

32. ASM, N.O., register. Sisters who, with Mother Austin Carroll formed the founding group of St. Alphonsus Convent of Mercy were Sisters Mary Teresa Gourrier, deSales Druhan, Philomene Butler, Agnes Moran, Angèle Brousse, Joseph Devereux (who had originally signed to go to St. Patrick's foundation), Henriette Briscoe, Liguori Duncan, Baptist Brophy, Aloy-sius Cook, Mercy Wiendahl, Genevieve O'Brien, and Barbara Pathack. Catherine Grant called the convent St. Catherine's, but after she left it was called St. Alphonsus. To avoid confusion about the various names, the convent has been identified by its location.

33. ASM, N.O., minutes. After Perché gave Giesen his consent to send out the two founda-tions and the two associates of Austin Carroll died of yellow fever, the archbishop appointed Austin the mistress of novices of the second community on St. Andrew Street. Perché had assisted in the canonical reorgnization of the Sisters of Our Lady of Charity of the Good

Shepherd of Angers, France, and had served as the chaplain of the Ursuline nuns in New Orleans for over twenty-five years. Hence, Austin Carroll trusted his judgment concerning the arrangements for the new Mercy community composed of only one professed sister and a group of novices and postulants.

34. ASM, N.O.; Carroll, *Annals* 4: 402. Catherine Grant's sisters remained within their convent during the yellow fever epidemics lest any of them get the fever and die. None of them took sick, but no local candidates entered their community, and Camillus Lucas went to New York to find some candidates.

35. McAuley to Moore, Jan. 13, 1839.

36. AAO, Carroll to O'Connor, Feb. 16, 1874.

37. McAuley to Delany, Nov. 15, 1838.

38. AAO, Carroll to O'Connor, April 16, 1874.

39. ASM, N.O., Austin Carroll Papers, memoirs and the O'Regan notes, 8-9.

40. AAO, Carroll to O'Connor, April 16, 1874.

41. ASM, N.O., Austin Carroll Papers, a medley of Memoirs with contributors listed in the order quoted: Sisters Mary Fredericka Turnbull, Paul McCarthy, Dominica Kimble, Borgia Walsh, Benita Pacheca, Catherine O'Regan, and Helena Curtin.

42. AAO, Carroll to O'Connor, April 16, 1874.

43. Ibid.

44. ASM, N.O., Austin Carroll Papers, memoirs and notes.

45. ASM, Birr, Limerick, London, and N.O.

46. Local newspapers which often carried items were: *N.O. Picayune, N.O. Times, N.O. L'Abeille, Le Propagateur Catholique, N.O. Morning Star*; and articles from these papers were sometimes reprinted in the *Boston Pilot*, the *Philadelphia Catholic Record*, and the *N.Y. Freeman's Journal*.

47. ASM, N.O. financial records, Austin Carroll Papers.

48. The Carroll *Life of Catherine McAuley* was printed in 1866, 1868, 1871, and 1874.

49. *Ave Maria* 3 (March 16, 1867): 172.

50. Early Carroll translations were *Margaret Mary* in 1867 and *Love of Our Lord Jesus Christ*, volumes in 1868, 1869, and 1871.

51. Early publications by Sisters of Mercy: Mother M. Catherine McAuley, *Cottage Controversy*; Sister M. Vincent Deasy: *Exhortations on the Vows, The Perfect Religious, Spiritual Conferences of St. Francis de Sales*; Mother Mary Anne Doyle: *The Religious Monitor, Instructions and Meditations Preparatory to the Reception and Profession of the Sacred Spouse of Jesus Christ*; Sister Mary Clare Agnew: *Illustrations of the Corporal and Spiritual Works of Mercy, Young Communicants*; Sister Mary Joseph Nugent: *The Virtuous Scholar, The Sacred Heart of Jesus, The Week Sanctified*; Anonymous: *Meditations and Considerations for a Retreat of One Day in Each Month, The Duties and Happiness of Domestic Service*; Mother M. Vincent Hartnett: *A Catechism of Scripture History*, (Hartnett's *Life of Rev. Mother Catherine McAuley* was published twenty years later).

52. Carroll, *Love of Our Lord Jesus Christ*, vii.

53. Carroll, *Spiritual Retreat of Eight Days* was selected from the Works of St. Alphonsus in 1872.

54. *Catholic World* 6 (Nov. 1867): 287.

55. Sources of reviews at this period: *American Catholic Quarterly Review, Ave Maria, Baltimore Mirror, Boston Pilot, Brownson's Quarterly Review, Catholic World, Catholic Record, Cincinnati Catholic Telegraph, Connecticut Catholic, Donahoe's Magazine, Guardian, Messenger of the Sacred Heart, Metropolitan Record, Western Watchman, Dublin Review, Irish Monthly, London Tablet, The Month, Tipperary Free Press.*

56. Carroll, *Angel Dreams* (N.Y.: Catholic Pub. Soc., 1868), 8.

57. Ibid.

58. Carroll, *Happy Hours of Childhood* (N.Y.: P. O'Shea, 1867); Carroll, *Glimpses of Pleasant Homes* (N.Y.: Catholic Pub. Soc., 1869); *By the Seaside* (N.Y.: Catholic Pub. Soc., 1872). Because early ads were located listing *Sunshine* and not *Happy Hours*, perhaps title and subtitle were exchanged.

59. ASM, N.O. Austin Carroll Papers, quotations from clippings in following sequence: *N.O. Morning Star*, n.d.; *N.Y. Metropolitan Record*, n.d.: *Baltimore Mirror*, n.d.; and *St. Louis Guardian*, Dec. 14, 1867.

60. *Brownson's Quarterly Review* (July 1873): 423.

61. Catholic World 4 (Oct. 1867): 576.

62. ASM, N.O.; Roger Baudier, *Catholic Church in Louisiana* (N.O.: Author, 1939), 137.

63. Carroll, *Annals* 4: 374.

64. Carroll, *Ursulines in Louisiana* (N.O.: Hyman Smith, 1886); Carroll, "Nuns in Louisiana," *Irish Monthly* 12 (June, Sept. 1884).

65. James A. Renshaw, "Lost City of Lafayette," *Louisiana Historical Quarterly* 2 (Jan. 1919): 47–55. Lafayette was incorporated in 1833, and merged with New Orleans in 1852.

66. Carroll, "In Memoriam—Reverend William Stack Murphy," *N.O. Morning Star*, Nov. 7, 1875.

67. AANO, Byrne to Blanc, Nov. 25, 1850; ASM, Carlow, Naas, and N.O.

68. Carroll, *Annals* 3: 328. The first Sisters of Mercy in New Orleans were Sisters Mary Teresa Farrell, Agnes Greene, deSales O'Keefe, and Stanislaus Farrell.

69. *N.O. Daily Delta*, Jan. 23, 1851.

70. Margaret Fitzpatrick from New Orleans entered the Mercy community in Little Rock on March 10, 1851, was received as mary Aloysius, and served until her death on Oct. 2, 1859, one hundred years after a New Orleans girl had become the first Ursuline from Louisiana.

71. ADJ, Browne to Elder, Feb. 23, 1874.

72. ASM, Vicksburg and N.O. Staying with the New Orleans Mercies were Sisters Mary Vincent Browne, Aloysius Houch, and Berchmans Petit.

73. Carroll, *Annals* 4: 79.

74. ACPF, Carroll to Pius IX, Sept. 4, 1872.

75. ACPF, Carroll's list of gifts. The original works sent were her *Catherine McAuley* and the four children's books. The translations were Margaret Mary and five volumes of Saint Jure's works.

76. ASM, Silver Spring and N.O. The crucifix which Pius IX gave to Austin Carroll is preserved in the Mercy Generalate. The letter from the Pope was dated Jan. 17, 1873, and was quoted in several papers upon its reception.

77. *N.O. Morning Star*, Feb. 25, March 2, 1873.

78. ASM. N.O., financial records; Teresa Maher to Carroll n.d.

79. ASM, Dublin, Birr, Limerick, Bermondsey, and N.O., Austin Carroll Papers. Correspondents: Xavier Warde and Gonzaga O'Brien in Manchester, Juliana Purcell in Providence, Jerome Shubrick in Worcester, Pauline Maher and Angela Fitzgerald in Hartford, Augustine McKenna of New York City, Patricia Waldron in Philadelphia, Elizabeth Strange of Pittsburg, Baptist Hearn of Buffalo, Teresa Maher of Cincinnati, Ignatius Walker of St. Louis and Louisville, deSales Brown of Vicksburg, Vincent McGirr and Genevieve Granger of Chicago, Francis Mulholland of Davenport, and Baptist Russell of San Francisco.

80. AUND, Carroll to Brownson, Nov. 26, 1872; John Francis Maguire, *Irish in America* (London: Longmans, Green, 1868), 492. For two books Austin had more than 24 approbations.

81. *Brownson's Quarterly Review* 1 in series 6 (July 1873): 399–400.

82. AUND, Giesen to McMaster, Dec. 12, 1873.

83. Ibid.

84. *N.O. L'Abeille*, July 17, 1869.

85. AAO, Carroll to O'Connor, April 15, 1874.

86. ASM, N.O. Austin Carroll Papers, memoirs of Curtin and Kimble.

87. Ibid.

88. ASM, N.O. chronicles of the branches in Belize and St. Martinville.

89. ASM, N.O. Austin Carroll Papers, memoirs.

90. Ibid.

91. *North British Review*, Feb. 2, 1862, quoted in Dominic, Murphy, *Sketches of Irish Nunneries*, 177–8.

92. Carroll, Foreword, 53.

93. ASM, N.O., Austin Carroll Papers, letters, memoirs.

94. *N.O. Times*, Dec. 9, 1873; *N.O. Daily Picayune*, Dec. 9, 1873; *N.O. Morning Star*, June 14, 1874, report the events of dedication.

NOTES – CHAPTER EIGHT

1. AAO, Carroll to O'Connor, Feb. 16, 1874.

2. ASM, N.O. Austin Carroll Papers.

3. Ibid.; Carroll, *Annals* 4: 404.

4. ASM, N.O. register.

5. ASM, N.O., N.Y., and Dublin.

6. On plan 1, property "J" on Constance Street purchased Aug. 19, 1871; and property "K" on St. Andrew Street purchased on Oct. 21, 1873.

7. ASM, N.O., *N.O. Morning Star*, Jan. 21, 1872.

8. *Western Watchman*, Feb. 24, 1872; *N.O. Times*, Jan. 20, 1872; *N.O. Morning Star*, Jan. 21, 1872.

9. ASM, N.O., *Western Watchman*, Feb. 24, 1872.

10. ADJ, Carroll to Elder, Dec. 10, 1878.

11. AAO, Carroll to O'Connor, Aug. 30, 1878; March 6, 1880.

12. B. M. Norman, *Norman's New Orleans and Environs* (N.O.: B. M. Norman, 1845), 110–6.

13. Carroll, *Catholic History*, 152, 210, 219, 224–5, 137; Carroll, *Ursulines in Louisiana*; Carroll, "Nuns in Louisiana;" Carroll, "Early Millionaire," *Magnificat* 1: 21–3; Carroll, "Don Alexander O'Reilly," *American Catholic Quarterly Review* 33: 87–97.

14. Earl F. Niehouse, *Irish in New Orleans, 1800–1860* (Baton Rouge: LSU Press, 1965), 118–9.

15. ASM, N.O., financial records.

16. *Battersby Registry or Irish Catholic Directory*, 1855 (Dublin: John Mullaney, 1855), 260, see list of dates for charity sermons. *Boston Pilot*, Dec. 24, 1953, announced that "the distinguished convert, Rev. H. Marshall," would be the "eloquent advocate in the Church of St. Francis Xavier, Up. Gardiner St., for the cause of the House of Mercy on Baggot Street."

17. ASM, N.O. and St. Louis.

18. AAO, Carroll to O'Connor, Nov. 4, 1875.

19. ASM, N.O., *N.O. Morning Star*, June 8, 1873.

20. ASM, N.O., n.Y., and Windham.

21. N.O. *Morning Star*, Oct. 25, 1874; Nove. 15, 1874.

22. Carroll, *Annals* 4: 405–6.

23. ASM, N.O., Austin Carroll Papers.

24. *N.O. Morning Star*, June 8, 1873; Jan. 21, 1873.

25. Carroll, *Annals* 4: 405.

26. ADJ, Browne to Elder, Feb. 23, 1874; ASM, N.O., Austin Carroll Papers.

27. Carroll, *Annals* 4: 408, 466-7.

28. C. B. White, MD, *Disinfection in Yellow Fever* (N.O.: John W. Madden, 1876), 15, *N.Y. Freeman's Journal*, Nov. 6, 1858; Nichols, *American Life*, 197-9.

29. ADJ, Elder to Carroll, March 10, 1874; ASM, N.O., Austin Carroll Papers.

30. ASM, N.O. Carroll, *Annals* 4: 418.

31. Carroll, "Southern Sketches," 2 *Irish Monthly* 11, 12 (Oct. 1883, Jan. 1884): 574-5; 14-15; Carroll, "Yellow Fever," in *For our Boys* 1879 (San Francisco: Bancroft, 1879), 67-75.

32. ASM, N.O.; AANO, Carroll to Leray, Oct. 15, 1883; ADJ, Browne to Elder, Feb. 23, 1874.

33. ADJ, Chevalier to Elder, Aug. 29, 1874.

34. ASM, N.O.: Carroll, *Annals* 4: 419; Carroll, "Southern Sketches" 2 *Irish Monthly* 11: 574-5.

35. ADJ, Carroll to Elder, Aug. 12, 1874.

36. ASM, N.O., Austin Carroll Papers.

37. ADJ, Elder to Carroll, Sept. 8, 1874.

38. ASM, N.O., financial records.

39. Carroll, *Annals* 4: 418. The square in which the Convent of Mercy was situated was that bounded by Reynoir and Fayard, and Jackson and Howard Streets.

40. ASM, N.O.; Carroll, *Annals* 4: 408.

41. AANO, Raymond to Perché, Feb. 12. 1876. See also chap. 7 nn. 15-16.

42. Sisters of Mercy taught in St. Patrick's schools as long as there was a building in which to teach. That point was reached in January 1878, when the schools were sold for the indebtedness of the church.

43. ASM, N.O., Austin Carroll Papers; AAO, Carroll to O'Connor, Feb. 16, 1874.

44. ASM, St. John's, Newfoundland, Dublin, and Carlow.

45. Carroll, *Annals* 3: 15-16, 43.

46. AAO, Carroll to O'Connor, Feb. 16, April 16, 1874; ASM, N.O. The portrait of Catherine McAuley was 36" by 28", and painted by N.O. artist, G. (?) D. Coulon.

47. AAO, Carroll, to O'Connor, June 17, 1874.

48. Ibid., April 21, 1875.

49. ASM, N.O. financial records.

50. AAO, Carroll to O'Connor, April 21, Nov. 4, 1875.

51. Carroll, *Annals* 4: 357, 373, 408-15, 409, 410-15.

52. Carroll, ed. "In Memory of the Rev. John B. Duffy, CSSR," *N.O. Morning Star*, Sept. 13, 1874; ASM, N.O. financial records.

53. ASM, N.O., Austin Carroll Papers, undated clippings; tribute in fragment of ms.; Carroll, *Annals* 3: 101–11, 134–5, 139–40.

54. Carroll, "Bishop Bacon and His Mother," *N.O. Morning Star*, Nov. 15, 1874; Carroll, "Right Rev. Dr. Bacon, Bishop of Portland, Maine, USA," *Irish Monthly* 23 (Jan. 1895), 27.

55. ASM, Bermondsey and N.O., Carroll, "Rev. Mother Mary Clare Moore," *N.O. Morning Star*, n.d., Bermondsey scrapbook.

56. ASM, N.O., Austin Carroll Papers, undated clipping.

57. Carroll, *Annals* 4: 375.

58. Ibid.

59. Ibid.; ASM, N.O. financial records.

60. Carroll, "In Memoriam Rev. William Stack Murphy, SJ," *N.O. Morning Star*, Nov. 7, 1875.

61. ASM, N.O., memoirs, and archival data from the Redemptorists, N.O.

62. The St. Vincent's Home for the newsboys was in the 300 block of Bienville, and each parish council was to pay the upkeep for its parish boys. The men of St. Vincent de Paul Society published an annual report on this home and other projects.

63. *N.O. Morning Star*, April 6, 1918; April 23, Sept. 26, 1875; April 10, 1876.

64. Archival data from the Redemptorists, N.O.

65. Ibid.; before the cemetery could be established, the suburb became part of N.O.

66. *N.O. Morning Star*, Sept. 26, 1875.

67. ASM, N.O., undated clippings.

68. *N.O. Morning Star*, March 21, 1875.

69. Archival data from the Redemptorists, N.O.

70. ASM, N.O. Austin Carroll Papers.

71. ASM, N.O., undated clippings; this one seems to be from the *N.Y. Freeman's Journal*, Aug. 22, 1875.

72. *N.O. Morning Star* regularly carried very complimentary articles.

73. *N.O. Morning Star*, March 2, 1873.

74. Ibid., May 31, 1874; Aug. 2, Oct. 25, 1874.

75. *Ave Maria* 3 (March 1867): 171–2; *Catholic World* 4 (March 1867): 855–6; *Brownson's Quarterly Review* (July 1873): 409.

76. Maguire, *Irish in America*, 363.

77. *Philadelphia Record* 11 (June 1876): 65–74.

78. *Connecticut Catholic*, July 1, 1876; *Western Watchman*, June 24, 1876.

79. *N.O. Morning Star*, March 21, 1875.

80. Ibid.

81. Ibid., Sept. 10, 17, 1876.

82. Ibid. Before the completion of the Irish asylum, Provincial Joseph Helmpraecht, who had authorized the project, was no longer the superior of the western section of the country because New Orleans had become part of the new western province. Helmpraecht had remained in the eastern section, and Nicholas Jaeckel, CSSR, became the first provincial in the new area.

83. McAuley to Delany, Nov. 15, 1838.

84. *N.O. Morning Star*, Dec. 3, 1876.

85. Jaeckel formed a board of laymen and chartered the asylum in their control, thus nullifying the previous Girardey-Carroll contract, which had arranged for the parish to assist with the support of the parish orphans.

86. *N.O. Morning Star*, April 16, 1918.

87. Ibid.

88. With the documentation available at this date, after some two dozen years of collecting documents, it is impossible to discern all the causes of the German antipathy toward Mother Austin Carroll. One obvious reason was her espousal of the Irish asylum, which through no fault of hers, was located on Redemptorist real estate for which the German priests had other plans. Other causes were, probably, Austin's independence of the priests and her great pride in her homeland, a pride which certainly matched that of the Germans for their own land and language. Another factor might have been the non-German Redemptorist, James Gleason, who shortly after his "Irish revolt," left the order. Although the Mercy archives do not indicate that Austin Carroll encouraged his public stance or nationalistic tendencies, it is quite likely that it was assumed that she did so. Unfortunately, there seemed to be a good deal of comparison by the German fathers of the old-world customs of the German School Sisters of Notre Dame and the more recent Rule and customs of the Irish Sisters of Mercy. The sisters themselves seemed to have no contact whatsoever, but the Redemptorists served as the ecclesiastical superiors for both. The Notre Dames, who taught in German in the Redemptorist parishes all over the country, asked permission of their priest director even to venture two blocks from the convent to purchase a pot or pan for their kitchen. Hence it must have been a great shock to the elderly German priests to see the Mercies, in highly visible contrast to the German nuns, visiting the hospitals and prisons clear across the city. Catherine McAuley's "walking nuns" also trudged all over the Irish Channel to visit the sick poor, and whenever they had the money, bought another Mercy Home as readily as kitchen utensils. Austin Carroll never established any new institution without the consent of the archbishop, but the Germans seemed to want the Irish nuns as firmly under their control as the other nuns were. Because Austin Carroll did not permit the priests to interfere in the internal affairs of the community, the priest who had been appointed their ecclesiastical superior upon their arrival began to work to get Austin out of office and out of the parish. There seemed to be the assumption that the next superior, one of the younger sisters could be more easily controlled. All of the Redemptorists of French, English, Irish, or American extraction were friendly with the Irish nuns, seemed to have no part in the opposition led by one German, and some were the staunchest of friends with Austin Carroll.

89. ASM, N.O., financial records. Helmpraecht arranged the contract in St. Louis with the superior, Ignatius Walker in 1869.

90. ASM, N.O., Jaeckel to Carroll, March, 1877.

91. ASM, N.O. Carroll to Jaeckel, March 15, 1877.

92. ASM, N.O., Jaeckel to Carroll, March 28, 1877.

93. Ibid.

94. ASM, N.O., Austin Carroll Papers, memoirs.

95. ASM, N.O., minutes, financial records.

96. ASM, N.O. Perhaps, Austin Carroll's decision to deal directly with the archbishop rather than with the German priests, caused hard feelings.

97. AAO, Carroll to O'Connor, Oct. 25, 1876; Nov. 14, 1876.

98. Ibid., ASM, N.O., register.

99. *Catholic Directories*, 1864–1877, the French Marianites or Sisters of Holy Cross from the New Orleans motherhouse taught in Pensacola for two years, 1869–1871. The Sisters of the Third Order of St. Dominic from Tampa taught in Pensacola for the next five years. The Sisters of St. Joseph from LePuy taught in Warrington 1874–1877, and left only after four of their five sisters died of yellow fever.

100. Carroll, *Annals* 4: 424.

101. According to the *Catholic Directories*, the missionary priest, Symphonian Guinand (or Guinaud) served most of the Gulf Coast, sailing from Pensacola or Bayou Battery from 1835 to about 1855, later restricting his course to the Mississippi Coast.

102. Carroll, *Annals* 4: 425.

103. Ibid., 425.

104. Carroll, "Southern Sketches," *Irish Monthly* 12 (Jan. 1884), 13–18.

105. Ibid.

106. Ibid.

107. Carroll, *Annals* 4: 425.

108. ASM, N.O. and Pensacola. One of the first lessons Austin Carroll learned in New Orleans was that there was rigid segregation between the blacks and the mulattoes in the late 1860s.

109. Carroll, *Catholic History*, 80.

110. Carroll, *Annals* 4: 425.

111. Carroll, *Catholic History*, 79–80; Frederick Faber, hymn to Our Lady of Mercy.

112. Carroll, *Annals* 4: 426.

113. Carroll, "Southern Sketches," *Irish Monthly* 12 (Jan. 1884): 79.

114. Ibid., 78.

115. AAO, Carroll to O'Connor, Aug. 20, 1877.

116. Ibid.

117. Ibid.

118. Carroll, *Annals* 4: 426.

119. AAO, Carroll to O'Connor, Sept. 17, 1877.

120. ASM, Carlow, Carroll to Catherine Maher, Aug. 13, 1877.

121. ADJ, Carroll to Elder, Feb. 6, 1877.

122. AAO, Carroll to O'Connor, Feb. 13, 1877.

123. Ibid., June 5, 1877.

124. AANO, Carroll to Leray, Oct. 15, 1883. The salary contract was cancelled in March, yet the St. Thomas mission was still on the schedule in June of that year. Hence, it does not seem that the broken contract caused the decision to change the plans and decline the Redemptorist mission in the West Indies.

125. AANO, Raymond to Perché, Feb. 12, 1876.

126. ASM, N.O. Pensacola, Warrington, and Mobile; Carroll, *Annals* 4: 426. ASM, N.O. and Warrington. In Warrington Austin Carroll staffed St. John the Evangelist Girls' School, St. John the Evangelist Boys', and St. Joseph's School for the blacks, which opened on Feb. 18, 1878.

127. ASM, N.O. financial records. Each sister had a copy of the *New Testament*, the *Following of Christ, Meditations and Considerations for a Retreat on One Day in Each Month* [Austin's copy of this was published in 1850 and was inscribed to her by Josephine Warde], the *Sayings of Catherine McAuley*, Carroll's *Spiritual Retreat for Eight Days* compiled from St. Alphonsus, besides her book with the office and prayers of the Sisters of Mercy.

128. ASM, N.O. financial records. The sisters themselves were the artists for the painted and embroidered materials used in liturgical services.

129. ASM, N.O. Austin Carroll Papers, memoirs; ASM, Manchester, Carroll to O'Brien, Sept. 18, 1884.

130. ASM, N.O. financial records, memoirs.

131. ASM, N.O., Pensacola, Warrington, Mobile, Biloxi, financial records.

132. ASM, N.O. memoirs. Leaflets for ordinary use contained the commandments and chief prayers of the Church. During yellow fever times, Austin Carroll had special novenas and prayers to St. Roch printed because he was the patron during such epidemics.

133. ASM, N.O., Austin Carroll Papers, memoirs, financial records.

134. ASM, N.O., Austin Carroll Papers, memoirs; Carroll, *Annals* 4: 418-23.

135. Carroll, "Southern Sketches," *Irish Monthly* 11 (Oct. 1883): 571-80.

136. Ibid., 375.

137. ASM, N.O., financial records.

138. Ibid., register, minutes.

139. *N.O. Morning Star*, June 10, 1877.

140. ASM, N.O. Austin Carroll Papers.

141. ASM, Dublin, N.Y., St. Louis, and N.O.

142. ASM, Savannah, Vicksburg, and N.O.

143. Carroll, *Pleasant Homes*, 82.

144. ASM, N.O. register, necrology.

145. ASM, N.O., Austin Carroll Papers, memoirs.

146. ASM, N.O., Pauline Maher died Aug. 7, 1876.

147. ASM, N.O. and Cincinnati, Teresa Maher died Nov. 29, 1877.

148. AAO, Carroll to O'Connor, Oct. 9, 1876.

149. Ibid., Oct. 27, 1877.

150. Mrs. William Carroll, neé Margaret Strahan, died Dec. 3, 1875, and the news reached New Orleans just before Christmas.

151. AAO, Carroll to O'Connor, June 20, 1878.

152. ASM, N.O., financial records. Coast schools were working to establish libraries as late as the 1890s.

153. ADJ, Carroll to Elder, Mardi Gras [Feb. 13], 1877.

154. Ibid., *N.O. Morning Star*, Nov. 15, 1874.

155. ASM, Bermondsey, McAuley to Marmion, March 20, 1841 [letter recently located by the writer and not included in the Neumann collection of *Letters*]. The Carroll account was published in the *N.O. Morning Star*, March 26, 1876.

156. Ibid.

157. Ibid.; ASM, Bermondsey, McAuley to Marmion, March 20, 1841, is quoted here as it had not been located in time for the published *Letters*:

> The delightful exhibition on Patrick's Day will never be forgotten — 70,000 Teetotallers marched in the most orderly manner — all wearing scarfs of Irish manufacture, the priests of each division attending in splendid carriages — Mr. [Daniel] O'Connell — four beautiful milk white horses dressed in blue and silver — four outriders in blue velvet jackets, caps, white overalls, Mr. [William] Yore — four jetblacks in crimson and gold, Mr. Flanagan — four bays with amber and blue, Dr. [Walter] Meyler — four dressed in scarlet and gold, His Excellency looking at them and Dr. [Daniel] Murry in his carriage at a corner of Merrion Square, standing till all passed — the servant saluting them. It is said there was never such a sight in the world — think of 70,000 without a single accident or window broken.

Before the description of the parade, Catherine had mentioned the health of several of the sisters and that she was coughing again. Eight months before her death she could laugh about herself, adding "I think three drinks of the 'Waters of Birr' would cure me." Catherine also told mistress of novices, Cecilia Marmion, how her charges were doing.

158. Ibid.

159. *N.O. Morning Star*, March 26, 1876.

160. Ibid.

161. Ibid.

162. Ibid.

163. ASM, N.O., Austin Carroll Papers, letters quoted in following sequence: Nov. 4, 1875, June 17, Feb. 16, April 16, 1874; April 21, 1875; July 9, Oct. 15, 1876; July 19, 1879; July 21, 1880.

164. ASM, N.O.; AAO, Carroll to O'Connor, April 21, 1875.

165. ASM, N.O.; Leray did not like religious visitors, AANO, Carroll to Leray, March 20, 1884. However, New Orleans had the tradition of hosting clerical and religious beggars, and Perché, unlike many bishops in other areas, did not forbid the frequent influx of clergy and religious seeking financial help to build a German school in Pennsylvania, a church in Canada, or a convent in Ireland. Thus it had always been in New Orleans since 1796, when Bishop John Carroll, in his letter of March 31, asked Bishop Luis Penalver for some assistance in order to build a "Catholic church in this town." The letter is quoted in *John Carroll Papers*, ed. by Thomas Hanley, SJ, (N.D.: Univ. of Notre Dame Press, 1976), 169.

166. ASM, N.Y. and N.O.

167. ASM, Worcester, N.Y., and N.O., minutes.

168. *N.O. Morning Star*, June 10, 1877.

NOTES—CHAPTER NINE

1. ASM, N.O., minutes; AAO, Carroll, to O'Connor, May 20, 1878.

2. ASM, N.O., Perché to Girardey, May, 1878.

3. AAO, Carroll to O'Connor, of the hundred-plus letters in the series, many ask his advice about community matters.

4. AAO, Carroll to O'Connor, May 20, 1878.

5. Ibid.

6. Ibid., June 20, 1878.

7. AAO, Carroll to O'Connor, May 20, 29, June 20, 1878.

8. Ibid., March 19, 1877.

9. Ibid.

10. Ibid.

11. Ibid., Oct. 25, 1876.

12. Ibid., June 17, 1874.

13. Ibid., Nov. 4, 1875; April 21, 1875.

14. Ibid., ASM, N.O., Chicago, Pittsburgh, and St. Louis had appealed to Rome, the first two with positive results, and the third in order to change the Mercy Rule in order to forbid certain academies. Carroll, *Annals* 3: 135-6, 269-70, 325-6; *Annals* 1: 153.

15. ASM, N.O. The Mercy communities in Natchitoches, Alexandria, and Pineville had been dissolved by Bp. Leray because they lacked funds, food, and candidates. Austin Carroll, as noted above, received these sisters and others from several groups that dissolved in the West.

16. AAO, Carroll to O'Connor, Sept, 22, 1883.

17. Ibid., April 22, 1881.

18. Ibid., Sept. 22, 1883.

19. Ibid.

20. Ibid., Feb. 6, 1879.

21. Ibid.

22. *Rule and Constitutions of the Religious Called Sisters of Mercy* (Dublin: James Duffy, 1863). Austin's copy is in ASM, Mobile.

23. *Customs and Minor Regulations of the Religious Called Sisters of Mercy*, in the parent house, Baggot Street, and its branch houses. (Dublin: J. M. O'Toole & Son, 1869). This was edited by Mary Magdalen Kirwan. Austin Carroll also had a copy of the *Rule and Constitutions of the Religious Sisters of Mercy* published in Providence in 1864.

24. ASM, Limerick. This was not a general meeting, as many houses did not send a representative, but the superiors who assembled in 1864 approved a set of customs which were published as *The Abridgment of a Guide for the Religious Called Sisters of Mercy* (London: Robson & Son, 1866). Unfortunately, a second unapproved *Guide* was published at the same time, and some communities bought it thinking it was the approved version. Edited by Mary Francis Bridgeman of fame in the Crimea, it was *A Guide for the Religious Called Sisters of Mercy Amplified by Quotations, Instructions, etc.* (London: Robson & Son, 1866). Many bishops directed their sisters not to attend a meeting that was not a general chapter and not attended by the Dublin motherhouse.

25. McAuley to Walsh, Nov. 6, 1840.

26. ASM, Manchester, Carroll to O'Brien, Feb. 20, 1886. Explaining that their customs were based in part on the Baggot Street *Customs* and part on the *Guide*, Austin added, "but we suit ourselves to the places where we live, and that is the secret of our great success here, T.G."

27. AAO, Carroll to O'Connor, Dec. 28, 1876.

28. Ibid., Aug. 30, Sept. 12, 1884.

29. Ibid., Oct. 1, 1884.

30. Decree from the Congregation of Bishops and Regulars, Dec. 17, 1890.

31. ASM, N.O. Austin Carroll's Mercy associates or affiliates, lay women who assisted by serving with the social works of mercy, were sometimes referred to as "out sisters" because they frequently accompanied the choir sisters as partners for the visitation of the sick or the imprisoned. An affiliate regularly shopped for the small items needed by the cook and bought the tickets for the sisters in the Gulf Coast branches. They were a great help in the Creche and the Mercy Home particularly.

32. ASM, N.O., register. Lay auxiliaries were Sisters Brigid Byrne, Ann McMeyler, Adele Trichette, Sarah Reilly, Monica Stewart, and Patricia Kelly. Distinct from the lay sisters in several ways, the Mercy affiliates made no vows, were usually none too young, tended to be educated and mannerly, and were free to leave at any time. The habit of the Mercy affiliates was similar to that of the choir sisters, but without the train and large outer sleeves. For the leather cincture they substituted a cord, but these slight differences were hidden by the long Mercy veil.

33. ASM, N.O., register. Two of the Mercy affiliates served for a few years, but the others, united in death as in life, were buried in the Mercy tomb.

34. ASM, N.O., register.

35. ASM, N.O. Not all Austin's successors had the same insight into the character and abilities of these sisters or underrated their qualities and limited them to household duties and tasks.

36. ASM, N.O. The same basic Mercy habit was worn by the lay sisters, but without the long train, and with the addition of a white apron in the house.

37. Carroll, *Annals* 3: 59.

38. *N.O. Morning Star*, Nov. 17, 1878.

39. *N.O. Daily Picayune*, July 27, 1881.

40. It was Catherine McAuley's friend, Bp. John Murphy of Cork, who suggested the addition of "the service of the poor, sick, and ignorant" as a distinguishing mark in the Mercy vow formula. The foundress agreed, but might have considered the phrase a part of the vow of obedience rather than a separate fourth vow. When Angela Dunn asked about a fourth vow in 1841, Catherine replied on Jan. 20, that the "fourth vow of enclosure has been added to Sisters of other communities."

41. ASM, N.O., Austin Carroll Papers, memoirs. Austin Carroll, like the Cork community among others, considered the phrase of service a fourth vow and so taught the sisters of her Southern communities. *N.O. Daily Picayune*, July 27, 1881.

42. ASM, N.O., Austin Carroll Papers, clippings, *N.O. Morning Star*, Feb. 11, 1872; June 17, 1877; Jan. 5, 1879, and many undated cuttings.

43. Ibid.

44. *N.O. Morning Star*, Jan. 2, 1881.

45. ASM, N.O., clippings, *Lake Charles Echo*, July 16, 1877.

46. AAO, Carroll to O'Connor, Aug. 20, 1877.

47. Carroll, *Annals* 4: 386–7.

48. Carroll, *Catherine McAuley*, 196.

49. ASM, N.O., Carroll Family Papers, Carroll to Fennessey, n.d.

50. Ibid.

51. Ibid.

52. *N.O. Morning Star*, Feb. 24, 1884.

53. Ibid., June 9, 1888.

54. Ibid.

55. ASM, N.O., register.

56. AAO, Carroll to O'Connor, Feb. 13, 1877.

57. Carroll, *Annals* 4: 353. Austin Carroll consulted the superior in Dublin.

58. AAO, Carroll to O'Connor, Feb. 13, 1877.

59. ASM, Savannah and Belmont, N.C. John England tried to bring sisters from Ireland on several occasions, and Catherine McAuley described his visit in 1841, when she had to refuse because of previous commitments. See McAuley to Scott, June 30, 1841. The diocesan community in Charleston, though entitled the Sisters of Our Lady of Mercy, was popularly referred to as "Bishop England's sisters." These are the religious Gibbons brought to Wilmington, N.C., in 1869, established as a separate foundation in 1872, and was planning to have Austin Carroll assist by teaching them the McAuley Rule in 1877. This community adopted the McAuley habit in 1893, but in deference to the wishes of their bishop, Leo Haid, deferred adopting the Rule until 1913. In Savannah, these same sisters of Our Lady of Mercy had served since 1845, separated from Charleston, and in 1890, wished to have a rule approved by Rome. Becker tried to get this approval, but the community was diocesan, and with the approval of Leo XIII, Becker gave the Savannah sisters the McAuley Rule on Sept. 24, 1892. The sisters and Becker asked Austin Carroll to assist them in acquiring an understanding of the McAuley Rule and customs. Austin agreed to their request, but delayed until she had the approval of Bishop O'Sullivan. She went to Georgia in February, remained for six weeks, and helped them to change into the new habit in March. Confusion about the date has arisen because of the reception of the Rule in 1892, and the assistance with the new Rule in 1893. The Savannah archives are quite clear on the sequence of events, and noted in their chronicles in Jan. 1893 that Mother Austin Carroll had "promised to come in answer to our appeal and" that of Bishop Becker. Austin arrived in Savannah on Feb. 1, 1893, and left for home on March 16, 1893. Shortly thereafter, Austin had the Savannah superior see a reception and profession ceremony in Selma, visit Mobile and the houses in New Orleans. After 1913, only the Charleston sisters continue as Bishop England's diocesan community with the Rule of the Sisters of Charity. Besides the archives of Belmont, Savannah, and Mobile, data was gathered in Mary Helen McCarthy, "History of the Sisters of Mercy of Belmont, N.C."

60. ASM, Savannah, San Francisco, and N.O., Austin Carroll Papers, memoirs.

61. ASM, San Francisco, McKenna to Russell, Aug. 15, 1893.

62. Ibid.

63. *A Little Book of Practical Advices and Prayers of Our Revered Foundress, Mother Mary Catharine McAuley* [compiled by Mary Clare Moore] (London: Burns, Oates, & Co., 1868). This first published collection of the sayings of the Mercy foundress was unavailable when Austin Carroll tried to purchase some for her sisters. So she acquired consent to put out an American reprint, which she did in 1877. A year later, she published a second collection as a companion to that of Clare Moore. Austin reduced the size of the volumes and the title. Small was cheaper, and she wanted to give them away in quantity. Clare Moore had decided to publish a small picture of Catherine McAuley at the same time as the book, and Bishop Thomas Grant suggested that she include a facsimile of Catherine's writing and signature. Perhaps the picture was tipped in as a frontispiece, though no such copies were located. Bermondsey archives had the printed picture with the printed facsimile clearly showing how the blessing and signature had been cut and mounted. To obtain the writing for this reproduction, Clare Moore must have used the complimentary closing from the letter to de Pazzi Delany dated Oct. 3, 1837. This letter is usually referred to as a fragment as only two of the four pages were available for the published letters. The writer recently located the remaining two pages and realized that the closing cut from the letter was that to be printed for all the Sisters of Mercy. Letters attesting to their gratitude for the collection of sayings, but especially for the picture and the facsimile of Catherine's writing are quoted in the chronicles in Bermondsey.

Several points about the letter became clear on examination. It is dated October 3, not October 4, and page two is marked private, not postscript. Mentioned in a way which illustrates the playful humor of the Mercy foundress is a note about Fr. William Delaney, later the bishop of Cork. He bore the same last name as de Pazzi Delany to whom Catherine was writing, so Catherine wrote, "We have a Father William Delaney as well as you. I have just been writing to him and found out his Christian name, and indeed he does not disgrace the Delaneys in any way, He has a true Irish countenance, abounding in 'gras' and good humour, an exemplary Priest." That was on page one with news of their former chaplain, Father Burke, who was preparing to go off to his foreign mission. Page two is in the collection of letters, page three is cut because the complimentary closing was on the other side and read, "May God bless you my Dearest Sister and preserve you in grace and health, Your ever affectionate, Mary C. McAuley." Page four contained the postscript on page 97 of the *Letters* and the address on the cover, which contained two postmarks.

64. *A Few of the Sayings, Instructions, and Prayers of the Foundress of the Sisters of Mercy*, [ed. for U.S. reprint by Carroll] (N.Y.: Catholic Pub. Soc. Co., 1877).

65. AAO, Carroll to O'Connor, May 19, 1878.

66. Ibid., Nov. 30, 1878.

67. *Sayings and Instructions of the Foundress of the Sisters of Mercy* vol. 2 [comp. by Austin Carroll] (N.Y.: Catholic Pub. Soc. Co., 1878).

68. Carroll, *Catherine McAuley*, 1866, 1868, 1871, 1874, and 1877.

69. *Love of Jesus Christ*, 1868, 1870, and 1875; *Spiritual Retreat*, 1872, 1875, 1878; *St. Alphonsus*, 1874, 1879; *Commandments and Sacraments*, 1873, 1875. The children's stories were printed in the 1860s, the 1870s, and later, in the 1890s.

70. *Clement Hofbauer* was printed in 1877 and 1879; and *L'Homme Spirituel* in 1878 and 1879.

71. AAO, Carroll to O'Connor, May 29, 1878.

72. Ibid., April 9, 1881.

73. ASM, Carlow, Carroll to Catherine Maher, April 10, 1878.

74. AAO, Carroll to O'Connor, March 19, 1877.

75. Ibid., April 9, 1881.

76. ASM, Limerick, chronicles.

77. Ibid.

78. ASM, N.O., Austin Carroll Papers, clippings.

79. AAO, Carroll to O'Connor, April 9, 1881.

80. ASM, Windham, Carroll to Warde, Feb. 2, 1882.

81. Ibid., Jan. 7, 1882.

82. Ibid.

83. ASM, Limerick, chronicles.

84. J. M. Toner, MD, "Statistics re Distribution and Natural History of Yellow Fever in the United States," 18-15, in reprint with John M. Woodworth, MD, "The Yellow Fever Epidemic of 1873," 42, 51. (Washington, DC: U.S. Marine Hospital Service, 1873).

85. ASM, N.O. register, necrology.

86. Carroll, "Southern Sketches," *Irish Monthly* 11 (Aug. 1883): 506.

87. Carroll, "Yellow Fever: Cross of the South," in *For Our Boys* 1879, ed. by A. Dietz (San Francisco: A. L. Bancroft, 1879), 68-9.

88. AAO, Carroll to O'Connor, July 24, 1878.

89. Ibid.

90. Ibid., Aug. 18, 1878.

91. Ibid., July 24, 1878.

92. Ibid., Aug. 18, 1878.

93. Carroll, *Annals* 4: 468-9.

94. Ibid.

95. Carroll, *Irish Monthly* 11 (Aug. 1883): 504-10.

96. AAO, Carroll to O'Connor, Aug. 30, 1878.

97. Ibid.

98. Ibid.

99. ASM, N.O., Browne to Carroll, n.d.

100. Ibid.

101. ASM, Carlow, Carroll to Catherine Maher, Sept. 17, 1878.

102. Carroll, *Annals* 4: 470.

103. AAO, Carroll to O'Connor, Aug. 18, 1878.

104. Ibid., Aug. 30, Sept. 30, Oct. 5.

105. ASM, N.O., financial records; *N.O. Morning Star*, n.d.

106. ASM, N.O., Carroll to Gibbons, Sept. 28, 1878; Carroll to Tuigg, Oct. 16, 1878.

107. ASM, N.O., Austin Carroll Papers, clippings; *Boston Pilot*, most undated, but Oct. 23, 1878 has a letter from Carroll to J. B. O'Reilly on page one.

108. ASM, N.O., Austin Carroll Papers, clippings; Austin Carroll's letters were printed in the *N.Y. Freeman's Journal*, and her vivid descriptions awakened sympathy.

109. ASM, Carlow, Carroll to Catherine Maher, Sept. 18, 1878.

110. ASM, N.O., Austin Carroll Papers, rough copy of Carroll to Morgan, Sept. 24, 1878.

111. ASM, N.O., Carroll to McKenna, Sept. 18, 1878.

112. Ibid.

113. ASM, N.O., Carroll to Morgan, Sept. 24, 1878.

114. Ibid.

115. ASM, N.O., Carroll to Catherine Maher, Sept. 17, 1878.

116. Ibid.; Rosaria Veesaert was revived from a dying condition by letter of the foundress.

117. AAO, Carroll to O'Connor, Oct. 5, 1878.

118. Ibid.

119. Carroll, "Southern Sketches," *Irish Monthly* 11 (Aug. 1883): 507.

120. AAO, Carroll to O'Connor, Sept. 30, 1878.

121. ASM. N.O., Austin Carroll Papers, clippings.

122. Ibid., Carroll to Gibbons, Sept. 28, 1878; AAO, Carroll to O'Connor, Sept. 30, 1878.

123. AAO, Carroll to O'Connor, Oct. 21, 1878.

124. ASM, N.O., Carroll to Titusville, Pa. donors, Oct. 21, 1878.

125. AAO, Carroll to O'Connor, Oct. 21, 1878.

126. *N.Y. Freeman's Journal*, Nov. 2, 1878.

127. Ibid., Oct. 21, 1878.

128. ASM. N.O., Austin Carroll Papers, Carroll to Tuigg, Oct. 16, 1878; Carroll to Gibbons, Sept. 28, 1878; Carroll to Titusville donors, Oct. 15, 21, 1878.

129. ASM, N.O., Carroll to J. B. O'Reilly, Oct. 23, 1878.

130. Carroll, *Annals* 4: 471.

131. ASM, N.O., Carroll to J. B. O'Reilly, Oct. 23, 1878.

132. Ibid.

133. Ibid.

134. AAO, Carroll to O'Connor, Sept. 30, 1878.

135. Ibid., oct. 21, 1878.

136. ASM, N.O., Carroll to J. B. O'Reilly, Oct. 23, 1878.

137. *N.O. Morning Star*, Oct. 20, 1878.

138. AAO, Carroll to O'Connor, Oct. 21, 1878.

139. Ibid.

140. Carroll, *Annals* 4: 470-1.

141. *Connecticut Catholic*, Sept. 7, 1878.

142. *N.Y. Freeman's Journal*, Sept. 21, 1878.

143. *N.O. Morning Star*, Jan. 5, 1879.

144. Carroll, *Annals* 4: 471-2.

145. *Boston Pilot*, Oct, 23, 1878.

146. Ibid., Oct. 12, 1878.

147. Ibid., Oct. 23, 1878.

148. Lillie Devereux Blake, *N.Y. Evening Telegram*, quoted in *N.O. Daily Picayune*, Oct. 22, 1878.

149. Ibid.

150. Ibid.

151. Ibid.

152. Carroll, *In Many Lands*, 389.

153. Carroll, *Catherine McAuley*, 1866, see chap. 1; Carroll, Preface, 1867, 13–56.

154. *N.O. Morning Star*, Jan. 5, 1879.

155. ADJ, Carroll to Elder, Dec. 10, 1878.

156. Carroll, *Sayings and Instructions of the Foundress*, 3.

157. Ibid.

158. AAO, Carroll to O'Connor, Dec. 3, 1878.

159. ADJ, Carroll to Elder, June 14, 1878.

160. Ibid., Dec. 10, 1878.

161. Ibid.

162. ASM, N.O., St. Joseph's Colored School, later known as St. Mary's, opened in the house next to the convent at the corner of Renoir and Jackson Streets. According to Julia Cook Guise, *Growth of the Biloxi Public School System*, (Biloxi: City, 1979), 6; the public school for blacks began seven years later in 1886 in a house rented from the Baptist Church.

163. ASM, N.O., register.

164. *N.O. Morning Star*, Nov. 24, 1878.

165. Ibid., Jan. 5, 1878.

166. Ibid., Nov. 24, 1878.

167. *N.O. Democrat*, Oct. 6, 1877.

168. Ibid., July 14, 1878.

169. *N.O. Morning Star*, Nov. 24, 1878.

170. AUND, Girardey to McMaster, Feb. 24, 1878.

171. AAO, Carroll to O'Connor, Jan. 3, 1879.

172. ASM, N.O., financial records.

173. ASM, N.O., Teresa Maher to Carroll, n.d.

174. AAO, Carroll to O'Connor, Oct. 15, 1876.

175. ASM, N.O. The only problem Austin Carroll had with the black parishioners of Notre Dame de Bon Secours Parish occurred when she planned that the mulattoes and blacks walk together as a unit in a procession. She soon learned that neither group would walk with the other. They had to be arranged into two separate units.

176. ASM, N.O. St. Joseph's School for the blacks opened Sept. 14, 1874; was burned down on Sept. 22, 1874; was reopened a month later, and lasted a semester before the arsonists struck again. A third attempt lasted a little longer before arson closed it permanently. *N.O. Daily Picayune*, Sept. 23, 1874; *N.O. Times*, Sept. 24, 1874.

177. AAO, Carroll to O'Connor, Sept. 5, 1883.

178. ASSJ, Baltimore, Benoit diary, 190–3.

179. Ibid., 193–4.

180. Ibid., 190.

181. Ibid.

182. Ibid., 190–4.

183. ASM, N.O., Austin Carroll Papers, memoirs, Curtin notes.

184. Ibid.

185. Ibid.

186. Ibid.

187. Carroll, *Catherine McAuley*, 125–6.

188. Carroll, *Annals* 1: 263.

189. ADJ, Carroll to Elder, June 14, 1878.

190. Ibid., Dec. 10, 1878.

191. AAO, Carroll to O'Connor, Jan. 14, 1879.

192. Ibid.

193. Ibid.

194. Ibid.

195. Ibid., Jan. 28, 1879.

196. ASM, Limerick and N.O., Limerick chronicles; N.O. financial records.

197. AAO, Carroll to O'Connor, Jan. 14, 1879; Abp. Purcell of Cincinnati was in distress because of the failure of the diocesan bank, and in New Orleans, several rectories and church buildings were on the verge of being sold in order to pay indebtedness.

198. ASM, N.O., financial records.

199. Ibid. The wood house which had served as the crèche seems to have been rolled off the Mercy lot to another across the street. The cleared lot, except for a small shed, became a part of the schoolyard.

200. ASM, N.O. The Boys' House of Refuge, in the Girod Asylum, was located on the lake side of St. Patrick's Cemetery No. 3 on Metairie Road, later called City Park Avenue.

201. Carroll, *Meditations and Contemplations on the Sacred Passion of Our Lord*, by Ven. Luis of Granada, OP, (N.Y.: Catholic Pub. Soc. Co., 1879).

202. AAO, Carroll to O'Connor, July 19, 1879.

203. *Little Companion of the Sisters of Mercy*, comp. by Mary Xavier Maguire.

204. Carroll, "Yellow Fever," *For Our Boys*, 67–75.

205. ASM, N.O. financial records. In 1879, because she had to go to New York on business with her publishers, she went to Manchester to see Xavier Warde and Gonzaga O'Brien, stopped in Providence to see Juliana Purcell. Those visits were a little farther than she had to go, but the other stops she made were along the train route and cost her nothing. This might be the appropriate time to mention that recent authors have mistakenly placed Austin Carroll in Ireland and all over the United States repeatedly, because they assumed that she went to each of the houses treated in the *Annals*. Not so, Austin received her information by mail, and only when a visit could be combined with necessary business, as in 1879, did she manage to visit some of the communities that had sent her historical information. Many sent nothing, but later berated her for omitting them.

206. Austin had extensive correspondence with many convents which she never saw, and had visitors from Nashville and Louisville, but did not get to either.

207. Austin Carroll did not return to Ireland for thirty-five years, but recent authors have placed her in Dublin, Cork, and other places while she was hard at work in New Orleans. She had correspondence, not only with Mercies all over England and Ireland, but she also wrote George's Hill to Brigid Carroll who knew Catherine McAuley. For the same reason, she wrote to the Byrn sisters, Fanny or Mary Louis Tighe, and even a servant who had worked for Catherine's family. She wrote, but was not there until 1889.

208. ASM, Cincinnati, Harrisburg, Philadelphia, Brooklyn, New York, Worcester, Manchester, and N.O., Austin Carroll Papers. Austin's companion was Mary Antonia McKinley, who was later to lead the Mercy community in New Orleans as either superior or assistant for several years.

209. AAO, Carroll to O'Connor, March 6, 1880.

210. ASM, Worcester, chronicles, Nov. 1879.

211. ASM, Cincinnati, chronicles, Oct. 1879.

212. Ibid.

213. ASM, Windham, Carroll to O'Brien, Sept. 14, 1885.

214. Ibid., Nov. 21, 1880.

215. Ibid., Sept. 11, 1884.

216. AAO, Carroll to O'Connor, March 6, 1880.

217. Ibid., Dec. 9, 1880.

218. Ibid., Sept. 12, 1884.

219. ASM, N.O., Austin Carroll Papers. Religion classes began in 1879, and regular school in 1880.

220. ASM. N.O., financial records.

221. ASM. N.O., Austin Carroll Papers, clippings.

222. ASM, N.O. The sisters commuted to St. Michael's from 1880 until Oct., 1883.

223. ASM, N.O., chronicles of St. Michael's. The brick school was dedicated March 7, 1875. The parish schools for boys and girls were staffed by lay teachers from 1871-1880, and by the Mercies, beginning on Sept. 1, 1880. Three years later, after the convent was established on Oct. 8, 1883, St. Michael's Colored School was opened on Oct. 8, 1883. Austin Carroll paraphrased the McAuley letter of Nov. 17, 1838.

224. AAO, Carroll to O'Connor, April 10, 1874.

225. ASM, N.O., financial records. On the strength of the Giesen words, the sisters spent thousands improving "their home." In 1869, William Meredith, CSSR, the pastor of St. Alphonsus Parish, collected from the generous parishioners and received the funds from the Irish congregation for the convent for "their nuns." Alexander Czvitkovicz, CSSR, made the plans for the combination school and convent, and then supervised the construction. When sending complaints to Rome a little later, Giesen said that the Redemptorists gave the convent to the sisters, but in New Orleans, the Germans demanded rent.

226. ASM, N.O., Austin Carroll Papers, memoirs, financial records, numerous letters, clippings, *N.O. Morning Star*, n.d.

227. ASM, N.Y., Providence, Worcester, and N.O., chronicles, minutes.

228. ASM, N.O., Purcell to Carroll, n.d.

229. Mary Juliana Purcell, *Meditations and Considerations for a Three Days' Retreat* (N.Y.: P. O'Shea, 1880), iii.

230. Carroll, *Marie Antoinette* (N.Y.: Catholic Pub. Soc., 1880); Carroll, *Mary Beatrice and Her Step-Daughters* (N.Y.: Cath Pub. Soc., 1880).

231. Carroll, ed., *Regle et Constitutiones des Soeurs Religieuses de la Misericorde*, trans. by Mary Xavier Durand (N.O.: T. Fitzwilliam 1881); Carroll, ed. *Meditations for a Novena to Our Lady of Mercy* (N.O.: T. Fitzwilliam, 1881).

232. Carroll, *Annals* 2: 531-2.

233. ASM, N.O., arrangements in process from Oct. 1880 to March 1881.

234. ASM. N.O., Austin Carroll Papers, clippings.

235. AAO, Carroll to O'Connor, Jan. 10, 1881. Both Teche towns changed the spelling of their names. The local postoffice stamped the mail "St. Martinsville" in 1881, just as contemporary records used "Jeannerette."

235. Ibid. Sisters arrived March 2, 1881, had convent blessed March 5.

236. Ibid., Carroll quoted the McAuley letter of Aug. 23, 1838. ASM, N.O., branch chronicles. The sisters opened St. Martin's Girls' Elementary and the Convent High School on March 7, St. Joseph's Colored School on March 21, and the Boys' Elementary, called "the College," on September 5—all in 1881.

237. AAO, Carroll to O'Connor, March 6, 1880.

238. Ibid.

239. Ibid.

240. ASM, N.O., Carroll to Jaeckel, March 15, 1877.

241. Leray, Bp. of Natchitoches and there only a year, was named coadjutor of New Orleans, where he began his duties as Administrator of Temporalities at the end of 1879.

242. AUND, Neithart to Leray, May 8, 1880; April 9, 1880; May 18, 1880.

243. Ibid.

244. AUND, Neithart to Leray, April 9, 1880.

245. AAO, Carroll to O'Connor, July 21, 1880.

246. Ibid.

247. AANO, Sisters of Mercy to Rouxel, May 10, 1880.

248. Ibid., April 9, 1880.

249. Ibid., May 10, 1880.

250. ASM, N.O., financial records.

251. AUND, Neithart to Leray, May 18, 1880.

252. Ibid.

253. ASM, N.O., financial records.

254. ASM, N.O. Community records and minutes show the signatures of the priest appointed by the archbishop to make visitation.

255. ASM, N.O., Girardey to Carroll, June 25, 1883.

256. Ibid.

257. Ibid.

258. ASM, N.O., minutes, Aug. 11, 1880.

259. ASM, Carlow, Carroll to Catherine Maher, April 10, 1878; Henry J. Coleridge, SJ, "The First Sister of Mercy," *The Month* 4 (Feb. 1866): 111-27.

260. ASM, Carlow, Carroll to Catherine Maher, Aug. 13, 1877.

261. Carroll, *Annals* 1: first several chapters.

262. ASM, Windham, Carroll to O'Brien, Nov. 21, 1880.

263. AAO, Carroll to O'Connor, Oct. 25, 1876.

264. Ibid., Nov. 14, 1876.

265. *Western Watchman*, Dec. 11, 1879, Rev. Theodore Clapp quoted.

266. ASM, N.O., Austin Carroll Papers, memoirs.

267. AAO, Carroll to O'connor, Oct. 27, 1877.

268. ASM, N.O., register, necrology, Angele Brousse entered in 1870 and died March 27, 1880.

269. ASM, N.O., Austin Carroll Papers, Dominica Carroll to Austin Carroll, n.d.

270. Carroll, *Annals* 1: 254-65.

271. ASM, Dublin and N.O., Clare Augustine Moore died Oct. 7, 1880.

272. ASM, Cork and N.O., necrology.

273. ASM, N.O., necrology, register. The average age of death for the first dozen Sisters of Mercy to die in New Orleans was not even 30.

274. AAO, Carroll to O'Connor, July 21, 1880. Carroll quoted McAuley to White, Oct. 17, 1837.

275. ASM, N.O., Carroll to Perché, Dec. 2, 1881; Perché to Carroll, Dec. 3, 1881.

276. Carroll, *Annals* 4: 476.

277. Carroll quoted McAuley to Fitzgerald, July 3, 1838.

278. Carroll, *Annals* 4: 475-6.

279. AAO, Carroll to O'Connor, June 16, 1882. Austin explained that, "Thanks to dear Sr. M. Elizabeth Strange, I learned that Mother McAuley published a little book called *Cottage Controversy*. I sent for it in all directions and succeeded in getting it. A copy goes to your Lordship by this post."

280. AAO, Carroll to O'Connor, Dec. 9, 1880.

NOTES – CHAPTER TEN

1. ASM, N.O., Austin Carroll Papers, memoirs.

2. ASM, N.Y., chronicles.

3. ASM, N.O., Newsboys to Carroll, July 11, 1881.

4. Ibid.

5. ASM, N.O., Austin Carroll Papers, *New Zealand Times*, Dec. 16, 1881; *West Australian Catholic Record*, n.d. [Dec. 1881].

6. AAO, Carroll to O'Connor. April 9, 22, Nov. 30, 1881.

7. Carroll, *Annals* 2: 452-3.

8. Ibid., 468-9, Mary Liguori Gibson died July 6, 1881; Mary Aloysius Consitt died April 28, 1882.

9. ASM, N.O., Austin Carroll Papers, clippings.

10. *Terra-Nova Advocate*, Dec. 15, 1881; *Connecticut Catholic*, Dec. 17, 1881.

11. ASM, N.O., Austin Carroll Papers, clippings, *N.O. Morning Star*, March 5, 1882.

12. ASM, clippings, *Boston Pilot*, Dec. 24, 1881; other cuttings contained poems by anonymous sisters in Hartford, Limerick, and Providence.

13. ASM, Limerick and N.O., Limerick chronicles; Carroll, *Leaves from the Annals of the Sisters of Mercy* vol. 1 (Catholic Pub. Soc., 1881).

14. ASM, Limerick, chronicles.

15. Ibid.

16. Ibid.

17. Ibid.

18. Carroll, Foreword, 15, 14.

19. Ibid., 30.

20. Ibid., 21.

21. *Dublin Review* 7 (Jan. 1882): 287.

22. *Irish Monthly* 10 (Sept. 1882): 616.

23. *Catholic Review*, Dec. 1881.

24. *N.O. Morning Star*, n.d.

25. AAO, Carroll to O'Connor, Sept. 5, 1883.

26. ASM, N.O., Hogan to Carroll, Dec. 5, 1881.

27. ASM, N.O., property list, deeds.

28. ASM, N.O., chronicles of St. Martinville; letters of Pere Jan or his lawyers, James Mouton and Robert Martin, to Carroll or Xavier Durand, Oct. 30, Nov. 4, 30, 1880; Jan. 26, Feb. 5, 9, 1881.

29. ASM, N.O., register, Marie Amelie Bienvenu entered March 23, 1881, and was professed on Oct. 6, 1883, and served until Oct. 11, 1934.

30. Carroll, "Southern Sketches," *Irish Monthly* 12 (April 1884): 173.

31. Ibid., 179-80.

32. Ibid., 173-81; Carroll, *Annals* 4: 430-9; Carroll, "Church of the Attakapas, 1750–1889," *American Catholic Quarterly Review* 14 (July 1889): 462-87.

33. The *Irish Monthly* published the series of "Southern Sketches" in six parts, 3 in 1883, and 3 in 1884. See individual listings in the Carroll Bibliography.

34. ASM, N.O., financial records.

35. Carroll, "Southern Sketches," *Irish Monthly* 11 (Aug. 1883): 510.

36. Ibid.; Carroll, *Annals* 4: 472.

37. Carroll, Foreword, 13-56.

38. ASM, N.O. Perché to Carroll, Dec. 4, 1882.

39. ASM, N.O., leaflets for the association. The eternal flame is still maintained although the oratory, like the original convent, fell before the destruction of the hurricane called Betsy.

40. ASM, N.O., association registry, financial accounts; Carroll, *Annals* 4: 402, 309; *Annals* 2: 347.

41. AAO, Carroll to O'Connor, June 15, 1882.

42. Ibid., ASM, N.O., Carroll to Perché, n.d.; reply April 1882. Bibliographical data is unknown on the first edition of *Cottage Controversy*, as no copy has been as yet located. If the letter of McAuley to Deasy were used as a preface in the original edition, then the publication date might have been 1838 or shortly thereafter. Austin received about six printed copies in 1882, then sent them out to friends, keeping only one to edit for the American reprint. Perhaps, one of the early convents in Ireland or England will discover their copy of the first edition.

43. ASM, N.O., Carroll to Girardey, n.d.; reply July 11, 1882.

44. Carroll to O'Connell, n.d.; reply, Sept. 15, 1882.

45. Austin's reprint, Catherine McAuley, *Cottage Controversy* (N.Y.: O'Shea, 1883), now rare, was tiny, only 3 1/2" by 5 1/2" and could easily slip between the stacks. Several New Orleans libraries used to have copies, but they seem to have been lost, as were many of the Carroll books once in the Library of Congress. The writer would be grateful to know of it if either the original Irish edition, or the Carroll 1883 edition were to be located. One of Austin's aims in compiling the *Annals* was to "preserve much that might otherwise be lost," and the wisdom of this purpose is certainly demonstrated in her preservation of this catechetical work by Catherine McAuley.

46. ASM, Windham, Carroll to Warde, Nov. 29, 1882.

47. Carroll, *The Tudor Sisters* (N.O.: T. Fitzwilliam, 1883); Carroll, ed. *Mary Queen of Scots* (N.O.: T. Fitzwilliam, 1882).

48. Carroll, "Nine Days' Queen," *American Catholic Quarterly Review* 1 (Oct. 1876): 680–712.

49. ATUL, Carroll to Cable, Sept. 16, 1882.

50. Ibid.

51. ASM, N.O., Carroll to Quinlan, Sept. 13, 1882.

52. ASM, Windham, Carroll to O'Brien, Nov. 29, 1882.

53. ASM, N.O., clippings, most unidentified like that quoted.

54. *N.O. Morning Star*, Oct. 15, 1882.

55. ASM, Windham, Carroll to Warde, Nov. 29, 1882.

56. *N.O. Item* quoted Letter from Warrington dated Oct. 15, 1882.

57. ASM, Windham, Carroll to Warde, Nov. 29, 1882.

58. Warrington letter, Oct. 15, 1882.

59. ASM, Windham, Carroll to Warde, Nov. 29, 1882.

60. Carroll, *Annals* 1: 230; McAuley to Elizabeth Moore, March 21, 1840.

61. ASM, N.O., register, Mary Rose Lee withdrew from the Mercy community in Oct. 1882.

62. Cosgrove to Sisters of Mercy, Nov. 2, 1882.

63. ASM, Windham, Carroll to Warde, Sept. 3, Nov. 16, 1882; Mary Stanislaus Donovan recovered from yellow fever to give long service in Belize. AAO, Carroll to O'Connor, Nov. 6, 1883.

64. *Escambia County Historical Quarterly* 6 (March 1976); *Brewton Banner*, Oct. 6, 13, 30, 1883.

65. ASM, Providence and N.O., Belize chronicles.

66. Ibid.

67. Ibid., the Belize chronicles open with the background in the decision to accept the Belize mission.

68. Carroll, *Annals* 4: 440; AUND, Carroll to Leray, Oct. 15, 1883.

69. ASM, Providence and N.O., Belize chronicles.

70. ASM, N.O., DiPietro to Carroll, Nov. 22, 1882.

71. ASM, Providence and N.O., Belize chronicles.

72. ASM, N.O., Teresa Maher to Carroll, n.d.

73. *N.O. Morning Star*, Jan. 14, 1883. Although the newspaper gives the departure date as the fourteenth, both the Belize chronicles and Carroll's *Annals* give Jan. 15.

74. Austin risked Leray's displeasure, though he was not the archbishop, to bring education to the girls in Belize. First group to be stationed in this foreign branch were Sisters Mary Evangelist Kearney, Raphael Woolfolk, Colette Baker, Paula Sebastian, and Gabriel Lavin. Companion to return with Austin was Henry or Henriette Briscoe.

75. From Buenos Aires Evangelista Fitzpatrick transferred her sisters to Adelaide, Australia, and ten years later, some of them returned to South America with Baptist O'Donnell. Austin met this group in Liverpool in 1890, as they prepared to take ship for Argentina.

76. ASM, Belize chronicles, St. Catherine's and Holy Redeemer both opened on Jan. 22, 1883.

77. The sisters visited the public institutions on Jan. 24, the sick in their homes on Jan. 25, 26, 28.

78. ASM, Belize chronicles.

79. ASM, N.O., deeds for the sale of the Cox property on Dean, later Gabourel Street, were dated Feb. 8, 1883; tinted plat accompanies deed.

80. ASM, Belize chronicles.

81. Assigned to Belize in the fall of 1883 were Sisters Mary Stanislaus Donovan, Rosina Bodkin, and Augusta Fitzpatrick. Assigned in 1884 and 1885 were Sisters Mary Rosaria Devlin, Mercedes Manning, Augustine McGuire, and Anita McDermott. Sisters who found the climate too difficult were reassigned elsewhere after 3 years, while those who enjoyed the mission work remained for long years of service, some for a lifetime.

82. ASM, Belize chronicles.

83. Ibid. The writer would like to have a sampling of Austin Carroll's letters to the Belize convent or any of the branch convents, or even copies of the school paper, *The Young Collegian*, which carried articles of the pupils in all the branches. Perhaps some fond parent preserved copies containing articles of a son or daughter. This school paper was printed on heavy paper, not newsprint, and would have preserved well.

84. ASM, Belize chronicles.

85. Carroll, "Nuns in Honduras," *Irish Monthly* 11 (July 1883): 446–551; Carroll, *Annals* 4: 440–6.

86. AUND, Carroll to Hudson, May 24, 1883.

87. ASM, Windham, Carroll to Warde, Jan. 7, Feb. 2, Nov. 29, Dec. 19, 1882.

88. ASM, Windham, Carroll to Clifton or O'Brien, Nov. 29, 1882; Jan. 8, July 22, 1883.

89. ASM, Windham, Carroll to O'Brien, July 22, 1883; Carroll dated *Annals* on April 30, the feast of the Mercy foundress.

90. *London Tablet* and other undated clippings; AAO, Carroll to O'Connor, Sept. 5, 1883.

91. ASM, Windham, Carroll to Warde, Dec. 19, 1882.

92. Ibid., Carroll, *Annals* 2: 44.

93. ASM, Carlow, Carroll to Catherine Maher, Aug. 13, 1877.

94. ASM, Limerick, chronicles.

95. AAO, Carroll to O'Connor, Aug. 20, 1877.

96. Ibid., Carroll, *Clement Hofbauer*, 239; see also chap 5, n. 42.

97. Carroll, *Clement Hofbauer*, 83.

98. ASM, N.O., minutes.

99. AUND, Rouxel to Perché, June 24, 1883; ACPF, Simeoni to Rouxel, June 5, 1883.

100. ACPF, Jaeckel to Eminence, May 25, 1883.

101. Ibid.

102. AUND, Neithart to Leray, April 9, 1880.

103. ACPF, Rouxel to Simeoni, July 10, 1883.

104. ASM, N.O., clippings; annual closing programs contain effusive praise for the Mercy teachers, usually given by the Redemptorist director.

105. ASM, N.Ol, Girardey to Carroll, June 25, 1883.

106. Ibid.

107. AUND, Ruland to Blanc, June 17, 1854.

108. Ibid.

109. ACPF, Simeoni to Rouxel, June 5, 1883; Rouxel appointed Theobald Butler, SJ, for the visitation on June 30, 1883. Records showed that the only year visitation was ever skipped was the year of the 1878 yellow fever epidemic.

110. ASM, N.O., Girardey to Carroll, June 25, 1883.

111. Ibid.

112. ACPF, Jaeckel to Simeoni, May 25, 1883.

113. ASM, N.O., Sisters of Mercy to Butler, June 30, 1883.

114. ACPF, Rouxel to Simeoni, July 10, 1883.

115. Ibid.

116. ACPF, Butler to Rouxel, July 3, 1883.

117. ACPF, Rouxel to Simeoni, July 10, 1883.

118. Ibid.

119. Ibid.

120. Ibid.

121. ASM, N.O., Austin Carroll Papers. The 1880 investigation of the Mercy Rule was made by Benedict Neithart, CSSR, who concluded that Austin Carroll could be elected according to the Rule in 1880 and 1883. Although Neithart was generally considered to be a brilliant man, Giesen and Jaeckel, who formed the anti-Austin clique, ignored his conclusions in their petitions and complaints addressed to Rome. From the correspondence of Neithart to Leray and the report of Rouxel to Simeoni, it is clear that Henry Geisen formed three-fourths of the clique. His earlier friendly attitude toward Austin changed drastically after she decided not to send a mission branch to St. Thomas Island and protested the lack of salary.

122. ACPF. The clique wanted to establish a community that would work only within the parish and be directed completely by the priests, not a diocesan congregation, but a parish one. This is spelled out in their Giesen/Jaeckel missive to Simeoni, May 25, 1883.

123. AAO, Carroll to O'Connor, Jan. 10, March 3, June 15, 1882.

124. ASM, N.O., Girardey and Sisters of Mercy to Perché, Feb. 6, April 9, 25, 1883.

125. *N.O. Morning Star*, Jan. 14, 28, March 6, 20, May 13, 1883.

126. ASM, Windham, Carroll to Warde and O'Brien, Jan. 7, Nov. 29, 1882.

127. Ibid., Aug. 13, Nov. 16, 1883.

128. ASM, N.O., Austin Carroll Papers.

129. AAO, Carroll to O'Connor, Oct. 25, 1876.

130. Carroll, "Nuns in Louisiana," *Irish Monthly* 12 (June, Sept., 1884): 344–55; 469–85.

131. Carroll, *Annals* 3: 335, 343. Margaret Fitzpatrick was received on June 22, 1851 as Mary Aloysius, was professed two years later, and died Oct. 2, 1859.

132. Carroll, *Annals* 2: 23–5. Maria Nugent was received as Mary Joseph, made her vows March 25, 1843, and died on June 24, 1847, the second Mercy to die in America.

133. ASM, N.O., clippings, *N.O. Morning Star*, n.d., quoted in Irish newspaper.

134. *N.O. Morning Star*, March 16, July 6, 16, and n.d., 1884. After Margaret Haughery's death, a fund was begun to raise a fitting memorial to this friend of the orphans. The tribute of Austin Carroll was written after the statue was installed on Margaret Place in July 1884.

135. ASM. N.O., Austin Carroll Papers.

136. ASM, N.O., Girardey to Carroll, June 25, 1883.

137. ACPF, DiPietro to Leo XIII, Sept. 1883.

138. ACPF, Eminence to DiPietro, Sept. 6, 1883.

139. AAO, Carroll to O'Connor, Aug. 4, 1883.

140. Ibid., Carroll to O'Connor, Aug. 4, 1883.

141. Ibid., Sept. 22, 1883.

142. Ibid., Sept. 5, 1883.

143. Ibid.

144. ASM, N.O., minutes; Perché to Sisters of Mercy, July 3, 1883; Rouxel to Sisters of Mercy, July 9, 1883.

145. AAO, Carroll to O'Connor, Sept. 22, 1883.

146. Ibid., Aug. 4, Sept. 5, 1883.

147. ASM, N.O., chronicles St. Michael's Convent of Mercy. The convent was established on Oct. 6, 1883, and the colored school on Oct. 8, 1883.

148. APIC, Carroll to Kirby, Oct. 17, 1883.

149. ASM, N.O., Perché to Carroll, Oct. 12, 1883.

150. ASM, N.O., Elder to Carroll, Oct. 26, 1883; ADJ, Elder to Leray, Nov. 15, 1883; AAO, Carroll to O'Connor, Nov. 6, 1883.

151. APIC, Carroll to Kirby, Oct. 17, 1883.

152. Ibid.

153. ASM, N.O., Perché to Carroll, Oct. 12, 1883.

154. ASM, N.O., Leray to Carroll, Oct. 6, 9, and 20.

155. AAO, Carroll to O'Connor, Nov. 6, 1883.

156. AUND, Carroll to Leray, Oct. 15, 1883.

157. Ibid.

158. AAO, Carroll to O'Connor, Nov. 6, 1883.

159. Ibid., Nov. 10, 1883.

160. ASM, Windham, Carroll to Warde, Nov. 16, 30, Dec. 25, 1883.

161. AAO, Carroll to O'Connor, Nov. 20, 1883; Feb. 29, 1884.

162. AANO, Gayarré to Rouquette, Nov. 22, Dec. 7, 1883; ALSU, Gayarré Papers, Nov. 1883.

163. ASM, N.O., Austin Carroll Papers, Austin sent tickets to Mercies from one coast to the other. AANO, Gayarré to Rouquette, Dec. 7, 1883.

164. Ibid.

165. ATUL, Gayarré letterbook.

166. ASM, Windham, Carroll to Warde, Nov. 30, 1883.

167. ACPF, Carroll to Simeoni, Dec. 12, 1883.

168. The Mercy Rule specified that the date of the election could be transferred, and the sisters wanted to have the election in Dec., when the Belize sisters could come during vacation. The change was approved by ecclesiastical director Girardey on April 25, 1883, by Visitor Butler on June 30, 1883, by Vicar Roussel on July 9, 1883, and by Archbishop Perché on July 3, 1883. The act of elections in December was signed by witnesses Rouxel and L. A. Chassé, and later by Archbishop Perché. Yet this is the election that Leray told Rome must be declared null and void.

169. ASM, Windham, Carroll to Warde, Dec. 25, Dec.28.

170. ASM, N.O., Carroll visited Perché Dec. 26, prayed with him, and he died the next day. Then Leray automatically succeeded him.

171. AAO, Carroll to O'Connor, Feb. 29, 1884.

172. AAO, Fitzgerald to O'Callaghan, Dec. 12, 1883.

173. Ibid.

174. AAO, Carroll to O'Connor, Feb. 29, 1884.

175. Ibid.

176. AAO, FitzGerald to O'Callaghan, Dec. 12, 1883; O'Callaghan to Propaganda Fide, Dec. 17, 1883.

177. Ibid.

178. ASM, Carlow, Carroll to Catherine Maher, March 12, 1884.

179. ASM, Windham, Carroll to O'Brien, April 19, 1884.

180. Bishop Manucy was transferred from Brownsville to Mobile in March, 1884.

181. ASM, N.O., Austin Carroll Papers, deaths: William Meredith, CSSR, March 1884; Jeremiah Moynihan, May 1884.

182. ASM, N.O., Austin Carroll Papers, deaths: Vincent Haire, March 1883; Augustine McKenna, Aug. 1883; Juliana Hardman, March 1884.

183. ASM, Windham, Carroll to O'Brien, Nov. 30, 1883; April 29, 1884.

184. ASM, N.O., Austin Carroll sent those who wanted sisters to Leray.

185. AUND, Carroll to Leray, Dec. 27, 1884; AANO, Manucy to Leray, June 23, 1884; Browne to Leray, Oct. 14, 1884.

186. ACPF, Leray to Simeoni, April 7, 1884.

187. ACPF, Leray to Simeoni, June 11, 1884.

188. AANO, Jaeckel to Leray, May 5, 1884.

189. ACPF, Leray to Simeoni, June 11, 1884.

190. AANO, Jaeckel to Leray, May 5, 1884.

191. ACPF, Bartolini to Propaganda Fide, Aug. 11, 1884.

192. Ibid.

193. AAO, O'Callaghan to Propaganda Fide, Dec. 17, 1883; ACPF, Rouxel to Simeoni, July 10, 1883; DiPetro to Simeoni, Oct. 24, 1884.

194. ACPF, Bartolini to Propaganda Fide, Aug. 11, 1884.

195. ACPF, Simeoni to Leray, April 7, 1884.

196. ACPF, Leray to Simeoni, June 11, 1884.

197. AANO, Manucy to Leray, June 23, 1884.

198. AAO, Carroll to O'Connor, Aug. 30, 1884.

199. ASM, N.O. and Mobile, property records. Note that it was in 1884 that Austin Carroll established a Mercy convent in the city of Mobile, but as early as 1877 she had opened branch convents in the Mobile diocese. Unfortunately, the Healy life of Warde perpetuated early errors by placing Carroll in Mobile early enough to have her founding Belize from Mobile. Mobile was established almost two years after Belize, and both were branches. Austin Carroll's forty years in the South were spent establishing branches. Mobile and the other convents in the diocese were branches until the bishops separated them from New Orleans, thus turning Selma or Mobile into a foundation, fourteen years after the Sisters of Mercy began serving in the diocese.

200. ASM, N.O. The Loewekamp/Carroll contract was signed before a notary public on Dec. 31, 1884.

201. Bernard Hafkenscheid, CSSR, had viewed the great work of the Redemptorists to be giving missions. Hence, he said the priests could not be tied down with the position of ecclesiastic superior as it would interfere with "the duties of the missionary life." AAO, Hafkenscheid to Michael O'Connor, Feb. 2, 1850.

202. ASM, N.O. The sisters served in the asylum from 1876 until 1926, when the various orphanages within the diocese were consolidated under the Commission of Charities.

203. Carroll received a telegram on Sept. 17, 1884, from Gonzaga O'Brien.

204. ASM, Windham, Carroll to O'Brien, Sept. 18, 1884.

205. Ibid.

206. Ibid.

207. Ibid.

208. *N.O. Morning Star*, Sept. 14, 21, Oct. 5, 1884; Carroll, *Annals* 4, chap. 29-30.

209. AAO, Carroll to O'Connor, March 3, 1882. Mothers Xavier Warde and Austin Carroll, though friends, differed in many respects. Each recognized in the other many fine traits and some faults. Neither of these Mercy leaders felt the need to claim that the other was perfect. In her books Austin was strong and positive in her praise of Xavier, and only in a private letter to her spiritual director did Austin ever question the actions of Xavier Warde. Austin's letters to Manchester, both to Warde and to O'Brien, illustrate her friendshiop and a growing tolerance of another's weaknesses.

210. Carroll, *Annals* 1: 255-6.

211. Ibid., *Annals* 4: 282-3.

212. ASM, N.O., Austin Carroll Papers, Walsh tribute.

213. AAO, Carroll to O'Connor, Jan. 5, 1889.

214. ASM, N.O., Carroll to Leo XIII, Nov. 27, 1884. Carroll appointed the first superior in each branch convent at the time of their establishment. Her choices must have been good, for these were the sisters elected as leaders of the whole community for many years and long after Carroll was dead.

215. *London Tablet*, Dec. 13, 1884, and *N.O. Morning Star*, Jan. 4, 1885 printed the letter from Leo XIII to Carroll, but the letter itself is no longer extant.

216. Carroll, "Southern Sketches," *Irish Monthly* 12 (Jan., April, Sept. 1884); Carroll, *Annals* 4, chap. 49-50.

217. Carroll, *Annals* 4: 402.

218. Carroll, *Lectures Delivered at a Spiritual Retreat* (N.Y.: Catholic Pub. Soc., 1885); Carroll, trans. *Principles of Government of St. Ignatius*, by Ribadeneira (N.Y.: Catholic Pub. Soc., 1885).

219. *N.O. Morning Star*, July 8, 1883. This paper regularly carried the reports on the special work of the Society of St. Vincent de Paul, like the Newsboys Home which they sponsored on Camp, then Bank Alley.

220. *N.O. Morning Star*, July 27, 1884.

221. *Report and Catalogue of the Woman's Department of the World's Exposition, New Orleans 1884-1885* (Boston: Rand, Avery, 1885), 192-3. Besides Alcott and Stowe, other authors on display were Julia W. Howe, George Eliot, Maria Edgeworth, Jane Austen, and the three Bronte sisters.

222. William T. Francis, "Convent Chimes — Reverie," (N.O.: Louis Grunewald, 1885), dedication is on the cover sheet. Unfortunately there is no extant record as to the act or charity which prompted the composition.

223. ASM, N.O., chronicles of the branch convents; clippings also mention it.

224. APIC, Carroll to Kirby, May 17, 1885.

225. ASM, N.O., clippings, many from the *N.O. Morning star*, which chronicled the arrival of each clerical visitor to the World's Centennial Exposition.

226. ASJ, Baltimore, the Benoit diary, April 5, 1875.

227. ASM, N.O., chronicles of the branch convents.

228. ASM, N.O., financial records, St. Martinville chronicles.

229. ASM, N.O., Providence, Belize chronicles. When Austin Carroll opened the convent in Belize in 1883, the administrator of the colony was the Lieutenant Governor, the Honorable Colonel, Sir Robert W. Harley, C.B., K.C.M.G., whose service in Belize had begun in 1871, and whom, Austin learned, was the brother of Sister Mary Caroline Harley one of the two companions professed with Catherine McAuley at George's Hill. The next governor was the Honorable sir Roger Tuckfield Goldsworthy, C.M.G., K.C.M.G., whose promised assistance for the building was not forthcoming. The titles and terms in office were contained in D. Morris, *The Colony of British Honduras* (London: Stratford, 1883), ix; and in L. W. Bristowe, *Handbook of British Honduras* (London: Blackwood, 1890), 14.

230. ASM, N.O., chronicles of branch convents.

231. ASM, N.O., register. While Carroll was superior, New Orleans gave permanent hospitality to Sisters Mary Vincent Labry, Teresa Vienne, Mercedes Vienne, Evangelista O'Rorke, Joseph Stapleton, Rosina Bodkin, Teresa Martyn, Alphonsine Lewis, Agnes Greene, and Gabriel Lynch. Austin Carroll frequently gave brief hospitality to traveling nuns, usually on a begging tour. Leray became angry that she took in one such pair, but she wrote on March 28, 1884 that she simply could not refuse them because they "came fatigued, hungry, and dirty."

232. ASM, N.O., chronicles; APIC, O'Connell to Kirby, June 17, 1885.

233. AAO, Carroll to O'Connor, Feb. 23, 1885.

234. Ibid., Jan. 10, 1882; Oct. 1, 1884; Feb. 23, 1885.

235. ASM, Merion, Waldron to O'Connor, Feb. 16, 1885.

236. AAO, Carroll to O'Connor, Feb. 23, 1885.

237. Ibid.

238. ADJ, Elder to Gibbons, April 23, 1879.

239. AAO, Carroll to O'Connor, Oct. 1, 1884; Feb. 23, March 2, 1885 re Robot et al.

240. Ibid., April 22, 1885; Feb. 23, 1884; March 2, 1885.

241. ACPF, Michael O'Connor to Barnabo, Oct. 3, 1852; Barnabo to Michael O'Connor, Dec. 4, 1852. The *Abridged Mercy Guide* so widely followed was used as a consultative reference by Austin. Pages 5 and 9 spelled out accepting payment for teaching: "If it is expedient that the children pay a trifle weekly ... it should be expended on school requirements or on works of charity," and the same went for the girls in teacher-training institutions "towards whose support a small sum can be paid."

242. AAO, Carroll to O'Connor, Oct. 10, 1884.

243. Ibid.

244. Ibid.

245. Ibid., March 2, 31, 1885.

246. Ibid., March 31, 1885.

247. ASM, N.O., chronicles, St. Martinville.

248. Sisters of Mercy to Leray in 1885; APIC, May 17, AUND, May 21, 25; AANO, May 26; [June].

249. ASM, N.O., Carroll to Leray, May 17, 1885.

250. Ibid.

251. Ibid.

252. AAO, Carroll to O'Connor, May 25, March 2, 31, 1885.

253. ASM, N.O., Leray to Carroll, May 23, 14, 1885.

254. AAO, Carroll to O'Connor, March 6, 1880.

255. AAO, Carroll to Leray, May 27, 1885.

256. AAO, Carroll to O'Connor, May 25, 27, 1885.

257. Ibid.

258. APIC, Carroll to Kirby, May 27, 1885.

259. Ibid.

260. Ibid.

261. Ibid.

262. Ibid.

263. Ibid.

264. AUND, Sisters of Mercy to Leray, May 21, 1885.

265. AANO, Ibid., May 26, [June], 1885.

266. APIC, Ibid., May 17, 1885.

267. AUND, Ibid., May 25, 1885.

268. AANO, Ibid., May 26, 1885.

269. AUND, May 21, 1885.

270. AANO, Woolfolk to Leray, [June], 1885.

271. AANO, Sisters of Mercy to Leray, May 21, 1885.

272. Ibid., [June], 1885.

273. Ibid.

274. AUND, Ibid., May 25, 1885.

275. Ibid., May 21, 1885.

276. APIC, Sisters of Mercy to Leo XIII, June 2, 1885.

277. APIC, Butler to Kirby, June 1, 1885.

278. Ibid.

279. ACPF, Simeoni to Leray, April 29, 1885.

280. Ibid.

281. ACPF, DiPietro to Propaganda Fide, Sept. 6, Oct. 24, 1883.

282. APIC, Carroll to Kirby, May 27, 1885; ASM, N.O., archival data from the Redemptorists, N.O.

283. AAO, Carroll to O'Connor, Aug. 22, 1885.

284. AAB, O'Connell to Gibbons, O'Connell was quoting Simeoni.

285. AUND, Leray to Simeoni, n.d., rough copy; ACPF, Ibid., June 11, 1884.

286. ACPF, Simeoni to Leray, April 29, 1885; Bartolini to Simeoni, Aug. 11, 1884.

287. ACPF, Leray to Simeoni, June 11, 1884.

288. ACPF, Simeoni to Leray, April 7, 1883.

289. Ibid., June 11, 1884; April 7, 1883.

290. ACPF, Simeoni to Leray, April 29, 1885.

291. ASM, N.O., elections held Aug. 7, 1885.

292. AAO, Carroll to O'Connor, Aug. 22, 1885.

293. Ibid.

294. Ibid.

295. Ibid.

296. APIC, Sisters of Mercy to Kirby, Aug. 13, 1885.

297. ACPF, Bartolini to Simeoni, Aug. 11, 1884; Franzelin, SJ, to Propaganda Fide, March 1885. Franzelin of the German College in Rome, suggested that no statement be made re the 1883 election of Austin Carroll because it was canonically proper, licit, and valid; and therefore, not suited to the request of Leray that she be put out of office. Since the common law favored shorter terms for superiors, the decision to hold a new election could be said to follow from that. Thus, in this report, unlike that of Bartolini, the aim was to please a certain side, the Germans and Leray. Report in the acta of April 1885.

298. ASM, N.O., minutes. The community was greatly embarrassed to have this private business of elections bandied about by those who seemed to wish them evil. Austin Carroll had requested that a Jesuit be one of the examiners. Neithart had judged in 1880 that Austin could, according to the Mercy rule be elected in 1883.

299. Butler, SJ, and Rouxel had also come to that conclusion.

300. ASM, N.O., third examination of the community and rule about elections was held Sept. 3, 1885, and among other findings of the visitors, Austin was canonically elected until 1886. ACPF, deCarrière/Bogaerts report, Sept. 29, 1885.

301. Ibid.

302. Ibid.

303. Ibid.

304. Ibid.

305. Ibid.

306. Ibid.

307. Ibid.

308. Ibid.

309. Ibid.

310. Ibid.

311. Ibid.

312. Ibid., deCarrière and Bogaerts made the protest against Leray's demand a part of the report itself.

313. Ibid., the visitors noted that the report was given to one party of the controversy only under protest.

314. ACPF, deCarrière/Bogaerts report to Propaganda Fide, Sept. 29, 1885.

315. Ibid.

316. AANO, Butler to Leray, Sept. 15, 1885; APIC, Carroll to Kirby, Sept. 18, 1885.

317. ASM, N.O., Austin Carroll Papers; APIC, Carroll to Kirby, Aug. 12, 1885.

318. ACPF, deCarrière/Bogaerts report, Sept. 29, 1885.

319. Ibid.

320. Ibid.

321. APIC, Carroll to Kirby, Sept. 29, 1885.

322. ACPF, Simeoni to Gibbons, July 15, 1885.

323. AAB, Janssens to Gibbons, Sept. 6, 1885.

324. ASM, N.O., Carroll Family Papers, Kirby to Carroll, Oct. 9, 1885, contained in Austin Carroll to William Carroll, Oct. 27, 1885.

325. ACPF, Simeoni to Gibbons, July 15, 1885; Acta, Nov. 16, 1885.

326. AUND, Loewekamp to Leray, Aug. 29, Nov. 16.

327. AANO, Chapelle notes, Nov. 23, 1885; APIC, Carroll to Kirby, Dec. 3, 1885.

328. AAO, Carroll to O'Connor, Nov. 30, 1885.

329. AAB, Leray to Gibbons, July 21, 1885.

330. ACPF, Gibbons to Simeoni, Dec. 17, 1885; AAb, Sisters of Mercy to Gibbons, Nov. 25, 1885.

331. ACPF, Gibbons to Simeoni, Dec. 3, 1885.

332. ASM, N.O., deCarrière/Bogaerts report, Sept. 29, 1885.

333. ACPF, Gibbons to Simeoni, Dec. 3, 17, 18, 1885.

334. AAO, Carroll to O'Connor, Aug. 22, 1885.

335. APIC, Carroll to Kirby, Dec. 3, 1885.

336. ACPF, Gibbons to Simeoni, Dec. 3, 17, 1885.

337. AAB, Sisters of Mercy to Gibbons or Leray, Nov. 26, 1885; Dec. 10, 1885.

338. AAB, Cook to Gibbons, Nov. 26, 1885.

339. ACPF, Gibbons to Simeoni, Dec. 3, 17, 1885.

340. APIC, D. O'Connell to Kirby, Jan. 22, 1886.

341. Ibid.

342. Ibid.

343. ACPF, Rouxel to Simeoni, July 16, 1883; deCarrieère/Bogaerts report, Sept. 29, 1885.

344. APIC, D. O'Connell to Kirby, Jan. 22, 1886.

345. APIC, Carroll to Kirby, Dec. 3, 1885.

346. APIC, D. O'Connell to Kirby, Jan. 22, 1886.

347. Ibid.

348. AAB, Gilmour to Gibbons, Dec. 20, 1886.

349. APIC, Carroll to Kirby, Dec. 3, 1885.

350. AANO, deCarrière/Bogaerts report, Sept. 29, 1885.

351. APIC, Carroll to Kirby, Dec. 3, 1885.

352. AAB, Leray to Gibbons, Jan. 6, 1887.

353. AAB, Gibbons diary, June 2, 1879, when he suggested Leray; Leray to Gibbons, Jan. 6, 1887.

354. APIC, Carroll to Kirby, Aug. 12, 1885.

355. APIC, Butler to Kirby, Aug. 13, 1885.

356. ASM, N.O., minutes.

357. APIC, Carroll to Kirby, Dec. 3, Aug. 13, Sept. 18, 1885.

358. Ibid., Dec. 3, 1885; Jan. 29, 30, 1886.

359. Ibid., June 2, 1886; Butler promise, June 2, 1886.

360. ASM, N.O., minutes; APIC, Carroll to Kirby, Jan. 29, 1886.

361. APIC, Carroll to Kirby, Jan. 29, 30, 1886.

NOTES – CHAPTER ELEVEN

1. APIC, Kirby Papers, about a dozen letters from Carroll.

2. ASM, Carlow, Windham, Limerick, San Francisco, about a dozen Carroll letters.

3. Mary Aulalia Herron, *Sisters of Mercy in the United States, 1843-1928* (N.Y.: Macmillan, 1929, 289.

4. ASM, Limerick, chronicles.

5. Ibid.

6. ASM, Windham, about two dozen Carroll letters.

7. ASM, Limerick, chronicles.

8. AAO, Carroll to O'Connor, Nov. 1885.

9. APIC, Carroll to Kirby, Jan. 30, 1886.

10. Ibid., Dec. 3, 1885.

11. AANO, Sisters of Mercy to Leray, Nov. 10, 23, 1885.

12. ASM, N.O., Carroll Family Papers, Austin Carroll to her father William Carroll, Oct. 27, 1885.

13. Ibid., Carroll enclosed Kirby letter of Oct. 9, 1885.

14. ASM, Windham, Carroll to O'Brien, April 29, 1884.

15. Ibid., Sept. 11, 1884.

16. Ibid., April 29, Sept. 11, 1884.

17. Ibid., June 9, 1884.

18. Ibid.

19. ASM, N.O., Austin Carroll Papers.

20. ASM, Birr, chronicles.

21. ASM, N.O., Austin Carroll Papers, clippings. Austin Carroll managed to have local papers print the death notice of each prominent Mercy who died.

22. ASM, Brisbane, Whitty to Marmion, Nov. 12, 1841. This letter, one of a series which presents details about the death of Catherine McAuley, surfaced when Mary Felicitas Powers visited the Mercy archives in Australia. The letter validates several points which Austin Carroll preserved for the Mercy community, like the legacy of charity and the cup of tea mentioned in the Carroll *Catherine McAuley*, 435-7.

23. ASM, Brisbane, Whitty letters.

24. ASM, Carlow, Carroll to Catherine Maher, about six letters.

25. ASM, Carlow, Naas, Little Rock.

26. ASM, N.O. and Little Rock. Mary Agnes Greene left Arkansas to help Teresa Muldoon, from St. Louis and Fort Dodge. Muldoon was trying to establish a foundation in Galveston in 1879. Then the group transferred several times in eastern Texas and southwest Missouri, and in 1883 to Fort Worth, where Agnes taught until the sisters transferred again five years later. Then, accompanied by Gabriel Lynch, Agnes Greene applied to Austin Carroll for hospitality. Agnes died in New Orleans in 1903.

27. ASM, Carlow, Carroll to Catherine Maher, Sept. 17, March 12, 1884. Francis Clare Cusack, a Poor Clare nun, became an activist at the time of the famine and collected money for food for the starving. When she began condemning the English authorities in newspaper articles both her community and the local church authorities insisted that she stop the public writing and work for the poor. Thus the condemnations adversely affected her efforts as her collections ceased altogether.

28. AAO, Carroll to O'Connor, Jan. 23, 1889.

29. Ibid., Jan. 5, 6, 23, 1889.

30. Ibid., Jan. 5, 1889.

31. Ibid., Jan. 6, 1889.

32. Ibid.

33. Francis Clare Cusack, *The Nun of Kenmare: An Autobiography* (Boston: Tichnor & co., 1889).

34. AAO, Carroll to O'Connor, Jan. 23, 1889.

35. In Dorothy Vidulich, *Peace Pays a Price* (Teaneck, N.J.: Garden State Press, 1975), 29, the author quotes Msgr. Gualdi of Propaganda Fide, who assured Cusack that "while many letters of complaint against her had passed through his hands, There was not one charge substantiated.' " He then continued in words that certainly could have been stated of the German letters as well, that "Propaganda Fide was used to this: letters full of complaints, rumors ... not one word of fact.' "

36. AAO, Carroll to O'Connor, Jan. 5, 23, 1889.

37. Ibid., Jan. 1887.

38. AAB, Keane to Gibbons, Dec. 29, 1886.

39. Ibid.

40. AAB, Gibbons diary, Nov. 24, 1886.

41. AAO, Carroll to O'Connor, Jan. 1887; Jan. 23, 1889.

42. AAB, Janssens to Gibbons, Sept. 6, 1885.

43. AAO, Carroll to O'Connor, Jan. 23, 1889.

44. Carroll, *Ursulines in Louisiana*. The booklet had run serially in local papers.

45. Carroll, "What Is True Education?" *Catholic World* 43 (June 1886): 404–13.

46. APIC, Carroll to Kirby, June 2, 1886.

47. Carroll, *Catholic World*, 404–13.

48. Carroll, "Education in Louisiana in French Colonial Days;" "Education in New Orleans in Spanish Colonial Days," *American Catholic Quarterly Review* 11, 13 (July 1886; April 1887): 396–418; 253–71.

49. Carroll, "Church of the Attakapas," *American Catholic Quarterly Review* 14: 462–87.

50. Carroll, "Twenty-Four Years in Buenos Ayres," *American Catholic Quarterly Review* 13 (July 1888) 478–92; Carroll, "Western Heroine," *Irish Monthly* 17 (May 1889): 242–54.

51. ASM, Windham, Carroll to O'Brien, Feb. 20, 1886.

52. Ibid., July 22, 1883; Dec. 4, 1885; Feb. 20, 1886.

53. Ibid., Nov. 21, 1880; July 22, 1883; April 29, Sept. 18, 1884; Sept. 14, 1885.

54. Ibid., April 29, 1884.

55. AAO, Carroll to O'Connor, May 14, 1886.

56. ASM, Windham, March 31, 1883.

57. APIC, Carroll to Kirby, June 21, 1888.

58. Ibid.

59. Ibid., June 2, 1886; June 21, 1888.

60. Ibid., June 2, 1886.

61. AUND, Butler to Leray, June 18, 1886, quoted Msgr. Capara.

62. Ibid., ASM, N.O., deCarrière/Bogaerts report, Sept. 29, 1885.

63. Ibid., APIC, Carroll to Kirby, June 2, 1886.

64. ASM, N.O., Carroll Family Papers, Mercy Carroll to Austin Carroll, Jan. 6, 10, 1887.

65. Ibid., AAO, Carroll to O'Connor, Jan. 1887.

66. ASM, N.O., Carroll Family Papers, Mercy Carroll to Austin Carroll, Jan. 10, 1887.

67. AAO, Carroll to O'Connor, Feb. 7, 1887.

68. ASM, N.O., Carroll Family Papers, Sisters of Mercy to Carroll, Jan. 15, 1887.

69. Ibid.

70. AAO, Carroll to O'Connor, Feb. 7, 1887.

71. ASM, N.O., minutes, Austin Carroll Papers, memoirs.

72. Ibid.

73. APIC, Carroll to Kirby, June 2, 1886; June 21, 1888; AAO, Carroll to O'Connor, Dec. 16, 1886; Jan., May 10, 1887.

74. ASM, N.O., Loewekamp to Butler, May 1887.

75. ASM, N.O., ibid., minutes.

76. ASM, N.O., Butler and Devereux to Loewekamp, June 1, 1887.

77. Ibid., minutes.

78. Ibid., financial records.

79. ASM, N.O., minutes, register.

80. ASM, N.O., financial records.

81. ASM, N.O., Austin Carroll Papers, memoirs, register.

82. ASM, N.O., register.

83. ASM, N.O., memoirs; ADJ, Colman to Janssens, n.d.

84. APIC, Carroll to Kirby, Aug. 12, 1885.

85. ASM, N.O., memoirs.

86. APIC, Butler to Kirby, Aug. 13, 1885.

87. ASM, N.O., register.

88. ASM, N.O., minutes. Austin Carroll served as mistress of novices from 1871–1880.

89. ASM, N.O., register. Teresa Gourrier was the first native Creole candidate; Xavier Durand was the first native Acadian candidate; and Margaret Mary Killelea was a lovely pupil from St. Alphonsus School. Gourrier died after 16 years in the community, Durand after 10, and Killelea after 8.

90. ASM, N.O., minutes, register, memoirs. Kate Imhoff had married Thomas Walsh, and the couple had five children. One baby had died in infancy in 1875, in 1878 Kate lost three children, one in an accident, two to yellow fever, and 1879 her husband. Her youngest child, just over a year, died of pneumonia in 1880. After a three-year friendship with Austin Carroll,

Kate Walsh entered the Mercy community, lived and worked with Austin ten years, and acquired her breadth of vision and compassion for others. Long after the death of Austin, Borgia Walsh served as a strong leader for the community.

91. ASM, Windham, Carroll to O'Brien, Feb. 20, 1886; AAO, Carroll to O'Connor, March 19, 1877.

92. Carroll, *Clement Hofbauer*, 160.

93. Carroll, *Annals* 2: 199.

94. Gaffney, 10.

95. C. C. Martindale, *The Queen's Daughters: a Study of Women Saints* (N.Y.: Sheed & Ward, 1951), 152-3.

96. Ibid.

97. Carroll, *Annals* 4: 519.

98. ASM, N.O., Austin Carroll Papers, letters: Nov. 27, 1889; Dec. 15, 1888; Nov. 29, 1882; Dec. 4, 1885; March 22, 1888; n.d.; Dec. 4, 1895; Jan. 14, Nov. 9, 1888.

99. ASM, N.O., clippings, most undated.

100. APIC, Carroll to Kirby, June 12, 1886.

101. AUND, O'Sullivan to Leray, April 30, 1886; AAM, O'Sullivan to Browne, May 31, 1886.

102. ASM, N.O., Carroll receipt for $1500, Jan. 4, 1886 [sic, actually 1887].

103. AAO, Carroll to O'Connor, Oct. 20, 1884; Dec. 6, 1886.

104. Ibid., Oct. 20, 1884.

105. Ibid., Dec. 6, 1886.

106. ADKC, Carroll to Hogan, Jan. 7, 1885.

107. Ibid.

108. AAO, Carroll to O'Connor, Dec. 9, 1880.

109. Ibid.

110. Ibid.

111. Ibid.

112. Ibid.

113. Ibid.

114. Ibid.

115. Ibid., Jan. 10, 1881.

116. Ibid.

117. Ibid., Nov. 14, 1876.

118. Carroll, *Lectures Delivered at a Spiritual Retreat*.

119. ASM, Silver Spring, Carroll to Ihmsen, Oct. 31, 1886.

120. ASM, N.O., financial records.

121. *Washington, DC, Church News*, June 5, 1887: "The President of Spanish Honduras, Don Luis de Brogan, through his prime minister, Fritzgartner, requested Mother Austin Carroll" to take charge of the schools and hospitals in his country. *Mobile Register*, Nov. 12, 1904: "Mother Austin Carroll considered the government too unsettled ... and the good work was indefinitely postponed."

122. ASM, N.O., clippings.

123. APIC, Carroll to Kirby, June 21, 1888.

124. ASM, N.O., deeds dated Nov. 5, 1887.

125. ASM, N.O., dedication, Dec. 12, 1887.

126. ASM, N.O., minutes, memoirs.

127. ASSJ, Carroll to Slattery, Nov. 24, 1888.

128. Ibid., 8 schools: 2 each in Pensacola and Belize, and one in Warrington, Biloxi, St. Martinville, and St. Michael's in New Orleans.

129. ASSJ, Carroll to Slattery, Nov. 24, 1888.

130. ASM, N.O. The Mercy foundation in Natchitoches failed in part because the sisters opened a school for the blacks. The whites dropped out of their school, and the sisters returned to New Orleans near to starvation.

131. ASM, N.O., chronicles of branch houses.

132. ASM, N.O., Habenicht/Carroll contract, Dec. 3, 1887.

133. *N.O. Daily Picayune*, Feb. 15, 1888; *N.O. Morning Star*, June 2, 1888; AAO, Carroll to O'Connor Jan. 14, 27, April 11, 1888.

134. *N.O. Morning Star*, June 2, 1888; ASM, N.O., charter.

135. ASM, Windham, Carroll to O'Brien, Jan. 26, 1885; Carroll, *Annals* 3: 362.

136. *N.O. Daily Picayune*, Feb. 15, 1888; Carroll, *Catholic World*, 43: 404–13.

137. AAO, Carroll to O'Connor, March 2, 1885.

138. ASM, N.O., financial records show salaries for tutors for the Mercy teachers; ASM, Windham, Carroll to O'Brien, Jan. 26, 1885; AAO, Carroll to O'Connor, Sept. 12, 1884.

139. Carroll, *In Many Lands*, 389.

140. Ibid.

141. AAO, Carroll to O'Connor, Jan. 14, 27, 1888.

142. ASM, N.O., memoirs; *N.O. Item*, Feb. 16, 1888; *N.O. Picayune*, Feb. 15, 1888.

143. ASM, N.O., Austin Carroll Papers, clippings.

144. AAO, Carroll to O'Connor, Feb. 18, 1888.

145. Ibid.

146. Ibid., Jan. 5, 6, 1889.

147. ASM, N.O., minutes, financial records.

148. ASM, N.O., Loewekamp to Butler, March 2, 11, 26, 1888.

149. Ibid. The sisters had purchased the property, paid the architect and contractor with their own funds, mostly literary profits from Austin Carroll.

150. Several of the correspondence series of Roman agents, having been microfilmed for ACUA or AUND, have seen extensive use by modern historians, but others have been restricted in use, such as that from which are quoted William McCloskey, Feb. 20, 1887, and Richard Gilmour, June 18, 1884, Jan. 29, 1887.

151. Ibid.

152. ASM, N.O., Austin Carroll Papers, Memoirs; AANO, Colman to Janssens, n.d.

153. AAO, Carroll to O'Connor, March 22, 1888.

154. ASM, N.O., clippings.

155. AANO, Rouxel to Janssens, July 30, 1888; Lowekamp to Rouxel, July 26, 1888.

156. AANO, Loewekamp to Janssens, Sept. 17, 1888; Rouxel to Janssens, July 30, 1888.

157. ASM, N.O., minutes; AANO, Rouxel to Janssens, July 30, 1888.

158. ASM, N.O., Sisters to Janssens, n.d. [July 1888].

159. AANO, Rouxel to Janssens, Aug. 1, 1888.

160. Ibid., Sept. 17, 1888.

161. ASM, N.O., chronicles of branch convents.

162. ASM, N.O. John D. Flanagan had tried repeatedly to get Mercy teachers. Then, after the death of Bartholomew Kenny, Flanagan was transferred to the pastorate of St. Peter and Paul in New Orleans. Having worked there as a young priest, he now served as pastor for 11 years. Michael Bardy had replaced Flanagan as pastor in Jeanerette in June 1885.

163. The convent opened in Jeanerette on Sept. 28, 1888. The Mercy secondary school, and the two elementary schools opened on Oct. 1, 1888.

164. ASSJ, Carroll to Slattery, Nov. 24, 1888.

165. ASM, N.O., financial records, contracts.

166. ASM, N.O. The election was postponed in Aug., Sept., and Oct.

167. AANO, Rouxel to Janssens, July 30, 1888; Loewekamp to Rouxel, July 26, 1888; Loewekamp to Janssens, Sept. 17, 1888.

168. AAB, Janssens to Gibbons, Sept. 6, 1885.

169. ASM, N.O. Sisters to Janssens, n.d. [July 1888].

170. ASM, N.O., minutes.

171. ASM, Dublin, McAuley Rule in manuscript, sec. 2, chap. 2, p. 31; ASM, N.O., minutes.

172. ASM, N.O., minutes, memoirs.

173. ASM, N.O., Austin Carroll Papers.

174. ASM, N.O., register, minutes.

175. Ibid.

176. Ibid.

177. ANNO, Carroll to Janssens, Dec. 11, 1893.

178. ASM, N.O., minutes.

179. AAO, Carroll to O'Connor, May 5, 1889.

180. AANO, Carroll to Janssens, Dec. 11, 1893.

181. ASM, N.O., Austin Carroll Papers, letters: July 28, Aug. 11, Oct. 5, Nov. 9, 12, 1888.

182. AANO, Carroll to Janssens, Dec. 11, 1893.

183. AAO, Carroll to O'Connor, May 5, 1889.

184. ASM, N.O., Austin Carroll Papers.

185. AAO, Carroll to O'Connor, May 5, 1889.

186. Whether the design originated with Carroll or was adopted by her from another community has not been established.

187. McAuley to Elizabeth Moore, March 21, 1840: "Some joyful circumstances will soon prove that God is watching over your concerns, which are all His own, *but without the Cross the real Crown cannot come.* Some great thing which He designs to accomplish would have been too much without *a little bitter in the cup.*"

188. AAO, Carroll to O'Connor, June 22, July n.d., Aug. 20, 1888; ASSJ, Carroll to Slattery, Nov. 24, 1888.

189. ADLR, Carroll to Fitzgerald, Nov. 21, 28, Dec. 3, 10, 1888.

190. Carroll, *Annals* 3, 43–49, 327–84.

191. ASM, N.O. *The Young Collegian*, 1887-1891. The writer is most interested in locating copies of extant issues. Since the school paper was printed on quality paper, not newsprint, issues stored in an attic would still be legible.

192. ASM, N.O., Austin Carroll Papers.

193. *Salve Regina,* St. Mary's Dominican Academy, n.d.; *Jeanerette Pilot,* Dec. 7, 1889.

194. AAO, Carroll to O'Connor, Jan. 27, 1888.

195. ASM, N.O., chronicles of Jeanerette. When the sisters went to Jeanerette, they rented temporarily a small house on Main Street. This served as a tiny leaking convent in 1888, served for the girls' elementary in 1889. Then the sisters were able to rent the Ring or Chaney residence early in 1889. This home on Church Street made an admirable convent and secondary school for four years until the Milmo home was purchased. This extensive property was just one block from the church and a much larger building. It was purchased in 1892, the year when the first high school students graduated.

196. ASM, N.O. When Joseph Gerlach, SJ, was working to establish a school for the children in the back half of the French Quarter, especially those near the parish of the Immaculate Conception, Mr. T. Philip Thompson donated a building, formerly a large residence, on Dauphine Street near Iberville. Though less than two blocks from the Jesuit church, the sisters

had quite a task escorting their ranks of students across Canal Street on occasions when there were services in church. As there was no convent attached to this school, tuition free for many years, the sisters commuted from the motherhouse.

197. AAO, Carroll to O'Connor, Aug. 22, 1885.

198. Ibid., Gayarré told her that she was the "Moses who struck the hard rock of his heart."

199. ASM, N.O., Austin Carroll Papers, letters: Feb. 24, March 22, April 11, May 23, 1888.

200. *Irish Monthly* 17 (May 1889): 242–54.

201. *American Catholic Quarterly Review* 14 (July 1889): 462–87.

202. Carroll, *Annals* 3, came off the presses in May 1889.

203. ASM, N.O., minutes; AANO, Carroll to Janssens, Dec. 11, 1889.

204. AAO, Carroll to O'Connor, May 5, 1889.

205. Ibid., March 19, 1889.

206. AAO, Carroll to O'Connor, May 23, 1889.

207. ASM, N.O., Austin Carroll Papers. She was definitely correspondent for the *N.O. Daily Item*, but probably for a number of other papers which regularly carried articles from her pen. Mary Cecelia Moran was Austin's companion, and the two graduates were Virginia Fairfax and Amire Macready.

208. Baptist Russell's brother, Matthew Russell, SJ, knew Austin Carroll well as a frequent contributor. He quoted some of the Carroll/Baptist Russell correspondence in his *Life of Mother Mary Baptist Russell* (N.Y.: Apostleship of Prayer, 1901), 119, 136-7.

209. In his *Three-Sisters of Lord Russell of Killowen* (London: Longmans, Green, 1912), Russell made numerous references to Carroll's *Annals*, and quoted her letters on 124-5.

210. AAO, Carroll to O'Connor, May 23, 1889.

211. Carroll, "From Sugar Fields to the Golden Gate," *Irish Monthly* 32 (Aug. 1904): 421-9; Carroll, "Some Haunts of the Padres," *Catholic World* 51 (April 1890): 76-87; and four articles on the Mormons, their customs, and history.

212. Carroll, "Joanna Reddan," *Irish Monthly* 20 (May 1892) 225-36.

213. Carroll, *Annals* 4: 1-65 re San Francisco; McAuley to Reddan, Nov. 1838, p. 13.

214. ASM, San Francisco, chronicles.

215. ASM, N.O., Austin Carroll Papers, chronicles of the branches, March 1890.

216. Russell, *Three Sisters*, 125; *Baptist Russell*, 124-5.

217. AAO, Carroll to O'Connor, Nov. 4, 1879; June 27, 1889.

218. ASM, Baltimore, Fitzpatrick to Carroll, Aug. 20, 1889.

219. ASM, N.O., clipping, n.d.

220. Carroll, *Annals* 3: iii, *Annals* 1: 268.

221. AAO, Carroll to O'Connor, Sept. 22, Nov. 6, 1883; Carroll, *Annals* 4: 198.

222. AAM, Carroll to O'Sullivan, Nov. 27, 1889.

223. AAO, Carroll to O'Connor, July 31, Aug. 15, Nov. 7, 1868.

224. Ibid., Aug. 30, Sept. 30, Oct. 5, 1878.

225. AAM, Carroll to O'Sullivan, Nov. 27, 1889.

226. Carroll, *Annals* 4: 201.

227. ASM, N.O. and Omaha, Austin Carroll Papers, memoirs.

228. AAO, Carroll to O'Connor, June 14, 1889; Carroll, *Annals* 4: 197-8.

229. Ibid., June 27, 1889.

230. Ibid.

231. Ibid.

232. Ibid.

233. AAM, Carroll to O'Sullivan, Sept. 21, 1889.

234. Ibid., Nov. 27, 1889.

235. Ibid.

236. Ibid.

237. AAO, Carroll to O'Connor, Nov. 27, 1889.

238. Ibid.

239. Ibid.

240. AAM, Carroll to O'Sullivan, Nov. 27, 1889.

241. ASSJ, Carroll to Slattery, Nov. 24, Dec. 15, 1888.

242. Archives of the Sisters of the Blessed Sacrament, checked through the courtesy of Mary Roberta Smith, but yielded no evidence of correspondence of Austin Carroll. AAO, Carroll to O'Connor, Nov. 27, 1889.

243. Ibid.

244. Mary Consuela Duffy, *Katharine Drexel* (Philadelphia: P. Reilly, 1966) names the bishops who visit Drexel as she tries to make her novitiate. AAM, Janssens to O'Sullivan, Dec. 12, 1888.

245. ASM, N.O., financial records. Occasionally, O'Sullivan sent Austin a donation for the needs of the black schools or the sick in black families. But neither Janssens nor any other local bishop gave any kind of financial help to the Sisters of Mercy for any purpose whatsoever. Austin Carroll's literary proceeds helped with the financing, and after she was gone, the black schools dwindled.

246. AAO, Carroll to O'Connor, Nov. 27, 1889.

247. Ibid., Dec. 21, 1889.

248. ASBS, O'Connor to Drexel, Feb. 16, Feb. 28, May 16, 1889.

249. Carroll, *Annals* 4: 198, 197-8.

250. AAM, Carroll to O'Sullivan, Nov. 27, 1889.

251. AAO, Carroll to O'Connor, Nov. 27, 1889.

252. Carroll, *Annals* 4: 199.

253. Ibid.

254. AAM, Carroll to O'Sullivan, Dec. 9, 1889.

255. Ibid.

256. ASM, N.O., Austin Carroll Papers, chronicles of St. Michael's.

257. Carroll, *Annals* 4: 200.

258. AAO, Carroll to O'Connor, Dec. 21, 1889.

259. Ibid.

260. AAO, Carroll to O'Connor, Dec. 23, 1889.

261. Ibid.

262. Ibid.

263. Ibid.

264. Carroll, *Annals* 4: 200.

265. Ibid.

266. ASBS, O'Connor to Drexel, Jan. 9, 1890, quoted in Duffy, 154.

267. AAO, Carroll to O'Connor, Jan. 7, 1890.

268. Ibid.

269. Ibid.

270. Ibid.

271. ASM, N.O., Hogan to Carroll, May 1890.

272. AAM, Carroll to O'Sullivan, May 27, 1890.

NOTES – CHAPTER TWELVE

1. ASM, N.O., financial account.

2. AANO, Carroll to Janssens, March 19, 1890.

3. APIC, Carroll to Kirby, June 21, 1888.

4. Sadlier released printings of Carroll's *Life of Catherine McAuley* in 1866, 1868 1871, 1874, 1877, 1880, 1884, 1887, and 1890.

5. ASM, Bermondsey, Willie McAuley to Camillus Byrn, July 9, 1884.

6. ASM, Dublin, N.Y., Providence, and Baltimore.

7. ASM, Bermondsey, Camillus Byrn to Margaret Byrn, Oct. 3, 1884.

8. ASM, Albany, papers of Bertrand Degnan.

9. ASM, Windham, Carroll to O'Brien, Feb. 20, 1886.

10. ASM, Dublin, Kate Byrn to Rev. Mother, Oct. 23, 1867.

11. Carroll, *Catherine McAuley*, 64, 67 n.

12. Ibid., 116-7.

13. ASM, Dublin, Willie McAuley, Notes re Carroll's *Catherine McAuley*.

14. Cusack, 20-1.

15. ASM, Dublin, Willie McAuley, Notes re Carroll's *Catherine McAuley*.

16. ASM, Carlow, Carroll to Catherine Maher, copied into the chronicles.

17. ASLU, Gayarré papers. The manuscript bears a few minor bits of editing in Austin Carroll's hand.

18. Gayarré, "Women of Louisiana," *Bedford's Magazine* 6 (January 1891): 176-86.

19. ATUL, CArroll to Cable, Sept. 16, 1882; ASM, N.O., Austin Carroll Papers, memoirs and notes.

20. AAO, Carroll to O'Connor, Oct. 21, 1878.

21. ASM, N.O., Austin Carroll Col. A few of the many Vincentians who worked for the maintenance and rent of the home and school for the newsboys were J. V. Donovan, Dr. E. Doumeing, P. A. Finney, T. Fitzwilliam, P. Gillen, J. Grehan, T. Loftys, J. McCaffrey, G. T. McCune, T. Moroney, Thomas Rapier, and J. Rice. Numerous others assisted by their regular donations, but most of the above served on the committee for the particular work for the newsboys. Chaplains who served in sequence in the Newsboys' Home were Jesuits from Immaculate Conception Rectory: Thomas McElligot, Alphonse Dufour, Edward Gaffney, William Tyrell, Albert Biever, Eugene Nicolet, and Augustine Porta. All were heartily involved with the boys, Fathers Gaffney and Porta for the longest assignments.

22. ASM, N.O., legal papers. William Castell attended to convent legal matters until his untimely death.

23. ASM, N.O., records of property.

24. Thomas Rapier was one of the newspapermen who welcomed Austin Carroll's contributions to his columns. As the manager of the *N.O. Morning Star* and later the *N.O. Picayune*, Rapier was generous with space for publicity to aid the Newsboys' Home. As one of the officers of the society of St. Vincent de Paul from the time that Austin Carroll inaugurated the Mercy ministry to the prisoners in 1869 until long after her death in 1909, Rapier supported the special works of the Vincentians with the Penal institutions, the Boys' House of Refuge, and the Newsboys' Home.

25. On July 10, 1890, the building which has served formerly as the Planter's Hotel, was purchased for the Newsboys' Home in the name of the Jesuit Corporation for $14,000, largely through the efforts of Rev. Edward Gaffney, SJ, the chaplain of the Home at that time. Encouraged to make this purchase because of the difficulty of gathering the monthly expenses for the matron's salary and the rent for the Bank Alley building, the committee of Vincentians which sponsored the work, in union with the chaplain, decided it would be better to buy the

Baronne Street Facility with several substantial donations, like the $1,000 bequest left for the Home shortly before that by Charles Macready. Gaffney's charitable friend, Mary Denègre, made the initial payment in the name of the corporation to be repaid over a three-year period. Gaffney and the Vincentian committee sponsored successful fairs, charity sermons, and other fund raisers and repaid the sale price and the cost of improvements. Then in 1894 the Home was put under the management of the Sisters of Mercy, the deeds presented shortly thereafter in gratitude for their many years of unsalaried teaching and motherly encouragement which assisted the young orphans and street waifs to become exemplary citizens. In 1913, Abp. Blenk transferred the management of the Home to his Commission of Charities, demanded that the sisters hand him the deeds without remuneration, and cancelled the home completely after three years. A decade later, when the property in the heart of the central business district was sold for $135,000, the financiers of the diocese did not see fit to share any of this generous price with the nuns who had taught the newsboys for thirty-four years. Of course, this work for destitute youngsters, like the fifty years of mothering in St. Alphonsus Orphan Asylum, was dedicated by the Sisters of Mercy to God's interests rather than to their own. Religious sisters serving in orphanages for nothing was an ordinary service in the nineteenth century, just as it was fairly common for a prelate to demand the deeds from the nuns, sometimes for property which they had purchased with funds accrued over a long period.

26. Albert H. Biever, SJ, *The Jesuits in New Orleans and the Mississippi Valley* (New Orleans: Author, 1924), 116.

27. ASM, N.O., Austin Carroll Papers, clippings.

28. Ibid.

29. ASM, N.O.; AAO, Carroll to O'Connor, Jan. 23, 1889.

30. ASM, N.O., Donahoe to Carroll, Jan. 14, 1889.

31. Carroll, *Catholic History*, 168.

32. ASM, N.O., library records.

33. ASM, N.O., Austin Carroll knew both the editor, Eliza Nicholson, and the reporter, Martha Field. She assisted the latter for a time with the education of her daughter, Florence, who followed her mother in the field of journalism.

34. AUND, Onahan Papers, Conway to Onahan, April 12, 1893.

35. ASM, N.O., Barry to Carroll, Jan. 31, 1891.

36. Kate Madeleine Barry, *Catharine McAuley and the Sisters of Mercy: a Sketch.* (Dublin: Fallon and Son, 1896).

37. Lawrence Kehoe died suddenly on Feb. 20, 1890, four years after James McMaster. John Boyle O'Reilly died on Aug. 10, 1890, just as Austin left for Ireland.

38. ASM, Silver Spring, MD., Carroll to Nelligan, February 4, 1889.

39. ASM, N.O., the register. Sister Veronica Nelligan died May 27, 1941, after 66 years of Mercy Service.

40. ASM, N.O., chronicles of the branch convents.

41. AANO, Carroll to Janssens, March 19, 1890.

42. AAO, Carroll to O'Connor, Sept. 12, 1884.

43. ASM, N.O., Carroll Family Papers, Carroll to Margaret Mary and Clare [Byrne], May 11, 1894.

44. Carroll, *In Many Lands* (N.Y.: O'Shea & Co., 1904).

45. Ibid.

46. The itinerary is not apparent from *In Many Lands*, as Austin Carroll rearranged the order of the various places treated. The archival data from the various convents she visited tend to clarify the plan.

47. ASM, Liverpool; Carroll, *In Many Lands*, 24–5.

48. Carroll, *In Many Lands*, 27.

49. Carroll, "Ancient Monastic Town — Shrewsbury," 554–62, 308–16.

50. Carroll, *In Many Lands*, 28.

51. ASM, N.O., Stanislaus Ward to Rev. Mother, Aug. 11, 1888. Prelates approving the suggestion were Cardinal Henry Edward Manning of Westminster, Bishop Edmund Knight of Shrewsbury, William Vaughan of Plymouth, William Smith of Edinburg, John MacEvilly of Galway, Angus Macdonald of Argyll and the Isles.

52. ASM, N.O., Austin Carroll Papers.

53. ASM, Birmingham, chronicles. Mary Juliana Hardman's appointment as superior was made by Catherine McAuley and formalized by the bishop on Sept. 6, 1841. She served in that position for almost three dozen years and died in 1884.

54. Carroll, *Annals* 2: 347.

55. Carroll, *In Many Lands*, 50.

56. ASM, N.O., Austin Carroll Papers. In June 1882, Austin Carroll established the perpetual lamp in the Sacred Heart Oratory in the Convent of Mercy in New Orleans.

57. Mary Elizabeth Watkins: *Contemplations and Meditations, Public Life of Our Lord Jesus Christ* (London: Washbourne, 1885), *Feasts of the Blessed Virgin & Saints* (London: Burns & Oates, 1887), *Passion and Death of Our Lord Jesus Christ* (London: Burns & Oates, 1889).
The editor for most of the volumes was Rev. W. H. Eyre, SJ, and he was thought by some to have translated the works since Watkins was not named in the books.

58. Carroll, *In Many Lands*, 47.

59. Neuman, *Letters*, 371. McAuley to Warde, Aug. 25, 1841.

60. Carroll, *In Many Lands*, 49.

61. Ibid., 48.

62. Ibid., 49.

63. Ibid., 343.

64. Ibid.

65. Ibid., 317–33.

66. Ibid., 334–8.

67. Carroll, "Pisa and Its Four Fabrics," 268–71; Carroll, "The Superb City: Genoa," 119–24.

68. Carroll, *In Many Lands*, 347–54.

69. Ibid. 356–7.

70. Ibid., 358–9.

71. Archives Little Company of Mary, Rome. Sister Mary John to writer, Feb. 28, 1984; Carroll, *In Many Lands*, 440.

72. Carroll, *In Many Lands*, 364.

73. Ibid.

74. Ibid., 364–5.

75. Ibid., 365–6.

76. Ibid., 366–9.

77. Ibid., 369.

78. Ibid., 413.

79. Archives Little Company of Mary, Rome. Logbook started 1892; Carroll, *In Many Lands*, 418.

80. Carroll, *In Many Lands*, 440, 456.

81. Ibid., 457.

82. Ibid., 421–30.

83. Ibid., 417, 434.

84. Ibid., 437–8.

85. Ibid., 451.

86. Ibid., 451–2.

87. Ibid., 449.

88. AAM, Carroll to O'Sullivan, Sept. 24, 1890; Carroll, *In Many Lands*, 449–50.

89. Carroll, *In Many Lands*, 451.

90. ASM, Bermondsey, McAuley to dePazzi Delany, Oct. 3, 1837; McAuley to Cecilia Marmion, March 20, 1841. Because these letters have not been previously published in their entirety, one not at all, they are contained in notes above.

91. ASM, Bermondsey. Catherine McAuley's article on the spirit of the Mercy Institute is usually referred to as the "Bermondsey Manuscript."

92. ASM, Bermondsey, chronicles. The opening excerpt from the Bermondsey chronicle, usually referred to as the "London Manuscript," was one of Austin's primary sources for her life of Catherine McAuley in 1866.

93. ASM, Bermondsey, scrapbook; ASM, N.O., Austin Carroll Papers, "A Truly Valiant Daughter of Erin."

94. ASM, Bermondsey, chronicles.

95. Ibid. The sisters left England Nov. 26, 1890, and as so often happened with Sisters of Mercy in the Americas, arrived at their destination in Alpha on the Feast of Our Lady of Guadalupe, Dec. 12, 1890.

96. ASM, St. Edward's Convent, chronicles.

97. ASM, Crispin Street Night Refuge, guest register.

98. Carroll, *In Many Lands*, 109.

99. Ibid., 60 pages on London, 62–122.

100. Ibid., 112.

101. Ibid., 113.

102. Ibid., 54.

103. Ibid., 56–57.

104. Ibid., 60.

105. ASM, Sunderland. Archives checked by Sr. M. Enda; Carroll, *In Many Lands*, 60–61.

106. ASM, Newcastle-upon-Tyne, chronicles. Archives checked by Sister Mary Rose.

107. ASM, N.O., Austin Carroll Papers.

108. ASM, Bermondsey, Night Refuge, and St. Edward's in London; Liverpool, Birmingham, Coventry, Newcastle-upon-Tyne, and Sunderland.

109. ASM, Dublin, Birr, Carlow, Cork, Ennis, Kinsale, Limerick, Passage West, and Westport; Athy, Charlesville, Clifden, Galway, Moate, Naas, Tuam, Tullamore, Waterford, and Wexford.

110. ASM, N.O., and Belfast. Sister Mary Genevieve interviewed the senior sisters and forwarded that material to the writer, July 1963.

111. ASM, Derry, manuscript usually referred to as the Derry Manuscript; Carroll, *In Many Lands*, 170–1.

112. Carroll, *In Many Lands*, 187–9.

113. Ibid., 178–181.

114. Ibid., 186.

115. ASM, N.O., Austin Carroll Papers, Carroll to Emmanuel Russell, Shrove Tuesday 1882.

116. Carroll, "The Battle of the Boyne and the Sieges of Limerick, 1690–1691," 845–62. Carroll, *In Many Lands*, 195–203.

117. Carroll, *In Many Lands*, 198.

118. Ibid., 203–4.

119. AAM, Carroll to O'Sullivan, June 2, 1890.

120. Ibid.

121. ASM, Dublin, Moore Papers, containing the Moore letters and the Clare Augustine Moore history of the foundress and the Mercy Institute, usually referred to as the Dublin Manuscript.

122. Mary Clare Moore, *A Little Book of Practical Sayings, Advises, and Prayers of Our Revered Foundress, Mother Mary Catherine McAuley*. Edition 1: (London: Burns, Oates & Co., 1868); edition 2: the Carroll American reprint (N.Y., Catholic Publication Soc., 1878); edition 3: (Dublin: M. H. Gill & Sons, 1886).

123. ASM, Dublin.

124. ASM, N.O., Austin Carroll Papers, references are to "injured arm," or "serious injury," but not anything more specific.

125. ASM, N.O., Carroll to O'Sullivan, June 2, 1890.

126. Ibid.

127. ASM, Tullamore.

128. ASM, Birr.

129. Archives of the Religious of the Sacred Heart, through Sisters Mary Nuala O'Higgins in Ireland and Marie Louise Martinez in this country.

130. ASM, Naas.

131. ASM, Wexford. Sister Mary Ignatius Walsh was Austin Carroll's friend, and it was through Wexford sisters that the writer was put in touch with the Carroll family. When Sister Mary Benedict Branigan heard the request in Dublin that all sisters be asked if they knew of any relative of Mother Austin Carroll, she followed through, learned that Sister Mary Augustine Twomey knew a grandniece, Mrs. Kitty Cullen. The writer's thanks have gone to the principals through the years since the contact in 1964.

132. ASM, Waterford.

133. ASM, N.O., Carroll Family Papers, Carroll to the Byrne nieces, May 1, 1894.

134. Carroll, *In Many Lands*, 303.

135. Ibid., 301–5.

136. ASM, N.O. and Carlow, Carroll to Catherine Maher, n.d. [c April 20, 1890].

137. ASM, Carlow, chronicles.

138. ASM, N.O. and Carlow, chronicles.

139. ASM, Carlow, chronicles.

140. AAM, Carroll to O'Sullivan, September 24, 1890.

141. Ibid.

142. ASM, N.O., Kirby to Carroll, Aug. 28, 1890.

143. AAM, Carroll to O'Sullivan, Sept. 24, 1890.

144. Carroll, *In Many Lands*, 267–74.

145. ASM, Limerick, chronicles. Austin "had met a serious hurt in her journey and had to stay under medical care with our Sisters in Dublin."

146. Carroll never mentioned finding any kind of notes from the Hartnett work.

147. ASM, Westport, Mother Paula Cullen, the founding superior in Westport, was the sister of Cardinal Paul Cullen.

148. ASM, Clifden.

149. Chronicles, ASM, Limerick. Besides their archives, Limerick has a museum display of their relics of the foundress.

150. Carroll, *In Many Lands*, 295.

151. Ibid., 296.

152. ASM, Kinsale, chronicles.

153. Carroll, *In Many Lands*, 283.

154. ASM, Passage West.

155. Chronicles, ASM, Cork. Sisters Mary Patricia and Austin Murphy were founding superiors in Passage West. Sisters Mary Baptist Crean and Paul Keyes were serving in St. Maries of the Isle.

156. ASM, Cork. Mary deSales Lane died Aug. 25, 1890, three months before her fiftieth anniversary.

157. ASM, Charlesville, Crimean manuscript of Mother Joseph Croke.

158. Carroll, *In Many Lands*, 297–300.

159. ASM, N.O., the register. Margaret Mary Killelea died on Sept. 12, 1890, in her 20s.

160. ASM, N.O. From the time of her death, her family and the sisters prayed to Margaret Mary as a saint in heaven. Her holiness and been apparent to all during her life.

161. AAM, Carroll to O'Sullivan, Sept. 24, 1890.

162. Carroll, *In Many Lands*, 279.

163. ASM, N.O., Carroll Family Papers, Carroll to Byrne nieces, May 1, 1894.

164. Ibid.

165. See the Carroll bibliography for the articles, twelve of those from 1890 were based on the trip, and the book, *In Many Lands*.

166. Carroll, *In Many Lands*, 383.

167. Ibid., 361.

168. Ibid.

169. Ibid., 48–9.

170. Ibid., 61.

171. Ibid., 24.

172. Ibid., 27.

173. Ibid., 233.

174. Ibid., 231–4.

175. Ibid., 131–2.

176. APIC, Carroll to Kirby, Dec. 6, 1890.

177. AAM, Carroll to O'Sullivan, June 2, 1890.

178. ASM, N.O., register.

179. AAM, Carroll to O'Sullivan, Sept. 24, 1890.

180. ASM, N.O. necrology and register.

181. Carroll, *In Many Lands*, 459-60.

182. ASM, N.O., Enumerator Certificate, signed Robert P. Porter, Superintendent of the Census, May 20, 1890.

183. ASM, N.O., U.S. Department of the Interior, per J. C. Stoddard, to Carroll, Nov. 7, 1890.

184. ASM, N.O., Carroll to and from P. O'Shea and Catholic Publication Society, 1890-1891.

185. APIC, Bentley to Kirby, Jan. 13, 1891. She reminded him of having met him when she was some months in Rome in 1873.

186. APIC, Corrigan to Kirby, March 9, 1891.

187. ASM, N.O., Kirby to Carroll, Sept. 24, 1890.

188. AAM, Collins to O'Sullivan, April 24, 1890.

189. AAM, O'Sullivan to Collins, March 2, 1891.

190. Request evident in later letters.

191. AAM, N.O., O'Sullivan to O'Shanahan, April 28, 1891.

192. ASM, N.O., O'Sullivan to Joseph, May 10, 1891 contains quotations from Janssens to O'Shanahan, May 9, 1891.

193. AAM, O'Sullivan to O'Shanahan. April 28, 1891.

194. Ibid.

195. ASM, N.O. By May Janssens had told both Joseph Devereux and Austin Carroll that he was determined to have a total division of the New Orleans Sisters of Mercy into two separate communities and that each sister would have to choose to serve permanently in one diocese or the other. If he and O'Sullivan agreed, they could not stop him, and if O'Sullivan would not agree he intended to appeal to Rome to accomplish it.

196. ASM, N.O., Janssens to Joseph, April 30, 1891.

197. Carroll, *In Many Lands*, 97-98, 157-8.

198. ASM, N.O., Austin Carroll Papers. This generosity is mentioned repeatedly in numerous letters from New Orleans to Austin's friends elsewhere.

199. APIC, Carroll to Kirby, March 23, 1891.

200. Ibid.

201. ASM, N.O., Austin Carroll Papers, memoirs and Pacheca reminiscences.

202. APIC, Carroll to Kirby, March 23, 1891.

203. ASM, N.O., Austin Carroll Papers, Pacheca reminiscences.

204. APIC, Carroll to Kirby, March 23, 1891.

205. *N.O., Morning Star*, Dec. 19, 1885.

206. APIC, Carroll to Kirby, March 23, 1891.

207. ASM, N.O., O'Sullivan to Joseph, May 10, 1891.

208. Ibid.

209. AAM, Janssens to O'Shanahan, May 25, 1891.

210. AANO, Devereux to Janssens, Aug. 30, 1891.

211. ASM. N.O., Devereux to Janssens, Aug. 16, 30, 1891.

212. AAM, O'Sullivan to Janssens, July 25, 1891.

213. AAM, O'Sullivan to Janssens, July 25, 1891.

214. AANO, O'Sullivan to Janssens, Aug. 4, 1891.

215. Ibid.

216. AAM, O'Sullivan to Carroll, July 25, 1891.

217. APIC, Carroll to Kirby, March 23, 1891.

218. AANO, Carroll to Janssens, Aug. 6, 1891.

219. ASM, N.O., Carroll to Devereux, Aug. 7, 1891.

220. McAuley to White, Feb. 3, 1841.

221. APIC, Carroll to Kirby, Nov. 7, 1891.

222. Ibid.

223. Ibid.

224. Ibid.

225. ASM, N.O., and Mobile. Community in the diocese of Mobile in 1891: Sisters Mary Austin Carroll, Clare Fitzpatrick, Joseph Stapleton, Henry Briscoe, Gertrude O'Leary, Francis Vitteman, Scholastica Ward, Caroline Macready, Augusta Fitzpatrick, Gonzaga Nugent, Camillus McDermott, Mariana Clery, Benito Pacheca, Loyola Kelly, Bernard Dowdal, Berchmans Kelly, Justina Bogue, and Stanislaus Fox.

226. ASM, Baltimore, deeds registered April 1893.

227. AAM, O'Sullivan to Carroll, Oct. 7, 1891.

228. APIC, Carroll to Kirby, Nov. 7, 1891.

229. AAM, Carroll to O'Sullivan, Nov. 12, 1891.

230. Ibid.

231. Ibid.

232. Ibid.

233. ASM, Silver Spring Md., Carroll to Byrne, July 22, 1891.

234. ASM, Buffalo, Providence, Omaha.

235. ASM, N.O., Austin Carroll Papers, Memoirs.

236. ASM, N.O., Carroll to N.O. sisters, n.d.

237. ASM, N.O., register, minutes, Sisters Mary Francis Vitteman, Caroline Macready, and Henry Briscoe.

238. See the Carroll bibliography.

239. Ibid., Carroll articles of 1892 contained material to be treated in *Annals* 4.

240. National Convention of the Apostolate of the Press was held in Columbus Hall in New York City on Jan. 6–7, 1892, under the general direction of the Paulists.

241. Carroll, "The Experiences of a Sister of Mercy," *Reports of Papers of the Convention of the Apostolate of the Press* (N.Y.: Columbia Press, 1892), 165–72.

242. Ibid., 168.

243. AUND, Conway to Onahan, Feb. 12, 1893.

244. ASM, Mobile, register.

245. AAM, Carroll to O'Sullivan, Nov. 12, 1891.

246. Ibid.

247. Ibid.

248. ASM, N.O., Austin Carroll Papers.

249. ASM, Limerick, chronicles.

250. AAM, Carroll to O'Sullivan, Nov. 12, 1891.

251. ASM, Limerick, chronicles.

252. ASM, Dublin, Limerick, Kinsale, and N.O., Austin Carroll Papers, memoirs.

253. ASM, N.O., Austin Carroll Papers, undated clippings. The *N.O. Times* and *Boston Pilot* seem to have been the papers which published most of the interviews.

254. ASM, N.O., Carroll to Devereux, Aug. 15, 1892; Carroll, *In Many Lands*, 113.

255. ASM, N.O., Austin Carroll Papers.

256. AAM, Carroll to O'Sullivan, Nov. 12, 1891.

257. ASM, N.O., Austin Carroll Papers.

258. ASM, Mobile, register. Candidates became Sisters Mary Genevieve Moylan and Alberta Cody.

259. ASM, Mobile, register.

260. Ibid.

261. ASM, Mobile, necrology, register; Sisters Mary Henry Briscoe, Frances Vitteman, and Caroline Macready.

262. ASM, Mobile, register; ASM, Big Rapids, Mich., Carroll to Bertrand, Oct. 18, 1898; Dec. 4, 1899.

263. AAM, O'Sullivan to Drexel, Jan. 8, 1892.

264. ASM, Carroll to O'Sullivan, June 2, 1890.

265. AAM, O'Sullivan to Carroll, Nov. 26, 1892.

266. ASM, Savannah, Becker to Carroll, Jan. 12, 1893.

267. See also, chap. 9, nn. 55–62.

268. AAM, O'Sullivan to Carroll, Dec. 27, 1892.

269. ASM, Savannah, Becker to Carroll, Jan. 12, 1893.

270. ASM, Savannah and N.O.; AAM, O'Sullivan to Carroll, Nov. 26, Dec. 27, 1892.

271. AAM, Carroll to O'Sullivan, Nov. 7, Oct. 15, 1891; Jan. 19, Nov. 26, 1892.

272. ACUL, Onahan directions to speakers, received by Carroll in April.

273. ASM, San Francisco, Ignatius to Russell, Aug. 15, 1893.

274. AAM, O'Sullivan to Carroll, Dec. 14, 1892.

275. AANO, Browne to Leray, Oct. 14, 1884; Holaind to Leray, May 21, 1885.

276. AAM, O'Sullivan to Carroll, Dec. 14, 1892.

277. ASM, Mobile, necrology, Sisters Mary Clare Fitzpatrick, Feb. 24, 1895; Augusta Fitzpatrick, Feb. 19, 1896; Gertrude O'Leary, July 24, 1896.

278. AAM, O'Sullivan to Carroll, Feb. 21, 1894.

279. AAJ, Heslin diary.

280. Ibid., the sisters returned to Mobile after the death of L. A. Dutto in 1902.

281. Rev. L. A. Dutto was pastor from Dec. 1, 1897, until his death five years later.

282. AAM, O'Sullivan to Carroll, Nov. 15, 1893.

283. ASM, Mobile and N.O. In 1895, Austin Carroll resided in Mobile for the first time. In 1884, when the Convent of Mercy on St. Francis Street was first established, she was not in the original community. As the superior in New Orleans she had assigned the sisters who first arrived, but was herself not among the number as several other records have reported erroneously. In 1891, her residence was in Selma, but she regularly spent a week in each of the other convents at intervals.

284. AUND, Onahan Papers, Conway to Onahan, April 5, 1893.

285. Ibid., July 7, 1893.

286. AUND, Onahan Papers, Carroll to Onahan, May 2, 1893.

287. Eleanor C. Donnelly, "Women in Literature," *Girlhood's Hand-Book of Women*, (St. Louis: Herder, 1898), 9–34.

288. Mary J. Onahan, "Catholic Women in Philanthropy," in Donnelly, ibid., 90–110; and Sister de Sales Chase, "Woman in the Religious Orders," by F. M. Edselas, Donnelly, ibid., 130–148.

289. ASM, N.O., memoirs.

290. Ibid.

291. ATUL, Kuntz Papers, Gayarré letterbook lists five or six letters and quotes one, Gayarré to Carroll, Jan. 20, 1892.

292. AANO, Carroll to Janssens, Dec. 11, 1893.

293. Ibid.; ASM, N.O., Austin Carroll Papers.

294. ASM, Mobile, Selma reception on April 15, 1893; visit to New Orleans followed.

295. ASM, N.O., Austin Carroll taught religion and prepared blacks for the reception of the sacraments from 1869 to 1874. From 1875 to 1900, she worked to establish schools for the blacks, and succeeded with ten permanent schools. With the exception of Pensacola, these were built, rented, and furnished by Austin Carroll.

296. AANO, Janssens journal speaks of "the separation proposed by the Rt. Rev. Bp. of Mobile and accepted by me." Yet his letters show that he forced O'Sullivan to accept the division of the Sisters of Mercy by threatening to appeal to Rome over O'Sullivan's refusal to comply with his wishes.

297. ASM, N.O., percentages figured and graphed in notes for Muldrey's *This Is the Day.*

298. AAM, Carroll to Allen, Jan. 22, 1898.

299. ASM, St. Mary's and motherhouse, Mobile.

300. ASM, Big Rapids, Mich., Carroll to Bertrand, Oct. 18, 1898.

301. AAM, Carroll to O'Sullivan, Nov. 26, 1892; Carroll to Allen, March 5, 1898.

302. AAM, Meurer to Allen, July 26, 1897; Carroll to Allen, Jan. 22, Aug. 23, 1898.

303. AAM, McCafferty to Allen, March 14, June 8, 1900.

304. ASM, Mobile, Bessemer, Apalachicola.

305. ASM, Mobile.

306. ASM, Mobile, register.

307. ASM, N.O. and Mobile, registers.

308. ASM, N.O., register.

309. ASM, N.O., chronicles of the branch convents.

310. Carroll, *Annals* 4 (N.Y.: P. O'Shea, 1895).

311. AAO, Carroll to O'Connor, Nov. 9, 1888.

312. ASM, N.O., Girardey to Carroll, June 25, 1883.

313. Carroll, *Essays Educational and Historic* (N.Y.: P. O'Shea, 1899).

314. ASM, Windham, Carroll to O'Brien, April 2, 1895.

315. See Carroll bibliography for all articles between 1891–1900.

316. Carrolls, "Right Rev. Dr. Bacon, Bp. of Portland, Me., U.S.A.," *Irish Monthly* 23 (January 1895): 27–38.

317. Carroll, "Joanna Reddan," *Irish Monthly* 20 (May 1892): 225–36.

318. Carroll, *Annals* 4: 16.

319. ASM, Grand Rapids, Carroll to Bertrand, July 7, 1899.

320. ASM, Windham, Carroll to O'Brien, April 2, 1899.

321. ASM, Grand Rapids, Carroll to Bertrand, Oct. 8, 1898.

322. Ibid., Dec. 12, 1898.

323. ASM, Windham, Carroll to O'Brien, April 2, 1895.

324. Ibid., April 23, 1895.

325. Ibid.

326. ASM, Grand Rapids, Carroll to Bertrand, June 14, 1898.

327. Ibid.

328. ASM, Windham, Carroll to O'Brien, April 23, 1895.

329. Ibid.

330. ASM, N.O., financial records, minutes, property book, and carefully preserved, the deed of sale of Feb. 8, 1883, and the plat drawn on Nov. 14, 1842.

331. The Belize "Tea Parties" brought in a few hundred dollars and the governor did not honor his commitment. Yellow fever among convent students and teachers were detrimental to enrollment for a number of years, thus further lessening resources.

332. The Belize mission was established by Rome as a branch attached to New Orleans until Rome gave consent for a separation, thus making Rome the source of DiPietro's hope for severance of the mission from the motherhouse. The Sisters of Mercy were not consulted, just as their opinion was not asked in 1910, when Abp. Blenk demanded that both Biloxi and Belize be separated from the New Orleans motherhouse. Biloxi was separated that year as the sisters had no choice but to obey. To separate Belize, however, Blenk had to work through Rome for three years before he accomplished his end. In both cases the New Orleans sisters suffered financial losses because their bishop had instigated the change. Blenk's plan was to have every member of any community centered in New Orleans or elsewhere in the diocese working within the boundaries of the archdiocese. Further, he put out of the diocese any nuns whose motherhouse was in another diocese.

333. ASM, Mobile, Devereux to Carroll, Oct. 28, 1893. AAM, AANO, ASM, and AANO have numerous letters to and from the principals and mediators in the property problem. Austin carefully avoided refusing to obey the bishops, as she always said she would willingly sign as soon as the conditions were met. She also tried to make the bishops understand that she simply held the title to the property in trust and that her conscience made it impossible for her to bestow upon others what was not hers to give. Austin seemed to be using delaying tactics, as the number of signatures required kept rising, and every exchange of correspondence caused another delay. Austin might have been awaiting the next superior. Joseph Devereux was dying by the summer of 1894, when three-fourths of the sisters consented. By the time that Austin signed, Philomene Butler, not Janssens, was in charge of the community and the deeds were kept in New Orleans.

334. AAM, Carroll to O'Sullivan, Dec. 27, 1893; Jan. 5, 1894.

335. AAM, O'Sullivan to Janssens, March 13, 1894; AANO, Carroll to Janssens, May 10, 1894.

336. AAM, O'Sullivan to DiPietro, May 16, 1894; O'Sullivan to Carroll, April 22, 1894.

337. AAM, O'Sullivan to Janssens, May 10, 1894; O'Sullivan to DiPietro, May 16, 1894.

338. AAM, O'Sullivan to Carroll, May 9, 18, 21, 1894.

339. AAM, O'Sullivan to Carroll, Aug. 11, 1894; O'Sullivan to Hugh, Aug. 15, 1894.

340. AANO, Carroll to Janssens, May 10, 1894.

341. ASM, Mobile and N.O., minutes.

342. ASM, N.O., minutes; AANO, Janssens to O'Sullivan, Dec. 11, 1894; Sisters of Mercy to Janssens, Dec. 16, 1894.

343. AANO, O'Sullivan conditions for the separation, Aug. 4, 1891; ASM, N.O., Janssens conditions in chapter book.

344. AANO, Carroll to Janssens, Jan. 2, 1894.

345. ASM, N.O., register, minutes.

346. AANO, Carroll to Janssens, Jan. 2, 1894.

347. AANO, Browne to Janssens, Dec. 18, 1894.

348. Ibid.

349. AAM, Sisters of Mercy to O'Sullivan, Dec. 16, 1894; AANO, O'Sullivan to Janssens, Dec. 12, 14, 1894.

350. AAM, O'Sullivan to Carroll, Feb. 12, 1895.

351. ASM, N.O., Austin Carroll Papers.

352. ASM, N.O. and Mobile, registers, Fitzpatrick died on Feb. 24, 1895; Gayarré on Feb. 11, 1895.

353. Carroll, *Pleasant Homes*, 52.

354. ASM, Grand Rapids, Carroll to Bertrand, Oct. 18, 1898.

355. ASM, N.O., Austin Carroll Papers, Memoirs.

356. ASM, Grand Rapids, Carroll to Bertrand, June 14, 1898.

357. ASM, Windham, Carroll to O'Brien, April 2, 1895.

358. Ibid.

359. AANO, Carroll to Janssens, Dec. 11, 1893.

360. AAM, O'Sullivan to Carroll, June 1, 1896.

361. There was a five-month delay between the death of Janssens and the appointment of Chapelle, and six months between the death of O'Sullivan and the appointment of Allen.

362. AAM, Allen to Carroll, May 9, 1900.

363. Ibid., Feb. 16, 1900.

364. Meurer to O'Sullivan and Allen, McCafferty to Allen.

365. ASM, Windham, Carroll to O'Brien, April 23, 1895; AAM, Allen to Carroll, June 15, 1900.

366. Mary Dominica Hyde, "Historical Sketch of the Sisters of Mercy, Mobile, Alabama," in *100 Years of Mercy, Mobile Diocese, 1877–1977* (Mobile: Sisters of Mercy, 1977), 14.

367. AAO, Carroll to O'Connor, Nov. 30, 1881.

368. Carroll to Matthew Russell, n.d., in Russell, *Three Sisters of Lord Russell*, 160–1.

369. ASM, Cork, chronicles; ASM, N.O., Austin Carroll Papers, obituaries.

370. ASM, N.O., Austin Carroll Papers, memoirs.

371. ASM, Windham, Carroll to O'Brien, May 21, 1895.

372. ASM, Mobile, Austin's successor, Mother Mary Patricia Ryan, was in the group of novices some years earlier when Austin said she saw her successor.

373. Carroll, "An Early Millionaire," *Magnificat* 1 (November 1907): 221–27.

374. Carroll, "Grave of Hernando de Soto," *Irish Monthly* 33 (December 1905): 670–3; Carroll, "Pedro Melendez," *Irish Monthly* 34 (February 1906): 102–5.

375. Carroll, "Don Alexander O'Reilly," *American Catholic Quarterly Review* 33 (January 1908): 87–97.

376. ALSU, Carroll to King, June 22, 1893.

377. Ibid.

378. Hartnett, *Reverend Mother McAuley*, 148–9.

379. Carroll, Foreword, 29.

380. ASM, Windham, Carroll to O'Brien, Feb. 5, 1894.

381. Ibid., May 14, 1886.

382. Ibid., Feb. 5, 1894.

383. ASM, Detroit, Carroll to Bertrand, June 14, 1898.

384. Carroll, *Angel Dreams*, 84.

385. ASM, Cork, Carroll to Crean, Jan. 23, 1903.

386. CArroll, *Angel Dreams*, 84.

387. ASM, Windham, Carroll to O'Brien, April 2, 1895.

388. ASM, Detroit, Carroll to Bertrand, Dec. 4, 1899.

389. ASM, N.O., O'Donnell to Carroll, n.d.

390. ASM, Windham, Carroll to O'Brien, April 23, 1895.

391. AANO, Carroll to Janssens, May 10, 1894.

392. ASM, Detroit, Carroll to Bertrand, Feb. 20, 1900.

393. Ibid., July 27, 1906.

394. See Carroll bibliography.

395. Carroll, *Catholic History*, 23.

396. AUAL, Carroll to Thompson, n.d.

397. ASM, N.O., Girardey to Sisters of Mercy, Sept. 8, 1905.

398. ASM, N.O., Austin Carroll Papers, clippings.

399. *Mobile Daily Register*, July 12, 1906.

400. ASM, N.O., Austin Carroll Papers, memoirs.

401. ASM, Detroit, Carroll to Bertrand, July 27, 1906.

402. ASM, N.O., Austin Carroll Papers, memoirs, chronicles from branches.

403. ASM, N.O. Regan to writer, March 16, 1883.

404. Ibid.

405. Degnan, *Mercy Unto Thousands*, xiii.

406. ASM, N.O., Austin Carroll Papers, memoirs; ASM, Silver Spring, notarized statement verifies the burning the trunk with all its contents.

407. ASM, N.O., Austin Carroll Papers, memoirs.

408. Carroll, *Catholic History*.

409. *Catholic Encylopedia* 16 vols. (N.Y.: Appleton Co., 1907–1914).

410. ASM, N.O., Austin Carroll Papers, memoirs.

411. AAO, Carroll to O'Connor, Jan. 6, 1889.

412. ASM, N.O., Carroll Family Papers, Carroll to Fennessey, n.d.

413. Russell, "Golden Jubilee," *Irish Monthly* 9 (Dec. 1881): 668.

414. ASM, Bermondsey, scrapbook.

415. *N.O. Morning Star*, n.d., [Dec. 1881].

416. *Catholic World* 4 (March 1867): 857.

417. ASM, N.O., Austin Carroll Papers, *Tipperary Free Press*, n.d.

418. *Catholic World* 6 (Nov. 1867): 287.

419. ASM, Bermondsey, scrapbook.

420. ASM, Albany, Foster to Degnan, Sept. 12, 1945.

421. ASM, Silver Spring, Degnan to Hartman, Aug. 7, 1950.

422. ASM, N.O., Austin Carroll Papers, memoirs.

423. Ibid.

424. Mary Borgia Walsh, tribute to Austin Carroll is the Foreword in the third edition and twelfth reprinting of Carroll's *Catherine McAuley*, (St. Louis: Vincentian Press) n.d. [1927 or 1928], vii–viii.

425. ASM, N.O., Austin Carroll Papers, memoirs.

426. Ibid.

427. Ibid.

428. Ibid.

429. ASM, Mobile, August 28, 1909.

430. ASM, Cork, Jan. 23, 1903.

431. ASM, N.O., Austin Carroll Papers, memoirs.

432. ASM, Mobile, register.

433. ASM, N.O., Austin Carroll Papers, memoirs.

434. Ibid.

435. Ibid.

436. *N.O. States*, Nov. 29, 30, 1909; *N.O. Times-Democrat*, Nov. 30, 1909; N.O. Daily *Picayune*, Nov. 30, 1909.

437. 1909: *Boston Review*, Dec. 4; *Boston Pilot*, Dec. 18; *America*, Dec. 4; *N.Y. Catholic News*, Dec. 4; *N.Y. Freeman's Journal*, Dec. 11, 18; *Irish world*, Dec. 11, 18; *Catholic Standard and Times*, Dec. 4; *Sacred Heart*, Dec. 11; *Brooklyn Tablet*, Dec. 18; *Ave Maria*, Dec. 11; *St. Louis Western Watchman*, Dec. 9; *St. Joseph, Mo., Catholic Tribune*, Dec. 11; *Kansas City Catholic Register*, Dec. 31; *Dallas Southern Messenger*, Dec. 9; *Clonmel Nationalist*, Dec. 11, 18; *America*, Jan. 1, 1910.

438. John O'Shanahan, SJ, "The Lesson of Her Noble Life," *Clonmel Nationalist*, Dec. 18, 1909.

439. Ibid.

440. Ibid.

441. *N.O. Item*, Feb. 21, 1851.

442. Carroll, Foreword, 21.

443. *N.O. Morning Star*, Sept. 1, 1906.

444. ASM, N.O., J. R. Coniff, Dept. of Ed., State of Louisiana, sent the college certification to Walsh, March 23, 1923.

445. ASM, Birmingham, Genevieve Bourke to Rev. Mother, March 9, 1910.

446. ASM, N.O., Austin Carroll Papers, Pius IX to Carroll, July 3, 1872. Before he was pope, Mastai-Ferretti served in Chile from 1823 to 1825 as auditor of the apostolic delegate.

447. Leo XIII opened the Vatican archives to historians in 1883, explaining that the Church has nothing to fear from historical truth.

448. ASM, N.O., Carroll Family Papers, Kirby to Carroll, Oct. 9, 1885; Austin Carroll to William Carroll, Oct. 27, 1885; APIC, Carroll to Kirby, Oct. 1885, Dec. 1890, March 1891, Nov. 1891; AANO, Sisters of Mercy to Leray, Nov. 10, 23, 1885.

449. *Boston Pilot*, Dec. 18, 1909.

450. *N.O. Morning Star*, Dec. 4, 1909.

451. *Dallas Southern Messenger*, Dec. 9, 1909.

452. *N.O. States*, Nov. 30, 1909.

453. Katherine E. Conway, "Golden Jubilee of a Great Sister of Mercy, Mother Austin Carroll of Mobile, Alabama," *Boston Pilot*, July 14, 1906.

454. Most accounts in chronicles mentioned zealous works of mercy, prolific literature, six considered Austin Carroll "great," seven called her "remarkable," and nine termed her "distinguished." ADJ, Heslin diary, Nov. 1909.

BIBLIOGRAPHY

Archives of the Sisters of Mercy of New Orleans, Louisiana:
Annals, chronicles, ephemera, historical manuscripts, notes, original letters and documents, rare publications, recollections of contemporaries, scrapbooks containing programs, newspaper and periodical clippings, and souvenirs complement bound volumes of chapter, corporation, and council minutes and financial records. The *Austin Carroll Papers* and the *Carroll Family Papers*, two special sets of archival photostats, contain reproductions of hundreds of letters, documents, and chronicle excerpts from the various archives listed below; copies of most of Mother Austin Carroll's books; reproductions of many of her published articles from periodicals and journals; original correspondence of the author with the members of several generations of the Carroll family; and copies of certificates giving the vital statistics of Mother Austin Carroll's family.

Photostats and copies of original papers in the *Austin Carroll Papers* and the *Carroll Family Papers* were located in the archives and the libraries of:

the Sisters of Mercy in:
Ireland: Baggot Street, Dublin, and Carysfort, Blackrock; Athy, Birr, Carlow, Charleville, Clifden, Clonmel, Cork, Ennis, Galway, Kinsale, Limerick, Moate, Naas, Passage West, Tullamore, Waterford, Westport, and Wexford.
Great Britain: Bermondsey, St. Edward's, and Crispin Street in London; Birmingham, Liverpool, Newcastle, and Sunderland in England; Belfast in Northern Ireland; and Lesmurdie and Adelaide in Australia.
The United States: Albany, N.Y.; Baltimore, Md.; Biloxi, Miss.; Buffalo, N.Y.; Burlingame, Calif.; Cincinnati, Ohio; Cresson or Loretto, Pa.; Dobbs Ferry, N.Y.; Farmington Hills or Detroit, Mich.; Frontenac, Mo.; Hartford, Conn.; Jeanerette, La; Laredo, Tex.; Little Rock, Ark.; Manchester or Windham, N.H.; Mercy Federation; Merion, Pa.; Mississippi City, Miss.; Mobile, Ala.; Omaha, Neb.; Pensacola, Fla.; Pittsburgh, Pa.; Providence, R.I.; Rochester, N.Y.; Savannah, Ga.; Silver Spring, formerly Bethesda, Md.; Slaton, Tex.; St. Louis, Mo.; St. Martinville, La.; Vicksburg, Miss.; Warrington, Fla.; and Worcester, Mass.

Pontifical, Diocesan, and Parish Archives and Special Library and Archival Collections in Seminaries, Universities, Colleges, and other Institutions in:
Rome: The Congregation for the Evangelization of Peoples or for the Propagation of the Faith, the Pontifical Irish College, and in Vatican City, the Vatican Library.
Ireland: In the Archidiocese of Cashel and Emly, the parish records and registers of Cashel; in the Diocese of Waterford and Lismore, the parish registers of the Holy Trinity Cathedral and St. Patrick's, Waterford; and St. Mary's, Irishtown, Clonmel, and Sts. Peter and Paul, Clonmel; the Tipperary (South Riding) Registry of Births, Deaths, and Marriages, Clonmel; the microfilm library of the Nationalist Newspaper, Clonmel, County Tipperary; in Dublin, the National Library, the Registry of Deeds, the Catholic Central Library, and the Office of the Registrar General; the library of St. Patrick's, Maynooth; the Cork City Library, Cork.
England: The British Museum Library, specifically the microfilm and collection of Irish newspapers contemporary with the subject; and the Public Records Office in Kew, Surrey.
The United States of America: The Archdiocese of Baltimore, Hartford, Mobile, New Orleans, and Omaha; and the Dioceses of Buffalo, Jackson, Little Rock, Richmond, and Savannah; the University of Notre Dame Library and the Archives, especially the episcopal papers of the Archdiocese of New Orleans and the Brownson, McMaster, and Onahan papers; the Archives, especially the Timon papers, of St. Mary's Seminary, Perryville, Mo.; and the Josephite Archives in Baltimore, especially the Benoit papers.

The libraries listed in this section, like those already enumerated in England and Ireland, were valuable in this research primarily for their collections of nineteenth-century newspapers and periodicals. These proved to be prolific sources for numerous articles about Mother Austin Carroll's social works and institutions as well as critical reviews of her books and tributes to her literary abilities.

The Archives and the Library of the Catholic University of America; Georgetown University Library; the Marist College Library; the Library of Congress; the National Archives; and the Immigration and Naturalization Service in Washington, D.C.; the Library of St. Charles Borromeo Seminary and the Records of the American Catholic Historical Society, Overbrook Pa.; the Libraries of Holy Cross College, Worcester, Mass.; Saint Louis University, St. Louis, Mo.; and the University of Southwest Louisiana, Lafayette, La.; the T. P. Thompson Collection in the Library of the University of Alabama, Tuscaloosa, Ala.; the Special Historical Collection of the Mobile Public Library, Mobile, Ala.; the Library and the Archives, especially the Grace King papers, of Louisiana State University, Baton Rouge, La.; and in New Orleans, the Library of Loyola University, the Library of Notre Dame Seminary; the Library, particularly the Howard Memorial collection, and the Archives, especially the Cable and Gayarré papers, of the Tulane University; the Historic New Orleans Collection, especially the riverboat photographs and the 1885 Cotton Centennial Exhibition materials; the Library and the Archives of the Louisiana Centennial Exhibition materials; the Library and the Archives of the Louisiana State Museum; and the Archives and the Special Collection of New Orleans and Louisiana materials in the New Orleans Public Library. These New Orleans libraries, like many of those listed above, contain some of the rarest of the publications of Mother Austin Carroll.

Except for the books of Mother Austin Carroll, the biography is based upon archival documentation and letters. Books mentioned, other than those of Austin Carroll, are listed in the notes with complete bibliographical data.

MARY AUSTIN CARROLL BIBLIOGRAPHY

The title page of each work identified the author, Mother Mary Teresa Austin Carroll, as "a Member of the Order of Mercy." Journals and other periodicals usually identified Mother Austin Carroll by the initials, "M. A. C."

Original Works:

Life of Catherine McAuley, Foundress of the Institute of Religious Sisters of Mercy. N.Y.: Sadlier, 1866, 1868, 1871, 1874, 1877, 1882, 1884, 1887, 1890; N.Y.: Kennedy, n.d., 1896; St. Louis: Vincentian Press, [1927].

Happy Hours of Childhood: a Series of Tales for the Little Ones. N.Y.: P. O'Shea, 1867, 1894.

Angel-Dreams: a Series of Tales for Children. N.Y.: Catholic Publication Society, 1868, 1869, 1871, 1894.

Glimpses of Pleasant Homes: a Few Tales for Youth. N.Y.: Catholic Publication Society, 1869, 1872.

By the Seaside: a Series of Tales for Young People. N.Y.: P. O'Shea, 1872, 1894.

Life of St. Alphonsus Liguori, Bishop and Doctor of the Church. N.Y.: P. O'Shea, 1874, 1879, 1882.

Life of the Venerable Clement Mary Hofbauer. N.Y.: Catholic Publication Society, 1877, 1879.

Mary Beatrice and Her Step-Daughters: an Historical Drama. N.Y.: Catholic Publication Society Company, 1880.

Marie Antoinette: an Historical Drama. N.Y. Catholic Publication Society Company, 1880.

Leaves from the Annals of the Sisters of Mercy. Vol. 1, *Ireland.* N.Y.: Catholic Publication Society Company, 1881, 1883, 1885.

The Tudor Sisters: an Historical Drama. New Orleans, La: T. Fitzwilliam, 1883.

Leaves from the Annals of the Sisters of Mercy. Vol. 2, *England, Scotland, Australia, and New Zealand.* N.Y.: Catholic Publication Society Co., 1883, 1885.

Scenes from the Life of Katharine of Aragon: an Historical Drama. New Orleans, La.: T. Fitzwilliam, 1885.

The Ursulines in Louisiana, 1727–1827. New Orleans, La.: Hyman Smith, 1886.

Leaves from the Annals of the Sisters of Mercy. Vol. 3, *Newfoundland and the United States.* N.Y.: Catholic Publication Society Co., 1889.

Leaves from the Annals of the Sisters of Mercy. Vol. 4, *South America, Central America, and the United States.* N.Y.: P. O'Shea, 1895.

Essays Educational and Historic or X-Rays on Some Important Episodes. N.Y.: P. O'Shea, 1899.

In Many Lands. N.Y.: P. O'Shea and Co., 1904.

The Father and the Son, St. Alphonsus and St. Gerard. St. Louis, Mo.: Herder, 1905.

A Catholic History of Alabama and the Floridas. N.Y.: P. J. Kenedy, 1908; Freeport, N.Y.: Books for Libraries Press, 1970.

Books translated, compiled, edited and/or reprinted in the United States:

Translated from the French with an original Foreward *History of Blessed Margaret Mary,* by Charles Daniel, SJ. N.Y.: P. O'Shea, 1867.

Translated from the French *A Treatise on the Knowledge and Love of Our Lord Jesus Christ*, by Jean Baptist St. Jure, SJ. 3 vols. N.Y.: P. O'Shea, 1868–1872. Vol. 1: 1868, 1869, 1875; Vol. 2: 1869, 1870, 1875; Vol. 3: 1872, 1875.

Compiled *Spiritual Retreat of Eight Days*, from St. Alphonsus Liguori. N.Y.: P. O'Shea, 1872, 1875, 1878.

Compiled *Instructions on the Commandments and Sacraments*, from St. Alphonsus Liguori. N.Y.: P. O'Shea, 1873, 1875.

Compiled *In Memory of Reverend John B. Duffy, CSSR*. New Orleans, La.: Morning Star, 1874.

Translated from the French *The Religious: a Treatise on the Vows and Virtues of the Religious State*, by Jean Baptist St. Jure, SJ. N.Y.: P. O'Shea, 1875. This title is listed in ads from O'Shea in 1875, but the earliest copy located seems to be a later translation in 1882.

Edited for U.S. reprint *A Few of the Sayings, Instructions, and Prayers of the Foundress of the Sisters of Mercy, Catherine McAuley* [compiled by Mother Mary Clare Moore]. N.Y.: Catholic Publication Society Co., 1877, 1878.

Translated from the French *The Spiritual Man or the Spiritual Life Reduced to Its First Principles*, by Jean Baptist St. Jure, SJ. N.Y.: P. O'Shea, 1878, 1879.

Compiled *Sayings and Instructions of the Foundress of the Sisters of Mercy*. Vol. 2. N.Y.: Catholic Publication Society Co., 1878, 1879.

Translated from the Spanish *Meditations and Contemplations on the Sacred Passion of Our Lord Jesus Christ*, by Venerable Luis of Grenada, OP. N.Y.: Catholic Publication Society Company, 1879.

Edited *Meditations and Considerations for a Three Days' Retreat* [by Mary Juliana Purcell]. N.Y.: P. O'Shea, 1880; Omaha, Neb.: Burkley, 1903, 1923.

Edited for U.S. reprint *One of God's Heroines*, by Kathleen O'Meara. N.Y.: Catholic Publication Society Co., 1880.

Edited *Regle et Constitutions des Soeurs Religieuses de la Misericorde* [translated by Sister Mary Xavier Durand.] New Orleans, La.: T. Fitzwilliam, 1881.

Edited for U.S. reprint *Meditations for a Novena to Our Lady of Mercy and Reflections for the Renovation Retreat* [by Mother Mary Francis Bridgeman]. New Orleans, La.: T. Fitzwilliam, 1881.

Edited *Four Days in the Life of Mary Queen of Scots: a Drama for Young Ladies*, by a Sister of Mercy. New Orleans, La.: T. Fitzwilliam, 1882.

Edited for U.S. reprint *Cottage Controversy in Six Conversations*, by Catherine McAuley. N.Y.: P. O'Shea, 1883.

Compiled *Lectures Delivered at a Spiritual Retreat*, from personal notes of the compiler. N.Y.: Catholic Publication Society Co., 1885.

Translated from the Spanish *Principles of Government of St. Ignatius*, from Pedro de Ribadaneira, SJ. N.Y.: Catholic Publication Society Co., 1885, 1895.

Articles in Journals and other periodicals:

"The Nine Days' Queen." *American Catholic Quarterly Review* 1 (October 1876): 680-712.

"Yellow Fever." *For Our Boys, 1879* (San Francisco: Bancroft, 1879), 67-76.

"Nuns in Honduras; Religion in Central America," series of Southern Sketches. *The Irish Monthly* 11 (July 1883): 446-51.

"The Cross in the South," series of Southern Sketches. *The Irish Monthly* 11 (August 1883): 504-10.

"Watering Places on the Mississippi Sound," series of Southern Sketches. *The Irish Monthly* 11 (October 1883): 571-80.

"In the Flowery Land—Pensacola," series of Southern Sketches. *The Irish Monthly* 12 (January 1884): 13-8.

"From Acadie to Attakapas—the Wanderings of Evangeline," series of Southern Sketches. *The Irish Monthly* 12 (April 1884): 173-81.

"Nuns in Louisiana; the Old Convents of Orleans Island," series of Southern Sketches. *The Irish Monthly* 12 (June, September 1884): 344-55, 469-85.

"Valiant Soldier of the Cross, Reverend William McDonald." *The Irish Monthly* 13 (November 1885): 598-606.

"What Is True Education?" *Catholic World* 43 (June 1886): 404-13.

"Education in Louisiana in French Colonial Days." *American Catholic Quarterly Review* 11 (July 1886): 396-418.

"Education in New Orleans in Spanish Colonial Days." *American Catholic Quarterly Review* 12 (April 1887): 253–71.

"Twenty-Four Years in Buenos Ayres." *American Catholic Quarterly Review* 13 (July 1888): 478–92.

"A Western Heroine: Mother Francis Mulholland." *The Irish Monthly* 17 (May 1889): 242–54.

"The Church of the Attakapas, 1750–1889." *American Catholic Quarterly Review* 14 (July 1889): 462–87.

"Forty Years in the American Wilderness." *American Catholic Quarterly Review* 15 (January 1890): 123–43.

"Some Haunts of the Padres." *Catholic World* 51 (April 1890): 76–87.

"When Brigham Young Was King." *American Catholic Quarterly Review* 15 (April 1890): 284–301.

"A Glance at the Latter-Day Saints." *The Irish Monthly* 18 (June 1890): 309–19.

"Ancient Monastic Town—Shrewsbury." *The Irish Monthly* 19 (May, June 1891): 254–62, 308–16.

"The Battle of the Boyne and the Sieges of Limerick, 1690–1691." *American Catholic Quarterly Review* 16 (October 1891): 845–62.

"The Experience of a Sister of Mercy." *In Reports and Papers of the Convention of the Apostolate of the Press*, 165–72. N.Y.: Columban Press, 1892.

"Alabama—Here We Rest!" *The Irish Monthly* 20 (February 1892): 69–78.

"Joanna Reddan." *The Irish Monthly* 20 (May 1892): 225–36.

"Some Episodes of the American Civil War." *The Irish Monthly* 20 (July 1892): 361–78.

"Right Reverend Dr. Bacon, First Bishop of Portland, Maine." *The Irish Monthly* 23 (January 1895): 27–31.

"Sisters of Mercy and the American Indians." *The Irish Monthly* 23 (June 1895): 301-6.

"About the Utah Saints." *American Catholic Quarterly Review* 20 (July 1895): 486-500.

"Pisa and Its Four Fabrics." *The Irish Monthly* 25 (May 1897): 268-71.

"The Superb City: Genoa." *The Irish Monthly* 27 (March 1899): 119-24.

"Mary of Modena—Her Descendants—the Jacobites." *Essays Educational and Historic*, 371-408. N.Y.: O'Shea, 1899.

"From Sugar Fields to the Golden Gate." *The Irish Monthly* 32 (August 1904): 421-9.

"Redemptorist Saints, the Earliest and the Latest: a Recent Pilgrimage." *The Irish Monthly* 33 (June, August 1905): 301-7, 400-6.

"The Grave of Hernando de Soto, Discoverer of the Mississippi." *The Irish Monthly* 33 (December 1905): 670-3.

"Pedro Melendez, Founder of St. Augustine, Florida." *The Irish Monthly* 34 (Febraury 1906): 102-5.

"Slavery in Its Mildest Form." *The Irish Monthly* 34 (November 1906): 643-6.

"An Early Millionaire." *Magnificat* 1 (November 1907): 21-7.

"Don Alexander O'Reilly, Field Marshall of Spain." *American Catholic Quarterly Review* 33 (January 1908): 87-97.

"Father John—a Sketch." *The Irish Monthly* 37 (January 1909): 27-31.

INDEX

Abbelen, Rev. Peter, 216, 246, n.348, 270

Alexandria, La., 118, n.31, 163, n.15, 231

Allen, Bp. Edward, 326-8, n.361, 329-30, 335

Appalachicola, Fla., 89, 320-21, nn.301.4, 327

Australia, 128, 181, 200, n.5, 253, n.22

Bacon, Bp. David, 51, 141, n.54, 322

Baltimore, Md., 59, n.36, 252-3, 264, 288

Barry, Kate Madeleine, 291, nn.35-36, 328

Bartolini, Cardinal Dominic, 226-7, 288-9, 240, 244

Becker, Bp. Thomas, 169-70, n.59, 317, nn.266-70

Beckett, Mother Anastasia, 252, 303, 328

Belfast, N. I., 301, n.110

Belize, C. A., 89, 207-10, nn.74-83, 212-3, 218-9, 224, 226-7, 231, n.229, 232, 238-9, 247, 266, 271, 323-4, nn.330-3

Benoit, Rev. Peter, 183, -4, n.178

Bentley, Mother de Pazzi, 75-80, n.9, 81-5, n.16, 92, 96, 161, n.4, 163, 308, n.185

Bermondsey London, 23, 55, 56, 77, 127-8, 170-1, n. 63-64, 200, 252-3, 288, 297, n.90-4, 299

Bertrand, Nother Gertrude, 316, n.262, 329, nn.383, 388, 392, 401

Bessemer, Ala., 320, nn.301-4

Bianconi, Charles, 1-2, 18, 296

Biloxi, Miss., 137-9, n.39, 151-4, 174, 176-7, 188, n.219, 282, 318, 324, n.332

Birmingham, Ala., 225, 264, 320

Birmingham, England, 23, 200, 204, n. 39, 224-5, 293, n.56

Birr, 12, 23, 127, 158, n.157, 252, 303

Blanc, Abp. Antoine, 51, 91, 105, 106, 107, n.65, 113, n.9, 252

Blenk, Abp. Hubert, 324, n.332, 329

Bogaerts, Rev. Jean, 240-1, nn.312-4, 244, 257

Brennan, Sister Josephine, 166, n.31

Brewton, Ala., 175, 207, 222

Brooklyn, N.Y., 38, 75, 188-9, n.205-8

Browne, Mother de Sales, 112, 117-8, n.29, 126, n.72, 127, n.79, 137, 159, 174, 221, 325, n.347

Brownson, Orestes, 32, 61, 80, 124, 128

Buenos Aires, 200, 209, n.75, 256, 328

Buffalo, N.Y., 39, 40, 45, 46, 47, n.55, 48, 49, 50, 51, 65, 313

Butler, Mother Philomene, 113, n.8, 119, n.32, 235-6, n.276, 239-241, 247,258-9, 262, 270-7, 321, 323-4, nn.330-3, 334

Butler, Rev. Theobald, 212-6, n.109, 218-23, n.168, 226, 236, 240, 257

Byrn, Kate (Sister Raymund, OP), 79, nn.31-32, 188, n.207, 287-8

Byrn, Sister Camillus, 56, n.23, 79, nn.31-2, 188, n.207, 253, 287-8

Bryn, Sister Margaret, 129, n.79, 188, n.207, 200, 252, 288, 297

Byrne, Bp. Andrew, 51, 91, 126, n.67, 275

Cable, George Washington, 59, n.34, 205, 289, 332

Callanan, Sister Elizabeth, 4607, n.55, 48, 76, n.15, 85, 175-6

Carlow, 12, 23, 83, 212, 253, 304, nn.136-9

Carroll, Abp. John, 13, n.66, 159, n.165, 302

Carroll, Anne (sister of Margaret) Sister Mariana, 4-5, n.23, 10, nn.53-4, 334

Carroll, Joanna (sister of Margaret) Sister Dominica, 4-5, n.23, 13, n.54, 18, nn.64-5, 127, 305-6, nn.155-6

Carroll, John (brother of Margaret), 4, n.20, 17

Carroll, Katy (sister of Margaret) Mother of Mercy, 3-5, n.20, 12-13, n.63, 18, 21, n.18, 23, 26-8, 127, 173, 257-8, 305-6, 325

Carroll, Margaret Anne (see also Mother Austin), 4, n.21, 6-8, n.38, 9-11, n.48; novitiate, 18-27, nn.12, 16-17, 40; missioning, 26-28

Carroll, Margaret Mary Strahan (mother of
    Margaret Anne), 1–5, n.17, 8–9, n.66,
    16–17, 21, 157, n.150
Carroll, Mary [Mrs. Charles Patrick Byrne]
    (sister of Margaret), 5, n.23, 9–10,
    nn.49–53, 54, 18, 306, n.163, 313
Carroll, Michael (brother of Margaret),
    3–4, n.19
Carroll, Mother Austin,
    annals, 171–2, 185–7, 251, 277, 321
    biography of foundress, 50, 54–56, 63,
        76–81, nn.31–33, 122–3, n.48, 287,
        330–3
    black schools, 61–62, 102, 138, n.39,
        150, n.108, 152, n.126, 157, 181,
        n.162, 153, nn.175–6, 187, n.219,
        190, n.223, 202–7, 224–5, 231, 234,
        267, n.130, 280–2, n.245, 313,
        317–320, n.295
    creche, 136, 153, 157, 165–6, 187,
        n.199, 263, 267
    honors, 127–7, n.76, 144–5, 229,
        n.221, 230–1, n.222, 243, 251, 255,
        314, nn.240–1, 318–9, nn.287–8,
        328
    newsboys, 153, 190, 197–9, 229–30,
        244, 276, 289, 309
    prison ministry, 70, 75, 85, 124, 153–5,
        167–9, 183, 229–30, 263, 276,
        309–11, 314, 322
    women, 16, 44–5, 50, 53, 80–1, 87–8,
        157, 167–9, 179–80, 197, 202,
        267–9, 337
    women's college, 232–3, 263, 267–9,
        274–6, 337
Carroll, Patrick (brother of Margaret) 4,
    n.23, 5, n.29, 18, 279–80
Carroll, William (father of Margaret) 1–3,
    n.17, 5–8, n.34, 10–13, n.66, 16–18,
    257–8, nn.64–68
Carroll, Willie Francis (brother of Marga-
    ret) 4, n.23, 5, 8, 18, 63
Castell, William, 229–90, n.22–3
Chapelle, Abp. Placide, 245, 255, 326,
    n.361, 329
Charleville, 12, 23, 306, n.155
Chicago, Ill., 38, 45, 59, 61, 66, 127, n.79,
    229, n.14, 264, 317, 328
Cincinnati, Ohio, 127, n.79, 156, n.147,
    182–3, 188–9, n.205–8, 205

Clifden, 115, n.16, 117, n.25, 200,
    252, 305
Clonmel, 1–2, 4–9, 16–17, 28, 43, 125,
    250–1, 269, 303–4, 327, 339
Coleman, Sr. M. Baptist, 39, 42, 43, 46, 47
Macon, Ga. (earlier Columbus, Ga. and St.
    Augustine, Fla.) 200, 265
Consitt, Sister Aloysius, 31, 200, 293
Conway, Katherine E., 212, 290–1, 318–9,
    nn.284–8, 328, 339
Cook, Mother Aloysius, 119, n.32, 262
Coolock House, 123, 303
Cork, 12, 18, 22, 23, 24, 25, 26, 34, 35, 56,
    81, 82, 91, 127, 175, 212, 305–6,
    315, 327
Cottage Controversy, 122, n.51, 197, n.279,
    204, nn.43–45, 229
Creedon, Mother Frances, 139–40, 200,
    218, n.132
Cullen, Mother Paula, 305, n.147
Cusack, Margaret Anne (Sister Francis
    Clare), 79–80, nn.31–32, 253, n.47, 254,
    n.35, 288

Davenport, Iowa, 127, n.79, 264, 277
Deasy, Mother Vincent, 24, 123, n.51,
    299–300
de Carriere, Rev. Philippi, 240–3,
    nn.297–300, 244, nn.312–3, 257
Delaney, Bp. William, 20–21, n.17, 34–35,
    n.10, 91, 171, n.63
Derry, 55, 77
Devereux, Mother Joseph, 115, n.14, 119,
    n.33, 260, 272–6, 284, 308, 310–2,
    321–4, nn.330–3
DiPietro, Bp. Salvatore, 207–8, 218, 226–7,
    231–2, 323–4, nn.330–333
Donahoe, Patrick, 127, 291
Donovan, Mother Stanislaus, 207, n.63,
    210, n.81
Doyle, Sister Mary Anne, 55–56, 123, n.51
Drexel, Mother Katherine, 280–1, nn.242–4,
    282, 285, 313, 317, 319
Dublin, 28, 55–56, 75–82, 113, 127–8, 132,
    135, n.16, 139–40, 156, 162, nn.22–24,
    200, 218, 288, 297, 302–4, 315–6, 337
Durand, Sister Xavier, 212, n.89
Duffy, Rev. John, 106, 134, 140–1, n.52,
    142–7, 194–5

Elder, Apb. William, 20, n.50, 59, n.36, 107, n.65, 133, 137-9, 157, 163, 217, 220

England, Bp. John, 169-70, n.56-59, 317

Faivre, Rev. Frederick, 148, 194-5, 264, 319, 325

Farrell (or O'Farrell), Sister Francis, 76 n.15, 94, n.14, 118, nn.27-30

FitzGerald, Bp. Edward, 217, 223, n.172, 275-6

Fitzgerald, Mother Angela, 37, 38, 44, 127, n.79

Fitzpatrick, Mother Evangelista, 200, 209, n.75, 253, 255-6

Fitzpatrick, Sister Aloysius, 126, n.70, 217, n.131, 318, n.277

Fitzpatrick, Mother Clare, 262, 312-5, n.218, 318, n.277, 325, n.352

Flanagan, Rev. John, 91, 92, n.3, 113, 117, nn.24-6, 118, 125-6

Flanagan, Rev. John D. 272, nn.162-3

Franzelin, Johannes Card., 240, n.297, 244

Gaffney, Rev. Edward, 289, n.24, 290, n.25

Gaffney, Rev. Myles (or Miletius), 16, n.3, 24, n.28, 56-57, nn.26-30, 78

Gayarré, Charles, 222-3, n.163, 229, 277, n.198, 289, n.17, 319, n.291, 325, n.352, 328, 332

Gaynor, Mother Ignatius, 115, n.16, 117, nn.25-26, 118, n.31

Gerlach, Rev. Joseph, 276-7, n.196

Gibbons, James Card., 169-70, nn.56-59, 175, 236-9, 243-6, n.348, 247, n.353, 254, 271-3

Gibson, Mother liguori, 31, 200, 293

Giesen, Rev. Henry, 92, 103-5, 115-7, 134, nn.88, 96, 152, n.124, 190, n.235, 212-6, nn.121-2, 220-1, 227, n.201, 234-6, 238-44, 259, 264

Girardey, Rev. Ferreol, 134, 142-6, n.62, 147-8, n.85, 161, n.2, 194-5, 213-4, 218, 227, 236, 321, 329

Gourrier, Mother Theresa, 103, nn.50-51, 108, n.69, 112, 119, n.32, 182, 232, 262, n.89, 273, 325

Granger, Mother Genevieve, 66, 127, n.79, 264-5

Grant, Mother Catherine, 76, n.16, 93, n.12, 94-6, 102-4, 109, 113, n.11, 117, nn.26-29, 118, nn.32-34, 148, 215

Grant, Sister Ignatius, 108, n.72-73, 115

Greene, Sister Agnes, 125-6, 231, n.231, 253, n.26, 303, 319

Hardman, Mother Juliana, 200, 224, n.182, 293, n.53

Harley, Sir Robert (brother of Sister Caroline), 231, n.229

Hartford, Conn., 23, 35-42, 51-54, 201, 228

Hartnett, Mother Vincent, 24, n.28, 29, n.47, 56, 78, n.31, 305, n.146

Haughery, Margaret Gaffney, 128, 134, 154, 218, n.133-4

Hearn, Sister Baptist, 49, n.66, 127, n.79

Helmpraecht, Rev. Joseph, 42, 142, n.82, 152, n.124, 228

Heslin, Bp. Thomas, 190, nn.222-3, 219, n.147, 283, 303, 317, 329

Hession, Sister Margaret, 115, n.16, 117, nn.25-26, 118, n.31

Hogan, Bp. John Joseph, 159, 175, 202, 236, 285

Ihmsen, Mother de Sales, 264, 266

Indianola, Tex., 117-8, nn.27-30

Indians, 115, n.16, 117, nn.25-26, 118, n.31

Jackson Barracks, 169, 176, 264

Jaeckel, Rev. Nicholas, 143-5, nn.65, 82, 146-7, nn.85, 88, 96, 212-6, nn.121-2, 225-8, 238

Jan, Pere Ange, 192, 202, 255

Janssens, Abp. Francis, 217, 224, 243, 255, 282, 309-13, 319, 323-5

Jeanerette, La., 192, n.235, 272, nn.162-3, 276-7, n.195

Kearney, Mother Evangelist, 210, n.81, 262

Kehoe, Lawrence, 128, 188, 290, n.37

Kelley, Bp. Patrick, 3, n.16

Kenrick, Abp. Peter Richard, 70, 83, 84, 92, 93, 94

Killelea, Sister Margaret Mary, 262, n.89, 306, nn.159-60, 308, 325

King Grace, 328, nn.375-6

Kinsale, 305, 315, 317
Kirby, Abp. Tobias, 220, 235-8, 243-8,
    251-2, 256-7, 294, 297, 304-5, 308-9,
    310-12, 325

Lancaster, William Blair, 146, n.50, 289,
    n.21, 290
Leahy, Bp. John, 24, n.27, 302, 306
Leo XIII, Pope, 17, 209, 218, 229,
    nn.214-5, 243, 251, 338, n.447
Leroy, Abp. Francis, 137, 192-3, n.241,
    207-9, 216-223, 225-7, 231, n.231-5,
    236-47, n.353, 251, 255-7, 264,
    267, 272-4
Limerick, 12, 23, 56, 117, n.25, 127, 162,
    n.24, 261, 251, 305, n.149, 315, 322
Little Rock, 125-6, nn.67, 70, 217, n.131,
    253, n.26, 265, 275
Liverpool, 31, 117, n.25, 200, 292-3
Loewekamp, William, CSSR, 227-8,
    nn.200-1, 234-5, 243-4, 271-3
Loretto, Pa., 264, 266, 313
Louisville, ky., 76, 93, 188-9, n.206
Lucas, Sr. M. Camillus, 94 n.14, 118,
    nn.30, 34, 139
Lynch, Mother Ignatius, 65, 68-70, 71-2

McAuley, Mother Catherine, 16, n.3,
    23-24, 75, 122, 129, 150, 156-8, 181,
    195-7, 218, 278, 301, 326, 334
    Quoted, 19-21, 27, 29, 38, 88, 116,
        120, 158, n.159, 166, n.40, 171,
        n.63, 190, 197, 275, n.187
McDermott, Sister Xavier, 93, n.13, 114,
    116, n.21
McDonald, Rev. William, 52, 53, 189
McGirr, Sr. M. Vincent, 127, n.79, 264
McKenna, Mother Augustine, 127, n.79,
    159, 175-6, 188-9, n.205, 191,
    224, n.182
McKinley, Sister Antonia, 188-9,
    n.208, 262
McMaster, James, 128, 175-6, 212,
    290, n.36
Madden, Sister Regis, 39, 42-45, n.42,
    46-48
Maguire, John Francis, 84-85, n.54, 128,
    145, 290
Maher, Sister Catherine, 304, nn.136-7,
    253, n.26-7

Maher, Mother Pauline, 36, 37, 38, 44, 127,
    n.79, 156, n.146
Maher, Mother Teresa, 127, n.79, 156,
    n.147, 182-3, 189, 208
Manchester, N.H., 35, 49, n.68, 51-54,
    58-59, 63-66, 83, 188-9, n.205-8, 205,
    211, 228, 252, 256, 321
Mandeville, La., 289
Manning, Henry Card., 293, n.51,
    297, 315
Martin, Bp. Augusta, 74, 113-5, 117,
    n.26, 118
Meade, Sister Francis, 27, 31, 34, n.9,
    35, 306
Meredith, Rev. William, 92, 103, 105, 114,
    294-5, 224, n.181
Mississippi City, 318, nn.379-81, 319-20
Mobile, Ala., 225-8, n.199, 280-4, 309-10,
    n.195, 310-2, n.225, 313, 318, n.283,
    318-20, 324-5, 330, 334-5, 339
Moore, Mother Clare, 29, 55-6, 141, n.55,
    170-1, nn.63-64, 298, 302-3, nn.121-2
Moore, Sister Clare Augustine, 55, 56,
    196-7, n.271, 302-3
Morgan, John P., 175-6, n.110
Moran, Sister Cecelia, 166, n.32
Mulholland, Mother de Sales, 66, 127, n.79,
    256, 277
Murphy, Rev. Dominic, 16, n.3, 20-21,
    n.17, 24, nn.27-28, 56-57, nn.26-30
Murphy, Rev. William Stack, 125, n.66,
    141-2, n.60
Murray, Abp. Daniel, 9, n.48, 16, n.3,
    158, n.157

Naas, 23, 28, 83, 125, 253, 303
Nagle, Honora (Nano), 80, 310, 365, 13,
    nn.66-67, 15, 21, 24, n.28, 56, 218, 256
Nagle, Mother Jane, 13, n.68
Nagle, Marguerite, 13, nn.67-68
Nashville, 188-9, n.206, 200
Natchitoches, 115, n.16, 118, n.25, 231,
    236, 267, n.130
Neithart, Rev. Benedict, 143, 194, 212-3,
    nn.121-2, 240
Newcastle-upon-Tyne, 229-400, n.106
Newfoundland, 139-40, n.44, 200,
    218, n.132
Newman, John Card., 3, 294, 207, 315

New Orleans, La., 51, 76, 81, 84, 88–89, 94, 102, 104, 108–9, 111, n.3, 119, 125–6, 133, 159, n.165, 159, 249, 309–10, 328, 336
Newry, 301–2, 316
New York, 25, 28, 33, 38, 46–48, 52, 61, 65, 75, n.9, 76–7, 81, 93–94, n.12, 113–5, 132–5, 156, 175–6, 188–9, 205–8, 288, 335
New Zealand, 58, 200, n.5
Notre Dame de Bons secours, 93, 105, n.57, 107–8, 112, 119, 136, 148, 150, n.108, 157, 183, n.175, 262, 273

O'Brien, Mother Gonzaga, 52, 63, 127, n.79, 188–9, n.205, 228, 252, 256, 321–2
O'Callaghan, Rev. C. T., 224, n.176
O'Connell, Bp. Denis, 238–9, n.284, 245–6, nn.346–8
O'Connell, Daniel, 8–9, n.48, 158, n.157, 295, 305
O'Connell, Sister Aloysius, 200, 299–300
O'Connor, Bp. James, 139, 161, n.3, 162–3, 188–9, n.205, 211, 218–20, 224, 232, 234–6, 238, 251, 275, 279–85, 292, 294, 307, 325
O'Connor, Bp. Michael, 45, 61, n.42, 134, 139–41, 228, 233, n.241, 279, 293
O'Connor, Mother Agnes, 25, 28, 46, n.55, 47–8, 65, 75, n.9, 76, n.15, 81–2, 96
Odin, Abp. Jean Marie, 74, 86, 92, 103, 104, n.51, 107, n.65, 113, n.9, 274
O'Donnell, Mother Baptist, 209, n.75
O'Gorman, Bp. James, 63–65, n.55, 66, 69, 70
Oliver, Mother Aloysius, 115, n.16, 117, nn.25–26, 118, n.31
Omaha, Neb., 35, 63–66, n.65, 67–71, n.91, 109, 205, 279–81, 284–7, 313
Onahan, W., 318–9, nn.284–8
O'Reilly, Alexander, 328, nn.375–6
O'Reilly, Bp. Bernard, 33, 38, 43
O'Reilly, John Boyle, 175–6, 212, 290–1, n.37
O'Shanahan, Rev. John, 309, 330, 334–5
O'Shea, Patrick, 128, 188, 290
O'Sullivan, Bp. Jeremiah, 169–70, n.59, 264, 279–85, 303–4, 309–19, n.296, 323–6

Ozanam, Frederick, 289, n.20–21

Passage West, Ireland, 21, n.18, 23, 26–28, 127, 173, 257–8, 305–6, n.155
Pass Christian, Miss., 126, n.72, 137, 149
Pensacola, 148–9, nn.99–101, 150–1, n.108, 152–3, 174, 202, 206–7, 217, 224, 317, 322
Perché, Abp. N. J., 113–114, n.9, 117, n.26, 119, n.33, 137, 139, 143, 148, 152, 161–3, 180–1, 194–5, 207–9, 213, 216–7, 219–23, n.168–70, 232, 236, 239–40, 246–7, 271–4
Philadelphia, 188–9, n.205
Pittsburgh, Pa., 38, 44, 49, 61, 188–9, n.205, 264, 280, 285
Pius IX, Pope, 126–7, n.75, 144, 229–30
Prendergast, Mother Genevieve, 317, 319, n.294
Providence, R.I., 27, 31–39, 41–42, 49–52, 54, 60, 109, 228, 288
Purcell, Sister Juliana, 17, n.10, 127, n.79, 191, 231, 269–70, 325

Quinlan, Bp. John, 74, 149–51, 163, 217, 317

Rapier, Thomas, 289–n.21, 290, n.24
Reddan, Sister Joanna, 278, 322, n.317
Rochester, N.Y., 34–35, 38–39, 40–42, 46–47, n.55, 48–50, 65, 108, 200
Rouquette, Rev. Adrien, 222–3, 332
Rouxel, Bp. Gustave, 212–4, n.109, 215–6, nn.121–2, 218–23, n.168, 225–6, 236, 240, 267, 271
Russell, Rev. Matthew, 56–57, nn.26–30, 79, 212, 278, nn.208–9, 313–4, 316
Russell, Mother Baptist, 127, n.79, 169, nn.59–61, 175, 201, 222, 277–8, 292, 302, 305, 316, 327
Russell, Sister Emmanuel, 302, 316
Ryan, Mother Patricia, 328, n.372

Sadlier, Mrs. James, 128, 145, 290
San Francisco, Cal., 127, n.79, 169, n.59–61, 175, 277–8, 322
Savannah, Ga., 74, 106, 169–70, n.57–59, 317, n.266, 319, 320
Selma, Ala., 309, n.195, 310–2, n.225, 313–5, 317–8, n.283, 319

Seton, Sister Catherine, 25, n.31, 75, n.10, 199, 325

Shields, Sr. Benedicta, 94, n.15, 116, 20

Shubrick, Mother Jerome, 107, n.15, 120, 121, 179, n.79, 225, 249, 268, n.205, 272, n.227, 330, 467

Society of St. Vincent de Paul, 133-4, 143, n.62, 190, 229, n.219, 240, 289, n.24, 290, n.25, 319

Stapleton, Sister Joseph, 115, n.16, 117, nn.25-26, 118, n.31

St. Alphonsus, 105-7, n.63, 112, 114-5, n.12-5, 119, 136, 140, 144, 148, 183, n.176, 190, n.225, 195, 203-4, 213, 217, 229, 273

Macon (earlier in St. Augustine, Lfa. and Columbus, Ga.), 62, nn.46-47, 200

St. Katherine's College, 232-3, 263, 267-9, n.149, 270-1, 274-5, 305, 337, n.444

St. Louis, Mo., 58, 70-71, n.91, 75, n.9, 76, n.15, 77, n.16, 78, n.17, 81-88, 93, 95, 97, 99, 134, 156, 335

St. Martinville, 192, nn.233-6, 202-3, n.29, 231, 255, 277

St. Michael's, 190, nn.222-3, 217, 219-20, 238, 283

St. Patrick's, 91-92, n.3, 113-4, 117, nn.24, 26, 139, n.42, 152

St. Philip's, 277, n.196

Strange, Sister Elizabeth, 29, 127, n.79, 175, 188-9, n.205, 201, 204, 327

St. Thomas Island, 151-2, n.124, 226

Sunderland, 200, 299-300, n.106

Thompson, T. Philip, 277, n.196, n.396, 329

Timon, Bp. John, 30, n.50, 38-40, 42, 45-46, n.55, 49, 51

Ursuline Nuns, 124-5, nn.64-65, 133, n.13, 217-8, n.130, 255-6, n.44, 364, n.48, 329

Vaughan, Herbert Card. 183, 281, 315

Verot, Bp. Augustin, 30, n.50, 62, 94

Vicksburg, Miss., 59, 62, 63, 73, 92, n.5, 100, n.37, 112, 118, n.29, 126, n.72, 156, 159, 174, 177, 265, 324-5

Waldron, Mother Patricia, 60, n.38, 61, 127, n.79, 188-9, n.205, 232

Walker, Mother Ignatius, 76, n.16, 92, 96, 127, n.79, 325

Walsh, Mother Borgia, 262-3, n.90, 276-7, 293-333, n.424, n.444

Walsh, Mother Ignatius, 303, n.132

Ward, Mother Stanislaus, 293, n.51

Warde, Mother Josephine, 18-19, 21-28, 36-38, 44, 52-54, 89, 127, 156, 164, 174, 185, 189, 196, 228-9

Warde, Mother Xavier, 24, 26-28, 33, 35-40, 42, 44, 43-50, n.68, 52, 54, 56, 58, 59, 60, 63-66, 76-77, 83, 89, 127, n.79, 139-40, 164, 188-9, n.205-6, 211, 223, 225-229, n.209, 256

Warrington, Fla., 148-9, nn.99-101, 150-2, n.126, 153, 206-7, 320

Waterford, 1, 3, nn.15-20, 6, 11-12, n.62, 23, 49, 141, 303

Watkins, Mother M. Elizabeth, 293, n.57

Wexford, 12, 23, 303, n.131

White, Mother Teresa, 200, 252, 305, 312

Whitty, Mother Vincent, 25, 200, 253, 325

Wiendahl, Mother Mercy, 119, n.32, 262

Wilmington, N.C., 169-70, n.57-59

Wildridge, Sister Teresa, 24, n.28, 56

Woolfolk, Sister Raphael, 207-8, n.74

Worcester, Mass., 127, n.79, 159, 175-6, 188-9, n.205-8